PRAISE FOR THE POLITICS OF THE DEAD IN ZIMBABWE, 2000–2020

Fontein makes a critical analysis and a major contribution towards the understanding of a complex and multifaceted cultural–political phenomenon called 'death'. ... Through close reference to colonial and post-colonial systemic violence and murders, spirits of the dead, spirit mediums and ongoing economic and political power dynamics in Zimbabwe, this book provides a robust analysis of the complex and dynamic interplay between the disappeared, tortured and mutilated bodies, the dead, spirits (ancestral, dangerous/evil and holy) and the living. ... Beyond doubt, this is a 'must-have' work for all interested in the relationship between death and the broader, intriguing Zimbabwean past.
Lesley Hatipone Machiridza, Great Zimbabwe University, *Journal of Southern African Studies*

This very important book offers valuable contributions to our understanding of the everyday politics of the dead in Zimbabwe. The author's theorization and discussion of the typologies of death, bones, and human remains are useful to a wider audience, within and beyond Zimbabwe, including academics and graduate students within the field of anthropology and sociology of death, political and contemporary history of Zimbabwe, and spirituality and religious studies.
Joshua Matanzima, *Death Studies*

original and exciting research, thinking, and writing. ... I can't think of a book that has this sort of innovative and reflective approach that offers a new interpretation of the way Zimbabweans view such 'accidents' and the politics of uncertainty for the past 20 years. ... a wonderful book.
Timothy Scarnecchia, Kent State University

[An] unusually good [work that] deals with the subject of 'death' in a manner that connects bodies, bones and souls to give an interpretation of contemporary Zimbabwean life its full meaning ... distinguished.
Gerald Chikozho Mazarire, National University of Lesotho

A valuable contribution ... Fontein brings together, under a single heading, the links between a diverse set of events and processes related to death ... It also opens the door onto the larger discussion of changing practices of death and memorialization in Africa.
Jeremy L. Jones, College of the Holy Cross

RELATED JAMES CURREY TITLES ON CENTRAL & SOUTHERN AFRICA

Roots of Rural Poverty in South Central Africa
ROBIN PALMER & NEIL PARSONS

Diamonds, Dispossession and Democracy in Botswana
KENNETH GOOD

Crossing the Zambezi: The Politics of Landscape on a Central African Frontier
JO-ANN MCGREGOR

Circular Migration in Zimbabwe and Contemporary Sub-Saharan Africa
DEBORAH POTTS

Remaking Mutirikwi: Landscape, Water and Belonging in Southern Zimbabwe
JOOST FONTEIN

The War Within: New Perspectives on the Civil War in Mozambique, 1976–1992
ERIC MORIER-GENOUD ET AL. (eds)

Faith, Power and Family: Christianity and Social Change in French Cameroon
CHARLOTTE WALKER-SAID

Land, Migration and Belonging: A History of the Basotho in Southern Rhodesia c. 1890
JOSEPH MUJERE

Manhood, Morality & the Transformation of Angolan Society: MPLA Veterans & Post-war Dynamics
JOHN SPALL

Protestant Missionaries & Humanitarianism in the DRC: The Politics of Aid in Cold War Africa
JEREMY RICH

Across the Copperbelt: Urban & Social Change in Central Africa's Borderland Communities
MILES LARMER ET AL. (eds)

Inside Mining Capitalism: The Micropolitics of Work on the Congolese and Zambian Copperbelts
BENJAMIN RUBBERS (ed.)

Namib: The archaeology of an African desert
JOHN KINAHAN

Competing Catholicisms: The Jesuits, the Vatican & the Making of Postcolonial French Africa
JEAN LUC ENYEGUE, SJ

Manufacturing in Colonial Zimbabwe, 1890–1979: Interest Group Politics, Protectionism & the State
VICTOR GWANDE

The Politics of the Dead in Zimbabwe, 2000–2020

Bones, Rumours and Spirits

Joost Fontein

UJ Press

© Joost Fontein 2022

Published worldwide excluding Southern Africa by
James Currey
an imprint of
Boydell & Brewer Ltd
PO Box 9, Woodbridge
Suffolk IP12 3DF (GB)
www.jamescurrey.com
and of
Boydell & Brewer Inc.
668 Mt Hope Avenue
Rochester, NY 14620–2731 (US)
www.boydellandbrewer.com

Published in Southern Africa
(South Africa, Namibia, Lesotho, Swaziland and Botswana) by
UJ Press
Room 311, Library, Auckland Park Kingsway Campus, Johannesburg, 2092

The right of Joost Fontein to be identified as
the author of this work has been asserted in accordance with
sections 77 and 78 of the Copyright, Designs and Patents Act 1988

All Rights Reserved. Except as permitted under current legislation
no part of this work may be photocopied, stored in a retrieval system,
published, performed in public, adapted, broadcast, transmitted,
recorded or reproduced in any form or by any means, without the
prior permission of the copyright owner

The publisher has no responsibility for the continued existence or accuracy of
URLs for external or third-party internet websites referred to in this book, and
does not guarantee that any content on such websites is, or will remain, accurate
or appropriate

British Library Cataloguing in Publication Data
A catalogue record for this book is available from the British Library

ISBN 978-1-84701-267-8 (James Currey hardback)
ISBN 978-1-84701-364-4 (James Currey paperback)
ISBN 978-1-7764341-1-4 (University of Johannesburg Press paperback)

This publication is printed on acid-free paper

For those still waiting;
and for Melissa.

CONTENTS

List of Illustrations ix
Acknowledgements x

Introduction 1
   Changing death and human corporeality across Africa and beyond 5
   The politics of the dead in Zimbabwe 15
   The power of uncertainty 29
   Sources and structure of the book 32

1. Liberation heritage: Bones and the politics of commemoration 40
   The burial of Gift Tandare 41
   Heritage and commemoration 46
   Heritage and commemoration in Zimbabwe 50
   Liberation heritage 64
   Unsettling bones 76

2. Bones and tortured bodies: Corporealities of violence and post-violence 84
   Resurfacing bones 85
   Emotive materiality, affective presence and transforming materials 93
   Tortured bodies 97
   Towards 'healing' and 'reconciliation' during the Government of National Unity 2009–2013 112
   Conclusions 117

3. Chibondo: Exhumations, uncertainty and the excessivity of human materials 121
   The Chibondo exhumations 125
   Too 'fresh', 'intact', fleshy, leaky and stinky? 138
   The torque of materiality and the excessive potentiality of human remains 147
   The politics of uncertainty 151
   Conclusions 157

Contents

4. Political accidents: Rumours, death and the politics of uncertainty	158
The death of Solomon Mujuru	159
Factionalism, rivalries and murky business dealings	160
The inquest	169
A particular kind of death	180
Conclusions	189
5. Precarious possession: Rotina Mavhunga, politics and the uncertainties of mediumship	192
Rotina Mavhunga – the diesel *n'anga*	196
Precarious occupation	204
6. Mai Melissa: Towards the alterity of spirit and the incompleteness of death	218
Towards the alterity of spirit	238
Conclusions	244
7. After Mugabe	247
Burying Bob	267
Conclusion	282
Bodies and spirits, change and continuity	285
AIDS, cholera, Congo, prisons, Chiadzwa, diaspora, Fast Track Land Reform, and charismatic Pentecostalisms	290
New directions for liberation heritage	298
Ambuya Nehanda returns?	302
Exhuming Bob?	312
Bibliography	316
Index	340

ILLUSTRATIONS

1.	Statue of Joshua Nkomo in Bulawayo (Author 2020)	22
2.	Alan Wilson Memorial, at 'World's View' in Matopos (Author 2020)	52
3.	Grave of Cecil Rhodes at 'World's View' in Matopos (Author 2020)	55
4.	Grave of Lookout Masuku, Lady Stanley Cemetery, Bulawayo (Author 2020)	57
5.	Grave of Mike Rukasha, Nemanwa (Author 2006)	107
6.	Burial of Mike Rukasha, Nemanwa (Author 2006)	108
7.	Entrance to 'Fallen Heroes' exhibition at National Heroes Acre (Author 2015)	156
8.	Grave of Solomon Mujuru at the National Heroes Acre, Harare (Author 2015)	168
9.	Mai Melissa (Author 2001)	219
10.	The empty grave next to Sarah (Sally) Mugabe, where it was long expected Robert Mugabe would be buried (Author 2015)	270

Note on the use of photographs: all the photographs used in this book are my own. Exploring the uncertain and excessive, affective, emotive and political salience of human remains and corporeal materials is one of the central purposes of this book. It is exactly because of these affects and the complex ethical issues they raise, that I have deliberately avoided any use of images of human remains or damaged bodies in this book.

ACKNOWLEDGEMENTS

All books involve collaborative effort. They also take a long time. The material for this book was collected over two decades, and over a series of other research projects (Fontein 2006a; 2015). There are far more people to thank than I could mention here. But let me try. Firstly, I acknowledge various funders whose financial support assisted periods of research and fieldwork from which this book draws. This includes the UK Economic and Social Research Council who funded my PhD (1999–2003), and the British Academy who funded my postdoctoral research fellowship (2004–2007). I am also grateful to the Munro, Tweedie and Hayter research committees whose assistance enabled a series of research visits in the 2000s and early 2010s. Thanks also to the British Institute in Eastern Africa, where I was director between 2014 and 2018, when I was able to make two short research visits, assisted by Nicholas Gakuu, Rodrigo Vaz, Julia Stanyard and Mercy Gitonga, to former guerrilla camps in Tanzania, to explore how liberation heritage is gaining traction in that country. Some of that material finds its way into this book. I am also grateful to the Faculty of Humanities at the University of Johannesburg who offered funds to enable a paperback version of this book to be available immediately across the region. It is impossible to overstate how important this is. I am also grateful to the anonymous reviewers of early versions of this manuscript for their incisive comments. Responsibility for what appears here remains with me.

The idea for this book first emerged in the late 2000s in Edinburgh, when, with my colleagues John Harries and Jeanne Cannizzo, we established the 'Bones Collective' research group, and held a series of collaborative workshops, publications and later exhibitions (Fontein & Harries 2009, 2013), as well as numerous less formal, coffee-fuelled discussions. Many others soon became involved, but I particularly treasure memories of working with Cara Krmpotich and Paola Filippucci (Filippucci et al. 2012; Krmpotich et al. 2010). Through these Bones Collective activities, I first experienced the great value of collaborative intellectual effort. Many of the theoretical insights carried in this book derive from those conversations and collaborations. Since I left Edinburgh in 2014, the Bones Collective has continued to develop exciting new collaborations under the insightful tutelage of John Harries,[1] who remains my closest intellectual buddy and

---

[1] For some of the Bones Collective's continuing activities, see www.san.ed.ac.uk/research/research_themes/bones_collective, accessed 8/7/20.

Acknowledgements

something of a seer. There are many others to whom I remain grateful for intellectual stimulation and friendship, including Terence Ranger, Richard Werbner, Florence Bernault, Finn Stepputat, Elisabeth Hallam, Elisabeth Anstett, Layla Renshaw, Zoe Crossland, Isak Niehaus, Tim Ingold, Rebekah Lee, Meghan Vaughan, Steffen Jensen, Howard Williams, Dimitri Tsintjilonis, Peter Lockwood, Constance Smith, Sam Derbyshire, Diana Espirito Santo, Katerina Kerestetzi, Anastasios Panagiotopoulos, Marianne Sommer, Pamila Gupta, Mark Lamont, Jean-Pierre Warnier and Joni Brenner, to name only some. It was also a great pleasure to work with Laura Major – whose PhD on the politics of exhumations and commemoration in Rwanda I was lucky to supervise – on a special issue of *Critical African Studies* in 2015 (Major & Fontein 2015).

In the late 2000s this project benefited from the assistance of several other postgraduate scholars, including Angela Riviera and Julie Hartley, who assisted in the preparation of literature reviews that fed into two large but unsuccessful European Research Grant proposals. Although these funding disappointments were consequential in the short term, in the long run their preparatory work proved invaluable. With hindsight this project benefited from being unhindered by the arduous administrative burdens that large 'mega-grants' involve. More recently Valerie Kondo, beginning her own PhD at the University of Johannesburg on biometric technologies and migration, helped bring order to my bibliography. In Nairobi I continue to be greatly inspired by Neo Musangi, Doseline Kiguru, Syowia Kyambi, Syokau Mutonga, Wambui Karanja, James Muriuki and many others.

I have also benefited from the opportunity to present some of the material in this book at university seminars and conferences, including Copenhagen, Zurich, Madrid, SOAS, Paris, Juba, Goldsmiths, Roehampton, Buenos Aires, Johannesburg, Duke, Pretoria, UCL, Oxford, Lisbon, Stellenbosch, University of the Western Cape, Witwatersrand, Bergen, and Cambridge. I remain grateful for the incisive comments I received on all these occasions. Some of these events led to publications, and therefore some of the chapters here include expanded and developed material that has been made use of before. Some sections of the Introduction were developed from material that appeared in a chapter (Fontein 2018) in Antonius Robben's *A Companion to the Anthropology of Death*; in Chapter 1, from a very early paper on *ASAonline* (Fontein 2009b); in Chapter 2 from an article in a special issue of the *Journal of Material Culture* (Fontein 2010); and in Chapter 3 from a contribution to Stepputat's excellent volume, *Governing the Dead* (Stepputat 2014). Chapter 4 is a revised version of a paper published in *Kronos* in 2019. In each case I am indebted to the editors for the work they did guiding those publications to fruition, and to the relevant publishers for allowing me to re-use, revise and expand that material here.

Over two decades of research in and on Zimbabwe I have accrued so many debts of gratitude that I cannot mention them all. I continue to be grateful to

Acknowledgements

the support of National Museums and Monuments of Zimbabwe, especially the Executive Director, Godfrey Mahachi, but also the regional director at Great Zimbabwe Lovemore Mandima, as well as Kundishora Chipunza, who kindly availed himself for a very useful interview in March 2020; and others, like Crispin Chauke, who I spoke to many years earlier, and have since left the organisation for new pastures. The now former curator at Great Zimbabwe, Munyaradzi Sagiya remains enormously helpful, and I have benefited much from various shared fieldwork and writing projects. This is also true of Joseph Mujere who remains a bastion of knowledge and insight. I have particularly fond memories of the work we did together in December 2013 in Gutu (Mujere, Sagiya & Fontein 2017). In Bulawayo I benefited greatly from the insights of Shari Eppel, over a series of conversations and interviews since the early 2010s, most recently in March 2020. There are few who have as much knowledge or experience of the intricacies of Zimbabwe's politics of the dead as her, especially what it looks like from Matabeleland. I was also very fortunate to have an opportunity to talk to Dumiso Dabengwa in 2015, who was extraordinarily accommodating. In 2011 I met with Zepheniah Nkomo of Mafela Trust, and more recently, in March 2020, with Strike Mkandla and Mbuso Fuzwayo. The unresolved legacies of the *gukurahundi* massacres in Matabeleland, of Matabeleland's still under-recognised contributions to Zimbabwe's liberation, and of continuing violence, exclusion and under-development, are all important aspects of Zimbabwe's politics of the dead, and weighs heavily on these people, as on many others. Much work remains, but I hope I have done some small justice to the great assistance I received.

In the penultimate chapter of this book I discuss the particular travails of the Rukasha family in Nemanwa in the mid-2000s, when I was doing fieldwork for a project on Lake Mutirikwi (Fontein 2015). I have known these people since 1995 and my debt to them does not diminish. I am particularly grateful to them for allowing me to discuss the story of Mai Melissa's hardships and emergent mediumship in 2005–06. When I asked them in March 2020 if they would be happy with me writing about this troubling story, they not only agreed but insisted I do not use pseudonyms or disguise their identities. To be sure I gave them drafts to read, but I was told 'it all happened, so tell the story'. And therefore I have done so.

The final stages of compiling this manuscript took place under the coronavirus-related lockdowns of 2020–21. During this tricky period my momentum was sustained by weekly meetings of our 'death cluster' research group, and particularly by the generous feedback of Jonathan Stadler, Thulani Baloyi and David Moore. My final thanks go to Mercy Gitonga, who has managed with good cheer to put up with me throughout the ups and downs of our drawn-out 'coronapocalypse'. *Asante*.

Introduction

In 1898, just before she was hanged for rebelling against Rhodesian settler rule, Charwe Nyakasikana, spirit medium of the legendary ancestor Ambuya Nehanda,[1] famously prophesised that 'my bones will rise again'. Over a century later bones, bodies and human remains have come to occupy an increasingly complex place in Zimbabwe's postcolonial milieu. From ancestral 'bones' rising again as guerrilla fighters and mediums co-operating in the struggle for independence, and later for land, to the resurfacing bones of unsettled war dead; and from the troubling, decaying but profoundly silenced remains of post-independence *gukurahundi* massacres in Matabeleland and the Midlands in the 1980s, to the leaky, tortured bodies of recent post-2000 election violence, human materials are intertwined in Zimbabwe's postcolonial politics in ways that go far beyond, yet necessarily implicate, contests over memory, commemoration and the representation of the past. In this book I examine the complex political efficacies of human remains in what I call Zimbabwe's politics of the dead. This, I will argue, is a multi-faceted, cultural-political phenomena which resonates widely and in diverse ways across the region and beyond, and yet has taken particular form in Zimbabwe in a way which turns on the demanding, problematic and uncertain presence of both human corporeal and immaterial remains and, ultimately, on the unfinished nature of death itself.

Existing scholarship has become increasingly sophisticated in its analysis of the politics of nationalist historiography, of contested memory, commemoration and heritage, and of the changing significance of 'traditional' practices relating to ancestors, chiefs and spirit mediums across the region and beyond. These all turn on contested and contingent processes of (re)constituting the past and the dead. But the political imbrications of human remains as material substances, as well as that of returning spirits, in these highly contested processes is only beginning to be understood, despite a growing recognition of the transforming significance of human corporeality. Based on fieldwork, research and reflection spanning two decades, this book seeks to redefine the parameters of this emerging scholarship by exploring how the politics of the dead in

---

[1] Discussions continue about whether the correct nomenclature is Ambuya Nehanda or Mbuya Nehanda. The latter is more common these days but both are to my knowledge correct, depending upon dialect. It is sometimes said that the latter implies a higher degree of respect. For sake of consistency I use 'Ambuya' throughout this book, except where quoting other sources.

Zimbabwe is necessarily intertwined with the changing and indeterminate materialities of human remains. Linking this indeterminacy of human substances to the productive but precarious uncertainties of rumours, spirits and death itself, it points to how the indivisibility, or uneasy mutual dependency, of the material and immaterial is not only inherently intertwined with but also constitutive of the stylistics of power and incomplete work of postcolonial politics.

An important year for this book was 2011, when two events took place that epitomised this politics of the dead and the power of uncertainty that is central to it. These are the highly politicised, contested and deeply corporeal war veteran-led exhumations from a disused mine shaft at Chibondo in northern Zimbabwe and the controversial, still unresolved death of retired General Solomon Mujuru in August that year. Of course, Zimbabwe's corporeal politics of death and uncertainty are not contained by these specific events, nor by the two decades that this book particularly examines. Robert Mugabe's death and contested burial in September 2019, and other recent changes, such as the emergence of a 'newish', not-so-post-Mugabe kind of ZANU PF politics under Emmerson Mnangagwa since 2017, and its attempts to draw a line under the unresolved legacies of the *gukurahundi* even as violent oppression of political opposition has continued, all underline the continuing salience of Zimbabwe's politics of the dead and the power of uncertainty; processes that have traction in the context of a wider, and perhaps older but nevertheless resurgent, corporeal politics across the region.

Theoretically, this book has two overarching purposes, constituting its contribution to wider scholarship. The first is to explore how the politics of commemoration – of 'what makes for a grievable life' (Butler 2004: 20) – turns on the transforming materialities of human remains. My argument moves beyond the burgeoning literature on the politics of commemoration, which has often assumed that corpses are only of symbolic or representational significance in the contested realms of who, what and how the past should be remembered (cf. Hallam & Hockey 2001). Rather it explores how this politics is profoundly animated, afforded and constrained by the transforming, emotive materialities and affective presence of human remains. I build on not only a resurgence of scholarly interest in the changing nature and politics of death and funerary practices, but also on recent anthropological debates about materiality, the 'agency of things' and the properties of materials (Miller 2005; Gell 1998; Latour 1999; Ingold 2007; Pinney 2005; Domańska 2006; Brown 2001), and how they relate to questions of ontology and alterity (Henare et al. 2007; Holbraad 2009, 2011), and ruination and affect (Navaro-Yashin 2009; Stoler 2008). These share a common purpose in problematising conventional distinctions between 'subjects' and 'objects', 'things' and 'concepts', 'materials' and 'meaning'. Moving beyond Verdery's argument about how 'a body's

Introduction

materiality can be critical to its symbolic efficacy' (1999: 27), I focus on the political affects of the excessive potentialities of human materials, which demand and yet defy stabilisation, containment and reconstitution into uneasy subjects/objects, as recognisable human 'bodies' and sometimes identifiable 'subjects'. The point here is not only to re-conceptualise the importance of human corporeality in the politics of commemoration but also to bridge a surprising but persistent gap between political anthropology – with its concerns with performances of sovereignty, state-making and the tensions of bio- and necro-politics (cf. Hansen & Stepputat 2001 & 2005; Mbembe 2001 & 2003; Das & Poole 2004) – and a growing anthropological literature on materiality and affect.

This is carried through the second purpose of the book. Here I chart how uncertainty can be a central but often overlooked dynamic of political processes and performances of power, in the gap between performances of sovereignty and claims to legitimacy; between the demands of 'bio-politics' and those of 'necropolitics' (Mbembe 2003). If politics is often assumed to turn on contested processes of determination, containment and the stabilisation of meaning and affect, the second half of the book explores how the uncertainties provoked by the indeterminate potentiality of human substances echoes the productive uncertainties that surround rumours, spirits and death (cf. White 2000 & 2003), as key dimensions of the stylistics of power in African postcolonies and beyond. This link between the 'politics of the dead' and the 'power of uncertainty' is made explicit through a discussion of the intense public controversies that surrounded the war veteran-led, 'vernacular' exhumations from the abandoned mine in Chibondo in March 2011. These turned on the indeterminate nature of the human materials themselves, as their surprisingly 'fresh' and 'intact' nature provoked unprecedented debate about whether these were in fact victims of Rhodesian atrocities and therefore liberation 'heroes', or victims of post-independence ZANU PF violence. This uncertainty allowed, I will suggest, the dominant ZANU PF party to both celebrate their 'heroes' and remind everyone of their own capacity for violence. Yet in the end, the uncertainties provoked by the excessive potentialities of these remains defied their political utility, and by August 2011, the hundreds of remains exhumed at Chibondo were reburied in a new memorialised grave onsite in an effort to contain and stabilise these unruly dead.

The uncertainties provoked by these human materials therefore resonate with the duplicitous[2] but productive political imbrications of

[2] Here, and throughout this book, when I refer to a thing, a spirit or a rumour as 'duplicitous', I do not necessarily use that term in the sense of a conscious or intentional agent deliberately deceiving someone or something else, but rather in the sense that they have double or multiple possible meanings and effects which are in tension, where one could undermine the other, so that the uncertainty of what a thing is doing or means has a deceptive and fraught

rumours and of spirits, which also turn exactly on their indeterminacy and uncertainty. This sets the scene for a discussion of some of the different ways in which this power of uncertainty has manifest itself in Zimbabwean politics in the post-2000 period. Using as a central hook the death of veteran ZANU PF figure, Solomon Mujuru, in a mysterious fire in August 2011, I examine the political productivity of rumours that have often surrounded the (rather common) 'accidental' deaths of senior politicians since independence. These date back to Herbert Chitepo's assassination in 1975 (White 2003) and the still unexplained death of the immensely popular guerrilla leader Josiah Magama Tongogara in late 1979, and have some commonality with the similarly unexplained deaths of high-profile figures elsewhere in the region (cf. Cohen & Odhiambo 2004). Linking the uncertainties provoked by such 'political accidents' to the uncertainties that all death in Zimbabwe (and perhaps beyond) can reveal, I explore how there may be much to gain politically, as well to risk, by deliberately leaving such deaths un-foreclosed and unresolved. This argument about the power of uncertainty is then further developed by reconsidering assumptions long carried in the literature on spirit mediums and ancestral possession – a form of the politics of the dead which has long been at centre of anthropological studies in Zimbabwe (cf. Lan 1985) – and examining the *precariousness* of spirit possession and mediumship, particularly as implicated in political events. In so doing, I critically re-assess the significance of ancestors and spirit possession in Zimbabwean politics by exploring the inherent uncertainties that surround mediumship, which both attracts yet can also undermine efforts by politicians and others to acquire the ancestral legitimacy that spirit mediums offer. This exemplifies (as with the controversies surrounding the Chibondo exhumations and Solomon Mujuru's death) the unfinished nature of death in Zimbabwe and perhaps everywhere; a political, social, cultural, epistemological but also ontological claim that hinges on a profound uncertainty in which everyone, to differing extents and in diverse ways, is imbricated.

This returns the discussion back to the central themes threaded throughout the book, which are the open-ended and ultimately indeterminate – and therefore highly contested – material, discursive and performative processes through which the past and the dead are (re)constituted, and come to have an 'ambivalent quality of felt presence' (Filippucci et al. 2012: 199) that animates and shapes the ongoing work of politics and power. By linking the political productivities and risks of the uncertainties of human

consequentiality. Such double or multiple meanings/effects can be useful and productive but also dangerous and subversive, and derive from their uncertainty, their indeterminacy and ultimately from their excessivity to fixed, stable meanings and affects. I am grateful to one of the anonymous readers for pushing me to clarify my use of this term.

Introduction

substances with those associated with rumours, spirits and even death itself, I seek to make an innovative and critical contribution to rethinking how the open-ended indeterminacy – and therefore, the alterity – of both the material and the immaterial, and the uneasy dependency between them, are intertwined in the work of politics, deepening our understanding of how the 'imbrication of the semiotic and the material' (Deleuze & Guattari [1980] 1987: 337) is inherent to and constitutive of the stylistics of power in the postcolony and beyond.

Changing death and human corporeality across Africa and beyond

Before a more detailed exegesis of this book's chapters, let me set something of the broader empirical and analytical scene within which it is set. As the complex entanglement of the politics of the past and of the dead with that of its material remains, performative practices and monumentalised forms (funerals, state commemoration, monuments, ruins, artefacts, graves, bodies, bones and so on) has received renewed scholarly attention (cf. Robben 2018), the significance of human corporealities or 'carnal fetishism' (Bernault 2010) has increasingly come into focus.[3] Aligned with a burst of activity exploring the changing nature of death across Africa (Lee & Vaughan 2008, 2012; Lamont 2009; Jindra & Noret 2011; Kalusa & Vaughan 2013) there has been a proliferation of new research devoted to the materialities of death (Posel & Gupta 2009; Krmpotich et al. 2010; Filippucci et al. 2012; Hallam & Hockey 2001). Sharing a focus on human remains and the 'political afterlife' of the dead, the ethnographic scope of these studies is vast, stretching from the changing significance of funerals, graves and reburials in localist politics of land, restitution and autochthony in South Africa, Kenya, Zimbabwe and elsewhere (James 2007; Fontein 2011; Cohen & Odhiambo 1992) to their importance as performances of 'cosmopolitanism' and 'festivals of belonging' in contexts of migration, diaspora and return (Geschiere 2005, 2009; Gable 2006). A related body of work has focused on 'missing' or 'hidden' bodies (cf. Rousseau et al. 2018; Harries 2017a; Casper & Moore 2009), sometimes intersecting with new studies examining worldwide movements for the repatriation of indigenous human remains from museum collections in the 'north' (Fforde 2004; Fforde et al. 2002; see also Krmpotich 2008); such as, in an African context, the remains of Sara Baartman (Crais & Scully 2009) and Hintsa's skull in South Africa (Mkhize 2009); victims of Germany's Namibian genocide (Dobler 2012);

---

[3] See for example the Human Remains and Violence book series and journal edited by Jean-Marc Dreyfus and Elisabeth Anstett, published by Manchester University Press (see www.manchesteruniversitypress.co.uk/journals/hrv, accessed 23/9/19).

'El negro' in Botswana (Parsons & Segobye 2002; Gewald 2001); and the bones of Savorgnan de Brazza in Congo-Brazzaville (Bernault 2010).

Parallel to such demands for the return of human remains collected under dubious colonial circumstances, concerns have grown with the 'commodification' and illicit trade of body parts, 'trophies', relics, occult substances, medical organs and human tissues (Scheper-Hughes & Wacquant 2002; Jenkins 2010; Harrison 2012; Sharp 2000; Geary 1986). At the same time, the propagation of both state-led and vernacular exhumations and reburials – framed as rituals of 'reconciliation' and 'transitional justice' as often as forms of 'national commemoration' – has come under increasing academic scrutiny in post-conflict contexts as varied as Rwanda (Cook 2009; Mamdani 2002; Richters et al. 2005; Caplan 2007), Uganda (Jones 2007; Meier 2013), Kenya (Branch 2010) and South Africa (Rousseau 2009); and further afield, in Yugoslavia (Petrovic 2005/06; Denich 1994), Spain (Renshaw 2010, 2011), Vietnam (Kwon 2006), the former Soviet Union (Paperno 2001) and Argentina (Crossland 2000, 2009a, 2009b).

In Zimbabwe demands for and examples of such 'post-conflict' exhumations, vernacular or otherwise, have increased over the last two decades, and this forms a key aspect of the politics of the dead discussed in this book. Yet it is important to remember that exhumations do not always involve war dead. One example cited by Ranger (2010b) involves the 2009 exhumation and return of the remains of Pasipamire, medium of the great spirit Chaminuka – who was famously killed on the orders of the Ndebele king Lobengula in 1883 – from Matabeleland to his shrine in Seke near Harare by his descendants, which has brought them into dispute with National Museums and Monuments of Zimbabwe (NMMZ) who manage the shrine.[4] Another example are the 2006 exhumations that accompanied the return of Nswazwi people to their ancestral lands in Botswana, from where they had been removed during the colonial period.[5] Also, NMMZ have been involved in exhumations to do with the resettlement of people displaced by the Tugwi-Mukosi dam.[6] Such examples illustrate how exhumations and reburials can be deployed to engage with a diversity of unresolved pasts and futures, from pre- and colonial-era conflicts and dispossessions to more-recent land appropriations, as well as the unsettling legacies of anti- and postcolonial violence.

Conversely, however, efforts to deal with recent, unsettled violent pasts, or to commemorate Zimbabwe's 'liberation heroes', do not necessarily involve exhumations. For example, local community and war veteran-led efforts in the early 2010s to 'monumentalise' the sites of two war-time massacres by Rhodesian soldiers during the 1970s in Gutu

---

4   'Chaminuka: The Resurrection?' *Sunday Mail* 14/12/09.
5   'First Nswazwi group arrives from Zimbabwe' *Mmegi* 12/12/06, www.mmegi.bw/index.php?sid=31&aid=53&dir=2006/December/Tuesday12, accessed 23/9/19.
6   Interview with Mr Mandima, Regional Director, NMMZ, Field notes, 13/12/13.

Introduction

district, at Kamungoma and Hurodzevasikana, were marked by a relative absence of both bodies and spirits (Mujere et al. 2017), setting these efforts apart from similar war veteran-led events taking place elsewhere in the post-2000 period. Other such examples include the renaming of King George VI Barracks in Harare after the late liberation guerrilla leader, Josiah Magama Tongogara, and calls for the former internment camp, Gonakudzingwa, where many Zimbabwean nationalists were detained in the 1960s and 1970s, to be protected as a national monument.[7]

The growing literature on human corporealities across the African continent is inevitably intertwined with expanding scholarship charting the immense diversity of changing meanings and practices of death across the region (Kalusa & Vaughan 2013: xiii; Lamont 2009). It is hard to refute the enormous diversity of African death practices and the fact that 'changes in funerary rites on the continent have been considerable and complex' over the last century and more (Jindra & Noret 2011: 31). In *Funerals in Africa*, Jindra and Noret point to transformations in funerary practices provoked by a wide range of 'inter-related changes' and 'alterations of outlook and practice caused by colonialism and … the large scale adoption of world religions', and by the social and political turmoil caused by conflicts (cf. Jones 2007), disease (cf. Posel 2002), labour migrations, and the 'increased mobility and pluralism' of urbanising contexts, which have led to 'new processes of creating status', new forms of social association, and new mortuary technologies (Jindra & Noret 2011: 16). For example, Golomski (2018a, 2018b) has explored how, in the context of Swaziland's devastating HIV/AIDS pandemic, new forms of funerary and death insurance emerged – in part to ease the work of satiating changing but long-enduring demands to 'dignify' death. Importantly, such changes have longer histories and a greater variety of trajectories than those wrought in the relatively recent context of HIV/AIDS, dramatic as that has certainly been, and despite growing recognition that the social, cultural and political affects of HIV/AIDS have their own of specific historicities, diversities and changing trajectories (cf. Fassin 2007; Niehaus 2007a; Tomaselli 2009). Ranger (2004b; 2011a), for example, has examined the creative and contested emergence and co-existence of different 'traditional', 'modern' and 'Christian' ways to 'dignify death' amidst a plethora of new burial societies among African populations in colonial Bulawayo. Likewise, Droz (2011) and Lamont (2011) explore how the colonial imposition of burial and the banning of older practices of corpse disposal and exposure in Kenya engendered a new politics of 'dignifying burial' among Kikuyu peoples, even as the 'death pollution complex' of Meru

---

[7] 'KGVI to be renamed after Gen Tongo' *Herald* 29/1/15; 'General Tongo's legacy lives on', *Patriot*, 29/1/15; 'Gonakudzingawa: A Sinking heritage' *Patriot* 7/11/13.

peoples was reconstituted in new ways in the context of Christianisation and a politics of belonging provoked by colonial land alienation.

A related strand of work has reflected upon the flourishing of new funeral practices by exploring the emergence of new forms of ritual and funerary expertise. This is illustrated in South Africa by the growing popularity of new embalming practices by 'funerary entrepreneurs', exploiting changing demands and expectations for the handling, return and burial of the dead (Lee 2011). This echoes Golomski's discussion of new forms of death insurance and the surprising domestic politics of concealment and secrecy this has sometimes engendered in Swaziland (2018a, 2018b). Demand for such new forms of financial security as well as expertise emerges in the context of new kinds of mobility, as African migrants in urban areas, in neighbouring countries and in 'diaspora' much further away, go to great lengths to ensure the 'return' of the dead, or the near-dead, for 'proper' burial at home; even as state pathologists and medical professionals face problems with growing numbers of anonymous migrant corpses abandoned in morgues in border-towns like Musina (between Zimbabwe and South Africa), illustrating the uneasy, marginalised lives and deaths that illegal migrants and border-jumpers often endure (Nunez & Makukule 2009; Mbiba 2010).[8] In the context of its waxing and waning economic and political woes, broader regional transformations in funerary practices have also been driven and challenged in Zimbabwe by factors such as shortages of fuel (Chadya 2015) and, more recently, doctors' strikes.[9] Other studies point to increasingly 'lavish' and opulent funerals and 'death celebrations' in, for example, Cameroon (Jindra 2011) and Ghana (cf. Parker 2005), where the preparation of corpses prior to burial has sometimes achieved renewed significance for remembering and reconstituting the dead in novel ways (de Witte 2011).

The emergence of new kinds of funerary expertise, technologies and practices across diverse African contexts relates, in turn, to a broader zeitgeist of comparative work elsewhere, beyond the continent, which has re-conceptualised the politics of life, death and dying in terms of the 'modernisation' 'secularisation', distancing and medicalisation of death (Casper & Moore 2009; Kalusa & Vaughan 2013: xiii). Some have traced how the medicalisation of death and dying emerged in tandem with a much broader medicalisation of life, causing a disruption in the 'natural' process of dying and resulting in the loss of familiar, 'tame' death and its replacement with the 'dirty', 'wild' event of medicalised death (cf. Aries 1974, 1991; Seymour 1999). In this view, a feature of 'modern' death is to sequester away the 'reality' of dangerous unbounded bodies, the corpse being the epitome of this body (Elias 1985; Green 2008; Lawton 2000). Other anthropological studies have sought to explore the ambivalence of life and

---

[8] '8 Beitbridge bodies face pauper's burial' *Newsday* 15/11/19.
[9] 'Doctors strike haunting the dead' *Sunday Mail* 25/11/19.

Introduction

death as particular ways of being-in-the-world (Tsintjilonis 2006; Riviera 2009); a strand that has particularly pertinent resonances in the complexity of stigma and shame associated with HIV/AIDS in South Africa (cf. Niehaus 2007a; Posel 2002), where the 'walking dead', considered neither dead nor alive, move from life to the brink of death and back again, transforming how death is understood (Lee & Vaughan 2008: 357).

Some of the recent writing on changing death across Africa has stressed less the supplanting of old forms, meanings and practices by new technologies and expertise, than the prevalence of new syncretisms, pluralities and co-existent multiplicities, as old and new repertoires of meaning and practice to do with death are re-assembled into new contingent and often contested ways, in diverse, shifting contexts (cf. Langewiesche 2011; Lamont 2011; de Witte 2011; Roberts 2011). Ellis (2008), for example, examined the historical continuities of a contemporary shrine in Nigeria where 83 corpses were discovered in 2004. These shrines are both sites of power and of death, as repositories for corpses whose spirits could not be accepted in ordinary funeral ceremonies. While Ellis's historical analysis highlighted collusions between disreputable religious practices and national elites/politicians, Adebanwi (2008) focuses on contemporary ancestor worship and how the newly dead are linked with the long dead, in order to create conditions through which they can be memorialised as 'heroes'. Such arguments point to the diverse ways in which 'modern' forms and techniques of 'national' commemoration (and heritage – Rowlands & De Jong 2007) have been 'localised' in African contexts; and at the same time, to the ways that older African motifs, idioms and practices endure in new guises and contexts. However, my emphasis would be on how the epistemological uncertainties and contingencies such multiplicities and entanglements invoke, turn on and contribute to the ontological indeterminacies and uneasy mutual dependencies of the material and immaterial, matter and meaning, the living and the dead, that death often reveals or instigates.

The co-existence and fine entanglement of different repertoires of death no doubt feeds the prevalent cultural politics that surrounds death and burial (cf. Parker 2005), even as it animates the multiple contradictions that Vansina (2011: ix) suggests make funerary rituals so fascinating. Importantly, however, they also point to the significance of 'continuities-within-change' that Nugent (2008) stressed in the context of African ethnicities. Therefore, while it is hard to deny the large diversity and profound transformations of death across Africa throughout the 19th and 20th centuries, it is equally important to recognise that the salience of transforming and transferring human corporealities to do with death often do have deep enduring and recurring historical purchase across different, co-existent repertoires in changing historical and political contexts. One potentially productive line of enquiry in this regard has begun to explore 'disgust' provoked by the ugly aesthetic 'realities' of bodily disabilities and disintegration associated with death and dying in African and other, often palliative, contexts (Livingston 2008; Lawton 2000, 2001; Russ 2005). Another strand explores, across the particularities of changing social and political milieu, how death reveals the extent to which 'the ontological status of persons – the living as well as the recently dead – is typically, even necessarily, in flux' (Straight 2006: 102).

Kalusa and Vaughan (2013: xiii) may be right to emphasise, then, that 'the extent to which, before the advent of colonialism, death was associated with space and place, and territorial sovereignty, varied enormously', and that contemporary links between graves and claims to land restitution often do reflect how 'spaces of death' acquired 'new meanings' in colonial/postcolonial settings, especially in former setter colonies like South Africa (James 2007), Zimbabwe and Kenya (Lamont 2011). Yet the presence (or disquieting absence) of bodies in the ground, and particularly the merging substances of decomposing bodies and soil that burial involves, *has* long been central to 'materialities of belonging' and the performances of 'autochthony', status and authority linked thereto (Fontein 2011 & 2015; Geschiere 2009) in many African settings. Moreover the co-mingling of human and non-human substances linked to death and decomposition have recurring salience and efficacy, regardless of whether burials (now or in the past) take place beneath living houses, in the derelict dwellings of the dead, in cattle kraals, on the margins of settlements, in river beds, or in sacred groves or caves; or if dangerous polluting corpses were once normally abandoned to devouring hyenas (Droz 2011; Lamont 2011). Colonial officials in southern Rhodesia in the early 20th century, supervising the removal of Africans to 'native reserves' from what had been delineated as European farmland, were certainly often acutely aware of the social, cultural, political and moral significance of ancestral graves left behind, an issue which gained renewed significance in the context of Zimbabwe's Fast Track Land Reform (Fontein 2011 & 2015). Similarly, motifs to do with the pollution of death do have continuing (if transformed) salience amongst Kenya's Meru, even if the colonial banning of corpse exposure later led 'to a "secondary" use of burials' as markers of land possession in its central highlands in the 1960s (Jindra & Noret 2011: 9; Lamont 2011).

The transformation, flows and transference of human corporeal forms and substances has therefore long been of central significance to the diverse and changing material/symbolic processes through which the living are made safely dead, and through which social/political orders and living persons, bounded or unbounded, are reconstituted, 'regenerated' or reconfigured after the 'rupture' of death (Hertz 1960; Huntington and Metcalf 1991; Bloch & Parry 1982; Bloch 1988). Warnier has demonstrated how the 'enclosure, containment and expenditure' of human

Introduction

substances was key to constituting royal authority in the 19th-century grassland kingdoms of Cameroon (2007). More recently Salpeteur and Warnier (2013) have explored vernacular public autopsies in Cameroon by addressing how these hugely invasive public techniques reveal, and thereby reconstitute, 'the truth about the dead and the living' through opening up the corpse and close inspection of its organs. The remarkable historical resilience of these practices, they suggest, 'seems to lie in a specific and enduring symbolic system combined with historical situations that foster much doubt and uncertainty about the deep material, corporeal and social truth of any subject' (2013: 172).

Conversely, Bernault has shown how both Europeans and Africans, but from different perspectives, together contributed to the 'refetishising' and 'resacralisation of bodies as political resources' during the colonial encounter in Equatorial Africa (2006: 238). More recently she has developed the notion of 'carnal technologies' to further explore how both French colonials and Gabonese invested 'diverse forms of agency and value in human flesh' (2013: 173). While French officials espoused a vision of the body as a 'mechanical device', this vision was haunted by their own religious beliefs and a strong attachment to the sacred value of the body. At the same time, Gabonese in their own ways believed in the 'sacred agency of human flesh' (2013: 183) yet also participated in a trade of body parts as commodities; thereby illustrating something of the complex and ambivalent processes by which the stuff of human bodies has salience and efficacy between disparate repertoires, and can move between subject- and object-hood while never wholly becoming one or the other. As Fontein and Harries have discussed (2013), such examples show how human corporeality can be powerfully distributed across co-existent repertoires of meaning and materiality, caught in fraught historical tensions and proximities of continuities-within-change, exactly because its excessive potentialities and multiplicities are at once metaphorical, literal and metonymic.

A key question that must remain properly unanswered, then, is whether the recent expansion of academic interest in death and human corporeality across Africa and beyond, reflects changing cultural, social and political practices to do with death, as Ranger (2010b) has suggested, or whether it reflects changing academic foci. Probably it is both, and the two are most likely inter-related. The recent zeitgeist of concern with bodies, human remains and particularly forensic sciences, within and beyond academia (think of the popularity of forensic science in television dramas, for example) reflects and is reflected in both broader transformations in death and funerary rites, and the longer continuities through which such changes gain traction and meaning. Indeed, in some ways the renewed scholarly concern with corporeality represents a return to issues first raised by Hertz (1960) in his classic discussion of death, but which then became lost under a groundswell of structuralist, symbolic, interpretive and discursive turns in anthropology. The prevalent focus on meaning and social processes of meaning-making carried by these approaches meant that the study of things and stuff, and particularly the physicality of 'bodies' and human remains (cf. Hallam et al. 1999) was, for a long time, marginalised in social/cultural anthropology. The recent turn to corporeality may therefore reflect not only broader historical changes and continuities across the region and beyond, but also new and renewed theoretical concerns with questions of embodiment, materiality and the mutually constitutive relationships between matter and meaning, spirit and substance across the social sciences and humanities, and especially in social anthropology.

Indeed, alongside the renewed concern with death and bodies, the materiality of things and substances more generally has become a central anthropological concern (Fontein & Harries 2013; Filippucci et al. 2012; Krmpotich et al. 2010). As discussed elsewhere (Fontein & Harries 2013), the 'tyranny of the subject' (Miller 2005: 37) through which objects, things and materials were made 'shamed, mute and passive' (Baudrillard 1990: 111) has been profoundly questioned. This theoretical 'return to things' (Brown 2001; Domańska 2006) and the renewed interest in the ethnographic study of 'material culture' (Buchli 2002; Miller 2005; Lock & Farquhar 2007) that accompanied it, has turned on recognition of the 'agency', 'affordances' and 'effectivities' (Ingold 1992; 2007) of networks of human and non-human actors (cf. Knappett & Malafouris 2008) or 'actants' (Latour 1999), and on the indivisibility of the material and the conceptual (cf. Henare et al. 2007: 3–4; Holbraad 2009, 2011), meaning that *a priori* distinctions between 'mindful' subjects and 'passive' objects can no longer be assumed. As a result, attention is increasingly focused on the 'co-entanglement' of things and society (Hodder 2012) and the unfolding, relational and co-dependent processes of becoming, through which entities are contingently forged and stabilised as recognisable subjects and objects in particular historical and political contexts.

The renewed interest in questions of death and human corporeality we have been tracing emerges entangled with these new theorisations of material agency. A plethora of studies have focused on the materiality of the body and the ways in which the stuff of the body – organs, bones, blood, skin, hair and flesh – sometimes in tactile engagement with other kinds of non-human stuff, become socially animate in relational processes of making and unmaking various kinds and categories of persons and things. Crossland, for example, has considered the ways in which the body has been 'conceptualised as evidence' (2009a: 69) through techniques of forensic analysis by which 'the dead' are constituted in particular ways (2009a, 2009b). This echoes Hallam's study of how the 'articulation or making of skeletons by anatomists' reveals the 'interdependence of bones

Introduction

and embodied practices' with 'the bones of the dead and the bodies of the living both mutually shaping one another' (Hallam 2010: 265). In a related vein, Harries explores how 'in their discovery and handling, pieces of stone *become* artefacts that index the presence of an absent other', showing how tactical corporeal engagements between hands and found stone tools can generate 'historical sensation' and a 'feeling of pastness' that presences, anxiously, the 'absent other' of Newfoundland's exterminated Beothuk people for its contemporary inhabitants (Harries 2017b: 110). Elsewhere Renshaw has examined the ways in which exhumations of Spain's civil war dead reconstruct 'affective identification' for their living descendants many decades after their deaths (2010, 2011). Such studies show how 'anthropological attention has once again returned to the body not simply as the site of our phenomenal being in the world', but as problematic 'material stuff: leaky, fleshy, messy material stuff, which flows, mutates, dissolves and decays' (Fontein & Harries 2013: 118); and this is something of a return to the relationships between the decomposing bodies, funeral rites and the settling of the souls that preoccupied Hertz in his famous essay on death (1960).

In this respect it is significant to note that the recent proliferation of work on human corporeality is not limited to the study of death and funerals, but also focuses on questions of life and vitality (Kalusa & Vaughan 2013: xii), and the politics there of (Fassin 2007: 265–70). This builds on but also beyond the seminal work of Bloch and Parry (1982) which explored death in terms of the cultural constitution of personhood, questioning conventional ('Western') boundaries between individuals so that the notion of the 'unbounded person' emerged, where ties between persons are just as material and real as ties within a person (Kaufman & Morgan 2005; Lambek & Strathern 1998). This provoked new understandings of death and undermined older ontological assumptions that distinguished corpses from souls and understood the imperative of funerary practices was to separate them (Bloch 1971; Fabian 1972; Huntington & Metcalf 1991; Rosaldo 2004; Taylor 1996; Turner 1969; Walter 1994).

The materiality turn and the renewed focus on corporeality is pushing further in this direction so that the long-questioned stability of distinctions between life and death become still harder to maintain, just as the 'moment of dying' becomes difficult if not impossible to isolate, medically as well as ethnographically (Tsintjilonis 2000, 2004, 2006). This is reflected in the literature on the effects of HIV/AIDS on death and dying, already discussed. Similarly, Lock's comparative study of brain death (1996, 2002) examined how different epistemologies of death demonstrate how the margins of life and death are socially and cultural constituted rather than 'biologically' given, pointing exactly to the ontological uncertainties of matter and meaning, vitality and efficacy that death often lays bare. There is a growing body of research that has deployed a 'cultural phenomenology of flesh' to consider how organ donation and transplants have challenged assumptions about life, personhood and kinship (Papagaroufali 1999; Haddow 2000, 2005; Sharp 2001), and there are related studies exploring traffics, flows and transfers of blood (Copeman 2005, 2009; Carsten 2013). In a similar vein, emerging work looking at the efficacy, vitality and complex 'co-dependency' (Hodder 2012) of human substances, persons and things, focuses increasingly on questions of 'human-ness' itself, as well as of 'life' and 'death' (Fontein & Harries 2013; Niehaus 2013a; Nyamnjoh & Rowlands 2013; Salpeteur & Warnier 2013; Bernault 2013; Espirito Santo et al. 2013).

Of course, not all of this renewed concern with bodily substances necessarily encompasses much of a concern with bodies as matter proper. Just as the materiality turn has sometimes been criticised for failing to take account of properties and flows of materials (Ingold 2007), or failing to 'look more closely at things themselves' (Hodder 2012: 1), so there is an ambiguity about some writings that ostensibly take human substances as their subject yet appear to evoke materiality merely as a means of acknowledging the presence of things without their proper inclusion in any subsequent analysis (Fontein & Harries 2013: 118–9). The significance of 'blood' for example is still more often framed in terms of its symbolic or metaphorical resonance than for its material properties (cf. Carsten 2013), and too often when 'corpses do matter' it is still only as a 'natural metaphor for society', for their 'malleability' and 'saturation with meaning', and remains limited to 'their ability to function as windows onto ourselves' (Posel & Gupta 2009: 308). For all the noise about stuff, sometimes anthropology seems like it still has much to learn from archaeology's attention to materials, substances and things (cf. Gosden 2005; Shanks 2007; Hodder 2012).

Yet it is clear that the new theoretical attention focused over the last two decades on questions of materiality and the contingent relationalities, agencies, flows and properties of materials, things and stuff, is highly pertinent to the study of changing death across Africa. The two bodies of literature can hardly be taken in isolation anymore. Much of the new work exploring changing death across Africa does emphasise the entangled material/symbolic dimensions of transforming bodies and human substances in commemorative and funerary practices, and the open-ended, uncertain and indeterminate transformative processes whereby persons and groups, the living and dead, are mutually constituted and re-constituted, assembled and re-assembled, made present or absent. Whether the deepening political significance of bodies, burials and exhumations across the region is the result of changing historical processes and epistemologies across the colonial and postcolonial period, or whether the 'carnal fetishism' (Bernault 2006, 2010) so apparent lately, really reflects longer continuities to do with the ontological uncertainties

Introduction

that death reveals, is a question that clearly lies at centre of the broader terrain in which this book is situated, however difficult it is to answer definitively. At the same time, it is also clear that despite identifiable broader regional patterns of changing death practices, how these are manifest or gain political traction in particular historical and geographical contexts is always likely to be quite specific. So the politics of the dead in Zimbabwe that this book examines is likely to materialise differently across the southern African region, both between (and within) particular countries, and more broadly, between 'post-conflict' post-colonies and those which did not experience extended liberation struggles and wars of independence.[10]

The politics of the dead in Zimbabwe

In Zimbabwe, where the politics of heritage, memory and commemoration has been the subject of academic and public debate for some time, the emergent conjunction of meaning and matter in relation to death and corporeality outlined above has followed a broadly similar trajectory. While Zimbabwe's pre- and early colonial past had long been a site of 'rival attachments' (Lowenthal 1990: 302) and a 'scarce resource' (Appadurai 1980; Kuklick 1991; Fontein 2006a; Ranger 1967), particularly during the African liberation struggle of the 1960s and 1970s, after independence in 1980 the historiography and commemoration of the liberation struggle itself became the subject of profound contestation (Alexander et al. 2000; Ranger 1985, 2004a; Fontein 2006a; Lan 1985; Kriger 1992, 1995; Werbner 1998). An estimated 30,000 to 50,000 people died during Zimbabwe's liberation struggle, often known as the second *chimurenga*, which lasted from the late 1960s until late 1979. Since independence in 1980, the ruling party, ZANU PF (Zimbabwe African National Union, Patriotic Front) has dominated state commemoration through Zimbabwe's hierarchical and highly elitist system of district, provincial and national Heroes Acres, which quickly became the subject of intense contestation (Werbner 1998; Kriger 1995), and continues to be highly problematic.[11]

[10] I am grateful to one anonymous reader for emphasising this. I seek not to aggregate everything under the heavy imprint of similarity, but rather to point out that, across both broader historical transformations and enormous regional diversity, there are historical continuities and contemporary resonances around death, and particularly around the salience of corporealities. Golomski's recent work (2018a, 2018b) on death in Swaziland, illustrates well how the politics of death materialises differently in particular contexts even where broader regional patterns of transformation and endurance are evident.

[11] For just a few examples: 'MPS attack selection of national heroes' *Daily News* (SA) 2/3/01; 'Comment: Broaden selection of National Heroes' *Standard* 8/8/09; 'Mugabe must restore dignity to burial' *Zimbabwe Times* 6/11/09; 'Heroes Acre only for ZANU PF: Mugabe' *Newzimbabwe.com* 26/3/11, accessed

After 2000, the politicisation of the historiography of the liberation struggle intensified through the emergence of what Ranger (2004a) called 'patriotic history', ZANU PF's revived postcolonial 'master fiction' (Primorac 2007), by which it increasingly arrogated exclusively to itself the liberation credentials and 'languages of suffering' through which it polarised political debates, and effectively marginalised the various factions of the opposition Movement for Democratic Change (MDC) with which it briefly shared power during the 2009–13 'unity government'. As argued in Chapter 7, although this might be considered a defining feature of 'Mugabeism' (Ndlovu-Gatsheni 2015), the removal of Robert Mugabe from the presidency during the 'soft' coup of November 2017 has not (yet) led to a profound transformation of this deeply historiographical politics of narrowly defined heroism, and its constant harking back to the struggles of the 1960s and 1970s. In Chigumadzi's words, ZANU PF's normative, exclusivist 'Chimurenga politics' involves 'a complex management of time' through which it '"inappropriated the now", so that present struggles were a necessary sacrifice to the fulfilment of a revolutionary future which was a re-articulation of a glorious African past' (2018: 103). 'In twist of fate, it is this very Chimurenga legacy', she claims, that the military-led, 'internal coup' was 'claiming to defend against "enemies" and "criminal elements"' (2018: 27) allegedly surrounding the ageing Mugabe, in what they (tellingly) dubbed 'Operation Restore Legacy'.

While this 'patriotic history' has manifest in many guises,[12] and in diverse forms in particular local contexts (Mujere et al. 2017) – sometimes including scholar-led projects not *directly* driven by the ruling party's agenda[13] – a central dynamic has circulated around what Muchemwa calls ZANU PF's 'necropolitan imagination' and 'an aesthetics of heroism' (2010). This is apparent both through the contestations surrounding the selection of 'national heroes' (Werbner 1998; Kriger 1995), but also by a host of new state-driven oral history and heritage projects focusing on

---

19/7/20;'ZANU PF hypocrisy on liberation heroes exposed' *swradioafrica.com* 21/6/12, accessed 19/7/20.

[12] Including populist music galas, articles in government newspapers, a new wave of biographies (Tendi 2010; Ndlovu-Gatsheni & Willems 2009).

[13] One anonymous reader emphasised that some documentary projects which have been too easily airbrushed as '*Patriotic* history' (like the 'Capturing a Fading National Memory' collaboration between the University of Zimbabwe, the National Archives and NMMZ, and the regional SADC 'Hashim Mbita' Documentation Project) were carried out independently from ZANU PF. This nuances simplistic arguments about the politicisation of liberation history in Zimbabwe and the region, and points to complexity of other 'local initiatives of commemoration and memorialization' taking place, discussed in Chapter 1. I would maintain, however, that the political purchase of such efforts was often exactly due to the ruling party's obsession with 'chimurenga politics' (Chigumadzi 2018).

Introduction

the legacy of the struggle (Mujere et al. 2017; Mujere 2012: 204). While particular to Zimbabwe in its specific trajectory, there is much here in terms of the politics of remembering, celebrating and commemorating legacies of anti-colonial struggle that is mirrored around the region, in South Africa (Marschall 2010), Mozambique (Jopela 2017), Botswana (Gulbrandsen 2012), Malawi (Vaughan 2013), Namibia (Gewald 2004), Tanzania[14] and elsewhere. Through its enthusiastic adoption of the Southern African Development Community (SADC)-wide, UNESCO-sponsored[15] 'liberation heritage' project, National Museums and Monuments became increasingly involved in state commemoration, and has carried out excavations, exhumations, reburials and built monuments at former guerrilla camps in Mozambique, Zambia and other former 'frontline' states.

As discussed in Chapter 1, this 'liberation heritage' project not only matched ZANU PF's rhetoric of 'patriotic history' with NMMZ's need for state funding, as well as international trends redefining heritage and commemoration across the region, it was also a response to long-standing demands from war veteran groups, spirit mediums and relatives of the war dead, and even the unsettled dead themselves, for the return of human remains from anonymous graves across Zimbabwe's rural areas and former guerrilla camps in neighbouring countries. Over the last two decades there has been a proliferation of such demands, reflecting both the broader changing salience of human corporeality discussed above, and a complexity of diverse local interests and agendas which do not always perfectly match ZANU PF's political imperatives and rhetoric: including diverse war veteran groups pushing factional agendas; families haunted by the unsettled spirits of their dead; civilian survivors of war-time atrocities demanding recognition or compensation (Mujere et al. 2017); spirit mediums concerned about failing rains; and land occupiers seeking to (re-)establish land entitlements through appeals to 'autochthony' on resettled ancestral landscapes (Fontein 2011 & 2015). As noted by Mataga (2019: 277), while 'the public life of liberation heritage in Zimbabwe' illustrates how 'the conferment of official heritage status to spaces, sites, routes or personalities associated with liberation wars provides space for public performance of the state's narrative of the past

---

[14] Despite Tanzania's role during the 1960s–90s in hosting guerrilla armies and refugees from across the region, as well as the OAU Liberation Committee, its government was slow to get involved in liberation heritage. This changed in the 2010s, and the Dar es Salam building that housed the OAU Liberation Committee is now being turned into a Liberation Heritage Centre, while former camps across the country are now protected under heritage legislation (Fieldnotes, Tanzania, November/December 2015, May 2018).

[15] UNESCO's involvement in supporting liberation heritage projects around the region has not included supporting exhumations (Interview Chipunza, NMMZ, Field notes, 5/3/20).

… it also produces a fractured and highly contested heritage complex, stimulated by emergent counter practices that resist state-sponsored forms of memorialisation'.

In many cases exhumations have taken place without official permission and beyond the supervision of trained archaeologists from NMMZ or forensic scientists. Sometimes, such as when large war veteran groups have turned up unannounced at NMMZ's flagship heritage sites, like Great Zimbabwe, to carry out rituals or even to exhume dead guerrillas believed (erroneously) to be buried there, NMMZ and Zimbabwe's would-be vernacular exhumers have seemed at direct logger-heads. More often, however, NMMZ's archaeologists, war veterans and others have been caught up in complex relationships of ambivalent, mutual mis/trust and co-operation. This happened after NMMZ was instructed by government to intervene at the Chibondo exhumations in 2011, discussed in Chapter 3, but also at subsequent exhumations of mass graves in Rusape in 2013, at Guinea Fowl Mine in Mutare in 2014, at Herbert Mine and Matombo Six Mine in Mutasa district, and most recently at Odzi mine, elsewhere in Manicaland in 2019.[16] In Rusape in 2013, war veterans from the Fallen Heroes Trust (FHT) deliberately invited NMMZ to attend in order to 'legitimise' their exhumations, exposing tensions with archaeologists that lay only thinly below the surface of official proclamations of co-operation (Chipangura 2015; Mupira 2018).[17] Likewise during war veteran and local community-driven efforts to monumentalise two liberation-era massacre sites in Gutu in the early 2010s, desire for NMMZ's involvement and the public recognition this might bring, led to community-built structures being demolished and rebuilt (on two subsequent occasions) according to NMMZ's exacting 'professional' standards (Mujere et al. 2017).

Aside from such deliberate activities, however, there are also many cases of unidentified human remains re-appearing from hitherto undocumented mass graves and abandoned mines. Both such discoveries and the deliberate activities of war veterans, spirit mediums and relatives of the dead, have obliged government institutions to act, and in this context NMMZ's adoption of its 'liberation heritage' portfolio in the late 1990s can in part be understood as a response to the demands of relatives, living comrades, and even of the resurfacing bones and unsettled dead themselves. As Kundishora Tungamirai Chipunza (archaeologist and chief curator at NMMZ) put it, the

---

[16] Interview with Chipunza, NMMZ, Field notes, 5/3/20. See 'Rusape's Butcher camp relived' *Herald* 19/3/20; 'Heroes special: "The killing field of Mutare"' *Sunday Mail* 10/8/14; 'Govt. Fails to identify 114 exhumed bodies' *Newsday* 8/10/19.

[17] Field notes, 4/12/13; also NMMZ Preliminary report 'Rusape "Butcher" Site Exhumation Project', June 2013; NMMZ 'Technical Report on Work done at Rusape Butcher Site' November 2013.

Introduction

liberation heritage project was really just thrust upon us ... Liberation heritage is not covered by the National Museums Act of 1972, [so] there was no legislative framework for NMMZ to be involved in that ... we found it thrust upon us from different angles, including from the war vets, and from communities, who wanted to know where their dead were buried, and of course from government'.[18]

NMMZ's 'liberation heritage' activities have often appeared reactive to events already taking place, even if they, as with other national heritage organisations across the region, have embraced the notion of 'freedom' or 'liberation' heritage with deepening enthusiasm.

Although heightened over the last two decades, the issue of the return of the war dead has animated politicised debates about state commemoration in Zimbabwe since independence (Kriger 1995; Werbner 1998; Daneel 1995). Indeed, the demands for the return of war dead for proper (re)burial may have an even longer history. In his autobiography Wilfred Mhanda described how even during the war, guerrilla fighters felt it was important that the remains of an influential medium of Ambuya Nehanda, who died 'in exile' in Mozambique, be returned to Zimbabwe for burial before the struggle could be continued (2011). Chigumadzi relays a similar account of a group led by the spirit medium Chidyamauyu who went to Zambia in 1982 to recover the remains of a Nehanda medium with whom he worked during the war, 'fulfilling the spirit's wish that her remains be returned to the soil of the ancestors' (2018: 88–9). Some official reburials were carried out after independence in the 1980s and 1990s (Daneel 1995; Kriger 1995), but demands for such events intensified as Zimbabwe's political and economic situation worsened dramatically after the end of the 1990s.[19] During field work in rural Masvingo during the early 2000s (Fontein 2006a; 2015) – long before FHT exhumations and NMMZ's liberation heritage project gained widespread publicity – I frequently heard accounts of war veterans and families being disturbed by angry, unsettled spirits killed during the war. As explained in later chapters, this phenomena reflects the importance of conducting 'proper' burial and funeral rites through which dead people are transformed into benevolent ancestors, the failure of which can leave

[18] Interview with Chipunza, NMMZ, Field notes, 5/3/20.
[19] Many early efforts were thwarted. In the 1980s plans for a 'cleansing ceremony for war veterans ... in which material from the Rhodesian massacre site at Chimoio (Mozambique) would be brought to be buried at Great Zimbabwe' (Matenga 2011: 111) were scuppered after the violent eviction of the Nehanda medium, Ambuya Muchini (Fontein 2006a: 156–63). In 2011, war veterans and mediums visited Great Zimbabwe unannounced during journeys from Matopos and to former Mozambican camps causing problems for local NMMZ staff required to pass all requests to hold ceremonies at the site to head office.

the deceased as dangerously unsettled, angry spirits, and 'incomplete' ancestors (Bourdillon 1987b: 233–5; Werbner 1991: 151–6, 188–90).

These unhappy spirits are often said to haunt the 'nation' as a whole, and spirit mediums often complain that Zimbabwe's recurring droughts, economic and political crises, and even the AIDS pandemic, are due these unhappy spirits.[20] Their troubling presence can also intertwine with the politics of regionalism, 'traditional authority' and factional disputes between rival war veteran groups. For example, in April 2011, even as war veteran-led exhumations in northern Zimbabwe were attracting huge media attention, reports emerged of a visit 'by hundreds of [other] war veterans to the sacred Njelele shrine in Matobo', who 'wanted to rid themselves of "evil spirits" dating back to the liberation war', provoking the ire of both 'traditionalists from Matabeleland' and former ZIPRA (Zimbabwe People's Revolutionary Army, the armed wing of the Zimbabwe African Peoples Union) war veterans in that region, who complained that 'it is taboo to visit the at this time of year'. Even leaders of the dominant Zimbabwe National Liberation War Veterans Association 'distanced' themselves from that event, amid rumours that its true purpose was 'for a cleansing ceremony after … the bloody 2008 presidential election run-off', in order 'to get national ancestors to wash their bloodied hands and cursed spirits', dating not to the liberation struggle but much more recent political violence.[21]

This example illustrates how the perceived failure of official commemoration to respond to the demands of the war dead for proper (re)burial, can intertwine with the equally contentious history of hindered commemorations of other nationalist parties; especially in Matabeleland of Zimbabwe African People's Union (ZAPU)'s and ZIPRA's war dead (Alexander et al. 2000; Brickhill 1995) which continued despite the 1987 unity agreement, the incorporation of ZAPU history into ZANU PF's re-imagined rhetoric of 'patriotic history' during the 2000s (Ranger 2004a), and the 1999 burial of ZAPU's late leader Joshua Nkomo at National Heroes Acre.[22] For many

---

[20] '56 war vets reburied' *Daily News* 25/10/01; 'Mysterious deaths rock Kanyemba' *Sunday Mail* 3/6/08.

[21] 'War vets Njelele trip slammed' *Newsday* 29/4/11; 'Blood soaked war Vets' Njelele sacrilege' *Newsday* 2/5/11; War veterans fight over Njelele shrine' *Standard* 20/5/12.

[22] ZAPU's own commemorative efforts were deeply hindered by the confiscation of its war records in the early 1980s, despite the formation of the Mafela Trust to continue the work of its War Shrines Committee (Brickhill 1995). Since Nkomo's National Heroes Acre burial in 1999 there were repeated demands to exhume and rebury his remains in Entumbane (near King Mzilikazi's grave) or St Joseph's, where his mother was buried, in protest at ZANU PF's denigration of ZAPU's war legacy ('Plan to exhume Joshua Nkomo from National Heroes Acre' *ZimEye.net* 21/2/12; 'Joshua Nkomo's son wants his father exhumed from Heroes' Acre' *Zimdiaspora.com* 4/7/10, both accessed

Introduction

the legitimacy of ZANU PF's elitist heroes' commemorations continues to be deeply problematic due to such exclusions; worsened by its tendency to award hero status to younger ZANU PF loyalists with dubious liberation-era credentials.[23] Such continuing animosities about the recognition of national heroes was one of the grievances that provoked ZAPU's 2008 reformation.[24] Since then the issue of ZIPRA's war legacy and its dead re-emerged with particular salience, as demonstrated both by the Mafela Trust's renewed pressure for ZIPRA's war contributions to be recognised,[25] and by the furore that surrounded Joshua Nkomo's statue (see Figure 1), finally unveiled in Bulawayo in December 2013 after years of controversy.[26] For many the delays surrounding the erection of this monument epitomised the long-standing marginalisation of ZAPU's contribution to Zimbabwe's independence. Similarly (see Chapter 7) the shenanigans surrounding Robert Mugabe's burial in September 2019 powerfully illustrate the continuing salience of ZANU PF's politics of burial, albeit one that had turned in on itself, fuelled by its internalised factionalism after the 2017 'soft' coup had displaced not only Mugabe but also a swath of stalwarts associated with the so-called G40 group, and his second wife Grace.

Zimbabwe's politics of the dead, however, does not only revolve around the dead of the anti-colonial struggle, however disputed nationalist historiography and official commemorations have become. Zimbabwe's postcolonial milieu is also haunted by the victims of *postcolonial* violence.

19/6/12; 'Son wants Nkomo remains exhumed' *Standard* 3/7/12; 'MLF lobbies for Nkomo repatriation' *Newsday* 5/7/11).

[23] 'MPs attack selection of national heroes' *Daily News* 2/3/01; 'Zimbabwe needs an apolitical National Heroes Commission' *Zimbabwe Independent* 13/8/09; 'Redefine hero status conferment – MDC' *Zimnetradio.com* 7/8/09; 'Hero's acre must be closed' *Zimbabwe Times* 16/8/09; 'Broaden selection of national Heroes' *Standard* 8/8/09.

[24] In July 2009 'revived ZAPU officials wrestled control of a memorial service for former ZIPRA commander Ackim Ndlovu from Government officials, accusing ZANU PF leaders of hypocrisy', 'Parties Clash at Hero's Funeral' *Standard* 11/7/09; 'Ziyapa Moyo's family blasts ZANU PF' *Standar*, 6/2/10.

[25] 'ZAPU demands return of seized war records' *SW Radio Zimbabwe* 3/1/14; 'MDC official backs Zapu properties fight' *Newsday* 3/1/14.

[26] 'Joshua Nkomo supporters insulted by plans to put up his statues in Harare' *The Guardian* (UK – hereafter *Guardian*) 6/7/10; 'New twist in Joshua Nkomo statue saga' *Zimbabwe Independent* 17/4/11; 'Nkomo statues go up again' *Newzimbabwe.com* 14/5/11; 'No to Joshua Nkomo North Korean statue' *Newsday* 19/5/11; 'Govt fails to fund Nkomo statue' *Daily News* 21/11/11; 'Mugabe blames sanctions for Nkomo statue delay' *VOA Zimbabwe* 22/12/13; 'Mugabe honours man he "tried to kill"' *Newzimbabwe.com* 23/12/13; 'Mugabe's sincerity questioned as Nkomo statue unveiled' 23/12/13 *SW Radio Zimbabwe*; 'Nation honours Father Zimbabwe' *Herald* 23/12/13; 'Mysticism around Nkomo's Statue' *Financial Gazette* 19/9/13; 'Joshua Nkomo: Thin line between honour and dishonour' *Bulawayo24 News* 11/1/14.

The Politics of the Dead

FIGURE 1. Statue of Joshua Nkomo in Bulawayo (Author 2020)

This primarily takes two forms. Firstly, the escalating political violence by ZANU PF against opposition MDC supporters and civil society activists since 2000, and particularly during the 2008 elections (Sachikonye 2011; Solidarity Peace Trust – hereafter SPT – 2008a, 2008b; Masunungure 2009; Human Rights Watch 2008), manifest its own politics of the dead in the form of tortured, dismembered bodies, disappearances, disrupted funerals, avenging spirits, as well as alternative MDC registers of 'heroes'. This is discussed in more detail in Chapter 2. Just as newspapers over the last two decades have regularly reported new discoveries of mass graves and resurfacing bones from the liberation struggle, so too has there been a proliferation of reports of disappeared people, tortured bodies and the human remains of missing opposition activists re-appearing in odd places around the country. In the same way that ZAPU's efforts to deal with its war dead were long marginalised by ZANU PF's domination of state commemoration, so have the funerals of opposition supporters killed in

Introduction

political violence frequently been disrupted by ZANU PF supporters, police and war veterans.[27] In response, MDC factions established their own lists of heroes and commemorations,[28] even as ZANU PF ministers continued to challenge them to demonstrate their liberation struggle credentials.[29] This echoes the way that for many across Matabeleland, Lady Stanley Cemetery in Bulawayo has long been an alternative 'heroes acre' for ZAPU commemoration.[30] The rising cases of 'disappearances' alongside the brutal repression of public protests that have become a marked feature of President Mnangagwa's 'new' regime since Mugabe's removal from office in 2017, suggests the forms and motifs of postcolonial political violence established by ZANU PF under Mugabe have not been transformed, despite very deliberate efforts by the 'new dispensation' to present a 'softer face' to the international community.

Secondly, even more contentious than the tortured bodies of the last two decades, have been the unsettled legacies and resurfacing bones of the *gukurahandi* massacres in Matabeleland and the Midlands in the 1980s, when an estimated 20,000 civilians were killed by the notorious Fifth Brigade, during a reign of terror directed by the ruling ZANU PF against its minority rival ZAPU, under the auspices of rooting out 'dissidents' (Catholic Commission for Justice and Peace – hereafter CCJP – 2007; Eppel 2001, 2004, 2009; Alexander et al. 2000; Ranger 1999; Werbner 1991). This lasted from 1982 until 1987, when ZAPU was 'swallowed' into a unity pact with ZANU PF. It remains a massive scar on Zimbabwe's postcolonial milieu and a hugely sensitive topic. Community efforts to commemorate, rehabilitate, exhume and rebury victims in order to resolve deep legacies of violence amongst the living and the dead have long been obstructed by ZANU PF, just as ZAPU's war dead often remained un-commemorated (Alexander et al. 2000: 259–64). Even the

---

[27] 'Police bar memorial service' *Standard* 12/8/07; 'ZANU PF forcibly buries murambatsvina victim as police disrupt solidarity service' *Zimbabwean* 18/9/07; 'ZANU PF thugs disrupt MDC funeral in Harare' *SW Radio Africa* 22/5/08; 'MDC-T activists arrested at a funeral wake in Harare' *Zimbabwean* 20/5/11; 'Riot police and teargas at memorial for murdered MDC' *SW Radio Africa – swradioafrica.com* 6/4/11; 'Mutilated body found' *Herald* 11/6/08; 'MDC activist's decomposed body found' *Newzimbabwe.com* 20/6/08; 'CIO hid MDC activist's corpse' *Zimbabwemetro.com* 23/7/08; 'Ndira's mutilated body found in mortuary' *Zimbabwe Times* 24/5/08; 'MDC activist Ndira buried as another body is found in Goromonzi' *Zimbabwejournalists.com* 26/5/08; 'Abducted MDC-N director of elections found dead in Zhombe' *SW Radio Africa* 9/8/11; all accessed 19/6/20.

[28] 'MDC-T unveils own heroes' *Standard* 7/8/11; 'MDC-T commemorates own heroes in Bulawayo' SW Radio Africa 8/8/11, accessed 19/6/20; 'Speech by President Tsvangirai on the occasion of the memorial service and unveiling of the tombstones of heroes of democracy', MDC Information and Publicity Department, 6/4/11.

[29] 'Mohadi challenges MDC over hero status' *Newsday* 19/5/11.

[30] 'Lady Stanley Cemetery to be extended' *Newsday* 10/8/11.

AMANI Trust, which had some early success using Argentinian forensic expertise to quietly carry out exhumations and community reburials of *gukurahundi* remains in the late 1990s (Eppel 2001), were unable to continue after 2001 because of interferences and threats from the increasingly intolerant and belligerent ZANU PF government (Venis 2003).[31]

As the *gukurahundi* issue gained political salience in the late 2000s, members of the various MDC factions and other civil society groups increasingly deployed a rhetoric of *gukurahundi* for their own political purposes, particularly in disputes within the troubled Government of National Unity (GNU, 2009–13). This new 'politics of suffering' was often treated with great disdain among Ndebele activist groups in Bulawayo.[32] Meanwhile deepening concerns within ZANU PF's upper echelons about the increasing noise around *gukurahundi*'s unresolved legacies led to renewed historiographical efforts to justify the military operations in Matabeleland in the 1980s. In December 2012 ZANU PF's newspaper *The Patriot* carried a lengthy supplement detailing the violence of 'ZAPU dissidents' during that period. Claims earlier that year by Enos Nkala (a founding member of ZANU PF and Minister of Defence during the 1980s killings) that 'mass graves discovered in Matabeleland were not necessarily of Gukurahundi victims' had 'stirred a hornet's nest' as 'angry villagers ... described Nkala's remarks as offensive' and pointed out that 'survivors who were made to bury the victims after they were killed know the graves'. 'What made people to keep quiet about these issues was too much fear' claimed one unidentified respondent, 'but now that things are opening up' he continued, 'we can tell the nation where our brutally murdered relatives are buried'.[33]

Even as ZANU PF's top echelons became increasingly reticent about the issue, local government officials in Matabeleland sometimes acknowledged the significance of these unresolved deaths, occasionally turning a blind eye to localised efforts identify, exhume and rebury the *gukurahundi* dead. One of the difficulties faced by families of *gukurahundi* victims has been obtaining death certificates for disappeared relatives.[34] In the absence of formal legislation surrounding exhumations – because 'mass graves are not legal graves'[35] – some families were able to obtain formal burial orders, alongside less formal 'letters of no objection', which allowed them to exhume and then rebury their dead, and in turn get death certificates. This was one of the legal loopholes utilised by AMANI during their 'brief moment of opportunity' in the late 1990s, enabling some kind of 'official' permission for the exhumations and reburials they

---

[31] Field notes, 6/12/11.
[32] Ibid.
[33] 'Nkala remarks invite backlash' *Newsday* 21/2/12.
[34] Interview with Shari Eppel, 6/12/11.
[35] Ibid.

Introduction

carried out before 2001. Often such informal or even verbal permission was granted directly to families, 'because they [local officials] recognised that these were real problems', but they never granted written authority, 'nor would they have given permission to NGOs' directly.[36] Some *gukurahundi* reburials also took place under the auspices of liberation heritage in the mid-2000s, but as one senior NMMZ employee explained, this was 'never talked about' because 'people are afraid to open old wounds ... especially ... because at one point nearly the whole of Matabeleland was MDC'.[37] Reports in 2011 that Matobo district council had approved the construction of a *gukurahundi* memorial at Bhalagwe camp (where mass graves from that period are known to exist), reflected both the growing salience of the issue and perhaps a weakening of central ZANU PF influence in the region at the time but also, possibly, growing courage among local government officials.[38] The fact that a year later, in March 2012, the central government refused permission for the Bhalagwe memorial to go ahead illustrates how ZANU PF's obstruction of any *gukurahundi* commemoration continued despite the ever-growing calls for the issue to be properly addressed.[39] In fact, as seen in Chapter 7, attempts to hold commemorations and construct memorials at Bhalagwe in particular, have continued to be highly contentious even after Mnangagwa's 2019 announcement that *gukurahundi* commemorations, truth-telling and exhumations would now be permitted.[40]

The prominence of the deeply troubling *gukurahundi* legacies was heightened by increasing calls across the 2000s for the issue to be attended to. The imposed silence surrounding what Mugabe himself (at Joshua Nkomo's funeral in 1999) had obfuscated as a 'moment of madness' became very noisy. This occurred in the wake of the MDC's growing support in the region after 2000, ZAPU's 2008 revival and the ineffectual 'Organ for National Healing' established by GNU. A host of new pressure groups and websites commemorating *gukurahundi* emerged calling for formal apologies, justice and resolution.[41] As a result of this growing

[36] Ibid.
[37] Field notes, 2006.
[38] 'Go-ahead for Gukurahundi monument' *swradioafrica.com* 1/3/11, accessed 19/6/20.
[39] 'Govt turns down application for Gukurahundi monument' *radiovop.com* 13/3/12 accessed 19/6/20.
[40] Interview with Mbuso Fuzwayo, 12/3/20; Interview with Shari Eppel, 11/3/20. Social media reports circulating in March 2019 indicated that a memorial erected at Bhalagwe the year before was destroyed by suspected ZANU PF agents.
[41] For example the Matabeleland Freedom Party ('Gukurahundi graves are "war crime sites"' *ZWNEWS* 18/7/09), the Mthwakazi Liberation Front ('Discovered 280 remains not victims of Rhodesian war: MLF' *Zimdiaspora.com* 19/3/11), and the Mthwakazi Action Group on Genocide in Matabeleland and Midlands

public pressure the massacres were finally recognised as a 'genocide' by *Genocide Watch* in 2010.[42] Yet despite (or perhaps because of) the dramatic increase in public demands for the *gukurahundi* issue to be dealt with, particularly from a younger generation of Ndebele activists and separatist movements, senior ZANU PF ministers continued throughout the GNU years (2009–13) to refuse to engage with such demands, arguing that the *gukurahundi* was a 'closed chapter'.[43] Two government reports on killings in Matabeleland in the 1980s – the Dumbutshena Report on the so-called 'Entumbane Uprising' of 1980/81, and the Chihambakwe report on the 'Matabeleland disturbances' 1983/84 – have still not been released.[44] And popular efforts to raise the issue continued to be forcefully quashed; as happened, for example, when Owen Maseko's art exhibition was closed down in 2010, or when Moses Mzila-Ndlovu, GNU co-minister for 'national healing' (and member of the smaller MDC-N) was jailed for a month in 2011 for attending a church service commemorating the *gukurahundi* in Lupane.[45]

(MAGGEMM – 'Gukurahundi memorial website launched' *Zimbabwemetro. com* 30/5/08, accessed 19/6/20). 'Dabengwa wants "unqualified apology"' *Nehandaradio.com* 12/8/09; 'Dabengwa says Mugabe must apologise' *Zimbabwe Times* 12/5/09; 'Push to classify Gukurahundi as genocide' *ZWNews* 8/6/09; 'Nkala denies contributing to Gukurahundi, wants Mugabe prosecuted' *swradioafrica. com* 18/12/09; 'Msika speaks out on Gukurahundi' *Standard* 15/10/06; 'Moyo says Gukurahundi Bill ready by September' *Zim Online* 16/5/07; 'Gukurahundi fears split Zanu' *Standard* 29/4/07; 'Calls for Gukurahundi justice' SW Radio Africa 14/11/11); online sources accessed 19/6/20.

[42] 'Zimbabwe: Gukurahundi finally classified as genocide by leading experts' *SW Radio Africa* 15/9/10, accessed 24/9/19. The campaign for gukurahundi to be classified a genocide made the argument that its purpose had been to annihilate the political opposition represented by ZAPU. Interview with Strike Mklanda, 12/3/20; Interview with Mbuso Fuzwayo, 12/3/20; Interview with Shari Eppel, 11/3/20. See also 'Gukurahundi was a political strategy with a genocidal outcome – Sipho Malunga', 28/11/18, see www.cite.org.zw/gukurahundi-was-political-not-ethnic-malunga, accessed 1/4/20.

[43] 'Gukurahundi, closed chapter – Charamba' *Daily News* 7/10/11; 'Mnangagwa wades into gukurahundi row' *www.new.zimbabwe.com* 18/7/11, accessed 19/6/20; 'Mnangagwa: Gukurahundi wounds have not healed' *Zimbabwe Independent* 21/7/11; 'ZANU(pf) desperate to stop probe' *Zimbabwean* 29/7/11;

[44] Interview with Mbuso Fazwayo, 12/3/20; 'Gukurahundi inquiry reports lost' *Newsday* 19/4/19.

[45] See 'Supreme Court readies itself for artist Owen Maseko's case' *Sokwanele*, www.sokwanele.com/thisiszimbabwe/archives/6505, accessed 28/6/12; 'I will not be silenced, vows artist' *Standard* 10/4/10; also 'Anti-gukurahundi activist survives abduction attempt in Bulawayo' *Zimdiaspora.com* 11/4/10; 'Gukurahundi playwright arrested in Lupane' radiovop.com 31/3/12; 'MDC Minister traumatised by Lupanne detention horror' SW Radio Africa 26/4/11; 'Minister acquitted of Gukurahundi case' radiovop.com 16/5/12); online sources accessed 19/6/20.

Introduction

The legacies of the *gukurahundi* continue to fester, perhaps more than ever. Although some *gukurahundi* sites are known, many are not. People across Matabeleland continue to complain that their lives are marred by the unsettled *gukurahundi* dead and the unresolved legacies of these atrocities (Eppel 2001; Werbner 1991). Like the mass graves of the liberation struggle, *gukurahundi* bones and graves continued to be discovered.[46] One example came in 2011 when human bones resurfaced from a football pitch at a Lupane school.[47] Pressure to allow *gukurahundi* exhumations, reburials and commemorations continued across the 2010s but were usually met with a firm rebuttal by the Harare government. Although some exhumations did take place, more often such efforts were immediately blocked by police.[48]

It is therefore enormously significant that some recent signs suggest that the new Mnangagwa government may be keen to find resolution to this immensely problematic past: by finally signing the National Peace and Resolution Bill in 2018, establishing the National Peace and Reconciliation Commission (NPRC) and by various 2019 announcements that *gukurahundi* commemorations and exhumations should now go ahead.[49] This recent turn of events is discussed in the last chapter. Some public 'hearings' and exhumations have already taken place.[50] Nevertheless, and very understandably, many in Matabeleland and the Midlands remain

---

[46] 'We want to know where our loved ones are buried' Letters, *Daily News* 3/9/01; 'Give us money not treatment: Gukurahundi survivors' radiovop.com 23/5/11; 'Mass graves from Gukurahundi era located in Matabeleland' *SW Radio Africa* 19/10/05; 'Evidence of "dirty war" lies far below' *Zimbabwe Independent* 29/9/00; 'Film reveals horror details of Ndebele massacre' *Nation* (Kenya) 11/11/07; 'Tracking down a massacre' *BBC news* 7/5/08; online sources accessed 19/6/20.

[47] 'Suspected fresh Gukurahundi remains discovered in Lupane' *Newsday* 11/8/11; '60 bodies in school mass grave' *Newzimbabwe.com* 5/10/11, accessed 19/6/20; 'Mass graves found at police training camp' *Zimbabwean*, 27/1/12.

[48] 'Youths defy govt, bury Gukurahundi victim remains' *Daily News* 24/3/13; 'Gukurahundi victims won't be re-buried, Govt. Says' *Zimbabwe Focus* 13/10/13; 'Government urged to rebury Victims of Gukurahundi Massacres' *Zimbabwean* 15/10/13; 'Commemorating Gukurahundi' OSISA 17/1/14; 'Mugabe's death not regretted before Gukurahundi apology' *Bulawayo24 News* 19/1/14; 'The case for the reburial of Gukurahundi Genocide Victims' *Bulawayo24 News* 19/1/14; 'Outrage as police bar Gukurahundi prayer meeting' *SW Radio Africa* 21/1/14; 'Police Block another Gukurahundi Memorial' *SW Radio Africa* 4/3/14; online sources accessed 19/6/20. Also Fieldnotes 18/12/13, 5–6/12/11.

[49] 'ED pledges support for Gukurahundi victims' *Standard* 24/3/19; 'Govt to facilitate Gukurahundi exhumations, reburials' *Newsday* 10/4/19; 'NPRC starts consultations on Gukurahundi atrocities' *Daily News* 16/4/19; 'Zimbabwe has started exhuming the remains of those killed in a massacre in the 1980s' *SBS News* 1/5/19.

[50] Field notes, March 2020; 'Gukurahundi exhumations process starts' *Bulawayo Chronicle* 10/3/20.

deeply suspicious. This is particularly because Mnangagwa is personally implicated in the atrocities, which took place when he was Minister of State Security; not to mention his previous assertions that the killings were 'an act of "self-defense" on the part of the "Zimbabwean people"' (cf. Chigumadzi 2018: 101, 133). For many, Mnangagwa's deliberate reversal of ZANU PF's long-held policy of obstructing and silencing all attempts to deal with the legacies of *gukurahundi* has much to do with his own (perceived or real) culpability in the atrocities, and his efforts to present his administration as a moderate, reformed government, keen to re-engage the international community, rather than any genuine desire to resolve this deeply problematic aspect of Zimbabwe's postcolonial past.

References to the *gukurahundi* and its continuing unresolved legacies loom large throughout this book, as they do in Zimbabwean postcolonial politics. They are an essential part of Zimbabwe's politics of the dead. But this is not primarily a book about the *gukurahundi*, nor is there a chapter devoted to it. There is no way this book could do justice to the enormity or complexity of this issue, or to the many thousands of people, young and old, relatives and the dead who have and are still suffering its affects. The *gukurahundi* deserves its own book, or indeed several, based on grounded, in-depth and long-term research across Matabeleland North and South, and the Midlands. There is neither space here, nor am I the right person to write this. There are many other researchers, in Matabeleland and elsewhere, better placed to do this work, some of whom have been quietly collecting data, or waiting patiently to do so,[51] in order to carry out exhumations and reburials in a more conducive time and context that will enable a more authoritative and empathetic reckoning with the past. Given the attention now, at last, being drawn to this enormous unresolved issue, that time may be approaching. It is urgent and long awaited. I hope that the insights offered in this book are useful to the important work that remains to be done.

---

[51] Alongside new generation of Ndebele activists there is a new generation of scholars devoted to this subject. See Nompilo Ndlovu 2019 'The Gukurahundi "Genocide": Memory and Justice in Independent Zimbabwe' Doctoral Thesis, University of Cape Town, https://open.uct.ac.za/bitstream/handle/11427/30431/thesis_hum_2019_ndlovu_nompilo.pdf?sequence=1&isAllowed=y, accessed 1/4/20; Cynthia Chigwenya, 2019 'Can we borrow peace building mechanisms? An examination of Zimbabwe's National Peace and Reconciliation Act, juxtaposed with Rwanda's Organic Law of 2001', Hons Dissertation (University of Johannesburg); Aaron Rwadzi 'Whose fault was it anyway? Gukurahundi (1982–1987) and the politics of blame and denial', www.researchgate.net/publication/330900743_Whose_fault_was_it_anyway_Gukurahundi_1982-1987_and_the_politics_of_blame_and_denial, accessed 1/4/20; Isheanesu Gusha 2019 'Memories of gukurahundi massacre and the challenge of reconciliation', www.scielo.org.za/pdf/she/v45n1/10.pdf, accessed 1/4/20.

Introduction

The power of uncertainty

Zimbabwe's politics of the dead discussed in this book is therefore deeply animated both by the bones of past (colonial and postcolonial) massacres, resurfacing from shallow and mass graves around the country and across international borders, and by the tortured bodies of much more recent political violence, mainly by ZANU PF supporters against Zimbabwe's MDC opposition parties since 2000. Moreover, this politics of the dead is deeply animated by the spirits of the dead themselves, as deeply frightening *ngozi* [Shona] spirits or ambivalent ghosts, whose presence is intimately intertwined with the 'affective presence' and 'emotive materiality' of bones, bodies and human substances. As developed in Chapter 2, these are linked through the simultaneously symbolic and material processes whereby people, living and dead, are properly constituted, and the proper ritual and material processes through which people are made safely dead. In this respect the resurfacing bones of people killed in the war or during the 1980s, the leaky, tortured bodies and disrupted funerals of people killed much more recently, and the frightening presence of unsettled *ngozi* spirits, all reveal and manifest the transgression of normal and normalising processes where by people (living and dead) are constituted, and the living transformed into benevolent ancestors, and sometimes avenging spirits. Moreover, this dynamic shapes the corporeal forms that political violence can take, so that a comparison between what resurfacing bones from troubled pasts do politically, and what leaky bodies from much more recent events do, is instructive for what it reveals about how violence is efficacious. It is also in this context that exhumations and reburials are often understood, across very different registers of meaning and practice (Renshaw 2010, 2011; Crossland 2000; Eppel 2001), as forms of healing or commemoration – a way to make people safely dead, or to 'feed' (Rowlands 1999: 144), 'atone for' or 'finish the work of' the dead (Küchler 1999: 55).

Yet even where there is general agreement about the socially cathartic potential of exhumations, these processes are often unusually problematic (Renshaw 2010) and enormously contested. The exhumations and reburials of NMMZ's liberation heritage project have been subject to the rivalries of competing forms of 'expertise', as spirit mediums, church leaders, war veterans, archaeologists and others, each with their own perspectives, loyalties, interpretations and practices; reflecting the diversity of changing repertoires and epistemologies of death and corporeality that are in play. And as with many programmes of so-called 'transitional justice' (Baines 2010: 413–7; Lynch 2018), or 'truth and reconciliation' (e.g. South Africa – Hamber & Wilson 2002), local manifestations of larger (global or national) level interventions can have little resonance amongst ordinary people, or can be subject to the influence of government elites, or be problematically set against 'purportedly universal' legal standards, thereby ignoring local cultural, social and political complexities and specificities.

This is particularly the case where the identity of the dead and the manner of their deaths is uncertain, which is extremely common in post-conflict exhumations. Even in the exhumations of mass graves at Chimoio, Nyadzonya, Freedom Camp, and other former guerrilla camps in Zambia and Mozambique, where the political identity of the dead and the manner of their deaths was hardly in much dispute, the complex legacies of internal factionalisms, rebellions and betrayal that marred Zimbabwe's nationalist movements during the 1960s and 1970s continue to animate its contested histories (cf. Mhanda 2011), and are reflected in the rivalries that inevitably emerge between different actors involved in exhumations. Differentiating between the remains of freedom fighters, Rhodesian soldiers, mercenaries, the African auxiliaries who fought with them, civilians killed by them, and those killed by guerrillas as 'rebels' or 'sell outs', amongst the mass graves of the liberation struggle, is a problem that has long beset commemoration in Zimbabwe, as even President Mugabe himself acknowledged in the early 1980s (Kriger 1995: 144; Ranger 2010a).

By the same measure, exhumations within Zimbabwe can be much more problematic exactly because of intense uncertainties about whether such exhumed remains date from the liberation struggle or different episodes of ZANU PF-instigated violence since independence. This was exemplified at the Chibondo exhumations in Mt Darwin in 2011, discussed in Chapter 3, which were shown to thousands of visitors, reporters and school children bussed to site, reported on extensively in the state media, and broadcast repeatedly on state television, in what many saw as a grotesque performance of 'patriotic history'. Here the ambivalent materialities of the human remains being disinterred provoked profound controversy about the identity of the dead, the manner of their deaths, and who was responsible for them, which meant that frictions between different ways of reconstituting the past and remaking the dead came sharply to the foreground. Tensions between those calling for 'scientific' forms of archaeological and forensic exhumation, and others defending the use of 'African' methods of divination and spirit possession to identify the dead, in particular, animated debates between war veteran exhumers, opposition and minority parties, and human rights activists, which played out through the media, often leaving NMMZ in an awkward position in between. The indeterminacies of the human materials being exhumed and the profound uncertainties they provoked, on which these debates turned, may have afforded, if only for a short time, an opportunity for ZANU PF to simultaneously reinforce its rhetoric of 'patriotic history' and remind everyone of their capacities for violence. In the end, however, these uncertainties were excessive to any political utility derived from the opportunity to exploit the tensions between the

Introduction

reinforcement of particular liberation legacies and re-assertions of necropolitical sovereignty, and therefore required the contingent containment and stabilisation that reburial in a new state memorial offered.

The arguments I develop in this book make sense of the intense controversies surrounding Zimbabwe's politics of the dead in terms of the excessive potentialities of human remains – what Pinney (2005) calls the 'torque' of human substances – which demands yet ultimately defies the stabilisation of human stuff into recognisable objects and identifiable subjects. This argument about the demanding yet defying uncertainties and profound indeterminacies of human remains both exemplifies why exhumation and reburial are often demanded as cathartic and healing processes – because of the promise of stabilisation, resolution and a 'final' remaking of the dead that they offer – and why these processes can in the end never be entirely complete; that there can be no entirely final 'closure'. Indeed, it is conceivable that were the diverse demands for exhumations and reburials in Zimbabwe ever met – until very recently, an extremely unlikely scenario – the troubling legacies of past violence would still remain for many unresolved and unforgotten, or at least retain the potentiality to return again to unsettle the present in new forms and contexts; just as ancestors, ghosts and unhappy *ngozi* spirits can always cross generations to afflict the present with new or unknown unresolved pasts.

The uncertainty of human substances reflects, in the end, the uncertainty that all death instigates, exactly because death brings the indeterminate and uneasy mutual dependencies of bodies and spirit, presence and absence, matter and meaning, material and immaterial existence, even life and death, to the foreground and leaves them ultimately unresolved. Such ontological uncertainties are amplified by the epistemological uncertainties provoked by the contested co-existence of different, changing repertoires of death and transforming funerary practices, in shifting historical, political and social contexts. Indeed, death in Zimbabwe nearly always provokes debate, controversy and rumours of foul play and the occult. Very rarely is it considered 'natural' and unproblematic. As a result, funerals often become very contested events. In a sense death always remains potentially incomplete (Nyamnjoh 2017a), uncertain and unfinished, and therefore open to enduring or recurring rumour, controversy and dispute.

This is exemplified by frequent controversies that surround the (unusually common) 'accidental' deaths of politicians, army officers and other public figures within ZANU PF, which have often provoked a fraught myriad of rumour and conspiracy about the ruling party 'eating their own'.[52] This is particularly the case because such 'political accidents' have produced an unusual proportion of 'national heroes', an observation frequently noted by critics and commentators. This is the subject of Chapter 4,

---

[52] 'Mystery surrounds deaths of national heroes' *Nehandaradio.com* 15/8/12, accessed 19/6/20.

The Politics of the Dead

which uses the controversial death of retired General Solomon Mujuru (the then Vice-President, Joice Mujuru's husband, long-time confidante of President Mugabe, and former ZANLA commander and chief of the army) in a mysterious fire in August 2011, as a way into exploring the efficacies of rumours surrounding what I call 'political accidents'.

As with the controversies provoked by Chibondo's indeterminate human materials, the rumours and conspiracy that surround the 'accidental' deaths of public figures can afford political opportunity, forged in the uneasy space between the celebration of 'national heroes' and the assertions of hierarchical necro-political sovereignty. Building on Mbembe's work (2001, 2003), the power of uncertainty that I pursue in Chapter 4 suggests that political actors may have much to gain from being associated with (but never formally held culpable of) such unresolved 'political accidents', illustrating how the indeterminacies of rumour can be a fundamental feature of the stylistics of postcolonial power. But the useful 'affordances' of rumours surrounding the unexplained deaths of public figures are not entirely divorce-able from the profound ontological uncertainties that all death can precipitate, especially in the context of rapidly changing, multiple regimes of death across the region. These uncertainties defy the ultimate containment, stabilisation, or 'fixing' of definitive narratives, and any final 'remaking' of the dead into 'heroes', 'victims' or 'ancestors'; and they easily 'leak' the confounds of space and time, as leaky bodies and troubling ghosts contaminate the troubled landscapes of militia camps, mass graves and car wrecks; and as unhappy, avenging spirits return to afflict kin across generations; or as new witness accounts, or even new confessions to murder (cf. White 2003), appear at odd moments, defying normative narratives and regulated temporalities.

All this points to the potential excessiveness of death itself, its open-ended incompleteness, and its profound lack of finality and closure. Death, it seems, is rarely entirely finished with, and this has important implications for the politics of the dead in Zimbabwe and elsewhere, and particularly for the potential for 'resolution' and 'closure' often assumed to be offered by commemorations, exhumations and reburials, or indeed by public inquests and 'truth' commissions. It is by pointing to the productive yet risky indeterminacies of matter and meaning, that death and human corporeality reveal how the power of uncertainty is, in many respects, constitutive of postcolonial politics and power.

Sources and structure of the book

The arguments developed here are mainly (but not exclusively) drawn from field, archival and secondary research between 2000 (when I began doctoral research in rural Masvingo, Southern Zimbabwe) and 2015,

Introduction

when I began another ongoing research project in Nairobi, Kenya. During that period, I conducted two large research projects in rural Masvingo, looking at the politics of heritage and landscape around Great Zimbabwe (Fontein 2006a), and at the political materialities of land and water in the context of Fast Track Land Reform around Lake Mutirikwi (2015). It was during these other projects that the idea for this book emerged, and much (but not all) of its material was collected. Collaborative fieldwork with Joseph Mujere and Munyaradzi Sagiya in December 2013, focusing on war veteran-led, community efforts to monumentalise two liberation-era massacre sites in Gutu district (Mujere et al. 2017) also fed into this project, as did several shorter research visits in late December 2014 – January 2015, August 2015 and March 2020.

This book makes use of a lot of documentary materials in the form of newspaper articles, NGO reports and other written sources, in critical engagement with ethnographic and interview data collected over many years of fieldwork and research in, on and across Zimbabwe. Obviously, the use of such a plethora of different sources requires critical nuance. In the context of Zimbabwe's long political and economic crises, its media landscape – as well as its NGO and parastatal sectors – have been marked by sharp polarisations and we should hesitate to take any individual report at face value. I have, therefore, tried to be thorough and critical in my use of documentary sources, in much the same way as I also do for ethnographic and interview data. In most cases, when discussing widely publicised events I have deliberately relied on a proliferation of diverse sources, from different sides of Zimbabwe's media divides, because I am interested in developing an empirically thick understanding and interpretation of the phenomena being reported on. Very rarely have I relied upon singular interpretations offered by particular media, or NGOs, or individuals. Where singular reports, commentaries or statements are used, they are contextualised (in much the same way as interview and other ethnographic data is) because the status, history, political or professional positionality of particular people and organisations is obviously significant. What I do not offer is a systematic discursive analysis of different kinds of media or NGO reporting. Other scholars have done this to much greater effect already (Mukasa 2003; Rønning 2003; Moyo 2005; Melber et al. 2004; Mpofu 2014; Chuma 2005).[53] Rather I use material collected from diverse documentary and ethnographic sources to make my own interpretations, very often based on my own long history of fieldwork in Zimbabwe, and my familiarity with secondary academic literature about it. This is particularly true in Chapter 5 on the controversies that surrounded Solomon Mujuru's death in 2011, but also Chapter 6,

---

[53] I am grateful to Blessing Vava for these links (personal communication – hereafter pers. com. – 31/3/20).

which discusses the controversial case of the so-called 'diesel *n'anga*' in 2007. Because rumours, stories and what they *do* are exactly part of what is under consideration, very often the veracity of any particular report is less relevant, and sometimes much less significant, than the fact that the report exists amid, and contributing to, a wide plethora of reporting on particular events. In a sense, therefore, I take a 'thick description' approach – in both the manner that Geertz intended, that is as 'interpretation', but also in the more everyday sense of empirical thoroughness – to documentary, ethnographic and secondary materials about the multi-faceted, diverse cultural-political phenomena that I call Zimbabwe's politics of the dead.

I have structured this book into seven chapters. The first explores the ambiguous agency of bones as both 'persons' and 'objects' in the politics of heritage and commemoration in Zimbabwe. It discusses how the emergence of 'liberation heritage' as a new 'commemorative' project adopted by Zimbabwe's NMMZ in the late 1990s, shifted focus from precolonial archaeology onto the identification, reburial, and memorialisation of the human remains of the liberation war dead at former guerrilla bases and battles sites within Zimbabwe and across its borders. Although related to the ruling party's rhetoric of 'patriotic history' (Ranger 2004a), this 'liberation heritage' project also drew on wider, UNESCO-sponsored efforts to identify, define, celebrate and preserve so-called 'African Freedom Heritage' across the region. At the same time, NMMZ has attempted to be responsive to highly localised and increasingly salient critiques of previous state-driven commemorative projects, so that 'liberation heritage' often sits awkwardly in the middle of two related but distinct nationalist projects of the past: heritage and commemoration.

Exploring the tensions that both commemorative and heritage processes can provoke between the 'objectifying' effects of professional practices, the reworkings of contested 'national' histories, and the often angry demands of marginalised communities, kin and the dead themselves, the central argument developed here, setting up the arguments pursued in following chapters, is that the politics of the dead is not exhausted by contested representations of past deaths, but is rather intertwined with the 'emotive materiality' and 'affective presence' of human bones in themselves. Engaging with recent anthropological discussions about materiality and the 'agency' of objects, as articulated in the work of Alfred Gell (1998), Bruno Latour (1999) and others, it is suggested that both as extensions of the dead (as avenging *ngozi* spirits, rain-providing ancestors or other kinds of spirit 'subjects' making demands on the living), and as unconscious 'objects', 'things' or 'materials' retorting to and provoking responses from the living, bones in Zimbabwe not only challenge normative processes of state commemoration and heritage, but also animate a myriad of personal, kin, clan, class and political loyalties

Introduction

and struggles. And it is through this dual and ambiguous agency of bones, both as extensions of the dead and as unconscious 'things' that the contradictions of commemoration, heritage and the politics of the dead in Zimbabwe are revealed.

Chapter 2 is about the corporeal dimensions of violence and examines how Zimbabwe's politics of the dead does not only circulate around the troubling presence of resurfacing bones and unsettled spirits marking the unresolved legacies of its liberation struggle or of the *gukurahundi* massacres of the 1980s in Matabeleland and the Midlands. Political violence since 2000 indicates that it is not only dry bones but also the fleshy materiality of tortured bodies that are entangled in Zimbabwe's troubled postcolonial milieu. Here I explore and contrast the complexity of agencies entangled in the affective presence and emotive materiality of both bones and bodies in Zimbabwe. Focusing particularly on the violence of 2008 (Sachikonye 2011), and the new 'corporeal' politics of disrupted funerals, denied burials, disappeared or dumped bodies that accompanied it, this chapter examines how violence against the living is materially and symbolically linked to violence against the dead. Engaging particularly with Ingold's critique (2007) of materiality in favour of proper exploration of the flows, properties and transformations of materials, I argue that violence against the living and the dead is linked through the simultaneously symbolic/material processes whereby people, living and dead, are properly constituted, and the proper ritual and material processes through which they are made safely dead. Resurfacing bones, leaky tortured bodies, and disrupted funerals of people killed much more recently, as well as the frightening presence of the unsettled dead as *ngozi* spirits, all manifest the transgression of normal/normalising processes whereby people (living and dead) are constituted and transformed, revealing both how the efficacy of violence in the present is often inherently related to its corporeal forms, but also why in the wake of lethal violence, exhumations and reburials are often understood, across very different registers of meaning and practice, as forms of healing, resolution or commemoration.

This sets the scene for Chapter 3's focus on the controversies that surrounded the highly publicised, war veteran-led exhumations at Chibondo in northern Zimbabwe in 2011, the most high profile of a series of such events which have continued to take place. Apart from the grotesque displays of human remains involved, and the crude politicking around them, this chapter discusses how fraught questions about the identity of the dead and the manner of their deaths, and who has sovereignty over them – i.e. by whom and how they should exhumed and reburied – were provoked by the excessive potentialities of the human substances being exhumed; by their profoundly evocative and affective, yet unstable, uncertain, and ultimately indeterminate materialities. I focus on how the stinking, intermingling, leaky, half-decaying bodies and bodily substances being disinterred and separated – being remade imperfectly and contingently into particular kinds of 'political bodies/subjects' – both demand and enable, and yet ultimately defy the very reconstitution of the dead and past lives, and the complex politics of commemoration in which they are entangled. The uncertainties of these remains may have afforded a particular political utility, allowing ZANU PF for a time to both celebrate their 'liberation legacies' and remind everyone of their capacities for coercion and violence. Yet ultimately they were unsustainable. By the end of the year the exhumations had been stopped, the remains reburied and the mine sealed off. If the resurgence of recent scholarly interest in death across the region has increasingly recognised that the transforming materialities of bodies and lives matter, then the Mt Darwin exhumations illustrate, I suggest, how human remains exemplify the excessive potentialities of stuff, and how the 'alterity of an enfleshed world' (Pinney 2005) defies easy reading, and therefore makes possible the very politics of uncertainty and (un)becoming in which they are entwined.

Chapter 4 uses the death of retired General Solomon Mujuru in a mysterious fire in August 2011 as a way into exploring the efficacies of rumours that surround what I call 'political accidents'. While Zimbabwe's postcolonial milieu has long been punctuated by the controversial deaths of public figures, dating back to the still unresolved deaths of Herbert Chitepo and Josiah Tongogara in the 1970s, Mujuru's mysterious demise is useful for further substantiating arguments developed in the preceding chapters, because a substantial part of the inquest that followed turned on questions about how to interpret Mujuru's desiccated remains, amid continuing family demands for them to be exhumed and re-examined. This again illustrates how proliferating rumour and dissent can turn on the indeterminacy of corporeal substances. My main purpose, however, is to explore such 'accidental' deaths in terms of the intertwined epistemological, ontological and social/political uncertainties that all deaths in Zimbabwe can provoke. I argue that 'political accidents' are particular kinds of death that exemplify the uncertain incompleteness that can surround all death. Their key elements include the high-profile (usually ZANU PF) status of the 'victim', which is then cemented through burial at National Heroes Acre, and the apparently 'accidental' nature of the death (often car accidents, but not always) which remains subject to unresolved controversy amid a plethora of continuing rumours of assassination, party factionalism, and malign intent. These rumours are never stabilised into any singular authoritative account. Where public inquiries have been held, as with Mujuru's death, they have managed neither to demonstrate that malign intent was involved (let alone identify responsibility), nor to successfully establish public confidence in the 'accidental' nature of the death. I argue that such high-profile deaths are nearly

Introduction

always left indeterminate and unfinished, and they would lose their political saliency if they were ever fixed. The uncertainty that surrounds them is key to their efficacy.

Chapters 5 and 6 continue to explore the uncertain and unfinished incompleteness of death by reconsidering the political significance of ancestors and spirit mediums in post-2000 Zimbabwe. Here I develop an approach implicit in the previous chapters, which demands that ethnographic accounts of spirit encounters, whether ancestral possession events, divination, frightening cases of witchcraft, or angry *ngozi* spirits – and although I do not focus upon it, we could perhaps include ecstatic Christian experience in this list – are not reduced to 'social functionality', 'mimesis' or 'cultural texts' in anthropological analysis in order to fully grasp their experiential, ontological and political dimensions. In particular I question assumptions often carried in scholarship on spirit possession about the over-determinations common to mediumship, by emphasising the uncertainties inherent to possession that confront not only politicians and others seeking ancestral legitimacy or guidance, but also mediums themselves.

These chapters use two very different case studies to explore the uncertainties and precarities inherent to mediumship and spirit possession, and the serious consequences as well as opportunities these can have for mediums. The first, in Chapter 5, is the famous story of the so-called 'diesel *n'anga*'; a spirit medium who in 2007 courted public controversy and government ministers with her claims to be able to procure refined diesel from rocks. The second, discussed in Chapter 6, is that of Mai Melissa in rural Masvingo District, and her emergent possession by her own dead father, Sekuru Shorty, before her own death from an AIDS-related illness in 2007. If the diesel *n'anga* story achieved great publicity, news coverage and notoriety across Zimbabwe in the late 2000s, then that of Mai Melissa is unheard of outside of a very small and particular family circle in rural Masvingo. And yet it probably reflects much more common everyday experiences of spirit possession across parts of rural Zimbabwe. Both the case of Rotina Mavhunga (the diesel *n'anga*) and that of Mai Melissa illustrate how the uncertainties of performance, agency and authenticity at the heart of mediumship turn, in many respects, exactly on the unfinished, incomplete and indeterminate nature of death.

While earlier chapters examined how the excessivities of human corporeality – which we could understand as a kind of 'alterity' – animates their profound indeterminacy, so that processes of determination, constitution and stabilisation (of 'remaking the dead') are inherently incomplete, imperfect and contingent; and if this profound uncertainty can muster political traction in ways that imbricate human corporealities with the productive/duplicitous affects of rumours, then the argument presented here points less to the 'alterity' of the material than to the 'alterity' of spirit and the immaterial. In other words, there is an 'otherness' to the immaterial remnants of past lives that matches the 'torque' of corporeality, and similarly demands but always defies processes of stabilisation, fixing and determination, accentuating the uncertainties that death reveals but rarely resolves. A key point here is that although 'otherness' could be (and often has been) construed as a kind of categorical fixing of opposing, polarised meanings and identities, the kind of 'alterity' we are concerned with here, deriving from the excessivities of stuff and the uncertain contingencies of how the material and immaterial are entangled, is marked exactly by the impossibility of any final determination, categorical stability, or completeness. This is illustrated by the way that the incompleteness of highly specialised efforts to 'remake the dead' through often contested, technical processes of exhumation, reburial, forensic pathology and archaeology are matched by the similarly contested, uncertain and ultimately incomplete practices of divination, spirit possession and mediumship through which the immaterial remnants of past lives are made known, present, fixed and authenticated. All this points to how the alterity of both the material and immaterial aspects of life, and the uncertainties of their entanglement, are foregrounded and revealed yet ultimately left unresolved through the rupture of death.

The final chapter considers events since Robert Mugabe's removal from office in November 2017, and his replacement by the new regime of President Emmerson Mnangagwa. I examine recent indications that the Mnangagwa government may now, and perhaps meaningfully, engage with the unresolved legacies of the *gukurahundi*. I consider (tentatively, as events were still unfolding at the time of writing) the mixture of enthusiasm and contestation that have surrounded the establishment of the National Peace and Reconciliation Commission, and Mnangagwa's promise that commemorations, exhumations and 'truth-telling' about the *gukurahundi* should now proceed. This chapter also looks at the recent deaths and burials of other significant political players, such as Morgan Tsvangirai (of the MDC) in 2018 and Dumiso Dabengwa (ZAPU) in 2019. It ends with a discussion of the controversies that surrounded the death and burial of Robert Mugabe in September 2019, which manifest perfectly the continuing salience of Zimbabwe's politics of the dead that Mugabe had himself played such a significant role in shaping.

Bringing together the main strands of the book, the Conclusion discusses further areas of contemporary significance which could be fruitfully explored in terms of the arguments made here about the politics of the dead and the power of uncertainty in Zimbabwe and beyond; as animated by the excessivities of human corporealities, the alterity of spirits and immaterial remnants of past lives, and the demanding but ultimately unresolvable incompleteness of death that

Introduction

their uneasy, uncertain entanglement exposes. It ends by considering two unfolding events to do with, firstly, highly publicised efforts by NMMZ to secure the repatriation from UK museums of Zimbabwean human remains believed by some to date to the 1896 rebellions, and some say include the remains of Ambuya Nehanda's medium Charwe Nyakasikana herself, alongside other first *chimurenga* 'heroes'. And secondly, to do with the controversies that have surrounded a new statue to Ambuya Nehanda erected in Harare in early 2021. The former is an issue that has become particularly salient over recent years and points to new directions being taken within NMMZ's larger liberation heritage portfolio, even as it remains situated within ZANU PF's 'chimurenga politics', while the latter recalls the controversies that have surrounded other statues and monuments across Zimbabwe's postcolonial period. Both take us back to the story of Ambuya Nehanda with which we have begun, reiterating the unfinished incompleteness of death; which is perhaps exactly to what Nehanda's 1896 prophesy that 'my bones will rise again' had always alluded.

1

Liberation heritage: Bones and the politics of commemoration

This chapter begins to explore the ambiguous or dual agency of bones as both 'persons' and 'objects' in the politics of heritage and commemoration in Zimbabwe. It discusses the emergence of a new commemorative project known as 'liberation heritage' in the 2000s which increasingly focused on the monumentalisation of sites dating to the liberation struggle (1965–1979), and particularly on the identification, reburial, ritual cleansing and memorialisation of human remains of the war dead, within Zimbabwe and across its borders (Mozambique, Zambia, Botswana, Angola and Tanzania). Although related to ZANU PF's rhetoric of 'patriotic history' (Ranger 2004a), which became a key feature of Zimbabwe's political crisis in the 2000s, and which the new dispensation under Mnangagwa since November 2017 has continued to lay claim to, this liberation heritage project was also positioned awkwardly in the middle of a tension between two related but distinct pre-existing nationalist projects of the past – heritage and commemoration. Exploring the tensions that both commemorative and heritage processes can provoke between the 'objectifying' effects of professional practices, the reworkings of contested 'national' histories, and the often angry demands of marginalised communities, kin and the dead themselves (for the restoration of sacred sites or for the return of human remains), the argument that this chapter pursues (setting up what follows in later chapters) is that the politics of death is not exhausted by essentially contested accounts or representations of past fatal events. It must also recognise the emotive materiality and affective presence of human bones in themselves. This is picked up in Chapter 2 which engages further with anthropological discussions emergent in the 2000s about materiality, in order to explore how different ways of thinking about the 'agency' of objects and particularly the flows and properties of materials are salient to understanding the corporealities of violence and post-violence in Zimbabwe's politics of the dead.

Liberation heritage: Bones and the politics of commemoration

The burial of Gift Tandare

In early March 2007, while the international media was focusing on the highly publicised, brutal beating by soldiers and police of Zimbabwe's main opposition leader, Morgan Tsvangirai of the MDC and several other well-known political activists including the lawyer Lovemore Madhuku,[1] the dramatic events surrounding the funeral of Gift Tandare – a little-known MDC activist shot by police on the same day – was being reported in the local independent media. The events unfolded as follows.[2] Soon after the fatal shooting during a peaceful prayer rally in Harare's Highfields suburb on Sunday 10 March, mourners began to congregate in large numbers at the deceased's residence in the high-density suburb of Glen View.[3] Apparently fearing further protests, armed police and soldiers were sent to disperse the mourners, resulting in more injuries and people being shot.

A few days later it emerged that Chief Kandeya, the 'traditional authority' in Mashanga village (Mt Darwin) where the Tandare family's *kumusha* (rural home) lies, and where his family sought to bury him, was refusing to allow the funeral to take place because Gift Tandare was an MDC activist and 'burial in his area is reserved for ZANU PF supporters only'.[4] Later, when the chief demanded payment of four cows for the burial to go ahead, Tandare's family, being unwilling or unable to pay this, decided Gift would instead be buried in Harare's Granville cemetery.[5] This decision, Gift's elder brother said, 'has been welcomed with joy as everyone wanted to attend his burial'.[6] But it was not to be. On the Saturday night before the funeral, a heavily armed police convoy turned up at the Tandare house to take only close relatives for a hastily prepared private burial. While mourners fled, the family were told that 'the chief had been talked to'.[7] The police wanted Gift's wife to sign another burial order granting permission to bury Gift in Mt Darwin, as originally planned.

---

[1] 'Tsvangirai assault was "attempted murder"' *Mail & Guardian* 13/3/07.
[2] 'MDC national hero Gift Tandare – How ZANU PF murdered and buried him in a mafia type ceremony' *MDC News Brief*, www.zimbabwesituation.com/mar20b_2007.html#Z4 19/3/07; 'MDC discover name of policeman who shot and killed Tandare' *SW Radio Africa* 16/3/07; 'Chief refuses permission to bury Gift Tandare' *SW Radio Africa* 16/3/07; 'Tandare burial set for Monday in Harare' *SW Radio Africa* 17/3/07; 'CIO agents seize Tandare's corpse' *Standard* 18/3/07; 'Zim police defy order to return Gift's body' *Cape Argus* (South Africa) 19/3/07; online sources accessed 19/6/20.
[3] 'MDC national hero Gift Tandare – How ZANU PF murdered and buried him in a mafia type ceremony' *MDC News Brief* 19/3/07.
[4] Ibid.
[5] 'Tandare burial set for Monday in Harare' *SW Radio Africa* 17/3/07, accessed 19/6/20.
[6] Ibid.
[7] 'MDC national hero Gift Tandare – How ZANU PF murdered and buried him in a mafia type ceremony' *MDC News Brief* 19/3/07.

The Politics of the Dead

The following morning reports from the funeral parlour explained that 'men in suits' (i.e. Central Intelligence Organisation [CIO] agents) had come in the early hours and 'forcibly removed the body … for burial', coercing 'Gift's sister in the presence of her fearful uncle to sign the burial order'.[8] While this was going on, Gift's wife had gone to get a court order barring the police from interfering with the funeral, an order that was granted but ignored by officials[9] who proceeded to bury the body in 'the absence of his wife and children' in a 'mafia style ceremony'.[10] According to *The Standard* (18/3/07), orders to remove the body and carry out the burial 'as quickly as possible' had come from the President's Office, because authorities were worried 'the activist's burial could be turned into a platform for an anti-Mugabe tirade by opposition supporters, already angered after the brutal attack on MDC President Morgan Tsvangirai'.[11]

The events surrounding Gift Tandare's burial illustrate how intense the politics of the dead, and what to do with their remains, can be in the context of Zimbabwe's ongoing post-2000 political turmoil. They have been replicated many times in Zimbabwe's postcolonial period, both long before Gift's death and afterwards, notably during the violence of 2008 (see Chapter 2), but also more recently after Robert Mugabe's 2017 removal from power and two years later his death (see Chapter 7). It is well documented that the funerals of people killed in political violence often become sites of protest and further violence (cf. Allen 2006; Feldman 1991 & 2003), hence it is no surprise that the police and ZANU PF government were concerned to avoid a public funeral in Harare. But the controversies surrounding Tandare's burial also point to a deeper complexity of contests that can be involved in the politics of the dead (cf. Cohen & Odhiambo 1992; Verdery 1999). Efforts to 'dignify death' can often provoke a complex politics of burial, which, in the case of colonial Bulawayo discussed by Ranger, revealed 'the existence of multiple and contesting agencies' that crosscut existing tensions not just between 'colonial' and 'African' efforts to control city space, or between 'traditional African' and 'modern Christian', or 'rural' and 'urban' mortuary practices, but also between the dictates of rival churches (whether African Independent, missionary or Pentecostal), burial societies and the entangled demands of class, wealth, labour, kin and gender loyalties, or even those of divergent imaginaries of cultural and ethnic nationalism (Ranger 2004b: 110–44). Golomski has made similar arguments more recently, in the context of changing 'funeral culture' in Swaziland in the wake of its devastating HIV/AIDS epidemic (2018a).

---

[8] Ibid.
[9] 'Zim police defy order to return Gift's body' *Cape Argus* 19/3/07.
[10] 'MDC national hero Gift Tandare – How ZANU PF murdered and buried him in a mafia type ceremony' *MDC News Brief* 19/3/07.
[11] 'CIO agents seize Tandare's corpse' *Standard* 18/3/07.

Liberation heritage: Bones and the politics of commemoration

Chief Kandeya's initial refusal, and later hefty financial charge, for permission to bury Gift in Mashanga village is perhaps less remarkable for the political motivations that apparently lay behind it, and more so for the simple fact that chiefs have the authority to decide who gets buried within their territories. This relates both to a past colonial ordering of land and authority in which commercial/European and communal/African areas of land were administered under separate regimes of rule (cf. Alexander 2006; Mamdani 1996), but also to a new streak of 'traditionalism' emergent in Zimbabwe in the 2000s, which saw the functions of 'traditional' leaders expand out of communal areas into resettlement schemes, farms, rural district councils and land committees (Fontein 2006b & 2015; Mubvumba 2005); a trend mirrored across the southern African region (Buur & Kyed 2006; Kyed & Buur 2006; Maloka 1996). The different burial orders being handled and signed and the subsequent court order, granted but ignored, barring police interference in the funeral arrangements, all indicate how complex struggles over sovereignty and rule can emerge in disputes over how to handle human remains. Although often manipulated by chiefs and ruling clans for their own local (and financial) interests, the jurisdiction of so-called 'traditional' rural authorities over the burial of the dead in the landscape relates closely, in cultural terms, to their function as living guardians of the soil, as descendants of the ancestral, often autochthonous, owners of the land, who must be appeased to ensure rain, soil fertility and prosperity (Lan 1985; Bourdillon 1987b). Hence, it is no surprise that both the existence of past graves and the burial of the recently dead became central to the complex restructuring of authority over land in Zimbabwe that emerged in the context of Fast Track Land Reform in 2000 (Fontein 2011, 2015; Marongwe 2003; Chaumba et al. 2003a & 2003b; Mubvumba 2005).

Reports about Gift Tandare's controversial burial also suggest the existence of tensions among his close relatives, as often emerge in Zimbabwe particularly between paternal and affinal kin, over funeral arrangements, the inheritance of property and the care of dependents. Some reports stated that it was Gift's paternal sister and uncle who left with the police and later signed, under duress, the burial order that 'allowed' the secret 'mafia style' burial, while his wife and her mother (both affines) hid. And it was the wife who later applied for and was granted the ineffectual court order.[12] Without drawing too much out of scant information, these references do suggest a subtle subtext of family tensions intermeshing with the political manoeuvres of the ruling and opposition parties. (Chapter 6 returns to discuss the kinds of family tensions which often erupt around funerals.) At the very least, belief in the dangerous liminality of a deceased's spirit during the immediate period after death and before burial, which

[12] 'MDC national hero Gift Tandare – How ZANU PF murdered and buried him in a mafia type ceremony' *MDC News Brief* 19/3/07.

anthropologists have noted is common among Shona peoples (Bourdillon 1987b: 119–208; Ranger 1987: 174; Lan 1985), particularly after violent death, must have made the political circumstances surrounding the burial even more troubling for Gift's family.

While the authorities may have been concerned about the threat to public order that a high-profile funeral in Harare's volatile suburbs could provoke, Gift's 'secret' burial may also have functioned as a means of circumventing the creation of a memorial landscape to work against ZANU PF's own highly politicised commemorative project, as exemplified by its monopoly of the North Korean-built National Heroes Acre. The MDC, for their part, firmly inscribed Gift Tandare on their counter-register of 'national heroes' amongst all the other 'innocent Zimbabweans who have been murdered for merely asking for a better life in a free and democratic Zimbabwe'.[13] While state interference in the death and burial of Gift Tandare and others[14] seemed to highlight the insecurity of the ruling regime, a longer view of commemoration in Zimbabwe since independence in 1980 (Kriger 1995; Werbner 1998, Brickhill 1995, Alexander et al. 2000) indicates that attempts to manipulate the representation of the recent past, and memories of violence, had been part of the ruling party's strategic historical project since independence, far pre-dating the renewed exclusionary, nationalist political rhetoric that some have identified as key to 'Mugabeism' (Ndlovu-Gatsheni 2015). As Werbner (1998) and Kriger (1995) have described, the controversies engendered by the efforts of the 1980s and 1990s to appropriate the dead for political purposes often provoked tensions not only between the ruling party and any opposition parties (then ZAPU, and in the 2000s, the MDC), but also between political elites and commoners, and between state and kin, and even within the fractious ruling party itself. The thwarted attempts in Matabeleland to commemorate both the unacknowledged dead of ZIPRA's military campaigns during the liberation struggle and the *gukurahundi* victims of the 1980s (see CCJP 2007) illustrate the extent of the ruling party's interference against alternative forms of commemoration going back to the 1980s and 1990s.

This chapter considers this history of the politics of memory and commemoration in Zimbabwe in relation to both the emergence of liberation heritage, as a new 'commemorative' project in the 2000s focusing attention and resources on the identification, exhumation, reburial, and monumentalisation of the human remains of the liberation war dead within Zimbabwe and across its borders, and that other older 'nationalist' project of the historical imagination centred on 'heritage' (Fontein 2006a). The liberation heritage project, with its emphasis on reburials, sits awkwardly between the two related but distinct nationalist projects

---

[13] Ibid.
[14] 'Abducted Zimbabwean journalist found dead' *SW Radio Africa* 6/4/07, accessed 19/6/20.

of the past; commemoration and heritage. It is, after all, NMMZ, the parastatal responsible for cultural heritage, which was primarily charged with carrying out the exhumations and reburials involved in this larger, UNESCO-sponsored, SADC-wide project of so-called 'Freedom War heritage'.[15] I suggest that for them involvement in this project was not merely playing lip service to the political demands of the ruling party's rhetoric of 'patriotic history', or the opportunities for research funding this offered, but also related to developments in the late 1990s and early 2000s in concepts of 'African', 'intangible heritage', which increasingly emphasised its living, ritual and spiritual aspects.

Like the contested burial of Gift Tandare, the exhumations and reburials of liberation war dead engage with sometimes competing, more often intermeshing attachments to the dead – by close kin, clans, ethnic and regional communities, or work and war comrades, political affiliates or rivals, as well as political parties and parastatal organisations. This chapter argues that this politics of the dead is not limited to contested *representations* of problematic deaths in the past. It is also animated by, and entangled with, the emotive materiality or affective presence of human bones and remains in themselves. This perspective builds on Verdery's discussion of the complex ways in which bodies can animate politics but moves beyond it by suggesting that the political efficacy of human remains is not limited to their 'symbolic effectiveness' (1999: 27–29). As I discussed with my colleague John Harries during the first of a series of 'Bones Collective' workshops[16] organised around the theme of

---

[15] Although officially launched in March 2007 ('Zimbabwe begins implementing the African Liberation Heritage Project' *Cluster Newsletter*, UNESCO Harare Cluster Office edition 3/2007, 8/3/07 and 'Zimbabwe launches the African Liberation Heritage project' *Cluster Newsletter*, UNESCO Harare Cluster Office edition 4/2007, 5/4/07), it can be traced back to a SADC initiative discussed at the UNESCO Windhoek office in August 2004 ('Preservation of Africa's liberation heritage' http://portal.unesco.org/en/ev.php, also 'Independence in Africa: the African Liberation Heritage' October 2006, http://portal.unesco.org/culture/en/ev.php); both accessed 19/6/20. In July 2004 Nick Katanekwa of the Zambia National Heritage Commission delivered a paper 'SADC Freedom War Heritage in Zambia' at a conference in Livingstone (McGregor & Schumaker 2006: 656). By then, National Museums and Monuments was already co-operating with its counterparts in Zambia and Mozambique in the re-habilitation and memorialisation of mass graves at former guerrilla and refugee camps ('Shrines are of great historical importance' *Bulawayo Chronicle* 17/9/05). Programmes related to liberation heritage have been adopted in other SADC countries, including Mozambique, South Africa, Namibia and Tanzania. National Museums and Monuments has also begun working closely with Rwandan authorities, where a very particular kind of corporeal politics of exhumations and reburials from the 1994 genocide has been taking place (Major 2015).

[16] See www.san.ed.ac.uk/research/research_themes/bones_collective/events, accessed 26/9/19.

the affective presence and materialities of human remains, 'in Verdery's work on bodies, the 'thereness', the material presence, is critical only to the symbolic efficacy of human remains – in the way they make the past present. But this ignores the stuff of corpses in themselves – material presence merely reinforces layers of cultural meanings' (Fontein & Harries 2009: 5). Setting the scene for further discussion of how the materialities of bones and bodies animate Zimbabwean politics in Chapters 2 and 3, here I argue that it is in the ambiguous or dual agency of bones both as extensions of the consciousness of the dead, as spirit 'subjects' or persons which make demands *on* the living, but also as unconscious 'objects' or 'things' that retort to and provoke responses *from* the living, that the tensions and contradictions of commemoration, heritage and the politics of the dead in Zimbabwe are revealed.

Heritage and commemoration

In many ways heritage and commemoration are very similar. Both involve processes of selective remembering and forgetting – or of representing and silencing, presencing and obfuscating – the past, which are fundamentally political, contestable and often controversial. Both have been central to nationalist projects and both have often involved the marginalisation not only of different representations of the past, but also of other ways of remembering, managing or dealing with it and its physical remains. Both reify particular ways of remembering or recounting the past, but also of dealing with its material remains, in the form of objects, ruins, landscapes and bones.

Apart from the similarities, there are also important differences or divergences. In very general terms, if heritage represents an inheritance from the past, then commemoration involves a response to the demands of the dead. Commemoration often relates to more recent, and sometimes very traumatic, events, involving the death and sacrifice (Rowlands 1999) of an individual or a group for, or on behalf of, a 'nation' or another large 'identity group', while 'heritage' – at least in its more old-fashioned, 'monumentalist' manifestations – may appeal to achievements, constructions or practices in the 'deeper' past for the purposes of the (often nationalist) present or future. Indeed, this focus on different time periods in the past was often enshrined in law. For example, in Zimbabwe, now out-of-date legislation prescribed that for a site to be declared a national monument, and therefore afforded legal protection, it must have existed before 1890 (Ndoro & Pwiti 2001: 24). This, therefore, excluded recent liberation war sites.[17]

---

[17] In South Africa even places like Robben Island are 'protected not because of the famous or infamous prison, but in part because of the colonial history

Liberation heritage: Bones and the politics of commemoration

Both 'heritage' and 'commemoration' inevitably involve selective forgetting (Forty & Küchler 1999) or silencing in order to legitimise a cause in the present through references to the past but, while commemoration often urges the living not to forget a debt to the dead (even as war memorials may seek to foster a simultaneous forgetting of the grim actualities of death – Rowlands 1999: 137), heritage more often seeks to narrate and represent the practices and achievements of the past in order to inform or entertain the living. In more material terms, while state commemoration often involves the massive construction of monuments to encourage or cajole the living into particular forms of remembrance, heritage processes commonly involve selectively preserving, conserving, representing and managing *existent* remains of the past, for the purpose of informing and educating the present. Commemorative sites and events are often more serious affairs, akin to a funeral, with an emphasis on the loss and sacrifice of the dead, the ongoing debt of the living and their requirement to 'feed' (Rowlands 1999: 144) or 'finish the work of the dead' (Küchler 1999: 55), while heritage sites can be more frivolous, less emotive of sacrifice and loss, and much more amenable to commodification. If heritage is a celebration of – or declaration of faith in – the past (Lowenthal 1998: 121) that, selectively, seeks to inform the present about it, commemoration often carries not only demands for an atonement or acknowledgement of the debt of the living to the sacrifices of the dead, but also functions of reconciliation, healing and the resolution of suffering, even if it is not always 'obvious how they do this' (Rowlands 1999: 142).[18]

Of course, these distinctions between heritage and commemoration can be very murky indeed. This is exemplified by examples such as Auschwitz Concentration Camp in Poland, Robben Island in South Africa, and the Old Bridge of Mostar in Bosnia, all of which are world heritage sites. Heritage can take on the commemorative functions of post-conflict reconciliation, although at times, as with the first two examples just mentioned, they almost appear as 'anti-heritage' in the

---

represented on the island dating back to the occupation of the Cape by the Dutch East India Company' (Ndoro & Pwiti 2001: 24).

[18] This 'healing' aspect of commemoration is demonstrated by examples from Rwanda (Caplan 2007; Eltringham 2004; Pottier 2002), South Africa (Coombes 2004) and Northern Ireland (L. Purbick, 'Without walls: A report on Healing Through Remembering's open call for Ideas for a Living Memorial Museum of the conflict in and about Northern Ireland' *HTR Report* November 2007; K.R. Ensor & M.T.I. Salvado, 'International experiences of days of remembrance' *HTR Report* January 2006; 'The report of the Healing Through Remembering project' *HTR Report* June 2002; 'All truth is bitter: A report of the visit of Doctor Alex Boriane, Deputy Chairman of the South Africa Truth and Reconciliation Commission, to Northern Ireland, February 1999' *HTR Report* March 2000; all at www.healingthroughremembering.org/d_pubs/publications.asp, accessed 22/5/09.

sense that such monuments demonstrate not an historical precedence for the present, as a symbol of past achievement, but rather examples of something not to be repeated. Such 'anti-heritage' can be deftly reconfigured in different ways, as, in the example of Auschwitz, a 'symbol of humanity's cruelty to its fellow human beings in the twentieth century' (http://whc.unesco.org/en/list/31, accessed 9/6/20), or at Robben Island, to 'symbolize the triumph of the human spirit, of freedom, and of democracy over oppression' (http://whc.unesco.org/en/list/916, accessed 9/6/20). As Macdonald's work on Nuremburg has shown (2009), such forms of 'difficult', often architectural, kinds of 'heritage' can raise very awkward questions about how to handle the remnants of pasts deemed not to be repeated, in such a way that does not allow the work they were originally designed to achieve, like instilling particular kinds of fascist ideology and constituting particular kinds of political subjectivity, to continue, yet at the same time without allowing them to be forgotten and thereby risking their repetition.

While these examples illustrate how foggy the distinction between heritage and commemoration can be, it should be remembered that these are only three out of 1,154 world heritage sites. The definitions of heritage espoused by UNESCO's 'world heritage system' (cf. Fontein 2000) did, for a long time, largely exclude the commemorative sites and processes which form that other highly conspicuous backbone of national imaginative investments in the past everywhere, alongside heritage, indicating that an exploration of convergences and divergences of heritage and commemorative processes is worth pursuing. There is also evidence that UNESCO remains unsure of exhumations in its support of liberation heritage across the southern African region.[19] One possible line of enquiry may be to explore of how the passage of time facilitates the transformation of sites of memory and commemoration into places of heritage. If, as Rowlands has suggested, 'memorials become monuments as a result of the successful completion of the mourning process' (1999: 131), then maybe, by extension, it is as objects of commemoration fade into a deeper past, that space is opened up for technologies of heritage to activate. Paola Filippucci's work on landscapes and memory on the Western Front in Argonne, France, has, for example, suggested that it is the fading of immediate memory with time that has provoked increased interest in experiencing, through re-enactments and by sensual exposure to the battle-scarred landscapes, what life in the trenches might have been like (Filippucci 2004: 44–5). So World War I landscapes long dominated by the monumentalism of state commemoration become increasingly suffused with heritage paraphernalia such as re-enactments, trench tours and tourist centres.

---

[19] Interview with Chipunza, 5/3/20.

Liberation heritage: Bones and the politics of commemoration

Perhaps we could suggest a similar temporal dimension to commemorative and heritage processes in Zimbabwe. If the 1980s and 1990s were marked by growing emphasis upon 'healing the wounds' of Zimbabwe's liberation struggle, as reflected in a proliferation of literature on spiritual healing and the resolution of suffering by churches, 'traditional' *n'anga* healers, *sangoma* possession cults and the *Mwari* cult of the Matobo hills (Ranger 1992; Reynolds 1990; Schmidt 1997; Werbner 1991), then perhaps it was the resolution offered by these processes which enabled the emergence of NMMZ's and indeed SADC's 'Freedom Heritage' Project in the 2000s. But, of course, this does not quite work. Not only is it far from clear that the scars of Zimbabwe's liberation struggle had been satisfactorily healed or resolved (much evidence points to the opposite), far more disturbing are the terrible legacies of the 1980s *gukurahundi* massacres which continue to trouble Zimbabwe's postcolonial situation. Throughout the 2000s, while the bones of unidentified dead from both these violent periods of Zimbabwe's recent past continued to resurface from the earth of unmarked shallow graves and mass burial sites across the country, relatives of the *gukurahundi* dead in Matabeleland and the Midlands too continued to demand 'to know where our loved ones are buried'.[20] As the 2000s progressed, a new generation of 'angry young men' emerged in Matabeleland, who, unencumbered by the 'fear that their parents' generation have' (those who experienced the *gukurahundi* first hand) to talk about the 1980s, energised a new politics of Matabeleland successionism that was partly centred on demands to find formal resolution for the *gukurahundi* atrocities.[21]

National Museums and Monuments' liberation heritage project – at least the reburials that it has involved – must therefore, in part, be understood as a response to the still unresolved legacies of both pre- and post-independence violence, even as it fits both with UNESCO's turn towards intangible, ritual and spiritual heritage, and ZANU PF's revitalised but narrowed nationalist historiography in the 2000s. If the murkiness of distinctions between heritage and commemoration defies the usefulness of arguing in such general terms, it may be more profitable to think in terms of very specific examples of where commemorative and heritage practices have coincided, overlapped, confronted or excluded each other. In order to do this, I turn briefly to Great Zimbabwe national monument in southern Zimbabwe, the country's most well-known heritage site from which its name derives, which was the subject of my first field research in Zimbabwe (Fontein 2006a).

[20] 'Mass graves from Gukurahundi era located in Matabeleland' *SW Radio Africa* 19/10/05, accessed 19/6/20; 'Evidence of "dirty war" lies far below' *Zimbabwe Independent* 29/9/00; 'We want to know where our loved ones are buried', letter from Z. Omphile, Bulawayo, *Daily News* 3/9/01.

[21] Interview with Shari Eppel, 6/12/11; Interview with Dabengwa, 18/8/15.

The Politics of the Dead
Heritage and commemoration in Zimbabwe

In his account of what he calls the 'heritage crusade', Lowenthal (1998: 94) discussed the difficulty of defining 'heritage'. He did not attempt to draw a distinction between commemoration and heritage, preferring rather to focus on the disjuncture between 'heritage' and 'history'. As he put it:

> Heritage diverges from history not in being biased but in its attitude toward bias. Neither enterprise is value-free. But while historians aim to reduce bias, heritage sanctions and strengthens it. Bias is a vice that history struggles to exercise; for heritage, bias is a nurturing virtue. (Lowenthal 1998: 122)

In my research into the politics of heritage at Great Zimbabwe (2006a), I found this distinction between 'history' and 'heritage' hard to maintain. In relation to what I called the professionalisation of the representation and management of the past at Great Zimbabwe, one key problematic aspect of heritage processes was precisely their reliance on, and reification of, 'modern' academic, 'objectifying' approaches to dealing with the past, such as history and particularly archaeology but also museum practices of conservation and preservation. Following Walsh (1992), I argued that archaeology has often appeared as a kind of distancing, disembedding mechanism, which appropriates the authority to represent and manage the past from those individuals and groups who have other ways of understanding and relating to it – other perspectives on the past, its relationship to place and the materialities of landscape, and its demands on the present (Sagiya & Fontein 2021). At Great Zimbabwe it was the dominance of archaeological narratives of the past following the infamous *Zimbabwe Controversy* of the early 20th century (Kuklick 1991), and later the gradual professionalisation of the management/conservation of its remains, which in effect appropriated and alienated the site from disputing local clans; each with their own attachments to the site, their own historical narratives or *history-scapes*, and their own needs and means of responding to the demands of the past in the form of tributes and rituals for the ancestral spirits and the *Voice* associated with it (Fontein 2006a: 19–45).

Increasing after independence in 1980, the growing professionalism of NMMZ – reinforced by what I called the anti-politics of world heritage (2000; 2006a: 185–212) – meant that local communities were unable to carry out ancestral rituals to ensure rain, fertility, and the welfare of the living. It was not only the competing interests and practices of local clans which were increasingly marginalised as heritage management was professionalised. After 1980 Great Zimbabwe became subject to a whole host of attempts by spirit mediums and 'traditionalists' from across the country to hold rituals there to thank the 'national ancestors', such as Nehanda, Kaguvi and Chaminuka, for the successful liberation

Liberation heritage: Bones and the politics of commemoration

of the country from colonial rule, and to appease the spirits of dead guerrillas killed during the war. These high-profile 'national' rituals to appease the ancestors, settle the spirits of the war dead, and cleanse the perpetrators of violence, were also prevented by NMMZ as they increased their 'professionalising' control over Great Zimbabwe during the 1980s and 1990s.

In terms of the tension between commemoration and heritage proposed above, this professionalisation of the past meant, at least for those whose rituals and ceremonies were being excluded, that the site was *not commemorative enough*. Heritage processes objectified and distanced the past to the exclusion of other perspectives which are less concerned with archaeological narratives about the achievements of Great Zimbabwe's 'original' builders between the 12th and 15th centuries (a primary concern of NMMZ archaeologists) and more with the need to respond to the ancestral spirits and the *Voice* associated with it. If commemorative processes involve rituals, memorials and monuments that are understood as a response by the living to the demands of the dead – however the dead are (re)imagined or constituted, however the response is structured, and regardless of whether at the level of the 'nation', clan or kin – then any kind of commemoration or 'feeding [of] the dead' (Rowlands 1999: 144) at Great Zimbabwe was increasingly frowned upon throughout the 20th century.

The distancing effects of heritage processes against commemoration at Great Zimbabwe has a long history. Alongside Rhodesian efforts to claim the site as their own 'heritage' to justify colonial conquest, based on fallacious beliefs about its 'ancient', 'non-African' origins, there were also early attempts to make Great Zimbabwe the centre of Rhodesian commemoration of its pioneer heroes. Most spectacular was the burial of the bones of the Alan Wilson Patrol in the late 1890s in a monumentalised grave at Great Zimbabwe, on the order of Cecil Rhodes 'to await his own death and burial' (Ranger 1999: 30; Kuklick 1991). But these remains were later removed, on the subsequent order of Rhodes's will, to accompany his own heavily monumentalised burial in (see Figures 2 and 3) and posthumous appropriation of the Matobo hills (Ranger 1999: 30–32, 39–42).

Perhaps it was, in part, due to the problematic nature of appropriating Great Zimbabwe as Rhodesia's ancient and exotic heritage that led to the Matobo hills being turned into 'the monumental centre of the white Rhodesian "nation"' (Ranger 1999: 40), and the site of many subsequent Rhodesian commemorative efforts. However, given the well-known significance of those hills to different African groups – as the site of the hugely important *Mwari* cult shrines (Daneel 1970; Nyathi 2003; Ranger 1999; Werbner 1989); the grave of the great Ndebele leader Mzilikazi at Entumbane; as well as those of earlier, pre-Ndebele rulers (Ranger 1999: 19) – Rhodesian commemoration in Matobo must also be understood

FIGURE 2. Alan Wilson Memorial, at 'World's View' in Matopos
(Author 2020)

as an appropriation of an already sacred landscape; a point that was deliberately 'impressed upon the minds of local Africans' (Ranger 1999: 31, 1987). Ndebele *indunas* were pledged to guard Rhodes's grave and remember their 'surrender' to Rhodes in 1896, even as memories of past Ndebele successes in battle or revolt against colonial rule were supposed to be forgotten. As Ranger discussed (2007a), then, if Great Zimbabwe suffered a lack of ritual and an 'abundance of archaeology', then the opposite could not be more true of Matobo, where cultural heritage and archaeology have been minimal in contrast to an 'abundance of ritual' in the form of the *Mwari* shrines, Rhodesian commemoration at the grave of Cecil Rhodes, and African rituals at the graves of both Mzilikazi and those of earlier, pre-Ndebele *Banyubi* rulers.

Liberation heritage: Bones and the politics of commemoration

But if Great Zimbabwe did not become the centre of Rhodesian commemoration as it might have done, commemorative efforts did on several occasions surface uneasily at the site. One extraordinary example was the 'psychic' séances of H. Clarkson Fletcher (1941) held in the Great Enclosure at Great Zimbabwe in the 1930s, when contact was made with the spirits of several dead Rhodesian heroes, including Alan Wilson and Richard Hall, alongside more 'ancient' fictional characters such as 'Abbukuk' the 'high priest', 'Utali' the 'last of the Queens of Great Zimbabwe' and, of course, her lover 'Ra-set'. More lasting than these white settler attempts to communicate with the spirits of Rhodesian heroes, was the naming of parts of the ruins after early European explorers. Soon after independence, as part of official efforts to rub away any last traces of the colonial commemorative appropriation of Great Zimbabwe, these names were replaced. Great Zimbabwe's Director at that time, Cran Cooke, anguished about this, suggesting cynically that 'at some future time Karanga names will be invented or perhaps some areas named after important visitors since independence'.[22] But Cooke misunderstood the continued professionalisation of heritage management that was to follow. Shona terms were allocated alongside neutral English terms for parts of the ruins (like Great Enclosure, *Imba Huru* [great house], Valley ruins, Eastern ruins, Hill complex) but no parts of the ruins have taken on the names of high-profile visitors or even the names of famous local or national ancestors. After a Rhodesian pioneer memorial in the nearby town of Fort Victoria (now Masvingo) was defaced shortly after independence, a plaque marking the site of the removed Alan Wilson memorial at Great Zimbabwe also became the subject of controversy and was subsequently removed (Fontein 2006a: 170–71).

It was not only the traces of Rhodesian commemorative efforts that were banished from Great Zimbabwe after independence. Expectations that Great Zimbabwe would be elevated to a national sacred site – which emerged in the discourses and spiritual practices of spirit mediums, war veterans, chiefs and others during the liberation struggle in tandem with nationalist use of the name 'Zimbabwe' as a 'useful rally point' for the imagination of a new nation – were also undermined and ultimately thwarted by NMMZ (Fontein 2006a: 117–66). The predominance of a 'heritage' perspective continued to exclude commemoration of any kind. Immediately after independence, the medium Sophia Muchini, who claimed to be possessed by the legendary Ambuya Nehanda, lay claim to the ruins, squatting on site and carrying out rituals and sacrifices amongst its stone walls. Her calls for a national ceremony at Great Zimbabwe to thank the ancestors for independence, to settle the spirits of dead guerrillas killed and to cleanse the perpetrators of violence were ignored.

[22] Letter from Regional Director Cran Cooke to T. Huffman, 11/6/81, NMMZ File H2.

Eventually she was imprisoned after being implicated in several high-profile murders of white settler farmers in the district (Fontein 2006a: 156–62, 2015: 256–62). (We will return to her story in Chapter 5.)

Muchini was not alone in her efforts to campaign for a national cleansing ceremony at Great Zimbabwe to thank the ancestors for their support during the struggle. In the early 1980s another high-profile event was organised involving chiefs from across the country, as well as prominent spirit mediums and members of ZANU PF, during which hundreds of cattle were to be slaughtered (Fontein 2006a: 40). This event was eventually called off, some allege on the orders of the then Prime Minister himself (Robert Mugabe), and thereafter NMMZ thwarted any further attempt to hold national commemorative or cleansing ceremonies at Great Zimbabwe. In 1985, just as Great Zimbabwe was being considered for the World Heritage list, calls for the local district Heroes Acre to be erected within the boundaries of the Great Zimbabwe estate were rejected by NMMZ on the grounds that this was not an appropriate use of a world heritage site.[23] Even the smaller, localised ceremonies of neighbouring communities, whose historical relationship with Great Zimbabwe was acknowledged by NMMZ, if scarcely celebrated or represented, were forbidden after fights nearly broke out between rival claimants from the Nemanwa and Mugabe clans during an early event in the 1980s (Matenga 2000). By the mid-1990s, Great Zimbabwe had become a heritage 'palimpsest' of past activities, and rituals of any sort, commemorative or not, were banned.

But if commemoration of any sort was not permitted at Great Zimbabwe that does not mean the new government did not invest heavily in national commemoration. Just as the last vestiges of Rhodesian memorabilia were removed at Great Zimbabwe, so across the whole country the commemorative landscape of Rhodesia was side-lined and, in many cases, physically removed, to be replaced by the commemorative symbols and rituals of the newly independent state. Zimbabwe's postcolonial commemorative project has been controversial in many ways. Kriger (1995) described in some detail the disputes that surrounded the removal of Rhodesian monuments in Harare, Bulawayo and elsewhere after independence. Many Harare streets were renamed not just after the dead heroes of Zimbabwe's liberation struggles, from the rebellions of 1896 to the struggle of the 1960s–70s, but also of still living politicians. Debates even raged about World War II memorials which some local politicians considered emblematic of colonial rule and felt should be removed, while central government argued that they signified, primarily, the fight against fascism, and should therefore remain in place (Kriger 1995: 143). In the event, central Harare's World War II memorials were not removed and they remained where they are today.

[23] Minutes of 24th meeting of local trustees, 4/8/85. NMMZ file C1a 'Trustee correspondence'.

Liberation heritage: Bones and the politics of commemoration

FIGURE 3. Grave of Cecil Rhodes at 'World's View' in Matopos
(Author 2020)

If debates about the removal of Rhodesian monuments stirred tensions between urban councils and the central state, they also revealed deep fissures between the commemorative priorities of the white community and the ZANU PF government. It is no surprise that the presence of Cecil Rhodes's grave only a few hundred yards from the sacred graves of *Banyubi* ancestors, was (and remains) deeply controversial (Ranger 1999: 30–32). In the context of the #RhodesMustFall movement in South Africa in the mid-2010s, it became the source of new debates, derision and contestation, fuelling renewed calls for his remains to be exhumed and returned to Britain. During a visit to South Africa in 2015, President Mugabe referred to the renewed controversies around Rhodes' grave,

The Politics of the Dead

saying 'I don't know what you want us to do with him ... do you think we should dig him up? ... but perhaps his spirit may rise again. We have decided to keep him down there'.[24]

Despite Mugabe's central role in Zimbabwe's broader politics of the dead (which I reflect on in Chapter 7) and the prominence of liberation-heritage-related exhumations in the 2010s, evidence suggests that Mugabe himself was not particularly enthusiastic about exhumations.[25] This may have informed his reticence about removing Rhodes's grave from Matobo. Just as important, however, was the listing of the hills as a 'cultural landscape' in the World Heritage List in 2003. This means that Rhodes's grave (see Figure 3) is unlikely to be disturbed (Ranger 2004a; Ndlovu 2003).

But most controversial of all the Zimbabwean government's commemorative work since independence has been the National Heroes Acre in Harare, and the accompanying hierarchical structure of provincial and district Heroes Acres across the country that later followed it. Apart from how this memorial landscape reinforced a particularly Zimbabwean, indeed ZANU PF, kind of elitism – with its grading of district, provincial and national heroes, and in its hard distinctions between the *chefs* and the *povo*, the elite and the people[26] – this memorial project has also involved a highly politicised nomination process, dominated by ZANU PF and its determination to present the kind of national past that suits its political interests. As the late ZAPU leader, Dumiso Dabengwa, explained in 2015:

> That heroes memorial? – We agreed, right at the beginning when we set up that thing, that yes, anyone declared a national hero must be someone who had performed outstandingly in the liberation struggle. That would include the national executive members of the NDP [National Democratic Party], of ZAPU and ZANU, and all those who continued from there to play a role in the liberation struggle and who performed outstandingly and consistently from there to the end of the struggle, would be given hero status. And at one time it was re-debated in the 1990s. I remember Mugabe asking me to give that precise definition. That definition laid 70% emphasis on what one did during the liberation struggle, and only 30% on what happened afterwards. A hero is supposed to be a liberation hero. So with that definition, it does not matter if someone played no role after independence, they could still be hero. But they changed it, without ever defining how they changed it. They change it when it suits them. The original definition was supposed to include all the people in the high command of ZIPRA and of ZANLA, but that has changed.[27]

[24] 'Mugabe: We won't dig up Rhodes' *Southern Eye* 9/4/15, https://Nehandaradio.com/2015/04/09/mugabe-we-wont-dig-up-rhodes, accessed 3/4/20.
[25] Interview with Chipunza, 5/3/20.
[26] This, as Werbner (1998: 73) pointed out, profoundly reworks the emphasis on the common soldier that exemplifies 'modern' commemoration in Western Europe.
[27] Interview with Dabengwa, 18/8/15.

Liberation heritage: Bones and the politics of commemoration

FIGURE 4. Grave of Lookout Masuku, Lady Stanley Cemetery, Bulawayo (Author 2020)

During much of the 1980s, before the unity agreement of 1987, this meant the marginalisation of the role played during the liberation struggle by the other nationalist movement, ZAPU (Zimbabwe African People's Union) and its armed wing ZIPRA (Zimbabwe People's Revolutionary Army). As a result, very few ZAPU/ZIPRA heroes have been buried at Heroes Acre and right up to the unity accord of 1987, and since, ZAPU leaders continued to protest against the ZANU PF-dominated process of selecting national heroes, by boycotting national heroes celebrations (Werbner 1998; Kriger 1995; Brickhill 1995). Most famously, Lookout Masuku, the commander of ZIPRA, who had been detained along with Dabengwa by the government during the 1982 'arms cache' crisis that later precipitated the ravaging *gukurahundi* period, was denied national hero status after his death in 1986, despite his well-known contribution to the liberation struggle (Brickhill 1995: 164–5). Instead he was buried in Lady Stanley Cemetery in Bulawayo, where many royal Ndebele clans and leaders are buried (Nyathi 2007).

As Dabengwa explained,

> When Masuku was declined national hero status, [Joshua] Nkomo went to Bulawayo council, and all the members there were ZAPU then, and he said we need a respectable place to bury Masuku. So he asked for a plot in Lady Stanley Cemetery next to the WWII cemetery there. So Nkomo said to council 'can you give us a place', and that is how they gave us that spot. Later on, each time they rejected our ZAPU leaders be awarded national hero status, we decided to put them in that place. We even stopped making requests for their national hero status to be awarded. For all prominent ZIPRA leaders we refuse national hero status.[28]

An estimated 20,000 people attended Lookout Masuku's funeral when a furious Joshua Nkomo, leader of ZAPU, demanded 'if Lookout Masuku is not a hero, who then is a hero in this country?' (Kriger 1995: 153). Many senior ZAPU figures have refused to be buried there, including in 2019, Dumiso Dabengwa, who told me in 2015 that 'I will never be buried at any of those heroes acres. I prefer to be buried at my family cemetery at Ntabazinduna communal area … our clan we have a plot there where we bury our dead, of the Dabengwa clan.'[29]

If ZAPU boycotts of national heroes celebrations during the 1980s challenged the legitimacy of the ZANU PF government's commemorative project, then during the same period, the government's actions also severely hindered ZAPU's own attempts to commemorate its war dead. As well as the detention of ZAPU leaders such as Lookout Masuku and Dumiso Dabengwa, the confiscation of ZAPU war records meant it was not able to publish lists of its war dead as ZANU PF did on Heroes Days in 1982 and 1983, making the party vulnerable to criticism in the public press (Kriger 1995: 151). But much more significant were the military activities against civilians, ZAPU ex-combatants and so-called 'dissidents' that took place in rural areas across Matabeleland during the *gukurahundi* period (CCJP 2007), which made any efforts by ZAPU to locate and commemorate its war dead absolutely impossible before the unity agreement of 1987. The urgency of the issue of the un-commemorated ZAPU war dead was certainly recognised, and even as negotiations between ZAPU and ZANU were still in progress, ZAPU's central committee appointed the ZIPRA War Shrines Committee to 'resume its programme of identifying the ZIPRA war dead' (Brickhill 1995: 166). In the 1990s, its successor, Mafela Trust, began a process of

[28] Ibid.
[29] Ibid.

Liberation heritage: Bones and the politics of commemoration

identifying and commemorating ZIPRA's dead combatants from the liberation struggle, a programme that continues today.[30]

After the unity accord, ZAPU's war legacy was increasingly acknowledged in state commemoration, albeit often scantly and very much in 'second place' to ZANU PF. When Joshua Nkomo (who became Vice-President after unity in 1987) himself died in 1999, he was buried at Harare's National Heroes Acre with a record 100,000 people paying their respects (Government of Zimbabwe 2000). Some deceased ZIPRA commanders who had previously been denied national hero status, including Lookout Masuku, were retrospectively granted that status, which is accompanied by not insignificant benefits (pensions and education costs) for immediate relatives.[31] Few (if any), however, were exhumed and reburied at the National Heroes Acre. According to Dabengwa, Masuku's family 'refused to move his body from his grave in Lady Stanley Cemetery' after he was latterly declared a national hero, illustrating how ZAPU/ZIPRA resistance to incorporation into ZANU PF's commemorative project continued after 1987. Ironically, there have been occasions when former ZIPRA/ZAPU commanders have been buried within regional Heroes Acres against their own wishes and those of their relatives and comrades. This happened, for example, in August 2015 when Charles Ndlovu, a former Lieutenant Colonel, was buried in Nkulumane provincial heroes acre after the burial was 'hijacked' by 'old ZAPU' elements still within ZANU, excluding members of 'reformed' ZAPU (who left ZANU PF in 2008, led by Dabengwa) from the arrangements.[32] Clearly after the 1987 unity accord, there were some attempts to incorporate elements of ZAPU/ZIPRA's war legacy within the ZANU PF-dominated commemorative complex, but this continued to be problematic.

In contrast, the estimated 20,000 *gukurahundi* deaths (CCJP 2007: xi) in Matabeleland have never been officially commemorated, and the late President Mugabe's 'moment of madness' apology continues to be grossly inadequate for many people, as even the late Vice-President Joseph Msika implied in a 2006 statement while attending a Mafela-organised event at Jotsholo to commemorate the 1979 killing of 11 ZIPRA cadres by Rhodesian forces.[33] Despite some incorporation of ZAPU history into the state's postcolonial narrative, local Ndebele commemorative efforts (of both the liberation struggle and the *gukurahundi*) continued to be strictly

---

[30] Zephaniah Nkomo discussed Mafela Trust's continuing efforts to have ZIPRA's liberation war contributions properly recognised, which included an exhibition of new ZIPRA photographs and archives previously held in former East Germany, Field notes, 6/12/11; 'Mafela Trust hosts ZIPRA exhibition' *Daily News* 14/10/11. See also Interview with Dumiso Dabengwa, 18/8/15.
[31] Interview with Dumiso Dabengwa, 18/8/15.
[32] Ibid.
[33] 'Msika speaks out on Gukurahundi' *Standard* 15/10/06.

controlled after the unification of ZANU and ZAPU in 1987. Alexander et al. described how two different efforts in Northern Matabeleland in the 1990s to commemorate both ZAPU's liberation war effort and the *gukurahundi* massacres were prevented after organisers were put under considerable political pressure and intimidation from CIO agents (2000: 259–64). Both an initiative to commemorate ZAPU war dead at Pupu shrine in Lupane – famously the site of not only liberation-era violence but also of Lobengula's last successful stand against the doomed Alan Wilson patrol in 1893 – and a more localised event to commemorate *gukurahundi* victims at Daluka, were subject to 'heavy-handed obstruction', illustrating how 'the rigid, top-down control of the nation's "heroes" could not be easily relinquished' because 'they symbolized the ruling elite's legitimacy' (Alexander et al. 2000: 264). Linking either an Ndebele past of resistance to colonial rule in the 1890s at Pupu, or a post-independence past of violence suffered at the hands of ZANU PF-controlled state forces at Daluka, to formal state commemoration of the liberation struggle continued to be unacceptable to the ruling elite, even if that now included former ZAPU leaders.

Commemoration at National Heroes Acre also continued to be beset with other problems, aside from and despite the government's limited incorporation of ZIPRA's war history in its 'patriotic history' in the 2000s (Ranger 2004a). Many other founding nationalists have also been left out of Heroes Acre (and the financial benefits that this accrues for their relatives), as part and parcel of ZANU PF's determination to control Zimbabwe's state historiography. The exclusion of Rev. Ndabaningi Sithole (a co-founder of ZANU in 1963, who later became a strong opponent to Robert Mugabe after taking part in the flawed 'Internal Settlement' negotiations with Ian Smith in 1978) from Heroes Acre in 2000 was particularly remarked upon, causing opposition MPs to question the role of ZANU PF's politburo in the selection of national heroes, arguing that 'hero's acre did not resemble a national shrine but a ZANU PF shrine'.[34]

Similar criticism was made of James Chikerema's exclusion from Heroes Acre in 2006, which many perceived to be due to Robert Mugabe's long grudge against his cousin (Chikerema) also due to his involvement with the 'Internal Settlement' in the 1970s. In 2015 Dabengwa explained that he and late Vice-President Msika tried to insist 'in the politburo that he should be recognised as a hero' because 'he was in the struggle from the very beginning with the NDP and long before Mugabe! Never mind his later involvement with Zimbabwe-Rhodesia'.[35] However, Chikerema himself allegedly told his friends that 'the last place on earth he wanted as a resting place was Heroes' Acre in Harare', because 'I do not want to be buried among thieves and murderers'.[36] The venom of such critiques was

---

[34] 'MPs attack selection of national heroes' *Daily News* 2/3/01.
[35] Interview with Dabengwa, 18/8/15.
[36] 'Death of a hero – James Chikerema 1925–2006' *Zimbabwean* 30/3/06;

Liberation heritage: Bones and the politics of commemoration

further fuelled by the burial of many ZANU PF stalwarts with dubious national hero credentials, such as the late minister for youth, Border Gezi, who set up Zimbabwe's notorious youth militia in 2001; the war veterans Chenjerai Hunzi and Cain Nkala in 2001; and Solomon Tavengwa, a former Harare Mayor in 2004, to name but a few.[37] Even former ZANU PF heavy-weight Eddison Zvobgo declared in 2001 that 'the heroes acre we have come to know has lost its glory';[38] before his wife's death and burial at Heroes Acre preceded his own subsequent death and burial as a national hero in August 2004.[39]

Apart from the controversies engendered by ZANU PF's highly politicised control of state historiography and selection of national heroes, official commemoration in Zimbabwe has also been beset by problems to do with *practices* of reburial associated with the structured hierarchy of national, provincial and district Heroes Acres across the country. Sometimes these had specific cultural dimensions. In the 1980s, besides protesting its partisan commemorative project, ZAPU leaders also rejected the government's 1982 decree that the remains of dead guerrilla fighters 'that had surfaced from shallow graves dug during the war' (Kriger 1995: 144), should be exhumed and reburied at local Heroes Acres. Joshua Nkomo argued that Ndebele traditions did not permit the exhumation of the dead, rather they had to be commemorated in their original graves (Kriger 1995: 150). As a result, the ZIPRA War Shrine Committee and its successor Mafela Trust, in their work documenting ZIPRA and ZAPU deaths during the struggle, both within Zimbabwe and at former camps in Zambia and Tanzania, have tended to emphasise the construction of shrines and memorials in situ, rather than exhumations and reburials, 'except in exceptional cases' (Brickhill 1995: 166). As Dabengwa described,

> we tend to avoid doing exhumations unless we absolutely must – if the graves are debilitated, or the bones are exposed or if we are under a lot of pressure from the families. There are many families who want to know what happened to their sons, their children, their relatives. We get a lot of pressure from the families. And sometimes then we do exhumations, especially if we have family members who we can compare the dead with, so we can identify them ... The problem also is that if you end up exhuming one person as a result of pressure from the relatives, then very soon you have a whole host of other demands

---

'Chikerema's punishment continues even after death' *Zimbabwe Independent* 15/9/06.

[37] 'Heroes?' *Sokwanele* 21/11/04, www.sokwanele.com, accessed 19/6/20.

[38] 'Heroes acre has lost its glory, says Zvobgo' *Standard* 19–25/8/01.

[39] 'Obituary' *Zimbabwe Independent* 30/8/04. Both Zvobgo and Cain Nkala's burial at Heroes Acre (and some would include George Nyandoro and Joshua Nkomo in this list too) illustrates how ZANU PF's tightly controlled commemoration sometimes celebrates in death those whom it denigrated in life.

from other families. We mainly only exhume those people who are easily identified, whose graves are already known, and then usually only single graves, because they are easier to deal with.[40]

It is interesting to note that the few exhumations and reburials of *gukurahundi* victims (as far as these were possible) which the AMANI Trust (Eppel 2004: 57) carried out in the late 1990s, before it was shut down in the early 2000s, seem not to have raised such 'cultural' objections, suggesting that this taboo may not be as rigid as Nkomo argued. Perhaps the ongoing political controversies around ZANU PF's obstruction of any kind of reckoning with the *gukurahundi* issue, negated or overwhelmed such anxieties. It is also possible that as the *gukurahundi* became subject to increasingly vocal debate in the 2000s – or even as part of a wider renewed 'carnal fetishism' (Bernault 2010) discussed in the Introduction – older taboos identified by Nkomo no longer held much traction. Alternatively, maybe it is the demands of the spirits of the *gukurahundi* dead themselves 'to be returned home' which has made any 'cultural taboos' around their exhumation less applicable. Dabengwa told me that in Mafela Trust they rarely came across cases where spirits of the dead from the liberation struggle demand 'to be returned' home, which is far more common in Shona-dominated areas of the country. 'Stories that we hear like that are only coming from the *gukurahundi*', Dabengwa explained; it is 'those who died in the *gukurahundi* [who] are not resting'.[41]

In other areas of the country, the reburial of dead guerrillas in district Heroes Acres in the 1980s and 1990s did sometimes offer meaningful resolution. A good example is offered by the 1989 Gutu reburial ceremony described in Daneel's (1995) thinly fictionalised *Guerrilla Snuff*. Yet in such cases too, the national heroes complex has been problematic. Often the hierarchism and elitism of the state's commemorative project meant that 'grassroots disinterest in the official commemoration of heroes acres has manifest itself in low party interest in organising reburials, in reluctance to contribute to reburial projects, and in low turnouts at official functions' (Kriger 1995: 148). Rural disinterest in district Heroes Acres also often derived from anxieties about offending local ancestral spirits by burying non-local guerrillas, of different or unknown totem and clan identity, in the areas where they fought and were killed during the war, rather than in their own rural areas. As illustrated with Gift Tandare's burial discussed at the beginning of this chapter, there are often multiple tensions in play around funerals and deaths, which means the politics of burial are complex and multi-dimensional. In rural Masvingo I often encountered controversies surrounding the burial of perceived 'outsiders' or 'non-autocthons' in lands claimed by particular chiefs, lineages and clans,

[40] Interview with Dabengwa, 18/8/15.
[41] Ibid.

Liberation heritage: Bones and the politics of commemoration

particularly in historical contexts of land alienation and resettlement, as old and new local forms of authority were (re-)established on resettled farms throughout the 2000s (Fontein 2015). This theme is picked up again in Chapter 6.

While some rural communities may have felt ill at ease with the burial of 'foreign' guerrillas in their ancestral territories, living relatives, friends and former comrades haunted by the spirits of the unsettled war dead have often demanded the return of human remains from shallow and sometimes mass graves in other parts of the country and across national borders in Mozambique and Zambia, to be interred in the soil of their own ancestors, to become ancestors themselves (Fontein 2006c: 185–8; Cox 2005; Shoko 2006). As developed more in the next chapter, a key part of both Ndebele and Shona mortuary rituals is some sort of 'bringing home' ceremony, to return a deceased's spirit back into the family home a year or more after death to become protecting ancestors. Failure to perform such rituals of return, whether involving the reburial of actual remains, or the symbolic return of soil from graves elsewhere, is understood to anger and trouble the spirits and can precipitate great personal or family misfortune. So it is no surprise that even as official Heroes Acres did not receive the popular support that had been envisaged, demands which first emerged soon after independence (Kriger 1995: 149) for the repatriation of human remains or symbolic soil from neighbouring countries have continued. These have often intersected, in the context of drought and growing political and economic strife, with the demands of mediums and chiefs for a national cleansing ceremony at Great Zimbabwe (or elsewhere) to thank the ancestors for independence, and to cleanse those who fought in the struggle, discussed above. These issues gained more national salience as different war veteran groups became increasingly disaffected during the early 1990s (Kriger 2003), and subsequently, as their courtship by the ruling party was renewed in 1997, particularly after 2000 when Zimbabwe's political crisis deepened and ZANU PF's nationalism became increasingly authoritarian (Raftopoulos 2003).

Clearly then, Zimbabwe's official commemorative efforts have been as controversial as its heritage processes. For much of the early independence era, at least until the mid-1990s, a sharp distinction between heritage and commemoration was maintained. Yet both involved normative processes in which particular narratives of the past and particular ways of dealing with its remains have been promoted, while the perspectives and demands of others about the past, and what to do with its remains, human or otherwise, have been marginalised, silenced and excluded. As a result, both official commemoration and heritage have remained problematic and subject to intense contestation.

The Politics of the Dead

Liberation heritage

The move towards 'liberation' or 'freedom' heritage challenged this earlier separation between commemoration and heritage. Or more accurately, it found its resonance precisely in the middle of the tension between them. Originally state memorials and commemoration at Heroes Acres in Harare and across the country were under the control of the Zimbabwe National Army. In 1994 NMMZ became officially involved after it was recognised that the army needed its 'professional input'.[42] After a lively parliamentary debate in 1995 about the poor state of many Heroes Acres across the country, NMMZ became increasingly focused on answering the 'deafening call' for 'decent burials of our heroes' and 'decent heroes acres'.[43] But it was only after 1997/1998, when former bases at Chimoio (Mozambique) and Freedom Camp (Zambia) were surveyed by NMMZ, and formally 'commissioned' by the President, that this involvement in state commemoration was extended to become known as 'liberation heritage', involving not only the exhumation and reburial of war dead from shallow graves within Zimbabwe, but also excavations and the rehabilitation of mass graves, memorial monuments, museums and 'shrines' at former guerrilla and refugee camps in Mozambique, Zambia, Botswana, Angola and Tanzania.[44]

Unsurprisingly, many tensions already affecting official commemoration lingered on and through this liberation heritage project. Although Kundishora Tungamirai Chipunza, NMMZ's chief curator (who has been deeply involved in its liberation heritage portfolio), emphasised that 'NMMZ is very conscious of the need to do a balancing act, so that it cannot be blamed for being partial or biased, or "patriotic"'; for many, partisan party politics became inevitably entangled with it whatever the professional ethos of NMMZ itself.[45] As Dabengwa explained:

> When I was Minister of Home Affairs, we were working on that. I was due to visit Tanzania for that purpose when I left the ministry [in 2000]. We had gone as far as communicating with the Tanzanian embassy … about making such a visit … I blame John Nkomo [who succeeded him

---

[42] Interview with Chauke, 5/4/06.
[43] NMMZ Monthly Report November 1995, NMMZ file O/1 'Monthly Reports'.
[44] NMMZ Monthly report, November/December 1997, NMMZ file O/1 'monthly reports'; 'RE: The freedom camp and Chimoio commissioning' Memo from Executive Director Dawson Munjeri to all Board members, 3/8/98, NMMZ file C1a 'Trustee correspondence'. Also 'Shrines are of great historical importance' *Bulawayo Chronicle* 17/9/05; Shoko 2006.
[45] Chipunza also qualified: 'Sometimes this just becomes a game of numbers. The fact that there were more Shona guys who died in the war … means that the balancing act is very hard to achieve. That is why Chimoio [the museum constructed at the site] came first, because it concerns bigger numbers'. Interview with Chipunza, 5/3/20.

as Minister of Home Affairs] because when I left the ministry, I gave a proper hand over. I wrote down everything that we were in the middle of, all the projects we were involved in, and I included that in the list and stressed its importance, but for some reason he did not pursue it, nor did Mohadi who came after him ... I explained that we needed to make arrangements to visit Botswana, Angola and Tanzania, but nothing came of that. Perhaps it was because if they had done that, then they would have to acknowledge that these were places where ZIPRA had camps ... They could not go to Tanzania with ZIPRA. Even the late [Solomon] Mujuru had arranged for such a visit, before he died, for that purpose. He wanted those shrines to be built, he was arranging to visit those countries. He told me that he had wanted me to recommend two or three ZIPRA guys to go with him. So we had it all arranged. We were just waiting for a signal for what date Mujuru wanted to go to Zambia and Tanzania, but then he was gone, he died. That was one of the issues that he was coming to discuss with me when he was on his way to visit his mining company, on the day that he died.[46]

Whether there was official reticence for following through with the development of monuments or shrines at former ZIPRA camps abroad, as Dabengwa's comment suggests, it is clear that between the late 1900s and early 2000s the 'liberation heritage' project offered a new way forward for national commemoration in Zimbabwe; one that might appeal across different sides of the nationalist struggle as well as gaining traction with other regional nationalist movements. 'Right now', Dabengwa explained, 'what needs to be done is that shrines need to be built at the former camps in Zambia'. 'That needs to be done for us, and for the Zambians, so we can honour our past co-operation and struggle, and the people who died there'.[47]

Liberation heritage also offered something new for NMMZ, particularly given its deepening economic woes in early 2000s. As Crispin Chauke, then acting deputy Executive Director of NMMZ, put it, 'the whole issue of liberation heritage has quite a lot of potential importance ... as a new direction for us to take',[48] offering new opportunities in government funding for research, and cultivating renewed public and political interest in NMMZ's work. With this growing involvement by NMMZ, the liberation war and its material remains were no longer just the subject of state *commemoration* but also of formal *heritage* processes. This is clear from the four phases of the project identified by NMMZ's curator of militaria, retired Lieutenant Colonel Edgar Nkiwane in 2004, which included 'the identification of the liberation war sites, traditional acknowledgement of the souls of fallen freedom fighters, physical rehabilitation of burials, erecting memorial shrines and site museums or interpreting centres, as well as conservation and promotion of

---

[46] Interview with Dabengwa, 18/8/15.
[47] Ibid.
[48] Interview with Chauke, 5/4/06.

Zimbabwe's Liberation Heritage'.[49] National Museums and Monuments soon became involved in building a new museum at the National Heroes Acre in Harare, to contain objects retrieved from its excavations, and to represent an authoritative account of the liberation struggle.[50] At its military museum in Gweru, NMMZ carried a display containing objects and photographs from its research and excavations at former guerrilla camps.[51] More recently, a site museum was established at the former ZANLA camp at Chimoio, based on extensive documentary and oral history research amongst local Mozambicans and former guerrillas as well as archaeological excavations. As Chipunza described, it is built over the remains of the former headquarters of the camp, which was known as the 'white house', with 'the original floor of the building which still has the marks of the bombs that were dropped on it, protected by varnish, so you can see the remains of the attack that took place there'.[52] In order to achieve NMMZ's desired 'balancing act', Chipunza also explained, another museum is now being planned for Freedom Camp in Zambia, from where ZIPRA operated.[53]

As well as archaeological projects and museumification at former liberation sites in neighbouring countries, NMMZ also became involved, alongside the National Archives and the University of Zimbabwe, in a project called 'Capturing a Fading National Memory' to collect oral histories of the struggle within Zimbabwe (Mujere et al. 2017). Simultaneously, the Zimbabwean National Army ran a parallel project also collecting oral testimonies of the struggle, which it evocatively called 'Operation *mapfupa achamhuka*' ('the bones will rise') in reference to Ambuya Nehanda's famous prophecy before she was hanged in 1896. As my colleague and historian, Gerald Mazarire (then at the University of Zimbabwe) put it, the new drive for the collection of oral histories of the liberation struggle, as well as the archaeological excavations of war sites, derived from a recognition of 'the requirement for there to be a narrative to go along with commemoration'.[54]

Of course, this need for a narrative to run alongside commemoration undoubtedly had serious political dimensions. Although some of the new documentary projects that began during the 2000s, like 'Capturing a Fading National Memory', and likewise the SADC-wide 'Hashim Mbita' Documentation Project, were led and carried out by scholars independent of the ruling party, and did generate significant archives of new oral material relating to the struggle in Zimbabwe and across the region, their political purchase during this period is hard to entirely

---

[49] *Herald* 18/03/04, cited in Shoko 2006: 8–9.
[50] Field notes, August 2015.
[51] Field notes, 26/10/05.
[52] Interview with Chipunza, 5/3/20.
[53] Ibid.
[54] G. Mazarire, pers. com. June 2007.

Liberation heritage: Bones and the politics of commemoration

divorce from what Chigumadzi (2018) has called the ruling party's 'chimurenga politics'.[55] Indeed these projects fitted well with the ruling party's efforts to re-imagine Zimbabwe's past ('patriotic history', Ranger 2004a), as a means of re-asserting its own legitimacy while undermining any claim to 'liberation credentials' by the opposition MDC and its factions. It is clear that much of the controversy which emerged around the 2011 Chibondo exhumations (see Chapter 3) had to do with the political instrumentalisation of the exhumations and human remains by ZANU PF. Likewise, the exhumations in Rusape in 2013 were also closely politicised by local and regional ZANU PF members for the elections of that year (Chipangura 2015; Mupira 2018). This politicisation of liberation heritage also manifest itself in other forms, most conspicuously in a series of populist 'cultural galas' held across the country in the early 2000s, to commemorate the lives of nationalist leaders such as Simon Muzenda and Joshua Nkomo,[56] the unity pact of 1987, and other significant Zimbabwean events. Two particularly problematic galas were held at Great Zimbabwe, until pressure from angry local elders assisted NMMZ in their efforts to prevent any further galas at the site (Fontein 2006a: 217–8). In 2004 one was held at Chimoio in Mozambique, the site of one of the Rhodesian army's worst atrocities during the liberation struggle.[57] More recently, in the context of growing *gukurahundi* activism in Matabeleland, suggestions have been made that the annual 'Unity day' public holiday held every December to celebrate the 1987 unification of ZANU and ZAPU, should be renamed 'End of Genocide Day'.[58]

But the emerging liberation heritage project in the 2000s was not only about ZANU PF's need to re-forge its particular 'chimurenga politics' (Chigumadzi 2018: 103). It can also be seen as a response to a diversity of other interests in Zimbabwe and beyond. For many the new focus on oral histories of the struggle offered an opportunity to recount their own experiences, wrestling control of the representation of the war away from both the elite accounts of nationalist leaders, and those of academic historians who had dominated the study of the war since independence. These oral histories sometimes offered profound challenges to the dominant narratives of ZANU PF, as for example when rural people describe atrocities and violence they suffered at the hands of both Rhodesian forces

---

[55] I am grateful to one anonymous reviewer for emphasising that these projects were not directly led by ZANU PF's ideologues and could therefore be understood to represent 'other', non-ZANU PF driven historiographical efforts to engage with Zimbabwe's liberation history. (See also footnote 13, Introduction).
[56] Shoko 2006: 4.
[57] 'Minister blows $1.5 billion on musical galas' *ZIM Online* 2/11/04, accessed 19/6/20; 'We're not broke, say Zim propagandists' *Mail & Guardian* 24/10/04.
[58] Interview with Mbuso Fuzwayo, 12/3/20.

and 'freedom fighters' during the struggle.[59] In other cases, war veterans formed groups like *Taurai Zvehondo* [lit. 'talk about the war'], and later the Fallen Heroes Trust (FHT), which according to its late leader, the prominent war veteran Comrade Rutanhire, should

> be a platform where all living fighters and heroes talk about their experiences. We want the unknown ex-combatants whose voices have never been heard, whose stories are still missing, to come forward and participate in this very important event of recording our national history. This is very important because it is the only way future generations will know what really happened.[60]

The liberation heritage project also obviously engaged with the continuing demands of spirit mediums, war veterans, relatives and others, for the repatriation and return of the war dead, and the settling of their spirits. The high-profile presence of spirit mediums, chiefs and other 'traditional' leaders at reburial events in Zimbabwe and abroad,[61] illustrate the extent to which this project not only merged existing commemorative and heritage structures/processes, but also responded to ritual demands previously marginalised or excluded by both these state-dominated processes at Great Zimbabwe, Heroes Acres and elsewhere (Fontein 2006c). It can also be seen as part of a wider response to long-running demands for national ritual events to thank the ancestors for independence and cleanse the nation's troubling legacies of violence, which became more insistent as the 2000s progressed in relation to drought, food shortages, recurring political violence and deepening economic crisis.[62]

Indeed, in 2005 and 2006, the government sponsored nationwide *bira* [ancestral ceremonies] in every chiefdom, which according to some were meant to, finally, thank the ancestors for independence, settle the spirits of the war dead, and ask for rain.[63] Immersed in highly complex localised contests, and with Zimbabwe's macro economic and political situation still deteriorating, it was always doubtful whether these national *bira* events could have forestalled continuing calls for national ceremonies at Great Zimbabwe or elsewhere. Nevertheless, they did indicate how NMMZ's

---

[59] Interview with Chauke, 5/4/06.
[60] Comrade Rutanhire, quoted in 'Mt Darwin's killing fields' *Sunday Mail* 13/1/08.
[61] '15'56 war vets reburied' *Daily News* 25/10/01; 'Independence war mass graves unearthed in Zimbabwe' *New Zimbabwe* 8/7/04; 'Remains of liberation war fighter exhumed' *Herald* 10/7/04; 'State to probe discovery of mass graves' *Herald* 16/7/04; 'Efforts to locate 2nd Chimurenga mass graves continue' *ZBC News* 12/1/08; 'Mt Darwin's killing fields' *Sunday Mail* 13/1/08. See also Cox 2005, Shoko 2006, Chipangura 2015.
[62] 'Mysterious deaths rock Kanyemba' *Sunday Mail* 3/6/08.
[63] 'Celebratory biras reach climax' *Sunday Mail* 25/9/05. Also Fontein 2006c: 185–8, 2015; Shoko 2006.

Liberation heritage: Bones and the politics of commemoration

liberation heritage project tried to engage with 'traditionalist' concerns across Zimbabwe. It is equally important to note that liberation heritage was not been entirely monopolised by spirit mediums and other adherents to so-called 'traditional' religion; representatives of mainstream churches and prophets from African Independent churches, as well as charismatic Pentecostals have also been involved. This was illustrated by the role played by Comrade Jimmy Motsi, one of the founders of the FHT and a 'prophet' (as well as a *n'anga* or healer) in the United Apostolic Faith Church, during the location of war graves in Mt Darwin.[64] Likewise, when the FHT began exhuming human remains from Guinea Fowl Mine in Mutare in 2014, local churches agreed to 'assist in providing decent burials'.[65] The complexity of actors and institutions involved in these events reflects the co-existence, in close proximity (Fontein 2011), of multiple, overlapping and intertwining repertories of death, and the diverse funerary practices associated with them, all of which are entangled in Zimbabwe's politics of the dead.

For NMMZ, the new liberation portfolio also came precisely at a moment when it had begun to take seriously a new interest in the intangible, living and spiritual aspects of heritage. This manifest itself in the easing of restrictions against local ceremonies at Great Zimbabwe – and even a NMMZ-sponsored event to reopen a sacred spring there in 2000 – as well as promises to involve local communities in the management of all of its heritage sites, and the successful 2003 world heritage nomination of the Matobo hills as a cultural landscape, thereby recognising the spiritual significance of the *Mwari* shrines at Njelele and Matonjeni, and of Mzilikazi's grave, founder of the Ndebele nation. Whether these important changes to NMMZ's approach to cultural heritage derived from UNESCO's determination to overturn the monumentalist and Eurocentric biases of the 1972 World Heritage Convention (Fontein 2000), or if the reverse is true, that changes to the world heritage system were provoked by the demands of practitioners in African contexts and elsewhere, is hard to say and perhaps beside the point. What is clear is that the broader, international imperative towards transforming definitions of world heritage, increased recognition of 'intangible', 'ritual' and 'living' forms of heritage, and a mounting desire for notions and practices of world heritage to be responsive to African milieu, and to particular 'local' forms of management, all provided a

---

[64] 'Mt Darwin's killing fields' *Sunday Mail* 13/1/08. Apart from leading the activities of the Fallen Heroes Trust (including at Chibondo in 2011), Motsi was also drawn into a bizarre internal ZANU PF witchcraft/murder plot in Buhera in 2011–12, which failed when Motsi informed the potential victims ('Chinotimba "marked" for death in ZANU PF witchcraft case' *Newsday* 15/11/11). Motsi died in 2014 and was replaced by Anymore Chinyani as the Fallen Heroes Trust's 'Chief Exhumer'.

[65] 'HEROES SPECIAL: The Killing Fields of Mutare' *Sunday Mail* 10/8/14.

context within which Zimbabwe's liberation heritage project could gain traction across the southern African region.

Although it undoubtedly complemented ZANU PF's emerging 'patriotic history' in the 2000s, the salience of 'liberation heritage' across the region and for UNESCO should not be understated. This was evidenced by the substantial, continuing co-operation between national heritage organisations across the region, between SADC countries as a whole, and the role of UNESCO's Windhoek office in this programme.[66] The significance of the international dimension of NMMZ's liberation heritage project was also revealed by the existence of related, regional programmes such as ALUKA's 'Struggles for Freedom in Southern Africa' which sought to create a digital library of oral and archival sources on anti-colonial movements in the region.[67] Of course liberation heritage was always likely to have particular salience for countries in the region whose independence was achieved 'over the barrel of a gun' (like Namibia, Zimbabwe, Mozambique, Angola and South Africa); or those 'frontline states' who hosted others' guerrilla armies (like Zambia and Tanzania); or both (Mozambique and Zimbabwe). For other countries in the region, it has less salience, and there the politics of the dead is likely to be very different (cf. Golomski 2018a, 2018b). Amongst the former, however, considerable levels of regional collaboration have been achieved, sometimes echoing patterns of collaboration manifest during the liberation period. As Chipunza explained,

> Officially we have an MOU with our counterparts in Mozambique, which allows us to take care of our liberation heritage in Mozambique. We also have an MOU with the Zambian authorities, and that has allowed us to rehabilitate former camps in Zambia. We have initiated the signing of an MOU with Tanzania, but that has not yet been completed. We are trying to extend the same approach to Angola, where there were also some Zimbabwean fighters based, especially from ZIPRA. We don't have an MOU with South Africa though. The ANC has approached the government, because they want to work with NMMZ on two sites: one in Hwange, and one in Guruve, where ZIPRA and the ANC worked together, and where some ANC/MK guys were killed and buried. So we are working towards that, but we don't [yet] have an MOU with South Africa.[68]

[66] 'Museums team rehabilitating graves in Zambia' *Herald* 12/7/06; 'Zimbabwe begins implementing the African Liberation heritage Project' *Cluster Newsletter*, UNESCO Harare Cluster Office edition 3/2007, 8/3/07; 'Zimbabwe launches the African Liberation Heritage project' *Cluster Newsletter*, UNESCO Harare Cluster Office edition 4/2007, 5/4/07); 'Preservation of Africa's liberation heritage' http://portal.unesco.org/en/ev.php; 'Independence in Africa: the African Liberation Heritage' October 2006, http://portal.unesco.org/culture/en/ev.php; all accessed 19/6/20. See also Katanekwa 2004 and McGregor & Schumaker 2006: 656.
[67] See www.aluka.org, accessed 19/6/20.
[68] Interview with Chipunza, 5/3/20.

Liberation heritage: Bones and the politics of commemoration

Aside from these significant regional and international dimensions, there is also a sense in which this new liberation heritage project was a response to events already happening on the ground within Zimbabwe. 'The liberation heritage project was really just thrust upon us at NMMZ', Chipunza explained. 'Liberation heritage is not covered by the National Museums Act of 1972' so 'there was no legislative framework for NMMZ to be involved'. But 'because of what was going on at that time' he continued, 'we found it thrust upon us from different angles, including from the war vets, and from communities, who wanted to know where their dead were buried and of course from Government'.[69]

Apart from collaborating with the prominent NGOs like Mafela Trust and AMANI Trust in Matabeleland (before it closed down under political pressure in the early 2000s),[70] NMMZ also began working with the War Veterans Association, and other (sometimes rival) war veteran groups, who all had obvious interests in the project. Cox (2005) and Shoko (2006) both describe events that followed the 2004 discovery of mass graves containing the remains of people killed by Rhodesian forces during the liberation war in the Mt Darwin area of north-eastern Zimbabwe. Here war veterans along with relatives, spirit mediums, and in some cases members of the CIO, led efforts to locate, identify, exhume and rebury individual human remains from mass graves. In some reported cases, the spirits of the dead themselves were involved as they possessed spirit mediums, or war veteran comrades, or even relatives, and then identified their own specific bones from the remains of the estimated 5,000 people buried in the 19 graves and abandoned mines in the area (Shoko 2006 & Cox 2005). In January 2008, *Taurai Zvehondo* and the FHT, which had both already been involved in identifying mass graves in Mt Darwin, were reported to be 'awaiting assistance from the Government which should lead the exhumation process'.[71] Similarly, in 2006 Crispin Chauke told me that local community groups had reported the existence of a site on a purchase area farm in Gutu where more than 100 people died during the war, and requested 'some sort of museum or memorial to be built there'.[72] This later led to NMMZ being drawn into community and war veteran-led efforts to monumentalise two liberation war massacre sites in Gutu, at Kamungoma and Hurodzevasikana (Mujere et al. 2017). National Museums and Monuments also became involved in numerous other, singular burial sites, where the identity of the individual concerned was known to local communities. For example, in Chivi, people reported a site to NMMZ where the bones of a guerrilla fighter buried during the war

---

[69] Ibid.
[70] Interview with Shari Eppel, 6/12/11.
[71] 'Mt Darwin's killing fields' *Sunday Mail* 13/1/08; 'Efforts to locate 2nd Chimurenga mass graves continuing' *ZBC News* 12/1/08.
[72] Interview with Chauke, 5/4/06.

'are now visible', and as Chauke put it, 'there will have to be museum's intervention at that site'.[73]

By the end of the 2000s, and throughout the 2010s, NMMZ found it itself increasingly called to assist with, or legitimise (Chipangura 2015), or offer their professional archaeological (but not forensic) expertise for, exhumations projects initiated and led by different war veteran and community groups, often working with different religious leaders and denominations, and sometimes with the armed forces. There are numerous examples of this, but the highly publicised and rather grotesque 2011 exhumations at a disused mine in Chibondo, northern Zimbabwe, and the enormous public furore this generated (see Chapter 3) were the epitome of a process that was much more widespread, and had begun more than a decade earlier. Another prominent example came in 2014 when the FHT, led by their then new 'Chief Exhumer' Anyway Chinyani (who replaced Jimmy Motsi after his death earlier that year), began exhuming remains from Guinea Fowl Mine outside Mutare, after they were discovered by an artisanal gold miner called Jacob Nyambundu, who claimed to have been told by a spirit medium 'that I was going to stumble upon an important discovery' and believed that that the freedom fighters were 'calling me to liberate them'.[74] More recent exhumations across Manicaland, such as at Herbert Mine, Matombo Six, and at Odzi mine in late 2019, illustrate that this is an ongoing process.[75]

As well as working closely with war veteran organisations and local communities, NMMZ also worked with the families of the unsettled dead themselves, who sometimes approached them asking for help in identification, exhumation and reburial of their dead relatives. Crispin Chauke described a reburial that took place at the request of a close relative of a man killed by a landmine in Gaerezi in eastern Zimbabwe. In that case, the dead person's identity and the details of his death were known by witnesses, but in many cases local knowledge about the identity of dead guerrillas is limited to the *noms de guerre* that guerrillas adopted during the struggle to ensure the safety of their kin. Such problems are frequently confounded in cases where people were buried far away from their own home areas, such as in camps in Zambia and Mozambique, or in distant operational zones within Zimbabwe. In 2015 I asked Dabengwa what was done with people who died at ZIPRA camps in Zambia during the struggle.

> JF – So if people were living there, then they were also dying there. What did you do with people who died there?
>
> DD – We buried them. We had burial sites at the camps, and [sometimes] we buried them in local cemeteries especially around Lusaka. Except for ... the transit camps nearer the border, there we buried them in

---

[73] Interview with Chauke, 5/4/06.
[74] 'HEROES SPECIAL: The Killing Fields of Mutare' *Sunday Mail* 10/8/14.
[75] Interview with Chipunza, 5/3/20.

other places. But there were not that many people who died there, except where there were mass killings and mass graves from where camps were attacked, that was something else.

JF – Are they still there, or were they returned after the war?

DD – They are still there. It is part of Mafela's work to identify these graves, especially of comrades who were killed ... But with those people who were killed in the mass bombardments, those mass graves in Zambia, those dead become very difficult to identify.[76]

The difficulties of identifying individual human remains from mass burial sites is very well known and would later confound the FHT who led exhumations at Chibondo in 2011, at the so-called 'Butcher's Site' in Rusape (Chipangura 2015; Mupira 2018) and elsewhere. In some cases at Chibondo, human remains were found with identification documents and cards in the pockets of their clothes.[77] There have also been some notable cases when the careful collection of oral histories and close co-operation with relatives in these exhumations has led to the positive identification of individuals. Chipunza described one moving story of an old woman who participated in the Chibondo exhumations and was able to identify the remains of her 12-year-old daughter who had been killed during an attack by Rhodesian forces on an all-night *pungwe* vigil at Karina, in Mt Darwin during the war.[78] But in the large and complex exhumations that took place during the 2010s this was fairly exceptional. More often human remains have never been identified.

It is perhaps exactly in such cases that the role of prophets, *n'angas*, diviners, Christian prophets and possessed spirit mediums came into their own, complementing and sometimes contesting (Chipangura 2015: Mupira 2018) both the empirical collection of oral histories that Mafela Trust, the History Department at University of Zimbabwe (UZ), the National Archives, and certain branches of the military were all becoming involved in in the 2000s, as well as the archaeological (although not forensic)[79] approaches that NMMZ offered. In some cases described by Shoko (2006) and Cox (2006) it was the living relatives themselves (in one case a 14-year-old girl) who, possessed by the restless spirits of their dead parents, brothers and children, have located, named and identified the particular bones of their relatives to be returned and buried into the soil of their own ancestors in their rural homes. Mediums were also heavily involved in the case of the 'Butcher site' exhumations in Rusape, led by

---

[76] Interview with Dabengwa, 18/8/15.
[77] Interview with Chipunza, 5/3/20.
[78] Ibid.
[79] Interview with Shari Eppel, 6/12/11; Fieldnotes, conversation with Shari Eppel, August 2015.

the FHT and supported (although not without contestation) by NMMZ archaeologists (Chipangura 2015: Mupira 2018). In 2011 this issue became part of the controversies that surrounded the Chibondo exhumations (see Chapter 3), during which NMMZ came under increasing pressure to demonstrate (and build capacity in) its forensic expertise.[80]

Although there were some obvious continuities with previous state commemorations and reburials (e.g. Daneel 1995), it did seem, then, that this new heritage project in the 2000s had more potential to deal with the complex, overlapping demands of the dead themselves, and those of living relatives, war veterans, and others haunted by them, than that afforded by the highly problematic commemorative efforts of the 1980s and 1990s. This did not mean that the new project was not contentious. Some spirit mediums I spoke to in Masvingo District in 2006 derided both the national *bira* ceremonies held in September 2005 and the reburials carried out at former camps in Mozambique for being politically motivated, or for not following correct procedures, or not involving the proper ancestral representatives (Fontein 2006c: 186–7). Of course, like nearly all 'traditional' events in Zimbabwe, these reburials were subject to the different interpretations, political and clan loyalties, and religious beliefs of people involved. It was also unclear exactly to what extent NMMZ (and the other national and international bodies involved, not to mention ZANU PF) would be able to continue to allow the rather ad hoc involvement of war veterans, spirit mediums, *n'anga*s, church prophets and relatives in these reburials, without stamping some of its own more conventional, bureaucratic imprint upon the processes. Nor was or is it clear to what extent NMMZ would be able to successfully deal with the intensely troubling legacies of Zimbabwe's *gukurahundi* (cf. Eppel 2004), the commemoration of which had been subject to increasingly stringent control since 1987, and yet the demands for which grew increasingly noisy throughout the 2000s and early 2010s. As Chipunza noted, these too have now been 'thrust' upon NMMZ in the post-Mugabe context – to which Chapter 7 returns.[81]

The proliferation of non-state-led exhumations and reburials illustrates how the issue of the unsettled and resurfacing war dead became increasingly salient throughout the 2000s, while NMMZ's growing involvement points to deepening official recognition of the unsatisfactory nature of earlier state commemorations and the continued need to respond to the unhappy war dead. But NMMZ's involvement did not mean that commemoration became any less politically fraught. In February 2010 'riot police had running battles' at Great Zimbabwe with a group of local war

---

[80] The Chibondo exhibition at the National Heroes Acre, which I visited in 2015, sought to stress NMMZ's forensic expertise which human rights activists and forensic experts often denied it had, Field notes, August 2015.
[81] Interview with Chipunza, 5/3/20.

Liberation heritage: Bones and the politics of commemoration

veterans accompanied by spirit mediums, 'who were digging up ... the Zimbabwe Ruins to exhume remains of bodies of fighters of the liberation struggle, which they said had been buried there'.[82] The growing interest of NMMZ in 'liberation heritage' did not mean it could easily concede control over heritage sites like Great Zimbabwe to unofficial (even if politically influential) interested parties, nor would it simply allow such groups to determine how and where such exhumations and reburials took place. Even the secretary general of the War Veterans Association, Alex Mudavanhu, acknowledged that the arrested war veterans 'wanted to dig up bones for reburial but did not follow procedures'.[83]

Nevertheless it did seem as if NMMZ's new liberation heritage portfolio was qualitively different both from past state commemoration and the professionalised heritage processes that had been so problematic at Great Zimbabwe and elsewhere, even if this did not make it any less politicised or controversial. The liberation heritage project seemed to be located exactly in the middle of the tension between commemoration and heritage because the reburials of the war dead involved both the distancing, 'objectifying' and 'professionalising' processes of heritage and archaeology, as well as efforts to respond to the demands of *some* war veterans, traditionalists and kin, and even of the dead themselves, to be commemorated, memorialised and ritually 'returned' to Zimbabwe, and to the soil of their ancestors. In short, the reburials involved both efforts to narrate and objectify the past, and efforts to respond to the demands that the dead make on the living. In Chauke's words:

> We try to combine both forensic methods and traditional methods. At Nyadzonya [Mozambique] for example we had traditional people come there because it was felt that the spirits of the people killed were still there and needed to be returned to their home country. So the chiefs were sent there... they went to all the different burial sites at Nyadzonya and did rituals there and collected soils to be brought back to Zimbabwe so that the spirits could return home. Some of these soils are now in the tomb of the unknown soldier, to represent or take the spirits of the dead child back to his home country.[84]

Above all else, then, it was its efforts to respond to the demands of the dead which marked liberation heritage out as different from both the distancing effects of previous heritage processes and the earlier, problematic state commemorations of the 1980s and early 1990s. Pushing this analysis further in the next section to set up what follows in Chapter 2, I want to reflect on how, apart from or rather in conjunction with the *spirits* of the dead, it was the bones and physical remains of the dead, in their very

[82] 'Zimbabwean war vets dig up Great Zimbabwe ruins' *Zimbabwean* 14/2/10.
[83] Ibid.
[84] Interview with Chauke, 5/4/06.

presence and materiality, surfacing from the soil of shallow graves across the country and over its borders, that subverted the otherwise normalising aspects of commemoration and heritage in Zimbabwe.

Unsettling bones

If both heritage and commemoration in Zimbabwe have involved the marginalisation of alternative pasts and alternative ways of dealing with its material remains, then bones have often confronted and subverted these normalising processes. Building on the work of Howard Williams (2004) and others (Hallam & Hockey 2001; Tarlow 2002; Verdery 1999; Hertz 1960), I suggest that it is through their ambiguous agency as both 'persons' and 'objects' that bones can do this. The most obvious way in which bones can confront both commemorative and heritage processes is through the presence of the 'wrong' bones (or the absence of the 'right' bones), pointing to the alternative pasts otherwise silenced or forgotten. At Great Zimbabwe (Fontein 2006a) the presence of local African graves of the recently dead of the Mugabe clan who occupied the site when Cecil Rhodes's pioneer column entered the country in 1890, were a profound challenge to the antiquarian fantasies of colonial apologists, but provided no more comfort for the 'professional' archaeologists aligned on the other side of the *Zimbabwe Controversy* either. The recent date of the graves made them irrelevant for archaeological interests that were mainly concerned with identifying the 12th–15th century occupiers of the site. The failure to find graves, tombs and human remains dating to that period continues to confound archaeologists, much as the absence of any sign of 'ancient' 'exotic' remains frustrated the antiquarians before them.[85]

More recently, the presence of these local 19th-century graves has begun to unsettle the otherwise comfortable predominance of archaeologically informed heritage managers. For the Mugabe clan, the presence of the graves of key ancestors at Great Zimbabwe has continued to be the basis of their claims to the custodianship of the site, and efforts to gain access to carry out rituals there (Fontein 2006a: 30–34). As NMMZ increasingly adopted in-vogue notions of intangible, living and spiritual heritage the presence of these graves and other local claims to Great Zimbabwe's sacred importance meant that NMMZ had to reconsider the archaeological pre-occupation with the particular 'black-boxed' (Hodder 1995: 8) dates of the site's medieval construction and occupation. In a sense, then, these graves – the material presence of these 'wrong' bones – provoked profound challenges to the distanced, professionalised view of Great Zimbabwe as a national heritage site whose only relevant past lay

---

[85] New archaeological work on the hills surrounding Great Zimbabwe is beginning to address this issue; cf. Ezekia Mtetwa's ongoing post-doctoral research (Uppsala University).

Liberation heritage: Bones and the politics of commemoration

in the 12th to 15th centuries, forcing heritage managers to engage with the hitherto silenced *history-scapes* of local clans (Fontein 2006a: 19–45).

While the presence of graves has also featured prominently in widespread efforts to claim ancestral ties to land occupied and resettled during recent land reform (Fontein 2015; Shoko 2006), bones have also confounded, at different moments, the highly politicised commemorative efforts of the Zimbabwean state discussed above. One issue that affected earlier state-directed efforts to rebury the remains of the war dead at district and provincial Heroes Acres was determining which bones were which (Kriger 1995: 144, 149). In many cases dead guerrillas, Rhodesian soldiers and auxiliary forces, were buried together in anonymous graves. This caused problems for rural people tasked to rebury the remains of war dead that were resurfacing from shallow graves. Even President Mugabe realised this problem when he made a statement to the Zimbabwean Parliament in 1986 asking 'how do we distinguish good bones from bad bones, the heroic ones from the fascist ones and so on' (Kriger 1995: 144).

But in terms of the 'wrong' bones, much more problematic for the government has been the resurfacing of the bones of *gukurahundi* victims.[86] These other 'wrong' bones amount to a profound challenge to the ruling party's efforts to present a particular, narrow version of the violent struggles that followed independence in 1980. Although the two efforts described by Alexander et al. (2000: 259–64) in Matabeleland in the 1990s to commemorate other silenced histories were thwarted, the bones of *gukurahundi* victims, like those of the liberation war dead, have continued to resurface from shallow individual and mass graves, and abandoned mines, confronting government efforts to control representations of the past, and straining the precarious unity of former ZAPU and ZANU factions in ZANU PF.

In 2005, Jabulani Sibanda, then leader of the War Veterans Association, and before he became deeply involved in ZANU PF's 2008 election violence, acknowledged that 'he too would like to see the perpetrators of the massacres tried in international courts', as reports emerged of plans then being prepared for exhumations, reburials and cleansing ceremonies to take place 'once Mugabe leaves office'.[87] Recent announcements by the post-Mugabe Mnangagwa regime about the need to finally address the *gukurahundi* issue, suggest that these might now be allowed to take place, after years of official obstruction. Yet to a limited extent, the location and identification of *gukurahundi* remains had already been taking place. Apart from exhumations carried out by AMANI Trust before its closure

---

[86] 'Evidence of dirty war lies far below' *Zimbabwe Independent* 29/9/00; 'Mass graves from Gukurahundi era located in Matabeleland' *SW Radio Africa* 19/10/05, accessed 19/6/20; 'Film reveals horror details of the Ndebele massacre' *Nation* (Kenya) 11/11/07.

[87] 'Mass graves from Gukurahundi era located in Matabeleland' *SW Radio Africa* 19/10/05, accessed 19/6/20; Eppel 2004: 57.

in the early 2000s, in 2006 the acting deputy executive director of NMMZ acknowledged that many, if not most, of the liberation heritage exhumations NMMZ had already been involved in Matabeleland were of *gukurahundi* victims. But, I was told, 'this is very sensitive. VERY SENSITIVE. The *gukurahundi* stuff is never talked about' because 'people are afraid to open up old wounds … especially … because at one point nearly the whole of Matabeleland was MDC'.[88] The horrific memories of the *gukurahundi* massacres were then deemed still too recent, too emotive and too political, challenging ZANU PF's precarious unity in Matabeleland. Indeed in 2008 the unresolved *gukurahundi* legacies were a key factor in the reformation of ZAPU under Dumiso Dabengwa.[89]

Likewise, the resurfacing human remains of victims of the ruling party's violent excesses against opposition supporters since 2000 – such as the death of Gift Tandare with which I began this chapter, and many other examples, particularly from 2008 – have also confronted ZANU PF's claims about where responsibility for political violence lies. The likelihood that the unsettled dead of Zimbabwe's various periods of post-2000 violence would return in their demands for reburial, cleansing and commemoration fed into calls for a national programme of 'healing' and reconciliation which increasingly animated Zimbabwean politics since the short-lived Government of National Unity (GNU, 2009–13), and perhaps even more so since the Mugabe's removal from office in 2017. Perhaps NMMZ's chief curator was right when he told me in March 2020 that 'yes, something has changed', and 'there are now people in government who recognise the need to handle the *gukurahundi* issue; that it needs to be dealt with for people to get closure'.[90]

Yet if these examples illustrate how bones and bodies can confront heritage and commemorative processes by retorting silenced or marginalised pasts back to the present, contesting or undermining the dominant narratives of political elites or heritage managers, then bones and bodies can also problematise heritage and commemoration in other ways, that have less to do with *representations of the past*, and more to do with what I call their *emotive materiality* as human substances and their *affective presence* as dead persons, spirits or subjects who continue to make demands on society. As Williams pointed out, bones and human remains have often been 'understood only as a set of materials without agency or the ability to affect the actions and perceptions of the living' (2004: 264). This

---

[88] Interview notes, 2006.
[89] 'Gukurahundi fears split ZANU' *Standard* 29/4/07; 'Moyo says Gukurahundi Bill ready by September' *Zim Online* 16/5/07, accessed 19/6/20; 'Msika speaks out on Gukurahundi' *Standard* 15/10/06; 'Zapu Breaks From Zanu PF' *Standard* 16/5/09; 'Dabengwa says Mugabe must apologise' *Zimbabwe Times* 15/5/09; Interview with Dabengwa, 18/8/15.
[90] Interview with Chipunza, 5/3/20.

approach fails 'to appreciate the close entanglement of the living with the dead in many societies ... [and] in turn it underestimates the complex engagements between people (both living and dead) and material culture in the production and transformation of social practices and structures' (2004: 264). Even Verdery's contribution (1999) which initiated new explorations of how dead bodies can animate politics in complex ways, was limited to the 'symbolic effectiveness' of human remains for the politics of the living. The new materiality debates (discussed in more detail in Chapter 2) have moved beyond these older approaches by providing opportunities to de-centre the agency of living human subjects in order to further explore how the political efficacy (or 'agency') of the dead is closely related to the emotive materialities and affective presence of their remains, and is not, therefore, limited merely to the symbolic.

As suggested above, at Great Zimbabwe in the 2000s there was a growing sense that 'professionalising' heritage practices had not been 'commemorative enough'; in that they have not allowed local clans, or 'traditionalists' and spirit mediums from elsewhere across the country, to carry out the rituals and rites they considered necessary to appease the dead and ensure the welfare of the living in terms of rain, prosperity, and so on, be that at the level of the nation or local clans and kin groups. Similarly, although it sounds odd, state commemorative processes had also for many not been 'commemorative enough', by not taking into account the 'entanglement of the living with the dead' and the specific cultural and historical needs to respond to the dead in particular ways to ensure the welfare of the living.

In terms of the burgeoning recent anthropological literature on questions of materiality and the agency of objects, things and materials, this relationship between the bones of dead people and the benevolent ancestral spirits that they become if correctly 'commemorated' – returned and reburied into the 'right' landscape, in the 'right' way, by the 'right' living relatives – seems to exemplify Alfred Gell's theory of 'object agency', as developed in his influential book *Art & Agency* (1998). As Miller (2005: 12–13) discussed, Gell's is a 'theory of abduction' and 'inferred intentionality ... behind the world of artefacts', in which objects, in his case art, function as the 'distributed minds' of their creators, affecting or influencing the minds and actions of others. Here 'art objects' have 'agency' because they carry the 'abducted agency' of the artist. In the example I have been developing, the agency of bones to affect the living seems to derive, in part, from the consciousness of the spirits whose bones they were when they were alive. This is illustrated powerfully by common accounts of unsettled spirits of the war dead demanding exhumation and reburial, and sometimes leading artisanal miners, war veterans and relatives to identify their dumped bodies in abandoned mines, events which were part of a complexity of issues that fed into Zimbabwe's liberation heritage project.

The Politics of the Dead

But what bones do does not necessarily depend upon belief in spirits, or in the need for specific rituals to 'return the dead' and transform them into benevolent ancestors. It is not dependent on particular repertoires of death. There is also a sense in which bones can do something that is not necessarily related to the deferred or disembodied conscious of the dead themselves. The phenomenological qualities of the dead body, the corpse – particularly as it rots/disintegrates – also affects the living (Williams 2004), suggesting a kind of non-conscious agency of bones, closer to that suggested by Latour (1999) who, unlike Gell, looks for 'the nonhumans below the level of human agency' (Miller 2005: 13). Although a kind of non-human agency, separate from the consciousness of the dead people they once were, it does, nevertheless, relate to the uneasy fact that bones are at once both objects/things and subjects/persons. This 'nonhuman' agency of bones does, in part, depend on recognition by the living of the bones as dead or absent human subjects rather than simply as objects, yet exists regardless of any personal knowledge, memory or relationship between the living person affected and the dead individual.

If the looting of local graves at Great Zimbabwe by early Rhodesian antiquarians in late 1890s profoundly disturbed locals employed in the work, whose relatives they probably were, then even these explorers themselves sometimes admitted to being disturbed by what they had done (Bent 1896: 79; Hall 1905: 43, 94). Bent describes how a 'man came to complain' after he opened the grave of a man who had died that year. Despite being 'horrified', Bent nevertheless 'took scientific research as our motto' and ignored 'the old Chief Ikomo's' efforts to prevent further excavation of graves (1896: 79). Twelve years later Hall did get Chief Mugabe's consent to open and move several graves, provided the remains 'were properly reinterred' and the local labourers were 'allowed to go to their kraals to purify themselves' afterwards (Hall 1905: 43). Similarly, anthropological studies of archaeological excavations carried out at battlefield sites along the Western Front in Belgium (Filippucci 2010; Brown 2007) suggest that even people involved in the otherwise 'distancing' and 'objectifying' processes of archaeology can be deeply affected by the discovery and excavation of human remains. This suggests that archaeological processes do not necessarily 'distance' the past, as I argued above. Where human remains are involved archaeological processes can bring the past much closer to the present. In a sense, the emotive materiality of bones can challenge the normally distancing effects of archaeological and heritage processes. Here, archaeology becomes an emotive practice that provokes an experiential sense of the past through its engagement with human corporeality. But more than this, those involved in excavations on the Western Front that Filippucci describes, 'see their work as a scientific

Liberation heritage: Bones and the politics of commemoration

enterprise that ... also fulfils an obligation to the fallen'. Archaeology therefore becomes a 'form of tribute to the dead and so also ... a form of commemoration' (2010: 177).

Crispin Chauke described exactly the same thing in 2006 when I asked him whether digging up human remains at liberation war sites was different to other archaeological excavations. I quote him at length here because his words capture exactly the overlapping agencies of archaeologists, families, politicians, spirits and bones that I have been trying to describe.

> Yes it's different. I have participated in a lot of archaeological excavations but digging up human remains is very different. There are different reasons for this. First of all, people's beliefs that, for example, the dead should just rest and not be disturbed. Secondly, apart from academic interest, and satisfaction from such an excavation, there is another kind of satisfaction too. If it were simply the bones of an animal then perhaps there would be an academic interest ... to find out what sex the animal was, and the bones would be taken to a lab and tests done, and there would be an academic interest in the results ... But that would not be of much interest to the commoner, and such an excavation is not really relevant to most people. But if you take something like the Chimoio projects: that is very relevant to common people. In a way you feel like you are contributing your part to make sure all the people who have died in those camps are buried properly. Often it is the first time that those bones have been treated in such a way.
>
> So it can be very emotional, and this is especially so where relatives and the family members have requested the exhumations take place. Often it is the family members who are experiencing problems, their family things are not going very well and so it is they who request that the bodies of relatives killed during the war are reburied. They may say for example that the spirit of their killed relative is complaining that he is still in the bush, he has not been brought home yet.
>
> And doing these exhumations does feel like opening up old wounds, the whole atmosphere is like that of a funeral. This is a funeral.
>
> Even touching the bones creates a personal bond. Sometimes I have found that when people start the exhumations they are using gloves, when I started I was wearing gloves, but with time you find yourself asking, why am I wearing gloves? Would I be wearing gloves if I was greeting these people? How is this different? So I stopped wearing gloves and you find yourself just using your hands. Even other people like assistants who I have seen come to help, many start off using gloves but after maybe a week or two the gloves come off.
>
> I had a particularly emotional moment at Nyadzonya where we exhumed the skeleton of a woman who still had her baby strapped to her back. That was a very emotional experience for me.

So yes excavating human bones is very different from animal bones. When you are excavating human bones you want to know straight away whether it was a man or a woman. That is something you can't run away from, as soon as you see the skeleton. Also questions like was it an old person or a young person. These are questions that you begin to think about straight away, and urgently not like with animal bones where you might take them to a lab to find out and then you have information for an academic paper. No, with human bones you want to know these things the same day, before you sleep. After digging up human remains you can't just leave it there overnight to finish the next day, you want to finish everything there, unlike an excavation of animal bones which you easily leave there to finish tomorrow. The difference is like, with human bones you are dealing with a living individual.[91]

This illustrates perfectly how the ambiguous agency of bones as both 'persons' and 'objects' can confront normative means of dealing with the past, in complex ways that go beyond mere 'symbolic effectiveness' or simply challenging dominant representations of the past. For my purposes here the claim that archaeological excavations of dead people killed during the war were 'like a funeral' illustrates not only how commemorative and heritage processes came together in Zimbabwe's recent liberation heritage project, but also how, apart from undermining dominant narratives of the past by pointing to other silenced histories, it is in the ambiguous agency of bones – both channelling the 'distributed' subjectivities of the dead as challenging and insistent spirit 'subjects' or persons, but also as unconscious, defiant material stuff confronting the living – that the tensions and contradictions of commemoration, heritage and the politics of the dead are revealed. After all, at sites like Great Zimbabwe, bones can promote recognition of the 'living' and ritual values of heritage, and it is during excavations and exhumations of war graves that normally distancing archaeology becomes 'like a funeral', and human bones become like a 'living individual'.

I started this chapter with an account of the controversies that surrounded the burial of Gift Tandare in 2007, after his violent death at the hands of the Zimbabwean police. In the context of the complex emergence and multiple origins of Zimbabwe's liberation heritage project in the 2000s that we have discussed, set within the broader politics of the dead that this book addresses, it seems likely that this would not be the last we hear of Gift Tandare or the other victims of ZANU PF's political violence in the 2000s, many of whom lie in unmarked graves around the country. The story of Gift Tandare's violent death and contested burial shows how in Zimbabwe's postcolonial milieu it is not only the dry resurfacing bones of the liberation war dead or of un-commemorated

[91] Interview with Chauke, 5/4/06.

Liberation heritage: Bones and the politics of commemoration

gukurahundi victims, but also the fleshy, leaky bodies of much more recent victims of political violence, which animate its commemorative politics. This is what the next chapter turns to, as we consider in greater depth how human corporeality, substances and materials are entangled in Zimbabwe's politics of the dead.

2

Bones and tortured bodies: Corporealities of violence and post-violence

In Chapter 1 we began to explore how bones occupy a complex place in Zimbabwe's politics of the dead. As both extensions of the dead (spirit 'subjects' making demands on the living) and as unconscious 'objects' or 'things' (provoking responses from the living), bones in Zimbabwe not only challenge state commemoration and heritage but also animate a myriad of personal, kin, clan, class and political loyalties and struggles. Political violence since 2000 – especially the troubled elections of 2008 – indicates, however, that it is not only dry bones but also the fleshy materiality of tortured bodies that are entangled in Zimbabwe's troubled postcolonial milieu. This chapter explores the complexity of agencies entangled in the affective presence and emotive materialities of both dry bones and leaky, fleshy bodies in Zimbabwe, in order to understand how the corporeal dimensions of violence and of post-violence are intertwined. If bodies inscribed with torturous performances of sovereignty do have significant, if duplicitous, political affects, how does this contrast with the unsettling presence of the longer dead? What does the passage of time – both the material and leaky decomposition of flesh, but equally the transformative processes of burial – do to the affective presence and emotive materiality of the dead? And how does the corporeality of physical violence – interrupting the bodily boundaries and processes of containment through which persons are normally constituted – relate to post-violence efforts to remake and safely settle the dead and resolve troubling pasts. How, in short, do broken bodies become bones?

To address these concerns, I consider how anthropology's turn towards questions of materiality, the properties of materials and the 'agency' of objects over the last two decades, can be usefully deployed to consider how both bones and bodies do things in Zimbabwe's politics of the dead. Developing the discussion initiated in the previous chapter, here I explore how the different theoretical perspectives offered by Alfred Gell and Bruno Latour about 'object agency' are complemented by the work of Tim Ingold; and how all three can be usefully engaged to examine the affective presence and emotive materialities of bones and bodies. In particular, while the uneasy ambivalence of bones as both subjects and objects can help us understand what bones in Zimbabwe do in terms of both Gell's notion of deferred human agency carried through objects, and Latour's notion of things as non-human, non-conscious and unintentional actants in complex networks of subjects and objects, Ingold's critique of recent approaches to 'materiality' in favour of the properties and flows of materials, helps us to understand how political violence gains efficacy exactly through its violation of normal bodily processes of containment and transformation by which people are normally constituted. It also shows how violence against the living is entangled with violence against the dead, as demonstrated through the proliferation of interrupted funerals and dumped or disappeared bodies that have accompanied periods of violence in Zimbabwe; and by ongoing demands that the resolution of past violence should take place through material and corporeal processes of exhumation and reburial to make those killed safely dead. In short, Ingold's emphasis on the properties and flows of materials helps us to understand how Zimbabwe's politics of the dead is finely intertwined with, and gains traction through, the ritual and material transformations of fleshy, leaky bodies into dry bones, of people into ancestors, and the living into the safely dead. The chapter ends by considering efforts made during the years of the Government of National Unity (2009–13), in the wake of the 2008 violence, to initiate programmes of national 'healing' and reconciliation; efforts which failed, in part, because they could not accommodate the entangled material, symbolic, social and political processes that the remaking of the dead of Zimbabwe's many periods of colonial and postcolonial violence demands.

Resurfacing bones

It is clear that bones occupy a peculiar place in Zimbabwe's postcolonial imagination. This can be traced back to Ambuya Nehanda, the much mythologised ancestor whose medium played a key role in instigating rebellions against colonial conquest in the 1890s (Lan 1985; Ranger 1967). As mentioned in the opening paragraph of this book, after the 1896–97 rebellions, as she was being hanged, Nehanda is said to have made the now famous prophecy that '*mapfupa edu achamuka*' – 'our bones will rise'. This story became hugely important in Zimbabwe during the 1950s, '60s and '70s, when histories of these early rebellions, known as the first *chimurenga*, fed readily into cultural nationalism, mobilising people for armed nationalist struggle (1965–79), which became known as the second *chimurenga* (Fry 1976; Lan 1985; Ranger 1985). After independence, Nehanda and other (re-imagined and elevated) 'national' ancestors inspired a host of postcolonial literature, perhaps best exemplified by Chenjerai Hove's classic books *Bones* (1988) and *Ancestors* (1996), and

Ivonne Vera's *Nehanda* (1993). This literary fascination with Nehanda continues, as exemplified by Panashe Chigumadzi's recent book, *These Bones Will Rise Again* (2018). But Nehanda's significance (and that of other ancestors) during the second *chimurenga* was not just as 'nationalist mythology' with which to imagine a postcolonial nation, providing historical/ancestral legitimacy for armed struggle. It also related to how the war was fought on the ground (Fontein 2006a: 141–65). One of the most remarkable aspects of Zimbabwe's liberation struggle was the close collaborations that sometimes existed between guerrilla fighters – *vana vevhu*, 'sons of the soil' – and spirit mediums (Chitukutuku 2019; Daneel 1995, 1998; Lan 1985; Ranger 1985).

A remarkable degree of 'ethnographic thickness' now characterises historical accounts of localised and regional differences, specificities and social tensions that played out during the struggle (Kriger 1992; Linden 1980; McLaughlin 1996; Maxwell 1999). And it is clear that nationalist mythology of ancestrally inspired struggle did not, alone, account for the rural support that guerrilla fighters relied upon. This was also often the result of coercion. Yet the significance of relationships forged between guerrilla fighters, spirit mediums and ancestors continued to be celebrated in the ruling party's revived postcolonial 'master fiction' (Primorac 2007), 'patriotic history' (Ranger 2004a), 'necropolitan imagination' (Muchemwa 2010) or 'chimurenga politics' (Chigumadzi 2018) throughout the 2000s and beyond. Moreover such 'war legacies', and the 'convivial relations' they can involve (Fontein 2006c), continued sometimes to be invoked by both mediums and war veterans, in (often heavily localised) struggles over authority, legitimacy and – most importantly – land, as well as in the pursuit of shared 'moral agendas' such as the return and reburial of the bones of war dead. The significance of Nehanda's prophecy that 'these bones will rise' for recruits in guerrilla camps in Mozambique during the 1970s, but also for these same people in 2000s, now as war veterans involved in Zimbabwe's recent land reform (dubbed, significantly, the third *chimurenga*) was captured perfectly during an interview with three war veterans in 2001:

> When we were in the camps in Mozambique ... we were told about how Sekuru Kaguvi and Ambuya Nehanda led the struggle to fight against these new colonisers ... it inspired us ... So there was a phrase that she [Nehanda] said, when she was being hanged. 'Our bones will rise, you can kill me now, but our bones will rise against you'. As I speak that phrase it sort of gives you an inexplicable feeling of wanting to take it from there and go forward ... We were told that we were the bones, the very bones that Ambuya Nehanda was saying. So that inspired us to say, whatever happens, we will fight till the end
>
> [...]

Bones, tortured bodies and corporealities of violence

We have not yet fulfilled the mission that was left by our ancestors ... that we, the bones, were tasked to fulfil ... to liberate all the land that we were given by our ancestors. The land of our ancestors must be free ... That is why you see that this present stage of going into the farms is still headed by the war veterans.

[...]

Sometimes you have no control over what you do ... some kind of invisible possession happens that forced us to do the farms ... that is the spirit that sent us to war. The same spirit that made us go across the border ... So unless we fulfil this task ... then there is not going to be any peace in this country ... Even our comrades in arms, who died beside us when we were fighting the war, they are now the spirits that are driving us forward, you see. So we have got a lot of pressure from behind ... that we cannot resist, to do these things to liberate our country, to go forward, for our people.[1]

I have used this quote elsewhere to illustrate the relationship between nationalist mythology of the first *chimurenga* and the complex alliances of guerrillas/war veterans and mediums during the struggle (Fontein 2006a) and since (Fontein 2006b, 2006c). Here, my purpose is slightly different. My focus is bones and their association with ancestral spirits, and the way in which they are connected to the subjective experiences and choices through which individual agency is denied and subjected to the spirits 'driving us forward' in the struggle and the 'third *chimurenga*'. What particularly interests me here is the last section, about the spirits of the liberation war dead pushing their living comrades forward to proceed with land redistribution. This is significant for my concern with what bones and bodies do in Zimbabwe's politics of the dead, because it points to how its postcolonial situation, as well as its literature, has long been animated by the spirits of the liberation war dead, to a similar, if not greater extent, to how ancestral spirits of the 1896 rebellions animated the second *chimurenga*.

This notion of the liberation war dead becoming the bones and spirits that haunt Zimbabwe's postcolonial milieu is one that the author Chenjerai Hove already anticipated in his novel 1988 *Bones*, which he dedicated to:

> For women whose children did not return,
> sons and daughters
> those who gave their bones
> to the making of a new conscience
> a conscience of bones, blood
> and footsteps
> dreaming of coming home one day
> in vain. (1988: 5)

---

[1] Interview with VaKanda, VaMuchina and Madiri, 16/3/01.

Perhaps the spirits and bones of the liberation war dead haunt Zimbabwe in much more profound ways than Nehanda's bones ever did. This is hinted at in the last lines of Hove's dedication: the dead 'dreaming of coming home one day', but 'in vain'. As discussed in the Chapter 1, this issue – the return of war dead from mass graves in former camps abroad (e.g. Chimoio and Nyadzonya in Mozambique, or Freedom Camp in Zambia), or in hastily dug shallow graves or stuffed down old mines shafts within the country's borders – has long been at the centre of highly politicised debates about state commemoration in Zimbabwe (Kriger 1995; Werbner 1998), and continued to be deeply contentious as the country's social, political and economic crises deepened after 2000 (Fontein 2009b). For me, this was best captured by Ambuya VaZarira, an influential (and now late) spirit medium in Masvingo with whom I worked for much of the 2000s (Fontein, 2006a; 2015):

> Some comrades [war veterans] came to me here, telling me that … their fellow comrades who died in Mozambique are continuously giving them problems, harassing them, saying that they should be collected from Mozambique. Some see them in their wardrobes, telling them their names, asking us to take our guns and come and fight. We tell them that our country is already in our hands, but they refuse to believe that we have taken the country. They are saying 'we are having problems in Mozambique, we want to come back home'. So the *masvikiro* [spirit mediums] … agreed that we will work with all the *masvikiro* and we will see how they can collect these dead from Mozambique.[2]

VaZarira echoed concerns raised by others about war veterans and relatives haunted by the spirits of dead comrades yearning to return to the soil of their ancestors, to become ancestors themselves and look after their living relatives and descendants. The importance of 'bringing home' rituals, held a year or more after death and a funeral, to return the spirits of the deceased home from a liminal period in 'the bush' to become benevolent ancestors – *kugadzira* or *kurova guva* in Shona or *umbuyiso* in Ndebele – is well known across Zimbabwe. The need to perform such mortuary rituals is pervasive across cultural, ethnic and religious divides in Zimbabwe, however diverse these rituals often are in different contexts. Failure to perform these rites leaves the deceased unsettled and incomplete in their transformation into ancestors. Such rituals cannot be held when the location or identity of the material remains of the dead are not known. These ritual processes therefore often require the identification of the dead and return of their remains, whether physically or symbolically through soil (Cox 1998: 230–32). If these rituals are not done, that can constitute a bad death (cf. Hertz 1960) – as in cases of people murdered and their bodies dumped in the bush, or those killed in war and buried

[2] Interview with Ambuya VaZarira and VaMoyondizvo, 16/8/01.

in unmarked graves, whose spirits remain troubled, unhappy, and even angry, haunting relatives and friends in dreams, demanding to be returned home, and tormenting the families of those responsible for their deaths as dangerous and terrifying, avenging *ngozi* spirits (Bourdillon 1987b: 233–5; Werbner 1991: 151–6, 188–90).

The presence of these frightening, unsettled *ngozi* spirits haunt Zimbabwe's postcolonial milieu.[3] Mediums and others often complain that droughts, economic and political crises, and even the AIDS pandemic are all the result of these unhappy spirits demanding that their bones be returned to Zimbabwe, and to their home areas, to be buried amongst the bones of their own ancestors. These concerns have long been an issue in Zimbabwe, despite early efforts after independence (Daneel 1995) to rebury the remains of slain guerrilla fighters in district and provincial Heroes Acres, not the mention the hugely problematic, elitist and partisan National Heroes Acre in Harare (Kriger 1995; Werbner 1998). The country's continuing political and economic strife have often been understood to be the result of these unhappy, haunting spirits, which spirit mediums told Andrew Ndlovu (then secretary of the War Veterans Association) back in 2001, were 'the result of rituals not being carried out for the liberation fighters and civilians who died in the war throughout the country'.[4] As Ranger noted, '*ngozi* spirits feature frequently in the Zimbabwean press (and in Zimbabwean novels)' and 'many ex-guerrillas and ex-members of the Fifth brigade [associated with the *gukurahundi* violence] have been terrified of the spiritual revenge of the restless dead' (2010c: 3). Some have even suggested that the proliferation of Nehanda mediums who have emerged since independence in 1980, are possessed not by the ancestor Nehanda herself, but by the angry *ngozi* spirits of her previous mediums, especial Charwe, the medium hanged in 1896.[5] While the inadequacies of state commemoration have often left rural communities, war veterans and family members deeply disturbed by the unsettled spirits of the unreturned dead, the wider political implications of these unresolved war legacies are perhaps best illustrated by common rumours that the late President Mugabe himself was haunted by *ngozi* spirits, particularly that of Josiah Magama Tongogara, a hugely popular ZANLA leader who died in a mysterious (some say suspicious) car accident on the eve of independence. We return will return to this in Chapter 4.[6]

[3] See for example, 'Mysterious deaths rock Kanyemba' *Sunday Mail* 3/6/08
[4] '56 war vets reburied' *Daily News* 25/10/01.
[5] Ruramisai Charumbira, cited in Ranger 2010c (also Charumbira 2008).
[6] 'Paranoid Mugabe dines with a ghost' 2/9/01; 'Mugabe eats supper with spirit of dead rival' 12/8/01, both *Sunday Times* (UK). This rumour has appeared in theatre productions (e.g. *Breakfast with Mugabe* by Fraser Grace, 'Review' *Guardian* 15/4/06) and in 2001 Mark Chavunduka, the editor of *The Standard*, was arrested for writing that Mugabe was haunted by Tongogara's ghost

The Politics of the Dead

It is important to note here that we have moved away from bones in the postcolonial literary imagination, towards real, physical bones and genuinely affective and consequential encounters with the spirits of the dead, demanding their bones be returned, reburied and/or correctly commemorated. Apart from spirits demanding their bones be exhumed from *known* graves,[7] there are also many cases of unidentified human remains resurfacing from *unknown* grave sites, or of being discovered in abandoned mineshafts, dating back to the 1970s. Numerous newspaper reports over recent years attest to this common occurrence.[8] Before the widely publicised war veteran-led exhumations at Chibondo mine in northern Zimbabwe caused enormous controversy in 2011 (see Chapter 3), a potent example came in January 2008 when, after particularly heavy rains, farmers in Mt Darwin, northern Zimbabwe, reported human bones re-emerging from the soil as they ploughed their fields.

> 'We thought the heavy rains were a good omen, but we got more than we bargained for when we began discovering skeletons as we tilled our lands. Some of the bones have been exposed through soil erosion, particularly after the heavy rains', said headman Doffah Dembezeko at a homestead where human remains had just been found in Dembezeko village last Thursday morning.[9]

One dimension of such discoveries, and of the exhumations and reburials they have often provoked (Cox 2005; Shoko 2006), differentiating them from earlier, problematic state commemorations, is that they have frequently been instigated (initially at least) by non-state actors and groups, including war veterans, relatives, mediums, prophets and other religious or 'traditional' leaders; even if significant state actors (CIO agents, local administrators and archaeologists from NMMZ) have subsequently become involved. In a sense, such discoveries and reburial activities, have obliged government agents and institutions to act. In this context, NMMZ's adoption of liberation heritage in the 2000s can be understood, in part, as a response not only to the demands of relatives and living comrades, but even to the resurfacing bones and unsettled spirits themselves. Examples of the spirits of the dead possessing the living bodies of mediums, veterans,

---

('Mugabe Still Fears Chitepo's Legacy', Trevor Grundy, Africa Reports: Zimbabwe Elections No. 16, Institute for War and Peace Reporting, 17/3/05).

[7] Or sometimes in the absence of an identifiable body a sample of soil (Cox 1998: 230–32).

[8] '56 war vets reburied' *Daily News* 25/1/01; 'Independence war mass graves unearthed in Zimbabwe' *New Zimbabwe* 8/7/04; 'Remains of liberation war fighter exhumed' *Herald* 10/7/04; 'State to probe discovery of mass graves' *Herald* 16/7/04; 'Efforts to locate 2nd chimurenga mass graves continue' *ZBC News* 12/1/08; 'Zimbabwe discovers 4000 in Mass graves' *New York Times* 7/3/84.

[9] 'Mt Darwin's killing fields' *Sunday Mail* 13/1/08.

Bones, tortured bodies and corporealities of violence

relatives, even children (Cox 2005; Shoko 2006) to identify their own specific bones to be exhumed from mass graves in northern Zimbabwe are indicative here, as are similar accounts of possessed mediums identifying human remains during war veteran-led exhumations in Rusape, provided by Chipangura (2015; Mupira 2018).

But as the case of Gift Tandare discussed in the previous chapter exemplifies, Zimbabwe's politics of the dead revolves not only around the dead of the anti-colonial struggle, however disputed nationalist historiography and commemoration has become. Zimbabwe is also haunted by the victims of *postcolonial* violence. Apart from escalating political violence since 2000 that we turn to below, the unsettled spirits and resurfacing bones of the *gukurahandi* massacres in Matabeleland, and the Midlands too, continue to be active and affective. This is reflected by the rapidly growing number of calls for the issue to be addressed. During the troubled, violent 2008 elections, the website of the government-controlled newspaper *The Herald* was hacked and all its news headlines were replaced with 'GUKURAHUNDI'.[10] Since then new pressure groups and websites commemorating the *gukurahundi* have been formed calling for formal apologies, justice and resolution.[11] Families and communities in Matabeleland continue to demand to know where their relatives are buried, complaining that their lives are deeply impaired by the unsettled spirits of the *gukurahundi* dead, and the unresolved violence of the 1980s (Eppel 2001, 2013) and, as with the mass graves of the liberation struggle, *gukurahundi* bones and graves are still being discovered.[12]

The previous chapter began to discuss the role played by bones in this complex politics of the dead by focusing on the tensions between heritage and commemorative processes in Zimbabwe, and how such 'unsettling bones' sometimes subverted both these normalising processes. Neither

---

[10] 'Hackers target Herald website' *Newzimbabwe.com* 12/5/08, accessed 19/6/20.
[11] Such as the Matabeleland Freedom Party ('Gukurahundi graves are "war crime sites"' *ZWNews* 18/7/09) and the Mthwakazi Action Group on Genocide in Matabeleland and Midlands (MAGGEMM – see 'Gukurahundi memorial website launched' *Zimbabwemetro.com* 30/5/08). 'Dabengwa wants "unqualified apology"' *Nehandaradio.com* 12/8/09; 'Dabengwa says Mugabe must apologise' *Zimbabwe Times* 12/5/09; 'Push to classify Gukurahundi as genocide' *ZWNews* 8/6/09; 'Nkala denies contributing to Gukurahundi, wants Mugabe prosecuted' *swradioafrica.com* 18/12/09; 'Msika speaks out on Gukurahundi' *Standard* 15/10/06; 'Moyo says Gukurahundi Bill ready by September' *Zim Online* 16/5/07; 'Gukurahundi fears split Zanu' *Standard* 29/4/07; online sources accessed 19/6/20.
[12] 'We want to know where our loved ones are buried' Letters *Daily News* 3/9/01; 'Mass graves from Gukurahundi era located in Matabeleland' *SW Radio Africa* 19/10/05; 'Evidence of "dirty war" lies far below' *Zimbabwe Independent* 29/9/00; 'Film reveals horror details of Ndebele massacre' *Nation* (Kenya) 11/11/07; 'Tracking down a massacre' *BBC news* 7/5/08.

heritage nor official commemoration had been 'commemorative enough' because both failed to respond to the demands of the dead. Bones resurfacing from shallow graves point to other silenced histories and to other ways of handling the dead, their remains and their pasts; to other ways of doing heritage and commemoration. The adoption by NMMZ of 'liberation heritage' not only complemented ZANU PF's new highly politicised historiography, and a growing regional concern with memorialising struggles against colonialism. It also reflected recognition that neither national heritage nor state-led commemoration had been adequate. This is why, while NMMZ undoubtedly welcomed the new funding opportunities the political context offered, its adoption of liberation heritage should also be understood as a response to these demanding unsettled spirits and resurfacing bones. Heritage and commemorative processes came together. Former guerrilla and refugee camps in Mozambique and Zambia were surveyed, excavated and memorialised. Human remains have been exhumed and reburied, often with relatives, chiefs, mediums, veterans and Christian pastors closely involved. The remains of the liberation war dead are no longer just subject to problematic state commemoration, but also heritage processes that increasingly attempt to celebrate the intangible, spiritual and 'living' dimensions of heritage. Heritage became more commemorative in the way that it responds to the demands of the dead, as well as the living comrades, relatives and others haunted by them.

Of course, there were still likely to be problems with this new heritage project. As with many programmes of transitional justice, 'truth' and 'healing', local manifestations of higher-level (national or international) interventions can have little traction amongst ordinary people, by ignoring local cultural, social, political and historical contexts (Baines 2010: 413–7); or, as Lynch (2018) describes of Kenya's post 2007 'performances of justice', by being subject to political manipulation and even reinforcing the structures through which violence persists. Exhumations and reburials carried out under NMMZ's liberation heritage project have often been subject to the competing contestations of rival spirit mediums, church leaders, war veterans and others, each with their own perspectives, loyalties, interpretations and practices. It is also remains unclear whether this portfolio can deal with the mammoth question of the *gukurahundi*, even as new opportunities have emerged since Mugabe's 2017 removal from office.

Nevertheless, the liberation heritage project *was* different to what had come before. Involving efforts both to narrate/objectify the past, and to respond to the demands the dead can make on the living, 'liberation heritage' made heritage processes in Zimbabwe more commemorative, sometimes exemplifying what others (Filippucci 2010; Brown 2007) excavating war sites have also identified: that archaeology does not necessarily 'distance' the past, where human remains are concerned it can become an emotive practice that provokes an experiential sense of the past through its engagement with the materiality of bones. In such contexts, archaeology can become a form of tribute to the dead, and so a form of commemoration.

Emotive materiality, affective presence and transforming materials

Let us return now to the ambiguous or ambivalent agency of bones as both persons and things, or subjects and objects (Geary 1986; Williams 2004: 263–7), in order to explore how this quality animates how bones *do* things. While resurfacing bones are active in the way they retort silenced pasts back to the present, they also confront normative ways of dealing with the past, beyond merely challenging dominant representations of it. What bones do in Zimbabwe is not confined to questions about the representation of the past, or their 'symbolic efficacy' (Verdery 1999), but also has something to do with their 'emotive materialities' as human substances and their 'affective presence' as dead persons; spirit subjects which continue to make demands upon society.

As suggested in the previous chapter, the contributions of two theorists to recent debates about materiality and the agency of objects, Alfred Gell (1998) and Bruno Latour (1999), can be usefully applied to a consideration of what bones do in Zimbabwe, despite important critiques of both these approaches (Leach 2007; Navaro-Yashin 2009). Gell's notion of the deferred or abducted agency, or intentionality, of human subjects operating through objects, finds strong resonances in the notion that what resurfacing bones in Zimbabwe do derives ultimately from the intentionality of the human spirits to whom they belonged, or who they once were. This is powerfully illustrated by the examples of war veterans, mediums, relatives and others, even the President himself, haunted by the unsettled spirits of the dead demanding their bones be reburied, their deaths atoned, and their spirits returned. This, I suggest, reflects the 'affective presence of bones'. In Williams's words, 'as extensions of the deceased's personhood, actively affecting the remembrance of the deceased by the living and structuring future social action' (2004: 266).

Yet there is also a sense in which what bones do is not dependent upon any belief in spirits, ancestors or avenging *ngozi*, or the need to carry out specific rituals to respond to the dead or return them home. There is a sense that what bones can do, their 'agency', is not dependent upon the deferred agency, consciousness or intentionality of the dead themselves, or anyone else. Separate from the consciousness of the living people they once were, but still, in part, dependent upon the uneasy ambivalence of bones as objects/subjects, and their recognition as human, the phenomenological qualities of bones encountered in a ploughed field, an archaeological excavation or a forensic exhumation (Eppel 2001), can also affect the living, provoking and structuring their responses much more like Latour's non-conscious, non-human actants operating, as Miller (2005: 13) suggests, 'below the level of human agency'. This kind of 'agency', I suggest, relates to the notion of 'emotive materiality'. It is exemplified by the account of Crispin Chauke (see previous chapter) of excavating human remains at a former guerrilla camp in Mozambique; and by those of forensic scientists exhuming bone fragments from *gukurahundi* graves in southern Matabeleland (Eppel 2001: 11–15). In such moments, encounters with human bones provoke very different responses than animal bones or artefacts, and can turn forensic/archaeological processes into forms of commemoration (Filippucci 2010: 177). In this way, bones in Zimbabwe have an ambivalent agency which relates exactly to their uneasy subject/objecthood: both as extensions of the dead themselves, as restless, demanding spirit subjects/persons, and as unconscious 'objects'/'things' provoking responses from the living. And as Mattheeuws (2008) has identified in relation to burial practices in Madagascar, the two are often intertwined, so that the emotive materialities of bones points towards their affective quality of presence.

Indeed, Mattheeuws's (2008) example of burial practices among the central-east Malagasy is important because it exemplifies a third approach to questions of materiality that is pertinent to understanding how it is that bones (and indeed bodies) can *do* things in Zimbabwe. Among the central-east Malagasy, people create and shape ancestors by wrapping decomposing, leaking bodies in shrouds until only dry bones and fragments of cloth remain. These bones and cloth fragments are then re-wrapped in new shrouds which catch spirits drawn to the smells of funerary feasts that are captured in their very fabric. Such practices demonstrate the need to consider the efficacy and consequential materiality of the processes by which bones are formed from decaying bodies; how bodies become bones through the leaky decay and transferences of bodily substances. This third approach derives from Ingold's (2007) critique of approaches to materiality in favour of thorough investigation into the properties, flows and transformations of materials. It enriches our understanding of how it is that objects/materials do things, by highlighting for example how it is the merging of materials, of bodily substances into soil, that often animates the politics of the burial in Zimbabwe.

For Ingold (2007: 1–2), to talk of the materiality of an object is an abstraction which distracts attention from the properties of materials, and 'has become a real obstacle to sensible enquiry into materials, their transformations and affordances'. I am sympathetic because what Ingold helps us to understand is that what matters is not necessarily already contained, stabilised and fixed 'objects' like bones, 'the body', 'graves', or indeed the soil, but rather the properties and flows of materials between them. Ingold's perspective favours examination of the qualities and affordances of *bone*, over the materiality of bones. So, for example, the substance of bones is good for making fishhooks but not fuel; or (using Ingold's examples) the enduring qualities of bone affords the construction of long ancestral genealogies, and even simply touching bone involves a transfer of materials (Fontein & Harries 2009).

Yet one result of a determination to focus on materials and substances rather than objects (and subjects), is that inevitably attention is reverted back to how materials become fixed or stabilised as 'objects' (and 'subjects'), physically but also conceptually, historically and politically. This recalls Brown's emphasis (2001) on the work involved in the ongoing (re)constitution, becoming and maintenance of objects from the constant flows and transformations of undefined things, materials and stuff (Fontein & Harries 2009). We could ask how bones or even fragments of burnt bone sifted from the merged substances of decayed bodies, sand and soil, are recognised, fixed, (re)constituted, or remade as uneasy human/things, or ambivalent subject/objects, through archaeological excavation, forensic exhumation or indeed divination; and in turn, how these processes are thus transformed into commemorative rituals or funerals, responding to the demands of the (reconstituted) dead. What are the material, methodological and technical, as well as social, historical and political (not to mention conceptual), affordances and effectivities that enable such unsettling subject/objects to come into being; with their own subsequent consequences?

In this respect, it is interesting to note that among the dilemmas faced by NMMZ archaeologists and the vernacular 'exhumers' of the FHT collaborating at the Rusape 'Butcher site' exhumations in 2013 (Mupira 2018), was the advanced state of decomposition and co-mingling of many of the remains. This made determining the number of individuals buried in different mass graves at the site very difficult. As Mupira explains, 'the total number of people buried in the graves was therefore construed from the long bones using the 'minimum number of individuals (MNI) principle'. And yet, of the 104 individuals determined by such means to have been buried there, 'in 31 cases clothing found in body bags was used to estimate the minimum number of individual cases as it was clear that the bags were buried with people but the bones had been destroyed by micro-environmental elements' (Mupira 2018: 156). As at Chibondo and elsewhere, during the Rusape exhumations NMMZ archaeologists found themselves caught up in tensions with the FHT's vernacular exhumers, who had a tendency to inflate the numbers of people buried in mass graves. The 104 individuals that NMMZ archaeologists determined from their excavations was 'far below the preliminary figures of over one thousand people given by FHZT [or FHT] sources at the beginning of the project' (Mupira 2018: 158). Furthermore, the decomposition, seeping and mingling of fragments of human materials into the soil raised problems with how to distinguish corporeal from non-corporeal substances, and therefore in determining the boundaries of any particular body. Such difficulties provoked further tensions between NMMZ archaeologists and the FHT's vernacular exhumers, as each adopted different approaches to handling human remains and determining the extent of any body, and therefore the number of total individuals identified. As Mupira explains,

> The excavation and systematic removal of skeletal remains was complex due to the constraints exerted upon the exhumation team by the FHZT. The latter continued the argument that we could not remove all the soil covering the remains as this would be tantamount to throwing away the body as 'the soil was/is the person'. The excavation team was also barred from sweeping soil covering the skeletal remains as this was equated to sweeping a person/corpse which is culturally taboo and demeaning. The third prohibition was that the human remains could not be exposed to the sun for a long time, as you would not expose a corpse to the same conditions – the skeleton was equated to a corpse laying in state awaiting burial. These restrictions were of an ethical and cultural nature and in the end were respected but with a pinch of salt as they had professional consequences. This meant that skeletons could not be fully exposed to enable the use of careful archaeological provenience techniques to solve comingling issues … In the end, there was a lot of mixing of skeletal parts and this affected the scientific separation of individuals that were buried in the mass grave. Despite the argument from FHZT that the mixed up parts would be separated during so-called 'spiritual identification' this was never done convincingly. (Mupira 2018: 161–2)

This example illustrates why Ingold's emphasis on the flows and properties of materials is important, because it demands us to recognise and interrogate how processes of becoming and unbecoming, of fixing, stabilising and 'remaking' the dead, are at once material and symbolic, physical and cultural, phenomenological and political. It enriches our repertoire of tools with which to understand how things and substances *do* things; such as how the way that bones and bodies animate the politics of the dead is intimately related to both the material properties, transformations and transferences of human, corporeal and other kinds of substances, and to the social, cultural, technical and ritual processes through which these material transformations and leakages are contained, stabilised, fixed and managed. In other words, focusing on the transforming qualities of different materials can promote a better understanding of how Zimbabwe's politics of the dead is finely intertwined with, and gains traction through, the ritual and material transformations of fleshy, leaky bodies into dry bones, of people into ancestors, and of how the living become or are made safely dead. This helps to reveal how the politics that the exhumation of bones from the liberation war are implicated in, is linked to, or entangled with, that which surrounds the tortured, leaky bodies of more recent violence.

Tortured bodies

Since independence – through both the *gukurahundi* of the 1980s, and more recently, the recurring bouts of political violence since the early 2000s – it is not only resurfacing bones, but also the fleshy, leaky bodies of the victims of political violence that have animated the politics of the dead. From its formation in 1999, the MDC, and its various offshoots and factions, has borne the brunt of ZANU PF's periodic but escalating violence. There were other forms and targets of state and ZANU PF-directed violence in the 2000s and 2010s, such as that associated with the urban clearances of *Operation Murambatsvina* in 2005, and later the discovery of diamonds in Chiadzwa,[13] but violence against opposition parties has been the most extreme and pervasive. In particular, the violence that accompanied the 2008 elections (Masunungure 2009) marked a pinnacle of deepening violence since 2000, and has been followed by continuing, sporadic periods of localised and selective violence since, despite the cross-party unity government (GNU) of 2009–13, and more recently, the establishment of Mnangagwa's presidency in 2017.

The Government of National Unity (GNU) was established after the Global Political Agreement (GPA) of September 2008. This came about as a result of the extensive violence of the 2008 elections, which denied Morgan Tsvangirai victory in an election that most commentators agree he had won, but also denied Robert Mugabe legitimacy, especially from the Southern African Development Community (SADC), thus forcing him into a power sharing agreement with opposition parties. The provisions of the GPA included measures to report upon, investigate and prevent further political violence;[14] however, selective, localised and targeted outbreaks of violence by ZANU PF, and threats thereof, continued throughout this period.[15] After Mugabe's removal from office in the 'soft'

---

[13] 'Victims of diamond massacres buried in Chitungwiza mass graves' *swradioafrica.com* 19/5/09, accessed 19/6/20; 'Victims of Zimbabwean diamond crackdown to be dumped in mass grave' *Times* (UK) 13/12/08; 'Bodies pile up as Mugabe wages war on diamond miners' *Guardian* 11/12/08.

[14] See Raftopoulos 2013 for a detailed account of the GNU period.

[15] 'Another MDC activist murdered' *swradioafrica.com* 7/9/09; 'Zanu PF Youth Militia forces villagers to join party' *radiovop.com* 12/3/10; 'Masvingo villagers get a hiding for attending MDC-T Rally' *radiovop.com* 7/2/10; 'ZANU PF sets up torture bases' *radiovop.com* 25/1/10; 'MDC activist was murdered by police' *ZimEye.net* 5/2/10; 'Political violence growing in rural areas' *IRIN* 27/6/09; 'Soldiers beat resident for playing anti-Mugabe ringing tune' *radiovop.com* 17/8/09; 'Merchants of violence regroup' *Zimbabwean* 28/8/09; 'MDC-T activist

coup led by army chief Constantino Chiwenga in late 2017, the new regime of Emmerson Mnangagwa tried to re-engage the international community by distancing itself from the violence of the Mugabe period. However, after the July 2018 elections, in response to opposition-led protests contesting the results, elements of the army were deployed on the streets resulting in the deaths of six civilians, and many injuries. In January 2019, in response to public protests across the country against fuel price increases, there was further ZANU PF and state-linked violence which resulted in 17 deaths, many more gunshot injuries, and hundreds of beatings and rapes.[16]

Sporadic and targeted violence continued throughout the rest of 2019, including a series of abductions that fit a longer pattern of political disappearances and murders dating back to the 2000s and before. These included the high-profile case of union leader, Dr Peter Magombeyi, linked to doctors' strikes over pay and conditions in September 2019. In some cases, such as that of Magombeyi, abductees have later been found alive, although often injured and brutalised. In many others the bodies of disappeared people have never been found, or found much later, murdered, dumped and even dismembered. As the issue of increasing abductions reached the international media in September 2019 it even provoked a tweet from the US Embassy urging the Zimbabwean Government to hold to account those responsible for more than 50 abductions of civil society, union and opposition leaders it had identified since January 2019.[17] In response, Mnangagwa made several bizarre and unconvincing statements in October 2019, accusing opposition parties and activists of staging abductions in order to discredit the government.[18] In this context (see also Chapter 7), many civic activists (although not all), independent observers and opposition

murdered in fresh political violence' *radiovop.com* 31/8/09; online sources accessed 19/6/20.

[16] Solidarity Peace Trust, 'Resurgent authoritarianism: The politics of the January 2019 violence in Zimbabwe' 20/2/19, http://solidaritypeacetrust.org/download/report-files/resurgent-authoritarianism-the-politics-of-the-january-2019-violence-in-zimbabwe.pdf, accessed 9/4/20; David Moore, 'Fantasy that Mnangagwa would fix Zimbabwe now fully exposed' *The Conversation* 22/1/19; 'Joint Statement on the Escalating Human Rights Violations in Zimbabwe' *Zimbabwean* 19/9/19; 'State-sanctioned murders and abductions: The facts' *Zimbabwean* 20/9/19; 'Lawyers bemoan dearth of human rights' *Newsday* 17/9/19.

[17] See https://twitter.com/usembassyharare/status/1173550395316232192?s=03 16/9/19, accessed 16/9/19.

[18] 'Zimbabwean Dr Peter Magombeyi goes missing after leading calls for strike' *IOL News* 17/9/19; 'Pressure piles over missing doctor' *Newsday* 18/9/19; '"Missing" doctor Magombeyi found' *Herald* 20/9/19; 'Abducted doctor suffers brain dysfunction referred to SA' *Newsday* 25/9/19; 'Zimbabwe abductions: Dozens of protest leaders missing' *Al Jazeera* 23/9/19; 'Govt speaks on

supporters remain deeply sceptical of the new regime's attempts to distance itself from the violence associated with Mugabe's long rule, seeing instead a continuation or 'resurgence'[19] of ZANU PF's older propensity to violence and coercion.

Although the MDC and its factions too have been associated with outbreaks of (often internal) violence at particular moments, the vast majority of political violence since the early 2000s has been committed by ZANU PF supporters, militia or state security agents, including the police and armed services operating on behalf of ZANU PF, and directed against opposition MDC members, their relatives, or others whose loyalty to ZANU PF was in question. During the troubled elections of 2008 in particular, thousands of people were severely beaten, tortured and maimed, and hundreds were killed, and many disappeared.[20] The deepening violence of the 2000s was accompanied by a new wave of disturbances involving dead bodies – funerals interrupted, decomposing bodies found mutilated and dumped in the bush, or piling up unclaimed in overflowing morgues around the country.[21] Apart from Gift Tandare's case (see Chapter 1), such events were exemplified by the abduction, mutilation and murder of another MDC activist, Tonderai Ndira (Wilkins 2013), in May 2008, whose broken and 'difficult to identify' body was discovered in the morgue of Harare's Parirenyatwa Hospital by MDC

---

abduction reports' *Herald* 9/10/19; 'Of missing people, forced disappearances' *Newsday* 14/9/19.

[19] Solidarity Peace Trust, 'Resurgent authoritarianism: The politics of the January 2019 violence in Zimbabwe' 20/2/19, http://solidaritypeacetrust.org/download/report-files/resurgent-authoritarianism-the-politics-of-the-january-2019-violence-in-zimbabwe.pdf, accessed 9/4/20.

[20] HRW – Human Rights Watch (2008) '"Bullets for each of you": state-sponsored violence since Zimbabwe's March 29 elections' 9/6/08, www.hrw.org/en/reports/2008/06/19/bullets-each-you; SPT – Solidarity Peace Trust 'Punishing dissent, silencing citizens: The Zimbabwe elections 2008', www.solidaritypeacetrust.org/133/punishing-dissent-silencing-citizens; SPT – Solidarity Peace Trust, 'Desperately seeking sanity: What prospects for a new beginning in Zimbabwe?' www.solidaritypeacetrust.org/326/desperately-seeking-sanity; all accessed 11/12/19.

[21] 'Police bar memorial service' *Standard* 12/8/07; 'ZANU PF forcibly buries murambatsvina victim as police disrupt solidarity service' *Zimbabwean* 18/9/07; 'State agents want to dig up Tonderai Ndira's body' *SW Radio Africa* 29/5/08; 'ZANU PF thugs disrupt MDC funeral in Harare' *SW Radio Africa* 22/5/08; 'Mutilated body found' *Herald* 11/6/08; 'MDC activist's decomposed body found' *Newzimbabwe.com* 20/6/08; 'CIO hid MDC activist's corpse' *Zimbabwe Metro* 23/7/08; 'Another Zimbabwean opposition activist found dead after abduction' *VOA News* 21/5/08; Two dead bodies by the roadside' *Zimbabwe Times* 20/6/08; 'Decomposing body of MDC polling agent found' *SW Radio Africa* 11/7/08; online sources accessed 19/6/20.

members who had gone to retrieve the bodies of other slain activists.[22] Epitomising how violence against MDC supporters often continued after their deaths, 'state security agents' later visited Warren Hill cemetery, apparently 'furious that murdered MDC activists are being buried there', trying to find and exhume his unmarked grave.[23]

There have been numerous other disruptions to the funerals and burials of people killed by state agents or ZANU militia, and the disappearances of prominent or vocal opposition activists has continued, on and off, since 2008, with a notable rise in 2019 drawing adverse attention against Mnangagwa's new regime.[24] Sometimes such events became sites of new violence, as happened in 2008 when '300 ZANU PF thugs … armed with stones, knobkerries and machetes attacked mourners at the funeral of murdered MDC activists Godfrey Kauzani and Cain Nyevhe'.[25] At other times the funerals of people killed were deliberately blocked.[26] Elsewhere, murdered bodies were deliberately left in prominent places, along roads or pathways, echoing a corporeal, 'necro-politics' that was also used by Rhodesian forces with the bodies of guerrilla fighters during the liberation struggle (Mujere et al. 2017: 92–3). In other cases, relatives were forced to bury their dead in rushed circumstances before proper autopsies could take place.[27] If burying evidence was not the main motivation, then such disturbances sometimes sought to defy the MDC's own efforts to commemorate its murdered and brutalised members as an alternative to the ZANU PF-dominated Heroes Day commemorations, which continued even after the GNU was formed in early 2009.[28]

---

[22] 'Another violent loss for Zimbabwe's opposition' *Globe & Mail* 24/5/08; 'Death of a Zimbabwean activist' *BBC news* 23/5/08; 'Ndira's mutilated body found in mortuary' *Zimbabwe Times* 24/5/08; MDC activist Ndira buried as another body is found in Goromonzi' *Zimbabwejournalists.com* 26/5/08, accessed 19/6/20.

[23] 'State agents want to dig up Tonderai Ndira's body' *SW Radio Africa* 30/5/08, accessed 19/6/20.

[24] 'Zimbabwe abductions: Dozens of protest leaders missing' *Al Jazeera* 23/9/19; 'Govt speaks on abduction reports' *Herald* 9/10/19; 'Of missing people, forced disappearances' *Newsday* 14/9/19.

[25] 'Zanu PF thugs disrupt MDC funeral in Harare' *SW Radio Africa* 22/5/08, accessed 19/6/20.

[26] One report described how Tabitha Marume's funeral – a widow in Rusape who was shot dead in front of 200 terrified villagers – was blocked by the agents who killed her ('Another brutal murder of an MDC hero' *Zimbabwejournalists.com* 1/5/08, accessed 19/6/20).

[27] 'Family forced to rush burial of murdered MDC leader' *Sunday Tribune* 20/4/08.

[28] 'MDC names real heroes' *Zimbabwean* 9/8/07; 'Zimbabwe security forces disrupt opposition memorial service' *VOA News* 13/8/07; 'Police bar memorial service' *Standard* 12/8/07; 'Redefine hero status conferment – MDC' *Zimnetradio.com* 7/8/09; 'Tsvangirai calls for inclusive process to choose Heroes' *Radio VOP* 12/8/09; online sources accessed 19/6/20.

Bones, tortured bodies and corporealities of violence

Throughout the escalating violence of the 2000s, damaged, decomposing bodies of the 'disappeared' periodically re-appeared in odd places, akin to the resurfacing bones of older struggles and previous violence. In April 2007, the body of an abducted journalist was found in Darwendale, just outside Harare.[29] In the same month, engineers at Kariba Dam found the remains of three people whose 'bodies were in coffins stuffed with cement'.[30] These events were later mirrored by allegations in May 2008 – at the height of election violence – that 'ruthless ZANU PF killing operatives' were now 'taking away their dead victims and disposing of them quickly in order to destroy evidence', by putting them into 'extra large aluminium coffins ... covered by concrete before they are tossed in deep dams and lakes'.[31] The same report added that the 'Mugabe regime is also alleged to have a tank of highly concentrated and corrosive sulphuric acid' to deal with the bodies of their victims.

But many bodies were not successfully concealed. In March 2008, the stench of decomposition drew attention to the bodies of 20 MDC activists killed in Lupane district during the 2002 elections, which had lain unburied and unidentified in a morgue in neighbouring Nkayi ever since.[32] Later in 2008, decomposing bodies were found abandoned in hospitals and morgues by relatives and friends too afraid to go anywhere near them. In many cases access to such bodies was deliberately denied.[33] In Goromonzi, after several consecutive discoveries of dead MDC bodies all with 'similar gunshot and knife wounds', the wife of one deceased was 'picked up by the police ... interrogating her on how the families ... discovered the bodies'.[34] More than a year after the 2008 elections, the remains of victims were still being found, as happened in December 2009, when a hunter in Unze mountain in Buhera found the remains of MDC activist, Paul Zimunda, who disappeared in 2007 and is believed to have been killed by ZANU PF militia.[35]

If Zimbabwe's postcolonial milieu is haunted by resurfacing bones and troubling, unsettled spirits of unresolved past violence, then this more recent political violence, and the disrupted burials, mutilated corpses and decomposing bodies that accompanied it, illustrate how it is also the leaky, fleshy materials of the damaged bodies of the recently dead – as

[29] 'Abducted journalist found dead' *SW Radio Africa* 4/4/07, accessed 19/6/20.
[30] 'Zimbabwe: ZESA engineers recover three bodies from Kariba Dam' 12/4/07 ZimDaily.
[31] 'Another brutal murder of an MDC hero' *Zimbabwejournalists.com* 1/5/08, www.zimbabwesituation.com/old/may2_2008.html#Z18, accessed 11/12/19.
[32] 'The revenge of the dead' *Zimbabwe Today* 13/3/08.
[33] 'Corpses rot as ZANU PF terror moves a gear up' *Standard* 3/5/08; 'ZANU PF militia blocking access to dead MDC activists in centenary' *SW Radio Africa* 14/5/08, accessed 19/6/20.
[34] 'Two more MDC activists callously murdered' *Zimbabwean* 19/5/08.
[35] 'Hunter finds activist's remains' *Radio VOP* 6/1/10, accessed 19/6/20.

well as of the many thousands who were tortured and/or raped but not killed – that are entangled in Zimbabwe's troubled postcolonial politics. Deeply disturbing images, widely circulated by human rights organisations in 2008, of the maimed, tortured bodies of victims of ZANU PF's 2008 election violence,[36] illustrate how the emotive materialities of broken bodies can be easily manipulated for ulterior motives. Not just by the perpetrators of violence – as visible signs of 'the ultimate expression of sovereignty ... the power and the capacity to dictate who may live and who must die' (Mbembe 2003: 11) inscribed in flesh – but also by human rights activists and even living victims themselves, choosing to circulate graphic images of bodily violence in order to de-legitimise, subvert and challenge such extreme performances of sovereignty. Here bodies, and images thereof, carry a complexity of 'distributed agencies' as Gell described (1998) – of the perpetrators, the victims and of third parties, not to mention the spirits of the dead themselves who threaten, like the unsettled spirits of war dead and the *gukurahundi*, to return as frightening, avenging *ngozi* – even as the affectivity of these images and these bodies turns on their emotive materialities much more like Latour's unconscious, non-human 'actants'. The political potency, and ambivalence, of such images was demonstrated again in Harare in 2010, when an exhibition of photographs showing torture victims organised by a human rights NGO was abandoned after police harassment.[37] More recently, during the 2019 fuel protests, internet services were deliberately disrupted to prevent the circulation of such images of violence and torture on social media.[38]

One important dynamic of the disruptions of 'normal' burial and funeral processes accompanying the periodic but escalating political violence of the last two decades, has been the deliberate refusal by some relatives to bury victims until their demands for atonement and formal settlement have been met. This is a long-established practice in Zimbabwe (Bourdillon 1987b: 235), where burial is deliberately delayed until grievances are settled – whether through the payment of overdue *lobola* (bride wealth) or more serious atonements for murder or unlawful death. As in northern Uganda, where some 'bodies of murder victims are disposed of ... in a manner intended to encourage the vengeance of the dead' (Baines 2010: 422), the refusal by relatives to bury the dead properly

---

[36] SPT – Solidarity Peace Trust, 2008, 'Punishing dissent, silencing citizens: The Zimbabwe elections 2008', www.solidaritypeacetrust.org/133/punishing-dissent-silencing-citizens; SPT – Solidarity Peace Trust, 2008, 'Desperately seeking sanity: What prospects for a new beginning in Zimbabwe?' www.solidaritypeacetrust.org/326/desperately-seeking-sanity; both accessed 11/12/19.

[37] 'ZimRights forced to abandon photo exhibition after launch' *swradioafrica.com* 25/3/10, accessed 19/6/20.

[38] 'How Zimbabweans stayed online when government shut down the internet' *Times* (SA) 18/1/19.

risks provoking terrifying *ngozi* to haunt the perpetrators of violence. This threat is perhaps powerful enough to explain some of the efforts that went into hiding bodies and 'disappearing' people, as well as cases of rushed, forced burials.

In March 2010, the independent newspaper *The Standard* reported that 'the vengeful wrath of [the] aggrieved spirit' of Moses Chokuda, killed in March 2009, was 'taking personal vengeance on the perpetrators' in Gokwe, after his family deliberately refused to bury him, leaving 'the body of the victim rotting in an inefficient mortuary … until the families of the murderers admit to the crime and perform traditional rites'.[39] According to that report, the alleged murderers were closely linked to high-ranking provincial and district ZANU PF officials, and included Farai Machaya, the son of the Governor of Midlands province, and provincial ZANU PF chairperson, Jason Machaya. Chokuda was last seen alive being bundled into an official ZANU PF vehicle. Police initially recorded but refused to investigate the murder, instead 'harassing' the dead man's relatives to force his burial. But Moses's father

> vowed the family would not bury the body, believed now to be a mere skeleton, until Machaya and his cronies seek forgiveness. And he believes his dead son is helping him 'sort them out' … 'They tried to send a councillor and two other people to secretly remove the body from the mortuary, but when they got there they found my dead son sitting on top of his metal coffin' … 'Very often, people tell me he [the dead Moses] has been seen at some places. They [the families of the alleged murderers] have tried to exorcise the avenging spirit by enlisting the services of different traditional healers, but all this has not worked.'[40]

Eventually, 'after inordinate delays in their case', and several years after Moses's death, the perpetrators of Moses Chikuda's death – Farai Machaya, Edmore and Bothwell Gana and Abel Maphosa – were convicted and imprisoned for the murder in October 2011. But it was not until the Midlands governor, Jason Machaya, paid '35 head of cattle and US$15 000 to compensate Chokuda's family' that his 'remains were finally buried in Gokwe … after the family performed some rituals'.[41]

In the context of efforts during the GNU, and again more recently (since Mugabe's 2017 removal from office) to initiate reconciliation and post-conflict healing in Zimbabwe, the controversies surrounding Chokuda's death, and the *ngozi* provoked by his long-delayed burial, have sometimes been cited as an example of how, as Gordon Chavunduka (President of the Zimbabwe National Traditional Healers Association, now late) put it, 'traditional systems can work in fostering healing' – as he claimed had

---

[39] 'High drama as ngozi fears grip Gokwe' *Standard* 6/3/10.
[40] Ibid.
[41] 'Chokuda case: Avenging spirits exact justice?' *Standard* 30/10/11.

been done by 'traditional experts' around the country after the liberation struggle.[42] Some argued the 'case could be used as a template to address the problematic issue of political violence and impunity', particularly in the context of what the Organ for National Healing, Reconciliation and Integration (ONHRI) co-minister, Moses Mzila-Ndlovu, himself described in 2011 as the GNU's 'flawed' reconciliation programme. Pathisa Nyathi, a prominent Ndebele historian, said it was 'a lesson that whoever spills blood should face the music', demonstrating that 'if you allow yourself to be used, it does not affect the person who gave the order, but it affects you the murderer'. He continued:

> When such things happen in our culture, what is important is to re-establish the lost equilibrium, the lost harmony, the injured social relations. 'The Shona have the best solution to this; the operation of *ngozi* where the murderer has to pay.' While serving a jail sentence would go a long way in punishing the murderers, Nyathi said the avenging spirit would have continued to torment them after prison had they failed to 'make amends with the injured'. He cited the example of the Gukurahundi atrocities in the 1980s, which he said 'will never affect those who gave orders, but willing agents and their families'.[43]

For our purposes, this example illustrates the complexity of agencies at play in the death and after-death of Moses Chokuda – of the victim and his relatives, the perpetrators, their relatives and the police, but also of his avenging *ngozi*, and his transforming body and its substances themselves, rotting in the inefficient mortuary. In this complexity the emotive materialities of the rotting corpse are linked to the affective and deeply disturbing presence of the dead, deployed by the victims or their relatives against the perpetrators or their kin. One purpose of contrasting what bones do and what fleshy, leaky bodies do is to explore this complexity of agencies and affordances entangled in the affective presence and emotive materialities of human remains in Zimbabwe. It provokes a series of questions: if bodies inscribed with violent performances of necro-political sovereignty (Mbembe 2003) do have substantial, if two-sided, political affects, how does this contrast with the unsettling presence of the longer dead? What do the leaky decomposition of flesh and the transformative processes of burial do to the affective presence and emotive materiality of the dead? How do damaged, violated bodies become bones?

The implication of these questions is that, while both bones and bodies in Zimbabwe point towards the affective presence of dead people and their spirits, it is in the differing flows of their materials that their emotive materialities become most apparent. And yet as Mattheeuws's (2008) work on Malagasy funeral shrouds suggests, the two (affective

[42] Ibid.
[43] Ibid.

presence and emotive materialities) are necessarily intertwined. As Ingold (2007; Fontein & Harries 2009) forcefully insisted, there is a need to move away from the notion of composed and contained bodies, towards an understanding of the flows of materials that link people, artefacts and landscapes. There are echoes here of Bloch's unbounded persons (1988), except that incorporating Ingold's insistence upon the properties and flows of materials requires an acknowledgement of the fine-grained entanglements of the material and symbolic, and stretches far beyond the social. Images of and encounters with maimed and fleshy bodies of victims of violence are more disturbing and more emotive exactly because they transgress normal procedures of containing/transforming the leaky flow of bodily materials into the affective presence of dry bones.

As Lan described in his account of symbolic oppositions between wet and dry, young and old, living and dead amongst Korekore-speaking Shona people in the Zambezi valley, 'the process of human ageing is imagined ... as a process of drying out'. 'The older people get, the closer to the ancestors and the more authoritative they become. They are dryer, harder and bonier' (Lan 1985: 93–4). So in Dande dead chiefs were placed on a platform, with 'pots placed beneath to collect the bodily fluids as they emerge. Only when all the wetness of life has drained away and nothing but hard, dry bones remain may the head of the royal lineage be placed in the earth with his ancestors' (Lan 1985: 93–4). Similarly, in the past in southern Zimbabwe some Duma groups dried their dead chiefs before burial in order to ensure their proper transformation into ancestors,[44] while the bodies of young, often unnamed, children, or those who do not yet have teeth (Lan 1985: 93) were buried in wet, flowing river beds. Conversely, if an adult 'is buried in wet soil, the spirit will become a dangerous *ngozi* rather than a kindly *mudzimu* (family ancestor) and this must be prevented at any cost' (Lan 1985: 93). Lan's structuralist leanings are revealed by his tendency to identify static binary oppositions – between wetness and dryness, young and old, living and dead – where we might prefer to see complex material and (simultaneously) symbolic processes of becoming and transformation. Likewise Lan's interpretation of the powerful ritual prohibitions that prevent senior spirit mediums from any contact with blood (whether from a dead body, menstruation or childbirth) might be better understood in terms of the transgression of the appropriate rituals, procedures and processes of bodily containment and transformation through which the living are made properly dead, and people become ancestors.

---

[44] This no longer happens but Duma chiefs are still often buried differently. In 2004/05 Chief Murinye was buried in the wet skin of a slaughtered bull, in an ancestral grave in the Boroma hills, substantiating belonging to the landscape and materialising an important totemic link (Fontein 2015).

The Politics of the Dead

Even 'normal' funerals in Zimbabwe today point to such intricate entanglements of material and symbolic transformations, particularly at those inherently dangerous, liminal moments when the leaking body fluids of a transforming cadaver materialise and threaten the living with the contamination of death, even as they can also be read as indicating the frightening displeasure of the recently deceased hovering around them. So the cloths, mats and other items touched by the fluids of death are safely buried deep in graves with the dead, even as the 'tears' of a corpse or its mouth dropping open during a funeral are read as disturbing signs of the unhappiness of the dead spirit.

In 2006, I attended the funeral of a young man, Mike, who had died of AIDS-related illnesses in southern Zimbabwe (see Figures 5 and 6). As discussed in more detail in Chapter 6, it was a year when there were many deaths in the household in rural Masvingo where I was living at the time. In part because of the nature of his afflictions, which included terrible open lesions, there was a profound sense of 'disgust' (Livingston 2008) and fear of the contamination of death (Niehaus 2007a) that surrounded the treatment of his clothes, his mattress and other personal items. This included not only those items usually 'safely' buried with the dead, but also items of value normally distributed amongst relatives and friends sometime after the funeral. Unusually I noticed some of the women washing his body in preparation for burial were wearing gloves.

During the funeral the body-viewing was dramatically cut short and the burial hastened along when 'tears' came from his eyes and his mouth dropped open; signs, I was later told, of the frightening unhappiness of the dead man's spirit. This illustrates how the emotive materiality of bodily substances can be linked to the affective presence of the dead, and more broadly, how death lays bear the uneasy entanglement of material and immaterial existence which funerary rituals are charged with resolving, but which can make them dangerous events. The evening before, during the all-night funerary vigil commonly held before any burial, I experienced a disturbing, 'uncanny' experience, when, in dim candle light and with tired eyes, I glanced at Mike's sister who was among the funeral entourage, and for a moment, saw Mike's face staring back at me. When I told Francesca, the mother of the household, what had happened, she told me quietly but firmly to not mention it to anyone else.[45]

The kind of structured, symbolic oppositions of wet and dry, purity and pollution, safety and danger that are easily identifiable here, and in the wider ethnography of Zimbabwe, may reflect organising metaphors of thought or society (Douglas 1966), but are also primarily, or at least

---

[45] Field notes, 21/5/06.

FIGURE 5. Grave of Mike Rukasha, Nemanwa (Author 2006)

The Politics of the Dead

FIGURE 6. Burial of Mike Rukasha, Nemanwa (Author 2006)

simultaneously, phenomenological experiences of the emotive materialities of the dead body and its leaky materials. As Williams (2004: 267) pointed out, citing Hertz (1960),

> the body undergoing decomposition and transformation affects memory through a response of fear, revulsion and avoidance ... [and] the experience of the cadaver creates such a unique and powerful impact on the senses that it can form the very basis of the way the dead person is remembered.

Yet as Mike's funeral showed, in Zimbabwe (and Madagascar, Mattheeuws 2008) this emotive materiality of human corporeality is often finely entwined with the affective presence of the dead as spirits that demand recognition, atonement, and 'proper' ritual and material transformation. In this important sense the material disposal of the dead really is a 'technology of remembrance' (Jones 2003 cited in Williams 2004: 267) that 'finishes the work of the dead' (Küchler 1999).

It is pertinent to note here that ancestors are often referred to as *ivhu*, meaning the *soil*, reflecting how proper funerary rites contain and transform the fleshy and leaky emotive materialities of the dead into dry, relatively stable bones through the flows and exchanges of bodily substances into the very material substances of the soil. In this way a dead person is transformed into a benevolent ancestor. Of course, it must be the right soil, where the dead's own ancestors were buried. Not only do these ritual, symbolic and material transformations and transferences of forms, substances and persons animate the politics of exhuming, reburying and commemorating the dead – as the example discussed above of the contestations between NMMZ archaeologists and FHT exhumers at the Rusape exhumations illustrate – they are also reflected in Zimbabwe's troubled politics of land, animating how guerrilla fighters, now war veterans, celebrated (or denigrated) as *vana vevhu* ('children of the soil'), or as Nehanda's arisen bones, appeal to ancestral authority 'to liberate all the land that we were given by our ancestors'.[46]

Far more disturbing is the way that the emotive materialities of bodily substances, and the transgression of normal processes of their material and ritual containment and transformation, appears to have shaped the forms and efficacies of Zimbabwe's political violence. All physical violence engages with and interrupts the containment of bodies and interferes with bodily boundaries and processes. This is particularly apparent in the different forms of torture, violence and the 'techniques of cruelty' that were deployed during the *gukurahundi* (CCJP 2007) and during the 2008 violence. Beatings, rape, shootings and burnings (and sometimes horribly extreme dismemberment) are forms of violence that occurred widely in both these periods, as well as during the violence of the liberation struggle, and to differing extents, around all election periods since 1980 (cf. Sachikonye 2011).

Detailed information about the full nature and extent of violence during the *gukurahundi*, the 2008 elections (cf. Masunungure 2009), and of more recent violence in 2018 and 2019,[47] remains incomplete and emergent. This is often a feature of large-scale episodes of violence and death, hence the common call for 'truth-telling', 'truth commissions' and 'public inquests' as forms of 'healing' and 'reconciliation'; or we could say, of 'remaking the dead'. This is a particular (but not exclusive) problem around the *gukurahundi* however, as the few authoritative accounts that have been written about that period remain very incomplete, and inaccessible to many people and activists in Matabeleland. As Shari Eppel put it:

> That generation of angry 40-somethings has very little information about what actually happened during the *gukurahundi*. There are these 'giant tomes' like *Violence and Memory* [Alexander et al. 2000] and *Breaking the Silence* [CCJP 2007] – but these are not very accessible. So for many of that generation the events of the GK are largely imaginary

---

[46] Interview with VaKanda, VaMuchina and Madiri, 16/3/01.
[47] Solidarity Peace Trust, 'Resurgent authoritarianism: The politics of the January 2019 violence in Zimbabwe' 20/2/19, http://solidaritypeacetrust.org/download/report-files/resurgent-authoritarianism-the-politics-of-the-january-2019-violence-in-zimbabwe.pdf, accessed 9/4/20.

because they don't have access to what knowledge there is – and of course even those large 'tomes' are very incomplete. There is much that is not known.[48]

Yet even with much information remaining outstanding or inaccessible it is clear that particular forms of violence have marked particular periods of Zimbabwe's past. The extreme nature of the 'atrocities and the level of callousness involved' during *Gukurahundi* is well known.[49] These horrors included pregnant mothers opened with bayonets, their babies removed and killed; people thrown alive into mineshafts; or forced to dig their own graves and then shot; while others were burnt to death in locked huts; and there were extensive beatings, interrogations, systematic rapes and sexual torture at camps such as Bhalagwe, where bodies were dumped and burnt.[50] During the 2002 elections, rape gained particular notoriety in relation to youth militia widely deployed for political mobilisation.[51] Rape was also widespread during the 2008 violence; and again more recently during the violence that followed fuel protests in early 2019.[52]

The photographs of torture victims and their injuries that were circulated at unprecedented levels on social media during the 2008 election 'run off' made the widespread access to information about this period unusual.[53] It is something which state authorities clearly learnt from,

---

[48] Interview with Shari Eppel, 11/3/20.
[49] Interview with Strike Mkandla, 12/3/20; Dangarembga et al. 2014.
[50] 'Matabele slaughter: CCJP report expose' *Standard* 4–10/5/97; see also CCJP 2007.
[51] '"Green bombers" using rape as political weapon' *Financial Gazette* 4/10/03; 'Rapes linked to groups tied to ruling ZANU PF party' *UN Wire* 21/3/03; 'Zimbabwe: Focus on rape as political weapon' *IRIN* 8/4/03.
[52] See 'Electing to rape: sexual terror in Mugabe's Zimbabwe' AIDS-Free World, December 2009; 'Outrage over reports of rape by Zimbabwe soldiers' *IOL* 25/1/19, www.iol.co.za/news/africa/outrage-over-reports-of-rape-by-zimbabwe-soldiers-18963713, accessed 10/4/20; 'Zimbabwe's violent crackdown continues amid reports of rape' *Al Jazeera* 25/1/19, www.aljazeera.com/news/2019/01/zimbabwe-violent-crackdown-continues-reports-rape-190125184915333.html, accessed 10/4/20; 'Exclusive: Zimbabwe soldier says he committed rape and broke legs in government-sanctioned crackdown' *Daily Telegraph* (UK) 25/1/19.
[53] Hundreds of graphic images of brutalised bodies and individual stories of violence were circulated on websites and social media; many have since been taken down. For an example see http://solidaritypeacetrust.org/image-gallery/nggallery/spt-main-album/desperately-seeking-sanity, accessed 10/4/20; also 'Political Violence Report' December 2008, Zimbabwe Human Rights NGO Forum, www.hrforumzim.org/wp-content/uploads/2010/06/200812MPVR.pdf, accessed 10/4/20; '"Bullets for Each of You": State-Sponsored Violence since Zimbabwe's March 29 Elections' Human Rights Watch Report, June 2008, www.hrw.org/sites/default/files/reports/zimbabwe0608.pdf, accessed 10/4/20.

as evidenced by the shutdown of internet services during violence in 2019.[54] The 2008 violence was perhaps most marked by the extreme and sometimes bizarre forms of violence that interfered with and disrupted bodily boundaries, and particularly the skin, of living victims.[55] As well as shootings, widespread rape, head injuries and abductions, one NGO reported 'literally thousands of cases of soft tissue damage',[56] reflecting widespread 'techniques of violence' that created extensive and painful sores, open wounds and lesions, which revealed, exacerbated and agitated bruised and damaged bodily flesh. Sometimes extensive bruising and open wounds from extreme beatings and stabbings with sticks, iron bars, knives and barbed wire were supplemented by forms of torture including *falanga* (beatings on the sole of the feet), the use of weed killer to aggravate wounds and prevent healing, or burning plastic and grasses to exacerbate deep flesh wounds.[57] Like rape, such violence invasively and demonstratively violates normal processes of bodily containment through which bodies and persons are constituted.

If writings on the symbolic and cosmic dimensions of ethnic and genocidal violence in central Africa (Appadurai 1998; Maalki 1995; Scott 2005; Taylor 1999) have sometimes suggested that ontologically specific notions of 'chaos', linked to uncontrolled 'postcolonial ethnic hybridity' (Appadurai 1998), 'blocked bodies' (Taylor 1999), or physical 'body maps' (Maalki 1995) lay behind the techniques of cruelty and bodily dismemberments witnessed during the genocidal horrors of Rwanda in 1994, or Burundi in 1972, then the attention to material qualities, transferences and flows of bodily substances that Ingold urges, warns against over-interpretation of the symbolic causes of such extreme violence. Rather it pushes for a better understanding of the entangled symbolic and social, political and material consequences of violent interruptions and transgressions of the normal, even normalising, processes of containment and transformation through which things and materials are (re)constituted as objects/subjects, bodies and persons, and through which fleshy bodies become bones, persons can become spirits, and the living become dead.

[54] 'Zimbabwe imposes internet shutdown amid crackdown on protests' *Aljazeera.com* 18/1/19, accessed 10/4/20; 'Zimbabwe orders second internet shutdown in a week of deadly protests' *npr.com* 18/1/19, accessed 10/4/20; 'Zimbabwe orders a three-day, country-wide internet shutdown' *accessnow* 15/1/19 www.accessnow.org/zimbabwe-orders-a-three-day-country-wide-internet-shutdown, accessed 10/4/20.

[55] SPT – Solidarity Peace Trust 2008 'Punishing dissent, silencing citizens: The Zimbabwe elections 2008', www.solidaritypeacetrust.org/133/punishing-dissent-silencing-citizens, accessed 11/12/19.

[56] SPT – Solidarity Peace Trust 2008 Desperately seeking sanity: What prospects for a new beginning in Zimbabwe? p. 35, www.solidaritypeacetrust.org/326/desperately-seeking-sanity, accessed 11/12/19.

[57] Ibid.

In this way the 'techniques of cruelty' and even 'ritualised' forms of Zimbabwe's 2008 violence, and of earlier and subsequent periods (cf. Sachikonye 2011), link the torture of living victims to 'post-violence' disruptions to processes of dealing with and burying those who were killed. Unidentified bodies dumped in the bush, people disappeared, funerals disrupted or prevented became a kind of second violence that had similarly marked the *gukurahundi* killings (Eppel 2001; CCJP 2007), when relatives were often prevented from burying their dead, forced to dump bodies in abandoned mines, dance on their shallow graves or, as happened at Sitezi, when human remains were later dug up and burnt to conceal evidence. Just as beatings and violence interfere with, reveal and disrupt normal processes through which bodily substances are contained and bodies and persons are constituted, so disrupted funerals and prevented commemorative efforts disturb the material, social and symbolic processes and techniques through which things and substances become human remains, bodies become bones, and living people become or are made safely dead.

Towards 'healing' and 'reconciliation' during the Government of National Unity 2009–2013

In the aftermath of the violence of the 2008 elections, the reformation of ZAPU that followed, the 'Global Political Agreement' (GPA) of September 2008, and the fragile Government of National Unity (GNU) formed in February 2009 (Raftopoulos 2013), there were some signs that the unresolved legacies of both the *gukurahundi* and of post-2000 political violence had gained renewed salience and might be addressed. The 2008 violence had denied electoral victory to Morgan Tsvangirai, the main opposition MDC leader, after he withdrew from the presidential run off due to unprecedented levels of coercion by ZANU PF, but it also 'simultaneously denied Mugabe legitimacy' after the images of tortured, violated bodies circulating across international media prevented SADC (Southern African Development Community) leaders from acknowledging and legitimising his presidency (Eppel 2013: 211). Those who suffered during that violence 'were therefore hopeful that their needs would be taken into account by the GPA' (Eppel 2013: 211). The formation of the cross-party ONHRI also generated some hope that the complex *gukurahundi* legacies and its troubling remains could now begin to be dealt with – just as the liberation war dead were receiving renewed attention as 'liberation heritage' – although ONHRI's main political purpose was the more immediate aftermath of the 2008 elections.[58]

---

[58] 'GNU crafts bill to 'guide national healing' *Standard* 18/7/09; 'Taking transitional justice to the people' *Zimbabwean* 13/08/09; 'Gov. dedicates three days to national healing' *swradioafrica.com* 21/7/09, accessed 19/6/20; 'Leaders to

However, as Eppel (2013: 241) has shown in her detailed analysis of the GNU's 'half-hearted commitment to "healing"', such hopes soon eroded due a variety of factors, including continuing political violence in some areas, and a general lack of political will among the leadership of the GNU's different political parties, and therefore little official support or clear direction for ONHRI's activities. The complexities of what 'reconciliation' and 'healing' – let alone truth-telling, acknowledgement and 'justice' – might actually amount to in the wake of Zimbabwe's different, unresolved histories of violence were swamped by the gritty inter- and intra-party politics of the GNU years. A new 'obstructive politics' by ZANU PF hindered the implementation of the GPA's various 'democratising provisions', including constitutional reform and the Zimbabwe Human Rights Commission, as well as ONHRI (Raftopoulos 2013: xvii). These 'obstructive measures' created 'formidable obstacles' for the MDC factions in the GNU, who increasingly lost political credibility and support due to ongoing internal rivalries and sometimes violence, and deepening corruption among its ranks in government, as well as the wider failure of the 'inclusive government' to deliver on its social and economic promises (Raftopoulos 2013: xix–xx). As the MDC factions were increasingly overwhelmed by GNU politics, ZANU PF focused on successfully re-establishing its political hegemony ahead of new elections in 2013 (which it later won), expanding its patronage networks and tightening its control of the government's security arms, as well over new diamond revenues from eastern Zimbabwe. Continuing and new forms of selective violence and coercion, or threats there of, remained part of ZANU PF's strategy during the GNU years (Raftopoulos 2013: xix), reflecting the long history of military-ZANU relations dating back to the liberation struggle (Mazarire 2013; Tendi 2020b), but also its renewed efforts to seize control of urban spaces through ZANU PF-linked gangs and militia, like Chipangano in the Mbare area of Harare (McGregor 2013). However, ZANU PF has never solely relied on violence and coercion (or on memories thereof) and during the GNU it also forged new political platforms around 'indigenisation' and opposition to international sanctions, to complement its existing 'chimurenga politics' and land redistribution.

'One of the dilemmas facing the ONHRI', Eppel explained, was 'the tension about what "healing" entails and what route TJ [Transitional Justice] should take, with the predominant TJ paradigm of the truth commission/justice model standing in juxtaposition to a notion of homegrown "ubuntu", or reconciliation' (2013: 215). ZANU PF's line on these issues reflected a position adopted by other African leaders across the region (for example, Uhuru Kenyatta in Kenya, and Paul Kagame in

launch national healing Friday' *Zimbabwe Times* 22/7/09; 'National Healing begins' *Herald* 15/6/09.

Rwanda), who have often been suspicious of international justice mechanisms, particularly as manifest at the International Criminal Court in The Hague, perceiving them to be biased, selective and a challenge to national sovereignty. During GNU discussions around the formulation of a policy for 'national healing and reconciliation', ZANU PF pushed against the demands of many Zimbabwean civic organisations for the ONHRI to involve a 'truth commission', reparations and 'retributive justice' mechanisms, as have become fairly standard aspects of international truth and justice programmes (although not without critique). Neither side of this juxtaposition between modular, 'international' forms of truth-telling and justice versus 'African' forms of reconciliation, can necessarily accommodate the complexity and diversity of contentious demands that deep, unresolved legacies of violence can invoke, particularly in the absence of accompanying social and economic re-address, or without genuine, long-term and ongoing 'grassroots' community-based involvement (Eppel 2013: 217–23). During the GNU discussions about the proposed functions of the ONHRI, the space needed for critical consideration of what might constitute effective 'healing' and 'reconciliation' was scarcely afforded.

Given the fragility of the GNU arrangement, it was not surprising that the 'National Policy Framework for National Healing and Reconciliation' commissioned by the UNDP and later approved by the GNU cabinet in early 2012, closely matched ZANU PF's preferred approach. It focused mainly on establishing district- and ward-level 'peace and reconciliation' committees, involving training programmes for 'traditional leaders', women and youth groups, but excluded any discussion of truth commissions, reparations, compensation or restorative justice. It also excluded any discussion of commemoration or memorialisation which might have opened 'the way for monuments, exhumations and reburials of the dead' (Eppel 2013: 216–17). It thereby again denied victims of postcolonial violence access to transformative, material processes of exhumation, return and reburial – funerary processes involving the material containment and transformation of bodies, so that people violently killed or disappeared could be made safely dead – even as these were, at the same time, becoming increasingly prominent ways of dealing with the surfacing bones and unsettled sprits of the independence struggle through NMMZ's liberation heritage programme. The GNU's ONHRI therefore did or could not effectively challenge the secondary 'post-violence' of disrupted funerals and dumped or disappeared bodies that had marked both the 2008 violence and the *gukurahundi* two decades before; nor did it challenge established hierarchies of what constituted a life worth commemorating in ZANU PF's postcolonial 'necropolitan imagination' and 'aesthetics of heroism' (Muchemwa 2010). Given the

GNU's flimsiness it was 'only the most non-threatening of TJ policies that could possibly be adopted and advanced' (Eppel 2013: 217).

Whatever the resonances with wider, regional critiques of international justice mechanisms, ZANU PF's motivation for pushing for an approach based on 'African' forms of 'reconciliation', avoiding modular, international, 'truth and justice commissions', was also clearly based on their desire to avoid accountability for past violence, and to maintain control over historical narratives of violence and victimhood which continue to be a key aspect of its postcolonial 'master fiction' (Primorac 2007) and 'chimurenga politics' (Chigumadzi 2018). In this respect, the arrest of Moses Mzila-Ndlovu, the MDC's co-minister of healing in the ONHRI, after attending a 2011 commemorative service for *gukurahundi* victims, indicated how for ZANU PF 'in Matabeleland "healing" should take place without "revealing"' (Eppel 2013: 215). As with NMMZ's 'liberation heritage', ZANU PF could not allow the GNU's ONHRI to attempt to accommodate the *gukurahundi*'s complex legacies. After Ndlovu's arrest relations between the ONHRI's three co-ministers became increasingly strained and its activities noticeably stalled.

Therefore, like 'transitional justice' and 'reconciliation' programmes elsewhere (Baines 2010: 413–17; Lynch 2018) the GNU's 'national healing' efforts were problematic and ineffectual for a myriad of complex reasons, not least the contested and unclear motivations of its main architects.[59] Recurring bouts of localised violence throughout that period constantly threatened to materialise further waves of political violence, especially with new elections in 2013 approaching. Such threats were effectively utilised by ZANU PF to regain electoral dominance when those elections did take place. As Marongwe (2012: 236) and Raftopoulos (2013: xix) have noted, memories of ZANU PF's 'history of violence' were politically affective not only through instigating fear of more violence, but also through complicity. 'The widespread involvement of people in ZANU PF's coercion and violence' Raftopoulos (2013: xix) explained, 'has created a constituency with a stake in such violence'.

Nevertheless, and whatever its limitations, some investment in the promise of 'reconciliation' and 'healing' was made by different parties in the unity government, and by civic groups across Zimbabwe's human

---

[59] Eppel 2013: 213. Also 'Tsvangirai wants Gukurahundi probe' *Zimbabwean* 25/7/09; 'Zim healing process flawed' *Zim Online* 24/7/09, accessed 19/6/20; 'Gukurahundi victims confront Nkomo' *Standard* 28/11/09; 'Amnesty is way to national healing: Gono' *Zimbabwean* 7/8/09; 'Sunday View: State's celebration of denial: Political uses of national healing' *Standard* 8/8/09; 'Hurdles lie in wait for national healing process' *Zimbabwe Independent* 30/7/09; 'National healing elusive, as torture bases re-emerge' *Zimbabwean* 16/2/10.

rights sector during this period.[60] At the very least, a conversation was begun which would regain broader political salience in the wake of Mugabe's 2017 removal from office and the new regime's attempts to differentiate itself from its predecessor (see Chapter 7). Whatever the flaws, the GPA and GNU, and its stalled ONHRI did 'facilitate some useful discussions among Zimbabweans on what they believe TJ processes should include in the future'. In some areas a reduction in violence allowed 'community TJ processes to take place that have facilitated resolution of old conflicts', even if at a national level the GNU's fragility precluded 'a transitional space in which meaningful reconciliation among all parties can take place' (Eppel 2013: 241–2).

If the ONHRI turned out to be contested and ineffectual, other structures linked to the GPA were sometimes able to promote co-operation and resolution to violence at local levels, particularly the Joint Monitoring Committee (JOMIC), formed in 2009 to investigate violations of the GPA. Having established credible cross-party mechanisms for collaboratively investigating incidents of violence, JOMIC extended its structures into district levels in 2011 with the explicit purpose of developing a 'proactive conflict prevention strategy and to build tolerance at the grassroots' (Eppel 2013: 239). Although later both JOMIC and the Human Rights Commission (established in 2010, and later carried over into the new 2013 constitution – see Munguma 2019) were subject to obstruction and accusations of bias by ZANU PF (Raftopoulos 2013: xviii–xix), early 'pilot' efforts around Harare to constitute 'peace liaison committees' did 'persuade local political actors to cooperate better' and resulted in significant 'reductions in political violence' in those areas (Eppel 2013: 239). Therefore, however frustrated wider hopes were for the possibility that Zimbabwe's complex legacies of postcolonial violence might be addressed, there were some significant, localised opportunities emergent during the GNU period giving some cause for optimism for future peace-building initiatives. As Eppel said (hopefully) in early 2013 (before elections that year restored ZANU PF's electoral hegemony) 'for the first time in over three decades of transitions, the opening to address and redress the violence and other injustices of the past in a broad and creative way, may be about to materialise' (2013: 242). Seven years later, in March 2020, she and other Matabeleland civic activists and politicians were much more circumspect about the possibilities for 'redress', 'truth-telling', 'reconciliation' or even 'restorative justice' that the National Peace and Reconciliation Commission (NPRC) established in 2018 by Emmerson Mnangagwa purported to offer.[61]

[60] Zimbabwe Human Rights NGO Forum, 2009, 'Taking transitional justice to the people', Harare: ZHR NGO Forum.
[61] Interview with Shari Eppel, 11/3/20; Interview with Mbuso Fuzwayo, 12/3/20; Interview with Strike Mkandla, 12/3/20.

Conclusions

The arguments developed in this chapter suggest that the politics of the dead involved in Zimbabwe's post-2000 political violence, as with the resurfacing bones and troubled spirits of the *gukurahundi* and the liberation war, reaches beyond (even as it necessarily implicates) contests over memory, the representation of the past and the 'symbolic efficacy' of dead bodies (Verdery 1999). Rather, it gains traction exactly through, and as a consequence of, the flowing materials and transforming properties of bones, bodies and bodily substances, and the material and corporeal processes through which living bodies are contained and transformed, or not, into the different kinds of dead. This sheds new light on how corporealities of violence, of the secondary violence of disturbed and interrupted funerals and burials, and of mechanisms of post-violence resolution and 'remaking the dead', are entangled and have political efficacy. The complex ritual, symbolic and material processes through which human substances are (re)constituted and transformed from bodies to bones, through which persons are remade to become ancestors, and the living are made safely dead, are precarious and can have long consequences.

Resonating with similar cases in northern Uganda (Baines 2010; Branch 2011), some efforts at localised levels by individuals, communities and religious leaders during the GNU years, and since, to implement community-based processes of reconciliation – such as the case of Moses Chokuda – suggest that dangerous *ngozi* spirits from recent political violence have joined the unsettled spirits of Zimbabwe's liberation war and the *gukurahundi*, in their demands for atonement, resolution and remaking. Whatever its obstruction of the GNU's 'healing' and 'reconciliation' efforts, the violence of 2008 continued to 'haunt ZANU PF' long after it re-established its electoral dominance in 2013.[62] Indeed, before Moses Chokuda's *ngozi* began haunting the Gokwe mortuary in 2010, similar concerns had been raised after the violence of the 2002 presidential election, when Chavunduka had warned of 'a wave of psychotic problems' akin to the 'vast numbers of cases … in 1980, when the freedom fighters returned from the war, because of people they killed'.[63] Even before the 2002 election, Oppah Muchinguri, then a ZANU PF Provincial Governor, had 'warned ZANU PF supporters … that if they killed opposition supporters they – and not the party – would be haunted by evil spirits'.[64] Since then, perhaps because of their abandonment by the instigators of their violence,

---

[62] '2008 murder haunt ZANU PF' *Daily News* 22/12/06; '2008 abductions haunt VP Mohadi' *Nehanda Radio* 10/1/20, https://nehandaradio.com/2020/01/10/2008-abductions-haunt-vp-mohadi, accessed 10/4/20.

[63] 'Political thugs to pay for murderous acts through mental illness' *Daily News* 27/4/02; 'The wage of torture is torture' *Standard* 20/3/10.

[64] 'Political thugs to pay for murderous acts through mental illness' *Daily News* 27/4/02.

The Politics of the Dead

numerous accounts have appeared of former CIO agents and ZANU militia haunted by the enormity of their violent atrocities, coming forward to confess.[65] In 2007, for example, 'John', a former member of the CIO, admitted that 'the things I have done haunt me every day'. Two years later, Biggie Chitoro, a war veteran leader from the Midlands, called for a Truth and Reconciliation Committee, because 'people need to forgive each other. I also need to be forgiven by my victims'.[66]

Aside from ONHRI's stalled activities during the GNU, and alongside JOMIC's early successes, in some rural areas local efforts by 'traditional leaders' were already taking place. In July 2009 a headman in Chimanimani organised a 'traditional cleansing exercise' at a local training centre that had been used as a 'torture base' the year before, in which he and his sons took part. According to one person 'this place has bad memories for the villagers. We hope that the headman is sincere when he is talking about cleansing this place. At times you see strange things if you pass the centre during the night'.[67] Elsewhere similar efforts were less successful, as in Chipinge in August 2009, when Headman Chichichi fled his homestead after angry ZANU PF supporters threatened him for 'presiding over cases of political violence committed during the run up to last year's presidential run off elections'.[68] Yet such localised efforts do suggest that Morgan Tsvangirai (then GNU Prime Minister) had been right when he said 'the blood of political violence victims that have been murdered by ZANU PF supporters will one day … haunt Mugabe and his people'.[69] Even some *gukurahundi* activists acknowledge a need for the perpetrators of those atrocities to be recognised as 'victims', especially those who

> have gone to those communities to try to apologise, because they are being haunted by spirits', but were prevented by 'state agents … from doing that, because there has been no [government] acknowledgement of the *gukurahundi* … They have tried to suppress the matter as much as possible.[70]

If the unsettled spirits of Zimbabwe's older histories of violence are anything to go by, the leaky bodies, resurfacing bones and unsettled spirits of electoral violence in 2008 and of more recent killings since Mugabe's

[65] 'Confessions of a Zimbabwe CIO ZANU-PF thug' *Harare Tribune* 22/3/09; 'Zimbabwe's terror: how I raped and tortured for Mugabe' *Independent* (UK) 7/6/07.
[66] 'Confessions of a Zimbabwe Torturer' *BBC news* 6/7/07; 'I need forgiveness – Biggie Chitoro' *Zimbabwean* 6/5/09.
[67] 'Headman cleanses torture base' *Zimbabwean* 22/7/09.
[68] 'Headman in hot soup with ZANU PF' *Radio VOP* 13/8/09.
[69] 'MDC activist Ndira buried as another body is found in Goromonzi' Zimbabwejournalists.com 26/5/08, www.zimbabwesituation.com/old/may26a_2008.html, accessed 11/12/19.
[70] Interview with Mbuso Fuzwayo, 12/3/20.

removal, will continue to trouble its political milieu until efforts to resolve Zimbabwe's multiple troubling pasts are taken forward again. It is not yet clear what will come of President Mnangagwa's 2019 announcement that *Gukurahundi* exhumations, reburials and commemorations would now go ahead, particularly given the continuing violence associated with his regime; although some *gukurahundi* exhumations have taken place.[71] Nor is it clear, if such measures do proceed, what form they will take, who will be involved, and if they will amount to the meaningful processes of resolution or even justice that many demand. It is still to early to say whether the NPRC[72] has learnt from the difficulties that ONHRI faced, or if it has been empowered sufficiently (politically, financially and organisationally) to effectively deliver its wide mandate. Many remain sceptical.[73]

As Rowlands argued (1999: 142), it is 'by no means obvious' how commemorative monuments and rituals can provide 'healing' and the resolution of suffering. The arguments developed here suggest that in Zimbabwe not only should the demands of the dead as well as of the living be taken seriously, it is also necessary to pay close attention to the transforming materials of dead people, and the complex ritual and material processes through which bodies and persons, bones and ancestors are transformed, contained, stabilised, (re)constituted and remade. If the efficacy of violence itself relies in part on the violation and interruption of corporeal processes of containment and bodily boundaries though which bodies and persons are constituted, then attempts to address such unresolved legacies of violence too must engage with the corporeal forms and transformations through which the living are turned into the safely dead. Baines (2010), like Eppel (2013), makes a compelling argument for taking seriously the complex localised 'socio-cultural processes of reconstruction' taking place amongst ordinary people and 'intimate enemies' in Uganda, Rwanda (Chigwenya 2019) and elsewhere, beyond the scope (and 'universalist' premises) of formal state or international programmes of national reconciliation. The argument presented here suggests attention must also be paid to the changing and diverse materialities of bodies and bones involved in such processes.

The material transformations of bodily forms and substances clearly inhere in very complex ways to the social, symbolic and political

---

[71] Some were led by Shari Eppel's Ukuthula Trust, involved in AMANI trust exhumations in the late 1990s and a leading author of the CCJP Gukurahundi report (2007). See 'Gukurahundi Horrors Relived, The Big Interview' *ZimEye.net* 5/5/19, accessed 11/12/19. Also 'Govt to facilitate Gukurahundi exhumations, reburials' *Newsday* 10/4/19; 'ED pledges support for Gukurahundi victims' *Standard* 24/3/19; 'Gukurahundi victims need closure, redress' *Standard* 14/4/19; 'NPRC calls for Gukurahundi truth-telling' *Herald* 17/4/19.

[72] See www.nprc.org.zw, accessed 10/4/20.

[73] Interview with Mbuso Fuzwayo, 12/3/20; Interview with Strike Mkandla, 12/3/20; Interview with Shari Eppel, 11/3/20.

The Politics of the Dead

transformations of the living into the dead. This is manifest in 'normalising' funerary processes, but also in the forms, shape and practices of particular kinds of political violence, as well as in the 'secondary', 'post-violence' of disrupted funerals and disappeared or dismembered bodies, which characterised, in particular, the violence of 2008. Therefore attention to the material dimensions, flows and entanglements of the social, political, ritual, symbolic and substantive processes by which the living become or are made safely dead, can offer useful insight for those trying to understand how corporeal violence has political efficacy, and for those concerned with the resolution of legacies of past and recent violence, which by all accounts Zimbabwe still so desperately needs (Eppel 2001, 2004, 2009, 2013).

Whatever the flaws, limited successes and important lessons learnt from the GNU's stalled 'reconciliation' initiatives in the 2009–13 period, careful attention to the entangled processes of material, social, political and symbolic containment and transformations of living bodies and persons into the safely settled dead, will need to be part of whatever future efforts to resolve Zimbabwe's troubled pasts are embarked upon. Such efforts will also need to heed the lessons learnt from those processes of exhumation, reburial and remaking the dead already taking place under NMMZ's 'liberation heritage' project, as well as those *gukurahundi* exhumations conducted by AMANI Trust in the late 1990s and early 2000s, and much more recently by Ukuthula Trust.[74] As demonstrated by the 'grotesque politicking' that took place around the war veteran-led, vernacular exhumations at Chibondo mine in 2011 (to which Chapter 3 turns), the uncertain 'duplicity' and excessivity or 'alterity' of human materials – demanding but also defying any stability of meaning or semantic closure – suggests that such processes of containing and transforming leaky bodies, fragmented human remains and resurfacing bones into the safely stabilised dead, however much demanded, are also often deeply contested and ultimately incomplete. This raises important questions about the unfinished nature of all death, and the possibilities for any complete or final kind of 'healing' and 'resolution' which processes of exhumation and reburial in post-violence contexts are often purported to offer.

---

[74] See footnote 71.

3

Chibondo: Exhumations, uncertainty and the excessivity of human materials

The previous chapters have begun to explore the multi-faceted nature of Zimbabwe's politics of the dead, and the complex efficacies of bones, bodies and material properties and flows that animate it. Chapter 2, in particular, focused on how the corporeal transformations that are essential to 'proper' funerary processes, through which people are made 'safely' dead, can also be a key feature of the violence that precedes death, and of the 'secondary violence' that can follow it, both of which interrupt and disrupt normal processes of containment and transformation through which people, living and dead, are bounded, stabilised and constituted. Managing, containing and stabilising these corporeal transformations are, as a result, also often part of the contested processes that are purported to offer resolution or 'healing' to troubling past legacies of violence, disrupted funerals and unresolved death, by 'remaking' the dead; processes that are always potentially unfinished or incomplete. This is how the long-standing politics surrounding state commemoration, and more recently 'liberation heritage', are connected to and intertwined with the troubling and increasingly noisy silence surrounding the *gukurahundi* massacres of the 1980s, and with the recurring, deepening violence of the post-2000 period.

This chapter pushes this analysis further in two ways. Firstly, by considering how the excessivity of human remains – animating their 'alterity' or 'otherness', and which demands but ultimately always retains the potential to defy resolution, stabilisation and 'closure' – provokes or reveals a profound uncertainty that is central to Zimbabwe's politics of the dead. And secondly, to begin to explore how this uncertainty, provoked by the alterity of human corporeality but often manifest in a myriad of rumours and competing, contested accounts of past lives and unresolved deaths, can have its own duplicitous political utility as part of a performative stylistics of power located between the tensions of bio- and necro-politics. This question about the politics of uncertainty and the 'incompleteness' of death will then be further discussed in Chapter 4 looking at what I call 'political accidents'.

The Politics of the Dead

Here I focus particularly on the much publicised controversies, rumours and contestations that emerged in 2011 around the war veteran-led, vernacular exhumations of hundred of bodies from a disused mine at Chibondo, in northern Zimbabwe. As discussed, these were not the first exhumations of human remains dating to the liberation struggle that war veteran groups like the FHT, or indeed NMMZ, had been involved in since independence. Nor were they the last. The exhumations of mass graves dating from the war, led by mixed teams of war veterans, mediums, relatives and NMMZ archaeologists, amongst others, have continued to take place since the highly publicised Chibondo exhumations of 2011; now often formalised and legitimated under NMMZ's liberation heritage portfolio, such as at Rusape in 2013 (Chipangura 2015; Mupira 2018), and later at Herbert and Guinea Fowl mines, and most recently at Odzi mine in Manicaland in 2019.[1] What makes Chibondo important and different, however, is not only the unprecedented scale of the exhumations – over 700 bodies were exhumed at the site[2] – but also the often quite grotesque media publicity and crude ZANU PF politicking that surrounded the events there, and the intensity of rumours, speculation and public contestation they provoked. Chibondo was the largest, most publicised and most controversial of the war veteran-led exhumations that had taken place in Zimbabwe up to that point, since independence, and the events and controversies it provoked inevitably led to changes in how subsequent war-related exhumations have been managed, controlled, and publicised since, which have received much less media attention and provoked much less controversy.

In March 2011, Zimbabwe's politics of the dead took a decidedly macabre twist when reports, accompanied with graphic photographs and video footage, emerged of massive war veteran-led exhumations taking place at the disused Monkey William mine at Bembera village in Chibondo in Mt Darwin, where the remains of hundreds of people apparently killed by the Smith regime during the liberation war of the 1970s, had been discovered. These events attracted enormous media attention and an unprecedented furore of angry responses from different political parties, civil society organisations, human rights groups and public commentators within Zimbabwe. The criticisms that these grisly exhumations provoked offer key insight into the topography of Zimbabwe's complex politics of the dead, and the difficult questions that can arise about who has sovereignty over human remains. But apart from the grotesque displays of human remains involved, and the crude politicking taking place around them by the war veteran group, the FHT, who were closely linked to the then former ruling and still dominant party,

---

[1] Interview with Chipunza, 5/3/20.
[2] Ibid.: Chipunza explained that they were able to do 'a minimum count of 700 people … by counting all the left femurs'.

Chibondo: Exhumations, uncertainty and human materials

ZANU PF (during the years of the GNU), who used the exhumations to reinforce its anti-colonialist rhetoric of 'patriotic history' (Ranger 2004a; Tendi 2010), perhaps the most striking aspect of these events was the way in which the forms and qualities of the human materials themselves animated the heated debates that ensued.

As discussed in detail in the rest of this chapter, many objections stressed the 'unscientific', 'chaotic' and 'destructive' nature of the exhumations, which were decidedly 'un-forensic', and led by war veterans and spirit mediums who emphasised 'African' ways of dealing with the dead, as they paraded villagers, reporters and TV crews through the mine, past tangled piles of indistinct human remains laid out on plastic sheets, to illustrate the horrors inflicted by Rhodesians. But the nature of the materials themselves caused many to question the true identity of the people whose remains were re-emerging from the abandoned mine. Did they really date from the late 1970s? If so, why were some of the remains still apparently fleshy, leaky and stinking? Might they include more recent human remains – from the *gukurahundi* massacres of the 1980s; or ZANLA purges of ZIPRA comrades around independence? Or from more recent political violence against MDC supporters since 1999? Or even the missing bodies of military purges at the Chiadzwa diamond fields in 2008/09? These questions about the identity of the dead were closely linked to questions about who should be in charge of the exhumations and how they should be carried out. Former members of ZIPRA argued that because the remains may be of their former comrades, they should have been consulted, and they were able to acquire a high court order from Bulawayo to suspend the exhumations, which was effectively ignored by war veterans in Mt Darwin until the government intervened and suspended operations. Recognising the links with existing government programmes of exhumation and reburial under the auspices of its liberation heritage project, NMMZ were drafted in to assist with the war veteran-led exhumations, but they could only offer (limited, given their poor budgets) archaeological rather than forensic expertise. Prominent commentators and human rights activists complained that ZANU PF was deliberately 'silencing the bones', arguing that the crude and decidedly un-forensic nature of the exhumations was not simply a travesty against a moral imperative 'to respect the dead', but possibly an effort to destroy evidence of other more recent deaths, purges and atrocities. Given these uncertainties about identities of the dead, and the manner of their deaths, questions were also raised about whether the grotesque displays of human remains paraded to villagers, teachers and even children, and on television, were really a thinly disguised threat, part of ZANU PF's more violent, demonstrative and performative politics, in the face of waning rural popularity and forthcoming elections.

The Politics of the Dead

In this chapter I explore how these questions about the identity of the dead and the manner of their deaths, and who has sovereignty over them (i.e. by whom and how they should exhumed and reburied) were provoked by the excessive potentialities of the properties of the human substances being exhumed; by their profoundly evocative and affective, yet unstable, uncertain, and ultimately indeterminate materialities. It focuses on how the mass of stinking, intermingling, leaky, half-decaying bodies and bodily substances being disinterred and separated – being remade imperfectly and contingently into particular kinds of 'political bodies/subjects' – both demand and enable, and yet also ultimately defy the very reconstitution of the dead and past lives, and the complex politics of commemoration in which they are entangled. It is likely that some in ZANU PF saw the political usefulness of the uncertainties provoked by the excessive potentiality of the human materials being exhumed from the Mt Darwin mines. They could both celebrate their 'liberation heroes' and reinforce the anti-colonialist rhetoric through which they had very effectively polarised Zimbabwean politics and marginalised opposition political parties, NGOs and Human Rights organisations over the previous decade, and at the same time, demonstrate and remind Zimbabweans of their own capacities for violence. It is in this way the exhumations can be understood as part and parcel of ZANU PF's performative stylistics of power.

Yet ultimately the uncontained uncertainties about the identities of the dead, and the manner of their deaths, in part provoked by the indeterminate nature of the human materials, were unsustainable. By August 2011 the exhumations had been stopped, the mines sealed, and exhumed remains reburied at the site, and the issue largely disappeared from the news agenda, as the government became increasingly concerned that the matter had got 'out of hand', and sought to physically and discursively contain the issue and any political ramifications that may ensue. If the resurgence of scholarly interest in the politics of death and 'the dead' over the last decade, across Africa and elsewhere (discussed in the Introduction), has increasingly recognised that beyond and yet intertwined with both bio-politics and necro-politics (Mbembe 2003), the transforming materialities of bodies and lives matter (cf. Posel & Gupta 2009; Krmpotich et al. 2010; Jindra & Noret 2011), then the Mt Darwin exhumations and the responses they provoked illustrate how human remains can exemplify the excessive potentialities of stuff. This is what Chris Pinney has called 'the torque of materiality'; how the 'alterity of an enfleshed world' defies any easy reading and therefore makes possible the very politics of uncertainty and (un)becoming in which they are entwined (Pinney 2005: 270).

Chibondo: Exhumations, uncertainty and human materials

The Chibondo exhumations

Almost as soon as the discovery and exhumations of human remains at Chibondo were announced in March 2011, they became mired in controversies which reflected the topography of the politics of the dead described in previous chapters. Like state commemoration in the 1980s and 1990s, initial concerns circulated around the highly politicised, partisan nature of the exhumations. The enormous attention the exhumations received from the state-controlled, ZANU PF-aligned print and broadcast media, fed claims that this was an exercise in ZANU PF propaganda, in the face of waning popularity, worsening internal factionalism and forthcoming elections. According to the independent newspaper, *The Standard*, ZANU PF was 'whipping up peoples' emotions ahead of an election it dearly wishes to force through this year'.[3] Meanwhile another independent newspaper, the *Daily News*, explained how 'ZANU PF has sought to project itself as the sole structure concerned about the decent burial of the country's fallen heroes', arguing that through the 'gross politicization' of the exhumations 'Mugabe's party had made a huge play on the pre-1980 massacres to garner sympathy from people ahead of the expected presidential and general elections later this year'[4]. As ZANU PF politicians publicly visited the site, many such criticisms focused on the deeply disturbing images and video clips of disassembled, decaying bodies, bones and undefined human remains being crudely disinterred and chaotically laid out on plastic sheets, broadcast several times a day, like ZANU PF election jingles, on televisions across the country. One commentator wrote:

> this place of horror and tragedy has been turned into a prime ZANU PF propaganda venue … One after the other speakers are coming forward and castigating the MDC for not visiting the site and condemning Rhodesians. Speeches criticizing and rebuking Prime Minister Tsvangirai are being made alongside mounds of human remains and we sit and watch in stunned silence at the crass insensitivity and obscenity of it all.[5]

---

[3] 'Sunday Comment: Unearth truth on human remains' *Standard* 26/3/11.
[4] 'Exhume Gukurahundi massacre victims too' *Daily News* 18/3/11; 'Zimbabwe mass grave becomes political propaganda' *Associated Press* 31/3/11; 'Sunday Comment: Unearth truth on human remains' *Standard* 26/3/11. Elections eventually took place in 2013, which ZANU PF won decisively, but in 2011 there were already fierce debates about when they would be held, with ZANU PF pushing for early elections and the opposition MDC parties arguing that the all terms of the 2008 Global Political Agreement first needed to be satisfied.
[5] 'No respect' *cathybuckle.com* 26/3/11; 'Skeletons to the rescue' *Zimbabwe Mail* 23/3/11; 'Mass graves raise more questions than answers' swradioafrica.com 23/3/11; online sources accessed 19/6/20.

Yet even as such critiques of ZANU PF's 'gross politicisation' of the exhumations appeared in independent newspapers, the ZANU PF-aligned media was describing in detail, and extolling the virtues of, the war veteran and spirit medium-led tours being conducted for people, including school children, bussed to the Chibondo site from all over the country.[6] Claims were made in April that they were receiving 'between 1500 and 3000 visitors a day',[7] and local ZANU PF officials across Zimbabwe's different districts and provinces were mobilising high-profile visits to Chibondo for local chiefs, war veterans, mediums and other 'traditional' leaders. Ambuya VaZarira and her son Peter Manyuki told me that the new senator for Masvingo, Maina Mandava came to collect them, 'with two bus-loads of war vets and other chiefs from Masvingo to go to the exhumations in Chibondo in Mt Darwin', and that she was 'hugely shocked by what she saw there'.[8] It is also clear that such visits were careful choreographed, and that 'the war veterans … wanted journalists to interview people they had selected themselves so that they wouldn't "give out the wrong information"'.[9] Journalists visiting the site reported that 'Zanu PF slogans and songs were the order of the day' and that 'school children, teachers and villagers were forced to go underground and view the bodies so that they would appreciate the extent of the brutalities of the Rhodesian army'. One suggested that 'just like the anti-sanctions petition ZANU PF have carefully coordinated the exhumations, giving them prime time viewing on national television. The plan is said to involve whipping up emotions against the West for past atrocities committed by the Rhodesian regime'. 'This "propaganda at all costs mentality"' that report continued 'has been highly criticized as nothing more than child abuse. Children should never be subjected to the horrific viewing of dead bodies'.[10]

Such critiques of ZANU PF's crude politicking at Chibondo often asked why this was happening now.[11] This was compounded by contrasting reports about how long these mass graves had been known about. *The*

---

[6] See Supplement to ZANU PF's newspaper *The Patriot*, 'Remember: Chibondo liberation war mass grave exhumations' 30/4/11; 'Chibondo Exhibition' by Tawanda Mudimu, on *Herald's* website (www.herald.co.zw/index.php?option=com_phocagallery&view=category&id=6:chibondo-exhumations&Itemid=125, accessed 6/3/12).

[7] '848 fighters exhumed from Chibondo mineshaft to date' in 'Remember: Chibondo liberation war mass grave exhumations' Supplement *Patriot* 30/4/11.

[8] Field notes, 13/12/11.

[9] 'Row over fresh Mt Darwin human remains' *Standard* 20/3/11.

[10] 'Mass graves raise more questions than answers' SW Radio Africa 23/3/11, accessed 19/6/20.

[11] 'Exhume Gukurahundi massacre victims too' *Daily News* 18/3/11; 'Discovered 280 remains not victims of Rhodesian war: MLF' *Zimdiaspora.com* 19/3/11; 'Row over fresh Mt Darwin human remains' *Standard* 20/3/11; 'Skeletons to

Chibondo: Exhumations, uncertainty and human materials

Standard reported that (the now late) George Rutanhire, then FHT's leader and a member of ZANU PF's politburo, claimed the 'mass graves were first identified in the 1980s', but 'two other war veterans said the mass graves were discovered in 2001 and 2008'. ZANU PF's senator Mandiitawepi Chimene 'said the graves were first discovered in 2001' while ZANU PF minister Kasukuwere said 'the Chibondo remains were discovered in 2008 by a gold panner who crawled into the shaft'.[12] When asked 'why it had taken so long to exhume the bodies and give the victims a decent burial', Rutanhire said that although they had known about these mass graves for a long time, they had recently come under threat from illegal gold panners, prompting FHT into action. Furthermore 'there were no resources', and 'people had also not organized themselves to carry out the exhumations'.[13] There is some evidence that this true. Shari Eppel told me in December 2011 that Dumiso Dabengwa, leader of the reformed ZAPU, had claimed that

> he always knew about those bones in Mt Darwin, and apparently soon after independence there had been discussion in government, and a decision had been made to cement over the mines and to put a monument there ... that was in the 1980s, but it was never done.[14]

Yet for the most part the FHT dealt with the 'why now?' question by pointing out the longue durée of their efforts to identify, exhume and rebury the remains of the war dead dating back to the early 1980s. Claiming that 'they were not going to rest until all freedom fighters buried in mass graves get decent burials', Rutanhire explained that they had conducted their 'first exhumation in 1980 of Kunzwana Chifamba at Chesa in Rushinga', and that, since then, 'they have exhumed more than 1300 freedom fighters countrywide and identified over 500 individual graves and 15 mass graves'.[15]

Many commentators recognised that the 'gross politicisation' of these human remains by ZANU PF fitted a long-established pattern of using a narrow and exclusivist legacy of the liberation struggle to buttress its own legitimacy, and undermine that of opposition parties, including 'old' (and 'new' or reformed) ZAPU, the fractious MDC factions with whom it was then sharing power in the GNU, and a host of new and emergent Ndebele pressure groups such as the Mthwakazi Liberation Front (MLF),

---

the rescue' *Zimbabwe Mail* 23/3/11; 'MDC calls for care, sensitivity in exhumations' SW Radio Africa 24/3/11, online sources accessed 19/6/20.

[12] 'Row over fresh Mt Darwin human remains' *Standard* 20/3/11; 'Zimbabwe mass grave becomes political propaganda' *Associated Press* 31/3/11.
[13] 'Row over fresh Mt Darwin human remains' *Standard* 20/3/11.
[14] Field notes, 6/12/11.
[15] '848 fighters exhumed from Chibondo mineshaft to date' in 'Remember: Chibondo liberation war mass grave exhumations' Supplement *Patriot* 30/4/11.

a radical group agitating for Matabeleland secession. It is not surprising therefore that the crude politicking at Chibondo provoked the anger of those linked to ZAPU and ZIPRA, who had long felt that their contributions to Zimbabwe's liberation had been ignored. This was particularly the case because other efforts, the year before, to exhume the remains of ZIPRA fighters in Lupane, spearheaded by Mafela Trust, had again been obstructed by ZANU PF.[16] On 26 March *The Standard* reported that 'ZAPU spokesman Methuseli Moyo said that Zanu PF wanted to distort the country's history by claiming that mass graves being exhumed in Mt Darwin contained the remains of only Zanla ex-combatants killed during the liberation war'. 'We are in the process of organizing a parallel process of exhuming the remains of our members to counter Zanu PF's attempts to distort history' he explained.[17]

Unsurprisingly the spectacle of the Chibondo exhumations also quickly provoked sensibilities about the unresolved *gukurahundi* legacies. Very soon, ZAPU and other Matabeleland-based pressure groups were calling for mass graves from the *gukurahundi* period to be similarly excavated and their human remains exhumed and 'given a decent burial'. Dumiso Dabengwa said 'ZANU PF should extend the programme to victims of *Gukurahundi* to prove its sincerity' and Methuseli Moyo added that 'ZAPU fully supports the exposure of wartime atrocities, but would be happier if the ... exhumation of mass graves of ZAPU supporters massacred during *Gukurahundi* between 1982 and 1987 is also done'.[18] As debates about the Mt Darwin exhumations raged on, reports of new mass graves found at Blanket mine in Matabeleland South province were hastily denied by the mine operators and local police, who stated that only known mass graves in the Gwanda area were at Mhangura and Bigben gold mines.[19] Nevertheless, as the *Daily News* reported, 'President Robert Mugabe is under pressure to order the exhumation of thousands of innocent civilians murdered and buried in abandoned mines during the *gukurahundi* massacres in the Matabeleland and Midlands regions'.[20] In the same report, the (now late) former ZANU PF strong man who became one its fiercest critics, Edgar Tekere, was quoted saying that the *gukurahundi* issue 'was swept under the carpet ... the Catholics did a very comprehensive report about this...[but] others don't want the report to be out because they know they will be exposed'. Likewise a ZAPU spokesperson said that while 'plans to rebury the dead "were commendable" ... ZAPU was worried about Mugabe's failure to acknowledge that

---

[16] Field notes, 6/12/11.
[17] 'Zapu threatens parallel exhumations' *Standard* 26/3/11.
[18] 'Gukurahundi evidence must be exhumed' *Newsday* 20/3/11.
[19] 'Police deny Mpofu claims on mass graves' *Newsday* 20/3/11.
[20] 'Exhume Gukurahundi massacre victims too' *Daily News* 18/3/11.

there were far more victims of his own "anti-terror campaigns" lying in unmarked graves all over the Midlands and Matabeleland'.[21]

Mthwakazi Liberation Front leader Maxwell Mkandla too expressed concern 'about ZANU PF plans to exhume and rebury victims of colonial war crimes, while ignoring those killed and maimed by *gukurahundi*', adding

> I am not surprised that they do not even acknowledge that Matabeleland has more people who were thrown alive into mines by the Fifth brigade, Central Intelligence Organisation, [police] support unit and the Zanu youth brigade than those killed by Smith.

'Smith's war was bad but *gukurahundi* was worse because it was black on black genocide' he continued, challenging 'Mugabe and his government to help national healing by ensuring that "high-ranking perpetrators of the massacres" were brought to book'.[22] This echoed Moses Mzila-Ndlovu (then MDC-N Minister of National Healing in the GNU) who said 'government was missing an opportunity to foster unity by embarking on partisan and selective commemorations of chosen war victims'. 'The national healing process' he continued, 'cannot happen because it is being undermined ... by the same parties that are supposed to be contributing to it'; adding that 'I hope by doing this the government is signalling that it will not interfere if we do the same with the victims of the *gukurahundi*'.[23] A good indication of ZANU PF's response to such demands came later that month when Moses Mzila-Ndlovu himself was arrested for addressing a church service commemorating the *gukurahundi*, and subsequently spent a month detained in prison.[24]

The prominence of the Chibondo exhumations in the context of the long obstruction of similar exhumations or any formal acknowledgement of the *gukurahundi,* meant that in 2011, as Eppel put it, Ndebele activists became acutely aware that 'the dead are not equal'.[25] These sentiments were echoed by Mzila-Ndlovu when he said that 'I will not be surprised if victims of the *gukurahundi*, who have been denied everything, from a simple acknowledgement of the genocide to justice, take this as the worst pinch of salt ever added onto their emotional injuries'.[26] Furthermore, he told *Newsday*, 'the people of Matabeleland were now suspicious that the grand plan of the exhumations project was to eventually go to

---

[21] Ibid.
[22] Ibid.
[23] Ibid.
[24] 'Minister arrested' *Daily News* 16/4/11;'Gvt Minister arrested over Gukurahundi-reconciliation speech' *ZimEye* 15/4/11; 'MDC Minister traumatised by Lupane detention horror' SW Radio Africa 26/4/11, accessed 19/6/20.
[25] Field notes, 6/12/11; 'Exhumations destroy gukurahundi evidence' *Newsday* 18/3/11.
[26] 'Exhume Gukurahundi massacre victims too' *Daily News* 18/3/11.

The Politics of the Dead

Matabeleland and the Midlands provinces to tamper with mass graves of *gukurahundi* victims and destroy crucial evidence of the atrocities'.[27] In Chapter 7 we shall see that these concerns about publicly administered exhumations damaging evidence and preventing future justice would re-appear later, in the context of President Mnangagwa's 2019 calls for the *gukurahundi* legacies to be finally addressed. In 2011, however, for many people in Matabeleland the Chibondo exhumations were just another way to distract attention away from the silenced legacies of the *gukurahundi*. As Mbuso Fuzwayo, of the Ndebele civil society organisation, *Ibhetshu LikaZulu*, put it:

> Those activities in Mashonaland are part of the government suppression, to equalise what happened in the liberation struggle with … the *gukurahundi*; to water down the *gukurahundi*. Those Chibondo exhumations were taking place during the constitution-making process. In Mugabe's era the government didn't want to hear about the *gukurahundi* at all. The Chibondo exhumations were an attempt to equalise the evils of the white regime with the *gukurahundi*, and to divert attention from the *gukurahundi*. I know this because in 2012 when I wanted to organise those [*gukurahundi*] commemorations, they [ZANU PF agents] asked me 'Why don't you want to talk about your war heroes?' I said: 'that is already emphasised in the Heroes Day celebrations, but nothing has been done about the *gukurahundi* killings, or any exhumations from the *gukurahundi*'.[28]

Apart from the unresolved *gukurahundi* legacies, the Chibondo exhumations also raised questions about the fate of much more recent victims of postcolonial violence. The (now late) political commentator John Makumbe asked, rhetorically, 'when will the group that is doing this work visit Domboshava to exhume the bodies of several soldiers that were "buried" there by night only a few years ago?'[29] Similarly in a press statement on 24 March, the largest MDC party (MDC-T) stated:

> The MDC … welcomes the exhumation, identification and proper documentation of any Zimbabwean whose fate was determined by the liberation struggle – a national project in which we all took part. For the exercise that is above party and sectional selfishness, a national budget administered by the relevant state institutions, led by the Ministry of Home Affairs, is imperative to cover the necessary costs of tracking down the genealogy and family trees of the victims through forensic science, carbon dating and indisputable DNA sampling. Such a process would reveal death details and murder methods. Zimbabweans have endured violence since colonialism and yearn for the day when the truth about the liberation war, *Gukurahundi*, Operation *Murambatsvina*,

---

[27] 'Exhumations destroy gukurahundi evidence' *Newsday* 18/3/11.
[28] Interview with Mbuso Fuzwayo, 12/3/20.
[29] 'Skeletons to the rescue' *Zimbabwe Mail* 23/3/11, accessed 19/6/20.

Chibondo: Exhumations, uncertainty and human materials

the 2008 atrocities – among others – is brought onto the surface for informed debate and reflection. Without such a concerted, nationally sensitive process, national healing and reconciliation shall be impossible. The MDC calls on ZANU PF to stop what it is doing and leave it to the nation to work out an appropriate way forward, beyond amateur propaganda antics and political carelessness.[30]

Apart from illustrating how complaints about ZANU PF's crude politicisation of the exhumations led to volatile questions being asked about other graves, other dead and other violent pasts still excluded by ZANU PF's partisan control of official commemoration, this statement also illustrates how quickly concerns were raised about the *manner* of the exhumations themselves. Some such complaints claimed the interests of relatives and families of the dead were being manipulated and ignored by the politicking taking place around them. For example, the GNU's deputy transport minister, Tichaona Mudzingwa, himself a war veteran and member of Morgan Tsvangirai's MDC-T, said that he was 'concerned since he personally lost relatives in the Mt Darwin area during the war but abhorred the manner ZANU PF was politicising the exhumations without making efforts to engage those who lost relatives during the war'. 'The exhumation of bodies' he continued 'was supposed to be a national event that should … involve forensic experts and relatives of people suspected to be buried in the mass graves'.[31]

Moreover these kinds of critiques often focused on the crude, unsophisticated way in which the exhumations appeared to be handled, and the absence of any trained 'archaeologists, pathologists or other specialists' supervising the events.[32] The widely circulated images of war veteran exhumers in overalls and gum boots piling up unsorted human remains on plastic sheets caused huge consternation about the lack of forensic expertise at the site. As John Makumbe put it:

> What is even more amazing is the manner in which these skeletons are being hauled from the mine shaft, stuffed into plastic bags and supposedly handed over to 'relatives' for decent reburial. There are no scientific methods of accurate identification of most of these victims. Some of the skeletons are literally just gathered by hand and lumped together as belonging to someone without any proof whatsoever of who that someone was. In the end some families are going to be forced to bury skeletons of people they had no relationships with. This could easily open Pandora's box as some spirits may visit these families with a

---

[30] 'MDC calls for care, sensitivity in exhumations' SW Radio Africa 24/3/11, accessed 19/6/20.

[31] 'Exhumations, reburials suspicious' *Newsday* 20/3/11; 'Muckraker: Look at me, see how useful I can be' *Zimbabwe Independent* 24/3/11.

[32] 'No respect', *cathybuckle.com* 26/3/11, accessed 19/6/20; 'Sunday Comment: Unearth truth on Human remains' *Standard* 26/3/11.

vengeance. Some opportunistic traditional leaders have suddenly come alive with all manner of tall tales about how some of these skeletons met their fate.[33]

In their defence, FHT emphasised their use of mediums and diviners to identify the dead and return their remains to their families. For them, as we have already seen, this was not a new practice. Given the long salience of the haunting, unsettled dead discussed in previous chapters, it is not surprising that FHT spokesmen placed much emphasis upon the resolution of suffering for communities and families and especially the dead themselves, that their exhumations at Chibondo offered.

However intense and public the controversies surrounding Chibondo were, it is likely that, at least for some people the exhumations did offer something like 'resolution', 'healing' or 'closure' to long-suffered legacies of loss. Kundishora Tungamirai Chipunza, one of the NMMZ archaeologists involved in several 'liberation heritage'-related exhumations over the 2010s, was at Chibondo for four months later that year, and described it as 'a very nasty one'. Yet despite the 'nastiness' of that event', there were moments when he was able to reflect 'that this work we are doing is not in vain':

> I remember ... at Chibondo this is one thing that has really stuck with me. We were working with the communities there, and there was one old woman, very humble, who was always there, working. We had different stations set up, for sorting, for labelling, for arrangement and for documentation and sign off, and so on. This old woman was always there, one of the volunteers working there, and I would always wonder to myself, why is this simple woman always here? She was working there everyday for over a month. So one day I invited her to lunch to talk to her. I asked her, why are you always here? Why are you so concerned with what is going on here? Then she explained that she was a victim or survivor of the Karina *pungwe* massacre, which was a *pungwe* [all-night] gathering in Mt Darwin that was attacked by soldiers during the war. That was where she had lost her 12-year-old daughter. After that massacre, the army collected all the bodies, and they were never seen again. No one knew what they did with those bodies. So this old woman suspected that her daughter had been buried in the mine at Chibondo with all those other bodies. She said she wanted to check if her daughter was there. Then one day when we were doing the sorting, we came across the body of a young girl, about 12 years old, wearing a dress. When I saw that I took a break and when I came back from my break, I saw that woman, and she was crying, because that body was her daughter. She identified her by the dress she was wearing.[34]

---

[33] 'Skeletons to the rescue', *Zimbabwe Mail* 23/3/11, accessed 19/6/20.
[34] Interview with Chipunza, 5/3/20.

Chibondo: Exhumations, uncertainty and human materials

For the archaeologists at the site such occurrences, although rare, were useful because they 'told us something about where those bodies in that mine had come from'. When 'there was another body that we found, of a man who had an ID in his pocket ... that same old woman was able to tell us who that man was, and where he had come from', Chipunza explained. 'So there were some volunteers working there' he continued, 'who knew some of the people who had died, and where they had been killed'.[35]

Official reports in the state-controlled and ruling party-aligned media about Chibondo sometimes told such stories of the 'resolution' and 'closure' that the exhumations had offered some people. But more often they emphasised the evidence of Rhodesian atrocities that was being unearthed with the human remains, including accounts of people being buried alive, the use of acid to destroy corpses and live grenades found amidst the mangled human materials.[36] Such accounts sometimes linked evidence of Rhodesian atrocities being revealed to the resolution offered by the 'traditional' 'African' approaches to identifying the dead that were being applied, which some argued meant that forensic approaches would not be necessary. For example, Saviour Kasukuwere, ZANU PF GNU 'Minister for Black Empowerment', stated 'Forensic tests and DNA analysis of the remains won't be carried out ... Instead, traditional African religious figures will perform rites to invoke spirits that will identify the dead'. 'Spirits of the dead had long "possessed" villagers and children in the district' he added, they have 'refused to lie still. They want the world to see what Smith did to our people. These spirits will show the way it's to be done.'[37]

Nevertheless, the crude and decidedly un-forensic nature of the exhumations did raise wider disquiet about 'disrespecting the dead'. Such concerns fed into a high court application made in Bulawayo at the beginning of April 2011 by lawyers acting for ZIPRA veterans, to 'stop the government from going ahead with its controversial programme of exhuming mass graves'. As these lawyers explained, 'our clients feel that the government has not followed proper channels in exhuming the graves. They also want the ministries of Home Affairs and National Healing to be involved in the exercise which also needs medical experts who will know how to preserve the evidence found'.[38]

The clearest statement criticising the unprofessional nature of the exhumations came, perhaps unsurprisingly given her previous work on *gukurahundi* exhumations in the late 1990s, from Shari Eppel of the

---

[35] Ibid.
[36] 'The untold story of Chibondo' in 'Remember: Chibondo liberation war mass grave exhumations' in *Patriot* 30/4/11.
[37] 'Zimbabwe mass grave becomes political propaganda' *Associated Press* 31/3/11.
[38] 'Zipra veterans challenge chaotic exhumations', radiovop.com 3/4/11, accessed 19/6/20.

Solidarity Peace Trust (SPT), who was closely involved, behind the scenes, in the high court application.[39] Her public statement, entitled 'The silencing of the bones', drew on her experience with AMANI Trust and its successor Ukuthula Trust, to argue that only the expertise offered by forensic anthropologists could provide evidence of the identity of the dead and the manner of their deaths, and thereby 'allow the bones to speak'.[40] In another subsequent SPT report, pictures of careful and minute forensic exhumations done in Matabeleland in the late 1990s with AMANI were deliberately juxtaposed to pictures of chaotic piles of human remains disinterred at Chibondo, to make this point.[41] She stressed the 'healing' effects that only proper forensic exhumation can provide, arguing that she had

> seen the voice of bones giving ... *themselves back with definite identities*, to be buried where they are supposed to lie, so that at long last ... their spirits can rest in peace, and the living, that have mourned them for so long, can have closure.[42]

'Yes, Zimbabwe desperately needs exhumations' she concluded,

> but there are experts in the world who are ready and willing to help ... such as the Argentinean Forensic Anthropology Team ... Before the voices of the Mount Darwin dead are irretrievable lost we need to call a halt to what is happening there and seek expert help.

The high court order was successful and by 7 April, Justice Nicholas Mathonsi had 'granted an interdict sought by the Zimbabwe People's Liberation Army (ZIPRA) war heroes who are demanding that any exhumations in Mt Darwin ... should be carried out in a government-led "legal process"'.[43]

Despite the claims of Kasukuwere, Rutanhire and others involved with the FHT exhumations, about there being no need for forensic expertise, it seems that others in ZANU PF and government did quickly recognise the need to legitimise the exhumations by bringing in professional archaeologists from NMMZ. If early on NMMZ had denied any involvement – the ZANU PF co-Minister of Home Affairs in the GNU, Kembo Mohadi, had

---

[39] Field notes, 6/12/11.
[40] Eppel, S. 'The silencing of the bones' SPT – Zimbabwe Update No. 2, 24/3/11 (www.solidaritypeacetrust.org/1015/spt-zimbabwe-update-no-2, accessed 24/3/11).
[41] See 'Violations of the rights of the dead', in SPT report, 'The hard road to reform', Johannesburg, 13/4/11.
[42] SPT – Zimbabwe Update No. 2 March 2011, 24/3/11, www.solidaritypeacetrust.org/1015/spt-zimbabwe-update-no-2, accessed 7/3/11, original emphasis.
[43] 'Judge halts Mt Darwin exhumations' Newzimbabwe.com 7/4/11, accessed 19/6/20.

even publicly stated that 'my ministry is not in charge of the project and we are not part of it'[44] – on 27 March (before the high court's decision), Mohadi announced that 'the government was taking over the exhumations from the Fallen Heroes Trust'.[45]

Despite claims by some members of Mafela Trust that 'we stopped those exhumations',[46] it is not clear if this government 'take over' was a direct result of the legal efforts made by ZIPRA war veterans in Bulawayo. The government and ZANU PF had not bothered to oppose the court application. It is likely the government's take over at Chibondo related equally to its own concerns that 'the government's tragic response to the crisis has further weakened its tattered credibility',[47] amidst the growing international attention the events were attracting. A statement by Amnesty International that 'the Zimbabwean government must ensure that the exhumations are professionally conducted according to international standards to properly establish cause of death, ensure proper identification and where possible, to return remains to family members'[48] must have caused some disconcertion, but it is also likely that not everybody with the higher echelons of ZANU PF was as keen on the exhumations as those closely associated with the FHT. Robert Mugabe himself, despite the significance of his particular stylistics of power (i.e. 'Mugabeism', see Ndlovu-Gatsheni 2015) in Zimbabwe's politics of the dead, was not a keen advocate of exhumations. As Chipunza explained, 'I went to Mugabe's office once, during the Chibondo exhumations, after NMMZ was drafted in ... I remember Robert saying to me, "those exhumations, you can do that, but the best thing is let the dead lie where they are buried"'.[49] It is also likely that differences on Chibondo within ZANU PF were aligned with its ferocious internal factionalism, already at that time (see Chapter 4) being fuelled by contests over Mugabe's succession. One rumour I heard in December 2011 was that the then Vice-President Joice Mujuru was deeply angered by the events in Mt Darwin, from where she herself originates, and raised the issue in cabinet, accusing the FHT war veterans of being greedy and only interested in retrieving gold from the disused mine. Apparently, no one contradicted her in that cabinet meeting, so perhaps her opinion carried the day.[50]

---

[44] 'No respect' cathybuckle.com 26/3/11, accessed 19/6/20.
[45] See 'Amnesty: Zim mass grave bodies must be exhumed by experts' Amnesty International Press release, 6/4/11.
[46] Field notes, 6/12/11.
[47] 'Chibondo mass grave cover up' *Zimbabwe Legal Affairs* 4/4/11.
[48] 'Amnesty: Zim mass grave bodies must be exhumed by experts' Amnesty International Press release, 6/4/11.
[49] Interview with Chipunza, 5/3/20.
[50] Field notes, 6/12/11.

After the court determination, it appeared at first that the Chibondo war veterans were going to defy the court order. The *Daily News* reported a war veteran claiming that 'the exhumations have continued uninterrupted' and 'its business as usual at Monkey William right now'.[51] Later, however, Rutanhire stated that 'our organization is no longer carrying out the exhumations. What I understand is that the government will rebury the bodies we exhumed at a mass grave that is being built next to the mine'.[52] Although initially relations between the vernacular exhumers, war veterans, spirit mediums and others of the FHT, on one side, and the NMMZ archaeologists drafted in by government to oversee the site, on the other, were very tense, eventually an uneasy rapport was established between them which would continue through subsequent exhumations in Rusape in 2013 (Chipangura 2015; Mupira 2018) and elsewhere in following years. As Chipunza described:

> At the beginning the FHT people were very suspicious of our involvement. They tried to block us from the site. They accused us of trying to be heroes of a war that we did not fight. But the chairman of the FHT George Rutinhare, he was a very good guy. He passed away now. He was very good, and soon the other FHT guys recognised our contribution to the exhumations and let us lead the activities there. So we struck a working relationship, even if it was not so easy to begin with. We were there for a long time, and we tried to be part of them, living there at the site in their grass huts, we slept there with them, and eventually they accepted us. Even the spirit mediums. The place was being controlled by the spirit mediums, who sanctioned who could go into the site and could go out. After seeing us work, those spirit mediums they welcomed us, and we got their support.[53]

Media politicking around the site continued, however, and on 9 April *The Herald* carried a typically vitriolic article by 'Nathaniel Manheru' (widely known to be George Charamba, former President Mugabe's press secretary and a key author in ZANU PF's 'patriotic history') entitled 'Mt Darwin: the wailing bones of Chibondo', in which the motives of critics of the exhumations were questioned with the threatening counter-claim that 'we know who seeks to gag the dead'. The same article was republished in *The Patriot*, on 30 April, alongside a more measured article explaining that only '848 fighters' had been exhumed (not the 1,700 claimed by 'Manheru'), and that the FHT were now complying with the high court order.[54] By May, it was clear that no new exhumations where taking place

---

[51] 'Govt defies court order' *Daily News* 12/4/11; 'Sunday Comment: Respect court ruling on exhumations' *Standard* 10/4/11.
[52] 'Body exhumations in Zim continues despite court ban' radiovop.com 12/4/11 accessed 19/6/20.
[53] Interview with Chipunza, 5/3/20.
[54] '848 fighters exhumed from Chibondo mineshaft to date' *Patriot* 30/4/11.

at Chibondo, and as security around the site was increased, efforts now focused on what to do with the human remains already disinterred.[55]

By this stage NMMZ was leading efforts to rebury the remains in new, individual memorialised graves at the site. In December 2011 NMMZ's Executive Director, Godfrey Mahachi, told me that he spent a great deal of time travelling back and forth to the Chibondo site over the months that NMMZ archaeologists were working there. At first 'these things were just happening but then the government took over' he explained, 'and then it is us, as NMMZ, who are tasked to do that work, so suddenly we had a whole new project on our hands'.[56] Clearly, as had often happened with its 'liberation heritage' portfolio, NMMZ and the government trailed behind events already taking place. 'Of course it's exciting' Mahachi continued, 'but it is also difficult when we are already so under resourced'.[57] He also acknowledged that NMMZ's forensic capacity was severely limited.[58] Indeed NMMZ was forced to draw heavily on the limited expertise of a visiting PhD researcher with forensic expertise from South Africa, who was working on archaeological collections in Harare's National Museum at the time, and was drafted in to provide hasty presentations and literature for NMMZ archaeologists.[59] On 13 August *The Herald* reported that the 'reburial of over 700 former liberation fighters' from 'the disused mine shafts at Chibondo' had begun. Kasukuwere said he hoped the area 'would become a national shrine' and that 'should remind Zimbabweans of the cruelty of the Ian Smith regime'. 'Over 24000 people' he noted, had 'visited the site since the exhumations started'.[60]

In many ways, then, the highly visible but crudely performed politics of the dead taking place at Chibondo mirrored and exacerbated the long-existing tensions of Zimbabwean commemoration: the narrow celebration of ZANU PF heroes, the marginalisation of other nationalist contributions, and the belated efforts to legitimise the operations through NMMZ's liberation heritage portfolio, as well as of course ZANU PF's continuing reticence about confronting its terrible *gukurahundi* legacy, or dealing with the dead of other postcolonial violence in which it is implicated. Importantly, however, these kinds of criticisms did not really question the need for the exhumations per se, nor initially, the identity of

[55] In May and June ZIPRA Veteran's Trust's attention turned to preservation of these remains and public statements were made suggesting a new court order forcing the government to act may be sought, although this did not materialise. 'War of words continues over exhumations' radiovop.com 7/5/11; 'ZANU PF urged to respect remains of liberation fighters' *SW Radio Africa* 22/6/11, both accessed 19/6/20.
[56] Field notes, 8/12/11.
[57] Ibid.
[58] Ibid.
[59] Ibid.
[60] 'Zimbabwe: Chibondo reburials in progress' *Herald* 13/8/11.

the remains being exhumed. Rather they questioned the crude politicking taking place around them, and the 'disrespectful', chaotic and 'unprofessional' manner of the exhumations.

Too 'fresh', 'intact', fleshy, leaky and stinky?

As ZANU PF's publicity machine went into overdrive using the exhumations to inflate its anti-colonialist rhetoric, controversies surrounding events at Chibondo quickly took on a much more sensitive dimension, which turned on the nature of the human materials themselves. Amid the proliferation of TV and press coverage, serious questions were raised about the true age and identity of the remains, and the cause of their deaths. Many reports suggested that the distorted bodies and disassembling remains being chaotically disinterred, laid out on plastic, and broadcast on television, were simply too 'intact', leaky, fleshy and too smelly to date back over 30 years to the liberation struggle. *The Standard* reported that suspicions were 'aroused' after 'journalists ... were shocked to see bodies that were still intact'. 'One of the bodies still had visible hair, while others had their clothes intact' the report continued, and another 'had fluids dripping from it', and a 'strong stench still permeates the 15-metre deep mine shaft'.[61] An unidentified pathologist claimed that 'there was no way there could still be a stench ... three decades after the bodies were allegedly dumped ... ordinarily by this time there should only be bone-remains', and numerous other news reports too carried articles citing pathologists claiming that the visual evidence of the Chibondo remains suggested they included 'fresh bodies'.[62]

It was not just the human remains that provoked this profound uncertainty but also the objects and artefacts associated with them: particularly the clothes, shoes and uniforms found entangled with the remains. Even Ambuya VaZarira and her son Peter Manyuki, when they were bussed there from Masvingo by ZANU PF officials, were shocked that 'some of these bodies were still wearing their clothes'. 'Is it possible that bodies would still be wearing clothes after 30 years?' Peter asked me rhetorically.[63] Some reports even suggested that cell phones, coins and (recent) plastic ID cards had been found amongst the remains, and in Bulawayo I heard rumours that Mafela Trust officials visiting the mine found Zimbabwe National Army ID tags amongst the remains.[64] The FHT dismissed as 'mischievous' and 'sad indeed' such claims that the bodies were 'too fresh' to date to the liberation

---

[61] 'Row over fresh Mt Darwin human remains' *Standard* 20/3/11.
[62] 'Mt Darwin mass graves contain fresh bodies: Pathologist' *Zimdiaspora.com* 27/3/11 accessed 19/6/20; 'Chibondo mass grave cover up' *Zimbabwe Legal Affairs* 4/4/11.
[63] Field notes, 13/12/11.
[64] Field notes, 6/12/11.

Chibondo: Exhumations, uncertainty and human materials

struggle.[65] But interestingly, they too pointed to the clothes, uniforms and other artefacts found in the mine to support their argument that these were victims of Rhodesian atrocities. In particular, great emphasis was placed on the 'super-pro' canvas shoes found amongst the remains, which were commonly worn by guerrilla fighters during the struggle. Similar references were also made to Rhodesian uniforms, Chinese 'rice camouflage', and even a 'farad uniform from Ethiopia' that was found in the mine, amidst more emotive descriptions of the barbed wire that strapped the hands and feet of another corpse, and the catapults that still hung around the necks of the remains of some children; and, in a few cases, to the ritual black beads worn by spirit mediums also found amongst the stinky mass of ill-defined human materials.[66] For people on both sides of the controversies provoked by the exhumations, the artefacts around them seemed sometimes to offer more stability of meaning then the remains themselves.

For her part, Eppel was careful to point out that what may appear like 'fresh' still-decomposing flesh, may actually be 'mummified' remains dating back to the 1970s. This is an effect that is, apparently, not uncommon in mass graves were many bodies have been densely buried on top of each other. She did however acknowledge that 'it is not impossible that these graves contained victims from the 1980s'. But her main argument emphasised that the uncertainty surrounding the material qualities of the remains could only be resolved and determined by professional forensic anthropologists. As she put it, 'whether these are mummified tissues or more recent, rotten soft tissues, needs an expert to decide'.[67] This was an argument she made in the SPT's reports, where she appealed 'to all those with long-standing desires for exhumations in their areas … not to follow the bad example of the "Fallen Heroes Trust", and rather to lobby for their right to expert exhumations undertaken by professionals'.[68] But it was also one she directed, behind the scenes, at Ndebele activists, ZAPU members, and former ZIPRA comrades, including Dabengwa himself, who approached her for contacts with the Argentinian forensic teams with whom AMANI had worked, wanting to use the context of ZANU PF's politicking around Chibondo, to push for similar exhumations at known *gukurahundi* sites.[69] In December 2011, Eppel explained how, when the Chibondo exhumations blew up in the media, she hastily organised a workshop in Bulawayo in order to explain to Ndebele activists why it was important a professional forensic approach and experts were deployed.[70]

---

[65] 'The pain of a historic village' *Patriot* 30/4/11.
[66] Ibid. p. 6.
[67] Solidarity Peace Trust, 'Hard road to reform' 13/4/11 p. 48.
[68] Ibid., pp. 48–9.
[69] Field notes, 6/12/11.
[70] Ibid.

These uncertainties about the age and identity of the Chibondo dead and the manner of their deaths – provoked by the unexpectedly fleshy and stinky nature of the human remains being disinterred – raised concerns not just about other graves that too need exhumation, but about whether these Chibondo remains themselves might include not only victims of Rhodesian violence, but also victims of more recent ZANU PF violence. Were these ZANU PF heroes or victims? Peter Manyuki's opinion that 'probably there are bodies from the liberation struggle there, but maybe also bodies from other periods of violence, like from the *gukurahundi* and maybe the elections of recent years, and even from Chiadzwa',[71] were repeated by others I spoke to in December 2011 and in many news reports. 'But they don't want the story complicated', Peter Manyuki continued, 'they just want a simple story to tell the public and the media, so they were just telling everyone that they were all heroes from the liberation struggle. But there are many periods in Zimbabwe's recent past when parents lost their children and don't know where they are buried'.[72] John Makumbe suggested a more sinister explanation:

> The truth of the matter is that not all of these skeletons are from atrocities committed by the Smith regime. There is a strong possibility that the Mugabe government may also have used the same 'burial' place to dumb some of its own skeletons. We know that there are many people who have disappeared ... as a result of the brutal work of the Mugabe regime. Perhaps Rashiwe Guzha's skeleton is among those that are being exhumed today. How convenient it would be for such a skeleton to be found amongst the hundreds that may have died at the hands of the Smith regime. Like all the others, the skeleton would not be identified, and so the desperate regime would not need to answer awkward questions.[73]

Very quickly, all the different constituencies of Zimbabwe's politics of the dead began suggesting that the Chibondo remains included 'their dead': including the MDC parties, ZAPU and ZIPRA veterans, Mafela Trust, and the new radical Ndebele groups such as the MLF. Indeed the MLF were first to suggest that the Chibondo remains included *gukurahundi* victims, stressing that 'thousands mysteriously "disappeared" in Harare, Chitungwiza and other parts of Mashonaland at the hands of the tribalistic Zimbabwe regime' in the early 1980s, and that 'the "discovery" of the said skeletons could as well provide a clue as to the fate of the said ethnic Ndebele people and ex-zipra force troops who disappeared during the same period'.[74] ZAPU's Methuseli Moyo was 'afraid that the ZANU PF-managed exhumations

---

[71] Field notes, 13/12/11.
[72] Ibid.
[73] 'Skeletons to the rescue' *Zimbabwe Mail* 23/3/11, accessed 19/6/20.
[74] 'ZAPU, MDC demand Gukurahundi exhumations' *Newzimbabwe.com* 19/3/11;

Chibondo: Exhumations, uncertainty and human materials

may be used to cover up evidence of the Gukurahundi atrocities'[75] and ZIPRA veterans 'alleged that remains could be of their colleagues and supporters who were abducted and murdered by ZANU PF militants and ZANLA guerrillas soon after independence'.[76] It is well known that ZIPRA guerrillas did operate across Mashonaland areas and that there was fighting between ZANLA and ZIPRA fighters during the war, and at assembly points during the ceasefire, notably at Entumbane,[77] and later when the Zimbabwe National Army was being forged after independence.[78] Indeed the basis of the court order successfully won by Mafela and the ZIPRA War Veterans Trust was that these Chibondo mines might contain the remains of ZIPRA dead, and they were therefore 'an interested party' who 'need to be consulted on the way forward'.[79]

Others raised similar questions about victims of recent violence, alleging 'the exhumations may be a cover up for crimes committed in the first decade of the new millennium when ... ZANU PF party is known to have committed gross crimes, such as the murder of political opponents'.[80] For these reasons the prime minster in the GNU, and MDC president, Morgan Tsvangirai, 'slammed' the exhumations while the MDC's deputy spokesman, Chihwayi, claimed 'these bodies look fresh; ZANU PF should come clean on the issue of these exhumations ... those remains are of MDC who were killed by ZANU PF [since] 2000 and especially during the run off elections of 2008'.[81] Tsvangirai also stressed that 'its illegal to exhume bodies' and that 'the police must investigate missing people and exhume them after carrying out forensic assessments'. 'The MDC' he continued, 'has its members missing and how do we know if those that being exhumed are not our members?'[82] Later he also acknowledged that the graves 'could include victims of the 1980s army campaign that left 20,000 minority Ndebeles dead in a purge by ZANU PF rivals'.[83]

Amid all these suggestions about who the remains might include, some even suggested that the Mt Darwin mines contained very recent

---

'Discovered 280 remains not of victims of Rhodesian war: MLF' Zimdiaspora. com 19/3/11; (both accessed 19/6/20).
[75] 'ZAPU threatens parallel exhumations' *Standard* 26/3/11.
[76] 'ZIPRA Veterans challenge Exhumations' radiovop.com 3/4/11, accessed 19/6/20.
[77] This was the subject of the Dumbutshena report which has still not been released.
[78] 'Audit human remains – colonel' *Zimbabwean* 30/3/11; also Field notes, 6/11/12.
[79] SPT 'Hard road to reform' 13/4/11, p. 48.
[80] 'Sunday Comment: Unearth truth on human remains' *Standard* 26/3/11.
[81] 'Hundreds of bodies removed from Zimbabwe mass grave' Ipsnews.net 25/3/11, accessed 19/6/20.
[82] 'Bob losing grip, says Tsvangirai' *Daily News* 27/3/11.
[83] 'Mt Darwin mass graves contain butchered Ndebeles: Tsvangirai' Zimdiaspora. com 7/4/11, accessed 19/6/20.

The Politics of the Dead

victims of the army's violent take over of the Chiadzwa diamond fields in late 2008 and early 2009, when it is alleged hundreds of illegal diamond miners and traders were machine-gunned from helicopters. Although this is perhaps unlikely, rumours were circulating about what had happened to the remains of people killed at Marange, just as the remains of many opposition supporters killed in 2008 were and are yet to be recovered. Earlier reports had suggested the bodies of 85 people killed at Chiadzwa had been surreptitiously buried in a cemetery in Chitungwiza, outside the capital, several years before.[84]

In this context the focus of criticism of the decidedly un-forensic methods employed by war veterans at Chibondo changed. No longer just deeply 'disrespectful to the dead', they were criticised as being a deliberate attempt to destroy or 'cover up' crucial evidence of violence and murder. Questions were raised about whether Chibondo was a 'war grave' or a 'crime scene', and for many using divination and spirit possession was no longer an acceptable means of identifying and settling the dead, but a deliberate obfuscation of the 'truth' about the dead; a way of 'silencing the bones'. When ZBC (Zimbabwe Broadcasting Corporation) footage was shown to forensic experts from Argentina in South Africa in June 2011, they 'condemned how ZANU PF has conducted the removal of the bodies'. ZIPRA's Magwizi, who was at that meeting, agreed that 'the archaic methods' applied at Chibondo mine were 'erroneous' and stressed that 'scientific methods have to be implemented rather than look up to *amadlozi* [ancestral spirits, in Sindebele] to detect the origins of the deceased'.[85]

In response, FHT complained, typically, that Tsvangirai's criticism of the exhumations were not 'in defence of African culture' and that he was 'talking cheap politics'.[86] Nevertheless by then the uncertain nature of the human materials being so publicly and visibly exhumed had changed the focus of the controversies, from the crude politicisation and 'disrespectful' nature of FHT practices to much more sensitive questions about the 'true' identity of the Chibondo remains and the 'real' purpose of the decidedly un-forensic exhumations. Having initially argued that similar exhumations should take place at other mass graves around the country, ZIPRA veterans, the MDC and other critics quickly changed

---

[84] 'Mass graves raise more questions than answers' *swradioafrica.com* 23/3/11; 'Victims of diamond massacres buried in Chitungwiza mass graves' *swradioafrica.com* 19/5/09; both accessed 19/6/20; 'Victims of Zimbabwean diamond crackdown to be dumped in mass grave' *Times* (UK) 13/12/08; 'Bodies pile up as Mugabe wages war on diamond miners' *Guardian* 11/12/08.

[85] 'ZANU PF urged to respect remains of liberation fighters' swradioafrica.com 22/6/11, accessed 19/6/20.

[86] 'Their bones shall rise' *Patriot* 30/4/11.

their focus towards the prevention of any exhumations without proper forensic expertise.

Clearly the Chibondo exhumations had raised far 'more questions than answers',[87] and perhaps this offers the best explanation for why, after initially supporting the war veteran efforts with enormous media coverage and aplomb, ZANU PF ministers in the GNU quickly moved to instruct NMMZ to 'take over' the exhumations, and then to rapidly close them down. It also explains why, as the controversies deepened, FHT became increasingly concerned to choreograph visits to and reporting at the site, and why once the government and NMMZ had taken over, security at the site was intensified and public visits stopped. Furthermore it explains why the question of professional forensic involvement came to dominate the ensuing debates, even though both those involved with FHT at Chibondo and those opposed to them – and not excluding NMMZ who were drafted in to mediate the controversies – all espoused the potentially cathartic, 'healing' nature of exhumations and reburials. Suddenly questions about *how* human remains are remade into dead (political) subjects, *how* the dead are made present, and *how* the past is reconstituted – how the cause and manner of these deaths was to be become known – became of central concern. And these sensitive and difficult questions turned, ultimately, on the indeterminate nature of the materials, substances, things – human and non-human – being reconstituted into particular kinds of subjects and objects. These are questions that were raised, in part, by the indeterminate yet demanding and excessive potentiality of the human materials themselves.

Much later, in March 2020, long after the Chibondo controversies had dispersed, Kundishora Chipunza explained to me how the archaeological work NMMZ subsequently did on the stratigraphy of the site challenged the rumours that had been circulating about 'wet', 'fresh' and 'recent' bodies.

> Despite the limitations that we faced – these were limitations of materials with which to do the work, and we didn't have a standard work model to follow, on how to do those exhumations in that mine – we did quite well despite those limitations. What we found in that mine was that there were three quite clear stratigraphies. There was the upper layer, which was almost dry. That layer was full of disarticulated bodies, which were all mixed up, civilians, bodies in uniforms, young and old people. This was a dry zone, and the bodies were almost or completely decomposed. Then there was below that the middle stratum, this was the wetter layer, the bodies here were better preserved. This consisted of mainly uniformed combatants, and a few civilians, but they were mainly adults, and many wearing uniforms. There were several wearing

---

[87] 'Mass graves raise more questions than answers' swradioafrica.com 23/3/11, accessed 19/6/20.

full Chinese uniforms. We were able to search in some of their pockets, and we found items like pieces of newspaper, folded to use for smoking tobacco, and sometimes we could read the dates of the newspapers, giving us a date we could use. Then there was the lower stratum, this was very wet, almost completely under water. The bodies here were very well preserved, and it was mainly male adults. We could see from what they were wearing that they were earlier mobilised people, often they were wearing several layers of clothes, several pairs of trousers and shirts on top of each other, because those earlier combatants, they did not have uniforms, and would often wear all of their clothes on top of each other. There was one body who had newspaper in his pocket that was a Rhodesian Herald dated to 1972. So there was quite a lot of archaeology there. Some of the bodies had their hands tied with wire, some had hospital drips, or were wrapped in hospital blankets. We also found some ID cards and were able to identify some of those bodies.[88]

The wet, fleshy, leaky bodies that had caused so much disconcertion and controversy were therefore probably not as 'recent' as the controversies they raised had surmised. In fact the stratigraphy, as well as the material culture found amongst the indeterminate human remains, suggested that the most recent bodies were those in the upper most 'dry zone', and the older bodies were those which were wetter, fleshier and more preserved, exactly because they were submerged under water; a possibility that Eppel had been careful to note during her critiques in 2011.

But Chipunza's comments also made it clear that the function that NMMZ and its archaeologists were sent to Chibondo to fulfil was to provide some kind of authoritative determination, certainty and stabilisation to the uncertain and excessive human materials being revealed by the exhumations, and to the fierce controversies they had ignited. They had clearly been handed a difficult task: to provide (at short notice, with little resources, expertise or experience) an authoritative account that would satisfy both the FHT's vernacular exhumers and their myriad supporters, including families and relatives troubled by their unsettled war dead, but also to counter or neutralise the fierce critiques levied by other political parties and interests, within and without the GNU, but also within ZANU PF itself, as well as from a myriad of local and international observers, civil society organisations, NGOs, and political commentators.

> JF – So what about the speculation going on at the time, about the bodies being 'too wet' – that they looked 'too recent', and were maybe victims of recent ZANU PF violence?
>
> Chipunza – There were lot of reports and a lot of rumours about that. But I think it was just speculation and politics. As I said, most of

[88] Interview with Chipunza, 5/3/20.

Chibondo: Exhumations, uncertainty and human materials

> those wet bodies came from the lower stratum of the exhumations at Chibondo – the lower layer. So they couldn't have been more recent bodies, because they were below the older bodies.
>
> But those were the kinds of questions we were being asked at that time. What are those fresh bodies there? And 'why are you working for ZANU PF?' There was a lot of people playing politics around that time with those exhumations. But there was nothing like that. It was a sealed context in terms of the archaeology. There was absolute clarity about each stratum. It was very clear. As I tried to tell our colleagues – our job is to provide the evidence, not to interpret. We have to provide the archaeological evidence. We even got a letter from the international human rights people, the international court of human rights or something, I don't remember exactly who it was from. They asked us about those exhumations, so we presented our evidence and after that they never came back to us, because the archaeological evidence was very clear. So from the evidence level, those rumours and reports about recent bodies, they were speculative. It was clear that those bodies were from the war period.[89]

And yet, even in 2020, almost a decade after Chibondo, some of the uncertainties that provoked the intense controversies surrounding those events inevitably remained.

> JF – What about the suggestion that some of those bodies might have come from the early independence period? It is known that there were quite a lot of cases, before the *gukurahundi* began, of people going missing, and violence against ZIPRA, even on this side of the country, and that was only a few years after 1979, the dates of some of the bodies from Chibondo. Is it possible some of those post-1980 bodies were there in that mine?
>
> Chipunza – Yes, it is possible. I would not discount the possibility that there maybe have been some individual incidents – some particular incidents of later bodies from those years, but if so, it would only be a few, one or two at most. But I doubt it. Because that mine was not known about by the government then. The new government did not know about the mine. No one knew about it. After all it was *makorokoza* [artisanal miners] who discovered the bodies in that mine. It wasn't even FHT. It was *makorokoza* … Not FHT and not the government.
>
> Also, after Chibondo, there have been other discoveries of mass burials in mines, at Herbert mine, Matombo 6, and recently at Odzi. So those burials in mine shafts, they fitted a pattern of dead people being thrown into mineshafts by Rhodesian forces. There was a clear pattern.[90]

---

[89] Ibid.
[90] Ibid.

The Politics of the Dead

The remaining uncertainties revolve around not only when Chibondo's terrible secret was known about, or re-discovered, and by whom, and what different interests were at play in the 'grotesque politicking' that surrounded the events there in early 2011, but also, still, who its dead are or were, and who was responsible for their unsettled and unsettling demise. The identification of a 'clear pattern' of Rhodesian forces using mines to dump bodies, to which Chipunza pointed, does likely reflect pervasive war-time practices, but the evidence of *gukurahundi*-era mass graves located in other abandoned mines in Matabeleland South indicates this was not solely the dubious preserve of Smith's supremacist regime in its last fading gasps. Such patterns could very possibly have been repeated or maintained into independence; as was also reflected in the post-mortem disruptions to the funeral rites and burials of much more recent victims of political violence, discussed in the previous chapter.

National Museums and Monuments *has* undoubtedly become much more knowledgeable and experienced in handling these kinds of exhumations, both technically and politically, since Chibondo in 2011. It was 'a sharp learning curve for NMMZ', Chipunza explained, but 'we have managed to improve our methods, and can be much more confident in how we handle exhumations'. Most importantly, however, there has been recognition that the identification of individual human subjects, communities and pasts that can be indexically linked to specific human materials exhumed from mass graves, remains, more often than not, deeply elusive and difficult to ascertain, demanding more specialised techniques of stabilisation, or of 'remaking the dead', than NMMZ's archaeologists can offer. Hence it is significant to note that NMMZ 'have slowly been introducing the use of DNA testing into exhumations', working with 'a DNA firm' – the African Institute of Biomedical Science and Technology (AiBST) at Wilkins Hospital in Harare – 'to build up a data base of DNA records from those exhumations'. This is so that when 'we get people coming to us looking for their dead relatives, we can send them to that data base, to see if their relatives have been recovered from any of these exhumations'.[91] While this does respond to some of the concerns raised by the 2011 Chibondo controversies, it remains to be seen whether such hugely expensive, technically specialised and still frequently not entirely conclusive, DNA testing will indeed be as widely available or effective as often promised. Whether such testing would also apply to the *gukurahundi* exhumations promised in 2019 by Mnangagwa's regime (if and when they go ahead) also remains unclear. For now, what NMMZ's turn to DNA testing reveals – as with the demands for the deployment of 'professional' expertise in exhumations that arose during the Chibondo affair, and to which NMMZ has clearly sought to respond – is a recognition of

[91] Ibid.

the excessivity and uncertainty of human remains, which demands but often defies efforts to stabilise meaning and 'closure'; efforts that can be enormously contested and controversial. This is what we turn to now.

The torque of materiality and the excessive potentiality of human remains

In previous chapters we began to examine Zimbabwe's politics of the dead (Fontein 2009b, 2010, 2011) through analytical lenses emergent from recent theoretical debates about materiality (Miller 2005) and what Domańska has called a 'return to things' (2006). What bones do in Zimbabwe is *not* confined to questions about their symbolic affects or contested representations of troubling pasts, but also relates to their 'emotive materiality' as human substances and their 'affective presence' as dead persons. Bones and bodies in Zimbabwe therefore have a dual agency as uneasy subject/objects that index restless, demanding spirit subjects/persons (Gell 1998) and as 'unconscious' but disturbing things and substances (Latour 1999) that provoke responses from the living. The two are often intertwined so that it is exactly the emotive materialities of human corporeality that can invoke or reveal the affective presence of dead spirits demanding recognition and proper 'ritual', symbolic/material transformation into ancestors, heroes or indeed victims.

In Chapter 2 I argued that Ingold's insistence upon the affordances, properties, flows and transformations of materials (2007: 1–2) is pertinent to understanding how the political efficacy of recently tortured bodies relates to that of older resurfacing bones by suggesting that what matters is not necessarily already contained and constituted objects like bones, 'the body', 'graves', or indeed the soil, but rather the properties and flows of materials between them. It highlights the simultaneously material/symbolic transformations and transferences involved in normal funeral processes – that is the ritual/material transformations of fleshy bodies into dry bones; how people become ancestors through the merging of bodily substances into soil; how the living become (safely) dead – and how transgressions of these 'normal' processes animate Zimbabwe's politics of the dead. This explains why this politics is not only about contested commemorations of people killed in the past but also about the shape of continuing violence against the living, as well as the 'second violence' of disrupted funerals and disappeared or dumped corpses, because both kinds of violence interfere with the normal corporeal processes of containment and transformation through which people – both living and dead – are constituted in particular ways. This is also why post-violence attempts at 'healing', 'closure' and the resolution of suffering often emphasise exhumations and reburials as processes that are akin to funerals, as forms of catharsis, of settling troubling spirits and problematic pasts, or of 'remaking the dead'.

Ingold's focus on materials and substances reverts attention back to how materials become or are stabilised and constituted (or in Latour's terms 'purified') into 'objects' and indeed 'subjects', physically but also conceptually, historically and politically. This recalls Brown's emphasis (2001) on the work involved in the ongoing (re)constitution, becoming and maintenance of 'objects' from the constant flows and transformations of undefined things, materials and stuff. How do bones – or fragments of bone sifted from the merged substances of decayed bodies, fibres, sand and soil – become recognised, 'articulated' (Hallam 2010), or (re)constituted as uneasy human/things, or ambivalent subject/objects, through archaeological excavation, forensic exhumation, or indeed divination? And how, in turn, are these processes turned into commemorative rituals or funerals, not only responding to the demands of the (reconstituted) dead, but actually 'remaking' them? Ingold's focus on materials (2007) and 'things' (2009) demands us to consider how exhumations are, in part, about remaking or reconstituting 'the dead' as particular kinds of 'objects' or 'political subjects' – specimens, ancestors, heroes or victims – afforded or enabled by the materials excavated from mass graves. This is an issue that others working on exhumations and human remains elsewhere have also explored (Hallam 2010; Renshaw 2010; Filippucci et al. 2012; Crossland 2009a, 2009b). Crossland, for example, has discussed how anthropological, archaeological and forensic 'practice brings the dead into being through exhumation and analysis' (2009a: 69 2009b), and Filippucci et al. have described 'unearthing' human remains as

> a transformative and relational process of becoming, involving soil, hands, trowels and brushes, and bones ... through which the flow of human materials with other substances is arrested and channelled, so that human remains are temporarily stabilized into recognizable objects and the work of cultural elaboration can begin ... it is a process of becoming by which traces of past lives are reconstituted and come to assert an ambivalent quality of felt presence, which has the capacity to unsettle the here and now, with an indeterminate alterity. (2012: 199)

Importantly, this emphasis on 'processes of becoming', or of 'remaking of the dead', points to the excessivity or 'otherness of human remains' (Renshaw 2010: 460); how 'things, materials and stuff are always both more and less than the objects and subjects that they constitute, substantive qualities that are in excess of, yet imbricated in their own becomings and unbecomings' (Filippucci et al. 2012: 11; Fontein 2011: 718). This is what Pinney calls the 'alterity (or torque) of materiality that can never be assimilated to a disembodied "linguistic-philosophical closure"' (2005: 270), which I suggest was exemplified by the excessive and uncertain qualities of the human remains exhumed at Chibondo, and which fuelled the controversies that enveloped those events. If scholars

Chibondo: Exhumations, uncertainty and human materials

of 'materiality' have often stressed the 'dialectics of objectification' (Miller 2005: 38), then for Pinney 'the dialectic of "subjects making objects making subjects" ... is not smooth but instead rife with disjunctures and fractures' (Filippucci et al. 2012: 204) exactly because stuff, substances and things always maintain an excessive potentiality to exceed their constitution, 'stabilisation' or 'purification', into recognisable objects or identifiable subjects. It is this material excessivity of stuff, and of human remains in particular, which constitutes their alterity. Pinney's insistence upon the 'enfleshed alterity' of the material world, means that processes of becoming, stabilisation, or (re)constitution are fraught, incomplete, uncertain and ultimately indeterminate, and this indeterminacy is what can make them so contested, as Chibondo exemplified.

This 'indeterminate alterity' of things or 'torque of materiality', has profound implications for older but recently re-invigorated anthropological questions about the nature of alterity and difference. It suggests, for example, that the possibility of 'radical alterity' emerges more from the excessive potentialities of stuff rather than from highly reified and abstracted philosophical notions of 'ontological difference', as some recent anthropological perspectives have tried (but largely failed) to advocate (Henare et al. 2007; Holbraad & Pedersen 2017; Graeber 2015; Fontein 2011: 719; 2020). It also indicates that the uncertainties surrounding how and what human remains do in Zimbabwe's politics of the dead, pre-exists or is immanent to questions about the ambivalent agency of bones and bodies as uneasy subjects/objects.

Furthermore, it raises important questions about what, then, is specific or unique about human substances that sets them apart from other kinds of things or materials. Filippucci et al. (2012) suggest that the distinction between metaphor and metonym might be useful here. They suggest that 'if initially human remains appear poignant because they seem more obviously "human" than other material objects and artefacts, then at second glance this poignancy does not easily or clearly make them more communicative as metaphors or objectifications of human beings or past lives lived' (Filippucci et al. 2012: 211). Rather, human remains often 'signal presence more than meaning; they denote more than they connote' and these 'excessive metonymic qualities defy, perhaps much more than other things, efforts to turn them into meaningful metaphors'.

> This excessive metonymic quality of human remains, over and above their metaphorical capacity, does not make then fundamentally different from or opposed to nonhuman remnants of the past but points to the autonomous and excessive affectivity, or 'torque' of materiality, of all materials and things; the abundant potentiality or alterity of thingness that is inevitably imbricated in and yet beyond the relational processes and flows of becoming through which all objects and subjects emerge, and which must be arrested and stabilized for entities such as the past,

> 'the body', a person, or an artifact to be constituted. What then appears to make human remains different from, and yet exemplary of, other things is their resistance to processes of 'purification' and stabilization. (Filippucci et al. 2012: 211)

'As a result', human remains 'can be subject to huge and often highly specialized efforts and dramatic over-determinations into particular types of subjects/objects, such as ancestors, victims, heroes or specimens – processes that are often unusually problematic, politicized and contested' (Filippucci et al. 2012: 211).

This discussion encapsulates how the controversies surrounding the Chibondo exhumations were provoked by the excessive potentialities of the human substances being exhumed – by their profoundly evocative and affective yet unstable, uncertain and ultimately indeterminate materialities. It also explains why the objects and artefacts – the clothes, uniforms, shoes, coins, grenades and so on – found with the tangled mass of stinking human substances took on such importance for the different sides of the debates that ensured; because they offered more stability of meaning. This echoes Renshaw's argument about the 'otherness of human remains' and the importance of 'other material traces pertaining to the dead' for reconstructing 'affective identification' with the dead of Spain's civil war (2010) for their living descendants 70 years or more after their deaths.

This argument also explains why many of the debates around Chibondo turned on the *manner* of the exhumations, particularly the tensions between demands for 'proper' forensic expertise and FHT's emphasis on 'African' ways of dealing with the dead, even as everyone appeared to agree that in principle exhumations and reburials can be cathartic, and offer resolution and 'healing'. Indeed this 'torque of materiality' and the 'excessive metonymic qualities' of human remains suggests that neither so-called 'professional', forensic or archaeological approaches, nor so-called 'African' divination or possession practices are necessarily very good at 'remaking the dead' in the absence of extensive contextual work by which human remains can be meaningfully reconstituted and made identifiable as specific kinds of political subjects, and even particular named individuals; whether through the collection of oral histories, DNA analysis, the archaeology of stratigraphy, or of material culture found with human remains, or through the performances of social relatedness by which divination and spirit possession often achieve or substantiate their moral authority.

Both reports of subsequent exhumations at Rusape in 2013, for example (Chipangura 2015; Mupira 2018), and Chipunza's discussions of the Chibondo exhumations indicate that such contextual work through the collection of oral histories and memories from families and communities affected by the dead – but also of the archaeology and material culture uncovered at those sites – was hugely significant for processes of stabilising the identities of the dead, and the reconstruction of the past events that lead to these mass graves, matching Renshaw's work on recent civil war exhumations in Spain (2010, 2011). Likewise Eppel emphasised that during forensic exhumations it is usually the material context of artefacts and personal effects found 'in vicinity of the bones' in burials that help to the date the 'era of death' and to identify the dead, while forensic examination of the human remains themselves may be better at identifying the cause of death. Furthermore, 'extensive interviews with possible relatives have to take place – preferably prior to exhuming'[92] – and 'normally we want to know who the dead are before we exhume'[93] exactly because the emotive but 'indeterminate alterity' of human remains often defies easy constitution 'into meaningful metaphors'. In some ways, therefore this emphasis on context further highlights the similarity of forensic approaches to forms of 'spirit possession' and 'divination' exactly because, as social anthropologists have long recognised, with such cultural practices it is often the social, historical and political context that grants particular actors and events significant meaning and moral authority. We will return to the subject of spirit possession as a way of 'remaking the dead' from material and immaterial human traces of the past in Chapters 5 and 6.

Ultimately, then, the excessive potentiality of human materials makes the remaking of the dead, however approached, a profoundly uncertain and indeterminate process, and it is this quality which often leads to highly 'specialized efforts and dramatic over-determinations' which, as the Chibondo exhumations exemplified, can be 'unusually problematic, politicized and contested'.

The politics of uncertainty

This argument about the excessivity and 'indeterminate alterity' of human remains provides explanation for the fierce controversies that surrounded the Chibondo exhumations. One issue remains to be explored however. Although the uncertainties about the identity of the Chibondo dead provoked by the indeterminacy of its human remains animated the most effective critiques of ZANU PF efforts to 'remake the dead' into their liberation heroes (and thereby reify its rhetoric of 'patriotic history'), there is also a sense that the profound uncertainties provoked by these human remains may have had (at least for a short time) some recognised political utility. If politics is often assumed to turn upon the (contested) work of determination, and the elimination of doubt, then recent work in political anthropology suggests that ambiguity and uncertainty – particularly on

---

[92] SPT 'Silencing the bones', 24/3/11, http://solidaritypeacetrust.org/1015/spt-zimbabwe-update-no-2, accessed 6/9/21.
[93] Field notes, 6/12/11.

The Politics of the Dead

the ubiquitous 'margins' of the state (Das & Poole 2004) – can also be part and parcel of performative stylistics of power. 'Uncertainty' has become something of a new 'buzz word' in anthropology of late; it is, if you like, the new 'ambiguity'.[94] References to 'uncertainty' and the analytical use of the term have been diverse (cf. Buyandelgeriyn 2008; Cooper & Pratten 2015; Fontein 2021), but here I make very specific use of it. I am keen to explore how we can relate the uncertainties and indeterminacies of stuff and material substance – Pinney's 'alterity' or 'torque of materiality' – to the productive duplicities and uncertainties that often surround rumours, gossip and political satire; what Ellis called 'pavement radio' (1989) and which Mbembe (2001) so effectively illustrated are often part and parcel of the 'stylistics of power' in African postcolonies.

For Mbembe, the satirical cartoons that attempt to ridicule and thus debase the vulgar excesses of the political elite in Cameroon are 'an integral part of the stylistics of power' (2001: 115) which do not check the power of the 'elite' so much as reinforce their omnipotent presence. Elsewhere I have used this argument to consider the political affects of rumours that circulated about the 'true' intentions behind ZANU PF's devastating urban clearances of 2005, known as *Operation Murambatsvina* (2009b). I argued that the plethora of rumours which circulated on the streets and sometimes in newspapers, about the 'true' intentions and 'hidden' political agendas behind *Operation Murambatsvina* acted in a way similar to Mbembe's cartoons, reinforcing the omnipotent presence of the ruling party elite, and reminding everyone of its ability to deploy devastating 'state power' at will. While White's *Speaking With Vampires* (2000: 312) showed how 'stories and rumours … mark ways to talk about conflicts and contradictions that gave them meaning and power', Mbembe points the way towards 'recontextualising' rumour 'as a quasi-material substance, as a hinge between the world of concepts and the world of bodily experience' (Weate 2003: 40). In a sense then, Mbembe does for political anthropology what recent theorising about 'materiality' has done for studies of material culture: that is exploring the 'mutual imbrication of the semiotic and the material' (Deleuze & Guattari 1987 [1980]: 37).[95]

Rumours then, like cartoons, and I would argue like bones, bodies and human substances, indeed any kind of 'thing' or material, not only carry or reveal a complexity of meanings; they can have duplicitous political affects. It is in this sense that the popular dubbing of *Operation Murambatsvina* as Zimbabwe's *'tsunami'* not only reflected attempts to

---

[94] See for example the 12th EASA Biennial conference on Uncertainty and Disquiet, Nanterre, France 10–13 July 2012.

[95] 314As Weate noted, the importance of Mbembe's approach lies in its 'hybrid amalgam of poststructuralist semiotics and existential phenomenology', aligned 'at some point between concrete lived experience and economies of the sign' (2003: 28–9).

make sense of its perceived arbitrariness in terms which resonated internationally that year (2005), and which subverted official justifications based on longer histories and aspirations for 'proper' urban planning and a functioning state, it also simultaneously reified the very powerful presence of the ruling party and its ability to deploy force ruthlessly, as it chose (Fontein 2009a). In the same way we could suggest that the controversies which surrounded the Chibondo exhumations, provoked by the uncertainties of the human substances being disinterred, and which challenged ZANU PF's crude efforts to 'remake' the dead into its own 'liberation heroes', actually also served the party's interests in another way: by reminding people everywhere of its profound capacity for violence. The significance of this point was recognised by some MDC critics at the time who 'accused its rival of trying to plant fear in the population that those who don't vote for it will end up dead'.[96] It was also reflected in the many critiques which linked the 'grotesque politicking' going on around Chibondo with fervent debates emergent at the time about when (and how) the next elections would be held.

If political authority must always depend upon a combination of legitimacy and sovereignty, consent and coercion, then perhaps the 'gross politicking' that surrounded the Chibondo exhumations were not just about reinforcing ZANU PF's anti-colonialist ideology and legitimacy, but also a performative exercise in demonstrating (again) that 'the ultimate expression of sovereignty resides … in the power … to exercise control over mortality'; what Mbembe calls 'necropolitics' (2003: 11–12). This argument gains strength if we bear in mind the increasingly troubled GNU politics of that time (Raftopoulos 2013), very much in the wake of the particularly violent excesses of the 2008 elections. In the context of ZANU PF's ultimately successful efforts to restore its electoral legitimacy two years later, the scars, memories and fears of the 2008 violence very much remained in the minds and bodies of thousands of brutalised people as debates were emerging in 2011 about the timing and conduct of future elections. Many people were worried that elections would provoke a repeat of the 2008 violence, and this was one reason why the MDC partners in the troubled unity government were insisting that elections could not happen until a new constitution was in place, and the other requirements of the GPA had been adhered to.[97] This argument about ZANU PF's performative necro-politics also provides explanation for the cruder, more grotesque dimensions of the politicking taking place at Chibondo: the school visits into the mine and people bussed in from around the country, broadcast like election jingles on national television. Similarly, in this perspective the ad hoc, chaotic and decidedly un-forensic

---

[96] 'Hundreds of bodies removed from Zimbabwe mass grave' *Ipsnews.net* 25/3/11, accessed 19/6/20.
[97] 'Voters still haunted by spectre of 2008 polls' *Zimbabwe Independent* 29/3/12.

conduct of the exhumations may have been less about deploying 'African' methods of identifying the dead, or about destroying evidence of ZANU PF atrocities, then about manifesting these performative and demonstrative stylistics of power and sovereignty. Indeed, this exact view was expressed by some commentators at the time. For example, in responding to reports that the FHT had 'forced school children, teachers and villagers from the surrounding area to view the decomposing remains so that they could "appreciate how evil whites are"', the MDC deputy spokesman, Kurauone Chiwayi, suggested that

> those villagers know that many of those remains are of MDC activists but they are too scared to say it ... that's why ZANU PF is now instilling fear by showing them those remains. This shows that we are again not going to have free and fair elections.[98]

Perhaps then ZANU PF's interests in the FHT exhumations at Chibondo may have lain not only in reinforcing its 'chimurenga politics'; a message dependent upon the remains being recognised as or successfully 'remade' into liberation war dead, and specifically ZANLA cadres. Importantly, this argument does not rely on the existence of any Machiavellian political intentions to provoke rumours and uncertainty; such political affects can operate regardless of any design. Yet ZANU PF, or at least some among its turbulent ranks, may have recognised the political purchase of the indeterminate nature of human remains, which makes them difficult to read, identify and recognise, and indeed defies such determination even as their emotive and affective qualities demand or insist upon it. It is likely that some in ZANU PF saw the political usefulness of such uncertainties because it allowed them to have it both ways: to celebrate their 'liberation heroes' and reinforce their anti-colonialist rhetoric, and at the same time remind Zimbabweans of their own capacities for violence. Furthermore, this kind of politics of uncertainty does have other historical purchase in Zimbabwe and fits an emerging pattern that circulates around the political efficacy of rumours. This dimension of ZANU PF politics may be less about controlling narratives of the past than about channelling the indeterminacies of meaning and matter to suit its political purposes. It is apparent not just around events like *Operation Murambatsvina* (Fontein 2009a) or the Chibondo exhumations, but also emerges from the continuing debates about the mysterious, accidental or otherwise, death of leading politicians, for which there are (too) many examples, stretching back to Herbert Chitepo's unresolved assassination in Lusaka in 1975, and the equally unresolved 'accidental' death of Tongogara in 1979, both of which are still subject to a great deal of rumour and debate. This is what is discussed

---

[98] 'Mt Darwin mass graves contain fresh bodies: Pathologist' Zimdiaspora.com 27/3/11, accessed 19/6/20.

Chibondo: Exhumations, uncertainty and human materials

in Chapter 4, where this argument about the politics of uncertainty is developed further in relation to what I call 'political accidents'. Indeed in August 2011, just as the Chibondo controversies were beginning to settle, the death of Solomon Mujuru in a mysterious fire again brought questions of death and uncertainty to the forefront of Zimbabwean politics.

Yet there is a limit to this argument about the political utility of the indeterminacies of matter and meaning. If the uncertainties of rumours and material remains are sometimes the site of the reinforcement of particular mechanisms or performances of 'state power', and if rumours that seek to subvert or 'reveal the truth' behind official representations can duplicitously reify the omnipotent presence they seek to undermine, then surely this can work both ways. There always remains the possibility that the politics of uncertainty provoked by rumours (and at Chibondo, by the indeterminate alterity of human remains) can subvert those other 'productive aspects of power', which appeal to moral and historical legitimacy and consent, and resonate with people's aspirations for good governance, a functioning state and, in Chibondo, with the long-held need to rebury the unsettled dead. Even in 2005, during *Operation Murambatsvina*, the Zimbabwean government was keen to demonstrate the legitimacy of its intentions, and there were indications of official uneasiness at some of the rumours circulating about the 'hidden agendas' behind the operation (Fontein 2009a: 390–94). In 2011, ultimately, the uncertainties about the identities of the dead unearthed at Chibondo and the manner of their deaths, were not sustainable or easily containable. By August the exhumations had been stopped, the exhumed remains had been reburied and the mineshaft apparently sealed, amid proclamations that a new national shrine was to be built at the site. The issue disappeared from the news. Perhaps the possibility and rumours that some of the Chibondo remains might be victims of ZANU PF's postcolonial atrocities were just too threatening to its legitimacy, outweighing any benefits that might have accrued from the grotesque displays of its ability to 'exercise control over mortality' (Mbembe 2003: 11–12). Perhaps, as several people in Harare and Bulawayo suggested to me later that year, some in ZANU PF's higher echelons became concerned that matters had 'got out of hand'. Perhaps, at its simplest, bio-politics outweighed necro-politics. Or as Eppel put it, 'they shut down those exhumations in Mt Darwin ... because their dead scare them'.[99] In the end, perhaps, the uncertainties provoked by the excessive potentiality of human remains exceeded or overwhelmed its own political utility.

Only much later, once Chibondo's problematic human remains had been safely reburied, and the controversies they raised had left the news headlines, was a carefully curated (and guarded) exhibition on the

---

[99] Field notes, December 2011.

FIGURE 7. Entrance to 'Fallen Heroes' exhibition at National Heroes Acre (Author 2015)

exhumations, entitled 'Fallen Heroes', established in a building at the entrance of the National Heroes Acre in Harare (see Figure 7).

Conclusions

In 2004 Judith Butler wrote that 'the question that preoccupies me in the light of recent global violence is: Who counts as human? Whose lives count as lives? And finally, what makes for a grievable life?' (Butler 2004: 20). In Zimbabwe these are familiar questions which demand answers that stretch beyond conventional analyses of how postcolonial commemoration across Africa, and elsewhere, is necessarily inflected with the politics of recognition, 'visibility' (Casper & Moore 2009) and the dynamics of inclusion and exclusion. Events at Chibondo illustrate how the 'alterity of an enfleshed world' (Pinney 2005: 270) is fundamentally imbricated in the 'disjunctures and fractures' of all human becomings (and unbecomings), in which the politics of commemoration (of 'what makes for a grievable life') are but one dimension. The grisly exhumations at Chibondo in 2011 illustrate how the excessive potentiality of human substances demands yet defies any easy 'reading', 'metaphorisation' or stabilisation, and therefore animates, affords and makes possible the kind of politics of commemoration to which Butler refers. It was, after all, the fleshy, leaky, stinking, maybe still decomposing or otherwise mummified, qualities of the human remains being disinterred and re-assembled from the Mt Darwin mine, which provoked much of the intense debate and criticism that enveloped the exhumations. Questions about the performative stylistics of power, the politics of uncertainty, and contestations over different techniques of determination – of remaking the dead – turn in part on these indeterminate material properties and transformations. And it is the excessive qualities of this human stuff, demanding yet defying easy determination or stabilisation into meaning, which both enabled and exceeded ZANU PF politicking around the dead, and the multiple, diverse responses provoked by it.

4

Political accidents: Rumours, death and the politics of uncertainty

In August 2011, just as the Chibondo controversies had begun to settle, another event took place that would prove even more contentious. On 16 August 2011 Zimbabwe awoke to the news that retired General Solomon Mujuru, aka Rex Nhongo (his war alias) – former deputy commander of ZANLA and Zimbabwe's first black army commander, husband of the (then) Vice-President, Joice Mujuru, long-term confidante of President Mugabe, and widely regarded as ZANU PF's 'kingmaker' – had died in a mysterious fire at his farm (Alamein or Ruzambo), in Beatrice, 60 km south-west of Harare. Only four days later, on 20 August, accompanied by public statements of grief from across the political spectrum, and amid growing speculation about the cause of his death, Mujuru's remains were buried at National Heroes Acre in Harare, attended by tens of thousands of people. After the 'inexplicable, horrendous fire accident' – as President Mugabe then described it[1] – there was only a 'small pile of charred bones and ash' to be buried, and workers reportedly needed 'shovels to scrape his remains off the floor'.[2] 'Burnt beyond recognition', unconfirmed reports suggested dental records were needed to confirm his identity;[3] and unusually the 'coffin remained sealed'.[4] But the closed casket could not contain the plethora of rumours of foul play that emerged in the months that followed, which remain unresolved despite police (and later 'private')[5] investigations and an official inquest.

This chapter uses Mujuru's death as way into discussing what I call 'political accidents' in Zimbabwe's recent history, in order to further explore the efficacies of rumours and the politics of uncertainty (begun

[1] 'Mugabe calls for peace as Mujuru is buried' *TalkZimbabwe.com* 20/8/11, accessed 19/6/20.
[2] 'Solomon Mujuru's death alarms moderates' *Mail & Guardian* 19/8/11.
[3] 'Mujuru death "accident"' *Times* (SA) 21/8/11.
[4] 'Doubts raised about Mujuru's cause of death' *Mail & Guardian* 6/2/12.
[5] Tendi refers to a private investigation carried out by a 'motley cluster of actors ... disgruntled with the manner in which the inquest into Solomon's death was conducted' (2020: 295–6) but provides scant details of how the account of Mujuru's death it produced was constructed and by whom.

Political accidents: Rumours, death and the politics of uncertainty

in the previous chapter) in relation to what I term the unfinished nature of death. My purpose is not to offer any kind of determination or commentary about what might actually have happened, or who might have been responsible, but rather to explore the political salience and efficacies of the rumours, conspiracy theories and uncertainties this unresolved death provoked. I am not interested (nor could I claim any such competence) in trying to offer an explanation for what actually might have happened, or in ascertaining responsibility. In fact, quite the opposite: I am interested in understanding what the uncertainties and unresolved or unfinished nature of this mysterious and gruesome death does politically, and how it fits into, and exemplifies Zimbabwe's broader politics of the dead. Mujuru's death is useful because the controversies that surrounded it and the official inquest that followed, which continue to be subject to great speculation both in print and on social media,[6] turned not only on the inconsistencies of different witness accounts, and the woeful incompetence of the police and the fire brigade's response to the fire, but also on their failure to secure forensic evidence properly, the contested role of the state-appointed pathologist, the unresolved mysteries of the fire itself, and the obscurities of Mujuru's burnt remains, which later provoked (unfulfilled) family demands that his remains be exhumed and re-examined. This illustrates further how, in the context of a long history of ZANU PF factionalism, proliferating rumour and dissent can turn on the excessive indeterminacy of material substances, as much as on, or rather in entanglement with, contested narratives and representations. The two are of course intertwined. This discussion leads to the suggestion that the productive uncertainties provoked by such 'political accidents' – which constitute a particular kind of death in Zimbabwe – reflect and reinforce broader (epistemological and ontological) uncertainties that can surround all death in Zimbabwe, and perhaps elsewhere, indicating that death is, in a sense, never finite, never complete, interminable, and potentially always in the (un/re)making.

The death of Solomon Mujuru

Let me begin by outlining the main events of Mujuru's death, and the controversies it provoked, before situating it in a longer history of unresolved 'political accidents' in Zimbabwe. Mujuru's death was undoubtedly an unusually controversial event and one that has already become subject to various academic and popular publications (Nyarota

---

[6] And academic writing (Tendi 2020a). I rely primarily on reports that appeared in local and international newspapers, many of which were published and accessed online. The veteran Zimbabwean journalist Geoffrey Nyarota (2018, chapter 7) has lamented how the media's political polarisation contributed to the 'rumour mill' of 'pure speculation' about Mujuru's death.

2018; Tendi 2016; George 2015); as well as (in the well-worn genre of Zimbabwean political biographies and autobiographies)[7] hagiography (Tendi 2020a), and equally politicised critiques thereof.[8] Nevertheless his death does fit a longer pattern of what I call 'political accidents'; a particular kind of death that points to the productive and potent, yet often disruptive, duplicitous and excessive indeterminacy that can surround all death. We will return to this below.

Factionalism, rivalries and murky business dealings

On the 16 August 2011, *The Herald* announced that 66-year-old Solomon Mujuru had died in a 'suspected fire outbreak at his farm in Beatrice'.[9] It described how a 'sombre atmosphere engulfed the farm' where his wife, Joice Mujuru, then Vice-President, other family members and a collection of senior ZANU PF officials had gathered.[10] *The Herald* carried quotes from these ZANU PF visitors that reflected both a sense of profound shock and of great loss, signalling the start of an intense period of hagiographic outpouring from across Zimbabwe's political divides. For State Security Minister Sydney Sekeramayi it was 'hard to believe' that 'one of Zimbabwe's greatest sons is no more', while Information and Publicity

---

[7] No one in Zimbabwe has had more (often problematic) biographies written about them, than Robert Mugabe (Chan 2019; Onslow & Plaut 2018; Holland 2012; Meredith 2003; Smith, Simpson & Davies 1981). There are also a series of biographies, sometimes equally problematic, of other political figures, like Joshua Nkomo (Ndlovu-Gatsheni 2015), Simon Muzenda (Bhebhe 2004), Eddison Zvobgo (Zvobgo 2017), the Samkange family (Ranger 1995) and Welshman Mabhena (Clarke & Nyathi 2016). There are also a series of autobiographies that sometimes take an even less thinly disguised political position (Chung 2006; Mhanda 2011; Tekere 2007; Coltart 2016; Nkomo 2001 [1984]).

[8] See article by Mutsvangwa ('Gen Mujuru portrayal – valiant, but misdirected' *Sunday Mail* 4/5/20), critiquing Tendi's recent (2020) biography of Solomon Mujuru as 'valiant but misdirected'. Mutsvangwa is a war veteran once associated with Wilfred Mhanda's ZIPA who later reaffirmed his commitment to Mugabe's leadership of ZANU in 1977, when the Vashandi movement was internally suppressed. More recently he was involved in mobilising war veteran support for the November 2017 'coup', and therefore aligned to Mnangagwa and not likely to be sympathetic to Tendi's 'hagiographic' portrayal of the former general (pers. com. David Moore, 3/5/20).

[9] 'Solomon Mujuru dies' *Herald* 16/8/11

[10] Including Home Affairs Minister Kembo Mohadi, State Security Minister Sydney Sekeramayi, Information and Publicity Minister Webster Shamu, Youth Development, Indigenization and Empowerment Minister Saviour Kasukuwere, Defence Forces Commander, Constantine Chiwenga, Air Force Commander, Perence Shiri, Director General of the Central Intelligence Organisation, Happyton Bonyongwe, ZANU PF spokesman Rugare Gumbo and ZANU PF Mashonaland East provincial chairman Ray Kaukonde ('Solomon Mujuru dies' *Herald* 16/8/11).

Political accidents: Rumours, death and the politics of uncertainty

Minister Webster Shamu described it as 'a tragedy which is difficult to fathom' as Mujuru was 'synonymous with the history of the whole liberation struggle ... a very brave fighter and illustrious son of the soil'. Such sentiments were not reserved to ZANU PF. In his 'condolence message', Morgan Tsvangirai, the (now late) MDC leader (then Prime Minister in the GNU) described as 'tragic' the loss of 'a patriot who served his country with honour and distinction', a 'true and gallant son of the soil'.[11] For his part, Dumiso Dabengwa – the (now late) ZAPU supremo – stated that Mujuru 'never feared criticising the party' and had 'played no part in massacres of opposition supporters in the Matabeleland provinces in the 1980s'.[12] Others described Mujuru as not only Zimbabwe's most highly decorated general, but a respected businessman and successful farmer. At the same time, for many international diplomats and others, he represented a 'moderate' face for ZANU PF, particularly as international efforts increased during the GNU years to re-engage with Zimbabwean politics.

Yet even on that first day, not all reports were quite so hyperbolic. One described Mujuru as 'among Zimbabwe's most feared men'[13] and even Ibbo Mandaza, an academic and political commentator close to Solomon Mujuru, described him as 'Machiavellian' in his behind-the-scenes efforts to secure presidential succession for his wife, then the Vice-President.[14] The reporter Lance Guma suggested Zimbabweans were 'divided' over Mujuru's 'mixed bag' legacy, pointing to the 'empire of farms, mines, properties and other business interests' he had 'amassed' since his retirement from the army in the 1990s. This included the farm where he died, which was acquired 'violently' from Guy Watson-Smith, who was made to leave 'with only his briefcase' in 2001 before all his farm assets, furniture and irrigation equipment was sold off by Mujuru. Later lawyers acting for Watson-Smith 'were attacked and assaulted' when they filed a high court application against Mujuru. Guma also discussed a defamation case Mujuru had brought against *Horizon* magazine, when he allegedly told the court that 'if I had known white people [i.e. *Horizon*'s editor Andy Moyse] had defamed

---

[11] 'Prime Minister Morgan Tsvangirai's condolence message' 16/8/11, www.zimbabwesituation.com/old/aug17_2011.html, accessed 10/9/18.

[12] 'Zimbabwe "king-maker" general dies in fire' *Telegraph* (UK) 16/8/11. Dabengwa repeated this claim in 2015, Field notes, 18/8/15, although he noted that as head of the armed forces, Mujuru would likely have been involved in organising logistics for the operations. Others point out that Mujuru was involved in purges of ZIPRA towards the end of the war, during outbreaks of fighting between ex-ZANLA and ZIPRA combatants at Chitungwiza and Entumbane in 1980/81, and during the amalgamation into the Zimbabwean National Army in the early 1980s (Tendi 2020: 186–8).

[13] 'Mujuru was among Zimbabwe's most feared men' radiovop.com 16/8/11, accessed 19/6/20.

[14] 'Mujuru: A leader who made, unmade history' by Ibbo Mandaza *Zimbabwe Independent* 18/8/11.

me, I would have shot them'.[15] Others pointed to alleged involvement in dubious business deals around the establishment of Zimbabwe's mobile phone networks in the 1990s; the controversial acquisition of the River Ranch diamond mine; and alleged laundering of 'diamond plunder' and illegal gold from the Democratic Republic of Congo.[16]

These emerging uncertainties about the nature of Mujuru's 'legacy' would continue for months and years later, particularly when family inheritance struggles loomed after it emerged Mujuru, a notorious womaniser, had a second wife, and more than 20 children out of wedlock.[17] But even more prominent in reports emerging that first morning after his death, were multiple questions about the 'mysterious circumstances'[18] of the death, and its potential consequences. 'It's a huge shock. The suspicion of power play is everywhere' said Eddie Cross of the MDC, 'Everybody's talking about it … it's a huge event and could spark violence between factions of ZANU PF'.[19] For the *Mail & Guardian* (16/8/11) the news came at 'a politically sensitive time … as the country grapples with a timeline for its next general election', pointing to intensifying ZANU PF factionalism then aligning differently around when to hold the next elections, as well as the thorny question of who might eventually succeed Robert Mugabe. Unlike Musila's book on the 1988 murder of Julie Ward in Kenya (2015), which identifies a sharp differentiation between UK and international discourses about Ward's death and those taking place within Kenya, both international and Zimbabwean media reports quickly linked Mujuru's death to internal factionalism and the looming succession debate. While the UK's *Daily Telegraph* (16/8/11) suggested that Mujuru's death 'could intensify turmoil in ZANU PF over who will succeed Mr Mugabe, 87', the (now late) Zimbabwean political analyst John Makumbe told the BBC that the death of 'Zimbabwe's "king-maker"' would likely result in 'more fragmentation in Zanu-PF', pointing to the 'fierce rivalry' that existed between Mujuru

---

[15] 'General Solomon Mujuru legacy divides opinion' Lance Guma SW Radio Africa 16/8/11, accessed 10/9/18.

[16] Ibid.

[17] 'Mujuru spills the beans' *Daily News* 6/5/12; 'Mujuru most patient woman in marriage: Mugabe' *Newzimbabwe.com* 5/5/12; 'Tempers flare over Mujuru estate' *Newsday* 21/3/15. Some reports implied that as many as ninety children had come forward to make a claim on Mujuru's estate, and this even fed back into rumours about his death, with some insinuating Joice Mujuru was involved because she wanted to control his vast wealth ('CIO accused by Baba Jukwa of killing Solomon Mujuru admits that Mujuru's death was planned' 9/4/15, www.myzimbabwe.co.zw/videos-pics/3526-man-accused-by-baba-jukwa-of-killing-solomon-mujuru-admits-that-mujuru-s-death-was-planned.html, accessed 19/6/20).

[18] 'Zimbabwe's General Solomon Mujuru dies in fire' *Mail & Guardian* 16/8/11.

[19] 'Zimbabwe's ruling party shrouded in suspicion after ex-military chief dies' *Guardian* 16/8/11.

and Emmerson Mnangagwa, then defence minister. Indeed many quickly suggested that the 'the most obvious beneficiaries [of the death] are the rival faction of Emmerson Mnangagwa',[20] while others pointed to the weakened position the Vice-President, Joice Mujuru now found herself in.[21]

Looking back from the time of finalising this text (July 2021) – almost ten years after Mujuru's death; seven years after Joice Mujuru's unprecedented 2014 removal from the vice-presidency and ZANU PF (in a large part because of Grace Mugabe's vitriolic interventions); three and a half years after Mnangagwa's own removal from the vice-presidency in November 2017 (after Grace turned her crass attention to her new rival); and after the spectacular, military 'non-coup' that followed, which removed Mugabe from office (vanquishing Grace and her so-called G40 faction) to be replaced by President Mnangagwa with General Chiwenga as his deputy; and three years after yet another controversial election (July 2018); and less than two years after Robert Mugabe's own death and contested burial – these particular predictions about Joice's vulnerability appear, at least for the moment, to have been shown as correct. Certainly in the wake of Solomon Mujuru's death, ZANU PF's succession disputes followed a decidedly changed trajectory, and any confidence that may once have existed that Joice Mujuru would succeed Mugabe has long since evaporated.

But at the time, the abundance of possibilities, rumour and uncertainty meant that 'the way he has gone' was indeed 'difficult to comprehend', as General Chiwenga, put it the morning after the death. Simply (or perhaps especially) *within* ZANU PF, let alone outside of it, there is 'so much in-fighting ... now that if its foul play', Makumbe commented, 'it's anybody's guess who might have done this'.[22] Chiwenga was himself was later fingered in rumours about Mujuru's death in an unconfirmed internal report allegedly compiled by Zimbabwe's Central Intelligence Organisation (CIO),[23] amid suggestions that he harboured his own presidential ambitions but had encountered deep opposition from an 'old guard' within the armed forces. Tendi (2016: 203–24) has since argued that factionalism between Mnangagwa and Mujuru was reflected in long-running tensions between Zimbabwe's military intelligence, allegedly aligned to the former, and elements of the civilian CIO linked to the latter – a point that at once reaffirms the efficacy of, and yet casts doubt on the veracity of, the unconfirmed CIO report. The noticeable suppression of the police and the CIO, and the increasing prominence of the military

---

[20] 'General's death opens Mugabe succession race' *Financial Times* 16/8/11.
[21] E.g. 'Zimbabwe's ruling party shrouded in suspicion after ex-military chief dies' *Guardian* 16/8/11.
[22] 'Zimbabwe's ruling party shrouded in suspicion after ex-military chief dies' *Guardian* 16/8/11
[23] 'Chiwenga ordered Mujuru assassination' *Nehandaradio.com* 13/1/12, accessed 22/6/15.

since the 'non-coup' of November 2017, particularly as witnessed by the shooting of opposition protestors by soldiers after the July 2018 elections, supports Tendi's argument, although recurring rumours of a new, alleged split between President Mnangagwa and his now Vice-President Chiwenga, reiterates the complex and deeply fractured nature of ZANU PF factionalism and internal strife. In August 2011, however, some quickly linked Mujuru's demise to a shooting incident involving (the now late) Air Marshal Perence Shiri three years earlier, as rumours circulated that Chiwenga was running a 'hit squad' to 'assassinate anyone that he views as an obstacle'.[24] As suspicions about Mujuru's death quickly reached fever pitch, Zimbabwe's *Independent* reported that 'a senior Zanu PF politburo member said Mujuru's allies were almost certainly sure he was murdered'. 'This is political murder, call it assassination, by other definitions', the anonymous source said. 'You must put this death in the context of the attempted murder of (Air Marshal Perence) Shiri a few years ago.'[25]

'Accusations of foul play are never far from Zimbabwe's political discourse',[26] and this involves allegations of treason and assassination plots almost as often as they do actual deaths. The prominent use of such accusations by ZANU PF to marginalise perceived threats, both within its own ranks (such as against Joice Mujuru before her 2014 ouster and against Mnangagwa in November 2017, but also in counter-attack by Mnangagwa against Grace Mugabe during the same period), and against opposition parties, Bishop Muzorewa in 1980, Ndabaningi Sithole in 1997 and Morgan Tsvangirai in 2002, illustrates the long histories of factional intrigue and nefarious subterfuge which quickly drew from, slotted into and contributed to rumours surrounding Mujuru's death.[27]

Yet ZANU PF factionalism and succession debates were not the only factors discussed the morning after Mujuru's death. Questions were also immediately raised about Mujuru's relationship with the President. The question of whether Mugabe had sanctioned an attack loomed very large. Although Mujuru had long been one of Mugabe's closest confidantes, dating back to the role he played cementing Mugabe's authority within the guerrilla movement in the 1970s,[28] 'there were reports two years ago that he may have fallen from grace after apparently meeting top US and UK diplomats in Harare'.[29] Not only had Solomon Mujuru been indirectly

[24] Ibid. See also 'Head of Zimbabwe air force shot in assassination attempt on close Mugabe ally' *Daily Mail* (UK) 16/12/08.
[25] 'Mujuru allies cry "murder most foul"' *Zimbabwe Independent* 23/8/11.
[26] 'Zimbabwe's ruling party shrouded in suspicion after ex-military chief dies' *Guardian* 16/8/11
[27] 'Mugabe's bitterness towards Mujuru thickens murder plot' *Zimbabwe Independent* 19/8/16. Also Tendi 2016: 219.
[28] 'Mugabe's bitterness towards Mujuru thickens murder plot' *Zimbabwe Independent* 19/8/16.
[29] 'Solomon Mujuru: Obituary of a Zimbabwean "king-maker"' *BBC news* 16/8/11.

Political accidents: Rumours, death and the politics of uncertainty

implicated in the US Embassy cables scandal[30] – which revealed that many senior ZANU PF figures (including Joice Mujuru) had been secretly meeting with US and other international diplomats – there were also suggestions that Mujuru was forging relations with the MDC opposition in anticipation of a more 'moderate' post-Mugabe dispensation targeted to head off ZANU PF hardliners such as Mnangagwa and Chiwenga. Suspicions also circulated that he had been a key actor in Simba Makoni's flawed bid to stand as an independent candidate against Mugabe in 2008, on behalf of his *Muvambo/Kusile/Dawn* movement. Mujuru, many surmised, had been against Mugabe's candidacy in the 2008 presidential elections.[31] More recently, Tendi (2020) suggested that Mujuru had been opposed to Mugabe's continued leadership since as far back as 1990. Although Makoni's 2008 efforts were ineffective, and never received the public support from Mujuru, or any other senior party member, rumoured to lay behind it, in 2011 many blamed Makoni and his 'hidden' supporters for ZANU PF's disastrous results at the March 2008 elections.

All this suggested the relationship between the two men had indeed soured. Mugabe was said to fear Mujuru's influence in the military and politburo. Mujuru, it was often claimed, was the only man who dared to challenge or question Mugabe directly. In other words, for many, it was Mugabe himself who stood to gain most from Mujuru's untimely and mysterious demise. This was extenuated by a particular rumour that began with a Facebook post by Elliot Pfebve, an MDC-T activist, which claimed, erroneously, that two cabinet ministers, Saviour Kasukuwere and Supa Collins Mandiwanzira had been the last to talk to Solomon Mujuru alive, on Sunday 14 August, at a cricket match at Harare Sports Club. As Nyarota (2018: 106, 108) discusses, this post 'perhaps fuelled most of the speculation that Mujuru was assassinated by people linked to Mugabe'; especially after it was published by *Zimbabwe News Network*, thereby also illustrating how news and social media became entangled in the 'habit of presenting idle speculation as the verified truth'. Tendi has further contributed to such rumours more recently by reflecting on how 'after his death, Solomon was publicly vilified by Mugabe and state-controlled media' (2020: 8) in the period around Joice Mujuru's expulsion from the vice-presidency and then ZANU PF in 2014. He (2020: 268–72) also discusses a series of unusual and contradictory comments and actions soon after Solomon Mujuru's death, made separately by both Robert and Grace Mugabe, to members of Mujuru's family and to a cabinet meeting the morning after the fire; to Morgan Tsvangirai and

---

[30] 'Zanu-PF ponders retribution for WikiLeaks "traitors"' *Mail & Guardian* 16/9/11.

[31] In February 2008 it was reported that Mujuru was under 'house arrest' after he was linked 'to rumours that the former finance minister Simba Makoni was planning a new party', 'Mujuru under house arrest' *Zimbabwean* 13/2/08.

Arthur Mutambara (leaders of different MDC parties in the GNU at the time) during a government visit to Luanda later that day; and subsequently to Didymus Mutasa (then a minister in the President's Office, but expelled from ZANU PF in late 2014 for his close association with Joice Mujuru's faction).

Aside from ZANU PF's insidious factionalism and his deteriorating relationship with the late president, Mujuru's shady business dealings, particularly in relation to diamonds, also quickly became the subject of intrigue after his death. 'The plot further thickens', Zimbabwe's *Independent* reported, 'when it is taken into account Mujuru's most trusted diamond dealer Bothwell Hlahla died in a car accident in Mutare a few days before' the fire, and on the evening that Mujuru himself died, he was on his way down to Beitbridge to meet international diamond dealers to 'resolve a dispute over payment for gems already sold'.[32] But the world of murky diamond deals is rarely separate from the intrigues of ZANU PF's internal politics. It is well known that various branches of the party, military and security services received controversial concessions at Marange's diamond fields, and that different 'companies' run by party heavy-weights have jostled to secure government-determined access over the last decade. Mujuru's business dealings undoubtedly meant he had many enemies and these are hard to divorce from the *political* intrigues provoked by his mysterious death. All these different rumours intertwine in obscure ways, reflecting both how the uncertainty of rumours can have the effect of making almost anything seem possible or conceivable, and how the politics of patronage, securocracy, corruption and factionalism are often perceived as deeply entangled.[33]

These rumours would persist, wax and wane in the following months and years, and remain unresolved. But it is both the speed with which they emerged in August 2011, and the trajectory they subsequently took that I draw attention to here. Indeed, if on 16 August questions were being raised about the mysterious circumstances of the fire, by the next day, media reports became much more direct, asking whether Solomon Mujuru had been assassinated and if so, by whom.[34] On the same day, Mujuru was declared a national hero and his state funeral on Saturday 20 August announced. But tensions within ZANU PF were becoming a problem. Joice herself was forced to publicly appeal for calm the following

---

[32] 'Mujuru allies cry "murder most foul"' *Zimbabwe Independent* 23/8/11.
[33] 'Who killed Solomon Mujuru?' Blog post by Robert Rotberg, 13/9/11, https://robertrotberg.wordpress.com/2011/09/13/who-killed-solomon-mujuru, accessed 7/1/17.
[34] 'Questions over Mujuru death' *Daily News* 17/8/11; Clifford Chitupa Mashiri, 'Was General Solomon Mujuru assassinated? *Zimanalysis* (blog) 17/08/11; Mujuru death raises more questions than answers Lance Guma, SW Radio Africa 17/08/11, accessed 10/9/18.

Political accidents: Rumours, death and the politics of uncertainty

day, after ZANU PF youth marched to her home demanding government answers for her husband's mysterious death.[35] Official denials that it could have been anything other than a terrible accident were considered unconvincing. As ZANU PF alarm about the explosiveness of the situation appeared to grow, *The Herald* was forced to pull a controversial article about the death,[36] and the politburo issued a directive banning any party member, except press secretary Rugare Gumbo, from commenting to the press (Tendi 2020a: 274). During the funeral itself, President Mugabe made an appeal for peace and calm, but this intervention did little to halt the intrigue, particularly because he himself expressed his own reservations after visiting Mujuru's burnt remains at One Commando barracks in Harare, an odd detail which would only emerge months later during the inquest in early 2012.[37]

On 20 August Solomon Mujuru was buried (see Figure 8) at the National Heroes Acre, attended by tens of thousands people.[38] The funeral did little to dampen suspicions. A few days later Tendai Biti, MDC Finance minister in the GNU, directly accused ZANU PF of orchestrating the death, claiming they had now taken to 'roasting' their internal opponents. He later withdrew his remarks.[39] Within a few days Joice announced that she too was deeply suspicious about the death, and called for a new, more thorough police investigation.[40] Within months, the Mujuru family would call for the exhumation of Solomon Mujuru's remains and a new autopsy, as details of the police's bungled forensic investigations were revealed. The apparent rush to bury Mujuru within four days of his death caused further controversy. Only after Solomon's burial were DNA tests confirming his identity carried out and, as a result, the identity of the deceased became a major subject for the inquest's deliberations in early 2012.

---

[35] 'Hold your guns: Acting president' *Newsday* 18/8/11.

[36] 'Herald pulls the plug on Mujuru story as tensions run high' 19/8/11 SW Radio Africa accessed 7/1/17.

[37] This detail was first publicly revealed during the inquest by the Cuban pathologist, discussed below. It subsequently turned out that Mugabe diverted his motorcade to the barracks to view Mujuru's remains on his way to the airport to fly to a meeting in Luanda. This is where he made the odd move of appointing Joice Mujuru (present at the body-viewing) acting president during his trip away. This episode was told to me by Arthur Mutambara, who accompanied Mugabe on his trip to the morgue and to Luanda (pers. com. 2/2/20); see also Tendi (2020: 269–70).

[38] 'Thousands of Zimbabweans Mourn Mujuru' radiovop.com 20/8/11, accessed 10/9/18.

[39] 'Mugabe has the most to gain from Mujuru death: analyst' Lance Guma SW Radio Africa 23/8/11, accessed 10/9/18; 'The mysterious death of Solomon Mujuru and fears for the future of Zimbabwe' *Telegraph* (UK) 27/8/11.

[40] 'Zimbabwe vice president suspicious about husband's death' voanews.com 24/8/11, accessed 10/9/18; 'Zim's Mujuru demands probe into husband's fiery death' *Mail & Guardian* 24/8/11.

Figure 8. Grave of Solomon Mujuru at the National Heroes Acre, Harare (Author 2015)

Rumours and intrigue therefore did not cease after Mujuru's funeral, especially as more details about the fire and events around it were leaked to the press. The farm's former owner, Guy Watson-Smith, contributed to the ferment by expressing his disbelief that Solomon Mujuru could not have easily escaped the burning building, given that it 'had more windows than holes in a colander'.[41] Joice expressed similar sentiments, describing how their grandchildren used to play climbing in and out of the windows of the house.[42] Police tried repeatedly to quell such speculation, as

---

[41] 'Mujuru allies cry "murder most foul"' Nehandaradio.com 23/8/11, accessed 10/9/18.

[42] 'Zimbabwe vice president suspicious about husband's death' voanews.com 24/8/11, accessed 10/9/18.

Political accidents: Rumours, death and the politics of uncertainty

criticism mounted over the delay in releasing their investigation's findings. Concerns about these delays mounted to such a degree that it was debated in parliament, and a new police investigation was launched in November, but as before, no details were released for public scrutiny.[43] The police, it seemed, did not want to take responsibility and many suspected this reflected political pressure they were under. Some suggested the delays mirrored the March 2008 elections, when the official results were delayed while ZANU PF regrouped to unleash a terrible wave of violence to secure their cling to power in the June 2008 presidential run off.[44]

While 'in a country with a history of politically suspicious deaths'[45] it is not surprising that suggestions of foul play emerged quickly, it is striking how many of the rumours circulated around existing intrigues. Part of the context for the controversies enveloping Mujuru's death was therefore already in situ long before the fire took place. In the first few months after the death, official efforts to keep a lid on the rumours only added fuel to public speculation. This changed, however, with the public inquest in 2012, when details of the fire, the events around it and of the police investigation, were finally made public. Then, as with the leaky, stinky human materials exhumed from Chibondo's mine earlier that year, the particular materialities of the death and its context – the farm's layout; the unexplained fire; the human remains burnt beyond recognition; guns apparently found next to the body; missing keys; contradicting witness statements; the flawed autopsy and problematic state pathologist; the failures of his VIP security and of the local police, fire service and so on – all added further traction to the political uncertainties already surrounding Mujuru's demise.

The inquest[46]

After months of speculation in early January 2012 Attorney-General Johannes Tomana announced that police investigations 'are now complete and an inquest is set to begin soon'. The police report had been 'kept a

---

[43] 'How did Solomon Mujuru die? Zim MPs demand answers' *Mail & Guardian* 6/10/11; 'Mujuru's death dominates parly debate' *Herald* 11/10/11; 'Mujuru frustrated by police investigations over husband death' *Zimbabwe Daily* 7/11/11, www.thezimbabwedaily.com/news/9562-mujuru-frustrated-by-police-investigations-over-husband-death.html, accessed 10/9/18.

[44] Clifford Chitupa Mashiri, 'Mujuru death probe is like the 2008 presidential results' 29/08/11, www.zimbabwesituation.com/old/aug30_2011.html#Z20, accessed 10/9/18.

[45] 'Zimbabwe's ruling party shrouded in suspicion after ex-military chief dies' *Guardian* 16/8/11.

[46] Here I deliberately draw on a wide array of news reports which came out as the inquest was ongoing, rather than just the inquest report itself, because I am particularly interested in how the inquest fed into public debates about Solomon Mujuru's death.

closely guarded secret' and Tomana 'appealed to all interested parties ... to be patient and let the judicial process take its course'. The inquest would 'bring finality to a tragedy that shocked the entire nation'.[47] As with other inquests into unexplained deaths (White 2003; Musila 2015; Cohen & Odhiambo 2004), it would do nothing of the sort, but it gripped Zimbabweans' attention for the following three months. If anything, the inquest only fuelled suspicions of foul play by offering, in its revelations, multiple points of traction through which the plethora of rumours could gain purchase.

The inquest began on 16 January 2012, presided over by Magistrate Walter Chikwanha. The courtroom was spruced up, polished, toilets cleaned, water was running, and heavy security deployed in anticipation of the Vice-President's attendance.[48] Forty-two witnesses had been summoned to give evidence, including the Vice-President herself. When the inquest opened objections were immediately aired by the Mujuru family lawyer, Thakor Kewada, that they had not seen the police findings or witness statements as they were legally entitled. The magistrate postponed the hearing for 'to allow her time to peruse the report'.[49] When it reopened the police came in for heavy criticism from Kewada's cross-examination, particularly the three guards who formed Mujuru's official security. It emerged that none of them had airtime to call the fire brigade when they discovered the fire, and their police radios had not been working for six weeks.[50] Furthermore, they did not know the layout of the homestead and upon discovering the fire, had 'opted to run three kilometres to the farm compound to get information on the location of his bedroom, instead of smashing windows to rescue him'.[51] Evidence emerged that Solomon Mujuru had 'frosty relations' with them after they had beaten up one of his farmworkers. He had told his maid, Rosemary Short, 'not to give them food because he was unhappy with the way they were carrying out their duties' and 'that there was virtually no security at the farm and that we were actually guarding ourselves'.[52] Two of the policemen admitted they had been asleep leaving their colleague on duty alone, who awoke them when he

---

[47] 'Mujuru probe complete but ...' *Newsday* 4/1/12.
[48] 'Heavy police and security agents presence at Mujuru inquest' radiovop.com 18/1/12, accessed 10/9/18; 'Mujuru inquest changes face of courts' *Daily News* 29/1/12.
[49] 'Mujuru inquest temporarily halted' *swradioafrica.com* 18/1/12, accessed 10/9/18.
[50] Ibid.; 'Mujuru cop makes shocking statement' *ewn.co.za* 18/1/12, accessed 10/9/18.
[51] 'Mujuru inquest raises more questions' *Standard* 22/1/12.
[52] 'Police left Mujuru to die – Lawyer' *Daily News* 21/1/12; 'I heard gunshots, says Mujuru maid' *Daily News* 20/1/12; 'Gen Mujuru feared Chihuri and his officers: Maid' *Zimbabwe Mail* 19/1/12.

Political accidents: Rumours, death and the politics of uncertainty

discovered the fire.[53] The farm's southern gate was also unguarded[54] and police stationed at Beatrice had had no working vehicle for six months and had to be assisted by a nearby white commercial farmer to reach Mujuru's farm, after the alarm was raised.[55]

More serious were contradictions between police statements and those of Mujuru's staff, particularly Rosemary Short and Clemence Runhare, a private security guard. Both claimed they heard gunshots that evening, before the fire, which they assumed at the time was the police guards shooting snakes or warning off intruders, or came from poachers on nearby farms. The police had, later that night, dismissed these as the sound of asbestos roofing cracking in the fire.[56] Runhare also claimed that when Solomon Mujuru had arrived at the farm's outer perimeter fence earlier that evening, he was sober and accompanied by an unknown man. Yet the policeman stationed 'at the inner perimeter gate testified Mujuru was drunk, alone in the vehicle with a suit draped over the passenger seat'.[57] Short insisted 'Mujuru was not that drunk that he could not appreciate what was happening', adding that 'when he came home drunk' he would usually 'fall asleep upon parking his car'.[58]

The inquest also scrutinised Mujuru's actions before arriving at the farm, when he stopped off at a Beatrice motel on his way home from Harare. Several witnesses claimed Mujuru, known to be fond of whiskey, was not drunk when he left the bar. The bar lady Portia Kamvura, stated Mujuru had four whiskeys, before setting off saying he had to drive to Beitbridge early the next day for business.[59] Details emerged about a mysterious phone call Mujuru received, which had appeared 'serious going by his facial expressions and hand movements', according to Douglas Nyakungu, a ZESA (Zimbabwe Electrical Supply Authority) employee who drank with Solomon Mujuru that night (and would later re-appear as an expert witness).[60] Further questions were raised about timing: why had it taken Mujuru 40 minutes to reach his farm from Beatrice, a journey that would normally only take ten minutes?

---

[53] 'Mujuru wanted police guards fired' *Newzimbabwe.com* 19/1/12, accessed 19/6/20.
[54] '*Independent* comment: Mujuru inquest exposes police' *Zimbabwe Independent* 19/1/12.
[55] 'New evidence suggests Mujuru fire not an accident' *swradioafrica.com* 24/1/12, accessed 10/9/18.
[56] Mujuru inquest raises more questions' *Standard* 22/1/12; 'Police left Mujuru to die – Lawyer' *Daily News* 21/1/12; 'I heard gunshots, says Mujuru maid' *Daily News* 20/1/12.
[57] 'Mujuru inquest adjourned with anti-climax heading towards a white-wash' *Zimbabwe Mail* 20/1/12.
[58] 'Mujuru sensed death' *Daily News* 19/1/12; 'Mujuru inquest raises more questions' *Standard* 22/1/12.
[59] 'Fresh evidence on Mujuru's death' *Daily News* 17/1/12.
[60] 'Family doubts remains belonged to Gen Mujuru' *Zimbabwe Independent* 26/1/12.

Other details from farm staff raised further questions. Short stated Mujuru had come to ask for her keys to the house, because he had left his own in Harare. His keys were later found in the burnt-out bedroom.[61] He had not parked in his usual parking spot, and far from the kitchen door he would have used to get in, nor was it like him to leave his mobile phone, groceries and medication in the unlocked car.[62] Short also contradicted suggestions that the fire had started by a candle or a cigarette, saying Mujuru was not carrying matches, was not a smoker, and there were no candles in the bedroom where the fire was believed to have started.[63]

Amid the tension of the inquest there were lighter moments. Another security guard, Samuel Lewis, 'raised laughter in the courtroom' when he claimed he 'ran more than 300 metres in half a minute' to raise the alarm after the fire was discovered.[64] But the inquest's first week was dominated by critical scrutiny of the police. The pressure on them was intense, and 'most of the witnesses ... appeared visibly frightened ... speaking in very low tones' such that 'the magistrate had to ask ... the police officers, to speak up more loudly'.[65] One was 'driven to the verge of tears under cross-examination by Joice Mujuru and her relatives'.[66] Indeed emotions ran high for everyone. When Short claimed Mujuru had 'sensed that his death was coming', Solomon Mujuru's brother Joel and sister Elizabeth 'failed to hold back their tears'.[67]

Although Tendi suggests that the magistrate was particularly concerned to discredit the evidence of Mujuru's private security guard, Clemence Runhare, in favour of that provided by the police guards, during the course of the first week of the inquest (2020: 279–82) it was the 'shocking shortcomings in the calibre of personnel in the Zimbabwe Republic Police',[68] that was particularly scrutinised by the independent media. Pedzisai Ruhanya, former news editor for the *Daily News*, commented that 'Mrs Mujuru was now seeing first hand how incompetent the police

---

[61] Tendi (2020: 296) suggests Mujuru's keys had been stolen a few days before the fire and, referring to the results of an undisclosed 'private investigation', were instrumental in his assassination; using this to imply that Mujuru 'was betrayed' by 'a member of Solomon's inner circle'.
[62] 'Mujuru "wanted police guards withdrawn"' *Zimbabwe Independent* 19/1/12; 'I heard gunshots, says Mujuru maid' *Daily News* 20/1/12.
[63] 'I heard gunshots, says Mujuru maid' *Daily News* 20/1/12.
[64] "Gen Mujuru feared Chihuri and his officers: Maid' *Zimbabwe Mail* 19/1/12.
[65] 'Mujuru inquest temporarily halted' *swradioafrica.com* 18/1/12, accessed 10/9/18. According to Tendi, the Mujuru's lawyer, Kewada told him that Rosemary Short was intimidated during the trial by state agents (2020: 283).
[66] 'General's ghost haunts ZANU-PF' *Mail & Guardian* 20/1/12.
[67] 'Mujuru sensed death' *Daily News* 19/1/12.
[68] '*Independent* comment: Mujuru inquest exposes police' *Zimbabwe Independent* 19/1/12.

Political accidents: Rumours, death and the politics of uncertainty

force was'.[69] But such criticism was not reserved for the police alone, particularly when it emerged that the fire brigade had taken hours to arrive, and when they did, they had no water because the tanks on their fire engines were leaky.[70] Beyond exposing how 'disaster preparedness' was 'in a shambles',[71] the independent media also criticised the police for failing 'to properly investigate this gruesome murder of our liberation war hero' and for obstructing 'all possible leads and evidence to uncover what sounds like a political killing'.[72] Clearly, as more details emerged, suspicions were further fuelled that the inquest was 'heading towards a white-wash'.[73] Complaints also focused on state media coverage, prompting some to remark that the inquest could 'not be of any significance to ZANU PF', who were, the lawyer Lovemore Madhuku claimed, 'not taking it seriously'.[74] Others noted that politically motivated deaths were 'not new in ZANU PF'. 'Remember when Tongogara died', the civic activist Charles Mangongera explained, 'there was suspicion ... but after that the party soldiered on'. 'What we already have is a seeming case of cover up ... I doubt if there is going to be conclusive evidence'.[75]

If week one failed to calm rumours, this was enormously amplified in the following weeks as the inquest turned to the fire, Solomon Mujuru's corporeal remains and the state pathologist's report. Evidence was drawn from various expert witnesses, including the fire brigade, ZESA officials, the pathologist, and forensic scientists from South Africa. All raised further criticisms of the police's conduct at the scene and subsequent investigations. Early suggestions by police that a candle might have started the fire had already been undermined by Short's evidence. Later testimony by both fire brigade and ZESA officials ruled out an electrical fault. Douglas Nyakungu (the same ZESA official drinking with Mujuru that night, before the fire) explained that investigations showed 'no ZESA equipment had started the fire' and there was no evidence of overloading by 'high currency appliances'. The fire had 'destroyed the electrical set up in the house' and not vice-versa.[76] Meanwhile 'fire fighters testified that the flames ... were too intense to have been "just a normal fire"', and 'no ordinary fire could have caused the roof to drop as it did'.[77] Harare's Chief Fire Officer, Clever

[69] 'Mujuru inquest temporarily halted' *swradioafrica.com* 18/1/12, accessed 10/9/18.
[70] 'Mujuru cop makes shocking statement' *ewn.co.za* 18/1/12, accessed 10/9/18.
[71] 'Mujuru inquest: Zim disaster preparedness in a shambles' *Zimbabwe Independent* 19/1/12.
[72] 'Mujuru inquest temporarily halted' *swradioafrica.com* 18/1/12, accessed 10/9/18.
[73] 'Mujuru inquest adjourned with anti-climax heading towards a white-wash' *Zimbabwe Mail* 20/1/12.
[74] 'Mujuru death crisis' *Daily News* 29/1/12.
[75] Ibid.
[76] 'Family doubts remains belonged to Gen Mujuru' *Zimbabwe Independent* 26/1/12.
[77] 'Fire brigade testimony fuels suspicion over the Mujuru fire' *swradioafrica.com* 25/1/12, accessed 10/9/18.

Mafoti, explained that their investigations had proved inconclusive, but had identified 'two sources of the fire in the main bedroom and the lounge', adding that fires with two sources usually point to arson or an electrical fault'.[78] But, Mafoti noted, the 'fire brigade could not definitely prove that theory because the crime scene ... had been contaminated by too many people'.[79] By 'the time that we eventually arrived most of the leads had been destroyed', he added.[80] Therefore, 'the cause of the fire could not be determined', Bothwell Mutandiro, director of Zimbabwe's police forensic section later admitted to the inquest.[81]

This uncertainty about the fire's cause and concerns about compromised evidence was echoed by forensic scientists from the South African Police Service (SAPS). They suggested 'the handling of evidence at the scene ... fell below professional standards'.[82] Lieutenant Colonel Kgotlakgomang Ariel Lenong, Chief Forensic analyst at SAPS, ruled out explosives, and Seomyatseng Jack Maine said that tests on materials retrieved from the scene to ascertain whether 'accelerants' had been used, also showed no evidence. But 'that was not to say any were not used', he stated, pointing to factors that could have 'compromised' the results, including how the samples were collected, the intense heat of the fire, and the incorrect storage bags used by the police.[83]

These uncertainties about the fire were directly linked to uncertainties provoked by Mujuru's corporeal remains. Again critical questions were raised about the competence of state investigators. Many witnesses spoke of unusually large, intense blue flames covering the burning human remains 'to a radius of about 30cm around the body', which was discovered 'lying face down with both legs and arms severely burnt' in a passage near the main bedroom.[84] Tawanda Madondo, gardener at the farm, described finding a burning 'black object ... the shape ... of a human being', which needed 'a number of buckets ... to be extinguished'.[85] The number of buckets needed to douse the remains escalated from two to ten in different witness accounts.[86] Constable Cletwell Garisai and Inspector Simon Dube 'told the inquest they poured at least ten buckets of water to douse the blue flame which was intense and became ferocious when

---

[78] 'ZESA rules out electrical fault in Mujuru farm' Newzimbabwe.com 26/1/12, accessed 10/9/18.
[79] 'Arson cause of Mujuru blaze: fire expert' Zimbabwe Mail 25/1/12.
[80] 'Mujuru evidence destroyed' Daily News 26/1/12.
[81] 'Zimbabwe general's killer blaze mystery' News24.com 30/1/12.
[82] 'Mujuru evidence "compromised": expert' Newzimbabwe.com 2/2/12, accessed 10/9/18.
[83] Ibid.
[84] 'Mujuru inquest: More questions than answers' Zimbabwe Independent 26/1/12.
[85] 'Police left Mujuru to die – lawyer' Daily News 21/1/12.
[86] 'Rescuers found Mujuru's body in flames' Newzimbabwe.com 20/1/12, accessed 10/9/18; 'Gen Mujuru died before fire: Allies' Standard 29/1/12.

Political accidents: Rumours, death and the politics of uncertainty

water was poured on it'.[87] Later Mafoti, from the fire brigade, explained that in fires above 500 degrees a 'triangle of combustion' could cause body fat to spontaneously combust with a blue flame, and that water poured on such an intense fire would immediately evaporate, causing the hydrogen in it to explode and intensify the flames.[88]

Gruesome descriptions were heard about the burnt remains, which were not easily identifiable as Solomon Mujuru. Indeed his identity had not been confirmed until DNA test results came out several weeks after his burial. This was a point that Solomon Mujuru's brother Joel had repeatedly raised, even before the inquest began, claiming that he could not be confident that the body they had buried was that of his brother. Joel's doubts were shared by many Zimbabweans in the country, and abroad.[89] Even the inquest report later agreed that the police's decision to authorise burial, before DNA tests confirmed Solomon Mujuru's identity, had 'made no sense', was 'inappropriate' and an 'oversight' on their part.[90]

As the inquest continued more questions emerged. As the *Zimbabwe Independent* noted, 'the expert witnesses did nothing but raise more questions',[91] for example, about why 'Mujuru's body burnt to ashes in two hours yet it takes over 11 hours to do an ordinary cremation'.[92] Others referred to a curious hole in Mujuru's stomach, and missing organs.[93] Doubts were also raised by differing accounts of the extent to which his body had been burnt, the position it lay in and whether the arms were raised.[94] There were suggestions the body had been moved before the investigators arrived.[95] Others queried why the carpet under the body was un- or less damaged by fire, indications for some (including Mutandiro, director of Zimbabwe's police forensic section) 'that Mujuru died before the fire spread into the room where his remains were retrieved'.[96] Equally contentious were the number of guns kept in the house: were there 14, 15 or 17?[97] Were they all registered? And what about

---

[87] Ibid.
[88] 'Findings of Mujuru inquest' *Herald* 29/3/12.
[89] 'Mujuru death crisis' *Daily News* 29/1/12; see comment by 'mdcsoutheastlondon' to article 'Zimbabwe general's killer blaze mystery' *News24.com* 30/1/12.
[90] 'Findings of Mujuru inquest' *Herald* 29/3/12.
[91] 'Mujuru inquest: Contradictions, more suspicion' *Zimbabwe Independent* 9/2/12.
[92] 'Gen Mujuru died before fire: Allies' *Standard* 29/1/12.
[93] 'Mujuru inquest: More questions than answers' *Zimbabwe Independent* 26/1/12.
[94] Ibid.
[95] 'New evidence suggests Mujuru fire not an accident' SW Radio Africa 24/1/12, accessed 10/9/18.
[96] 'Mujuru inquest: Contradictions, more suspicion' *Zimbabwe Independent* 9/2/12.
[97] 'ZESA rules out electric fault in Mujuru fire' *Newzimbabwe.com* 26/1/18; 'Mujuru: family wants second opinion' *Newzimbabwe.com* 28/1/12; '17 Burnt Firearms Discovered at Mujuru's House: Makedenge' radiovop.com 27/1/12, accessed 19/6/20.

The Politics of the Dead

the guns allegedly found next to his body[98] – and suggestions that spent ammunition had been found?[99] These tied into comments about why a soldier of Solomon Mujuru's experience could not have escaped the burning building, something President Mugabe had raised at Mujuru's funeral.[100]

The pathologist, Dr Gabriel Alviero Gonzalez, a Cuban doctor working at Parirenyatwa Hospital, drafted in to carry out the autopsy at Harare's One Command barracks on 16 August 2011, received particular attention during the inquest.[101] The *Zimbabwe Independent* summarised his testimony as follows:

> A postmortem carried out by Dr Gabriel Alvero deduced the cause of death as 'carbonation due to open fire, origin unknown. The tracheal mucosa was red and black with carbon inside demonstrating that the deceased was alive when the fire started,' he said. Postmortem findings were: The right arm was complete but left arm was burnt to ashes up to the elbow level. Both lower limbs were burnt to ashes up to the knee level. The lungs were severely burnt and could not be recognized. The large vessels such as the aorta and vena cava were burnt and could not be recognized. The teeth were present but fragile and breaking off. The esophagus was severely burnt and could not be recognized. The stomach was burnt and absent. The pancreas was absent. The liver and gall bladder were present but severely burnt and charred. A portion of the bowel was present but damaged by action of the fire and heat. The kidneys were absent. The bladder was absent. The prostate was absent. The spleen was absent. No endocrine organ was found.[102]

---

98 'Zimbabwe general's death marked by many mysteries' *Monstersandcritics.com* 8/2/12; 'Two guns found next to Mujuru's body' SW Radio Africa 26/1/12; both accessed 10/9/18.

99 'Two guns found next to Mujuru's body' SW Radio Africa 26/1/12; 'Mujuru: family wants second opinion' *Newzimbabwe.com* 28/1/12, accessed 10/9/18.

100 'Rare unity at funeral for Zimbabwean hero Solomon Mujuru' .voanews.com 19/8/11. Later Mugabe told the *Independent* that he thought Mujuru's 'careless' smoking must have caused the fire, as had happened during a well-known incident at a Geneva hotel in 1976: 'Robert Mugabe finally speaks on Solomon Mujuru's death', www.pazimbabwe.com/zimbabwe-45876-robert-mugabe-finally-speaks-on-solomon-mujurus-death.html, 24/3/18; 'Robert Mugabe refuses to jump from the fourth floor of Geneva hotel after Solomon Mujuru started a fire: Fay Chung book reveals chilling details' www.pazimbabwe.com/zimbabwe-45957-robert-mugabe-refuses-to-jump-from-the-fourth-floor-of-geneva-hotel-after-solomon-mujuru-started-a-fire-fay-chung-book-reveals-chilling-details.html, 26/3/18; both accessed 10/9/18.

101 'Mujuru inquest: Contradictions, more suspicion' *Zimbabwe Independent* 9/2/12; 'Mugabe at Mujuru post mortem, inquest told' *Newzimbabwe.com* 3/2/12, accessed 10/9/18.

102 'Mujuru inquest: Contradictions, more suspicion' *Zimbabwe Independent* 9/2/12.

Political accidents: Rumours, death and the politics of uncertainty

While Gonzalez had identified no external injuries, others suggested that one of Mujuru's legs was broken.[103] Solomon Mujuru's missing feet later led some members of ZANU PF and relatives of Mujuru to surmise they had been removed by Solomon's assassins in a ritual attempt to stop his spirit becoming a *ngozi* that would haunt them (Tendi 2020a: 294). As the inquest continued, some questioned why the autopsy had pointed towards smoke inhalation as a possible cause of death, due to evidence of carbonisation in the mouth and throat, while other indications implied his lungs were still pink.[104] The pathologist's status was also questioned when it emerged that he was not formally registered in Zimbabwe (Nyarota 2018: 110). Furthermore, the autopsy had been done without the proper equipment,[105] and there were no tests on the blood or organs because they were all burnt out. Amid this barrage of criticism of the bewildered Cuban pathologist, who was giving evidence through an interpreter, one of the oddest details to emerge was that President Mugabe had himself turned up, unannounced, just moments before the autopsy began, later telling journalists 'I have never seen a person die in such a horrific manner, we are all shocked'.[106] The pathologist testified that 'Mujuru appeared to have died from inhaling smoke', but added that his findings were inconclusive 'considering the state of the body'.[107]

The many official failings that the inquest revealed obviously fed the feverish rumour mill, and especially the Mujuru family's demands for an exhumation and a new post mortem by an independent pathologist from South Africa, Dr Reggie Perunel, who was in court alongside Mujuru's lawyer.[108] Their court application was made even before the state pathologist had given evidence. Kewada questioned the Cuban pathologist's autopsy 'saying he had been in the country for only seven weeks and had a poor command of English', had been ill-equipped, and had 'bungled' the post mortem.[109] Initially, Magistrate Chikwanha delayed responding to this request, saying it was 'premature', and evidence from the 'local pathologist' needed to be heard first.[110] Later, Chikwanha denied the request altogether in an extraordinary outburst accusing Kewada 'of "violating" the Inquest

---

[103] 'Gen Mujuru died before fire: Allies' *Standard* 29/1/12.
[104] Ibid.
[105] 'Mugabe at Mujuru post mortem, inquest told' *Newzimbabwe.com* 3/2/12, accessed 10/9/18.
[106] Ibid. See footnote 37 above.
[107] 'Mujuru exhumation request rejected' *Newzimbabwe.com* 6/2/12, accessed 10/9/18.
[108] 'Mujuru evidence "compromised": expert' *Newzimbabwe.com* 3/2/12, accessed 10/9/18.
[109] 'Mujuru exhumation request rejected' *Newzimbabwe.com* 6/2/12; 'Mujuru coroner blasts lawyer' *Newzimbabwe.com* 6/2/12; both accessed 10/9/18.
[110] 'Magistrate dismisses request by Mujuru family' SW Radio Africa 30/1/12, accessed 10/9/18.

Act', arguing that for him 'to conclude that Dr Alviero [Gonzalez] had not carried out a proper job' was 'highly inappropriate'. Kewada, Chikwanha claimed, was not 'qualified' to 'address the magistrate over facts provided by witnesses', and would have to await until 'after the court has analysed all evidence', had made its 'conclusions on how the deceased met his death' and sent its 'recommendations to the AG's office'.[111]

After three weeks of testimony from 39 witnesses – the last being Joice Mujuru herself, who did not testify but submitted a signed affidavit[112] – the inquest ended with 'sharper contradictions and inconsistencies' and 'deepening suspicions of foul play', than it began with.[113] Chikwanha's report was published at the end of the following month. It concluded that there was no evidence of 'foul play', and that Solomon Mujuru had died of 'carbonisation' from smoke from an open fire whose cause could not be determined.

> Despite the suppositions, speculations, conjectures and suspicions by various people including the deceased's relatives, nothing concrete and no evidence at all was placed before the court to show that there was foul play in the death of the deceased. In addition to that there is evidence from the doctor that deceased did not suffer any other injuries besides that caused by fire and there is also the evidence from the lead Investigator, Chief Superintendent Makedenge to the effect that they carried out exhaustive investigations but there was nothing to show that there was foul play leading to the death of the now deceased.
>
> The facts and evidence presented before the court, therefore, do not show that there was foul play and consequently the court concludes that there was no foul play.
> **W. Chikwanha**
> **PROVINCIAL MAGISTRATE**
> **14 March 2012**[114]

Following Chikwanha's report, the attorney-general told police to close the case (Nyarota 2018: 109). Mujuru's lawyer called the result a 'mockery' that failed to 'bring closure to the case'.[115] Despite continuing uncertainties and persistent demands from Joice Mujuru and the family, an exhumation and re-examination of Mujuru's remains has never taken place.[116]

---

[111] 'Mujuru coroner blasts lawyer' *Newzimbabwe.com* 6/2/12, accessed 10/9/18.
[112] 'Inquest into Zimbabwe general's death ends' *The Africa Report* 7/2/12, www.theafricareport.com/7686/inquest-into-zimbabwe-generals-death-ends, accessed 29/4/20.
[113] 'Mujuru inquest: Contradictions, more suspicion' *Zimbabwe Independent* 9/2/12.
[114] 'Findings of Mujuru inquest' *Herald* 29/3/12.
[115] Mujuru inquest results a mockery: Family lawyer' *radiovop.com* 17/3/12, accessed 10/9/18.
[116] 'Exhume Mujuru, demands family' *Standard* 23/3/12; 'Family still wants

Political accidents: Rumours, death and the politics of uncertainty

These continuing uncertainties link Mujuru's death to other unresolved, high-profile deaths in Zimbabwe and elsewhere. Indeed, they are a key aspect of the kind of 'political accident' that Mujuru's death epitomises, which I turn to below. The inquest left the cause of death profoundly unresolved, and if anything, only further extenuated uncertainty by offering in its minutely detailed account of the known and unknown aspects of the death, multiple points of traction for the swelter of suspicion and rumour to gain purchase. Indeed, as several commentators had already surmised, the inquest was never 'likely to bring [the] finality' the attorney-general had promised. This is partly because public inquests of this sort, although judicial, are usually not charged with identifying culpability, but merely the cause of death and the identity of the dead. This is important in a Zimbabwean context where deaths are very rarely understood as 'natural', whatever their immediate cause, and usually provoke difficult-to-resolve questions about intent and culpability (Fontein 2018; Bourdillon 1987b). Pushing further, however, one could question whether the political and social functions of such public inquests really are about offering the kind of finality and closure the attorney-general had promised; a position that is akin to older anthropological arguments that see the function of death rituals as being about remaking society after the rupture of death (Hertz 1960; Bloch & Parry 1982). The argument that 'the state allowed an inquest in Solomon's death in order to dispel lingering speculation that there was any foul play in his demise' (Tendi 2020a: 292), misses the political salience of the uncertainty that surrounds 'political accidents' in Zimbabwe, just as the claim that Mugabe himself 'attempted to superimpose a hegemonic version of Solomon's death as a fire accident' in his statements before and after the inquest, ignores Mugabe's own statement at Mujuru's funeral, that 'for some events we can never get answers that satisfy us' (Tendi 2020a: 276).

In contrast, I suggest that the inconclusive nature of the Mujuru death inquest, and others like it elsewhere, whatever the official pronouncements, is important for two reasons. Firstly, because this is how the politics of uncertainty surrounding death works. Situated contingently between necro-politics and bio-politics – between the need for political legitimacy and the need to demonstrate necro-political sovereignty, impunity and capacity for fatal violence – such deaths must remain unresolved. They cannot be fixed as a named party's culpability as that would undermine the need for political legitimacy, yet by keeping rumours and suspicions of malevolent intent in circulation, this uncertainty contributes to 'necro-political power' by making rumoured culprits (or even just the very possibility that such a party exists) appear powerful, sovereign and above the law. As argued in the Chapter 3, this double effect was also key to the political efficacy of the war veteran-led 'vernacular' exhumations at

---

Mujuru exhumed' *Herald* 29/3/12; 'They murdered my husband – Mujuru' *Daily News* 23/2/16; 'We'll find Gen Mujuru killers' *Daily News* 27/8/15.

Chibondo earlier in 2011. Here I suggest it is equally key to the efficacy of 'political accidents' as particular kinds of death in Zimbabwe. In both cases, this uncertainty turns, in part, on the 'excessivity', 'indeterminate alterity' or 'otherness' (Renshaw 2011) of human materials, which demands but ultimately elides easy determination or stabilisation into meaning. As discussed, Filippucci et al. (2012: 211) argue that the 'excessive metonymic qualities' of human materials often 'defy ... efforts to turn them into meaningful metaphors', and this explains why they 'can be subject to huge and often highly specialised efforts and dramatic over determinations into particular types of subjects/objects, such as ancestors, victims, heroes or specimens – processes that are often unusually problematic, politicized and contested'. This was apparent both during the Chibondo controversies and the Mujuru inquest; how the *manner* in which human remains in both cases were handled, interpreted and 'reconstituted' was what provoked particular attention, debate and critique.

Secondly, and related to this, the unresolvable and inconclusive nature of the Mujuru inquest is important because it exemplifies something that may be a feature of all death in Zimbabwe, and maybe all death in general: that it is never, or very rarely, entirely contained, stabilised, resolved, finished, or over and done with. That there always remains a contingent potentiality and uncertainty to death which defies material, semantic and temporal closure, and has to do with the way that death raises but cannot resolve difficult ontological questions about the imbrication of matter and meaning, and the entangled material and immaterial aspects of life. This argument is picked up again in Chapters 5 and 6 through an examination of the politics of spirit mediumship in Zimbabwe, and what I call 'precarious possession', which are another important aspect of its politics of the dead. For now it suffices to say that, of course, the two reasons mentioned above are intertwined: therefore the profound ontological problems that death raises are what give the uncertainty of death its political traction, even if it also, ultimately and necessarily, defies attempts to channel such political utility. While the key point here is that the uncertain or unfinished nature of death is politically productive, it also seems unlikely that any inquest (or any new investigation, exhumation, book or biography) *could* have resolved the burgeoning questions and intrigue surrounding Mujuru's demise.

A particular kind of death

Mirroring what has frequently been reported within research on road and traffic accidents across the region (Lamont 2012, 2013; Melnick 2013; Klaeger 2013; Sanders 2008b) – part of the new literature re-assessing meanings and practices of death across sub-Saharan Africa discussed in the Introduction – fatal accidents in Zimbabwe, on roads or elsewhere, are often the subject of dissent and rumour, and sometimes accusations

Political accidents: Rumours, death and the politics of uncertainty

of the occult. Links between rumours, gossip, sorcery and 'witchcraft' are well established in anthropological literature (Stewart & Strathern 2003), as are the political imbrications of witchcraft accusations (Jensen 2012). A key point here is that the uncertainties surrounding such deaths often leak across different social, symbolic, discursive and political realms, and the uncontained materialities of bodies and persons can destabilise things, place, time and landscape just as they question official, normative accounts of fatal events. This is what Jensen (2013), in a different but not unrelated context – rape in South Africa – refers to as 'shimmering', as different possible explanations and categories constantly fade into and out of clear view.

Traces of past accidents are highly visible in the carcasses of vehicles on roadsides, but also appear through the uneasy presence of unsettled spirits and indeterminate ghosts said to haunt accident 'black spots' (cf. Melnick 2013), themselves becoming dangers to be avoided or encountered at great risk. There is an important link here to landscapes of terror associated with militia 'bases' and election violence, which are also often haunted by frightening *ngozi* spirits of people killed, demanding atonement and reparation (Chitukutuku 2017, 2019; Mujere et al. 2017; Eppel 2013, 2014; Fontein 2010). Accidental and violent deaths are therefore linked by the haunted landscapes of terror they co-produce (at once literally and metaphorically) through the spilling of blood, exemplifying the profound uncertainties that all deaths provoke. Indeed, as already pointed out, death is only very rarely considered 'natural' in Zimbabwe, and is therefore very often accompanied by an excess of intrigue and contestation exactly because of the instabilities of personhood and society, bodies and spirit, material and immaterial, matter and meaning, that it can reveal (Hertz 1960). This is part of what I call the unfinished nature of death in Zimbabwe (Fontein 2018).

These dynamics are reflected in how Zimbabwe's postcolonial milieu has long been punctuated by the 'accidental' deaths of politicians, army officers[117] and other senior ZANU PF figures, such as Solomon Mujuru in 2011, which have provoked a fraught myriad of rumour and conspiracy about the ruling party 'eating their own'.[118] Although unusually high profile, the controversies surrounding Mujuru's death echo very many other examples, including (to name only a few) the deaths of ZANU PF ministers and senior figures like Chris Ushewokunze in 1994, Zororo Duri in 1996; Border Gezi and Moven Mahachi in 2001; Brigadier General

---

[117] 'Mugabe honours alleged victims' *Zimbabwean* 17/8/09. The death of former ZNA Chief of Staff, General Trust Mugoba from an 'undisclosed ailment' on the same day that Mugabe died also generated much suspicion, Field notes, March 2020.

[118] 'Mystery surrounds deaths of national heroes' *Nehanda Radio* 15/8/12 accessed 19/6/20.

Paul Armstrong Gunda in 2007; and Elliot Manyika in 2008.[119] Some examples from the 1960s, such as the death of Parirenyatwa in 1962, when his car was allegedly hit by a train (but unlikely), and of Paul Mushonga in a car crash a few months later, suggest this motif, sometimes known as 'the phenomenon of the "black dog"', may have nefarious Rhodesian origins.[120] If so, then (as may also be true of the practice of dumping bodies in mines), it has long since become firmly associated with ZANU PF. Another prominent example came just before the June 2013 elections when the outspoken ZANU PF MP Edward Chindori-Chininga died in a car accident only a week after the parliamentary committee he chaired released a 'damning report' into 'the abuse of diamond revenue from the Chiadzwa diamond fields'.[121] All these cases involved 'mysterious' accidents accompanied by rumours of foul play and assassination plots.

Although I am mainly focused here on the 'accidental' deaths of high-profile ZANU PF officials, because this status is key to the 'political accidents' I am describing, there are also examples of suspicious deaths beyond the party which feed into the swelter of intrigue that can surround fatal car accidents, such as of senior ZAPU and ZIPRA figures in the 1970s and 1980s,[122] and especially of the outspoken opposition MP Sydney Malunga in 1994;[123] and more recently Susan Tsvangirai's death in a car accident which some suspected was a botched attempt to assassinate her husband Morgan Tsvangirai on the eve of the GNU's 2009 formation.[124] Another example illustrating how the unexplained deaths of much less high-profile party members can provoke similar controversy was that of aspiring ZANU PF parliamentary candidate Bruno Mugabe, just before the 2000 elections, when his car was washed away in a flash flood in Masvingo, which many suspected was intertwined with that province's infamous factionalism, and possibly occult interference.[125] Likewise, Moore (forthcoming A: 80) discusses how Wilfred Mhanda – aka 'Dzino'

---

[119] 'Mystery Zim car-crash deaths haunt Zanu-PF' *Mail & Guardian* 27/6/13.

[120] B. Marmon 'The controversial life and death of Paul Mushonga' *New Frame* 29/1/20, www.newframe.com/the-controversial-life-and-death-of-paul-mushonga; 'Dr Samuel Parirenyatwa assassination: new details emerge' *Nehanda Radio* 12/3/20; both accessed 1/5/20.

[121] 'Secret insider warned ZANU PF "rebel" before his death' 21/6/13 *Mail & Guardian*.

[122] See Nyarota 2018; also 'Mystery Zim car-crash deaths haunt Zanu-PF' *Mail & Guardian* 27/6/13.

[123] I am grateful to one anonymous reviewer for suggesting this example. Also B. Marmon, 'The controversial life and death of Paul Mushonga' *New Frame* 29/1/20, www.newframe.com/the-controversial-life-and-death-of-paul-mushonga, accessed 1/5/20.

[124] 'Fatal Tsvangirai crash "was not accident", says MDC' *Telegraph* (UK) 7/3/09.

[125] 'Battle for Masvingo supremacy resurfaces', *Financial Gazette* 8/6/00; also Field notes, 2001.

Political accidents: Rumours, death and the politics of uncertainty

Machingura, the former Marxist guerrilla commander associated with the mid-1970s attempt to bring ZIPRA and ZANLA together under the ZIPA (Zimbabwe People's Army) banner, later disparagingly known as the *Vashandi* [lit. 'workers'] movement and imprisoned by Samora Machel (at Mugabe's request) for their efforts – showed him the severed brake cables of his car after he re-emerged into Zimbabwean politics through the Zimbabwe Liberators' Platform (a rival to the ZANU PF-linked War Veterans Association) in the 2000s. There continue to be suspicions that Mhanda's subsequent death from cancer of the colon was actually due to poisoning – another (perhaps less common) motif for alleged assassination plots in Zimbabwe which has gained traction recently in relation to Mnangagwa's alleged poisoning in 2017 during the intense internal factionalism that preceded the 'coup' of November that year. As with mysterious 'car accidents', alleged poisonings correlate closely with the shape that witchcraft accusations often take.[126]

The point I am making here is that these kinds of 'political accident' constitute a particular kind of death that can be used as a lens through which to make sense of the unfinished nature of death in Zimbabwe. Controversial deaths of senior ZANU PF politicians are not only a feature of the last two decades, since Zimbabwe's turn towards 'authoritarian nationalism' (Raftopoulos 2003). There are many older unresolved deaths dating to the 'struggles within the struggle' which beset nationalist parties and guerrilla armies during the 1960s and 1970s (Sithole 1979). As with so much of contemporary Zimbabwean politics, the past looms large, close and unresolved. Just as the burial of every new 'national hero' invokes recursive referral back to the nationalist politics of the 1960s and 1970s, so every new 'accidental' death renews the controversies of earlier unresolved deaths. Often these coincide exactly because such 'political accidents' have produced so many 'national heroes', an observation frequently noted in the media.[127]

Of all such deaths, the 1975 assassination of ZANU Chairman Herbert Chitepo in Lusaka (White 2003) and the car accident that killed the popular ZANLA commander Josiah Magama Tongogara in Mozambique in December 1979, on the eve of independence, remain subject to the fiercest controversies. Both are mired in rumours of ZANU power struggles and frequently the subject of media speculation. Zambia's deeply flawed 1976 Chitepo Commission Report blamed 'ethnic tensions' within ZANU, implicating Tongogara (and others) himself in Chitepo's death, a charge

---

[126] 'Mystery surrounds Mnangagwa poisoning' *Zimbabwe Independent* 18/8/17; 'Zimbabwe's Emmerson Mnangagwa criticised over poison claim' *BBC news* 4/10/17; 'Mnangagwa poisoning FRESH DETAILS' *Zimbabwean* 25/1/18; 'Mnangagwa poisoning; new details emerge' *Bulawayo 24News* 24/6/19.

[127] 'Mystery surrounds deaths of national heroes' 15/8/12 *Nehanda radio*, accessed 10/9/18.

The Politics of the Dead

he went 'to his own unexplained death in 1979 still denying' (White 2003: 87). In turn, President Mugabe was often rumoured to be haunted by Tongogara's ghost, implying his hand in the guerrilla commander's death.[128] Unlike other examples, Chitepo's death always was murder; it is hard to imagine how a car bomb could be reconstituted as an accident. Yet Chitepo's murder is perhaps the archetypal kind of 'political accident' – the exception that proves the rule perhaps – because as White (2003) showed, the multiple confessions it led to and the fact that its controversies not only endure but continually gain new meaning and salience, point exactly to the open-ended indeterminacy that death can provoke, even after 40 years. History is indeed 'a messy business' and 'there is no "perfect closure" to any event' (White 2003: 2).[129] Furthermore, that so many different people, at different times, for different audiences, continue to claim or assign responsibility for Chitepo's assassination – 'fixing blame' to make possible a litany of diverse but inevitable partial 'national narratives' (White 2003: 9) – illustrates something of the political salience afforded by being associated in 'pavement radio' (Ellis 1989) with particular deaths, without ever being held formally culpable or legally responsible.

Such confessions can be made to do different things in changing historical contexts, like presenting a 'Rhodesia more powerful in memory that it ever was in practice' or portraying Chitepo and Tongogara 'as more heroic, more charismatic and more judicious than they had ever been considered in their lifetimes' (White 2003: 85, 97). They operate across, as well as within, diverse discursive registers, and often appear like a means of evading legal responsibility. Indeed perhaps the efficacy of rumours lies exactly in their multiplicities, so that like confessions and secrets-revealed they can best be understood *both* as 'tools of increased surveillance' (in Foucault's terms), and as 'spectacles', 'made so that we – their audience – can know all about the state' (White 2003: 84). This reflects the productive duplicity of rumours discussed in the previous chapter in relation to the indeterminate alterity of human remains at Chibondo, which enables the celebration of 'national heroes' and the reinforcement of anti-colonialist rhetoric at the same time as reasserting hierarchies of necro-political sovereignty.

One problem that any discussion of rumours faces, like studies of jokes and humour, is that what they mean or rather *do* is so context dependent; their efficacy is dependent upon their performance and reception as much as on their 'content' per se.[130] The rumours surrounding Mujuru's death illustrate this very well. The immediate suspicions about murder

---

[128] White 2003: 93; Nyarota 2018; also 'Mugabe still fears Chitepo's legacy' IWPR Srdan – Zimbabwe Crisis Reports ZIM Issue 16 10/4/08, http://iwpr.net/global-voices/mugabe-still-fears-chitepos-legacy, accessed 14/9/21.

[129] White cites Trouillet's (1995) study of the Haitian revolution.

[130] I am grateful to Justin Willis for raising this and making me think harder

Political accidents: Rumours, death and the politics of uncertainty

(and who might be responsible) engaged with a wide host of pre-existing intrigues to do with ZANU PF factionalism, its deepening succession disputes, the still rebounding repercussions of its 2008 electoral failures, of the Wiki-leaks scandal, and Solomon Mujuru's alleged fallout with the President, as well as various conspiracies involving diamonds and murky business interests. In August 2011, and even months afterwards, each rumour seemed possible or even likely. Nine years later, however, after his wife Joice Mujuru's 2014 eviction from the vice-presidency, and Mnangagwa's ascendency to and then removal from the same position, followed by President Mugabe's own removal in late 2017 in favour of Mnangagwa and Chiwenga, ZANU PF's deepening factionalism around the succession issue has become the most likely intrigue lying behind Solomon Mujuru's death. Other explanations now appear less convincing, less salient, less obvious, even if other possibilities do continue to circulate. Rumours surrounding such uncertain, high-profile deaths make each of those deaths both unique events in and of themselves, and unique to any moment in which they are (re)considered, reconstituted, and given new or renewed significance, meaning and value. In other words, they are historically situated.

Mujuru's death was, therefore, like Chitepo's assassination, Tongogara's accident and all Zimbabwe's other mysterious deaths: a unique event that is necessarily of changing significance and meaning in changing circumstances, and perhaps therefore best judged on its own (historical) terms. And yet all these different deaths *are connected*; in people's minds and conversations, but also in their form, their uncertainties and the responses they provoke; each new mysterious death immediately indexing the last. 'Political accidents' are, I suggest, a particular kind of death in Zimbabwe. And although they resonate across the region, where the death of public figures is often surrounded by a wealth of intrigue,[131] there is something particular about this form of unfinished Zimbabwean death that has to do with the profound uncertainty that surrounds them; a productive and potent, yet often disruptive, duplicitous and excessive indeterminacy.

Most obviously, what unites these 'political accidents' – distinct from the unresolved violence and deaths of the liberation struggle, of the *gukurahundi*, and of more recent political violence (Sachikonye 2011) – is both the senior ZANU PF status of the dead, and the speed and public grief with which so many were immediately declared National Heroes, despite (or maybe because of) the controversies surrounding their deaths. This has often been remarked upon by the media who gleefully report the 'mysteries' surrounding the 'litany of sinister deaths'

---

about what it is that usefully defines these kinds of rumour as political significant in particular ways.

[131] For an example in Kenya, see Cohen & Odhiambo 2004.

of national heroes.[132] While the apparent contradiction of a ruling party engineering the 'accidental' deaths of its own 'heroes' contributes to the broader contestations long surrounding ZANU PF's elitist control of state commemoration (Werbner 1998; Kriger 1995; Muchemwa 2010), it also offers a coherence to these particular kinds of death. In this respect, it is instructive to note that aside from the multi-layered politics of exclusion surrounding the selection of national heroes – marked by elitism, hierarchism and the exclusion of high-profile members of rival parties (such as ZAPU/ZIPRA) and former ZANU/ZANLA 'rebels' and perceived 'sell outs' (such as Ndabaningi Sithole, James Chikerema, Joseph Taderera or Wilfred Mhanda), in favour of recent political actors with questionable liberation credentials – another less remarked upon dynamic is the phenomena of former party 'insiders' who later became critical voices against the party, but who are none-the-less still interred as national heroes after their deaths. This includes both Eddison Zvobgo (d. 2004) and Edgar Tekere (d. 2011) who were both buried at National Heroes Acre despite having expressed specific critiques of the national heroes selection process and denying any wish to be buried at the site.[133]

These two examples are, of course, different from each other and from what I am calling 'political accidents'. Nevertheless they are informative. Edgar Tekere was a more outspoken and longer-standing adversary of President Mugabe than Eddison Zvobgo's much more measured and careful critiques in the later years of his life. And although both were awarded National Hero status, President Mugabe's response to each death was different. Highly unusually, he avoided attending Tekere's Heroes Acre burial at all in 2011 but had sung Zvobgo's praises at his funeral almost a decade before, describing him as a 'fearless and dedicated gallant freedom fighter'.[134]

Both Tekere and Zvobgo had in their own ways challenged Mugabe during their lives, and at different moments harboured ambitions to succeed him. Both died after long illnesses, so neither death was surrounded by controversies common to 'political accidents', although Zvobgo had survived a car accident in the mid-1990s that for many 'looked suspiciously like several others in which challengers to Mugabe have died'.[135] Yet they do illustrate the opportunities that the deaths of

---

[132] 'Mystery surrounds deaths of national heroes' *Nehanda Radio* 15/8/12; 'Mystery car-crash deaths haunt ZANU-PF' *Mail & Guardian* 27/6/13; 'Litany of sinister deaths' *Times* (SA) 8/3/09; 'Mugabe honours alleged victims' *Zimbabwean* 17/8/09.

[133] 'Heroes acre has lost its glory, says Zvobgo' *Standard* 19–25/8/01. 'Mugabe avoids Tekere Heroes Acre burial' *Nehanda Radio* 12/6/11, http://nehandaradio.com/2011/06/12/mugabe-avoids-tekere-heroes-acre-burial, accessed 28/12/15.

[134] 'President Mugabe pays tribute to Eddison Zvobgo' *Herald* 30/8/04.

[135] 'Eddison Zvobgo – Obituary' Andrew Meldrum *Guardian* 24/8/04.

Political accidents: Rumours, death and the politics of uncertainty

high-profile ZANU PF politicians can offer to contain, stabilise and fix disruptive political legacies and potential alternative historical narratives within an acceptable 'heroic' and 'patriotic' mode; attempting to fix in death what was difficult to contain in life. Although decidedly not a ZANU PF figure, Tsvangirai's 2018 state-assisted funeral is another more recent example also illustrative here.[136] Such examples are instructive about the political affordances that accrue from the uncertainties that surround all deaths, but perhaps particularly 'political accidents', creating new opportunities for the (re)stabilisation, containment and determination of particular pasts, particular necro-political orders and particular kinds of dead. It is, after all, not simply sentimentality that has made Heroes Acre funerals and annual celebrations such key events for the (re)making of ZANU PF's nationalist historiography over the last three decades.

If the achievement of 'national hero status' is a defining feature of 'political accidents', then of course this also differentiates them from the killings and disappearances of different periods of political violence since independence, such as the *gukurahundi* of the 1980s and the election violence of the 2000s. 'Political accidents' are distinct exactly because they index struggles *within* ZANU PF, establishing a more exclusive strand of 'necropolitan' (Muchemwa 2010) order internal to the ruling party itself. Furthermore, unlike the dismembered, unburied, leaky or disappeared bodies of *gukurahundi* and post-2000 election violence, 'political accidents' are less about the *disruption* of normal processes of containment and transformation through which people (dead or alive) are constituted (discussed in Chapter 2), than about the making of very particular kinds of dead. And in so doing, the 'mysterious' accidental deaths of ZANU PF figures transformed into national heroes turn, like the indeterminate human remains exhumed at Chibondo, on a fundamental tension between necro- and bio-politics – between the demands of sovereignty and of legitimacy – exactly because these dead are such high-profile political actors, ZANU PF insiders, and because they nearly always become national heroes.

Partly then, 'political accidents' are about stabilising and containing in death that what may have been perceived as troublesome and difficult to contain in life; and the conspiracy theories that surround the mysterious accidents of ruling party politicians do often point explicitly in this direction. But this alone is not enough. Equally important are the duplicitous affects of uncertainty at play in the way such deaths can be made to reify ZANU PF's exclusivist, 'heroic' forms of nationalist belonging while simultaneously reaffirming a concentrated hierarchy of necro-political sovereignty within its own ranks, by pointing to where the capacity to 'exercise control over mortality' (Mbembe 2003: 11–12) ultimately lies. We

---

[136] 'State funeral for Tsvangirai' *Herald* 16/2/18; 'Hundreds pay their respects to Morgan Tsvangirai at funeral' *Times* (SA) 19/2/18.

can therefore see how rumours about 'dodgy' accidents can do political work that turns on their productive uncertainty, just as the excessive potentialities of human remains from the Chibondo exhumations did.

A key issue here is that rumours of foul play surrounding 'political accidents' can only ever remain allegations. They cannot be substantiated or fixed through more authoritative mechanisms, judicial or otherwise, because that might mean issues of legitimacy would outweigh any necro-political advantages. Any such fixing, however contingent, could undermine the productive uncertainties at play in these situations. 'Political accidents' must therefore, almost by definition, remain unfinished and unresolved in order to be politically efficacious. In this respect it is no surprise that the inquest into Solomon Mujuru's death, although officially concluding it was accidental, hardly offered resolution to anyone's satisfaction; just as NMMZ's reburial and memorialisation of the Chibondo remains, and the sealing of the mine, ultimately only delayed rather than resolved the controversies provoked by those exhumations; and just as the 1976 Chitepo Commission report failed decidedly to curtail decades of subsequent intrigue surrounding Chitepo's assassination.

Reflecting more broadly across the region and beyond, what marks Zimbabwe's 'political accidents' off from a plethora of other rumoured assassinations is that they are (nearly) always officially framed as 'accidents' (Chitepo's death being the obvious exception). Moreover their 'accidental' nature although questionable (and usually questioned) always remains a possibility. The unresolved uncertainties surrounding these deaths are not confined to why and by whom someone is killed, but whether malevolent intentionality was involved at all. Therefore despite the continuing fervour of intrigue around both Tongogara and Mujuru's deaths, for some evidence of 'foul play' in either case remains thin and unconvincing (e.g. Nyarota 2018). In comparative examples across the region, such as Kenya, it is more common for rumours to surround the death of someone recognisably a victim of intentional killing (having been shot, for example) so that any unresolved issues revolve around the question of *who* lies behind it, and *why*.[137] With Zimbabwe's 'political accidents', by contrast, the possibility of 'chance' and misfortune (as well as 'occult' intervention) always retains potential traction.[138] This makes the uncertainties surrounding these deaths more profound, in turn extenuating the potential political efficacy deriving from the duplicity

---

[137] A good example was the torture and death of Chris Msando, a senior election official, a few days before Kenya's 2017 election. See 'Kenya election official tortured, murdered before vote, officials say' *Reuters* 31/7/17, www.reuters.com/article/us-kenya-election-death-idUSKBN1AG1B5, accessed 10/9/18.

[138] An informative counter-example here is the considerable effort, described by Musila (2015), spent by Kenyan authorities trying to persuade Julie Ward's father that her death was accidental, a very unlikely scenario.

Political accidents: Rumours, death and the politics of uncertainty

of rumours in which they are immersed. Because a possibility always remains that any particular individual's 'accidental' death really was an accident (even as it is assumed not all of them were) the duplicitous salience of this kind of death is amplified, fuelling both the necro-political affects and enabling 'patriotic' proclamations of heroism to be endlessly reinforced. Of course, such uncertainty also means that any political affects remain potentially disrupt-able. The indeterminacy surrounding such deaths is both of great potential political salience and yet, in the end, excessive to it.

Conclusions

'Political accidents' are therefore particular kinds of death in Zimbabwe, the key elements of which include: the high-profile status of the 'victim', usually within the ruling ZANU PF party; which is then cemented (although rarely without controversy) through burial at National Heroes Acre; and the apparently 'accidental' nature of the death – most usually car accidents, but not always – which remains subject to unresolved controversy amidst rumours of assassinations, internal party politics and suggestions of malign (sometimes occult) involvement linked to individual interests, agendas and ambitions. Most important, however, is that these rumours are never stabilised into any singular authoritative account. Where public enquiries have been held, they themselves, as with Mujuru's inquest, have been subject to feverish and continuing rumour and conspiracy, and have managed neither to demonstrate malign intent was involved in any particular case (let alone identify responsibility), nor successfully establish public confidence in the 'accidental' nature of the death. In short, these high-profile deaths are always left indeterminate and therefore unfinished. Moreover, they would lose their political saliency if they were ever fixed. The uncertainty that surrounds them is key to their saliency.

The argument developed here turns on the notion that the uncertainties of these kinds of death, can offer political salience and opportunity even as they must remain, by their nature, duplicitous, indeterminate and ultimately excessive to any intentional scheme, containment or 'fixing'. Building on Mbembe's work (2001), this suggests that political actors may have much to gain from rumours that circulate around 'political accidents'. It illustrates how uncertainty can be a fundamental feature of the stylistics of postcolonial power, particularly as forged in the ambivalent space between the legitimating dimensions of 'bio-power' and assertive demonstrations of 'necro-political' sovereignty. But it also suggests that the 'useful' rumours surrounding unexplained deaths of public figures are not entirely divorce-able from the profound uncertainties that all deaths can precipitate, particularly in Zimbabwe and especially in the context of rapidly changing, multiple regimes of death across the region, discussed at the beginning of this book. Such uncertainties defy containment, stabilisation, or the 'fixing' of definitive narratives and any final 'remaking' of the dead into 'heroes', 'victims' or 'ancestors'. And they easily 'leak' the confounds of space and time, as leaky bodies contaminate the troubled landscapes of militia camps, mass graves and car wrecks, and as unhappy, avenging spirits, troubling ghosts, or new witness accounts, or even new confessions to murder, appear at odd moments to defy regulated temporalities. All this points to the potential 'incompleteness' (Nyamnjoh 2017a, 2017b) of death itself, its open-endedness, and its profound lack of finality and closure. It is, in this sense, that death is rarely entirely finished with, and this has important implications for the potential resolution that is often assumed to be offered by exhumations and reburials.

Therefore, even if the Mujuru family's demands to exhume and re-examine Solomon Mujuru's remains are ever actualised – an unlikely scenario for now – it seems also unlikely that this would offer any more closure or finality than the inquest into his death did in 2012. It is also in this respect that those still seeking the publication of the two, allegedly lost, official inquest reports (Dumbutshena; Chihambakwe) into killings before and during the *gukurahundi*,[139] might in fact be disappointed should they ever be released. Likewise, as we discuss in Chapter 7, many in Matabeleland remain understandably circumspect about the 2019 promises of new *gukurahundi*-related 'truth' hearings and exhumations made by President Mnangagwa; not only because of continuing suspicions about the new regime's motivations, but also, perhaps, because of the inevitable incompleteness of any attempts to stabilise or fix meaning and resolution to problematic pasts.

This is not to deny that 'truth commissions', exhumations and reburials can sometimes play an important role in processes of post-conflict resolution, it is rather a warning against overstated expectations of the 'justice', 'healing' and 'closure' often assumed to derive from them. Indeed Verdery's (1999) account of how such processes fed into ethnic and nationalist violence in Yugoslavia in the early 1990s, illustrates how they can precipitate turbulence and violence as often as they offer resolution. The controversies that surrounded the vernacular exhumations at Chibondo in the months preceding Mujuru's death, discussed in the previous chapter, likewise undermine any suggestion that exhumations and reburials are necessarily cathartic, even if they can be for some

---

[139] 'Gukurahundi inquiry reports lost' *Newsday* 22/4/19. The Dumbutshena Commission of Inquiry investigated violence between former ZANLA and ZIPRA guerrillas at Entumbane in Bulawayo between November 1980 and March 1981, and the Chihambakwe Commission of Inquiry into the Matabeleland Disturbances investigated the killing of civilians by the Fifth Brigade between 1983 and 1985.

Political accidents: Rumours, death and the politics of uncertainty

people and in some contexts. Creating the kind of 'mediated space in which grievances and conflicting versions of "truth" about ... violence can be shared', which Eppel (2013: 238) identifies as essential for processes of post-conflict resolution and reconciliation (of which exhumations and reburials may be a part) is very difficult to achieve in the best of circumstances, and requires huge amounts of careful documentation and community work. Such difficulties point exactly, as with the inquests that followed both Solomon Mujuru and Chitepo's deaths (and more recent attempts to re-assess them – Tendi 2020a; White 2003) to the unfinished nature of death that this book seeks to highlight.

As we shall see in the next chapter, the uncertain and unfinished incompleteness of death in Zimbabwe is not just a matter of the excessivity of human remains from unresolved periods of past violence, demanding but defying stabilisation into meaning; nor of inconclusive inquests into unexplained deaths and the plethora of rumours and conspiracy that they can provoke. It also can also appear in the form of ancestors, *ngozi* and other spirits, sometimes of unknown provenance or recognition, appearing unpredictably to disrupt people's lives, family relations and politics with unexpected insistence and opportunities. Turning our attention to the political significance of ancestors and spirit mediums in postcolonial Zimbabwe, Chapters 5 and 6 reveal how there is something equally excessive to encounters with the immaterial remnants of past lives intruding into the present as there is to encounters with material human remains, and it is exactly in the nexus of material and immaterial existence that the uncertain, incompleteness of death and its political efficacy is manifest and revealed.

5

Precarious possession: Rotina Mavhunga, politics and the uncertainties of mediumship

The purpose of this chapter and the next is to continue to explore the uncertain and unfinished incompleteness of death (which we began in Chapter 4) by reconsidering the political significance of ancestors and spirit mediums in postcolonial Zimbabwe. The link between mediumship and politics has long animated scholarship on Zimbabwe (Matereke & Mungwini 2012; Lan 1985; Fry 1976, Garbett 1977, 1992; Ranger 1967, 1982b, 1985; Werbner 1991; Shoko 2007; Mawere & Wilson 1995; Mafu 1995; Fontein 2006a, 2015), particularly in the Shona-dominated eastern and northern provinces, but also in relation to the *Mwari* cult shrines of Matobo in Southern Matabeleland (Nyathi 2003; Ranger & Ncube 1996 Werbner 1989; Ranger 1999; Daneel 1970), and the wider region (Sanders 2008a; Bertelsen 2004; Ranger 2003; Jedrej 1992; Werbner 1989; Akong'a 1987; Packard 1981; Schoffeleers 1979; James 1972; Southall 1953; Krige & Krige 1943). Previous chapters have sought to nuance this by focusing on the transforming materialities of death with which it is imbricated. Implicit in those previous chapters is an approach further developed here, which demands that accounts of spirit encounters – whether ancestral possession events, witchcraft or frightening *ngozi* spirits – are taken seriously and not reduced to 'social functionality', 'mimesis' or 'cultural texts' in anthropological analysis (all of which over-emphasise meaning or explanation) in order to fully grasp their experiential, ontological and political dimensions. Questioning assumptions about the over-determinations common to spirit mediumship, I emphasise the uncertainties inherent to spirit possession which confront everyone involved, including not only politicians and others seeking the ancestral legitimacy or guidance that spirit mediums can offer, but also mediums themselves. In particular, I examine links between the precariousness of mediumship – both the conditions of precarity that often precede mediumship but also that which results from it – and the uncertainties which characterise relations between mediums and the spirits possessing them, which is often obscured by the historical narratives of successful initiation into mediumship offered by mediums themselves.

Rotina Mavhunga, politics and mediumship

The larger purpose here, linking it the broader politics of the dead this book examines, is to explore how the uncertainty of death – its unfinished incompleteness – is not just a matter of the excessivity of human remains, demanding but defying stabilisation into meaning, such as revealed by the controversial Chibondo exhumations of 2011 discussed in Chapter 3. It is also not limited to the resurfacing bones and haunting spirits of the unsettled dead indexing unresolved periods of past violence, such as the liberation struggle, the *gukurahundi*, or the election violence of 2008, discussed in Chapters 1 and 2. Nor is it limited to the controversies that frequently circulate around unresolved deaths, as illustrated by Mujuru's death in 2011 and many other 'political accidents' in Zimbabwe's postcolonial past, but which the ethnographic literature suggests are also common to more prosaic everyday deaths (Bourdillon 1987b: 206). Beyond concerns around questions of cause and responsibility, this uncertainty of death also appears in the not infrequent occurrence of ancestors, *ngozi* and other spirits, sometimes of unknown providence and recognition, or without previous salience, appearing unpredictably to disrupt people's lives, family relations and politics with unexpected demands and expectations.

The point here is that there is something equally excessive to encounters with the immaterial traces of past lives intruding into the present, as there is to encounters with material human remains, and this is salient in everyday contexts as much as it obviously is in relation to controversial and politically-implicated unresolved deaths from troubling pasts such as the *gukurahundi*, the liberation war, election violence, or 'political accidents'. In other words, there is an alterity to spirits (Fontein 2015: 15) – or what Ranger called a 'relative autonomy' of spirits (2010b) – which matches the excessivity (and therefore alterity) of human corporeality, and similarly demands processes of stabilisation and determination that are usually left incomplete and contested. This links forensic, archaeological, divinatory and vernacular exhumations and reburials (and public inquests such as followed Solomon Mujuru's troubling demise) as contested processes that seek to identify, stabilise or 'remake' the dead and resolve difficult pasts, to the contested uncertain and often precarious processes whereby mediums and those around them establish authentic possession and mediumship. All of this indexes, I suggest, the uncertainties of relationships between material and immaterial life which is foregrounded and revealed, yet left unresolved by death.

This chapter and the next use two stories of spirit encounters to explore how the longer dead can intervene consequentially into the lives and politics of the living. The first is the well-known story of the so-called 'diesel *n'anga*', Rotina Mavhunga, a spirit medium who in 2007 courted public controversy and government ministers with her claims to be able to procure refined diesel from rocks. I discuss this story, and

The Politics of the Dead

other similar cases, in order to explore the multi-faceted uncertainties and precarities that surround the authenticity of mediumship and possession in Zimbabwe, and the serious political consequences, dangers and opportunities that these can have for mediums. The second story, in Chapter 7, takes place at the other end of an imaginary continuum between such extremely politicised spirit encounters – involving senior clan ancestors, politicians, media publicity and a myriad of rumour and controversy – and much more everyday, highly localised spirit encounters which take place within particular families across Zimbabwe almost routinely, without the kind of publicity and controversy the 'diesel *n'anga*' provoked. It is that of a young woman – Mai Melissa – in Masvingo District, who I first met in 1995 and got to know well through a series of difficult personal trials until her death in late 2007. In the years before her death, but following the deaths of her husband and then her daughter, as she faced an increasingly impoverished life and deepening ill health, she became first a prophetess in a local Zionist church, before succumbing to spirit possession by her own late father, a Mozambican migrant, who had unexpectedly re-appeared first through the mental illness of her older brother in 2005 and then through her possession, in the context of a series of contested deaths and burials. Like the diesel *n'anga*'s intervention in Zimbabwean political life in 2007 – at a moment of deepening social, economic and political crisis in Zimbabwe – Mai Melissa's possession by her late father came at a moment of deepening personal and family crisis. Both stories show how the longer dead can intervene unpredictably – yet powerfully – into the lives of the living, illustrating how past and present lives, distant and impending deaths can entangle in uncertain yet consequential ways.

The claims of Rotina Mavhunga – the 'diesel *n'anga*' – were unusual, as was the government's apparent credulity, and her subsequent fall from grace extreme, once her fraud was finally uncovered. But behind the public story of her deception and fraud, lies a more familiar story indicative of the uncertainty of authenticity, presence and subjectivity that often characterises experiences of mediumship and spirit possession (cf. Steedly 1992; Lambek 2002a), including much less prominent 'everyday' examples like that of Mai Melissa. As already noted, spirit mediums and the territorial ancestral and *Mwari* cults they are often involved in, have long been implicated in Zimbabwean politics. This dates back to the rebellions against colonial rule in the 1890s, when Charwe, the Nehanda medium, made the famous prophecy that her 'bones would rise again'; a story with which this book began, that became central to nationalist mythology during the liberation struggle, and has continued to animate nationalist historiographies and literary imaginations (Hove 1988, 1996; Vera 1993; Chigumadzi 2018). Because their authenticity, legitimacy and authority as mediums, as both representatives and vessels of ancestors, exists beyond the limits of political or social control – their very presence

Rotina Mavhunga, politics and mediumship

pointing to other ancestral or divine sovereignties – Zimbabwe's postcolonial government has often treated spirit mediums with a great deal of ambivalence, even as some have become deeply imbricated in political events (Fontein 2015: 101–5). Elsewhere I discussed, with particular reference to drought and rainmaking, how the ambivalence with which the ruling party has engaged with prominent mediums is indicative of their uncertainty about water and especially rain, which in turn is linked to water's multiple material properties and the multiple regimes of rule within which it appears or are spun around it (Fontein 2015: 78–111). More broadly, however, the controversial case of Mavhunga, and that of others such Ambuya Sophia Muchini in the early 1980s and Ambuya VaZarira in the 1990s and 2000s (Fontein 2015, 2006a), illustrate how the ambiguities and uncertainties of performance, presence, agency and authenticity that lie at the heart of mediumship offer both opportunities and risk, making spirit possession in Zimbabwe an inherently precarious and uncertain occupation.

Earlier chapters examined how the excessivity (and therefore alterity) of human remains animates a profound indeterminacy which means that processes of determination, constitution and stabilisation (of 'remaking the dead') are inherently incomplete, imperfect and contingent. This uncertainty can have its own political utility; by linking, for example, the political imbrications of human materiality to the productive and duplicitous political affects of rumours. The argument in this chapter and the next about the uncertainties inherent to mediumship points to the equally uncertain alterity of spirits and the immaterial, which similarly demands but defies processes of closure and stabilisation. Indeed, the excessivity of one more often than not demands stabilisation through mechanisms and interventions in the other. Just as indeterminate human remains may require highly specialised 'immaterial' processes like divination and public inquest (as well as material processes like forensic archaeology, pathology, exhumation and reburial) to be stabilised and contained, so mediumship too is often confirmed (or not) through highly material processes of performance (Fontein 2006a: 58–62), initiation and tests of authenticity (Bourdillon 1987b: 236–42; Lan 1985: 49–56); or in Mavhunga's case the unlikely delivery of diesel. Yet unlike Miller's comfortable formula of 'the things that people make, make people' (2005: 38) – or of subjects-making-objects-making-subjects – or indeed Ingold's (2016) account of the 'correspondences' through which different materials and living forms constitute the shared world, Zimbabwe's politics of the dead points to the fractures, uncertainties and precarities, as well as opportunities that inhere to these incomplete processes.

Both the excessivity and alterity of human remains and of spirits index incomplete pasts but also unknown futures, illustrating how the uncertainties of death are necessarily entangled with those of life, as materialities and immaterialities, lives and deaths, pasts and futures intertwine in complex, incomplete and open-ended ways. This is another way of saying that the stories of Rotina Mavhunga and Mai Melissa are simultaneously historically and historiographically grounded (Fontein 2015: 8–9, 289);[1] both involved 'invention' in the sense that Wagner (1975) might have meant, and both take place, as all life does, on the frontier or precipice of time; which is also to say that they are consequential even if the consequences are not always immediately knowable. It is instructive to note, in this regard, that both cases involved the possibility of not only ancestral involvement but also charismatic Christian intervention (Pentecostal and African Independent), reflecting broader religious and spiritual fluctuations, the co-existence of diverse (sometimes competing) religious repertoires, regimes and loyalties, and the instabilities that these invoke, which have long marked Zimbabwean social, political and economic lives. All this sets the scene for Chapter 7, and the Conclusion which follows, where the different strands of argument presented in this book – about the dissonance, fractures and opportunities that mark the mutual 'imbrication of matter and meaning' and the power of uncertainty which animates in Zimbabwe's politics of the dead – are reconsidered in relation to more recent events, particularly the death and contested burial of Robert Mugabe in 2019.

Rotina Mavhunga – the diesel *n'anga*

In 2007 Zimbabweans watched with astonishment, bewilderment, amusement and not a small amount of ridicule as the so-called 'diesel *n'anga* saga' unrolled itself in newspapers, television and ultimately in court. The story began sometime in 2006, but newspaper reports first came out in early 2007 of claims that refined diesel had been discovered coming out of rocks in an area of northern Zimbabwe near Chinoyi.[2] At the centre of the story is a spirit medium (or *svikiro*), known as Rotina Mavhunga (but whose real name later turned out to be Nomatter Tagarira),[3] who quickly became known as the diesel *n'anga*,[4] and claimed to be possessed by a senior ancestor called Changamire Dombo (and also

---

[1] By which I mean, for sake of precision, that they are not just about different versions or narrations of the past, but also different techniques and mechanisms through which the past is conceived of, made present and constituted.

[2] 'Diesel-like liquid oozes from rock near Chinoyi caves' *Herald* 23/4/07; 'Zim heavies squabble over oil' *Zimbabwean* 17/5/07; 'Diesel-producing stone unveiled' *Sunday Mail* 20/5/07. Not all these early reports were free of scepticism; see 'Manna from heaven that never was' *Sunday Mail* 13/5/07.

[3] 'I lied to the nation – "Diesel" n'anga confesses' *Herald* 17/4/08.

[4] In some ways this was an anachronism because *n'anga* is a term that usually refers to a 'traditional' healer, herbalist or diviner, whose role may involve spirit possession (often by an animal or 'alien' 'shave' spirit) but not

took on that name, or alternatively Sekuru Muboni, another spirit who also possessed her). She claimed that her spirit had revealed where the diesel was, and that 'she could conjure refined diesel from a rock'.[5] In the context of Zimbabwe's deepening economic crisis and recurrent fuel shortages, but also recent discoveries of gold and diamonds elsewhere in the country, her claims drew the attention of ZANU PF governor of Mashonaland West Nelson Samkange and, not long after, the central government, who sent several high-profile delegations of party and government officials to explore the claims, including the 'security chiefs' of the Joint Operations Command (JOC).[6] One of the entourages included the then ministers of National Security, Didymus Mutasa; of Defence, Sydney Sekeramayi; of Home Affairs, Kembo Mohadi (who became one of Zimbabwe's two vice-presidents in 2017); and various police and intelligence officers.[7] This team apparently camped at Chinoyi for a fortnight investigating her claims, while she took them to visit other sacred sites in the area, and made them undergo various rituals to honour her spirit Changamire Dombo. She or her ancestral spirit must have made some impression, or charmed them in some way, because they reported back to the cabinet that 'she was indeed able to produce fuel out of granite rock',[8] and responded to her requests for cattle, buffalo and more. Despite some early doubts about the veracity of her claims,[9] the government continued to support and fund her activities well into the first half of 2007.

Later reports suggested she was given a farm, an armed guard, a car and Z$5 billion dollars, and at one stage led a convoy of 50 vehicles 'for 230km to Makuti and Kariba in a POINTLESS [sic.] trip as part of her elaborate con'.[10] As the magistrate adjudicating her later trial put it: 'the state channelled immense resources towards the diesel project. Many vehicles and at times helicopters were used on a wild goose chase'.[11] By May 2007, some of these ministers and particularly Governor Samkange were becoming frustrated by her failure to deliver diesel in tanker-full quantities, despite repeated promises. On one occasion a police tanker was sent to see how much diesel could be procured, but was 'disappointed when only 40 litres were produced'.[12] Amidst growing scepticism in May

---

necessarily. *N'anga* is rarely used to refer to a senior clan or lineage medium, even if such a senior *svikiro* might also be involved in healing.
[5] 'Saga could land Mudede in court' *Financial Gazette* 2/11/07.
[6] 'Diesel-like liquid oozes from rock near Chinoyi caves' *Herald* 23/4/07; 'Diesel n'anga: the true story' *Standard* 2/10/10.
[7] 'Diesel-producing stone unveiled' *Sunday Mail* 20/5/07.
[8] 'Diesel n'anga released from prison' *Standard* 8/4/12.
[9] 'Manna from heaven that never was' *Sunday Mail* 13/5/07.
[10] 'Zim learns: No diesel from a stone' *SA Times* 30/9/10; 'Diesel n'anga was sponsored by Tobaiwa Mudede' *ZimEye* 30/9/10.
[11] 'Diesel n'anga Mavhunga jailed' *Zimbabwe Mail* 29/9/10.
[12] 'Diesel n'anga: the true story' *Standard* 2/10/10.

2007 she invited a delegation of ministers and government newspapers, including *Sunday Mail* reporters, to the 'the launch of the "diesel" plant' constructed on a '"sacred" piece of land near the Chinoyi caves'. 'Getting in was cumbersome' reporters wrote, 'as one ritual after another had to be performed'; but inside they witnessed a remarkable scene where ministers and other officials were 'paying homage to her and taking off their shoes at her command to show respect' while being sprayed with diesel by Mavhunga.[13] These pictures later became the source of great ridicule.

Eventually, as doubts persisted, and Mavhunga continued to fail to deliver on her promises, other delegations were sent, apparently by Robert Mugabe himself. These included a visit by 'the minsters of energy, mines and science and technology' and various engineers and geologists, and later by 'top military and police officers'[14], who 'reported back … that Mavhunga had duped the government'.[15] It later turned out that a pipe and a tank had been hidden on the hillside, which would be fed with diesel acquired on the black market by accomplices in the spirit medium's entourage during official visits investigating the claims.[16] Mugabe ordered her arrest for fraud.[17] But the 'saga' did not end there. Initially Mavhunga went into hiding, and later it turned out she was being hidden by the Registrar-General Tobaiwa Mudede, a very senior ZANU PF official responsible for running Zimbabwe's problematic elections for much of the 2000s.[18] In late 2007 her trial started but it took a long time, partly because, after appearing in court several times, even going into trance in the court room on a number of occasions,[19] and changing her plea and her lawyers several times, she jumped bail and disappeared

13 'Diesel-producing stone unveiled' *Sunday Mail* 20/5/07
14 'Mugabe, top politicians paid woman now accused of fraud in fuel-from-rocks claim' *Associated Press* 16/11/07.
15 'Diesel n'anga saga: Justice must be done, says president' *Herald* 16/11/07.
16 Some reports suggested that the tank or tanks had been left by a white commercial farmer evicted during Fast Track Land Reform a few years before ('Witchdoctor sent to prison for duping Mugabe' *Saturday Nation* (Kenya), 2/10/10).
17 'Mugabe, top politicians paid woman now accused of fraud in fuel-from-rocks claim' *Associated Press* 17/11/07; 'Diesel n'anga saga: Justice must be done, says president' *Herald* 16/11/07.
18 'Diesel n'anga was sponsored by Tobaiwa Mudede' *ZimEye* 30/9/10, accessed 19/6/20; 'Witchdoctor sent to prison for duping Mugabe' *Saturday Nation* 2/10/10; '"Diesel n'anga" Mavhunga jailed" *Zimbabwe Mail* 29/9/10; 'Top ZANU PF official escapes prosecution in diesel fraud case' *swradioafrica.com* 28/7/09, accessed 19/6/20; 'Mudede role queried as diesel n'anga convicted' *Herald* 27/7/09; 'Mudede "directly linked" to Chinoyi diesel-from-rock rigging – court' *Zimbabwe Mail* 27/7/09.
19 'Diesel n'anga in trance' *Herald* 7/4/08; 'Top ZANU PF official escapes prosecution in diesel fraud case' *swradioafrica.com* 28/7/09, accessed 19/6/20; 'Mudede role queried as diesel n'anga convicted' *Herald* 27/7/09.

again.[20] Police searched for her while she apparently continued to work as a medium and diviner in northern Zimbabwe, where she would be finally re-arrested in 2010.[21] In July 2009, while still on the run, she was found guilty in absentia, along with two accomplices, 'of defrauding the state of about Z$500 billion dollars between March and June 2007 and misrepresenting to a public official that diesel was oozing out of a rock at Maningwa hills in Chinoyi'.[22] Over a year later, in September 2010, she was finally apprehended again and sentenced to 27 months in prison.[23] She was released in April 2012, having converted to Christianity in prison where she 'asked for prayers to strengthen her as she doesn't want to be associated with other witchdoctors who may want to harm her'.[24]

Obviously the 'diesel *n'anga* saga' was deeply embarrassing for the ZANU PF government, as it had, in the words of one journalist, 'blown the lid on how deep the belief in superstition and sorcery among the country's political leaders runs'.[25] Various commentators, authors and others heralded the events with enormous amusement and glee. The celebrated Zimbabwean author Petinah Gappah seconded a motion (apparently first suggested by Alex Magaisa in the *Zimbabwe Times*) to nominate Rotina Mavhunga for Person of the Year 2007, adding that 'my admiration for this

[20] 'Diesel conjurer convicted of fraud for fooling Mugabe's government' Monstersandcritics.com 27/7/09, accessed 19/6/20; 'Mudede role queried as diesel n'anga convicted' *Herald* 27/7/09; 'Top ZANU PF official escapes prosecution in diesel fraud case' swradioafrica.com 28/7/09, accessed 19/6/20; 'Mudede role queried as diesel n'anga convicted' *Herald* 27/7/09; 'Mudede "directly linked" to Chinoyi diesel-from-rock rigging – court' *Zimbabwe Mail* 27/7/09; 'Diesel n'anga fails to appear in court' *ZimDaily* 10/7/09; 'Government fails to locate diesel n'anga' *Zimbabwean* 13/8/09; 'Diesel mystic "unaware" police searched for her' ZimEye.net 28/9/10, accessed 19/6/20.
[21] 'Diesel n'anga: the true story' *Standard* 2/10/10; 'Diesel mystic "unaware" police searched for her' ZimEye.net 28/9/10, accessed 19/6/20.
[22] 'Mudede "directly linked" to Chinoyi diesel-from-rock rigging – court' *Zimbabwe Mail* 27/7/09. As the story circulated hugely different figures were mentioned for the amount Mavhunga was said to have defrauded the state, from 5 billion Zimbabwe dollars (about 165,000 US dollars at the time ('Diesel mystic "unaware" police searched for her' ZimEye.net 28/9/10) to 500 billion Zimbabwe dollars ('Mudede "directly linked" to Chinoyi diesel-from-rock rigging – court' *Zimbabwe Mail* 27/7/09), to 1 million US dollars ('Top ZANU PF official escapes prosecution in diesel fraud case' swradioafrica.com 28/7/09), and 1.7 million British pounds ('Zim learns: No diesel from a stone' *SA Times* 3/10/10); online sources accessed 19/6/20.
[23] Reports varied about the length of her sentence, from 27 months, to three years, to 39 months ('Diesel n'anga released from prison' *Standard* 8/4/12; 'Diesel n'anga: the true story' *Standard* 2/10/10; 'Zim learns: No diesel from a stone' *SA Times* 3/10/10; 'Diesel n'anga was sponsored by Tobaiwa Mudede' ZimEye.net 30/9/10, accessed 19/6/20.
[24] '"Diesel n'anga" released from prison' *Standard* 8/4/12.
[25] 'Saga could land Mudede in court' *Financial Gazette* 2/11/07.

woman's chutzpah mounts with everything I read'.[26] Such comments were mirrored across social media as Zimbabweans all over the world watched eagerly. 'Venhengo Ras', from Kwekwe, commented that 'Rotina, you are a star. more power to you!', while 'John Motsi' commented from the UK that 'the MDC should honor Rotina Mavhunga', and adding a day later 'whatever the case maybe, purified diesel from a rock !!!!!!!!!!!!!! hah ha ha ha – zanu is full of shit skunks. Still Rotina is a hero'.[27]

President Mugabe was clearly furious. He ridiculed his ministers who, he suggested, were 'blinded by her beauty', while acknowledging that some police had been 'afraid to pursue Mavhunga' because of her spiritual powers.[28] It was also deeply embarrassing for some individuals, particularly minister Didymus Mutasa who, reports claimed, had continued to visit the Mavhunga for private consultations with regard to his own ambitions to succeed Mugabe as President, long after her fraud had been unveiled.[29] Reports suggested President Mugabe was equally, if not more, furious about this, particularly given other earlier reports that ministers had been consulting *n'angas* in order to secure their succession.[30] In his defence Mutasa 'denied performing bizarre rituals to help him succeed President Robert Mugabe', or that 'cleansing ceremonies' were held for him, but insisted that 'while it turned out the diesel claims were a "hoax", it was unfair to criticize him for entertaining the alleged spirit medium'. 'Asked why he never doubted from the start that diesel could not gush out of rocks' Mutasa insisted 'he did right to listen to the alleged spirit medium' adding that 'from the days of the liberation struggle ... mediums offered guidance and counselling to freedom fighters and "could manage miracles and strange happenings" during the war'.[31]

Perhaps more significant, and problematic, was the implication that the Registrar-General Tobaiwa Mudede had been involved in the affair

---

[26] See www.petinagappah.blogspot.com, 8/4/08, 28/1/08, accessed 11/5/10.
[27] See comments (9/7/09 and 10/7/09) to 'Diesel n'anga fails to appear in court' *ZimDaily* 10/7/09.
[28] 'Diesel n'anga saga: Justice must be done, says president' *Herald* 16/11/07; 'Mugabe, top politicians paid woman now accused of fraud in fuel-from-rocks claim' *Associated Press* 17/11/07; 'Diesel n'anga fails to appear in court' *ZimDaily* 10/7/09; 'Mudede "directly linked" to Chinoyi diesel-from-rock rigging – court' *Zimbabwe Mail* 27/7/09; Diesel n'anga: the true story' *Standard* 2/10/10.
[29] 'Diesel n'anga in succession plot' *Zimbabwe Independent* 10/8/07; 'Mutasa defies Mugabe' www.denfordmagora.blogspot.com/2010/01/mutasa-defies-mugabe.html 2/1/10, accessed 19/6/20; 'Why I followed diesel n'anga – Mutasa' *Standard* 11/11/07. Mutasa's involvement with Mavhunga continued to provoke ridicule in the factional contests of the 2010s, after Joice Mujuru's removal from the vice-presidency in 2014 (see 'Kasukuwere throws "Diesel in Chinhoyi" insult at Mutasa' *Nehanda Radio* 22/1/15, accessed 19/6/20).
[30] 'No need for witchdoctors – I'm staying says Mugabe' *Telegraph* (UK) 17/7/06.
[31] 'Why I followed diesel n'anga – Mutasa' *Standard* 11/11/07.

from the very beginning, not just in protecting and sheltering Mavhunga after her fraud was uncovered, but long before. During the trial, it became clear that he had helped her to procure 125 litres of the diesel she had used in her fraud, and although the magistrate 'directly linked' him to the events, and that 'from evidence … it was abundantly clear that Tobaiwa Mudede had an interest in the matter', he avoided prosecution, and the purpose of his 'disturbing' involvement was never fully revealed.[32] Some rumours suggested he was involved in a love affair with Mavhunga. Although Mugabe had insisted the case should be 'thoroughly investigated and those responsible for giving the woman the idea to fool the government and the nation should also be brought to book'[33], Mudede's exact involvement has never been made clear.[34]

This untold part of the diesel *n'anga* story is important because it suggests that far from being a highly instrumental, clever trickster – the woman of 'chutzpah' that Petinah Gappah celebrated[35] – who successfully, for a time at least, manipulated government officials and ministers for personal material gain, and in the process revealed for public ridicule the shortcomings and absurdities of ministerial credulity, perhaps Mavhunga was herself being played or influenced by others around her, with ultimately quite serious consequences for her. Reading closer between the lines, a different and more complex picture emerges of Rotina Mavhunga, the spirit medium, which points, I suggest, to the way in which all spirit mediums can appear subject, and sometimes unusually vulnerable to, the demands, expectations and even deliberate manipulations of others around them. These might include not only politicians, as in Mavhunga's case, but also acolytes, communities, clans, families and others who seek guidance, divination and consultation from their spirits, and who are therefore invested for their own reasons in the mediumship concerned (Lan 1985: 49–56; cf. Lambek 2002a). Suggestions that Mavhunga continued to work as medium and diviner during her long period on the run from the police, some of whom allowed her to continue her work even as she was being sought by other police elsewhere, and the suggestion that various ministers had approached her for 'personal career advice', illustrate this point.[36] She also told the court in 2008, before going on the run, that she wished 'Government officials would

---

[32] 'Mudede "directly linked" to Chinoyi diesel-from-rock rigging – court' *Zimbabwe Mail* 27/7/09; 'Saga could land Mudede in court' *Financial Gazette* 2/11/07; 'Diesel n'anga was sponsored by Tobaiwa Mudede' *ZimEye.net* 30/9/10, accessed 19/6/20; 'Witchdoctor sent to prison for duping Mugabe' *Saturday Nation* (Kenya) 2/10/10; '"Diesel n'anga Mavhunga jailed' *Zimbabwe Mail* 29/9/10; 'Mudede role queried as diesel n'anga convicted' *Herald* 27/7/09.
[33] 'Diesel n'anga saga: Justice must be done, says president' *Herald* 16/11/07.
[34] 'Top ZANU PF official escapes prosecution in diesel fraud case' *swradioafrica.com* 28/7/09, accessed 19/6/20.
[35] See www.petinagappah.blogspot.com, 8/4/08, 28/1/08, accessed 11/5/10.
[36] 'Diesel mystic "unaware" police searched for her' *ZimEye.net* 28/9/10.

stop bothering me about wanting to consult Sekuru Dombo'.[37] However, as I will discuss below, beyond the implications for any medium of the expectations and demands others invest in their mediumship, we also need to include the manipulations, demands and expectations of the spirits themselves in this complicated equation.

This reading between the lines of the sensationalist media reporting of the story is actually rather difficult because most of the reports, including much of the evidence presented to the trial, were rather opaque about exactly how the fraud was enacted, what the involvement of different actors really was, or what Mavhunga's own actions and intentions were. The presiding magistrate admitted as much when he stated that 'there are inconsistencies in the evidence from the defence witnesses, which shows that the "discovery" of diesel was shrouded in secrecy such that "no two people came up with exactly the same position" on what transpired during the period'.[38] As may often be the case, the precise motivations of those involved remains unclear and uncertain.[39] In this respect, it is interesting to note that the various media accounts of the trial reported not only the dramatic moments when Mavhunga went into trance in the courtroom – which the magistrate dismissed as a faked 'bid to hoodwink the court into believing she could not give evidence'[40] – but also Mavhunga's own divergent statements at different moments in the long-drawn-out legal process. Such as, for example, that it was not her who deceived the government but her spirit Changamire Dombo himself;[41] and later, that she had failed her own spirit by going 'against the spirit of Sekuru Dombo when she decided to "play games" and started pouring diesel into a pipe that had been mounted on the rock ... and bought the fuel from truck drivers and a government official', after 'the spirit had initially showed her where the diesel was coming from'.[42] It is likely her changing accounts in part relate to the apparently turbulent relationships she had with her different defence lawyers, but may also have related to the harassment she received in police custody, and pressure exerted upon her by interested parties to the case.[43] But it may also have had to do with her own troubled relationship with the spirits who possess her – or least with her own 'mediumship' – a theme

---

[37] 'I lied to the nation – "Diesel" n'anga confesses' *Herald* 17/4/08.
[38] 'Mudede "directly linked" to Chinhoyi diesel from rock rigging – court' *Zimbabwe Mail* 27/7/09.
[39] See Clark (1985) for similar uncertainties about different participants' motivations at the trial of Ambuya Sophia Muchini's trial, discussed in more detail below.
[40] 'Mudede "directly linked" to Chinhoyi diesel from rock rigging – court' *Zimbabwe Mail* 27/7/09.
[41] 'Diesel n'anga in trance' *Herald* 7/4/08.
[42] 'I lied to the nation – "Diesel" n'anga confesses' *Herald* 17/4/08.
[43] 'Mudede "directly linked" to Chinhoyi diesel from rock rigging – court' *Zimbabwe Mail* 27/7/09.

developed further below. At any rate, during the trial she hardly appeared like the woman of 'chutzpah' that Gappah celebrated.

Equally interestingly, accounts of the trial indicate that she claimed to have been a spirit medium since she was 13 years old, when she was first possessed by a spirit from whom she derived the name Mavhunga, and that she only 'became Changamire Dombo's medium in 2003'.[44] This suggestion of a much longer history of mediumship and spirit possession, pre-dating the diesel fraud, is likely to be correct, at least in so far as it would be hard to imagine how her rather extreme claims of having discovered diesel in the hills of Chinhoyi would ever had gained any local traction without her credibility, authority, legitimacy and status as a medium having already been established, to some degree or for some people at least. Spirit mediums, particular ambitious ones, are often dependent upon a strong and consistent, local, kinship- or clan-based support base, from which they can launch wider projects; an absence or weakening of this can undermine their authority in serious ways (Fontein 2006a: 62–9). It is also not immaterial to the case that Changamire Dombo is indeed a real historical person and well-known Rozvi ancestor, long associated in oral history with 17th-century rebellions against Portuguese colonial trading outposts.[45] As with other (sometimes labelled as 'national') ancestors, like Nehanda and Kaguvi, hanged after the 1896 rebellions, Changamire Dombo is an ancestral figure who appears in Zimbabwean school text books (Sibanda et al. 1992). 'What school child growing up in Zimbabwe does not know of Changamire Dombo?' asked the author Petina Gappah, rhetorically.[46] All this points to the complex social, cultural, historical, moral, political and indeed performative mechanisms, techniques and 'habits' (Perman 2011) by which mediums – especially of senior 'clan' and lineage ancestors, or '*mhondoro*' (Lan 1985) – establish their authority and authenticity as genuine mediums of ancestral spirits, which I turn to below.

The picture that emerges from underneath the sensationalist but opaque reporting about the case therefore suggests that not only had Rotina been a medium for a lot longer than the 'diesel *n'anga*' saga itself – that her mediumship pre-dated her fraud – but also that there were a lot of other people implicated in the events and her mediumship. This was not, then, just a deliberate and well-executed – if ultimately flawed – fraud, to be denigrated and condemned or celebrated, according to your political and social positioning. There was a longer, social and political, not to mention personal, history to Mavhunga's mediumship, both in general and specifically in relation to the spirit Changamire Dombo. This points to how spirit possession and mediumship is always socially,

[44] Ibid.; 'I lied to the nation – "Diesel" n'anga confesses' *Herald* 17/4/08.
[45] Pers. com. Paul Hubbard, 20/4/08.
[46] www.petinagappah.blogspot.com, 8/4/08, 28/1/08, accessed 11/5/10.

historically, morally and politically, as well as culturally, determined and constituted. It raises questions about how Rotina Mavhunga came to find herself in a situation whereby this obvious fraud was a thinkable and doable opportunity, and the social, historical and political contexts that made her deception possible. Aside from the gleeful reporting on Mavhunga's creative instrumentality and the credulity of government ministers, lay familiar but difficult questions about the socially constituted nature of mediumship, and about what I call 'the alterity of spirit' that this involves. This amplifies the uncertainties of performance, agency and authenticity that lie at the heart of spirit possession, offering both opportunities and risk for mediums, and those associated with them, and making spirit mediumship in Zimbabwe an often precarious occupation.

Precarious occupation

Although the diesel *n'anga* saga was unusual because a clear fraud was involved and demonstrated – often 'fraud' can be as hard to demonstrate as 'authenticity' – it was not particularly unique. A huge literature indicates that Zimbabwe's diversity of mediums, ancestral and *Mwari* cults have long been implicated in its politics, drawing upon a longer history of rainmaking, fertility and the guardianship of land (Werbner 1989, 1991; Daneel 1970, 1998; Bourdillon 1987b; Shoko 2007; Schoffeleers 1979; Mawere & Wilson 1995; Mafu 1995), dating back (at least) to the anti-colonial rebellions of the 1890s, and probably long before, from whence colonial authorities became highly aware and anxious about the power of spirit mediums to mobilise opposition against colonial rule (Abraham 1966; Garbett 1977, 1992; Lan 1985; Ranger 1967, 1985, 1999, 2003; Matereke & Mungwini 2012). Although Rhodesian authorities kept records of known spirit mediums throughout the colonial period, concerns heightened in the 1960s and 1970s as African nationalist movements and later guerrilla armies began to agitate and then fight for liberation and independence.

As Lan (1985), Fry (1976), Ranger (1985) and others (Werbner 1991; Maxwell 1999; Daneel 1995; Fontein 2006a, 2015) have discussed in detail, spirit mediumship became hugely significant amid the 'cultural revival' provoked by African nationalism, and mediums themselves often became involved in guiding, supporting and raising popular support for the struggle within operational zones in Zimbabwe and across its borders.[47] The medium for Ambuya Nehanda famously escaped across the border to Mozambique, along with many other less well-known examples, to

---

[47] See Kriger 1992, Bourdillon 1987a and Maxwell 1999 for important critiques of both Lan 1985 and Ranger 1985, indicating that rural support for guerrillas varied greatly in different areas and times, and was often as much about coercion, churches and other factors, as about the ancestral legitimacy offered by mediums (Lan 1985) or rural aspirations for the 'peasant option' (Ranger 1985).

Rotina Mavhunga, politics and mediumship

join and provide spiritual guidance for guerrilla fighters in rear bases in Mozambique and Zambia (Mhanda 2011). When she died in exile, great effort was made to return her body for burial in Zimbabwe. Within Zimbabwe, spirit mediums not only assisted by providing local legitimacy for guerrillas operating in zones far from their own 'home' areas, but also provided support by guiding guerrillas through unknown areas of wilderness, by healing the wounded, by warning of future attacks, and by teaching guerrillas how to read ancestral warnings in the actions of birds and animals in the bush. They also often imposed taboos on guerrilla conduct in war zones in Zimbabwe, which Lan (1985) skilfully, if overly creatively (Bourdillon 1987a), interpreted as part of a symbolic process of associating guerrilla fighters with long dead Korekore ancestors in the Dande in northern Zimbabwe. In response to the re-emergence of mediumship during the 1960s and 1970s, Rhodesian intelligence began again to gather detailed information on spirit mediums and their political affiliations, producing the infamous 'Spirit Index' (Ranger 2003: 73). Elsewhere I explored how this played out around Great Zimbabwe and Lake Mutirikwi in Masvingo in the 1970s and early 1980s, immediately after independence, and later in the early 2000s when, during Fast Track Land Reform, mediums again became instrumental in a re-emergent local politics of land restitution (Fontein 2006a: 117–66, 2015: 230–87). Similarly, Daneel (1998) has discussed the role of mediums in new forms of 'community-led conservation' emergent in the 1990s, while Mawere and Wilson reported upon the impact of the short-lived Julianna cult during the devastating drought of the early 1990s (1995; Mafu 1995).

The scholarly picture of 'peasant-guerrilla' relations during the war has become much more complex since the early 1980s, when this aspect of the struggle was particularly celebrated by scholars like Lan (1985) and Ranger (1985). It is now well recognised that churches too, as well as coercion and violence, were also significant in garnering rural support for the struggle (Kriger 1992; Maxwell 1999). Yet spirit mediums continued, in particular places and contexts, to play a prominent role since independence, just as ancestral support for the struggle has continued to animate its postcolonial imagination. The role of ancestors, mediums and cult shrines in guiding guerrilla fighters remains a central aspect of nationalist, and particularly ZANU PF mythology and its 'necropolitan imagination' (Muchemwa 2010), as witnessed by their prominent role in war veteran-led exhumations of the liberation heritage project, and indeed by Mutasa's public defence of his consultations with Rotina Mavhunga in 2007.

At ZANU PF's December 2018 annual conference, in Esigodini, Umzingwane District, a resolution was passed that 'there should be ceremonies in honour of ancestral spirits that guided the nation during the armed struggle', to 'be conducted by the party and government', and, furthermore, that 'spirit mediums should ... lead the nation in correcting the wrongs that supposedly happened spiritually after independence in our country'.[48] Earlier the same year, ahead of the 2018 elections, and in the context of the opposition leadership wrangles that followed Morgan Tsvangirai's death, Welshman Ncube (leader of the smaller MDC-N) claimed that the appointment of Nelson Chamisa (who is an ardent Pentecostal Christian pastor) as the MDC Alliance's presidential candidate, had been 'endorsed by spirit mediums at Njelele shrine as evidenced by the rains that poured during his campaign rally in Plumtree on Sunday';[49] thereby illustrating both how mediums' political salience is not the sole resolve of ZANU PF, and how it easily defies 'containment' within specific religious boundaries.

The political significance that some spirit mediums have achieved has sometimes made their lives dangerous and precarious. Many of Zimbabwe's most high-profile mediums have come to a sticky end, whether through violence and death, intimidation, or through trial and imprisonment; or through having their credibility and authenticity questioned and undermined through allegations of fraud and deception (Fontein 2015: 101–5). Spirit mediumship in Zimbabwe is often precarious. Rhodesians famously executed the mediums of Nehanda and Kaguvi after the 1896 rebellions, and again, during the war of liberation, mediums were often targeted by Rhodesian forces. Mediums were also sometimes killed by guerrilla fighters, particularly if they had been revealed as 'frauds', or if it was suspected that they worked with Rhodesian forces. Pasipamire, medium for the legendary Chaminuka, was famously killed by guerrilla fighters in Makoni in the late 1970s – despite having been instrumental in amplifying the significance of his spirit for African nationalism through the writings of Rhodesian researchers like Gelfand (1959) and Abraham (1966) – after guerrillas became aware that he lacked local legitimacy and suspected he was working with Rhodesian forces (Ranger 1982b).

In the Dande, where guerrilla-medium relations during the war were made famous by Lan's research, Spierenburg reported that mediums opposing a post-independence land reform project in the 1990s, were subjected to heavy-handed surveillance by state agents, wary of the influence they could wield (2004: 222). After 2000, although the nationalist rhetoric of ZANU PF's 'patriotic history' often emphasised the importance of mediums and particularly rainmakers in its appeal to ancestral legitimacy and 'African authenticity' (Ranger 2004a; Fontein 2015: 93–101), mediums too sometimes suffered violence, evictions, beatings and murder amid ZANU PF's violent responses to growing political opposition. For example, in 2002 a 70-year-old medium was

---

[48] 'ZANU PF to consult spirit mediums to remedy post-independence wrongs' *Pindula News* 19/12/18, accessed 7/5/20.
[49] 'Pastor Nelson Chamisa gets third anointment from Njelele shrine' *Zimbabwe News* 13/3/18.

killed by suspected ZANU supporters for 'mobilising against President Mugabe in the presidential poll'.[50] At the same time, however, other mediums did become deeply involved in ZANU PF's land reform project, and sometimes in its violence. In 2010, a resettled farmer in Chinhoyi had his house burnt by police operating on instructions of a Nehanda medium called Lina Govera.[51] In Masvingo, in the early 2000s, a medium and war veteran called Mai Macharaga was involved in the district land committee overseeing Fast Track Land Reform until she became embroiled in a dispute with the provincial governor Josiah Hungwe (Fontein 2015: 104–5). Another more senior, and much more established (and now late) Masvingo medium, Ambuya VaZarira, with whom I worked throughout the 2000s (Fontein 2006a, 2015), was also frequently consulted by war veterans occupying farms in the east of the district. Later her links with the short-lived Liberators' Platform, an alternative war veteran's association led by Wilfred Mhanda (2011) meant that she too, like the Dande mediums Spierenberg discussed, came under close state surveillance, curtailing some of her ambitious plans and activities (Fontein 2015: 105).

Unsurprisingly, involvement in Fast Track Land Reform in the 2000s was not always rosy for Zimbabwe's spirit mediums. Sadomba has pointed to three different Nehanda mediums in northern Zimbabwe who were each evicted from farms they had resettled, as '*jambanja*' ('violence' or 'chaos', usually used in reference to the early land occupations of 2000–01) was inflicted 'on *jambanja*' (2011: 217) during the upheavals of that period. Yet there have also been moments when ZANU PF leaders, even President Mugabe himself, have publicly appealed to spirit mediums, not just during the ludicrous search for diesel in 2006/07 but long before. During the devastating 1992 drought, Mugabe appealed to rainmakers to bring rain, a request which was refused with firm insistence by mediums that they should be consulted by government at all times and not just when there was a crisis (Derman 2003: 71; Fontein 2015: 82). This fits a broader pattern of spirit mediums complaining of being marginalised by the government since independence, despite their contributions to the struggle, which I have often come across during fieldwork (Fontein 2006, 2015).

All this suggests that, although of immense political significance at times, spirit mediums have often been treated with a great deal of ambivalence by ZANU PF, which in turn has often amplified the precarity of mediumship on which I am focusing here. This ambivalent treatment of mediums by ZANU PF has a long history which relates in part to the fact that they are much harder to 'co-opt' into governmental or party structures than other forms of so-called traditional leadership (Fontein 2015: 78–111). Unlike chiefs and headmen, whose legitimacy often depends only partly

[50] 'Spirit mediums condemn terror' *Daily News* 7/3/02.
[51] 'Police destroy home on orders of spirit medium' *Zimbabwe Independent* 5/3/10.

upon descent from known 'founding' clan ancestors, and who derive much authority from their appointment within local state structures and from ZANU PF patronage, spirit mediums' authority derives not from the sovereignty of the state or the law, but from the ancestors as owners of the land, and ultimately from the divinity *Mwari*, the provider of rain. Ruling party stalwarts may desire mediums' ancestral and divine legitimacy, but they are also often wary of the political efficacy of spirit mediums' claims about where their authority derives from. This issue lies at the root of the ambivalence with which state authorities and politicians have treated spirit mediums. It explains why the senior Nehanda medium that Spierenburg (2004: 222) encountered in the Dande was under heavy guard or 'protection' by CIO agents, and why mediums with whom I worked in Masvingo too often reported being 'protected', chaperoned and monitored by state agents (Fontein 2015: 104–5). This kind of 'protection' is double-sided, reflecting both the significance that can be ascribed to mediums, and revealing the potentially dangerous ambivalence with which government and ruling elite regard them.

Evidence suggests that even during the liberation struggle different factions within Zimbabwe's nationalist parties and armies had divergent opinions on the importance of mediums, ancestral cults and the *Mwari* shrines, as well as different churches, for the liberation movement and the war (Chung 1995: 146; Ranger & Ncube 1996). This ambivalence became much clearer after independence with the controversies that surrounded the activities of another medium of Nehanda, Ambuya Sophia Muchini, at Great Zimbabwe in the 1980–82 period. Muchini's story has been covered in much detail elsewhere (Fontein 2006a: 156–63, 2015: 256–67; Garlake 1983; Clark 1985) and will not be rehearsed here in great detail except to point out where it reflects some of the controversies that embroiled Rotina Mavhunga two decades later.

During the latter stages of the war Muchini established herself near Great Zimbabwe but was soon implicated by Rhodesian authorities in efforts to support guerrillas in the area, which meant she was detained by them for some time. Shortly after independence she returned to Great Zimbabwe and gathered former guerrilla fighters from a nearby assembly point around her, offering them healing services and lobbying for national healing ceremonies to be held at the site. Although museum authorities found her presence difficult,[52] there is not much evidence that her initial intentions were particularly controversial or radical. The ex-guerrillas based with her did cause local disruption, particularly in the context of a wave of land occupations across the district, and there is some evidence she became caught up in the older struggles between local clans over Great Zimbabwe (Fontein 2006a: 159–60), but this was not enough for NMMZ to evict her, much as they

---

[52] NMMZ archives contain many gritty descriptions of bloody 'animal sacrifices' Muchini conducted within the site (Fontein 2006a: 158).

clearly wanted to. However, as with Rotina Mavhunga, Muchini too became involved with particular politicians who were invested in her activities for their own political purposes within the already fractious dynamics of the new government (Clark 1985: 153; Fontein 2015: 261–2). In particular, Herbert Ushewokunze, then Minister of Health, became a regular visitor and, some reports suggest (Clark 1985: 133), influenced Muchini to make much more radical calls for all white farmers in the district to be removed, to finish the incomplete struggle for independence. This found traction amidst the wave of land occupations taking place across the Masvingo area immediately after the war, as landless and previously evicted groups sought to acquire land or reclaim lost ancestral territories (Fontein 2015: 256–87). Muchini's increasingly radical position was ultimately implicated in the murders of two white farming couples in the district, and a third attempted murder, by ex-guerrillas gathered around her (Daneel 1995: 12–13; Clark 1985). Muchini's compound was stormed by armed police in a violent operation that left several people injured or dead. She was tried for murder and, after a similarly eventful trial to that of Rotina Mavhunga in late 2000s, was found guilty and sentenced to death. This was later reduced to life imprisonment and ten years later she was pardoned and returned to live in relative isolation in a forest on the nearby Boroma hills, where she lived till her death in March 2019.

There are several aspects to this story which pertain to my argument here. Firstly, the story marks the ambivalence and contradictions involved in ZANU PF's celebration and denigration of spirit mediums, particular those of Ambuya Nehanda. As Ranger noted (2010a: 10; Fontein 2015: 262), during her trial and in response to Muchini's claims that 'independence was a mockery' and 'Mugabe was a puppet of the whites', ZANU PF asserted 'that the party had made Nehanda rather than Nehanda the party' and 'it was treason to dispute Mugabe's right to determine peace', even as they continued to trumpet Nehanda's legendary contribution to Zimbabwe's liberation, as indeed ZANU PF continues to do. Secondly, contemporary accounts of the events and subsequent trial suggest that Sophia Muchini, like Mavhunga two decades later, was subject to the political machinations and possibly manipulation by senior ZANU PF figures, particularly Herbert Ushewokunze. Ushewokunze was a controversial political actor in the early 1980s, and at Muchini's trial he was directly implicated by the judge, who found his denials 'bald and unconvincing' (Fontein 2006a: 161). Before Muchini's trial was complete, Ushewokunze had been expelled from government, in part because of 'the publicity it caused' (Fontein 2015: 262). As with the diesel *n'anga* case, this material suggests that Sophia Muchini was perhaps, in part and like Rotina Mavhunga, being played.

It is important to emphasise immediately that this is not to denigrate or deny the creative 'agency', or moral potency (or 'chutzpah' as Gappah puts it) of mediums like Muchini, Mavhunga or less controversial figures like Ambuya VaZarira. Clearly mediumship can offer great opportunities for dynamic and creative actors to locate themselves in powerful and influential positions, to forge new moral languages or landscapes, and from which some, like Rotina Mavhunga, can acquire considerable benefits, material and otherwise. It is rather to acknowledge that however performative and creative mediumship is, and to whatever extent a medium might emphasise the ancestral or even divine basis of their authority, it is also always, to some extent, socially and politically constituted and dependent. Mediumship is about 'subjection to power, moral agency, and being the subject of one's own experience' (Lambek 2002a: 25).[53] Important as it may sometimes become, therefore, the authority and legitimacy of a medium is rarely entirely dependent upon the approval of those political actors who may seek to make use of them. In fact the effectiveness of a medium – their authority and their legitimacy – is, in many respects, the result of constant effort and careful negotiation, involving a shrewd and 'agentful' juggling of performance, personal narratives and behaviour, and of the clan loyalties and the multiplicity of projects in which ambitious mediums might often be involved (Fontein 2006a: 63–9).

Thirdly, and indicative of this larger point, it is also clear that Muchini's significance in the early 1980s, and her ability to effect her plans (for national ceremonies at Great Zimbabwe, for example), depended to some degree on local support. National Museums and Monuments archives indicate she did have some support from the Duma chiefs of the Mugabe and Murinye clans around that time.[54] The land question and the wave of occupations taking place around Masvingo in the early 1980s are significant here. This local support also caused her other problems, however, particularly with Chief Zepheniah Charumbira, of the rival Charumbira clan, and an influential senator, who (Matenga [2011] has suggested) opposed Nehanda's presence exactly because of her apparently close alliance with these Duma chiefs. Muchini had become involved, perhaps inevitably, in long-running local clan struggles over Great Zimbabwe that pre-date the colonial period but were markedly re-invigorated after independence (Fontein 2006a).

Fourthly, an important but not-oft remarked aspect of the Sophia Muchini case, was the fact that her credibility as a medium and the authenticity of her possession by Nehanda was never firmly established, and was often in some doubt. In 2001, Comrade Nylon – a guerrilla commander who operated in the area during the later war years – told me that he

---

[53] As Lambek puts it in his discussion of Nuriaty, a medium on Mayotte, a medium is always both 'subjected to power and history' yet 'nevertheless manages to constitute herself as a subject in her own right' (2002a: 25).

[54] Fontein 2006a: 159; Letter from Cran Cooke, Regional Director, 16/3/81, NMMZ Archives at Great Zimbabwe, file C5.

Rotina Mavhunga, politics and mediumship

and his comrades considered her a fake, and worried that she was a Rhodesian informer. They deliberately avoided her.[55] After independence, the ex-guerrillas who gathered around her, as well as some local chiefs, did find credibility in her mediumship, although apparently even this waned during the fire-fight that led to her arrest, as her claim to offer spiritual protection from bullets were proved dramatically wrong (Clark 1985: 118). In 2001, both the late chief Mudarikwa Murinye and the late Aiden Nemanwa told me that they had come to realise that she was mad, and that this was probably due to her possession by mischievous, malign *mashavi* spirits, rather than the great ancestor Nehanda as she believed and claimed (Fontein 2006a: 159–60). That is why, after her release from prison, she was left alone to live in a forest at the Boroma hills. When I interviewed her there in 1997 and in 2001, she was very wary of visitors but did eventually open up little (Fontein 2006a: 162). Murinye's view that she was mad due to mischievous *mashavi* spirits that possessed her was shared by many other locals who would often see her walking bare-footed and bare-breasted, in skins and bangles, along the road to Masvingo town.

This last point is significant because it raises the issue of authenticity which was even more prominent in Rotina Mavhunga's case. It amplifies the point that there is always a question mark over the authenticity of any medium; and if not over the medium, then over the spirits involved; and if not over the spirits themselves, then over their intentions, or even their actual presence at any particular possession event. This is well recognised in the ethnographic literature which highlights how even established mediums might occasionally fake possession (Bourdillon 1987b: 241). Even when there is confidence about the authenticity of possession and mediumship, people will often say that 'it is difficult to know what the spirit wants' (214). Most mediums find themselves accused of fraud or inauthenticity at some point in their lives, by somebody or some group, and this can have serious consequences; multiplying what I understand as the precarities of mediumship, as indeed both Mavhunga and Muchini's cases exemplify. It is perhaps of little surprise that the proliferation of Nehanda mediums that have emerged since independence have often given rise to accusations of fraud. In 2005, for example, the late president of the National Council of Chiefs, Chief Jonathan Mangwende 'accused people of falsely claiming to be possessed by prominent national spirit mediums [meaning ancestors] to get rich'.[56]

Aside from such obvious instrumentality, the commonality of fraud accusations against mediums also reflects the inherently social and historical constitution of mediumship. The importance of a medium's clan and local loyalties (and the particular ancestral genealogies these loyalties invoke), for example, often mean mediums are readily denounced as

[55] Interview with Comrade Nylon, 8/8/01.
[56] 'Bogus national spirit mediums hammered' *Herald* 8/3/05.

fraudulent by rival clans and rival mediums. Even Ambuya VaZarira, who was an unusually well-respected medium in Masvingo in the 2000s, was frequently accused of not being genuine by rival clans, or by rivals within her own clans, as well as by those aligned on other sides of various ambitious projects of which she was part (Fontein 2006a: 62).[57] As with the uncertainty that can surround human remains and exhumations, or suspicious 'political accidents', this uncertainty around mediumship and possession can have its own political utility. It means that mediums whose possessed pronouncements are perceived as dangerous or threatening might always be denounced as false or frauds. This is not uncommon, and many local struggles between chiefs, clans, mediums and others over land, territory, sacred sites (like Great Zimbabwe) or seniority, turn on accusations of inauthenticity and fake possession. This prevalence of fraud accusations amplifies the precariousness of mediumship, particularly for high-profile or controversial mediums like Sophia Muchini and Rotina Mavhunga, who court public and political attention. This is also why, in many respects, the really successful mediums of senior or prominent clan and lineage ancestors are those who, like Ambuya VaZarira, are able to juggle convincing performances, personal narratives and behaviour, and a multiplicity of wider projects, while maintaining a strong basis of close kin- and clan-based support. In this context it is also not surprising that mediums often express how much hard work is involved in mediumship, as Ambuya VaZarira and other mediums with whom I worked during the 2000s often said.

However, although accusations of fraud were part of Muchini's case, as with Mavhunga, her story also suggests that the profound uncertainties that circulate around spirit possession may not always, or only, have to do with the ongoing work of maintaining the authenticity of mediumship. They may also have much to do with what I call 'the alterity of spirits'. Indeed, the uncertainties that swirl around possession, and the precarities that can derive therefrom, also often turn on questions about the identity of the spirit(s) possessing any medium, and the possibility that mediums themselves may be misled or deceived by them. This uncertainty about who or what a spirit is, is reflected in the long, often arduous process of becoming a recognised *svikiro* [medium] for a senior clan spirit, and the various trials this can involve, which is well reported in the literature (Bourdillon 1987b: 236–42; Lan 1985: 49–56). These focus as much attention on the identity of any spirit, as on questions about the

---

[57] This is what some people told me lay behind her expulsion from a splinter group of the 'traditional' community conservation organisation AZTREC (Daneel 1998), after its late patron, an influential war veteran called Cosmas Gonese (one of the ex-guerrillas imprisoned after the Muchini affair in the early 1980s) accused her of being a fraud, although VaZarira herself gave a different explanation (Fontein 2015: 283 fn. 115).

authenticity of a medium, their performance or their social recognition. Likewise, it is also common for any possession ritual, or *bira*, even of well-respected, established mediums, to begin with questions about the identity of the spirits present (Lan 1985: 51).

All this suggests that the uncertainties that surround the authenticity of spirit possession are not just questions of effective and convincing performances by a medium, or of his/her ability to garner the social and political recognition and support required to be effective mediums. These uncertainties are also about the spirit him-, her- or itself, whose excessivity and alterity makes them hard to identify, discipline and make sense of. Murinye's comments about Muchini being deceived and made 'mad' by lesser *'mashavi'* spirits possessing her, and not the legendary Nehanda as she claimed, echo the contradictory statements and anxieties that Mavhunga expressed in court about her changeable relationship with the spirit Changamire Dombo. Even mediums claiming to be possessed by Nehanda herself might, it has been suggested (Charumbira 2008), be deceived by avenging *ngozi* masquerading as great ancestors. Another example, already cited, is that of Ambuya Julianna, who, as Mawere and Wilson discussed (1995), came to prominence in the context of the devastating 1992 drought. Her remarkable rise to influence, rapidly generating a movement that stretched across southern Zimbabwe, came on the back of her claims to be able to make it rain. Her equally sharp demise came when those rains did not arrive. In 2001, one of her former acolytes, who claimed she used to work as a *nyusa* (*Mwari* messenger) with Ambuya Julianna, organising *mikwerera* (rainmaking) events and travelling to the Matonjeni and Njelele shrines in Matobo, told me that she later came to learn that Ambuya Julianna was a fraud, or had been deceived, or was possessed not by powerful rainmaking spirits but rather by mischievous *mashavi* spirits.[58]

There is therefore a profound uncertainty that always surrounds spirit possession and mediumship which goes beyond simple questions of possible deception by self-proclaimed mediums, or their manipulation of or by (or under intimidation from) politicians and other interested parties. This is an uncertainty (and therefore a precarity) that derives from the alterity of spirits and from the possibility that, even if any possession event is judged as 'real', the identity or even just the intentions of any spirits involved remains obscure. Beyond the understanding that even a socially recognised 'genuine' medium might occasionally fake possession, a possessing ancestor may always turn out to be a lesser, more malign *shavi* or other 'alien' spirit, or even a witch, out to do mischief or harm. There may even be doubt about whether the intentions of a known spirit, possessing a recognised medium in an 'authentic'

[58] Interview with Ambuya Magura, 12–13/7/01.

possession event, are indeed benign or malign in any instance. Therefore, even the assumption that all senior ancestral spirits, unlike lesser *mashavi* spirits and witches, are always benign and well-intentioned towards his or her living descendants, or his/her medium, is not one that can always be entirely relied upon, unlike what Lan's (1985: 38) rather static, polarising and overly structuralist diagrams might have suggested (Bourdillon 1987b). It is also possible that a spirit can 'desert its human host', if the 'medium breaks his taboos, or behaves in a way not becoming to a medium, or when a rival claims mediumship of the same spirit'. This often leads to 'confusing and contradictory opinions' so that 'the only certain sign that the spirit has left its medium is when the medium does in fact die' (Bourdillon 1987b: 240–41). It is also believed that spirits may leave recognised mediums if they become too old. I was aware of one case like this in rural Masvingo in the early 2000s; an old blind woman – Ambuya Zonani – who was once said to have been a powerful healer and medium, but whose spirit had left her once she became too frail.

If politicians and others are inevitably both enticed by and yet wary of mediums, because their authority points to other higher sovereignties (of the ancestors and/or *Mwari*, the divinity that provides rain), then these issues about the authenticity of a medium, of the spirits and of any particular possession event are clearly troubling for everybody concerned, not excluding the mediums themselves. The case of the diesel *n'anga*, and of Sophia Muchini two decades before her, as well as of Julianna in the 1990s, perhaps illustrate this more starkly than other examples; how the indeterminacy that can surround all spirit possession provides additional impetus and explanation for the ambivalence with which mediums have often been treated by the ruling party. The indeterminacy of possession illustrates why and how mediumship in Zimbabwe – particularly the more public and controversial mediums and their claims are – can be very precarious. Importantly, the term 'precarious' is used here both in the sense of 'dangerous' or 'not securely held', and in the sense of uncertain and unknowable yet potentially consequential. While prominent mediums who court public attention and politics, like Mavhunga and Muchini, can get killed, 'unmasked', accused of fraud, or put in prison, they are also (like less prominent, more careful mediums) subject to the vagaries of their spirits, who can make them sick or cause misfortune, or make them powerful and strong, or mislead them, or leave them altogether.

Furthermore, not only is mediumship a precarious occupation in all these ways, often precariousness precedes possession, if you will. 'The medium does not wish to be possessed' notes Lan, because 'possession is a hardship and trial' (1985: 49). Moreover, 'the careers of all mediums develop out of a state of crisis' (1985: 49). This links us to the discussion in the next chapter, about Mai Melissa. Spirit mediums' own narratives of how they became mediums or *homwe* ('pockets', as they are sometimes

Rotina Mavhunga, politics and mediumship

referred to) often illustrate how a spirit's desire to possesses a medium is usually announced through sickness and ill-fortune long before possession and mediumship is established. This is well reported in the literature, even if such accounts are very often based on mediums' own narrative and performative mechanisms through which they constantly work to authenticate their own status. My long personal, historical and ethnographic relationship with Mai Melissa, from 1995 when I first met her, until her possession in 2006 and her death in late 2007 offers a glimpse, through my incomplete but extensive field notes across this period, of how mediumship comes about; of how the troublesome presence of the spirit of a significant dead family member can be recognised long before possession and mediumship are established; and of the personal difficulties and precarities this long process can involve.

Indeed, precariousness is almost a precondition for mediumship. This works both on an individual and family level; for example, how personal sickness or a series of unexplained deaths in a family, often precede becoming a medium. But it also operates at a larger societal scale. National crisis, drought, violence and war have often provoked the emergence of new mediums and new religious movements. Examples include African nationalism and the liberation struggle of the 1960s–70s, and how this led to a marked increase in mediumship reported by Fry (1976); the terrible 1992 drought and the rapid rise and demise of Ambuya Julianna in the early 1990s (Mawere & Wilson 1995; Mafu 1995); and of course Zimbabwe's post-2000 political and economic crisis. The fuel crisis of the mid-2000s was clearly significant for Rotina Mavhunga's remarkable, if short-lived, success (Matereke & Mungwini 2012: 427), just as Zimbabwe's struggle for independence, for land and over Great Zimbabwe were for Sophia Muchini. In her account of how she became a medium, Ambuya VaZarira too often discussed the personal trials, ill health and other tribulations she faced before the cause of her 'spiritual affliction' was identified and her mediumship established, which was also during the liberation struggle (Fontein 2004).

But the examples offered by the controversial cases of Mavhunga and Muchini, as well as other less flash-in-the-pan mediums like VaZarira, are still to some extent exceptional, exactly because they involve senior territorial ancestors whose status inevitably makes them politically significant. This means that formal, thorough and long processes of establishing 'authentic' mediumship are usually involved (Lan 1985; Bourdillon 1987b; Garbett 1977, 1992). Much more common forms of mediumship and spirit possession across Zimbabwe are those of much 'smaller', less significant, *vadzimu* or family ancestors, and of other *mashavi* or 'alien' spirits, who may turn mediums into powerful healers or *n'anga*, but who do not command the same kind of clan or territorial loyalties, and therefore rarely rise to the kind of political significance that Mavhunga, Muchini or

VaZarira achieve. The case of Mai Melissa and her emergent mediumship before her 2007 death, discussed in the next chapter, is one such example. Exactly because such cases involve less 'known' or historically significant spirits, these mediums rarely fall subject to long authenticating processes often associated with spirits like Nehanda, Zarira or Changamira Dombo. Therefore, the profound uncertainties that derive from the social constitution of mediumship and from what I call the 'alterity of spirit' can be much more marked. As Mai Melissa's case shows, such less high-profile but much more common experiences are useful for what they reveal about the profound uncertainties of mediumship and how this is entangled with the uncertain incompleteness of death, particularly in circumstances of rapid or marked social change and personal precarity.

One final point about the Muchini affair is worth mentioning, because it further links her case to those of both Mavhunga and Mai Melissa, and because it highlights the question of the alterity and uncertainty of spirits with which I am concerned. One interesting aspect of Muchini's claims – and one that some people in Masvingo in 2001 felt undermined her authenticity, but which others (Garlake 1983) have celebrated – was her efforts to synthesise a position between what we might call a 'traditionalist' perspective and a 'Christian' one. She described Great Zimbabwe's as 'God's place' and identified the spirit of Nehanda (who she claimed possessed her) with the biblical Eve. When I visited her in 1997, 2000 and 2001, she quoted verses from the Bible to us (Fontein 2006a: 162). There is nothing particularly contradictory about such efforts to synthesise across diverse, co-existent, and sometimes-but-not-always competing religious regimes and loyalties. Very many Zimbabweans have, for a very long time, maintained allegiances and commitments to both churches (of various denominations and forms) and diverse ancestral and other cult practices. Some churches – notably the Catholic church and some African Independent churches – raise no issues about such dual loyalties, or may even encourage them; while others, such as the Dutch Reformed church and especially Pentecostal churches, make great efforts to emphasise their difference from ancestral practices, often provoking mediums' wrath by describing them as *mweya wetsvina* (dirty/evil spirits). Of course, fervent devotees on all sides may maintain and reinforce such boundaries, but most people dibble and dabble across denominations and spiritual practices, seeking guidance and healing wherever it may be found.

Where these issues do often come to the fore is in mediums' own personal accounts of becoming mediums, or of leaving mediumship behind. After all that she had endured through the 'diesel *n'anga* saga', in court and in prison, it is perhaps not surprising that Rotina Mavhunga sought to turn her back on her troublesome spirit and converted to Pentecostal Christianity. More common, however, at least in experiences of rural life in Masvingo, are accounts of how emergent mediums may mistake or deny the presence of spirits seeking to possess them by becoming active members of church congregations; often African Independent churches, like the Zion Christian Church (ZCC). Bourdillon cites one such example (1987b: 238) which echoes many I have encountered, including Mai Melissa's story to which we now turn. Beyond the politics of synthesis and antithesis, of difference, resemblance and co-existence, that tensions between different church denominations and diverse traditionalist observance are often entangled in such accounts relates, I suspect, to the uncertain alterity of spiritual encounters, which demand but usually defy final stabilisation through either devout church adherence or spirit mediumship.

6

Mai Melissa: Towards the alterity of spirit and the incompleteness of death

I first met Mai Melissa, or Rosina, in 1995, when I was travelling through Zimbabwe during a break from my undergraduate studies. Approximately 16 years old, she was a dancer with a traditional *mbira* dance group performing at Great Zimbabwe, in Masvingo District, central southern Zimbabwe. She then lived in the Nemanwa communal areas nearby, at the rural homestead of her elder, half-brother, Peter Rukasha, whose wife, Francesca, was one of the *mbira* group's leaders. This was my first encounter with the Rukasha family, whom I grew to know very well as they hosted me over long periods of ethnographic fieldwork in the area (1997, 2000–01, 2005–06) and numerous other brief visits in between and since, most recently in March 2020. The story of Mai Melissa's possession by her own father, Sekuru Shorty, in 2006, until her death in late 2007 is very much a story about this family's complex kinship history, the migration of Peter and Mai Melissa's father from Mozambique many years before, and the many trials and struggles that this family have endured since settling in the Nemanwa area shortly after independence in 1980, as '*vatorwa*' or strangers, living under Headman Nemanwa, in what was then part of the Chief Charumbira's territory.[1]

By the time of my next visit to the area in 1997, then doing research for my honours degree, Mai Melissa had become a mother (to Melissa) and was married to Daniel Mutevedzi, the *mbira* group's lead dancer and a member of a prominent Charumbira family, where she now resided about one hour's walk from the Rukasha homestead. I visited her and her husband several times during this period, for personal visits or to attend family events, and became gradually aware of her change in status, from being a child living under the authority of her half-brother (then in many respects a proxy for their dead father, Sekuru Shorty), to being a *vatete* (paternal aunt) to the Rukasha household, and *muroora* (wife) to the Mutevedzi family. These changes in status were marked by new formalities of respect, and different obligations between the people involved,

---

[1] For a more detailed history of the complex local clan politics over landscape and autochthony in the area, see Fontein 2006a and 2015.

Mai Melissa, the alterity of spirit and the incompleteness of death

FIGURE 9. Mai Melissa (Author 2001)

but also sometimes tension as well as care between her and members of the Rukasha household, especially Francesca, Peter's wife, who herself, like all wives, is a *muroora* (to the Rukasha family). Mai Melissa was by then dancing less frequently with the *mbira* group, whose activities had anyway reduced during this period.

Although its significance did not become apparent to me until many years later, there was one memorable event during the months I spent at the Rukasha household that year, which would reverberate importantly with the subsequent events around Mai Melissa's possession by her dead father, Sekuru Shorty, almost a decade later. It happened during a family *bira* event in August 1997, held to find a solution to various troubles affecting the family to do with the misbehaviour of Peter and Francesca's eldest son Philip. During this event their second son Phillimon, then only a young teenager, was ritually given the name of his dead *sekuru* [grandfather], and offered gifts of 'seven-days' beer brewed for the event, rice and a chicken brought by Mai Melissa's husband, Daniel Mutevedzi, as *mukwasha* [son-in-law]. I was told these offerings were a sign of respect for Sekuru Shorty and a way to draw the dead man's spirit and his guidance closer to the family. Rice and chicken, in particular, were offered because (I was told) in Mozambique this is what a *mukwasha* would be expected to bring his father-in-law or *tezvara*. Phillimon was addressed as *sekuru* as a sign of respect, not because he was to become a medium for the spirit, but 'only as an offering to the spirit to ensure its continued help and support'. Even Sekuru Shorty's former wife, Ambuya Magumbo, Peter's mother, took up a seat next to him and addressed him as if he was her husband. Later, as music and dancing intensified in the round kitchen hut where such proceedings normally take place, she made a great performance of twice crawling on her knees through the rising dust and stamping feet of the dancers, as if in mourning for her dead husband, to the appreciative ululations of women present.[2]

For this small family it was a significant event for which beer was brewed and between 30 and 40 relatives and prominent locals were in attendance. The moment that would later become much more significant was when, quite late in the proceedings, after one woman had already become possessed by a spirit called Banda from Malawi, and during a period of intense music, singing and dancing led by some local elders singing Mozambican songs (deliberately, to entice the spirit of the dead Mozambican man), Mai Melissa suddenly became afflicted by something appearing like trance or even possession. As I recorded in my notes:

> As the drumming grew in intensity, so did the dancing and singing. Everybody participated, clapping etc. Ambuya [Magumbo] was very drunk now, and dancing with an intensity that surprised me. Similarly Rosina [Mai Melissa], whose dancing was very good, and her intensity grew and grew. It began to appear like a spirit was trying to 'come out'. Tears streamed from her eyes and she shook violently. Her dancing and expression was very intense, as she kept bumping into and pushing into the woman who had earlier been possessed. Now that woman was supporting Rosina, guiding her back to the group who were dancing ... Suddenly Rosina collapsed on the floor crying her eyes out, and she was taken to sit down on a mat. Later she was led outside.

> I sat down next to Calvin [or Baba Kenny, another *mukwasha* to Peter, and a *mbira* player], who I asked about Rosina. 'Rosina', Calvin said 'has *mudzimu*' [ancestral spirit].

> A short time later, Daniel signalled to me to go outside, and then he said 'let's go and smoke'. Calvin, Daniel, myself and another man went out behind the termite mound below the Muchechete tree to smoke a joint.

---

[2] Field Notes, 25/8/97. Bourdillon 1987b: 216 has an account of this naming practice.

Mai Melissa, the alterity of spirit and the incompleteness of death

I asked Daniel about Rosina and he said that the spirit of *sekuru* (Peter's father) was trying to come out. That was the first time, so therefore it could not come completely. But next time, the spirit would probably talk.[3]

When I returned to the area three years later to begin PhD research, Mai Melissa's circumstances had changed again. She was now the mother of a second child, Munashe, but her husband Daniel had died, and she was again living at her brother, Peter's household, with her children. After her husband's death, there were some tensions with her husband's family, as is not uncommon in relationships between a *muroora* and her in-laws, particularly around the unexplained death of her husband, who I was told, had died very suddenly in his field one day, after having complained of an intense headache. During that year a public health research team from the University of Zimbabwe (UZ) visited the area and tested all youth between particular ages for HIV, including myself, Phillimon and Mai Melissa. That was when Mai Melissa learnt that she was HIV positive, although, in what was an upsetting and emotional moment for everyone involved, she fiercely denied it, claiming that the result was incorrectly based on the fact that she had suffered from TB some years earlier.[4] During those two years (2000–01) of ethnographic fieldwork, there were also occasional tensions between Mai Melissa and her half-brother Peter, as he became increasingly sensitive to public ridicule that he, as *tezvara* (father-in-law), was looking after his *mukwasha*'s (son-in-law) children, his *muzukuru* – that is the children of the late Daniel Mutevedzi. Little Melissa's repeated ill health during this period was a cause of growing concern and added to these tensions. Eventually Mai Melissa would return to the Mutevedzi household, although she remained wary that her late husband's family wanted her to marry one of her late husband's brothers, or even one of his nephews,[5] in a contemporary form of what used to be known as *kugara nhaka*, a form of 'wife inheritance' (Bourdillon 1987b: 214–16).

Apart from a brief visit in 2004, I did not return to the area until 2005, when I began 18 months of fieldwork for a new project (2015). Sometime in 2004 little Melissa had passed away after a long illness, still only seven years old. This was a period in Zimbabwe's recent history when the economy was failing drastically, exacerbated by several years of drought and poor harvests amidst the turmoil of Fast Track Land Reform and ongoing political repression in the context of elections that year and the devastating urban clearances known as *Operation Murambatsvina* (Potts 2006; Vambe 2008; Bratton & Masungure 2007; Fontein 2009a). Mai Melissa was then living with her young son Munashe, in a small, still-standing house, in the largely ruined and almost abandoned Mutevedzi homestead.

---

[3] Field notes, 25/8/97.
[4] Field notes, 26/7/01.
[5] Field notes, 10/3/06.

The Politics of the Dead

As with many households in the area around that time – during the apex of the AIDS pandemic, and just before antiretroviral drugs (ARVs) became easily available – there had been many deaths in the Mutevedzi family,[6] and Mai Melissa and Munashe were living an impoverished life there. One remarkable thing was that she had become a very active member, even a prophetess, of a local Zionist church, and would regularly attend services wearing the white headscarf and gowns common to that 'African Independent' church denomination. Later, after her mediumship of Sekuru Shorty was established, others would explain this episode as part of Mai Melissa's efforts to deny the Mozambican spirit who was trying to 'come out'.[7] As Peter's eldest daughter, Epifania, told me in 2006,

> For quite some time Vatete Mai Melissa had denied that it was *Sekuru* who was trying to possess her, by ignoring dreams and other signs that she was getting. That was why she suddenly joined the ZCC. It was only after [Mai Candid's] death and the problems over her burial and then Baba's illness that she was finally possessed and then ... she stopped going to church.[8]

The year 2005–06 was a tumultuous year for the Rukasha family. They suffered a series of illnesses, deaths and other misfortunes,[9] many of which fuelled, but were also understood as reflecting, a series of intense family and kinship struggles that involved both the troubling presence of the Mozambican spirits of Sekuru Shorty (Peter and Mai Melissa's dead father) and of his father [Peter's grandfather] Sekuru Manico, and a series of controversies surrounding Shorty's former wife, Peter's mother, Ambuya Magumbo, who too lived locally, and who had had a series of other children by other men, both before and after her marriage to Sekuru Shorty. A lot of these tensions reverberated around the death and contested burial of different children and grandchildren of Ambuya Magumbo at Peter's homestead – people who were maternally related to

---

[6] Field notes, 22/7/05.
[7] I heard a similar story from another medium in Nemanwa, VaChikumbu, who explained how he 'tried several churches when I was running away from my *mudzimu* and *chikaranga* [loosely, in this context, 'tradition']. I tried the Zviratidzo Church, the Apostolics and even the Zion, but when I went to these churches as I arrived the lights would turn off, unexpectedly, and when I left they would turn on again. Ultimately I had no choice, one does not choose to be *svikiro* you are chosen, and it is often hard work ... you cannot run away' – Field notes, 18/11/05.
[8] Field notes, 9/3/06.
[9] These included continuing troubles with Philip (Peter's and Francesca's eldest son) who was now married, and a 'border-jumper' into South Africa, and rarely heard from or sending money home. In late 2005, during a rare visit home, Philip had quarrelled with his wife one night and set their small round thatched house alight – Field notes, 14/11/05.

Peter, but members of different clans because they had different fathers. These problems also had to do with Peter and his family's contested belonging in the area as *vatorwa* or strangers, not related to the autochthonous Nemanwa clan. Peter and his immediate family had been invited to live there after independence, but his maternal kin and other relatives of different clan and totemic identities had not, so burying them in Nemanwa soil risked upsetting local ancestral spirits (as well as, it would turn out, the spirits of Peter's father and grandfather in Mozambique), and would normally involve making requests to the *sabhuku* (village head) and some kind of compensatory payment and ritual offering to the spirits. Francesca, Peter's wife, *muroora* to the Rukasha family, had had similar troubles with Nemanwa elders when her father had died and was buried in the field at their homestead during the early 1990s.[10]

In 2005–06 when I was conducting fieldwork in the area there were four prominent deaths, all of which caused controversies. First was Mai Candid, Ambuya Magumbo's seventh child, by a subsequent husband to Sekuru Shorty.[11] Mai Candid died from an HIV-related infection after a long, painful wasting illness at Ambuya Magumbo's homestead, after she had been abandoned by her own husband. Against the wishes of Francesca Rukasha (Peter's wife), Mai Candid was buried at the Rukasha homestead, upon the insistence of Ambuya Magumbo and Mai Muchemwa (Ambuya Magumbo's eldest daughter by a much earlier relationship prior to her marriage to Sekuru Shorty). Mai Muchemwa was married into a prominent, politically connected family in neighbouring Gutu district, and had long used these connections to assume a senior role in the Rukasha family, much to Francesca's annoyance, particularly because Mai Muchemwa was not of the same paternal lineage as Peter.[12] As Francesca predicted, Mai Candid's burial at the Rukasha homestead caused problems for the family with the local *sabhuku* because she was not of Peter's totem, and therefore had not been invited to live or be buried

---

[10] Field notes, 20/4/06. The burial of *vatorwa* relatives in communal areas is not uncommon across rural Zimbabwe, despite potential problems with 'autochthonous' clans and offended ancestors. As with many such transgressions there are ways around such problems which usually involve some kind of compensatory payment to a chief, headman, village head, and/or a ritual offering of '*bute*' (tobacco snuff) or beer to an offended spirit (pers. com. Joseph Mujere, 13/2/20).

[11] In my notes Mai Candid is often referred to as '*Vatete* Mai Candid', because she was Peter's half-sister but, although this is not uncommon, a person in her position would not normally be afforded that status because she was from a different father, and not of the same paternal lineage and totemic group as Peter.

[12] The tensions between Mai Muchemwa and Francesca went back a long way, to the latter days of the war, when Mai Muchemwa had arranged Francesca's marriage to Peter, when Francesca was only 16 years old – Field notes, 14/5/06.

The Politics of the Dead

in Nemanwa's territory.[13] The second death came not longer after, in December 2005, when Mai Muchemwa herself died, very suddenly (and for some, suspiciously) after collapsing in a bar only a few days after attending the *nyaradzo* or memorial service for Mai Candid, in Nemanwa. Mai Muchemwa was buried in Gutu.[14]

Then, in early 2006, there was the death of Mai Effy, Ambuya Magumbo's sixth child by another father after Sekuru Shorty. Her case was unusual because she apparently died en route from Harare, having been sick there for a long time. She too was buried at Peter's homestead, and this too caused problems because she was also not of Peter's or his father, Sekuru Shorty's clan or totem, *tsoko* [monkey].[15] The last death that year, only a few weeks after Mai Effy, was that of Mike, whose funeral I discussed in Chapter 2. Mike was the son of Mavis (or Mai Rosy) who was Peter's younger sister by the same father (Sekuru Shorty from Mozambique) and his mother (Ambuya Magumbo), and who therefore, like Mai Melissa, was a paternal *vatete* to the Rukasha's family and of the same totem. Mavis herself had died just a few years earlier and had also been buried (albeit 'legitimately') at Peter's homestead. Mike was therefore Peter's *muzukuru*, that is (in this case) his sister's son. Mike's painful and traumatic illness and death was particularly difficult because he had turned up at the Rukasha's homestead a few months earlier, incredibly sick and afflicted by terrible skin infections, and a CD4 count of only four. He needed enormous amounts of care, which his immediate relatives in Gutu (where he had been living) were not able to provide. Great effort was spent caring for him and trying to get him enrolled on an ARV programme through a local clinic, being rolled out at that time, but he passed away only a week after finally beginning the drugs. Mike's burial at Peter's homestead too, as with Mai Effy and Mai Candid, also had the potential to cause problems due to his status as *muzukuru* to the Rukasha family.

Mai Melissa was deeply implicated in these family events not only because she was Peter's half-sister, but also because of the involvement of her dead father, Sekuru Shorty, the spirit from Mozambique, who would eventually 'come out' later that year. Mai Melissa shared Peter's totem – *tsoko* – from their father Sekuru Shorty, and therefore legitimately held the important status

---

[13] Field notes, 26/10/05.
[14] Field notes, 11/12/05.
[15] Field notes, 14/4/06, 16/04/05. I was told that Mai Effy was very sick in Harare and wanted to come to the hospital at Morgenster Mission near Nemanwa but died en route. Rumours suggested she may actually have died in Harare and then been immediately and secretly transported to Masvingo by relatives to avoid the administrative costs of getting a death certificate, burial order and a private ambulance as would be officially required. This is not uncommon in Zimbabwe, although rarely openly discussed, as it was not in this case.

Mai Melissa, the alterity of spirit and the incompleteness of death

of paternal aunt, or *vatete*, but she was unrelated to Ambuya Magumbo or her other children. Mai Melissa's mother had been Sekuru Shorty's second wife, and that is why, some people told me, Ambuya Magumbo had long disliked her.[16] In this context there were deep tensions between Mai Melissa and Ambuya Magumbo, and by extension with Mai Muchemwa, Ambuya Magumbo's eldest daughter, who had insisted upon Mai Candid's burial at Peter's homestead. Francesca was involved in these tensions not only because she was very close to Mai Melissa – they had lived and danced together for a long time – but also structurally because, as Peter's wife, she was *muroora* to the Rukasha household, and to Ambuya Magumbo (and by extension to Mai Muchemwa, Peter's elder half-sister) and therefore was often accused of being too bossy over Peter, or overstepping the bounds of her role as 'incoming' wife.

These tensions came to a head in October–November 2005, when Peter became very sick with an unexplained mental illness, shortly after Mai Candid's death. Given reports about increasing cases of meningitis related to the HIV pandemic, I was very concerned to ensure Peter received appropriate medical treatment. Peter's wife, Francesca, was clearly beside herself with worry and agreed with my suggestion to seek health care from nearby Morgenster hospital, and later Masvingo hospital in town, but also insisted we consulted a prominent local healer or *n'anga*, well known to the family, who was (confusingly) also known as Ambuya Magumbo. For clarity's sake I shall call her here, Ambuya Mai Matanda, after her husband, Sekuru Matanda, a *mbira* player and assistant in her work as a healer.

Francesca, Mai Melissa and I took Peter to Ambuya Mai Matanda's homestead on 3 November 2005 to seek advice on Peter's illness, on our way to Masvingo hospital.

> Presently Ambuya [Mai Matanda] and Sekuru [Matanda] both come in and Ambuya sits in front of us, facing side on, towards the back of the hut. Behind her and near the door Sekuru sits down and picks up a *mbira* and begins to play. Ambuya talks to us as she slowly puts on various strings of white, blue and black beads. She is old and shakes as she puts on the beads and arranges objects around her. She ties the animal skins round her and reaches for a small ceremonial staff; as the possession begins she lets out a low moan, shakes and trembles and begins to speak in a very squeaky voice. The movements of Ambuya and Sekuru playing *mbira* seem so smooth, so coordinated, as if they have done this many times before. As Ambuya becomes possessed Sekuru welcomes the spirit saying 'Mauya ...', etc. etc. [You have come ...] and puts the *mbira* down and reaches over to a snuff container and puts some on a wooden plate near Ambuya, who takes it ... Sekuru speaks to the spirit, and explains why we have come.

---

[16] Field notes, 10/3/06.

The Politics of the Dead

The spirit begins to speak and announces that he is Pfupajena the spirit of the Duma people who lived and died long ago. As the spirit speaks he dips the small staff into the wooden cup of water Sekuru has put beside him, and lets the water drip from it into a bowl in front of him hidden under the pile of clothes. The spirit begins to say that he can see a spirit in Mozambique, who is not happy, and who is responsible for what is happening. He repeats this over and over and Amai [Francesca] responds saying, yes, Baba's [Peter's] father is from Mozambique. The spirit possessing Ambuya says that something must be done so that this spirit knows and is told that his children are now living here in Zimbabwe, in Nemanwa. Amai explains that Peter's father came from Mozambique and lived on a farm in Gutu. But the spirit that Ambuya's spirit is talking about is of Peter's grandfather, the father of his father [Sekuru Manico], because (as Amai explains to me later) the spirit of a person rarely comes onto his or her own child but rather the grandchild – it skips a generation.

Peter's affliction is caused by this unhappy spirit, the spirit continues, saying that when he is well he must go to Mozambique to find his relatives there to tell them what has happened and to explain that they are living here in Zimbabwe and to find out what to do next. The spirit continues and says '*Ndiri kuona mukadzi mutema, chipfupi, chakashata*' ['I am seeing a short, dark ugly/evil woman']. Amai and Mai Melissa start saying who it could be. It is someone who is next to Baba [Peter], says the spirit. Very soon both Amai and Mai Melissa start mentioning Mai Muchemwa's name and get quite excited. The spirit says that person is doing wrong, she is trying to rule at the house which is not her own. She is of a different *dzinza* [clan], but she is trying to rule Baba Philip [Peter], and has no respect, but she is not of his *dzinza mukanya* [the *tsoko*/monkey clan].

Amai [Francesca] gets excited and explains that it must be Mai Muchemwa, and begins to explain the things that happened at the funeral, about Mai Candid being buried here at Mai Muchemwa's insistence even though Amai was refusing because she is not of our clan, and comes from a different father/husband of Ambuya Magumbo, and that this might cause problems in the future. And now it appears it has, as the spirit possessing Ambuya is getting very worked up. He talks about Ambuya Magumbo, Peter's mother as having been very wrong, sleeping and having children with four different fathers, so that the children are left not knowing the ancestors of their clan. He mentions [Mai Candid] who was buried recently, who is unhappy buried there and not with her own relatives. The spirit is so worked up that he is using very explicit language describing Ambuya [Magumbo] as '*mapeche embwa*' [vaginas of dogs] and '*mapeche akasviba*' [dirty vaginas] and so on, scolding Ambuya's conduct.

This goes on for a long time, at least half an hour or so. The spirit possessing Ambuya often repeats himself and sometimes refers back to

Mai Melissa, the alterity of spirit and the incompleteness of death

himself saying I am a spirit of the VaDuma, I am *Pfupajena*. He says that money will have to be collected and eventually a cloth will be bought (I later learn from Amai that this will happen later after Sekuru has 'come out' – either on Baba [Peter] or Vatete [Mai Melissa] – two of the three children left alive of Sekuru Shorty and Ambuya Magumbo – the other one is Mai Kenny in Chivhu).

The spirit also talks about a bull that needs to be given /offered to the spirit that has been angered and is causing these troubles. But most of the time the possessing spirit is giving out a very strong moral message about Ambuya's conduct and that of Mai Muchemwa, '*chikadzi chakashata*' [that small ugly/evil woman]. The spirit also asks where Ambuya [Magumbo] is and Mai Muchemwa. Amai answers and says that they had said they would come early this morning but did not turn up ... The spirit says that the problems are with them but also that we should not talk about what has been said today to them but they themselves must come here and the spirit will talk to them himself, and say what has been done wrong, so that things can be put right.

Eventually the spirit begins to go, after almost an hour of talking, Sekuru [Matanda] plays his *mbira* again, and in a similar way to how the spirit came, it leaves, Ambuya taking off her skins, beating herself on the back with her ceremonial staff, grunting and groaning, facing the other way.

Ambuya turns back to us and talks softly and asks how Baba [Peter] is feeling. Ambuya is putting down snuff and praying to the ancestors and specifically Peter's *sekuru* that the rain will come this year; that the ancestors will intercede for the people to *Mwari, Musikavanhu* [God] that the rains will fall this year. She also asks that Peter gets well soon, and that the problems effecting this *dzinza* [clan] will soon be over. When this is over some of the snuff is given to Francesca to put in water for Peter to drink. Also Sekuru [Matanda] digs into some of his pots and prepares parcels of *mushonga* [medicine] and explains to Amai that one needs to be put into Baba's porridge and the other in the water in which he washes. As what has been said is discussed, Amai cries to herself quietly, hiding her face in the 'Zambia' [serong] around her waist, before drying her tears and preparing to get up.[17]

A few days after this consultation with Ambuya Mai Matanda, rumours began circulating that Ambuya Magumbo and Mai Muchemwa were accusing Mai Melissa of using witchcraft against her brother, and that this was the cause of his unexplained illness. These rumours pointed to her activities with a local Zionist church, an African Independent denomination which has often been accused of malevolent witchcraft activities by members of other (especially Pentecostal) churches, older mission churches and by 'traditionalists'. As I recorded in my field notes:

---

[17] Field notes, 3/11/05.

The Politics of the Dead

The whole issue of Baba's [Peter's] illness, and the spirits and Ambuya Magumbo and Mai Muchemwa took a different twist yesterday when Joey said that he had heard Mai Muchemwa and Ambuya saying that they thought Baba was victim of witchcraft from Vatete Mai Melissa. This was connected to her joining the Zion church (ZCC) recently, so either they said she must have got *mushonga* there, or there was an unhappy spirit or something. Obviously Mai Melissa was very upset. She said that when she heard this the day before she almost went to hang herself. Why, she asked, would I want to kill my own brother who has helped me so much in the past, who I lived with for so long?[18]

Mai Melissa was understandably upset and visibly angry at these allegations, which were very serious. Although the tension was thick in the air, both Francesca and Mai Melissa on the one hand, and Ambuya Magumbo and Mai Muchemwa on the other, were careful to avoid direct confrontations. Francesca, as *muroora*, was limited in what she could actually say or do. Peter continued to be sick, and had been admitted to Masvingo hospital, but was then, unexpectedly, discharged. Medical doctors struggled to get a clear diagnosis. A local nurse told me that he thought that Peter's affliction was not medical but 'cultural' and would need to be solved 'in the village'. A day after the consultation with Ambuya Mai Matanda, Ambuya Magumbo came to the Peter's household to suggest that they should now go to consult a 'prophet' from a local church about Peter's illness. Francesca refused to go, but Mai Melissa agreed to attend the visit, which turned out to be not with a Christian 'prophet', as had first been implied, but rather with a young Ndau *n'anga* from Chipinge. From the account I was later told by Mai Melissa, the young Ndau *n'anga* confirmed what Ambuya Mai Matanda's spirit had said; that Peter's illness was the result of Mai Candid having been incorrectly buried in 'foreign soil', and that some kind of ancestral appeasement would need to be performed to reconcile the unhappy Mozambican spirits. As Mai Melissa herself put it: 'the issue of [burying] Mai Candid here in this *musha* [village] caused all the *vadzimu* who are in Mozambique to get up and become angry'.[19] Ambuya Magumbo seemed to accept this, because the following day she visited Peter's household to try to reconcile with Francesca and Mai Melissa, offering to assist in organising the necessary rituals to appease Sekuru Shorty, and his father Manico, the angry spirits in Mozambique.[20]

Later I learnt that during this intense period of family trouble in late 2005, between Mai Candid's burial and Peter's unexplained illness, Mai Melissa had, on a day when I was away in Harare, visited Peter's homestead and suddenly become 'spontaneously' possessed by Sekuru

[18] Field notes, 5/11/05.
[19] Ibid.
[20] Ibid.

Mai Melissa, the alterity of spirit and the incompleteness of death

Shorty, who was 'angry that there was this woman from another *dzinza* buried here and the fact that Ambuya [Magumbo] and Mai Muchemwa do not respect him'.[21] Although the presence of the offended spirits from Mozambique, Sekuru Shorty and his father Sekuru Manico, had already been recognised by this stage, uncertainty about exactly which spirit was responsible and what their intentions were remained for some time. Yet this event was the first indication since 1997 that one of those spirits wanted to 'come out' on Mai Melissa. It remains unclear to me why I was only told this story later, although I heard it independently from several different people at different times.[22] Although Peter was shuttled between Masvingo and Morgenster hospitals several times, and different medical tests were carried out, and various antibiotics administered, no medical cause for his mental illness, which lasted four or five weeks, was ever identified. Just as unexpectedly as he had become sick, Peter began to recover in December 2005, and within a few weeks had returned to his normal everyday self and was able to attend Mai Muchemwa's funeral in Gutu that month.

After Peter's recovery, Mai Melissa's mediumship of the spirit of her father, Sekuru Shorty, was quite quickly established. Within two or three months, Sekuru Shorty began to speak. After returning from Harare in early 2006, I was told that Mai Melissa was now regularly getting possessed, and her reputation as healer and medium was growing. Between March and July 2006, when that period of fieldwork ended, I visited Mai Melissa at her homestead in Mutevedzi several times, for personal visits and to attend consultations by members of the Rukasha family with the spirit of her father, Sekuru Shorty. These visits had to do with Mike's failing health, but also covered a wide range of family issues.[23] On 9 March 2006, I visited her with Mike, Peter, and his other *vazukuru* Fransy and Rosy (both Mike's sisters, daughters of Mavis), on our way to taking Mike to Morgenster hospital to see a doctor. I described these events at length in my field notes:

> Inside the hut there seem to be more pots and plates than I remember and I think to myself that Vatete [Mai Melissa] seems to be doing better for herself. She sits opposite and begins to groan and whistle softly and beats herself on her back with her fist. She pulls out a bag of *bute* (snuff), which she takes in her nostrils hastily.

---

[21] Field notes, 17/11/05, also 8/3/06.
[22] Ibid.
[23] Francesca told me that on a previous occasion Sekuru Shorty (possessing Mai Melissa) had foretold Mike's arrival at their homestead, and 'that he knew Mike was sick and had problems with blood in his urine, and that milk should be taken to him and Sekuru would provide *mushonga* to heal him' – Field notes, 9/3/06.

The Politics of the Dead

The spirit then comes out, and in a voice not that much different from her own, she stretches out her hand to Baba [Peter] and greets him as *mwanangu*, my child. She seems to have got possessed very quickly without any difficulty. The spirit gives Baba [Peter] *bute* snuff and later me too.

Baba says to the spirit that we have come because *muzukuru* is sick. The spirit turns around and says, so you *muzukuru* are sick … yes, let me see your hands. Mike stretches out his scabby hands, and Sekuru asks whether this rash is all over his body. Mike says yes. Then Sekuru asks quite forthrightly whether Mike has also suffered from pains in his stomach, and whether it hurts when he pees, and if when he pees only urine comes out. Mike seems a bit embarrassed as well as being in pain and says that sometimes it hurts and yes sometimes blood does come out. The spirit asks if he has suffered sores on his 'things down there', and Mike says yes that is so. He seems even more embarrassed now. The spirit says yes I can see what is wrong. Have you been with *vakadzi* [women]? the spirit asks. Mike answers – getting a different sense of the word *mukadzi* (woman or wife), and maybe also trying to evade a difficult question – no I don't have a wife. But the spirit is not fooled. No, I mean have you been with women? the spirit insists. Yes, Mike answers, a little sheepishly. The spirit says this is the problem, these young people who play with women and rather than staying with one as a wife. What you have is the *chiwere chevakadzi* (lit. 'the disease of women'). You have been made sick by being with women. Your problem is that you have been living in the bush, *unogara kusango, haudzoki kumusha* [you live in the bush, you don't come home]. You must come back to your *musha* [home/village] and respect *chikaranga* [tradition].

Then addressing Baba [Peter] the spirit says: I will give you *mushonga* [medicine] to make him better but you must also take him to the doctor or hospital. The spirit repeats this several times and says that these problems are being caused by young people not staying with one woman as their wife. The *mushonga* that I will give should be mixed with a little mazoe drink [orange cordial] because that will make it strong. This is important, the spirit emphasises several times. We explain that we are going to Morgenster hospital next, and the spirit actually seems to wonder out loud if there will not be a problem with giving Mike *mushonga* when he is in hospital. Baba and I both suggest that we can give it to him in mazoe drink the hospital people will not know that he is being given herbs to take. The spirit agrees.

After a while the conversation changes as the spirit turns to address Baba about other matters. Have you prepared the *nhumbi* (clothes/cloth) which I asked for? Or the beer which I said must be brewed? Baba says no we have not been able to do that yet. Although Baba looks serious, as indeed does everyone else, he also breaks into smiles every so often and even makes jokes with Sekuru, who is his dead father. For a while now the spirit is quite strict with Baba [Peter] saying that for too long he has ignored him, and that is why Sekuru made him sick last year.

Mai Melissa, the alterity of spirit and the incompleteness of death

[*It is not entirely clear whether it is Peter's father – that is this spirit here – who made Peter sick, or whether it was Peter's grandfather who was buried in Mozambique who made him sick – this evening* (as I was writing these notes) *Peter says it was this spirit – i.e. his father – but Epifania (who was not there today of course) explains that it was Baba's Sekuru, that is Manico, who had made him sick, as indeed the consultation with Ambuya Mai Matanda had also suggested.*] The spirit emphasises the need for *chikaranga chedu* [our tradition] to be respected and followed. At one point the spirit says emphatically it is important for a woman to listen to her husband. Women should not rule men, it is men who should be listened to. The woman should never be on top, the spirit stresses.

The spirit also mentions a cow that has been lost. You have been looking for one of your cows, haven't you? Baba says yes the *mhuru* [calf]. The spirit says that cow is ok, it is in the dam, but you will not find it if you just go looking it. It will stay there and be ok and come back to you. But the cows in the *danga* [kraal] are almost finished, aren't they? Yes, replies Baba, we have been losing cows. Yes, the spirit says, I have seen that there have been many arguments about the cows in the *danga* between you and Mai Magumbo. It is me that has decided to scatter your cows, *kuparadza mombe dziri mudanga*. Then I will give you your cattle, many of them. I will also give you much money which you must keep as I will tell you.

The spirit points at *muzukuru* Fransy and says that it was him who made her sick some time ago. You must follow *chikaranga chedu* he says to Peter. We are not *MaKaranga* [Karanga people], we are from Mozambique and you must follow our customs, *rudzi rwedu* [our type/identity] for that beer that I want you to brew. You must collect many chickens, I don't want *musoro wemhombe* [cow's head] or goat meat or anything else. You must take plenty of chickens and roast them on the fire, not cook them but really fry them up properly, *nyatso kanga huku idzo* [properly fry those chickens], and then make soup to go with the rice. We are from Mozambique we do not know *sadza* [maize meal porridge] we eat rice with chicken! *Rudzi rwedu* [our type/identity] is like that of the *varungu* [white people]. When we do our things we sit at the table and eat with rice with a spoon! *Tine ukama nechikomana icho* [we are related to that small boy] (pointing to me!).

The spirit also says that she wants Baba [Peter] to keep dogs because the spirit says: I used to have 25 dogs who I would hunt with, and I want you to do the same. And Baba must also come with a black and white cloth and another cloth of white, black and red colours mixed up (which *masvikiro* [mediums] often have). You must also bring my child (Mai Melissa) some blue beads, to go with these, as the spirit fingers the strings of black beads and a string of clear beads she is wearing explaining what each represents or is for. The spirit turns to me and says that I have already told my *muzukuru* here (meaning me) that I need a tail of a horse, a black one. You must also get for me a stool, she says to Baba. Then after that *bira* [traditional ancestral ritual/ceremony] with these things then I can begin to work with my child here. I used to be a big *n'anga* I would heal people and chase away bad spirits that were sent to them by *varoyi* [witches]. With these things I can begin to work with my child here and heal people and with the whisk of horse hair I will sweep away those bad spirits which witches send.

For a while the spirit returns to the subject of Mozambique. We are from Mozambique, the spirit says, that is our *kumusha* [home/village]. I came from Mozambique our *dzinza* [clan] is not Karanga and we should do things in our own way. The spirit also adds that recently he has been *kumusha*, in Mozambique and he saw Philip [Peter's paternal uncle, Sekuru Shorty's brother] there, who is still alive and now an old man with a bald head. [*Peter later tells me that Philip was his father's younger brother who came with him from Mozambique but later returned there, while Baba's father – i.e. the spirit Sekuru Shorty – remained here until he died and was buried in Gutu.*] I go there on my *rusero* (winnowing basket) he says. Baba [Peter] jokes and asks can I go there too on your *rusero* and everyone including the spirit laughs, but he adds: No, you cannot, because you are not dead like me.

The spirit then says that he can see a witch that has been bothering Mai Miriam [wife of Joey, Mike's brother]. A tall dark thin woman, and asks Baba [Peter] if he knows who that is, and Baba says yes he does. The spirit raises his voice again and says you must know that I can protect you but right now you have not been respecting me, your *musha* [home/village] is wide open, anything can happen. You people you must respect your *chikaranga* [tradition] and then I will protect you! The spirit also says that Joey will one day stop working, he will say he has had enough and then the spirit will give him work to do.

The spirit then turns to Rosy and says you I can see that you go to church, *unonamata handiti?* [you pray, don't you?] Rosy says yes I do. The spirit says to her, you must respect your traditions, *rudzi rwenyu* [your type/identity]. But don't worry, you are ok, but don't throw away your traditions. You can pray if you want to but listen also to me. One day you will be thankful to me. The spirit then says that she can see a tall dark lady who Rosy is often with and asks if that is a friend of Rosy. Rosy says yes I know who you mean. The spirit says be careful of her, she is a witch. Rosy says ok. The spirit warns her that she talks too much and that she scolds people too easily, *une pamuromo* [lit. 'you have it on your mouth' or 'you have a big mouth']. The spirit emphasises that he does not necessarily know what is going on, only that he is telling what he can see.

The spirit also mentions Rosy's mother Mavis [Peter's full sister, mother of Rosy, Mike, Joey and Fransy, who died a few year earlier and is buried at Peter's homestead], and asks whether a *nyaradzo* [memorial event usually done some time after burial] was done after she died.

Mai Melissa, the alterity of spirit and the incompleteness of death

Rosy and Baba both say yes there was a *nyaradzo* and the spirit, slightly surprised, says that it was not done properly, you need to prepare another *bira* [traditional ceremony] for her. The spirit is quite specific and says that Mavis (Mai Rosy) was not buried properly. She was buried facing west, but for us we should be buried facing east. Right now Mavis is not happy because every time she needs to go *kumusha kuMozambique* [home to Mozambique] she first has to turn to face the right way. So beer must be cooked to sort out that problem. After you have cooked the *bira* for me then you should go ahead and cook another beer for Mavis. The spirit implies that the spirit of Mavis is not settled, and certain things still need to be done for her. The spirit also mentions Rosy's father and asks rhetorically: you do not know him do you? He has died now hasn't he? Rosy says yes he is dead and I do not know him. The spirit says I can see maybe a soldier, someone in uniform, that is what I can see.

Every now and then the spirit repeats what he has already said and asks if there is anything else that people present want to ask him. At one point Fransy speaks up and asks the spirit for advice about the *mushonga* [medicine] for Mike, and he replies giving detailed instructions. Don't worry *muzukuru* [meaning, in this context, grandchild] the spirit says to Mike, I will help you.

At one point the spirit turns to me and says that this one, this *muzukuru* is good he is very helpful, and he must look after you *mwanangu* ['my child;' referring here to Peter] but you must also look after him. The spirit also mentions Amai [Francesca] and other people in the family. He stresses it is important for you to look after your *dzinza*, your relatives, our *dzinza* [clan]. Don't worry about other people but your family must be brought together. Like I have said at the moment your *musha* is wide open and anything can happen. Help me to close it. At this *bira* you must invite all the *vazukuru* [grandchildren, but also sister's children]. I don't know how you will do this but it is important that everyone is there. The spirit implies Baba's [Peter's] sons but also the other *vazukuru*, such as Rosy, Mike and Fransy who were there today.

The spirit also explains that he has come on this child now [referring to Mai Melissa], but before had wanted to come out through that young man, Phillimon [referring to Francesca and Peter's second son]. Phillimon used to do what I did, I used to go hunting with dogs and bring home meat and things like that, but these days he has changed, he is interested in girls and he is no longer doing those things, and that is why I have now come out on this child here. When he returns to do those things, when he has returned from working then I will come through him, but right now I am on this one here.

And so the conversation goes on. Sometimes the spirit is very strict and demanding and sometimes Peter and the spirit are making jokes, and the atmosphere relaxes. The spirit mentions several other people and what they should do, or what they do that is not good, some of which I do not catch. But before the spirit finally does leave, he repeats again what needs to be done for Mike, and what Baba needs to do for the spirit. With a cough, a wheeze and whistle the spirit departs and Vatete [Mai Melissa] gets up and walks outside, soon followed by all of us except Mike who stays inside.

Outside Rosy seems surprised and says: so Sekuru really does know, the way he described my friend was amazing. Baba and Fransy agree with similar comments. The atmosphere is light- hearted, but soon the conversation returns to Mike and the need to get him to hospital at Morgenster to see a doctor. Vatete is somewhere beyond our sight in the woods nearby and calls out for Fransy who goes to her. After few minutes they come back carrying different bundles of roots and plant stems, and Vatete begins to explain how each should be prepared in water and administered. It is not clear to me at this point whether Vatete has indeed returned or whether it is still the spirit speaking. At one point I notice her saying *'mwanangu'* but I am not sure whether she is saying it to Baba [Peter] or Fransy. I later ask Peter quietly as we walk to the car whether Vatete is now back, and he says yes smiling, Sekuru has gone.[24]

During subsequent visits with other family members other revelations and more instructions emerged from Sekuru Shorty. On 26 March that year, he repeated his instructions that a '*bira* that has to be brewed for him to welcome him into the *musha* [home/village]', adding that he didn't 'want beef or goat there, but chickens that have been properly roasted' and that he wanted 'to eat with a knife and fork which is what we used to do'. He also demanded that 'I want you to bring me a cow, and I need beads, blue ones', adding later, to much amusement, that he wanted 'some khaki shorts because right now *ndakashama* [I am naked]! I don't want these woman's clothes!' Sekuru Shorty instructed that 'Baba and Vatete [Mai Melissa] will have to go to Mozambique on foot to go and see Philip his younger brother, [because] there is something that will need to be arranged over there in Mozambique'. He also indicated that 'he will send his daughter [Mai Melissa] to see his son [Peter] and they will have to go to the Mutevedzi family where she was married ... to inform them that Sekuru has come out and wants to begin his work as a healer through her'.[25]

In the two hours that he possessed Mai Melissa on that day, as on previous occasions, he offered advice and *mushonga* not only to Mike, but to everyone present individually. Speaking to Epifania (Francesca and Peter's daughter), for example, he said that 'although she is ugly she has a good heart', and warned her 'about an old woman who lives next to them in town ... because she is a witch', explaining that she was the cause of the

---

[24] Field notes, 9/3/06.
[25] Field notes, 26/3/06.

breastfeeding problems Epifania was facing. Epifania was also warned to 'be careful of people who live next to [her husband's] *kumusha* [home] in Bikita, who are very dangerous'. He gave similar specific advice to every single person present. Later Sekuru Shorty spoke to Francesca's mother (who was visiting from Chirumanzi at the time) about Peter's wife (Francesca) and her problems with Mai Magumbo (Peter's mother and Shorty's former wife). Sekuru Shorty said he was

> very happy with his son's wife, because she is good for him, but there is a problem because she is hated by Ambuya Magumbo ... That wife of mine [Ambuya Magumbo] is wrong. Her child Philip, who was named after my brother there in Mozambique, died because soon after [he was born] she started to sleep with another man. That is what happens when a woman leaves her husband and takes another one, her children will die!
>
> Sekuru also mentions that [Francesca] is going to be possessed by her late father's mother, who wants to come out on her. Is that why my child [Francesca] is so rude to her husband, your son? asks Ambuya [Francesca's mother]. Sekuru says, yes that ambuya [the spirit] she has a lot of anger, isn't it that you have seen that this Ambuya has anger ... Yes say Ambuya [Francesca's mother] and Epifania. This ambuya [the spirit] also likes to drink. So when your child [Francesca] says roughly to her husband, I'm going to drink, don't worry, it's this ambuya [the spirit] who wants to come out on her.[26]

That day Sekuru Shorty ended, after talking for nearly two hours, by explaining that 'Mai Melissa will have no more children, [and] she will not marry again because he wants to work through her – *ndine basa guru rekuita* [I have big work to do]'. 'Soon' he continued 'there will be a goat that this child [Mai Melissa] will get for cleansing people's houses ... of evil spirits'. You should send Ray [Peter and Francesca's third son] to come and get the goat. I will bring many goats and cows to my son's *musha!*'[27]

During these months there continued to be some confusion over whether it was Sekuru Shorty, or his father Manico who had been the cause of Peter's unexplained illness the year before, and had been angered by the controversies surrounding Mai Candid's burial.[28] I heard different interpretations from different people, although most agreed that it was indeed Sekuru Shorty who was now possessing Mai Melissa. Undoubtedly, some likely suspected Mai Melissa's mediumship to be fraudulent. Others referred back to the events of 1997, when Phillimon had Sekuru's name ritually bestowed upon him, and when Mai Melissa had shown the first signs of her subsequent mediumship almost ten years later. Sekuru Shorty himself seemed to imply on several occasions that, in the past, he had wanted to

[26] Field notes, 26/3/06.
[27] Ibid.
[28] Field notes, 9/3/06, 26/3/06

'come out' on Phillimon – saying that he had caused Phillimon to be such a proficient hunter when he was young – although at other times he also suggested that the spirit of his own father, Manico, would in the future 'come out' on Phillimon or perhaps on his elder brother, Philip.[29] Sekuru Shorty also told Epifani [Philip and Phillimon's sister], that the spirit of his dead sister 'wants to come out on you', adding that 'yes, there are many of us wanting to come, you will see it!'[30]

What did emerge from the possession events I attended, and various conversations with others around this time, was a more detailed biography of Sekuru Shorty. This included details of his death; about how he had died after being severely beaten by pro-Muzorewa forces near the end of the war,[31] and had then been buried hastily in a cave in Gutu. During one possession event, Sekuru Shorty claimed he had 'finished off those thieves who killed me in 1979', and that he had shown Ambuya Magumbo in her dreams where he had been buried, promising Epifania that he would also soon show her the 'small pathetic grave where he was buried'.[32] Sekuru Shorty also explained that he had been born in 1904 and spent 40 years of his life in Zimbabwe, 'after he came here ... looking for his wives'.[33] Peter told me his father initially worked as a carpenter on a farm in Mutare owned by a white man, Mr Carter, before moving to Gutu and getting a place to live in the 'reserve' [communal areas].[34] Sekuru Shorty claimed he had had six wives, but only two bore him any children. His own father Manico (i.e. Peter's grandfather) had had ten wives and was buried in Mozambique. Shorty had been accompanied by his younger brother Philip when he first came to Zimbabwe but Philip had soon returned to Mozambique. This Philip was Peter's *babamunini* [younger paternal uncle], and it was his name which had first been bestowed on one of Ambuya Magumbo's sons who died young, before being given to Peter's own eldest son. It was this elderly uncle Philip, apparently still alive, whom Sekuru Shorty instructed Peter and Mai Melissa to visit, on foot, in Mozambique.

During those early months of 2006 Mai Melissa was able to rapidly establish herself not only as a medium in the Rukasha household, but also as a healer, as Sekuru Shorty promised. She began to be consulted by various local people seeking assistance with their problems, and there

---

[29] Field notes, 26/3/06.
[30] Ibid.
[31] Field notes, 9/3/06, 26/3/06, 20/4/06. Bishop Muzorewa was part of the so-called 'Internal Settlement' with Ian Smith's Rhodesian Front during the late 1970s. The main nationalist armies of ZANLA and ZIPRA refused to join this 'peace' initiative and the war continued until late 1979. Muzorewa gathered his own security forces, known as 'auxiliaries', who were responsible for much violence and many atrocities during the late war years.
[32] Field notes, 26/3/20.
[33] Ibid.
[34] Field notes, 9/3/06.

Mai Melissa, the alterity of spirit and the incompleteness of death

was a visible upturn in her earnings from the deeply impoverished state she had been in before, although she continued to work her fields, and sell fruits and vegetables at the market at Nemanwa. The way in which Sekuru Shorty addressed different family members during visits that I attended reflects how different people were drawn into Mai Melissa's mediumship, even if this never entirely eliminated the muted scepticism some had about what was going on. And yet everybody was involved, for different reasons and in different ways, in this collective exercise, including myself as both adoptive-son and resident anthropologist, and long-time friend of the family. Like others, I was also given instructions by Sekuru Shorty, to bring beads and a horse tail fly-wisp for Mai Melissa to use in her work as a *n'anga*, which I did.

The family struggles that had manifest a few months earlier in the form of Peter's illness were clearly part of this story. Francesca later told me, with a hint of glee, that it must have 'burnt' Ambuya Magumbo to know that her dead, former husband was now possessing Mai Melissa, his daughter by a second wife.[35] But Mike's devastating illness, and the deaths and contested burials of so many others were also important context to these events, illustrating what I call the precarities that often precede possession. But, as with the case of the 'diesel *n'anga*', mediumship also brings its own problems. It was clear that her mediumship brought not only rewards but also demands upon Mai Melissa, and others around her. One day Mai Melissa visited the Rukasha household to offer help with caring for Mike. The potential dangers of her new mediumship was brought up in a conversation between her and Francesca.

> Mai Melissa started telling us how she had been approached by an old and apparently quite influential man in the council for a consultation with Sekuru Shorty (or *Baba* as she refers to him because the spirit is her father, not her grandfather). The spirit told him that his *musha* [homestead] was wide open and is at great risk from witchcraft and *ngozi*. Sekuru [Shorty] told him that he is supposed to pay a white goat, which is supposed to be kept by her at this house [i.e. at Peter and Francesca's house]. Amai [Francesca] warns Vatete [Mai Melissa] that what she is now getting into is quite serious and she herself could find herself becoming a victim to witchcraft. Vatete says she knows this but it is nothing to do with her because it is *basa rasekuru* [Sekuru's work], and adds that the spirit keeps telling her that 'I am a big *n'anga* and I want to do my work'.[36]

Mai Melissa's mediumship by Sekuru Shorty did however mark, for a moment, a remarkable and positive change in her life circumstances. But it did not last. Before I left Zimbabwe in July 2006, I visited her

---

[35] Field notes, 10/3/06.
[36] Field notes, 19/3/06.

several times and urged her to enlist with one of the new IO clinics being established across the country, in order to access ARV medicines.[37] She remained reluctant, and her response was on one occasion, shortly after Mike's funeral, sharp and telling, saying that Mike had died from those pills and she did not want them. Only 18 months later, Mai Melissa died in December 2007, just a few weeks after Ambuya Magumbo (with whom she had so many troubles) had herself succumbed to cancer.[38] Several others too died in the interim period, and afterwards, including Mai Kenny, Peter's other sister, and later Philip, his eldest son. When I next returned to the area in 2008, I was told that sometime after I had left in 2006 Mai Melissa had remarried, to an old man living in the Mutevedzi area, and she had soon fallen pregnant, despite what Sekuru Shorty had said. It was that pregnancy, Francesca later told me, that had caused her to get sick, and her health quickly deteriorated after the birth of her third child, a daughter. I asked Francesca whether Sekuru Shorty had continued to 'come out' during this period, and if he ever said anything about Mai Melissa's illness.

> Amai [Francesca] explains that before she died, Mai Melissa was still getting possessed by Sekuru but that he never said anything about her illness, all he had said was that it was Mai Melissa's fault that she had been unable to find another husband since Daniel Mutevedzi had died, and that she needed to find another husband to live with.[39]

After she died, young Munashe came to stay with Francesca and Peter for some time, before a *vatete* from the Mutevedzi family came to take him back to their homestead. It is not clear if the spirit of Sekuru Shorty, or of Sekuru Manico, has re-appeared through any other family members, such as Phillimon, as he once claimed he was seeking to do. Since Mai Melissa's death, Shorty has been quiet. It is not clear if all of Sekuru Shorty's predictions came to be, or if all of his instructions were ever followed. There has been no visit to find Shorty's younger brother Philip in Mozambique that I know of. Peter, however, maintains that when he is buried, he will be buried facing east, towards Mozambique where his father came from.

Towards the alterity of spirit

It would be fairly straight forward to interpret Mai Melissa's emergent possession by Sekuru Shorty as a story about long-enduring family and (to some extent structural) kinship conflicts over authority, such as was evident in the tensions between Francesca and Ambuya Magumbo, which follows a predictable pattern of relations between *varoora* and their

---

[37] Field notes, 14/5/06, 27/6/06.
[38] Field notes, 22–24/8/08.
[39] Ibid.

Mai Melissa, the alterity of spirit and the incompleteness of death

mothers-in-law, and between wife-giving and wife-receiving families. It also reflects the struggles that *vatorwa* [incomers] can face establishing belonging and entitlement to land in resettlement areas; and the difficulties that people of 'foreign' background (especially Malawian, Zambian or Mozambican) have endured over citizenship and belonging in Zimbabwe, particularly in the post-2000 period (Raftopoulos 2003, 2007; Dorman et al. 2007). The story could also be understood as the long fall out from a marital dispute between Mai Magumbo and her late husband Sekuru Shorty, and the problems these have caused her other children, and in turn, their children – and perhaps orphans in general – about clan identity and belonging; all set in the context of deepening political and economic crisis, and the profound social effects of the devastating mortality of the AIDS pandemic at its peak. Yet to do so *only* in such terms risks ignoring the active presence of the spirits of dead people in this long saga, and threatens to reduce it to a kind of social, cultural, political or even moral determinism.

The story of Shorty's death at the end of the war at the hands of 'thugs' associated with Bishop Muzorewa's 'auxiliaries', and his apparently hasty burial in a cave in Gutu, links Shorty's possession of Mai Melissa in 2006 to the stories of haunting *ngozi*, and the unsettled, restless dead of Zimbabwe's liberation and post-independence struggles, which the earlier chapters of this book have focused on. It locates the lives of the people involved in this story, in Zimbabwe's broader, contested and unfinished histories. So this is also a story of how mediumship is socially and historically situated; of how wider, unresolved pasts find presence in and can disrupt lives in the present in open-ended and demanding ways. Yet to uncritically assume – as mediums' own accounts might do as part of the ongoing work of reinforcing their authenticity – that the presence of the dead as demanding spirits was always already historically determined, does not do justice to the uncertainties and precarities that mediumship and spirit possession actually involves. Mai Melissa's story, and that of the role played by Sekuru Shorty and his father Manico from Mozambique, in the events that led up to her possession, is hardly a romantic epic in which a hidden or obscured past, or spirits therefrom, find presence and recognition, or even redemption, for their role in shaping the present. There is no happy ending, no final resolution. Mai Melissa's story is one fraught with disjunctures, tensions, incomplete beginnings and endings, and a great deal of suffering. Mai Melissa herself put it well one day when she told me about the difficulties she was facing as a result of her mediumship by her father, Shorty: *vanhu vakafa vanonetsa*, she confided in me – 'dead people are troublesome' – a sentiment I have often heard from other mediums.[40]

---

[40] Field notes, 24/6/06.

These fractures and disjunctures have not only to do with the contested social and political constitution of mediumship, and the precarities that both precede and result from it, but also exactly with what I call the alterity or excessivity of spirit. This is what Ranger, by his own admission, somewhat romanticised as the 'relative autonomy of spirit' (2010b). Even in Mai Melissa's story, although the problematic presence (however obscure) of Sekuru Shorty's spirit, and/or that of Manico his father, was recognised as far back as 1997, the spirits' intentions remained for the most part uncertain and unclear; demanding yet defying stability and clarity. Mediumship may have assisted Mai Melissa and given her a new status, but it did not prevent her own sickness and death, or anybody else's. This alterity of spirits points, I will conclude below, to the uncertain incompleteness of death itself, which throws up difficult existential or ontological questions about the relationship between material and immaterial existence through time, and yet leaves them unresolved.

In previous writings on spirit possession in Zimbabwe (2006a: 47–72), I have focused upon how mediums *both* narrate, perform and try to demonstrate the ambiguous entanglement of their agency with that of the spirits possessing them, and at other moments (particularly during rituals when they become possessed) must perform an effective denial of their agency in order to demonstrate the authenticity of their possession, and of their mediumship. In effect mediums establish their authenticity and legitimacy by playing with, and on, the 'edgy double agency of spirit/medium' (Steedly 1993: 14–15). Such arguments focus attention upon the efforts and techniques mediums deploy to substantiate their claims to be authentic mediums in relation to others around them, but what they do *not* do is explore to any great depth the relationships that mediums forge with their spirits.

In a recent paper focusing on Ndau mediums in eastern Zimbabwe, Perman has put forward another approach to exploring spirit possession in Zimbabwe, which, in line with recent so-called ontological turns in anthropology (Holbraad & Pedersen 2017; Fontein 2021), demands attention upon the 'brute truth and factuality of Ndau spirits for local practitioners', and to defy the difficulties of 'translating' this into the 'agnosticism' of anthropological language (Perman 2011: 62). In many ways I am sympathetic to this purpose. I have always sought less to represent or analyse a *worldview* in which spirits exist, and more to explore what such a *world* might be like (Fontein 2011: 719). In setting up his argument, Perman delivers a succinct and productive critique of older anthropological approaches (citing Lambek 2002b; Boddy 1989; Comaroff 1985) that have tended to read or analyse spirit possession in terms of its social 'functionality' – 'as history, as therapy, as resistance', in order 'to elucidate broader sociocultural processes, practices and truths' (Perman 2011: 71). Or they have explored spirit possession as either 'cultural text'

Mai Melissa, the alterity of spirit and the incompleteness of death

or as 'mimesis', both of which he correctly observes 'rely on analytical detachment from the lived experience at hand' and therefore 'only allow for discursive reality' (2011: 73). Interestingly, because anthropologists like Taussig (1993) and Stoller (1995) have explored how mimesis and imitation 'can eventually engender and shape indexical relations' between an imitating medium and the spirit that they can become, he has more sympathy for these approaches. But in the end, Perman insists he is more interested in the 'indexical connection between a medium and his or her spirit' and as 'mimesis relies more on iconicity than indexicality ... even if mimesis were to lead to the foundation of an indexical relationship, as suggested by Taussig and Stoller (Taussig 1993; Stoller 1995), it relies on iconicity for its salience' (Perman 2011: 86).

Perman's insistence upon the need to explore the presence of spirits in the lives of the Ndau mediums he studies is productive. Many of his observations match my own ethnographic experiences among mediums in southern Zimbabwe, and his approach offers a fruitful way to explore large amounts of material I have collected. In particularly his focus on the mutually constitutive, 'intersubjective habits ... of relating to others that define one's subjectivity and one's sense of self' (2011: 78) between mediums and spirits, is useful for reinterpreting, for example, Ambuya VaZarira's long narratives of how she became a medium, in a way in which the significance of her spirits VaZarira and VaMurinye is properly recognised, as she herself would emphasise (Fontein 2004). It may also help us understand the longue durée of Mai Melissa's emergent mediumship in 2006. A focus on 'intersubjective habits' and 'habitus', 'between the living and the dead' might also help us to understand how spirit possession can be both involuntary and a learned or practised art at the same time, as ethnographic accounts of spirit possession often insist. All in all I am, therefore, very sympathetic to Perman's call to explore the role of spirits in the lives of mediums, and in constituting their possession and mediumship. This is why in the analysis above I have tried to leave space in the precarious lives of the mediums I have been discussing, for the demands and actions of the spirits themselves.

But where my approach departs from Perman's argument is the comfortable certainty with which he characterises relationships between mediums, their spirits and others around them. This does not match the fraught and incomplete, contingent and uncertain context of spirit possession and mediumship with which I am familiar, like Mai Melissa's emergent possession by Sekuru Shorty in 2006, or the contestations that often surround high-profile cases, such as that of Rotina Mavhunga, Sophia Muchini, Ambuya Julianna or Ambuya VaZarira. The picture that Perman paints of spirits who are easily known to their mediums, and of medium/spirit relationships mutually forged and imbricated through 'intersubjective habits' by which 'the living possess their spirit just as their spirits possess them' (2011: 86) – marked by an all-encompassing sense of certainty and a lack of doubt – simply does not reflect the uncertainties and precarities of mediumship I have been describing.

I am therefore not convinced that mediums' relationships with their spirits necessarily conform to Perman's comfortable descriptions. I suspect these relationships are much more fraught and uncertain than his analysis suggests. Of course, there may be significant regional differences at play here. Ndau mediumship in Chipinge may be very different from what mediumship looks like in Masvingo, where my ethnographic fieldwork took place, although the account of Mai Melissa's mediumship above suggests that such localised emplacement of ritual practices to do with spirit possession does not reflect ethnographic realities. Her story involves spirits and mediums from across Zimbabwe (including an Ndau medium) and beyond, most prominently from Mozambique. I would go further to argue that the excessivity of spirits and the uncertain presence of the dead in peoples' lives across Zimbabwe and its politics – in whatever diversity of ways this is made sense of and however it is actualised across multiple co-existent regimes of meaning – defies the rigidly localised cultural emplacement that anthropologists of an earlier generation might once have been partial to. Indeed, the politics of the dead that this book has discussed in its various manifestations in post-2000 Zimbabwe, speaks to phenomena that are replicated in diverse ways, across different contexts and scales, and in forms that defy containment within specific, locally, geographically, ethnically, culturally, religiously or politically defined frameworks of meaning and action.

I am therefore struck that the 'inter-subjective' relations of spirits and mediums that Perman encountered, do not appear to be fraught with the uncertainties and doubts, or the heavy and demanding expectations and obligations that spirits can impose upon their mediums, which my own encounters revealed. Nor do they reflect the multiple uncertainties about possession, mediumship and the identity, presence and intentions of the spirits involved, which much of the wider ethnographic literature on spirit possession in Zimbabwe (particularly among Shona peoples) describes. Furthermore, it might be argued that Perman overstates the mutually constitutive nature of the relationship between spirits and mediums, and neglects the key role that others, with complex divergent agendas and interests, have in constituting possession and mediumship, often from the very beginning of any initiate's mediumship. What of the acolytes, assistants, family members, relatives, clansfolk and members of wider 'society' or the 'community' more generally, let alone politicians, who were so important in the stories of the diesel *n'anga*, Rotina Mavhunga, Sophia Muchini, and Mai Melissa? Mediumship is necessarily socially, politically and historically constituted, and for these reasons alone it is therefore already contested and contingent.

Mai Melissa, the alterity of spirit and the incompleteness of death

Indeed throughout a new medium's emerging mediumship he or she is remarkably dependent upon others: from the *n'anga* who may first diagnose a dead spirit wanting to 'come out' as the cause of an illness or a misfortune, to the drawn-out processes whereby a person becomes recognised as an authentic medium of authentic and recognised ancestors, to the reliance that every medium always has on others around them, to inform them of what their spirit said when they were possessed, if nothing else. Establishment as a recognised medium of a senior ancestral spirit can take years. There are many people involved. Even Mai Melissa's mediumship of her father, an inconsequential spirit beyond immediate family and kinship circles, took years to be established. While this did involve her embodying, in relationship with the spirit, shared habits, techniques, skills and bodily practices of mediumship, it was nevertheless also a profoundly socially, politically, morally and historically constituted; not just an 'inter-subjective' process with her spirit. For these reasons alone, before we even consider the alterity of spirit and the profound uncertainties this engenders, mediumship is already contested, contingent and emergent.

In fairness, Perman does allow some space for the other 'people (and spirits)' who 'become mutually central to one another's inter-subjective habits and thus constitutive of each other's senses of self'. Yet for him, this is how 'community is created and confirmed' (2011: 85), not how it might be contested, challenged or left fractured and unresolved (Niehaus 2013b: 210–15). He does stress that the 'inter-subjective' relations of peoples and spirits implies that this constitution of the social is always emergent and becoming, yet the comfortable, easy image presented does not reflect the politically fraught imbrications and uncertainties of mediumship that I have been discussing, the precarities that often precede and can derive from it, or the difficulties mediums can face in their relationships with the spirits that possess them. Perman does acknowledge that 'one's relationship with one's spirit is personal, multifaceted and complicated', but 'rarely overwhelming' (2011: 81). Yet an example he cites of a man blamed and imprisoned for a murder that his spirit committed, suggests otherwise. More importantly, perhaps, he emphasises the 'lack of doubt on the part of practitioners that possession was real' and yet states 'that the only doubt was ever whether any particular instance was "faked"' (2011: 87). The examples of the diesel *n'anga*, Mai Melissa, and others discussed above and in the previous chapter, suggest that any question about the authenticity of a particular possession event is not so straightforwardly separated from the other uncertainties, doubts, social fractures, tensions and disjunctures that surround mediumship.

As Mary Steedly has put it in relation to spirit possession in Sumatra:

> Stories of spirit encounters raise with particular urgency questions of belief, agency, and authenticity – questions that lie at the heart of

ethnographic experience and its representation. What to believe? Do others believe? Do I? Is this experience (of mine, of others) real? How to evaluate the evidence of unseen experience, or of experience shared yet incomprehensible? This is not simply a matter of Western scientific rationality at its epistemic limits; Karo too are troubled, for reasons of their own, by the edgy double agency of spirit/medium. (1993: 14–15)

Likewise, in Zimbabwe, the questions of belief, agency and authenticity that 'spirit encounters' provoke do not just confront 'outside' ethnographers but all those participating, and including mediums themselves. Of course, in their own narratives mediums are likely to emphasise the certainty of their relationship with the spirits that possess them (Perman 2011: 87); such accounts are part of the process by which mediumship is constituted and authenticated. But longer biographies of the precarious lives of spirit mediums – like Mai Melissa's emergent possession which I was able to witness over nearly a decade – suggests mediums' relationships with their spirits can often be anything other than certain and assured.

Mediumship is therefore far more precarious than is often assumed and, for a variety of reasons, this is so even if the argument is well taken that 'the signs of a spirit in possession … are less imitative or mimetic of a social imagined spirit than they are indicative of spiritual presence' (Perman 2011: 87). Part of this precariousness is, I suggest, exactly due this spiritual presence and its alterity: the otherness of the spiritual and the immaterial, and of the past, which is both profoundly present yet exists or extends beyond the here and now, demanding but defying efforts of stabilisation, containment and determination; and which remains, in the end, unknowable and uncertain for everyone concerned. This is an ontological problem beyond questions of epistemic limits or difference, and therefore it applies across loyalties to, or histories of, particular cultural or political regimes of stabilisation and sense making, be they particular church denominations or cult allegiances, or particular regional ancestral practices. 'Spirit encounters', as Steedly puts it, 'provoke a way of reading narrative experience against the grain of credibility; as uncertain, duplicitous, always open to revision, bottomless' (1993: 14–15). This is what makes mediumship and spirit possession so riddled with uncertainties, doubt and fraught with contestation, even as this same quality can make the legitimacy that mediums and spirit possession promise – which derives from the 'relative autonomy' (Ranger 2010b) and sovereignty of the ancestors and the divine – so appealing.

Conclusions

The smooth and unproblematic mutual constitution of mediums, their spirits and society that Perman's analysis implies is reminiscent of the romanticism with which some scholars of materiality have envisaged

Mai Melissa, the alterity of spirit and the incompleteness of death

the dialectic of 'subjects making objects making subjects', through which people and things are always emergent, becoming in their mutual imbrication (Miller 2005: 38). As discussed in earlier chapters, other scholars question this (Pinney 2005), arguing that such processes of becoming, constitution and stabilisation are necessarily rife with fractures, disjunctures and incompleteness (Nyamnjoh 2017a; 2017b), which derive ultimately, I have argued, from the excessive potentiality of substances to exceed their stabilisation into recognisable objects and subjects. Pinney calls this the 'alterity (or torque) of materiality' (2005: 270).

Chapter 3 deployed these arguments about the excessivity of materials and stuff to think about human remains (particularly fraught substances exactly because of their uneasy subject/objecthood) and the way that their profound uncertainties can be politically productive. The argument presented here about the precarious, uncertain and often contested nature of possession and mediumship suggests that there is a comparable argument to be made about the alterity of spirit, and the problematic presence of the immaterial remnants of past lives, which exceed or defy, and yet demand, extraordinary efforts to determine, contain or stabilise into recognisable ancestral spirits and authenticated spirit mediums. Just as the (always incomplete) stabilisation and identification of human remains in contexts like the 2011 Chibondo exhumations, or after Solomon Mujuru's dramatic demise, often provoke highly specialised material *and* immaterial processes of determination, containment and ordering (from forensic archaeology and court-led public inquests to divination and possession, and much in between) so, too, processes of authenticating mediumship, spirit possession and the presence of a known, identifiable spirit, can involve very complex, specialised material and immaterial processes, performances and re-forged narratives. In this light, it is no coincidence that among Shona people in southern Zimbabwe, ancestral spirits are often described ambiguously as both wind (*mhepo*) and as soil (*ivhu*); and that, for mediums, their spirits are often described as both intimate to them, simultaneously in and of them, and key to the constitution of self and society, yet they also exist separate to, outside of and beyond them, and are ultimately unknowable. All of this makes spirit possession inherently uncertain, contingent and precarious.

In the end, both the excessivity and alterity of human materials and of spirits as the immaterial remains of past lives, intruding awkwardly, demandingly and problematically into the present, point to the uncertain incompleteness of death itself, as a (if not *the*) key moment when the material and immaterial aspects of life and existence, and the relationships between them, are wrought open, exposed and never fully resolved. In Mai Melissa's story, the prevalence of problematic deaths and contested burials in 2005–06 – that is unsatisfactory resolutions to death – was surely significant in her emergent mediumship, as was Sekuru Shorty's own difficult death long before, not to mention other previous and maybe subsequent deaths. As Mai Melissa herself put it, it was Mai Candid's incorrect burial which 'caused all the *vadzimu* ... in Mozambique to get up and become angry'.[41]

If funeral processes have been conventionally understood in (classic/Durkheimian) anthropology as part of a remaking of society after the rupture that death imposes (Hertz 1960; Huntington & Metcalf 1991), then perhaps it is the excessivity and alterity of both the material and the immaterial aspects of human lives which death reveals (but struggles to resolve) through this rupture, which makes death uncertain, incomplete and always potentially unfinished. Funerals (like exhumations and reburials or public inquests) may often look like, promise or purport to offer final resolution, but the alterity of both material and immaterial human remains, and their uneasy imbrication, revealed by the rupture of death, suggests they rarely entirely succeed. It is perhaps these excessive material and immaterial aspects of the uncertain, unfinished nature of death which gives the politics of the dead its salience and potency in Zimbabwe, and maybe elsewhere too; and possibly also (if we dare to be so bold) even everywhere.

---

[41] Field notes, 5/11/05.

7

After Mugabe

In this chapter I consider more recent events in Zimbabwe, and what they suggest about its politics of the dead, particularly in the wake of President Mugabe's two deaths: first his political death[1] after the so-called 'Military Assisted Transition' (MAT)[2] removed him from office in November 2017 (Tendi 2020b; Nyarota 2018; Ndlovu 2019; Moore 2018, forthcoming A), and then his subsequent physical death and burial in September 2019. My purpose is to consider how the multi-faceted politics of the dead discussed in this book has continued or been transformed by events in the late 2010s. It is hard to refute that many aspects of Zimbabwe's politics of the dead are closely linked to Mugabe's long dominance of the country's political sphere, even if much of the critical cultural, political and historical context through which it gained its particular form and traction in the post-2000 period have both a longer durée within Zimbabwe, and reflect phenomena of wider contemporary and historical salience across the region. There are features of Zimbabwe's politics of the dead that could be ascribed to 'Mugabeism' (Ndlovu-Gatsheni 2015), such as the National Heroes commemorative complex, the rise of patriotic history (Ranger 2004a), and the violent atrocities of the 1980s and again in the 2000s, and the increasingly 'noisy silence' imposed upon the terrible legacies of the *gukurahundi*. But other aspects may be less attributable to Robert Mugabe per se. For example, there is evidence that Mugabe was never a keen supporter of exhumations, whether related to the *gukurahundi* killings – where there were obvious reasons for his reticence – or to Rhodesian war atrocities (or indeed to Cecil Rhodes's dubious grave in the Matopos), where such actions had obvious political traction. If for Mugabe, as Chipunza (Chief Curator, NMMZ) explained, 'the best thing

---

[1] I am grateful to David Moore for pointing out that, by the time of his physical death in September 2019, Mugabe had already been politically dead for almost two years, since the 'coup' of late 2017.
[2] This, along with 'Operation Restore Legacy', was part of the official nomenclature for Mugabe's removal from office in November 2017 (Field notes March 2020), although it has also been referred to as a 'soft' or 'smart' coup, or simply the 'coup'.

is let the dead lie where they are buried',[3] then the increasing salience of exhumations in Zimbabwe suggest they are part of a wider phenomena not dependent on Mugabe's particular style of politics. Moreover, the approach developed here, looking at how the excessive uncertainties of bones, leaky bodies, spirits and rumours can animate, shape and give traction to particular kinds of politics, challenges the usefulness of looking for single or individual sources of complex, emergent cultural-political phenomena like Zimbabwe's politics of the dead.

Nevertheless, Mugabe's first death, the 'soft coup' or 'MAT' of 2017, and the emergence of Mnangagwa's regime thereafter, sometimes referred to as the 'new dispensation' or even the 'second republic', and events that followed, allow us to consider to what extent the form that Zimbabwe's politics of the dead took in the 2000s was partly attributable to Mugabe's rule, and what has continued or changed since. While there have been some important changes since 2017, there have also been some obvious continuities, or even expansions, upon the politics of the dead discussed in this book. In particular, as I discuss below, it was Mugabe's second death and the controversies surrounding his burial, that illustrated perfectly the continuing salience of the uncertain corporeal and immaterial dimensions of Zimbabwe's politics of the dead, and the unfinished, incompleteness of death it turns on.

The events that led up to and immediately followed the 'soft coup' of November 2017, when Robert Mugabe was forced to resign and Emmerson Mnangagwa, with his 'Lacoste' faction of supporters, backed by the military under Constantino Chiwenga,[4] was able to secure his succession to the leadership of ZANU PF and the government, have already been discussed in detail elsewhere (Moore 2018, forthcoming A, forthcoming B; Tendi 2020b; Ndlovu 2019; Rogers 2019; Nyarota 2018),[5] and will not be repeated here. It suffices to say that, although the way it

---

[3] Interview with Chipunza, 5/3/20.
[4] In 2016, Constantine Chiwenga changed his name to Constantino Guveya Dominic Nyikadzino Chiwenga ('Gen Chiwenga changes name' *Herald* 30/7/16), apparently in accordance with the death-bed wishes of his late grandfather. I am grateful to an anonymous reviewer for highlighting an article in the *Sunday Mail* ('General Chiwenga and the Nyikadzino Prophecy' 26/11/17) which details his reasoning. The date of its publication suggests it may have been part of Chiwenga's attempts to solidify his own nationalist credentials and to legitimise the 'coup' against 'the criminals who had surrounded Cde Mugabe'.
[5] Also: 'Zimbabwe minus Mugabe: Two books on his fall and Mnangagwa's rise' *The Conversation* 17/12/18, https://theconversation.com/zimbabwe-minus-mugabe-two-books-on-his-fall-and-mnangagwas-rise-107097, accessed 2/7/20; 'Contemplating Zimbabwe's recent "military interventions" and the repercussions for the country's future' – Fellows' seminar by David Moore 11/3/19, https://stias.ac.za/2019/03/contemplating-zimbabwes-recent-military-interventions-and-the-repercussions-for-the-countrys-future, accessed 2/7/20.

transpired seemed to catch many people off guard, it clearly came after a long period of unrest within the ruling party and must have been in the planning for some months. The weeks of increasingly vitriolic abuse before the 'coup', targeted against the then Vice-President by Grace Mugabe, which forced Mnangagwa into hiding and out of the country, were deeply reminiscent of the public denigration that Joice Mujuru had received in the weeks before her ouster from the same position three years before.[6] Mnangagwa and his allies must have seen the writing on the wall. Interviews in Masvingo in March 2020 revealed that many people were bussed to Harare from the provinces to take part in street protests during the 'coup',[7] suggesting the massive popular outpouring of anger against Mugabe was not quite as spontaneous as many suggested at the time. However quick the mobilisation of rural supporters and transport was, it must have taken some preparation.[8]

Another notable feature of the 'coup' – the form of which many observers now recognise as commensurate with an older pattern of how ZANU PF deals with internal factionalism and contested leadership and succession issues (Moore forthcoming A) – was the determination of its protagonists to frame the 'transition' as a defence of ZANU PF's 'chimurenga politics' (Chigumadzi 2018), for which Mugabe himself had stood and of which he was a figurehead. It was not for no reason that the 'smart coup' (as some refer to it) was given the designation 'Operation Restore Legacy' (Mudau & Dylan 2018: 179; Tendi 2020b). The coup leaders' targets were the 'Generation 40' or 'G40' sycophants surrounding the ailing president, led by his unpopular second wife Grace, who were presented as undermining the party's liberation credentials. The MAT was therefore carefully framed as a defence of Mugabe's own, and ZANU PF's liberation legacy, both because its leaders needed the political support of the region from SADC and the African Union (AU), but also because the coup leaders were themselves invested in this kind of politics, which they had played a big part in constituting over previous decades.

This already signalled that despite efforts to mark the 'new dispensation' as different, not much would change in the way the ruling party would do its politics. As well as the tacky material culture of election politicking – the

---

[6] See '"Angry" Grace says she wants Mugabe's VP Mnangagwa "gone before extraordinary congress"' *News24.com* 6/11/17, accessed 2/7/20; 'WATCH: Four times Grace Mugabe slammed Mnangagwa in scathing speeches' *The Citizen* 15/11/17, accessed 2/7/20. For examples of her attacks on Joice Mujuru three years earlier see: 'Mugabe's wife threatens Zimbabwe's vice-president in Zanu-PF faction fight' *Guardian* 17/10/14; 'Grace Mugabe claims Joice Mujuru plans to kill her "Gaddafi-style"' *Telegraph* (UK) 19/11/14; 'No grace in pursuing Mujuru' *Daily News* 21/11/14.

[7] Field notes, March 2020.

[8] This rural mobilisation, David Moore suggests, was mainly the work of war veterans aligned with the 'coup' leaders (pers. com. 5/7/20).

garish paraphernalia and regalia of t-shirts, hats, scarfs and suits printed with party logos and the new president's face, which have become prevalent across the region – there was much about the way that Mnangagwa (and Chiwenga)[9] tried to embellish his historical role during the liberation struggle[10] that clearly fits a 'Mugabe-esque' political style.

The repetitive accounts of the near-fatal poisoning he allegedly suffered during a ZANU PF youth rally in August 2017,[11] just months before the coup, may reflect a genuine fear of assassination on his part,[12] but they also fit well with the languages of victimhood, suffering and entitlement, as well as of liberation heroism, that increasingly marked ZANU PF's 'patriotic history' during the 2000s. Likewise, the way Mnangagwa narrated the story of his 'escape' from Zimbabwe, in fear of his life, across the border into Mozambique,[13] during the tumultuous weeks before the coup, bore more than a little resemblance to the much lauded story of how Mugabe himself, with Edgar Tekere, had escaped Rhodesia into Mozambique in 1975.[14] Similarly, the stories that circulated after the still-unresolved explosion at a ZANU PF election rally in Bulawayo before the July 2018 elections, which killed two people and injured 49 others, including both the vice-presidents, point to the continuing political productivity and duplicity of the uncertainty of rumours, akin to what has long surrounded 'political accidents' in Zimbabwe.[15] While some rumours about the 2018 'grenade

---

[9] See footnote 4.

[10] 'How ED helped ANC comrades during Apartheid' *Herald* 21/9/19; 'Zimbabwe: State House is far to arrive at – Mnangagwa' *Herald* 1/9/18. Even as Vice-President, Mnangagwa was often accused of embellishing his war past, see 'Mnangagwa cannot rewrite war history' *Daily News* 9/10/15; 'VP Mnangagwa's war credentials: The facts' *Patriot* 1/10/15.

[11] 'Zimbabwe's Emmerson Mnangagwa criticised over poison claim' *BBC news* 4/10/17; 'Mystery surrounds Mnangagwa poisoning' *Zimbabwe Independent* 18/8/17; 'Grace Mugabe denies plotting to poison rival for Zimbabwe presidency' *Guardian* 6/10/17; 'Mnangagwa poisoning; new details emerge' *Bulawayo News 24* 24/6/19.

[12] 'Paranoid Zimbabwe president Emmerson Mnangagwa haunted by fears of poisoning' *Telegraph* (UK) 7/9/19.

[13] 'Mnangagwa reveals 30km walk while escaping Mugabe's "hunting dogs"' *News24.com* 22/12/17, accessed 19/6/20; 'Army role in ED escape recounted' *Herald* 16/7/18; 'Mnangagwa tells of his greatest escape from Grace Mugabe through land mines in Mozambique' *Club of Mozambique* 15/1/18; 'Zimbabwe: Chiwenga exposes Mnangagwa's "great escape" yarn' *Newzimbabwe.com* 18/7/18, accessed 19/6/20; 'Ousted Zimbabwe vice president flees into exile, claiming assassination attempts against him' *Los Angeles Times* 8/11/17; 'Zimbabwe president-designate Emmerson Mnangagwa reveals "poisoning"' *SkyNews* 23/11/17.

[14] '40 years on: Retracing President Mugabe's journey into Mozambique' *Herald* 4/4/15.

[15] 'Zimbabwe Bulawayo blast: Two die after attack on Mnangagwa' *BBC news* 25/6/18.

After Mugabe

attack' pointed to tensions between military and police investigators in the aftermath of the attack, others, including Jonathan Moyo (now 'tweeting' from exile), suggested that the attack 'smacks of an inside job', implicating allegedly deepening tensions between Mnangagwa and his powerful Vice-President Chiwenga.[16] Mnangagwa himself quickly pointed to the G40 faction led by Grace Mugabe, adding that 'it was not my time' and anyway 'he'd had numerous attempts on his life in the past' and 'was used to them by now'.[17] It has been suggested that there is something particularly paranoid and insecure about the 'new dispensation'; perhaps for good reason. Yet we should not lose sight of the political productivity of such rumours and of the uncertainties they reflect and provoke. As with the duplicitous uncertainties surrounding Solomon Mujuru's 2011 demise, despite long investigations and a public inquest, we should look to the political utility and advantages that might derive from emphasising the insecurities of the new regime.

Given the centrality and length of time that the 'coup' plotters had operated within Mugabe's regime – and their deep complicity with some of its worst atrocities, and its 'chimurenga politics' – there were always likely to be some marked continuities in the new government's political style. For this reason too, however, they have been under pressure to demonstrate their difference from the previous regime. Attempts to mark the new government as new and different have been apparent in Mnangagwa's emphasis on re-engaging the international community to seek economic support for the state's empty coffers, and in his repeated claims that Zimbabwe would now be 'open for business'.[18] It was also manifest in Mnangagwa's lofty promises to bring peace and reconciliation across Zimbabwe's political divides,[19] as well as in the immediate marginalisation (in favour of the military and military intelligence) of the police and the CIO, both of which had long been implicated in ruling party violence and corruption, were deeply unpopular and seen as aligned with the now exiled G-40 faction.

---

[16] '"ED rally bombing an inside job"–Jonso hints at internal power struggle' *iHarare.com* 26/6/18, accessed 2/7/20; 'Zimbabwe police: Grenade attack at Zanu PF rally an attempt to assassinate Mnangagwa' *voanews.com* 3/7/18, accessed 19/6/20.

[17] 'Mnangagwa says "it is not my time" after escaping blast at rally' *Reuters* 23/6/18; 'Zimbabwe rules out state of emergency after Bulawayo blast' *Africanews.com* 24/6/18, accessed 25/6/18.

[18] 'Zimbabwe is "open for business," new president Emmerson Mnangagwa tells Davos' *CNBC.com* 24/1/18, accessed 19/6/20; 'Zimbabwe: Mnangagwa Takes "Zim Open for Business" Mantra to Australia' *263Chat* 3/6/19, https://263chat.com/49468-2, accessed 2/7/20; '"Zim is open for business" mantra now rings hollow' *Zimbabwe Independent* 28/2/20.

[19] 'Mnangagwa promises a "new democracy" in Zimbabwe' *Euronews* 22/11/17; 'Zimbabwe's Mnangagwa promises jobs in "new democracy"' *BBC news* 22/11/17.

Writing now, two and half years after the 'transition', it has become unavoidably apparent that in many respects very little has changed. Repeated bouts of state violence and killings; new political abductions and disappearances; continuing high-level corruption; as well as, once again, deepening economic crisis; have all undermined any unlikely goodwill Mnangagwa's government managed to garner internationally, regionally, and among local civic organisations, in the early months of the 'new dispensation'.[20] The violence that marred the aftermath of the July 2018 elections, when soldiers deployed onto Harare's streets to quell an opposition protest killed six people, gave clear indication that the ruling party had not relinquished its dependence on violence and coercion.[21] The confusion that followed about who exactly had ordered the troops onto the streets served only to aggravate rumours of internal dissent within the new regime, again fostering the kind of productive uncertainties which have long been core to how the ruling party does its politics. The widespread protests and violent state responses that followed fuel hikes announced a few months later, in January 2019,[22] caused more deaths but also raised reports of systematic sexual violence and rapes,[23] which recalled previous political violence dating back to

---

[20] 'How Mnangagwa squandered his goodwill' *NewZWire* 2/7/18; '"New Zimbabwe" looks an awful lot like the old one' *The Rand Blog* 11/3/20, www.rand.org/blog/2020/03/new-zimbabwe-looks-an-awful-lot-like-the-old-one.html, accessed 2/7/20; 'A looter continua: For how long can Emmerson Mnangagwa and his regime cling to power?' *Daily Maverick* 11/6/20; 'NCUBE: Mnangagwa squandered global goodwill over Mugabe ouster' *Newzimbabwe.com* 11/1/19; 'Zimbabwe's Mnangagwa govt engulfed in corruption scandals' *Anti-Corruption Digest* 8/6/20.

[21] 'Zimbabwe: At least 6 dead in post-election violence' Human Rights Watch 3/8/18; 'Zimbabwe election: Troops fire on MDC Alliance supporters' *BBC news* 1/8/18; 'Zimbabwe election unrest turns deadly as army opens fire on protesters' *Guardian* 1/8/18; Zimbabwe Human Rights NGO Forum, '2018 Post election violence monitoring report: 01–09 August 2018' 15/8/18, www.hrforumzim.org/publications/reports-on-political-violence/2018-post-election-violence-monitoring-report-01-09-august-2018, accessed 2/7/20.

[22] 'The Latest: Zimbabwe troops assaulting people in capital' *Associated Press* 22/1/19; Solidarity Peace Trust, 'Resurgent authoritarianism: The politics of the January 2019 violence in Zimbabwe', 20/2/19; also: Zimbabwe Human Rights NGO Forum, 'On the days of darkness – An updated report on the human rights violations committed between 14 January, 2019 to 5 February, 2019' 6/2/19, www.hrforumzim.org/press-releases/daysofdarkness2, accessed 6/9/21.

[23] 'Zimbabwe's violent crackdown continues amid reports of rape' *aljazeera.com* 25/1/19; 'Zim army responsible for murders, rapes – report' *Mail & Guardian* 30/1/19; 'Exclusive: Zimbabwe soldier says he committed rape and broke legs in government-sanctioned crackdown' *Telegraph* (UK) 25/1/19; 'WATCH: Zimbabwe's violent crackdown continues with reports of rapes' *News24.com* 25/1/19, accessed 19/6/20.

the *gukurahundi*, the Border Gezi youth militia camps of the early 2000s, and 2008 election violence. The complete shutdown of the internet that accompanied the violence of early 2019,[24] suggested the ruling party had learnt its lessons from 2008, when hundreds of images of brutalised and murdered opposition supporters were circulated internationally through social media, and arguably played an important role in forcing Mugabe to the negotiating table, leading to five years of GNU government with the MDC (Raftopoulos 2013).

The growing numbers of disappearances and abductions, both in the context of a doctor's strike in the second half of 2019, and later with the abduction and sexual torture of three female MDC officials in April 2020, similarly index deep continuities in ruling party methods.[25] If anything was unusual about these horrific events it was the considerable, repeated efforts by the state-dominated press to suggest that these rising abductions were untrue, 'fake news' or instigated by opposition parties in order to discredit the new government.[26] Such assertions and denials were hardly taken seriously by many people,[27] but again perhaps that was not the point, given how the political productivities of uncertainty have long been a feature of the ruling party's stylistics of power.

Therefore, if there has been something new or unique about Mnangagwa's politics, it has been in its efforts to present itself both as the obvious guardian of Mugabe and ZANU PF's liberation legacies and, at the same time, as moderate and reforming, keen to draw a visible line underneath the violence, exclusions and economic deprivations of the past.[28] The new

[24] 'Zimbabwe imposes internet shutdown amid crackdown on protests' *aljazeera.com* 18/1/19; 'Zimbabwe orders a three-day, country-wide internet shutdown' *accessnow* 15/1/19, www.accessnow.org/zimbabwe-orders-a-three-day-country-wide-internet-shutdown; both accessed 2/7/20.

[25] 'Of missing people, forced disappearances' *Newsday* 14/9/19; 'Culture of abductions must fall' *Newsday* 17/9/19; 'Joint statement on the escalating human rights violations in Zimbabwe' *Zimbabwean* 19/9/19; 'Lawyers bemoan dearth of human rights' *Newsday* 17/9/19; 'State-sanctioned murders and abductions: The facts *Zimbabwean* 20/9/19; 'Zimbabwean MDC activists "abducted and sexually assaulted"' *Guardian* 17/5/20; 'MDC-Alliance abductions unsettle top police officers' *Zimbabwe Independent* 22/5/20; 'Brutal attacks on women in Zimbabwe evoke memories of Gukurahundi tactics' *Daily Maverick* 21/5/20.

[26] '"Abductions" wave worries Zanu-PF youths' *Herald* 26/9/19; 'Govt speaks on abduction reports' *Herald* 9/10/19; 'Politburo, Youths League slam abductions' *Herald* 19/9/19; 'Zimbabwe accuses MDC activists of made up state torture claims' *Guardian* 4/6/20; 'Mangwana drags G40 into MDC activist abduction storm' *Newzimbabwe.com* 29/5/20.

[27] Although, surprisingly, some journalists and 'NGO-types' apparently did (David Moore, pers. com. 5/7/20).

[28] One could argue that Mugabe made a similarly duplicitous move after the 'Vashandi' rebellions of the mid-1970s, when he imprisoned ZIPA's 'Marxist' leaders, such as Wilfred Mhanda, and appealed to international liberal

dispensation's sense of insecurity in the face of possible, and repeatedly rumoured, subsequent coups from the military or any of the ruling party's marginalised wings,[29] its inability to achieve the kind of international fiscal support it was seeking, and its increasing recourse to violence and intimidation, all suggest it has failed to achieve this delicate balance.

An early moment when the 'new dispensation' sought to mark its difference to the previous regime came with the death (of cancer) of the opposition leader Morgan Tsvangirai in February 2018, only a few months after the coup.[30] In so doing, however, it also showed its continued imbrication in the politics of the dead that this book has described. At the front of political opposition against Mugabe and ZANU PF for nearly two decades, Tsvangirai had repeatedly suffered violent arrests, assassination attempts, assaults and debilitating charges of treason. His wife Susan was killed in a road accident in 2009 that many suspected was a 'political accident' of the type that had killed so many other Mugabe opponents in previous decades. Although Tsvangirai was Prime Minister during the flawed GNU years (2009–13), becoming implicated in the petty corruption and internal violence that marred MDC factions during that period, ZANU PF-aligned military leaders had repeatedly made it clear that they would not abide by a Tsvangirai presidency.[31] It was therefore to some surprise that Mnangagwa magnanimously offered to assist the Tsvangirai family with funeral arrangements and costs after his death, although he was not declared a national hero.[32] According to the state-owned *Herald*, Mnangagwa said 'Mr Tsvangirai remained a national figure who would

---

democrats such as the American congressman Stephen Solarz, while also telling his comrades to educate themselves in Marxist-Leninist-Mao thought (Moore 2011, 2014).

[29] 'Zimbabwe denies rumours of "imminent military coup"' *CGTN.com* 8/3/20, accessed 2/7/20; 'Another Zimbabwe army coup? Rumours swirl over Mnangagwa's future' *South African* 8/3/20. Mnangagwa accused G40 of the 2018 grenade attack, and there have been suggestions from ruling party members that they were also responsible for recent abductions, to discredit the government. Reports also emerged that G40 members funded the MDC Alliance's 2018 election campaign ('Jonathan Moyo confirms g40 members sponsored Chamisa's 2018 election' *Newzimbabwe.com* 13/2/20, accessed 19/6/20).

[30] 'Morgan Tsvangirai, Zimbabwe opposition leader, dies aged 65' *Guardian* 14/2/18.

[31] 'Mugabe vows MDC will "never rule Zimbabwe"' *Financial Times* 15/6/08; 'Zimbabwe Army chief calls Prime Minister Tsvangirai a security threat' *VOAZimbabwe.com* 23/6/11, accessed 19/6/20;' 'Army general, Nyikayaramba vows not to salute Tsvangirai' *Zimbabwean* 29/5/11; 'We will not let Mugabe be beaten, police and army chiefs warn' *Guardian* 15/3/08; 'Army deals blow to Mugabe rival' *BBC news* 9/1/02;

[32] 'Zimbabwe's new president visits ailing opposition chief' *New Vision* (Uganda) 6/1/18; 'President Mnangagwa mourns Tsvangirai' *Herald* 15/2/18; 'President Mnangagwa, the world mourns Tsvangirai' *nampapr.com* accessed 2/7/20;

be remembered for his strong fight for free and fair elections'.[33] A year later the government again assisted by financing a memorial service for Morgan Tsvangirai held in Buhera.[34] Despite opposition from more sceptical MDC members, Tsvangirai's relatives made their gratitude for the new government's assistance publicly known.[35]

Not long after the memorial service in 2019 Mnangagwa had another opportunity to demonstrate his regime's new tolerant overtures towards the political opposition, when Tsvangirai's daughter Vimbai, herself MP for Glen View South and secretary general of the MDC Alliance's Women's Assembly, died of her injuries after a car accident which also killed two other MDC members, and an army colonel travelling in the other vehicle. Suggestions were later made by Kudzai Mutisi (a lecturer and political analyst) that Nelson Chamisa, leader of the MDC Alliance, had been involved, because 'Chamisa doesn't want any remnant of Tsvangirai in the MDC'.[36] Others laid blame on the military, because army personnel had been driving the other car. All this suggested that Vimbai's death too, could become a 'political accident' of the type that may have killed her mother in 2009. For their part Mnangagwa and his wife, the new first lady, again took the opportunity to publicly demonstrate the new dispensation's commitment to tolerant and inclusive politics by announcing their commiserations for the Tsvangirai family.[37] Later, heckling broke out at Vimbai's funeral and burial when ZANU PF's Speaker of the National Assembly, Jacob Mudenda, conveyed the condolences of Parliament to Vimbai's relatives, and when Thokozani Khupe, leader of the other MDC-T faction, was acknowledged by the master of ceremonies.[38]

Although Mnangagwa's superficial overtures towards the Tsvangirai family might have appeared to demonstrate the new regime's fresh approach to multi-party politics, in fact such manoeuvres fitted well within the established pattern discussed in Chapter 4 in relation to Zimbabwe's 'political accidents'; particularly the ruling party's habit to celebrate, memorialise, contain and control in death those whom they had denigrated and violently opposed in life. The real proof in the pudding

---

'No national hero status for Morgan Tsvangirai – Mnangagwa' *African News Agency* 15/2/18.

[33] 'President Mnangagwa mourns Tsvangirai' *Herald* 15/2/18.
[34] 'EDITORIAL COMMENT: President Mnangagwa's support of Tsvangirai family laudable' *Bulawayo Chronicle* 6/5/19.
[35] 'Tsvangirai family thanks ED' *Sunday Mail* 22/4/18; LATEST: 'Tsvangirai family salutes ED' *Herald* 6/6/19.
[36] '"Chamisa's MDC plotted the death of Vimbai Tsvangirai-Java" – Mutisi' *ZWNews* 11/6/19.
[37] 'Zimbabwe: President mourns Tsvangirai daughter Vimbai' *Herald* 11/6/19; 'First Lady mourns Tsvangirai's daughter' *Herald* 13/6/19.
[38] 'Mudenda, Khupe heckled at Vimbai Tsvangirai funeral' *Newzimbabwe.com* 13/6/19, accessed 19/6/20.

came later in 2019 when an announcement was made about various roads to be renamed in honour of the new president and other dignitaries. This was the second renaming of infrastructure to occur since Mnangagwa took office, the first taking place only a few weeks after the coup, when the King George VI Barracks in Harare were renamed after Josiah Magama Tongogara, in what looked like an obvious early attempt by the new regime to indicate their continued adherence to ZANU PF's 'chimurenga politics'.[39] In 2019, apart from ten streets to be named after himself, other names honoured in this way included Patrice Lumumba, Oliver Tambo, Jomo Kenyatta, Abdel Gamal Nasser, Leonid Brezhnev, Fidel Castro and Mao Zedong, giving a good indication of Mnangagwa's sense of his own significance. Solomon Mujuru, John Nkomo, Joseph Msika, Julia Zvobgo, Josiah Tungamirai, and the veteran journalist Willie Musarurwa were also honoured, and the former Alan Wilson road became Mgagao Camp Road, after the famous guerrilla camp in Tanzania.[40] Except in Kwekwe,[41] Robert Mugabe's name adorning many roads (and since 2017, just before the coup, the airport) was not removed anywhere, although Harare's Central hospital was renamed after his first, still much respected wife, Sally Mugabe. Many interpreted this as a snub to Mugabe's second wife, Grace, who had so publicly vilified Mnangagwa in the weeks preceding the coup and, as we shall see, had again defied him after Mugabe's death a few months earlier.

The renamings in November 2019 caused some disquiet, with many commentators pointing out that the economic woes facing Zimbabwe were surely a higher priority for the government.[42] More to point, however, despite the much lauded overtures Mnangagwa had made after his death, Morgan Tsvangirai was noticeably absent from the list. Whatever use could and was made of Tsvangirai's death by the new regime, this did not entitle him to a place in ZANU PF's tightly controlled commemorative complex, either as National Hero or with a road renamed to memorialise him.[43] Indeed the duplicitous political use of Tsvangirai's death by Mnangagwa might have come straight out of the Mugabe rule book of political chicanery. The grim scenes that marred

---

[39] 'Mnangagwa piqued by spelling error at Tongogara barracks' *Zimbabwe Mail* 6/12/17.
[40] 'New names for streets, buildings' *Herald* 22/11/19; 'Zimbabwe uproar as roads named after Emmerson Mnangagwa' *BBC news* 22/11/19; 'Mnangagwa Street and Fidel Castro Road: Zimbabwe's president ditches colonial street names for tributes' *Telegraph* (UK) 22/11/19.
[41] 'Mystery over renaming of Mugabe Street' *Newsday* 20/2/20.
[42] 'Zimbabwe: streets, buildings renaming sparks uproar' 22/11/19, https://allafrica.com/stories/201911220749.html, accessed 3/7/20.
[43] 'Govt snubs Tsvangirai in new road names' *Newsday* 22/11/19; 'No national hero status for Morgan Tsvangirai – Mnangagwa' *African News Agency* 15/2/18.

After Mugabe

Tsvangirai's funeral,[44] when the MDC-T visibly played out its own nasty succession squabbles between rival deputy presidents seeking control of the party – the more populist Nelson Chamisa who later formed the MDC Alliance, and the more constitutionally legitimate Thokozani Khupe, who kept the MDC-T tag but garners little popular support – played straight into Mnangagwa's hands by effectively dividing the strongest opposition to the ruling party. Similar scenes were repeated a year later at Vimbai Tsvangirai's funeral.[45] This schism continues to undermine the credibility and capacity of the opposition, financially as well as politically, and was kept unresolved after a 2020 Supreme Court ruling declared Khupe to be Tsvangirai's legitimate successor; and a subsequent decision by the Parliament's Speaker to recall four MDC Alliance MPs at the request of Khupe's MDC-T faction.[46] Many people sensed ZANU PF's hidden hand behind the Supreme Court decision, which has played into the ruling party's ongoing strategy to divide and weaken the political opposition through legal means as well as violence and coercion.[47]

Another prominent person excluded from the 2019 list of renamed roads was Dumiso Dabengwa,[48] the former ZIPRA Intelligence supremo, who had been detained by the Mugabe government during the mid-1980s, but later became Minister of Home Affairs after the unity agreement, before re-forming ZAPU in 2008. Dabengwa passed away in Nairobi in May 2019, on his way back from India where he had been receiving treatment for liver disease.[49] He was declared a national hero, and a series of memorial events were held across the country and in Johannesburg before his burial at the end of the month. His exclusion from the list of renamed roads was quickly noticed, perhaps particularly because Lookout Masuku (the former ZIPRA commander, detained alongside Dabengwa in the 1980s) had been included, as had Edgar Tekere.[50]

---

[44] 'Succession wrangle at Morgan Tsvangirai's funeral' *Mail & Guardian* 21/2/18; 'Chaos at Tsvangirai's funeral as succession battle intensifies' *SA Times* 20/2/18.

[45] 'Mudenda, Khupe heckled at Vimbai Tsvangirai funeral' *Newzimbabwe.com* 13/6/19, accessed 19/6/20.

[46] Brian Raftopoulos, 'Mounting challenges for Chamisa' *Bulawayo24 News* 26/6/20, accessed 19/6/20.

[47] Ibid. See also, for example, Ringisai Chikohomero, 'Court ruling pulls the rug from under Zimbabwe's opposition' *ISS Today* 27/4/20, https://issafrica.org/iss-today/court-ruling-pulls-the-rug-from-under-zimbabwes-opposition, accessed 17/6/20.

[48] 'No national hero status for Morgan Tsvangirai – Mnangagwa' *African News Agency* 15/2/18; 'Govt snubs Tsvangirai in new road names' *Newsday* 22/11/19; 'Zimbabwe uproar as roads named after Emmerson Mnangagwa' *BBC news* 22/11/19.

[49] 'Dabengwa dies…1939~2019' *Bulawayo Chronicle* 24/5/19; 'Zapu liberation war hero Dabengwa dies, aged 79' *Daily Maverick* 23/5/19.

[50] 'Govt snubs Tsvangirai in new road names' *Newsday* 22/11/19.

The Politics of the Dead

Unsurprisingly, given ZANU PF's long marginalisation of ZAPU's war legacy, the issue of renaming roads in Bulawayo soon erupted into a dispute between Bulawayo City Council and the central government, after the city authorities unanimously rejected the central government's renaming of city streets, and made a formal decision to re-rename them after dignitaries from the region, including King Mzilikazi and Queen Lozikheyo Dlodlo, as well as Dumiso Dabengwa himself, and others like Sydney Malunga, who had died of a suspicious car accident in 1994.[51]

Perhaps appropriately, Dabengwa's funeral, attended by thousands of mourners, too became a much contested event, again illustrating some of the continuities in Zimbabwe's politics of the dead, albeit in different ways to Tsvangirai's death given his very different role in Zimbabwean history and politics.[52] Although, according to Vice-President Kembo Mohadi,[53] 'Dr Dabengwa's contribution to the liberation struggle was unquestionable' and 'we all agreed unanimously that he be conferred with the national hero status',[54] Dabengwa's relatives, at his own insistence, refused to let him be buried at Harare's National Heroes Acre. In 2015 he expressed to me his profound disillusionment with ZANU PF's partisan control of national commemoration, which, as we have seen, has been marked by consistent reticence to recognise ZAPU and ZIPRA's contributions to Zimbabwe's liberation. He had told me then that he would be buried at his rural home in Ntabazinduna.[55] Given this history and these sentiments it is perhaps not surprising that when he was buried in Ntabazinduna, Umguza District, in Matabeleland North, the family and other Ndebele politicians and activists refused to allow ZANU PF to control the proceedings. There were indications that the ruling party were concerned about what would happen at the funeral, and that the dreaded Joint Operations Command (JOC), who masterminded ZANU PF's 2008 election violence, tried to control of the funeral programme and 'to screen

---

[51] 'Govt, Bulawayo City Council headed for clash over street names' *Newzimbabwe.com* 17/3/20; 'BCC defies govt, changes street names' *CITE* 5/2/20, www.cite.org.zw/bcc-defies-govt-changes-street-names, accessed 3/7/20.

[52] 'Jittery military takes over Dabengwa burial programme, Chamisa set to attend' *Newzimbabwe.com* 31/5/19; 'Dabengwa burial: A story of defiance' *CITE* 1/6/19, www.cite.org.zw/dabengwa-burial-a-story-of-defiance; both accessed 3/7/20; 'Dabengwa burial snub cannot erase his legacy' *Zimbabwe Independent* 7/6/19.

[53] Mohadi was a member of ZAPU before the unity accord of 1987, but who remained in ZANU PF after other former ZAPU members left to reform the party under Dabengwa in 2008. He now occupies the 2nd vice-president's position, which has normally been reserved for former ZAPU members within ZANU PF.

[54] 'Dabengwa is national hero … His contribution unquestionable' *Herald* 27/5/19.

[55] Interview with Dumiso Dabengwa, 18/8/15.

After Mugabe

speakers at the late national hero, Dumiso Dabengwa's burial'.[56] But this was not to be, and as a result neither President Mnangagwa nor his two deputies attended the funeral.[57] The President's spokesman George Charamba later claimed that when National Heroes choose to be buried at their homes, the President never attends because that would distract from the family's privacy.[58] For some, this refusal to attend the funeral was seen as snub to Dabengwa's unquestionable liberation legacy, but for others it reflected how Dabengwa's funeral became a 'story of defiance'.[59] When government authorities tried to impose their programme onto the proceedings at the funeral itself, they were publicly told 'that Dabengwa's family would first go through their planned programme and when finished the government could do as it pleased'.[60] Later, when the Minister of State for Matabeleland North, Richard Moyo, who Mnangagwa had sent in his place, stood up to speak, he was booed and heckled.[61] When subsequent speakers, including Nelson Chamisa (who had been excluded from the VIP list but who Dabengwa's widow insisted should be allowed to speak) as well as Chief Ndiweni, sharply criticised the government, those senior ruling party and government officials who were present walked off 'in a huff'.[62]

For many in Matabeleland, it was a fittingly defiant funeral for Dabengwa. As Mbuso Fuzwayo explained:

> Dumiso defied ZANU in life and in death. It was a funeral attended by people from all over the country. It was a state funeral, and he was declared a hero. But it was presided over by ZIPRA and ZAPU, who put their foot down over the arrangements. They ran the programme. It gave the people of this part of the country something to celebrate. Whenever the government is resisted it's a good opportunity for people from this region.[63]

Dabengwa's funeral turned out, quite appropriately, to be a ZAPU affair, and the ruling party was denied any opportunity to make political mileage out of it. In the end, he may have been declared a national hero, recognising his immense contribution to the struggle, but Dabengwa's

---

[56] 'Jittery military takes over Dabengwa burial programme, Chamisa set to attend' *Newzimbabwe.com* 31/5/19.
[57] 'Dabengwa burial snub cannot erase his legacy' *Zimbabwe Independent* 7/6/19.
[58] 'Charamba clears air on Dabengwa burial' *Herald* 1/6/19.
[59] Dabengwa burial: A story of defiance' CITE 1/6/19, www.cite.org.zw/dabengwa-burial-a-story-of-defiance, accessed 3/7/20.
[60] Ibid.
[61] Ibid.
[62] 'Gvt and top Zanu PF officials walk out of Dabengwa burial as Chamisa and Chief Ndiweni speak' *iHarare.com* 3/6/19, accessed 3/7/20.
[63] Interview with Mbuso Fuzwayo, 12/3/20.

death was not available for political use by the ruling party. They, in turn, as with Tsvangirai, did not see it fit to rename any roads after him.

Alongside Dabengwa, Mnangagwa's regime has declared several other prominent people as National Heroes since November 2017, including the international musician Oliver Mtukudzi (who too was buried, at his family's insistence, at his rural home),[64] as well as Professor Phineas Mogorosi Makhurane and, more recently, Major General Trust Mugoba, who died (some say suspiciously)[65] on the same day as Robert Mugabe in September 2019. The new regime has clearly sought to maintain the ruling party's use and domination of national commemoration, as might have been expected given their careful commitment to maintaining Mugabe's 'chimurenga legacy' and politics, even if they have not always been successful. All of this came to a head with Mugabe's own death and the protracted contests that it provoked in September 2019 which, I suggest below, epitomised the continuing salience of Zimbabwe's politics of the dead.

But perhaps the most significant opportunity Mnangagwa's government has utilised to differentiate itself from Mugabe's long rule, has been its announcements and nascent efforts to initiate new processes of 'truth-telling', reconciliation and exhumations relating to Zimbabwe's troubling *gukurahundi* legacy. This began with his signing of the National Peace and Reconciliation Act in January 2018, a piece of legislation deriving from Zimbabwe's 2013 constitution, which had been awaiting President Mugabe's signature for a long time.[66] This formally constituted or defined the roles of various independent commissions that are, according to the National Peace and Reconciliation Commission's (NPRC) own documentation:

> mandated to support and entrench human rights and democracy; to protect the sovereignty and interests of the people; to promote constitutionalism; to promote transparency and accountability in public institutions; to secure the observance of democratic values and principles by the State and all institutions and agencies of government and government-controlled entities; and to ensure that injustices are remedied.[67]

---

[64] 'National hero status sought for Tuku' *Herald* 24/1/19; 'Tuku declared national hero' *Herald* 24/1/19; 'Tuku. The deserving national hero' *Herald* 25/1/19. Mtukudzi's death was followed, appropriately, by a concert in his honour: 'Tuku tribute concert set for Saturday' *Newzimbabwe.com* 18/7/19, accessed 19/6/20.

[65] Field notes, March 2020.

[66] Heal Zimbabwe, 'Statement on the enactment of the National Peace and Reconciliation Commission (NPRC) Act' 11/1/18, https://kubatana.net/2018/01/11/statement-enactment-national-peace-reconciliation-commission-nprc-act, accessed 3/7/20.

[67] National Peace and Reconciliation Commission website, www.nprc.org.zw, accessed 29/6/20.

After Mugabe

It was followed in early 2019 by government statements announcing that commemorations and exhumations, as well as a series of 'truth-telling' processes, related to the *gukurahundi* in particular would now go ahead.[68] As *The Herald* reported:

> Among key interventions, that are in line with President Mnangagwa's pledge during a meeting with civil society under the banner of Matabeleland Collective a fortnight ago, Government will issue birth and death certificates to those affected. Government will also facilitate the exhumation and reburial of victims of Gukurahundi while medical assistance will be availed for those injured during the time while other restorative justice measures will be rolled out, making good of President Mnangagwa's promise that his administration would not shy from confronting the ugly past.[69]

There is little doubt that these announcements seemed to mark a significant u-turn from the ruling party's previous position on the issue. They have been followed by a series of 'truth-telling' hearings run by the NPRC, and some exhumations.[70] For NMMZ, now approached by the Zimbabwe Human Rights Commission to lead exhumations, it did seem like much had changed from 2006 when the acting deputy director told me that any *gukurahundi*-related exhumations NMMZ had been involved under the auspices of liberation heritage, were 'too sensitive' to be discussed (see Chapter 1). Given the ruling party's long reticence to deal with what Mugabe had once dismissed, during Joshua Nkomo's 1999 funeral, as a 'moment of madness', it is not surprising that these announcements were met with much scepticism.[71] While some welcomed

---

[68] 'Gukurahundi healing measures announced' *Herald* 10/4/19; 'Zimbabwe to exhume, rebury thousands from 1980s mass killing' *AP News* 10/4/19; 'Zimbabwe to compensate victims of genocide that claimed 20,000 lives' *SA Times* 10/4/19; 'Zimbabwe to exhume, rebury Gukurahundi massacre victims' *IOL* 10/4/19, accessed 19/6/20.

[69] 'Gukurahundi healing measures announced' *Herald* 10/4/19.

[70] Interview with Shari Eppel, 11/3/20. 'Zimbabwe begins exhuming victims of Gukurahundi massacre' *Mail & Guardian* 30/4/19; 'Gukurahundi exhumations begin, one body set for reburial in Tsholotsho' *Newzimbabwe.com* 30/4/19, accessed 19/6/20; 'NPRC calls for Gukurahundi truth-telling' *Herald* 17/4/19; NPRC, 'National Peace and Reconciliation Commission launches 21-day outreach programme' 9/4/19, https://kubatana.net/2019/04/09/national-peace-and-reconciliation-commission-launches-21-day-outreach-programme, accessed 3/7/20.

[71] 'Gukurahundi: Can the man accused of opening the wounds heal them?' *African Arguments* 4/6/19; 'One year after: Has the National Peace and Reconciliation Commission Act failed Zimbabweans?' *Kujenga Amani* 7/2/19, https://kujenga-amani.ssrc.org/2019/02/07/one-year-after-has-the-national-peace-and-reconciliation-commission-act-failed-zimbabweans, accessed 3/7/20.

The Politics of the Dead

the moves with extremely guarded and cautious optimism,[72] many accused Mnangagwa of trying to 'whitewash' the *gukurahundi*.[73] Others were insulted by the government's statements, or argued that truth-telling hearings and exhumations should have been done long ago.[74] Mnangagwa's own perceived complicity with the *gukurahundi* atrocities, when he was minister for state security, made many people question his sincerity.[75] Others, perhaps more aligned with ZANU PF, suggested that the new government's permitted exhumations, truth-telling and fact-finding processes may reveal that far fewer people than the oft-stated number of 20,000 had been killed during the massacres; implying that these processes could thereby lead to a new kind of '*gukurahundi* politics'.[76]

On the other hand, some civil society organisations, locally and internationally, cautiously welcomed the moves towards resolving the complex question of the *gukurahundi* and saw them as evidence that Mnangagwa was indeed the moderate, reforming leader he claimed to be. This has been much trumpeted in the state-run press.[77] Unsurprisingly in Matabeleland, in particular, the government's announcements that the *gukurahundi* issue should now be addressed, and the early meetings, 'truth-telling' events and exhumations they led to in 2019, have had a decidedly mixed reception. Ukuthula Trust, for example, worked closely with the NPRC in exhumations that they carried out in Tsholotsho in 2019, even as they acknowledge the limitations the NPRC faces in terms of the breadth of its mandate and the limitations of its financial resources.[78] Later, however, in December 2019, plans to carry out another exhumation in Lupane, to which commissioners from the NPRC and representatives

---

[72] Strike Mkandla, 'ZAPU response to "Gukurahundi" moves by President Mnangagwa' *Bulawayo24 News* 24/4/19.
[73] 'Mnangagwa accused of trying to whitewash Gukurahundi' *Zimbabwe Independent* 21/2/20; 'Digging up the graves of Gukurahundi graves – and burying the evidence' *Mail & Guardian* 10/5/19.
[74] 'Interview with Strike Mkandla, 12/3/20; 'Gukurahundi should have been resolved decades ago: NPRC' *CITE* 31/7/19, www.cite.org.zw/gukurahundi-should-have-been-resolved-decades-ago-nprc, accessed 3/7/20.
[75] 'Gukurahundi: Can the man accused of opening the wounds heal them?' *African Arguments* 4/6/19; 'Gukurahundi ghosts haunt Mnangagwa' *Mail & Guardian* 24/11/17; Stuart Doran, 'Zimbabwe massacres: "You're all wrong on President Mnangagwa and the Gukurahundi killings"' *Daily Maverick* 29/11/19.
[76] Interview with Chipunza, 5/3/20.
[77] 'Mnangagwa, Matabeleland leaders seek Gukurahundi closure' *Herald* 15/2/20; 'Government explores legally, culturally acceptable processes … ED to meet Matabeleland leaders over Gukurahundi reburials' *Sunday News* 23/2/20.
[78] Interview with Shari Eppel, 11/3/20; also 'Gukurahundi exhumations begin, one body set for reburial in Tsholotsho' *Newzimbabwe.com* 30/4/19, accessed 19/6/20.

of NMMZ, the army, police, CIO and local chiefs had been invited, were abruptly cancelled at the last moment, for unclear reasons.[79]

Like the way that the MDC's internal succession squabbles have been fanned by the ruling party's overtures towards the Tsvangirai family, so too have the efforts of Mnangagwa's government to promote 'reconciliation' through the NPRC and other channels, led to deep divisions among Matabeleland's civil society organisations.[80] In particularly, the Matabeleland Collective – a loose amalgamation of different regional NGOs, organisations and interests formed to present coherent and unified representations about regional issues to the government, and whose meeting with Mnangagwa in early 2019 preceded his public statements about new *gukurahundi* processes – has been beset by a series of sharp internal leadership disputes. These circulate around the leadership and dictatorial style of Jenny Williams, who first came into the public limelight in the late 2000s as a founder of Women of Zimbabwe Arise (WOZA), and quickly became a leading critic of Mugabe. Many see her now as an apologist for Mnangagwa's government, and worry about her apparently close relationship to the President, as evidenced by a series of high-profile public meetings she had with him, and particularly about the way in which her activities have effectively co-opted the collective's mechanisms into the ruling party's agenda, thereby allowing ZANU PF to claim to be listening to regional concerns while still marginalising dissenting, alternative voices.[81] Particular concerns have been raised about how Jenny William's so-called 'implementation matrix' for measures to deal with *gukurahundi*-related issues was generated.[82] In response to these concerns, in early 2020 several leading, original constituent partners in the collective established a new group, the 'Matabeleland Forum', in order to distance themselves from her activities.[83] For many, these events reflect a continuation of the kind of 'divide and rule' tactics that the ruling party has often utilised with great effect against opposition movements, including the MDC.

---

[79] Field notes, March 2020.
[80] 'Mnangagwa splits Matabeleland NGOs, groups accuse each other of selling out' *Newzimbabwe.com* 8/2/20; 'Matabeleland Collective collapses, new coalition formed' CITE 7/2/20, www.cite.org.zw/matabeleland-collective-collapses-new-coalition-formed; both accessed 3/7/20; '"Matabeleland Collective was a Mnangagwa scam" Jonathan Moyo says' *Bulawayo24 News* 10/2/20;
[81] Interview with Shari Eppel, 11/3/20; Interview with Mbuso Fuzwayo, 12/3/20.
[82] 'ZimEye.com speaks to Jenny Williams leader of Matabeleland Collective live' *ZimEye.net* 15/2/20; 'Mnangagwa meets Mat civil society organisations' 13/2/20, www.cite.org.zw/mnangagwa-meets-mat-civil-society-organisations, accessed 3/7/20.
[83] Interview with Shari Eppel, 11/3/20; Centre for Innovation and Technology (CITE), 'Matabeleland Collective collapses, new coalition formed' 7/2/20, https://kubatana.net/2020/02/07/matabeleland-collective-collapses-new-coalition-formed, accessed 3/7/20; 'Why Matabeleland Collective collapsed' *ZimEye.net* 10/2/20, accessed 19/6/20.

The Politics of the Dead

Not surprisingly, given these circumstances, the few 'truth-telling' hearings and exhumations that took place in 2019–20, before the corona pandemic halted many things, were often beset by controversies and contestation. In March 2020 Shari Eppel explained how truth-telling hearings in Gwanda and in Bulawayo were disrupted by members of the Mthwakazi Front, who 'pulled out these pink posters they had prepared, on which it said that Mnangagwa had called the Ndebele cockroaches and the 5th Brigade were the DDT', and then continued 'toyi-toying for four whole hours, chanting "Shonas go home"', until the NPRC commissioners 'fled through the backdoor of the building'.[84] On the ground there is also, in some contexts, little evidence that ZANU PF's long obstruction of *gukurahundi* commemorations has in fact changed, despite Mnangagwa's announcements. Although he acknowledged that some things had improved, Mbuso Fuzwayo, founder of an organisation called *Ibhetshu LikaZulu*, which seeks to promote Ndebele culture and history, described the obstructions that he and his colleagues have faced since 2018 trying to hold annual commemorative events at Bhalagwe camp in southern Matabeleland, where many *gukurahundi* atrocities occurred, and where some of its victims are buried.[85] Eppel too described a 'very visceral battle' going on at Bhalagwe between Ndebele activists and ZANU PF supporters involving provocative commemorations, and the repeated construction and destruction of rival commemorative monuments and plaques.[86] Others have pointed to the way in which the NPRC commissioners have been selected, and raise concerns about the wide and indeterminate nature of their portfolio, their limited resources and capacity, and about its independence and that of other commissions established by the NPRC Act.[87]

Divisions have also emerged between Ndebele activists and other civil society actors working in the region around the question of exhumations. While some Ndebele activists are determined to hold out against doing exhumations in the current context, seeking to preserve any forensic evidence *gukurahundi* burials may contain for the promise of formal justice procedures in the future,[88] others have less faith that formal justice mechanisms will ever be deliverable. This is partly because of the prohibitive costs and complexity of forensic exhumations, but also, among other reasons,[89] because there is, as Eppel put it, 'often very little

---

[84] Interview with Shari Eppel, 11/3/20.
[85] Interview with Mbuso Fuzwayo, 12/3/20.
[86] Interview with Shari Eppel, 11/3/20.
[87] Interview with Strike Mkandla, 12/3/20; Interview with Mbuso Fuzwayo, 12/3/20; Interview with Shari Eppel, 11/3/20.
[88] 'Mnangagwa accused of trying to whitewash Gukurahundi' *Zimbabwe Independent* 21/2/20; 'Digging up the graves of Gukurahundi graves – and burying the evidence' *Mail & Guardian* 10/5/19.
[89] Shari Eppel explained some of the reasons why the promise of future justice is unrealistic, including: continuing amnesties for violence committed during

forensic evidence from exhumations of bones', especially after three or four decades. Ukuthula Trust, in particular, are seeking to work with the NPRC in order to use the limited and reluctant window offered by Mnangagwa's apparent détente to carry through exhumations and reburials for 'truth-telling' purposes; to bring resolution and 'closure' to the many families and communities still affected by the killings.[90] At stake here is a fundamental question about what exhumations are for, and what human remains do and are capable of doing, which has been a central concern of this book. The arguments developed here suggest that human remains are frequently of enormous significance for managing, stabilising and containing the proper transformations that death demands, and yet they are also often unusually elusive in delivering upon what they promise, especially in terms of forensic evidence, or in terms of resolution or final closure.

Among a younger generation of Matabeleland activists, many too young to have experienced the massacres, these debates have sometimes carried pronounced tribal or ethnic undertones. Some observers have noted how the violence that took place in Bulawayo in January 2019, in the context of fuel protests across the country, were – unlike elsewhere – not largely caused by state security forces and had marked xenophobic and ethnic dimensions.[91] Such tensions have been further fuelled recently by the MDC Alliance's deepening loss of popularity in Bulawayo due to its own perceived ethnic partisanship and the scandals that have surrounded the MDC-A controlled city council.[92] As Fuzwayo explained, 'the MDC is now showing signs of not being different from ZANU, especially on the

---

the *gukurahundi* and during later violence; the fact that the International Criminal Court was established in 1998, and is not empowered to investigate crimes dating to the 1980s; and a lack of any international appetite to establish special tribunal for the *gukurahundi*, as was done for Rwanda and Yugoslavia. For her the emphasis should be on 'truth-telling' and identifying the dead, and the urgency relates to the fact that the bones are beginning to disappear', particularly in the acidic wetter soils of northern Matabeleland (Interview with Shari Eppel, 11/3/20). Her position seems to have shifted from 2011, when she opposed the vernacular exhumations taking place at Chibondo on the principle that they were destroying evidence (see S. Eppel, 'The silencing of the bones' SPT – Zimbabwe Update No. 2, 24/3/11, www.solidaritypeace-trust.org/1015/spt-zimbabwe-update-no-2, accessed 24/3/11.

[90] Interview with Shari Eppel, 11/3/20.
[91] Ibid.; Solidarity Peace Trust, 'Resurgent authoritarianism: The politics of the January 2019 violence in Zimbabwe', 20/2/19. Not everyone agrees with this argument (Moore forthcoming B).
[92] 'Bulawayo chaos & corruption … MDC-A summons councillors to Harare' *Bulawayo Chronicle* 18/7/19; 'MDC MPs, councillors in $60m scandal' *Bulawayo24 News* 27/1/19; 'Ex-Bulawayo deputy mayor set to bounce back as court acquits him of theft' *Newzimbabwe.com* 16/6/20, accessed 19/6/20.

gukurahundi'.[93] Like other activists, however, he too warned against understanding Matabeleland's issues in ethnic terms, arguing that:

> The dominant narratives say that this is an ethnic division. But it is the government that killed people. Actually the Shona and Ndebele people have never fought each other since colonisation. We want to build our own narratives, to be able to define what affects us. The *gukurahundi* was genocide committed by the government. It is the government that created the story of the Ndebeles versus the Shonas. They have been hiding behind their divide and rule tactics – setting Ndebele against Shona. No one is focusing on the actual perpetrators, which is the government led by ZANU PF. *Gukurahundi* was a genocide by the government. So we need to correct the narratives.[94]

He also emphasised that the 'healing' and 'resolution' still required in the *gukurahundi*'s long wake, will need to focus on the perpetrators of the atrocities as well as upon its living survivors.[95] 'For the nation to be stable' he argued 'we need to think about the security of perpetrators as well as of the victims'.[96] For his part, the secretary-general of ZAPU, Strike Mkandla, too warned about the dangers of ethnic division. His statement below captured perfectly the scepticism that the ruling party's overtures have provoked:

> [T]he NPRC is a misnomer. NPRC assumes that there are people in conflict. But there are no people in conflict. It was genocide by one party against one group of people. What is there to reconcile? We must simply bring to book the killers. This is the kind of politics where I get really hot, and I am really unimpressed. If you look at what happened during the *gukurahundi*, the atrocities, and the level of callousness involved – opening up pregnant women, burning people in their houses, throwing live people down mine shafts. And the people responsible are in the government talking about peace and reconciliation. That is an insult to our intelligence. It also shows insensitivity to the danger of real conflict, the danger of actual rebellion against injustice. This might trigger something. There is now a large number of young adults who saw their parents killed in front of them. They [the government] are toying with the future of the country, anything can happen. It's only that we are lucky that we don't have inter-ethnic conflict in these streets.[97]

In Matabeleland, therefore, there remains a great deal of uncertainty around the new regime's 'real' intentions and motivations. Some have suggested that one way this new politics might pan out in the future is

---

[93] Interview with Mbuso Fuzwayo, 12/3/20.
[94] Ibid.
[95] Ibid.
[96] Ibid.
[97] Interview with Strike Mkandla, Field notes, 12/3/20.

that after a limited number of highly publicised events, hearings and exhumations – such as those at Tsholotsho in 2019 – Mnangagwa might declare the *gukurahundi* issue resolved, and move forward quickly to sweep outstanding issues (such as his own culpability) under the carpet once again, emboldened to silence or negate alternative disputing voices by accusing them of hampering national reconciliation.[98] Not only would this match the political shenanigans that often surround large 'national' efforts at transitional justice and reconciliation elsewhere (Lynch 2018), it would also, like the events surrounding Tsvangirai's death and the drawn-out MDC succession contests it provoked, fit ZANU PF's long-standing style of political chicanery and its engagement with Zimbabwe's politics of the dead. Much does seem to have endured across ZANU PF's change of leadership in 2017, with the uncertainty of Mnangagwa's intentions, as well as the instability of his administration, being perhaps the defining feature of his regime. Indeed, in some respects he may be performing the politics of uncertainty much more than Mugabe ever did. However, as we shall see below, Mugabe's role in Zimbabwe's politics of the dead did not end with his own death in September 2019. In many ways the furore that emerged around what to do with his remains epitomised the politics of the dead that he had played such an important part in fomenting during his life.

Burying Bob

The death of Robert Mugabe, or 'Bob' as he was irreverently known by many Zimbabweans, on 6 September 2019, was always likely to be something of an event. Having ruled Zimbabwe for 37 years, and as nearly the last of a whole generation of African liberation leaders in the region, Bob was in equal measures revered, feared, respected and despised across his country and beyond.[99] For many across the region, he remained a respected figurehead of anti-colonial struggle, perceived as a welcome thorn in the side of 'Western' and global interests, and an icon of widely resonating struggles for land and economic redistribution. For many ordinary Zimbabweans, on the other hand, both in Zimbabwe and the millions etching out precarious lives in its diaspora, after two decades of relentless economic crisis, political polarisation and numerous failed attempts to replace him electorally – often at enormous cost in terms of the violence such efforts provoked – Bob's death in office had long been anticipated as the only way that things were ever going to change; the only way that Zimbabwe's social, political and economic problems could ever be resolved.

[98] Interview with Shari Eppel, Field notes, 11/3/20; Interview with Strike Mkandla, Field notes, 12/3/20; Interview with Mbuso Fuzwayo, Field notes, 12/3/20.
[99] 'Mixed reactions to Mugabe death' *Newsday* 7/9/19; 'Mugabe death ignites an inferno of debates, discussions' *Newsday* 13/9/19.

Meanwhile, for a hard core of ZANU PF loyalists, across different sides of its complex and fiery internal factionalism, Bob remained very much the 'hallowed' father of Zimbabwean independence, as indeed those responsible for 'Operation Restore Legacy' which pushed him out of office in November 2017, have been at pains to maintain. For all these reasons, his death was always going to be significant, albeit in different ways for different people. And it was long anticipated. He was 95 and, until 2017, one of the world's oldest serving presidents. Since the early 2000s when I began fieldwork in Zimbabwe, people had been expecting, and maybe hoping, he would kick the bucket soon, and there were endless recurring rumours about his ill health, and his many, expensive trips to see doctors in Singapore. Yet he often seemed to rebound, fist waving and strong, still masterly manipulating ZANU PF's rivalries and factions, so that Zimbabweans grimly joked that maybe he would never die. It only became harder to conceal his evident frailty in his later years.

Bob could himself be seen as responsible for much of the anticipated significance that his death was supposed to generate. Ever playing the ideologue, Mugabe had been instrumental in establishing the National Heroes complex in Harare, and in forging ZANU PF's controversial control of state commemoration and its partisan selection of 'national heroes', which have been a key part of Zimbabwe's politics of the dead. Every year Bob would lead annual 'Heroes Day' celebrations and an increasing number of state funerals at Harare's National Heroes Acre (as more and more of the liberation generation passed away); opportunities he apparently relished a great deal, rambling and ranting at tedious length, endlessly recanting his own revised versions of history, over the deceased bodies of ZANU PF's designated heroes to bored bussed-in audiences, or broadcast on national television. Among the many hundreds of other graves, some Great Zimbabwe-style walling and some fairly garish North Korean sculptures, Bob's supposed burial spot had already long been marked out, on a top terrace next to his late, first wife, Sally (see Figure 10).

Given all of this anticipation, and preparation, it is therefore interesting that the first announcements of his death in Singapore on 6 September 2019, were met with notable ambivalence among many Zimbabweans.[100] Some of this ambivalence was predictable for a leader as controversial and polarising as Mugabe. The seemingly endless stream of obituaries, statements and commentaries by other politicians, journalists, commentators and scholars that quickly emerged, are easy to categorise into three

---

[100] 'Zimbabweans choose work over mourning Mugabe' *News24.com* 8/9/19; 'Zimbabwe's "end of an error"' *AFP Correspondent* 11/10/19, https://correspondent.afp.com/zimbabwes-end-error; Alex Magaisa, 'The death of Robert Mugabe' *Big Saturday Read* 6/9/19, www.bigsr.africa/big-saturday-read-the-death-of-robert-mugabe-d3; all accessed 3/7/20.

groups. There are those who continued to valorise Bob's liberation past, including respected international figures like Graca Machel, spouse to Samora Machel and later Nelson Mandela.[101] Another group are those who, for very good reason, continued to vilify him, both for the economic mess Zimbabwe has endured for two decades, but even more so, for the political violence of that period, and the atrocious, unresolved crimes of the *gukurahundi*.[102] The third group were those seeking to construct a middle path, between Mugabe's 'heroic' liberation past fighting Rhodesian belligerence in the 1960s and 1970s, and his markedly mixed postcolonial record.[103] Some of these accounts pointed to the enduring legacies of Bob's expansion of free education and health care in the 1980s[104], while others framed his complex past in a familiar narrative of 'hero' turned 'villain' under global pressures of neo-liberalism, or in the context of a wider disillusionment with the postcolonial dispensation across the region.[105] Sometimes such commentaries appealed to the necessity of 'not speaking ill of the dead' to euphemise their biographies and obituaries. While the injunction to not speak ill of the dead has particular, and powerful, cultural connotations in a Zimbabwean context (which we return to below) others, such as Ruth Murambadoro, countered that there is no such thing as an injunction against speaking of the dastardly deeds of someone like Bob.[106]

All of these kinds of ambivalence about Mugabe's complex legacy were to be expected. What struck me more, however, in speaking to Zimbabweans and reading newspaper reports, blogs, commentaries and Twitter feeds circulating immediately after his death, was a different kind of ambivalence,

---

[101] 'Graca Machel – appreciate Mugabe's role in Zimbabwe' *Newzimbabwe.com* 10/9/19; 'Thabo Mbeki hails Robert Mugabe as a true African patriot' *News24.com* 18/9/19; both accessed 19/6/20; 'Don't judge Mugabe on last days: General Sibanda' *Herald* 7/9/19; 'Mugabe was a towering figure against colonialism – Ramaphosa' *News24.com* 21/9/19, accessed 19/6/20.

[102] 'Bob owes us an apology' *Standard* 8/9/19; 'An evil legacy' *Zimbabwe Vigil Diary*, 7/9/19; 'Gukurahundi victims react to Mugabe death' *Standard* 15/9/19; 'Mugabe was unrepentant' *Standard* 15/9/19; 'Mugabe was no revolutionary. He was obsessed with power and control' *News24.com* 6/9/19, accessed 19/6/20.

[103] 'Mugabe: Hero or villain?' *Zimbabwe Independent* 13/9/19; '"Hero turned tyrant": international reaction to Mugabe's death' *Guardian* 6/9/19; 'Bob: As divisive in death as he was in life' *Newsday* 7/9/19; 'The other side of Mugabe' *Standard* 22/9/19.

[104] 'Contribution to education unparalleled' *Herald* 7/9/19; 'Coordinator's Note: Mugabe ... "The good men do is oft interred with their bones"' *Zimbabwe Briefing* 11/9/19.

[105] '"Hero turned tyrant": international reaction to Mugabe's death' *Guardian* 6/9/19; 'Robert Mugabe: Liberation hero turned despot' *eNCA* 15/9/19, accessed 19/6/20; 'Reflections' *Zimbabwean* 16/9/19.

[106] Mugabe and the tradition to not speak ill of the dead' *Mail & Guardian* 23/9/19.

The Politics of the Dead

FIGURE 10. The empty grave next to Sarah (Sally) Mugabe, where it was long expected Robert Mugabe would be buried (Author 2015)

bordering on resigned indifference or even disinterest. Like the young woman, Esther Moyo, for whom attending Bob's funeral was just an opportunity to sell more peanuts. 'Mugabe is the reason we are in this mess' she said, 'I just came here to sell my snacks to make a living … and to make sure the old man was really dead'.[107] For the many Zimbabweans scratching a meagre living in its informal sector, or forced abroad to work low-level jobs in the face of xenophobic violence in South Africa, or increasingly acerbic anti-immigration policies in the UK and elsewhere, Bob's death was just too far away, too inconsequential in their daily lives, and maybe far too late to really matter. This kind of ambivalence and indifference seemed to suggest that Mugabe's death was just a big anti-climax.

Given how long Mugabe had been expected to die in office, as he (and those around him) had often implied,[108] and how long it had been assumed that this would be the moment of Zimbabwe's long-awaited political change, perhaps it was his removal from office two years earlier,

---

[107] 'Pomp, thin crowds and mixed feelings as Robert Mugabe is buried' *Guardian* 15/9/19.

[108] 'Mugabe "is king and should die in office"' *News24.com* 8/3/12, accessed 19/6/20; 'Mugabe will die in office' *Daily News* 28/2/17; 'Robert Mugabe says "only God" can remove him' *Telegraph* (UK) 20/6/08.

and demise into political irrelevance soon afterwards, that meant that Bob's death was really not as big a deal as many had long expected. In a sense he was already dead politically, regardless of the continuing activities of the so-called G40 faction ousted with him in November 2017, and suggestions that Bob had switched his support to the MDC opposition in the 2018 elections.[109] Moreover, as the new regime's claims to offer a more tolerant, 'open for business' kind of politics rapidly lost credibility with new outbreaks of state-sponsored violence and killings in August 2018 and January 2019, amidst a new wave of disappearances, and as the economy again faltered, any promise that Mugabe's demise would offer meaningful change had already largely evaporated for many people. Conversely, for some, Bob's death could even be construed as meaningful only in so much as his successor had been shown to be even worse; with all of Bob's violence and intolerance and none of his eloquence.[110] If this kind of ambivalence can be represented, then perhaps it was best expressed in satirical memes that circulated on the social media in the weeks after Bob's death, reflective of a particularly kind of caustic political humour. My favourite is an image, entitled 'Pastor Lukau has done it again', of Bob photo-shopped onto a now famous photograph of a man sitting up in a coffin, surrounded by a church congregation, having allegedly been brought back to life.[111]

This kind of ambivalence bordering on resigned indifference seemed to be confirmed by reports that suggested that Mugabe's lying in state at two stadiums in the capital, and later at his rural home in Zvimba, were marked by poor attendance and a lack of public interest.[112] It is therefore notable that other reports, particularly (but not exclusively) in the

---

[109] 'Mugabe supports MDC – sort of – as propped up ex-dictator elbows his way into historic polling day' *Daily Maverick* 19/7/18; 'Mugabe supports MDC, will hand over power to me, says Chamisa' 3/7/18, https://ewn.co.za/2018/07/28/mugabe-supports-mdc-will-hand-over-power-to-me-says-chamisa, accessed 3/7/20; 'G40 bankrolled the MDC election campaign' *263Chat* 16/6/20, www.marketwatch.com/press-release/g40-bankrolled-the-mdc-election-campaign-2020-06-16, accessed 3/7/20; 'G40 funded MDC-A election campaign' *Herald* 14/2/20.

[110] As I completed this manuscript in mid-2020, the sentiment that Mnangagwa is worse than Mugabe was becoming increasingly common. Also 'Pastor Evan Mawarire says life after Mugabe is more brutal than ever in Zimbabwe' *CNN* 13/11/19, www.zimbabwesituation.com/news/pastor-evan-mawarire-says-life-after-mugabe-is-more-brutal-than-ever-in-zimbabwe, accessed 2/7/20.

[111] https://twitter.com/MayibongweBongo/status/1170272942376312832?s=20, accessed 3/7/20.

[112] 'Few turn out as Mugabe is returned to a Zimbabwe in crisis' *Associated Press* 11/9/19; 'Acres of empty seats as Zimbabwe says goodbye to Robert Mugabe' *news.sky.com* 16/9/19; 'Crowds shun Robert Mugabe's funeral in a stadium less than half full' *Daily Mail* (UK) 16/9/19; 'Pomp, thin crowds and mixed feelings as Robert Mugabe is buried' *Guardian* 15/9/19; 'Zimbabwe's Mugabe to lie in

government press, were keen to emphasise the large numbers attendant at the airport to welcome his remains home, at the different public vigils, and the number of international visitors who flew in to take part in the state funeral on Sunday, 15 September.[113] The actual numbers involved in these different events were always likely to vary, and are hard to measure. There is a history of inflated figures for such events, and of people being bussed in by the ruling party, as well as of people gate-crashing funerals simply for the promise of food or drink. More intriguing is the possibility that the prospect of Mugabe's death being a non-event for a hard-pressed, disinterested Zimbabwean public, might not have passed muster for those in Mnangagwa's regime for whom his death presented political opportunities too good or too problematic to ignore.

But if that was the case, there was no need for concern. The shenanigans that quickly emerged after his state funeral, about where and how to bury Mugabe, ensured that his death would, after all, become a memorable and controversial event, fitting for the politics of the dead that Bob himself had done so much to foster.[114] These burial controversies very much reflected what scholars working elsewhere have written about in terms of the 'political lives of dead bodies' (Verdery 1999; Cohen & Odhiambo 1992). Mugabe's burial turned out to be far more intriguing and revealing than the initial sense of general ambivalence and disinterest had promised, suggesting, as my favourite meme also implied, that it was Bob himself who had 'done it again'; ensuring that in death as much as in life, Zimbabwean politics would circulate around him.

Given the use that has been made of Mugabe's legacy by Mnangagwa's regime, it was not surprising that the new government would be keen to ensure Mugabe was interred at the National Heroes Acre, and appropriately enshrined as one of independent Zimbabwe's foundational heroes.[115]

state at 2 different stadiums' *Associated Press* 10/9/19; 'Mugabe gets low-key farewell in Zimbabwe home village' *News24.com* 17/9/19, accessed 19/6/20.

[113] 'Mugabe body for Rufaro' *Herald* 12/9/19; 'Thousands bid Mugabe farewell at Rufaro' *Herald* 13/9/19; 'Final salute for Cde Mugabe' *Sunday Mail* 15/9/19; 'Mugabe family pays tribute to nation for sharing grief' *Herald* 14/9/19; 'Massive send-off for Mugabe' *Daily News* 16/9/19; 'Mnangagwa calls on Zimbabweans to mourn Mugabe' *eNCA* 12/9/19, accessed 19/6/20; 'Stampede to view Uncle Bob's body' *Newsday* 13/9/19; 'Mourning for Zimbabwe's Mugabe marred by dispute, stampede' *Associated Press* 13/9/19; 'Leaders jet in for funeral service' *Herald* 14/9/19.

[114] For just a few examples: 'Mugabe's family clashes with Mnangagwa over plans for state funeral' *Guardian* 7/9/19; 'Impasse over Mugabe burial' *Newsday* 11/9/19; 'Family denies feud with government over Mugabe burial' *eNCA* 11/9/19; 'Mugabe lies in state as family rejects funeral plans' *BBC news* 12/9/19; 'Robert Mugabe's family rejects government burial plans' *Guardian* 12/9/19; 'Inside the fight over Robert Mugabe's body' *Standard* 16/9/19; 'Shocking details on Mugabe burial' *Sunday News* 29/9/19.

[115] 'Heroes Acre burial for Mugabe' *Herald* 13/9/19.

After Mugabe

As discussed above, although Mnangagwa was at pains to be seen to be creating distance from the previous regime in some respects, actually his politics is not one of radical rupture from Mugabeism. The 'soft coup' was carefully presented as an effort to preserve Bob's and ZANU PF's liberation legacy from the young miscreants gathered around him, and especially his deeply disliked second wife, Grace. Apart from needing regional legitimacy from SADC (Southern African Development Community) and the AU, the new leadership is very much invested in ZANU PF's 'chimurenga politics'. Its determination to preserve a claim on the legacies of Mugabeism is why great care was taken to ensure that Mugabe, his wife and his family, were well cared for and given a very generous 'retirement' package after his removal in November 2017.[116] It is also why efforts were repeatedly made to publicly reconcile with Mugabe and Grace following his ouster, notably after the death of Grace's mother, when Mnangagwa chartered a plane to enable her return from Singapore.[117]

Mnangagwa's government was therefore deeply concerned to ensure that Mugabe took his place at National Heroes Acre to bestow his liberation legacy, ideology and legitimacy onto the new regime.[118] Even as arrangements for Bob's funeral and burial were being discussed, Mnangagwa presided over the burial at the National Heroes Acre of another senior military commander, Major General Trust Mugoba, who had coincidently (and maybe suspiciously)[119] died on the same day as Mugabe, illustrating again (as with the deaths of Dabengwa, Mtukudzi and other recently declared 'national heroes') Mnangagwa's commitment to continuing the narrow politics of ZANU PF-controlled commemoration that his predecessor had forged.[120]

But it seems Bob had anticipated that his ZANU PF usurpers would try to make use of his death in this way. Bitter and resolute Mugabe apparently indicated before his death that he did not want to be buried at the National Heroes Acre, preferring instead to be buried at his rural home in Zvimba,[121] as has been common among many who have rejected

---

[116] 'Robert Mugabe's retirement package: 20 staff, private air travel and a fleet of cars' *Guardian* 29/12/17; 'Mugabe's generous "retirement" package is revealed' *BusinessDay SA* 28/12/17.

[117] 'Mugabe to meet Mnangagwa for first time since coup' *SA Times* 25/2/18; 'Grace reconciles with Mnangagwa following her mother's death' *SABC News* 6/9/18; 'Mnangagwa God-given: Grace' *Herald* 7/9/18.

[118] 'ED welcomes Mugabe's body' *Herald* 12/9/19; 'Cde Mugabe's body expected Wednesday' *Sunday Mail* 8/9/19.

[119] Field notes, March 2020.

[120] 'Ministry mourns Mugabe, Mugoba' *Herald* 12/9/19.

[121] 'Former President laid to rest in Zvimba' *Sunday Mail* 28/9/19; '"Shamed" Mugabe made choice to be buried in Zvimba – Family' *Newzimbabwe.com* 29/9/19; 'Zimbabwe ex-president Robert Mugabe buried in his native village' *Aljazeera.com* 28/9/19; 'Robert Mugabe buried in low-key ceremony with a

The Politics of the Dead

burial at National Heroes Acre. The ironies reverberate here. As we have seen, Mugabe had himself presided over the burials of many former ZANU PF stalwarts who, having fallen out with him in life, had publicly refused to be buried at National Heroes Acre before their deaths, but were subsequently interred there anyway. This reflects, as discussed in Chapter 4, ZANU PF's tendency to instrumentalise and contain in death those who had defied them in life. Through what he allegedly told his relatives in August before he died, Mugabe was now doing the same.[122] Understanding well how this politics works, he was not prepared to allow his former comrades who had so unceremoniously removed him from office less than two years before, to use his body to prop up their ideological cause, however much he himself had been an author of this style of politics in the first place.

Almost as soon as Mugabe's body touched down at Harare airport, if not before, reports began emerging of a dispute between the government and Bob's relatives, especially his wife Grace.[123] There was a sense of the frenetic about the plans being laid down for his body-viewing in two stadiums in Harare, his state funeral, and its journey to Zvimba for memorial services and body-viewing there, which all seemed to reflect the unsure direction in which his burial would proceed.[124] At first the tension about where he should be buried appeared to be, rather simply, between the government who wanted him interred at the National Heroes Acre, and the family, headed by Grace, and supported by chiefs and clan elders in Zvimba, who wanted him buried according to his own wishes, next to his mother, or according to local traditions amongst other 'chiefs' in a secret cave near his rural home.[125] Many recognised Bob's

---

no-show from senior govt officials' *News24.com* 28/9/19; all accessed 19/6/20. 'Mugabe buried in low-key ceremony as family snub national plans' *Guardian* 28/9/19.

[122] 'Former President laid to rest in Zvimba' *Sunday Mail* 28/9/19 'Mugabe finally laid to rest' *eNCA* 29; 9/19; '"Shamed" Mugabe made choice to be buried in Zvimba – Family' *Newzimbabwe.com* 29/9/19, both accessed 19/6/20.

[123] 'Mugabe's family clashes with Mnangagwa over plans for state funeral' *Guardian* 7/9/19; 'Impasse over Mugabe burial' *Newsday* 11/9/19; 'Mugabe lies in state as family rejects funeral plans' *BBC news* 12/9/19; 'Robert Mugabe's family rejects government burial plans' *Guardian* 12/9/19; 'Inside the fight over Robert Mugabe's body' *Standard* 15/9/19.

[124] 'Mugabe burial in 30 days' *Newsday* 14/9/19; 'Ex-leader's body expected in Harare' *Herald* 18/9/19; 'Family feuds over Mugabe body' *Newsday* 16/9/19; 'Funeral programme shifts to Zvimba' *Sunday Mail* 15/9/19; 'Zimbabwe's Mugabe to lie in state at 2 different stadiums' *Associated Press* 10/9/19.

[125] 'Mugabe set for Zvimba burial' *Newsday* 13/9/19; 'We forgive Mugabe coup leaders' *Newsday* 18/9/19; 'Zimbabwe chiefs demand Mugabe be buried according to traditions' *News24.com* 20/9/19; 'The dilemma of how to appease Mugabe's spirit' *BBC news* 28/9/19; 'Six traditional questions stalling Mugabe's burial' *Africanews.com* 18/9/19; 'Traditional rites fuel discord over Mugabe

After Mugabe

wishes as a deliberate last snub to those who had ousted him, aware that ZANU PF would find it difficult to impose its will having already publicly committed itself to respecting Mugabe's and his family's wishes. Evocative statements were circulating from some relatives, especially Leo Mugabe (his nephew), that Mugabe had been hounded to an early death by the way ZANU PF had treated him after the coup. These were later repeated by South Africa's firebrand, EFF (Economic Freedom Fighters) leader, Julius Malema, when he visited to pay his respects, and clearly upped the pressure on the ruling party.[126]

It was therefore with some surprise that news was received a few days after his funeral that the family had, reluctantly, agreed to allow Mugabe to be buried at the National Heroes Acre. The negotiations must have been tense and acrimonious, because the agreement arrived at was that Bob would not be interred in the long vacant spot next to Sally, his first wife, but rather in a new, still-to-be-built 'mausoleum' to be hastily constructed at a spot on the summit of the small hill at Heroes Acre identified by some of his immediate relatives.[127] This was going to take some weeks to build, and many began to wonder how long Bob's body would be lying in state, or ferried between Zvimba and the garish 'Blue Roof' mansion in Harare where he and Grace had lived.

As discussed in Chapter 2, according to common death beliefs and practices in Zimbabwe, the period between someone's death and their burial is often seen as a particularly anxious and unsettled time, when the spirit of the dead is believed to hover around the body dangerously. Grace Mugabe spent much of this period under a heavy black veil, maintaining a vigil around her late husband's corpse.[128] Nevertheless,

---

funeral' *HeraldLive* (SA) 19/9/19; 'Mugabe will be buried neither in a cave nor next to his mother' *ZimEye.net* 28/9/19; online sources accessed 19/6/20.

[126] 'ED hounded Mugabe to death: Malema' *Newsday* 24/9/19; 'Huge Mugabe send off planned' *Newsday* 9/9/19; 'Robert Mugabe died a "very bitter" man, nephew says' *BBC news* 9/9/19; 'In Mugabe's village, relatives say he was very bitter before death' *Reuters* 7/9/19; 'Mugabe died in a foreign land because Zanu-PF "tormented" him: Nephew' *SA Times* 12/9/19; 'Malema: Mnangagwa's government tormented Robert Mugabe until his death' *Eyewitness News* 24/9/19; 'Malema's Mugabe closing gambit' *Daily Maverick* 15/9/19.

[127] 'Mugabe to be buried in national monument' *News24.com* 13/9/19, accessed 19/6/20; 'Special grave for Mugabe' *Herald* 14/9/19; 'Work on Mugabe mausoleum begins' *Herald* 17/9/19; 'Mugabe burial in 30 days' *Newsday* 14/9/19 'Robert Mugabe family backs down over burial after "threat to Grace"' *Sky News* 15/9/19; 'Heroes Acre burial for Mugabe' *Herald* 13/9/19; 'Inside the fight over Robert Mugabe's body' *Standard* 16/9/19.

[128] 'Is grieving Grace behind Mugabe funeral plans drama?' *IOL.co.za* 14/9/19; 'Robert Mugabe buried in a steel coffin encased in concrete as family claims people are "after his body"' *Telegraph* (UK) 29/9/19; 'Mugabe feared body parts could be used for rituals … nephew confirms' *Nehandaradio.com* 29/9/19; online sources accessed 19/6/20.

some mused that Grace must have managed, in some way, to get her way by refusing to allow Bob to be buried next to his still-popular first wife, Sally. Others either applauded or strongly critiqued the decision to build a new separate and elevated mausoleum for Mugabe, as either befitting of his unique legacy, or as an obvious extenuation of ZANU PF's long-running politics of distorting Zimbabwe's liberation past by privileging some contributions and denigrating others. Clearer indications of the pressure that Mnangagwa's regime must have placed upon Grace and Bob's relatives became clearer when it emerged a few days later that the title deeds on the Blue Roof and another Harare house owned by the family were listed in ZANU PF's name, but would now, out of concern for the former first family's wellbeing, be transferred to them.[129] Suggestions that the threat of withholding these title deeds had been waved over their heads in order to get the Mugabe family's approval, revealed the extent to which ZANU PF were invested in ensuring Bob would be interred at Heroes Acre.[130]

Soon, however, the politics surrounding Bob's burial became even more complex after it emerged Grace had wanted Mugabe buried at the Blue Roof mansion in Harare, but the city authorities had refused permission, citing city bye-laws.[131] Not only is it likely that city authorities could have succumbed to ZANU PF pressure to refuse this request, but this detail also suggested that Grace, Bob's children, and the rest of Bob's family, let alone chiefs and other community elders in Zvimba, were not necessarily speaking with the same voice at all. This was later confirmed when it emerged that several Zvimba chiefs had fallen out with Grace, and were forcibly ejected from her ongoing vigil around the corpse at the Blue Roof, because they had sided with ZANU PF and argued Bob should in fact be interred at Heroes Acre in Harare.[132]

The controversies deepened further soon after, however, when, with building work on the mausoleum already proceeding, it was suddenly announced on 27 September that plans had changed again, and Bob would now be buried in Zvimba after all.[133] Robert Mugabe was then

---

[129] 'Zanu-PF owns Blue Roof, Bona Mugabe's residence' *Herald* 16/9/19; 'Zanu-PF regularises Blue Roof title deeds' *Nehandaradio.com* 16/9/19; 'Zanu-PF to transfer Blue Roof mansion to Mugabe family' *IOL.co.za* 3/10/19; 'Mnangagwa keeps his word, transfers title deeds of Blue Roof Mansion to Grace Mugabe' *HarareLive.com* 18/10/19; online sources accessed 19/6/20.

[130] 'President reassures Mugabe family of properties' *Herald* 1/10/19; 'Robert Mugabe family backs down over burial after "threat to Grace"' *Sky News* 15/9/19; 'Inside the fight over Robert Mugabe's body' *Standard* 16/9/19.

[131] 'Grace now wants Mugabe to be buried at the Blue Roof' *Zimbabwe Mail* 25/9/19; 'Shocking details on Mugabe burial' *Sunday News* 29/9/19.

[132] 'Chiefs kicked out of Mugabe mansion' *Newsday* 25/9/19; 'Chiefs snub Mugabe burial' *Sunday Mail* 29/9/19.

[133] 'ED loses Mugabe burial site tussle' *Newsday* 27/9/19; 'Mugabe burial for

hastily buried one day later, in a private, guest list-only event, which Mnangagwa did not attend, in a specially designed casket, in a concrete-lined grave at the centre of his family homestead.[134] What exactly had caused this change of mind on the family's part remains open to speculation, although the role of Julius Malema and his outspoken critique of ZANU PF's pressure on Grace and her family was quickly identified by some as a key factor.[135] That Mugabe was buried in the centre of his homestead and not in a secret burial location for Zvimba chiefs, as earlier suggested, confirmed that Grace and the family had indeed fallen out with local community elders as well as with the ruling party. It later emerged that Leo Mugabe – self-styled family spokesman – too had been excluded from the family burial, amid rumours that he and Grace had fallen out after she accused him of taking bribes from ZANU PF to ensure Bob's burial in Harare.[136] Whatever family intrigues were in play, however, the end result was a double riposte to Mnangagwa and his new regime, with the half-built mausoleum at Heroes Acre affirming that Bob was not only better than any other ZANU PF hero, he had also managed to defy his usurpers until the very end.[137] There were some rumours later that the family's longer term plan is for Mugabe's remains to be disinterred and reburied at the National Heroes Acre, once Mnangagwa's 'second republic' has been replaced. At any rate Bob had defied his successors' attempts to utilise his corpse to buttress their use of the 'chimurenga politics' he had himself propagated. Bob had indeed done it again.

As if all of this was not enough to show how the contestations that surrounded Mugabe's death epitomised many aspects of Zimbabwe's politics of the dead, there was yet another dimension to these controversies that is worthy of a final comment, because of the way it reveals how questions of corporeality too were part of the intense politicking going on. After the burial, reports and rumours began to emerge that throughout

---

Zvimba' *Herald* 27/9/19; 'Mugabe burial set for today' *Herald* 28/9/19; 'Former President laid to rest in Zvimba' *Sunday Mail* 29/9/19.

[134] Ibid.; 'Reinforced grave, tamper-proof casket: battle for Mugabe's corpse' *Eyewitnessnews.com* 30/9/19, accessed 19/6/20; 'Mugabe feared rituals' *City Press* 29/9/19; 'Mugabe looked after his own' *Newsday* 30/9/19; 'Robert Mugabe buried in a steel coffin encased in concrete as family claims people are "after his body"' *Telegraph* (UK) 29/9/19.

[135] 'Mugabe burial set for today' *Herald* 28/9/19.

[136] 'Bribery storm engulfs Mugabe burial' *Zimbabwe Independent* 4/10/19.

[137] Reports later in 2019 of various legal challenges facing Grace Mugabe's '*Gushungo*' businesses (styled thus by Grace Mugabe after her husband's clan name) suggest that it did not take Mnangagwa very long to respond. 'Grace faces eviction' *Newsday* 16/10/19; 'Grace's world crumbles' *Newsday* 23/10/19; 'Grace Mugabe fights diamond dealer lawsuit' *Sunday Times* (SA) 6/10/19; 'Once untouchable, now her world's crumbling' *East African* 2/11/19; 'Grace Mugabe's woes mount' *Nehandaradio.com* 11/3/20, accessed 19/6/20.

the troubled negotiations between Grace, the family and ZANU PF, great concern had been circulating about ensuring Bob's body was protected from any nefarious attempts to tamper with his corpse, or remove body parts.[138] This, some suggested, was the reason for Grace's apparent refusal to allow Bob's body be held at any city morgues or at One Commando barracks, where national heroes are usually kept preceding burial. It was this concern which had fuelled her exhausting, but well-performed, mourning vigil and her insistence that Bob's body could only be kept and displayed under careful guard at her home in Harare, and later in Zvimba. According to several reports Grace hardly left Mugabe's corpse at all during the weeks between his return from Singapore and his eventual burial.[139] Leo Mugabe stated that Bob had himself been concerned that his enemies might want to make use of his body parts for nefarious rituals to accrue 'occult' power, and it was this which led to the exhausting vigil around his body.[140] These suggestions were fed by rumours circulating in the press and on social media about the number of different coffins Bob appeared to have been displayed in during the weeks since his death, as well as reports that a special 'tamper-proof' coffin had been constructed for him to be interred in.[141] Reflecting the duplicity that is common to such rumours, accounts of Grace's long and tortured vigil performance around Bob's corpse soon sparked suggestions that it was she herself who had sought to make nefarious use of his potent corporeality.[142]

In the very crudest terms, there have long been whiffs of the 'occult' to ZANU PF's style of politics, and to its internal factionalism. This has manifest in various ways in its contributions to the politics of the dead discussed in this book. It is a dimension of political life that is as broad and diverse as religious and spiritual life is in Zimbabwe generally; ranging from the central role that mediumship, ancestral practices and

[138] 'Reinforced grave, tamper-proof casket: Battle for Mugabe's corpse' *Eyewitnessnews.com* 30/9/19; 'Mugabe feared rituals' *City Press* 29/9/19; 'Robert Mugabe buried in a steel coffin encased in concrete as family claims people are "after his body"' *Telegraph* (UK) 29/9/19; 'The dilemma of how to appease Mugabe's spirit' *BBC news* 28/9/19; 'Mugabe buried in secret ... mausoleum construction was a tactical diversion' *Nehandaradio.com* 23/9/19; online sources accessed 19/6/20.

[139] 'Grace foiled plans to use Robert Mugabe's body parts for rituals' *ZWNews* 6/10/19; People were after Mugabe's body parts, family spokesperson reveals' *The Citizen* 28/9/19; '"Grace blocked attempts to steal Mugabe's body parts," Mugabe family' *Zimbabwe News* 30/9/19.

[140] 'Mugabe feared body parts could be used for rituals... nephew confirms' *Nehandaradio.com* 29/9/19; 'Mugabe feared rituals' *City Press* 29/9/19.

[141] 'How many coffins does Mugabe have? Are they changing his clothes too?' *Nehanda TV* 26/9/19: 'Robert Mugabe buried in a steel coffin encased in concrete as family claims people are "after his body"' *Telegraph* (UK) 29/9/19; '"Mystery" of Mugabe's "multiple" caskets unraveled' *Sunday Mail* 6/10/19.

[142] 'Did Grace chop-off Mugabe's body parts?' *Zimbabwe Mail* 6/10/19.

After Mugabe

the cult of Ambuya Nehanda have and continue to play in anti-colonial African nationalism (Dube 2018), to the increasing overtures towards new charismatic Pentecostal movements in recent years (to which we return briefly in the Conclusion). It extends from both the ridiculous – such as the much mocked involvement of Mugabe's top ministers with the fraudulent 'diesel *n'anga*' discussed in Chapter 5 – to the downright malicious, such as the accusations of witchcraft levied at two previous vice-presidents, first Joice Mujuru and then Mnangagwa, as part of the intensifying factional politics of Mugabe's latter years in office.[143] Conversely, statements, rumours and claims associating Mugabe's rule with some kind of divine, ancestral or even occult providence, have often contributed to an aura of totalising, all-encompassing power and supremacy weaved around him (Chitanda 2020b).[144] Although sometimes the cause of ridicule, these dimensions of ZANU PF politics are extraordinarily effective and affective. Their efficacy derives again from their uncertain duplicity; their ability to both cast any opposition into an over-determined position of absolute malevolence, and conversely in making Mugabe appear transcendental, omnipotent and untouchable. Seen in this light, there is nothing particularly unusual, 'exotic' or 'occult' about this stylistics of power, nor about the wider politics of the dead to which they contribute. It is with this in mind that we can understand the corporeal politics that circulated around Bob's cadaver, which Grace performed so magnificently.

In this book, I have discussed the importance of recognising the enduring salience, however complex and emergent, of human corporealities in meanings and practices to do with death, across diverse religious registers and regional contexts, and enduring through the profound historical transformations that funerary practices experienced during the colonial period and the 20th century. The common belief and anxiety that corpses are dangerous between death and burial has not only to do with the hazardous presence of unhappy spirits of the dead said during this period to 'hover' around their corpses; it also has to do with the troubling potencies of their corporeal substances. Moreover, as I argued in Chapter 2, often these two concerns are deeply entangled. This is why, however contested they can often become, funerary practices across a wide range

[143] 'Joice Mujuru rejects Mugabe claims of bare-breasted witchcraft rituals' *SA Times* 3/3/15; 'Mujuru rejects Mugabe witchcraft claims' *IOL.co.za* 3/3/15; 'Mugabe says fired deputy plotted via witchcraft' *News24.com* 8/11/17; 'Zimbabwe president Robert Mugabe: My rival used witchcraft against me' *Newsweek* 8/11/17; 'Mnangagwa expelled from Zanu-PF, accused of witchcraft' *IOL.co.za* 9/11/17; 'Critics say Mugabe believes in witchcraft, not being truthful sorcery is alien to Zanu-PF Politics' *Newzimbabwe.com* 27/8/17; both accessed 19/6/20.

[144] 'Robert Mugabe is God's Angel Gabriel' *Eyewitness News* 2/6/17; 'Mugabe appointed by God' *eNCA* 5/2/13, www.youtube.com/watch?v=jsVuLsQNcd4, accessed 4/7/20.

of religious regimes can be understood both as processes of managing the transformation of life into death, and of dealing with and containing the dangerous corporeal substances that death involves. It is in both ways that funerals are about making people safely and benevolently dead. This is also why an injunction against speaking 'ill of the dead' can have particular potency in a Zimbabwean context, as dead people and their corporeal remains are considered dangerous before burial, and before these processes are complete. Indeed, as discussed in Chapter 2, there are well-known cases of people deliberately not burying their dead in order to force compensation or some kind of response from those deemed culpable for their deaths, who risk being haunted by the dangerous unsettled *ngozi* spirits of those killed. The fact that Mugabe himself was often rumoured to be haunted by the unsettled spirits of people whose death he was said to have orchestrated illustrates the intense political salience of such beliefs.

It is in this context that the long delays around Bob's burial were already political affective and anxiety provoking. Similarly, it is also common in Zimbabwe for people to be anxious about protecting the graves of the recently deceased, because witches and those who practice witchcraft are believed to eat human flesh (Lan 1985: 35–6; Simmons 2000: 2). Considered in many respects as 'the quintessential anti-social being' (Simmons 2000: 3), witches are often understood to substantiate this through consuming the dangerous substances of decaying corpses (Crawford 1967: 112–15; 124–5). So people commonly check graves for any signs of disturbance during the early days after a burial. Likewise, grandiose cemented grave mountings, which have become increasingly common throughout the region,[145] serve not only to monumentalise the continuing memory of the dead, but also to keep them contained and secure. Indeed, these two things reinforce each other; a heavily monumentalised grave, covered in concrete, bolsters the presence of a dead person as someone not only to be remembered, but whose corporeal substances are themselves potent and dangerous, in need of being contained and protected.

We can therefore understand how the controversies surrounding where and how Bob was to be buried were entangled with this corporeal politics. We can glimpse the efficacy of the rumours that suggested that Grace's exhausting vigil, Bob's tamper-proof coffin, and his concrete-lined grave, unusually placed in the middle of his rural homestead, were all a response to Bob's own fears that his body parts would be the target

---

[145] In March 2020 Chipunza mentioned that the Tonga equivalent to the Shona *kurova guva* ritual used to literally involve beating a grave 'until it disappears, to sink it into the ground, so that there would be no more trace. But now, like everyone else in Zimbabwe, there is this emphasis among Tonga people on monumentalising graves with large permanent stone head stones' (Interview with Chipunza, 5/3/20).

of nefarious interference by malevolent interests aligned against him and his family. These rumours and performances all served to reinforce Bob's omnipotent salience and corporeal presence in Zimbabwean politics, just as the refusal, then acceptance and then refusal again to bury Bob at National Heroes Acre had ensured that his death and burial would become as eventful and talked about as it was always supposed to be. Not only had Bob done it again, he also showed everyone that although the phenomena of Zimbabwe's politics of the dead is, as I have argued, necessarily bigger than any individual's intentional design, he could still be its most masterful player. Furthermore, the controversies around Mugabe's death and burial again demonstrated how in Zimbabwe's politics of the dead the corporeality of human materials matter. With rumours already circulating about Mugabe's spirit or ghost re-appearing,[146] as well as reports that Grace has secretly exhumed and reburied his remains to prevent 'Mugabe's political enemies from getting to his body',[147] or has begun turning his Zvimba grave into a museum or tourist attraction,[148] alongside speculations that Bob's remains might still, in some future moment, be moved to the National Heroes Acre, it seems likely that Bob's death, like all death perhaps, is not yet complete or finished with. Indeed, for many, including Mnangagwa, Mugabe's ghost had already been haunting Zimbabwe long before the politics that surrounded his burial emerged in September 2019.[149] Perhaps the priest overseeing his interment was right when he declared, 'this man lives for ever'.[150]

[146] 'Mugabe ghost spotted in attendance at his funeral service' *LuiSpot* 15/9/19, www.youtube.com/watch?v=end2TfocCtk, accessed 4/7/20; 'Shocking: Suspected Mugabe's ghost appears at National Sports Stadium' *Gambakwe* 14/9/19, https://gambakwe.com/2019/09/14/shocking-suspected-mugabes-ghost-appears-at-national-sports-stadium, accessed 4/7/20; 'Robert Mugabe ghost to haunt Zimbabweans?' *ZimEye.net* 10/9/19, accessed 9/6/20; 'The dilemma of how to appease Mugabe's spirit' *BBC news* 28/9/19.
[147] 'Grace Mugabe exhumes and reburies Mugabe's body: Spotlight Zimbabwe' *Gambakwe* 1/5/20, https://gambakwe.com/2020/05/01/grace-mugabe-exhumes-and-reburies-mugabe-s-body-spotlight-zimbabwe, accessed 4/7/20.
[148] 'Grace Mugabe dumps Blue Roof for Zvimba as she turns Robert Mugabe's grave into cash cow tourist attraction' *iHarare.com* 10/12/19, accessed 19/6/20; 'Grace Mugabe relocates to Zvimba' *Anchor* 13/12/19.
[149] 'Mugabe ghost haunts ED in Tanzania' *Standard* 1/7/18; 'Mugabe's Ghost?' *Ubuntu FM* 25/1/19, accessed 19/6/20.
[150] '"This man lives forever": Zimbabwe's Mugabe set for burial' *Associated Press* 28/9/19.

Conclusion

'Where there is life, death is a certainty; it's guaranteed' announced the opening line of a recent advertisement for a 'worldwide' funeral insurance policy offering 'body repatriation' services for diasporan Zimbabweans.[1] The odd mixture of morbidity and enthusiasm carried by that statement may be common to this peculiar genre of writing, and to the commercial activities it promotes, which have been the subject of a growing body of literature over the last decade or more (Golomski 2018a; Lee 2011). Although I have not focused particular attention here on the emergence of new commercial funerary activities in the context of broader, changing death practices across the region – a fascinating area of research where much remains to be done – the arguments developed in this book do suggest that, contrary to the statement above, there is much that is uncertain and unfinished or incomplete about death in Zimbabwe, and maybe elsewhere.

This book has focused on a particular, but multi-faceted, cultural-political phenomena in Zimbabwe that I call the politics of the dead. It is peculiar to Zimbabwe in so far as it animates, and is animated by, its particular colonial and postcolonial histories; especially the central role that legacies of violence from the liberation war, and from different post-independence periods, continue to play in its politics. But this phenomena is not limited to Zimbabwe's peculiar politics of violence and commemoration. It has both wider and more diverse salience *within* the country and *beyond* it; drawing on, feeding and gaining traction in the context of broader trajectories of change and continuity in meanings and practices to do with death. These include the rising significance of 'liberation heritage' across neighbouring countries that fought, or supported, struggles for independence, as well as broader patterns in the way that violence and post-violence has political efficacy in diverse contexts across the region. Zimbabwe's politics of the dead also resonates with a wider, revitalised 'carnal fetishism' and new (or renewed) concern with bodies and corporeality that scholars like Bernault (2010) and Ranger (2010b) also identified, and which the emergence of innovative funeral and mortuary practices similarly point towards, such as new insurance policies offering repatriation services which I began with above.

What this book has sought to show is that the uncertainties and incompleteness of death in Zimbabwe are politically productive, and that they

---

[1] 'Body repatriation – your bespoke policy' no date, https://diasporafuneral-cashplan.com/zimbabwe/news/123-dfcp-news, accessed 19/5/20.

Conclusion

ultimately derive from the problematic, entangled excessivities of human material and immaterial existence, which are wrought open, revealed and laid bare through death in ways that demand but usually (or even ultimately) defy stabilisation, fixing or resolution. This politics of the dead, and the uncertainties that lie at its core, are not unique or limited to particular cultural, religious, political or professional registers of meaning, or the regimes of knowledge and practice historically associated with them. Indeed, death's uncertainties are simultaneously compounded by and yet reflected in the multiple, co-existent, and always transforming and transformative, repertoires of meaning and practice that it invokes. The histories of diverse, changing and always emergent death practices across the wider continent discussed in the Introduction, which have received renewed scholarly attention over the last two decades, point exactly to, even as they reinforce, the profound uncertainties that swirl around death in Zimbabwe, and perhaps everywhere.

In 1972 Johannes Fabian argued that at that moment there had emerged a deep lacuna in the anthropological study of death; a void that had become filled by what he called 'parochialization'. This 'parochialization', he commiserated, 'had the effect of eliminating a transcendental and universal conception of the problem'. '"Death" (in the singular)' he argued, had 'ceased to be a problem of anthropological inquiry; there are only deaths and forms of death-related behavior' (1972: 545). The enormous amount of new research carried out over the last few decades on 'death-related' matters, and across a wide range of regional foci, suggests that this may no longer be the case. Death and 'death-related' practices have become the subject of a large new body of literature. However, the extent to which this new literature has answered Fabian's call to 'find or construct a [new] meta-level of interpretation', a new 'social hermeneutic' or 'interpretation of social reality which conceives of itself as part of the processes it attempts to understand' (1972: 567), remains to be seen. There still often seems to be a failure of nerve (or perhaps of ambition) among many scholars who 'came of age' in the long wake of our discipline's 'crisis of representation' in the 1980s, to say anything larger or beyond what Fabian identified as the 'parochial'. Much (but certainly not all) of the new work on death still seems focused on particular 'deaths' and particular 'death-related' practices, rather than death itself. Exceptions here might include new research into precarious lives (Butler 2004) and the 'governance of the dead' (Stepputat 2014) inspired by Mbembe's work on necro-politics (2003); or the new attention devoted to corporeality and the affective materialities of human remains (Fontein 2018; Harries 2017a; Filippucci et al. 2012; Krmpotich et al. 2010; Crossland, 2009a; Fontein & Harries 2009); as well as significant developments in medical anthropology and science studies critiquing the 'medicalisation of death', exploring organ transplants, palliative experiences and raising important questions about death as process (Haddow 2000, 2005; Green 2008; Lawton 2000, 2001; Seymour 1999; Lock 1996, 2002; Papagaroufali 1999; Sharp 2000, 2001).

This book has tried to grapple with the problem of how to understand the historical, cultural, social and political particularities of 'parochial deaths' in the wider context of death as shared human experience, by focusing on how the politics of the dead has emerged as a particular cultural-political phenomena in Zimbabwe exactly in traction with aspects of death that may have much wider social, political and historical purchase; such as the productive uncertainties that derive from the excessivity of human remains and from the unfinished incompleteness of death. In developing these arguments I have sought to engage recent debates about materiality, especially as applied to human corporeality, in critical discussion with developments in political anthropology that focus on the interplay of bio- and necro-politics in performative stylistics of power. The 'social hermeneutic' to which this has led, and that lies at the core of this book, centres the profound but productive uncertainties of death. It is this, I suggest in belated response to Fabian's 1972 call, which may have much wider interpretative significance than just Zimbabwe's peculiar politics of the dead. Indeed Fabian already anticipated this in his suggestion that 'sensitive ethnography may come to the surprising conclusion that "everything that touches upon death is equivocal, ambiguous"' (Fabian 1972: 565).[2] More recently this analytic finds powerful echoes in other anthropological and sociological work (Cooper & Pratten 2015; Rosa 2018, 2019) on unpredictability, indeterminacy and contingency; and what I call elsewhere an 'anthropology of the subjunctive' (Fontein 2021). It may also have much to say to Graeber's notion of 'ontological realism and theoretical relativism' as core to anthropology's purpose; that is 'the development of a rich diversity of (at least partly) incommensurable theoretical perspectives on a reality that, I believe, can never be entirely encompassed by any one of them – for the very reason that it is real' (Graeber 2015: 31). Such an analytic of profound uncertainty also resonates with Nyamnjoh's work (2017b: 253, 2017a) on notions of 'incompleteness' through the writings of the Nigerian writer Amos Tutuola, which he deploys to critique 'colonial and apartheid ideologies on being human and being African' by stressing 'conviviality, interconnections and interdependence between competing knowledge traditions' in Africa and elsewhere. In one passage Nyamnjoh specifically discusses how death appears in Tutuola's work:

> To die in life and live in death is part of the flexibility characteristic of Tutuola's universe. Death is a form of circulation and not a matter of permanent severance of links with life and the living. One is dead to

---

[2] He drew this from Theuws's mid-20th century work in Zaire (Theuws 1960, 1968).

Conclusion

> a particular context, as a way of becoming alive to prospective new contexts. Death is a form of adventure and exploration of the infinitudes of life. Death and dying are processes in gradations and by degree. There seems to be no end to dying, just as there is no end to living. People who die reappear elsewhere and are again available for death. There is no such thing as an ordinary mortal, just as there is no such thing as the fully dead. Death and dying are as much a reality for gods, spirits, ghosts and death itself, as they are for humans. (Nyamnjoh 2017b: 257)

Tutuola's 'universe' may seem far removed from the particularities of Zimbabwe's politics of the dead, yet the echoes here with my arguments about the unfinished, uncertainties of death suggest they may have far wider significance.

Although the way that Zimbabwe's politics of the dead has manifest since independence is undoubtedly related to ZANU PF's particular stylistics of power – forged between coercion and consent, bio- and necro-politics, and over several decades of political chicanery – it is, in the end, not limited to the ruling party's brand of politics. The co-existence and play of different regimes of death *within* Zimbabwe takes place across diverse loyalties, religious commitments and political allegiances, as well as across myriad cultural and ethnic boundaries, drawing in a multiplicity of different expert, vernacular and everyday forms of sense making, experience and knowledge. In short, there is no 'outside' to this phenomena; everyone is, to a greater or lesser extent, complicit within it. And just as I have argued that death always remains potentiality incomplete, unfinished and unresolved – open-ended and emergent, however latently – so too the politics of uncertainty which it provokes has few absolute boundaries. No one, not even (or perhaps least of all) an observing anthropologist, can claim a special positionality beyond it. This too was already anticipated by Fabian in 1972 in his evocation that 'Lévi-Strauss was right: the anthropology of death is a form of dying, or of conquering death – which, in the end, may be the same' (1972: 567).

Bodies and spirits, change and continuity

This book began by exploring what bones and bodies do in Zimbabwe's politics of the dead, and how they do it; taking as the entry point its troubled politics of commemoration and the emergence of liberation heritage in the 2000s. This was deliberate because so much scholarship has already been written about the role of ancestral spirits and mediums (Ranger 2010b) – not to mention holy spirits and churches (Maxwell 1999, 2006; Engelke 2007; Linden 1980) – in Zimbabwe's liberation and post-independence history and politics. I set out to explore the role of corporeality in Zimbabwe's politics exactly as a counterweight to this over-emphasis on the immaterial and the spiritual.

Furthermore, my aim has been to use emergent debates about materiality and corporeality to think through the ways in which politics more broadly turns not merely on the contested play of different meanings, symbols, narratives and representations, but rather on the stuff of stuff itself – particularly human stuff – as active problematic things, uneasy subject/objects and as difficult transforming materials and flows of substances that demand stabilisation, fixing and containment. In subsequent chapters the argument moved from a concern with the efficacy of bones and bodies as active, problematic things and materials that index unresolved, dangerous pasts, challenge normative state processes, animate forms of political violence before and after death – and demand resolution through interventions like 'proper' funerary rites or exhumations and reburials – to questions about how the uncertain, duplicitous excessivity of human corporeality and even of death itself can be politically productive and useful as well as subversive. In this shift, the argument moved from exploring how the demanding, uncertain, excessivity of bones, bodies and material substances animate and enable particular kinds of politics, towards questions about the excessive uncertainties that likewise envelop the immaterial, whether in the form of the myriad of rumours that surround the suspicious unexplained deaths of ruling party officials; or through the unexpected return of demanding ancestors; or of unknown, mischievous, possibly dangerous spirits – haunting but also providing opportunities for mediums, families and kin, as well as politicians. I suggested that there is something equally excessive, uncertain and incomplete to encounters with the immaterial remnants of past lives encroaching into the present as there is to encounters with corporeal human remains. It is this excessivity – of being always beyond any final containment and stabilisation – which constitutes the alterity of both the material and immaterial and binds them together. Furthermore, this is salient in everyday contexts as much as it obviously is in the case of controversial and politically implicated mediums, or the unresolved deaths of troubling pasts, like the *gukurahundi*, the liberation war, election violence, or 'political accidents', or the promise of ancestrally divined diesel in the context of deepening economic woes and fuel shortages. Mai Melissa's story, in Chapter 6, illustrates how the politics of the dead, and the uncertain incompleteness of death at its core, are an everyday problem and phenomena as well as sometimes an intensely political one.

The uncertainties of the material and that of the immaterial, to which I have drawn attention, are not just bound by iconicity and resemblance. They are rather bound by their normal yet uneasy entanglement and imbrication, and by the processes of containment, stabilisation, fixing and determination that their rupture and revelation through death demand, but which, I suggest, they ultimately defy. These processes of determination and fixing usually involve both material and immaterial aspects.

Conclusion

So problematic resurfacing human remains or the fleshy, leaky bodies of the recently dead can demand identification, stabilisation and fixing through what are often highly technical and specialised material processes of forensic archaeology, pathology and/or vernacular exhumations, and at the same time employ less material practices of divination and spirit possession, or the collection of oral histories, or indeed long-drawn-out, inconclusive police investigations and public inquests. Sometimes, as during the Chibondo exhumations (Chapter 3) – and others like it since – non-human objects and things provide much more stability of meaning than the human materials themselves, reflecting the unusually problematic nature of human corporeal stuff. At other times, only immaterial practices can offer any semblance or stability of meaning in these contexts. Likewise, the problematic re-emergence of the immaterial remnants of incomplete pasts intruding into the present in the form of unknown or long silent ancestors and kin, or angry *ngozi* spirits, often takes decidedly material forms through sickness, affliction, precarity and crisis, and demand, in turn, resolution through unusually material kinds of fixing and stabilisation.

The apparent synchronicity of the excessivity of both the material and the immaterial – the torque of materiality (Pinney 2005) and the alterity of spirit – and their deep entanglements, might recall the common and overly smooth adage of 'subjects making objects making subjects' (Miller 2005), or indeed of the easy 'correspondences' through which different materials and living forms constitute the shared world (Ingold 2016). Yet, in the contexts on which this book has focused, there is little that is smooth, coherent or comfortable about these entanglements, and much that is fractured, disjunctured, precarious and unresolved. The excessivity of both stuff and of spirits, their refusal to be contained or held still, is what animates their alterity. Yet it is in these fractures and disjunctures that the potential political productivities of uncertainty are located, and from where the possibilities of subversion and contestation derive. All of this indexes the productive but perilous uncertainties of relationships between material and immaterial life which is foregrounded and revealed yet left unresolved by death.

As Ranger pointed out during an unfinished conversation in the early 2010s,[3] just a few years before his death in 2015, for him there had been a marked cultural shift 'from spirit to body' over his five decades of research in/on Zimbabwe. Referring to pioneering work by Shoko (2006) and others, he suggested something had changed in Zimbabwean discourses and practices to do with the dead, from an emphasis on spirits

---

[3] Ranger mentioned our conversation during a lecture (2010b) at the University of Illinois in October 2010; see 'From spirit to body: Approaches to violence and memory in Zimbabwe', www.youtube.com/watch?v=hoZz7I4JnlA, Center for Advanced Study, University of Illinois at Urbana-Champaign 21/1/14, accessed 21/5/20.

to an emphasis on bodies, corporeality and materiality. As if we were re-enacting a classic discussion between historians and anthropologists, my instinct at the time was that stuff and materiality (in all of its emergent complexity) had always mattered, but had been constrained from scholarly view by deeply-located Cartesian assumptions that long over-emphasised the agency of human immateriality – whether in the form of 'the mind', 'social structure', 'culture' or 'discourse' – and relegated human materiality mute and passive to the mechanistic determinations of 'nature', biology and physiology. In my view human corporeality had always mattered in ways that defied these kinds of dichotomy, but we had been looking at the wrong things or in the wrong way.

Looking back at that unfinished conversation now, I see that we were both right, and maybe, as he suggested, we had both overstated our positions.[4] Something has changed, not just in Zimbabwe but much more broadly. The wider literature on changing death across the region outlined in the Introduction clearly attests to significant and diverse transformations in death culture. Ranger was right to suggest that there has been something of a (re)turn towards bodies and corporeality across the region and the beyond. This could be reflected in the deepening significance of monumentalised graves in the politics of autochthony, belonging and rights to land (Geschiere 2005, 2009; Fontein 2011); or in the emergence of novel mortuary, embalming and funerary practices that Lee (2011) and Golomski (2018a, 2018b) have discussed. Or using Ranger's own example (2010b), in the outrage raised in Zimbabwe in 2010–11 when the tree in Harare that had allegedly (but falsely) been used to hang Ambuya Nehanda's medium Charwe in 1898, fell down just as attempts were being made to monumentalise it;[5] not to mention more recent efforts to repatriate her alleged remains and those of other first *chimurenga* leaders from UK museums, which I return to below. According to Ranger, these kinds of concerns were not prominent in the 1960s when African nationalism, with the help of writings by scholars like himself (1967), first began appealing to Nehanda's legacy and spirit in their efforts to garner support for the struggle against white-supremacist Rhodesia. Perhaps even scholars' renewed interest in the materialities of death in the 2000s reflects such broader societal and cultural transformations more than recent theoretical developments, as I had inferred. In the end, I suppose, theoretical and wider cultural transformations do not take place in isolated silos and the two are undoubtedly intertwined.

[4] Ibid.
[5] Charumbira 2010; 'Council fells tree where Mbuya Nehanda was hanged' *Herald* 7/12/11; '"Mbuya Nehanda tree" falls' *Newsday* 8/12/11; 'Heroes denied hero status but mystery tree "buried" at Heroes Acre' *Bulawayo24 News* 21/12/11; 'Zimbabwe: Fall of "Nehanda tree" bad omen for Zanu-PF' *SW Radio Africa* 13/12/11, accessed 19/6/20.

Conclusion

But Ranger did not refer to the importance placed on returning to Zimbabwe the corporeal remains of Nehanda mediums who died in Mozambique in the 1970s, which both Mhanda (2011) and Chigumadzi (2018: 88–9) have discussed. Perhaps Nehanda's corporeality or that of her mediums, had in the past mattered more than he surmised. Furthermore, in the way that change only gains traction in the context of continuities (Fontein 2015: 6–7; Nugent 2008), recent transformations in funerary and mortuary culture across the region could surely only gain adhesion exactly in relation to longer continuities of meaning and practice. Work in diverse regional contexts such as Ghana (Roberts 2011) and Kenya (Droz 2011; Lamont 2011), for example, certainly supports the argument that intertwined with, or in the backdrop of, great transformations in funerary processes as a result of Christian missionisation and colonial administrators' 'hygienist polices' (Droz 2011), lay the persistence of older motifs, patterns and practices. Ranger's own work on the complex politics of 'dignifying death' in colonial Bulawayo shows as much, revealing not only 'the existence of multiple and competing agencies' in the shaping of African urban mortuary culture, but also how the creative tensions and entanglements of a wide diversity of African interests (including old Ndebele elites, migrants, 'traditionalists' and Christians of many different types, denominations and loyalties) were marked by the persistence and remaking of older forms, such as *umbuyiso* ceremonies (Chapter 2), in synthetic engagement with various 'new' Christian practices and 'the prestige of white memorial culture' (Ranger 2011a: 58, 2004b).

As Hertz (1960) identified in his classic work on the anthropology of death, human bodies and corporealities have long mattered in very complex and sometimes astonishingly diverse ways,[6] across very different contexts. There is significant evidence from across Africa that human substances – especially in decay – have long been considered potent, problematic and dangerous. In Zimbabwe this is exemplified by the longue durée of concerns about necrophagy by witches, or the use of human materials to concoct dangerous *muti* [magic/medicine], as well as by enduring practices through which corpses might be denied proper burial by relatives for the purpose of raising angry *ngozi* spirits to extract retribution from those responsible for their deaths. Such concerns long pre-date more recent and often problematically sensationalist concerns

---

[6] During a 2008 'Bones Collective' workshop, Magnus Course emphasised this by referring to endo-cannibalism in South America, in his well-judged warning against assuming that everywhere human remains and 'the dead' are necessarily respected or venerated. In some contexts they may be denigrated 'because they are seen to have failed' (Fontein & Harries 2009: 8). Of course, 'it could be argued that such rituals in themselves suggest there is an unsettling quality about human flesh and corpses which requires to be dealt with or transformed in some way' (ibid.).

about so-called *'muti* murders'[7] (Ranger 2007b; Kuper 2005) and are reported in literature dating back to at least to the mid-20th century (Crawford 1967: 112–15; 124–5).

Two other examples from the wider region (already discussed in the Introduction) by Bernault (2006) and Lamont (2011) on the colonial encounter in Equatorial Guinea and on Meru practices in central Kenya respectively, illustrate how problematic African notions of corporeal potency often were for colonial authorities and missionaries. This was despite the fact that these colonials were themselves in no way isolated from practices to do with the containment of dangerous, polluting human materials, however much they may have aligned themselves against them. Colonials were not immune from their own forms of 'carnal fetishism', whatever shape ('scientific', 'Christian' or otherwise) they may have taken. Likewise, as mentioned in Chapter 1, when those irascible early Rhodesian apologists, Theodore Bent and Richard Hall interfered with and removed graves during destructive excavations at Great Zimbabwe in the late 19th and early 20th centuries, not only were they challenged by locals whose relatives were buried there, they were sometimes 'horrified' by what they had done, and found themselves obliged to allow the African labourers they had employed 'to go to their kraals to purify themselves' afterwards (Bent 1896: 79; Hall 1905: 43, 94).

Whatever profound and diverse transformations have taken place in how death and human corporeality were handled and responded to in Zimbabwe and across the continent over the 20th century, under the complex weight of different colonial, missionary and other influences, human bodies and materials have long been central to funerary and mortuary practices, albeit in very diverse ways. Both bodies and spirits have always mattered, even if the nature and salience of each, and of their entanglement, has always been emergent and uncertain as well as contested and historically grounded.

AIDS, cholera, Congo, prisons, Chiadzwa, diaspora, Fast Track Land Reform, and charismatic Pentecostalisms

Given all of the above, there are further thematic areas beyond the limitations of this book that remain to be productively explored in terms of its arguments about Zimbabwe's politics of the dead, the excessivity of material and immaterial human remains, and the productive uncertainties of death. The detailed story of Mai Melissa's emergent possession

---

[7] See for example: 'Muti killings on the rise in KZN' *Daily News* 31/10/07; 'Death for Tanzania albino killers' *BBC news* 23/9/09; 'Nigeria "child witch killer" held' *BBC news* 4/12/08; 'Congo witch-hunt's child victims' *BBC news* 22/12/99. Ranger 2007b offers a strong critique of the problematic essentialisations often involved in such reporting.

Conclusion

by Sekuru Shorty in 2005–06 in Chapter 6 provides a useful counterweight to the highly-charged political situations that dominate much of the rest of the book. The complex details of that story also point to other areas ripe for further research.

Most obviously, Zimbabwe's AIDS pandemic – which was coming to a devastating crescendo in the mid-2000s – is a looming backdrop to Mai Melissa's story and to the period covered in this book. The effects of the enormous mortality of HIV/AIDS on practices and meanings of death across the region has already been discussed in much literature which charts how the trajectory of these transformations changed as experiences of the pandemic altered with the widespread introduction of ARVs (Niehaus 2007a, 2013a, 2013b; Golomski 2018a, 2018b; Stadler 2021). Quite a lot has been written about how experiences of AIDS-related illnesses challenged previously neat demarcations of the transition from life to death, as sufferers were visibly seen to move to the brink of death and back again, as the availability of or compliance with antiretroviral medication waxed and waned; and how this fuelled already existent and widespread associations between the pandemic and new 'moral panics' about witchcraft (Rodlach 2006). Yet not enough focus has yet been placed on the corporeal dimensions of these transformations, or on the question of what has changed and what has endured, and why. Even Golomski's work on the effects of AIDS on funerary culture in Swaziland, which does discuss changing material cultures of death, focuses little attention on the corporealities of life and death involved (Golomksi 2018a, 2018b; Fontein 2020: 104). During the funerals of people who had succumbed to HIV/AIDS-related illnesses that I attended in the rural Masvingo in the mid-2000s (such as Mike's burial, Chapters 2 and 6) there were often noticeable concerns about the unhappy, unsettled spirits of the dead and the possibility of their failed transition into ancestor-hood because of their youth or the problematic nature of their deaths. But these funerals were also often marked by overwhelming feelings of 'disgust', fear and horror that had to do specifically with the disturbingly unbounded, leaky and polluting corporealities of these particular kinds of bodies. One also wonders whether in years to come Zimbabwe's more than a million AIDS deaths will return in the form of terrifying *ngozi* spirits, like the liberation war dead, victims of the *gukurahundi* and of more recent violence have done. If so, what methods and techniques of resolution, stabilisation and determination might emerge, and to what kinds of politics and contestation may they give traction, or enable?

If the immense mortality of AIDS suggests it is an area ripe for further research in terms of the excessive corporealities and uncertain incompleteness of death, then the same could be said of the outbreaks of cholera that Zimbabwe suffered as a result of the infrastructural and economic crises it has experienced since the early 2000s. In 2008/09, shortly after the devastating election violence of that year, a cholera outbreak killed over 4,000 people. There have been subsequent outbreaks. These have been subject to some research (Chambers 2009; Chirisa et al. 2015; Nyandoro 2011; Chigudu 2019) which has tended to focus on their political and economic as well as medical, environmental and public health dimensions. The visceral and corporeal nature of this disease, its intense infectiousness, and the politics of citizenship, urban planning and control surrounding these outbreaks suggest that further research on cholera in Zimbabwe – in terms of notions of pollution, leakages and bodily containment, and its effects on funerary culture and the politics of the dead – is likely to be productive. The same will likely be true of the COVID-19 pandemic, still unfolding as I write,[8] which has already produced much debate on the politics of viral containment and contamination, the use and availability of protective masks and other 'personal protective equipment' (PPE), 'vaccine nationalism' (Gastrow & Lawrence 2021), as well as a multitude of images and much discussion of mass graves and the politics of burial elsewhere across the globe.[9] In early 2021, within the space of just a few weeks, at least six leading ZANU PF politicians, including sitting and former government ministers (Foreign Minister Sibusiso Moyo; Transport Minister Joel Biggie Matiza; Provincial Affairs Minister for Manicaland, Ellen Gwaradzimba; as well as the former Education Minister, Aeneas Chigwedere; former head of Prisons Paradzai Zimondi, and former deputy Finance Minister Morton Malianga) succumbed to COVID-19, producing four new national heroes and provoking a spread of jokes and rumours (as well as academic articles – see Falisse et al. 2021) about COVID 'finally' achieving what the political opposition had failed to do over the previous two decades.[10]

8   Ukuthula Trust, 'Stay home – or feed your children: A double edged sword – COVID-19 update, Bulawayo and Rural Matabeleland, 4–23 April 2020' 23/4/20, https://kubatana.net/2020/04/23/stay-home-or-feed-your-children-a-double-edged-sword-covid-19-update-bulawayo-and-rural-matabeleland-4-23-april-2020, accessed 6/9/21; Brian Raftopoulos, 'Politics, livelihoods, the pandemic in Zim' *Zimbabwe Independent* 18/4/20.
9   D. Vicki, 'Mass graves for coronavirus victims shouldn't come as a shock – it's how the poor have been buried for centuries' *The Conversation* 24/4/20, https://theconversation.com/mass-graves-for-coronavirus-victims-shouldnt-come-as-a-shock-its-how-the-poor-have-been-buried-for-centuries-136655, accessed 28/5/20; 'Why coronavirus burials are just the latest chapter in New York's plague history' *Guardian* 12/4/20; '"Utter disaster": Manaus fills mass graves as Covid-19 hits the Amazon' *Guardian* 30/4/20; 'Coronavirus: Are the bodies of victims undermining Iran's official figures?' *BBC news* 15/4/20; 'Sobering photos reveal how countries are dealing with the dead left by the coronavirus pandemic' *Business Insider* 13/4/20.
10   'ZINATHA warns of fake, harmful Covid-19 herbs' *Newzimbabwe.com* 16/1/21; 'Zimbabwe: Coronavirus claims transport minister' www.aa.com.tr/en/africa/zimbabwe-coronavirus-claims-transport-minister/2120095 23/1/21; 'Matiza,

Conclusion

As dissatisfaction with hastily imposed government restrictions on funerals and burials grew across Harare and elsewhere, the Zimbabwe Traditional Healers Association (ZINATHA) issued warnings about 'fake' and 'harmful' herbs being sold as 'traditional remedies' for COVID-19 treatment by 'unregistered and "ignorant" herbal traders'.[11]

Zimbabwe's complex social, political and economic crises since 2000, which many identify as lying behind its recent cholera outbreaks, are clearly also (like the AIDS pandemic, and maybe now COVID-19) a significant part of the backdrop to its politics of the dead. The 'chimurenga politics' of ZANU PF (Chigumadzi 2018), the 'patriotic history' (Ranger 2004a) and 'necropolitan imagination' (Muchemwa 2010) all so central to it, emerged in the context of these crises. Aside from the deliberate exclusions that ZANU PF's particular brand of necro-politics has involved – the silencing of the *gukurahundi* and of ZIPRA's war legacies; the narrow exclusivism of ZANU PF's domination of the National Heroes complex; and its recurrent violence against all perceived opposition – there are other problematic bodies and deaths from this period that remain largely unresolved and worthy of further study. These include the deaths of Zimbabwean soldiers from its misadventure in the Democratic Republic of Congo in the late 1990s and early 2000s,[12] as well as the missing dead from massacres allegedly carried out by the Zimbabwean National Army against informal diamond miners at Chiadzwa in 2009, whose fate remains subject to rumour and debate.[13]

Zimbabwe's drawn-out economic and political crises have also affected funerary practices in ways not always directly related to ZANU PF

Zimondi declared national heroes' *Newzimbabwe.com* 25/1/21; 'Former Zimbabwe prisons boss Paradzai Zimondi dies from Covid-19' *Newzimbabwe.com* 22/1/21; 'Ex-minister Chigwedere, businessman Chigumba succumb to Covid-19' *Herald* 23/1/21; 'Declare Gwaradzimba national heroine – Zanu PF Manicaland Province' *Newzimbabwe.com* 16/1/21, accessed 6/7/21.

[11] '"Buried by strangers": Funeral curbs raise ire in Zimbabwe' *Newzimbabwe.com* 19/1/21; 'Herbalists dismiss claims bute heals Covid-19' *Newzimbabwe.com* 19/1/21; 'ZINATHA warns of fake, harmful Covid-19 herbs' *Newzimbabwe.com* 16/1/21; all accessed 6/7/21.

[12] 'Battalion Destroyed in Congo' *AP News* 9/3/99, https://apnews.com/9159bcc8 27a5bfe6a230caf20986949b; 'Zim deaths in DRC revealed' *News24.com* 28/5/04; both accessed 29/5/20. Also Maringira 2016.

[13] 'Victims of diamond massacres buried in Chitungwiza mass graves' *swradioafrica.com* 19/5/09; 'Operation Hakudzokwi – What happened in Chiadzwa?' 23/11/16, http://aidc.org.za/operation-hakudzokwi-happened-chiadzwa, accessed 28/6/20; 'Bodies pile up as Mugabe wages war on diamond miners' *Guardian* 11/12/08; 'Chiadzwa killings sanctioned by the state – Maguwu' *Newzimbabwe.com* 28/2/18; 'Diamonds in the rough: Human rights abuses in the Marange Diamond Fields of Zimbabwe' Human Rights Watch 26/6/09, www.hrw.org/report/2009/06/26/diamonds-rough/human-rights-abuses-marange-diamond-fields-zimbabwe, accessed 28/6/20.

politics. These include the devastating prevalence of death and sickness in Zimbabwe's decrepit prisons (Alexander 2009), new struggles around urban burials to do with declining space in cemeteries[14] and with problems caused by Zimbabwe's recurrent fuel crisis (Chadya 2015), as well as challenges that have arisen due to its growing diaspora (Mbiba 2010). The nexus of financial crises, failing medical infrastructure and the dramatically increased but precarious mobility of Zimbabweans seeking economic opportunities elsewhere (South Africa particularly), has generated a myriad of complex, interconnected conditions that are likely to have significant lasting effects on funerary culture. In November 2019, for example, Beitbridge district hospital was facing a 'mortuary crisis following the suspension of morgue services' due to recurrent electricity cuts and the failure of the hospital's generator, forcing officials to apply for 'authority for pauper burials' for the unidentified bodies in its morgue, who included 'six minors, mostly stillbirth products and two adults'.[15]

The phenomena of unidentified, unclaimed decomposing bodies overwhelming dysfunctional morgues has become increasingly common in Zimbabwe over the last two decades, with the increasingly prohibitive cost of burials, the increased movement of people back and forth across international borders, and (see Chapter 2) as a result of political violence and intimidation which has sometimes made people reluctant to claim the bodies of killed relatives.[16] In late 2019, a protracted and acrimonious doctors' strike – during which a junior doctor leading the action was abducted and tortured by suspected state agents[17] – interfered with funerals too, as pathology services and the processing of burial orders was affected in several major hospitals. The state-run *Sunday Mail* complained that the doctors' strike was 'haunting the dead' as events became increasingly hostile and politicised.[18]

[14] 'Grave problem: No space for the dead in Zimbabwe's growing cities' *Thomson Reuters Foundation* 3/6/19; 'Rising costs and dwindling land leave Zimbabweans without traditional burials' *Global Press Journal* 15/3/20.
[15] 'Eight Beitbridge bodies face pauper's burial' *Newsday* 15/11/19.
[16] 'Zimbabwe: 25 bodies unclaimed at Harare Hospital morgue' *Herald* 22/6/04; 'Corpses rot as ZANU PF terror moves a gear up' *Standard* 3/5/08; 'Mortuaries stuck with unclaimed bodies' *Herald* 19/3/14; 'Chitungwiza hospital to conduct pauper's burials for 34 unclaimed bodies' *MyZimbabwe.com* 5/4/18; 'Thousands of anonymous bodies of migrants found in South Africa' APIMAGESBLOG.com 1/11/18; both accessed 29/5/20.
[17] 'Abducted doctor suffers brain dysfunction, referred to SA' *Newsday* 25/9/19; 'Zimbabwe govt panicky reaction to Dr Magombeyi abduction raises more questions' *Zimbabwean* 22/9/19; 'Pressure piles over missing doctor' *Newsday* 18/9/19; 'Striking doctors' leader "abducted"' *Newsday* 14/9/19. The government press denied the abduction and torture: '"Missing" doctor Magombeyi found' *Herald* 20/9/19; 'Magombeyi not tortured – ZRP' *Herald* 26/9/19.
[18] 'Doctors strike haunting the dead' *Sunday Mail* 25/11/19; 'Zanu-PF condemns health services strike' *Herald* 3/9/19.

Conclusion

Another area where further research into Zimbabwe's politics of the dead may prove productive will be the long-term effects of Zimbabwe's Fast Track Land Reform on meanings and practices of death. Existing literature has already documented how graves became increasingly significant as markers of belonging, land rights and sometimes autochthony through the 20th century, and particularly during the land occupations of the 2000s (Fontein 2015; Mujere 2011, 2012, 2019). As the rotund literature on land reform in Zimbabwe increasingly focuses on the political and social dynamics of life on resettled farms (Sinclair-Bright 2016, 2019; Dande & Mujere 2019; Mkodzongi 2016), 20 years after the 'invasions' of 2000 began, it will be interesting to explore how old and new forms of mortuary practice and regimes of death and corporeality are re-forged as the politics of belonging takes new forms in changing contexts. As Ranger might have warned, we cannot assume they will remain the same and we should be alert to the multiplicity of people, interests and divergent registers that will be invoked, even as any transformations will necessarily gain traction in entanglement with older and wider endurances of practice and meaning. It will be interesting to see if the graves of former farm workers and new farmers will be as affective and salient in future struggles over entitlement, authority and belonging as those of precolonial ancestors, colonial-era migrants and white farmers were in Gutu and around Lake Mutirikwi in the early 2000s (Mujere 2011, 2019; Fontein 2011, 2015).

Another aspect of Zimbabwe's politics of the dead which this book has repeatedly touched upon but deserves more attention in subsequent research, is to consider the effects of a remarkable, not yet fully understood (cf. Chitanda 2020a), feature of Zimbabwean society increasingly apparent over the last decade: the rising political influence of new forms of charismatic Pentecostalism. Pentecostalism has a very long history in Zimbabwe (Maxwell 2006), alongside older African Independent churches (AICs) and even older missionary churches, and their role in the transformation of death-related meanings and practices has been recognised in Zimbabwe (Ranger 2011a, 2004b) and across the region (Jindra & Noret 2011). The significance of diverse yet peculiarly Christian notions of the body, resurrection and the afterlife – and especially the monumentalisation of burials that this has often engendered – in transforming mortuary cultures across the region is undeniable and largely self-evident. It has a long history. Yet there is also a sense that Pentecostal and other 'pentecostalised' Christian movements, often led by charismatic pastors, have achieved increased political significance in Zimbabwe over the last decade or so, and taken up a more central political stage, out of the sedate corners of civil society activism where many had long resided. When the main political opposition is led by someone (Nelson Chamisa) who is also an ordained Pentecostal pastor, and who clearly makes much political mileage out of this, and when leaders of competing factions within the ruling ZANU PF (including the current president) too have made a point of publicly attending Pentecostal and AIC events, sometimes dressed in the appropriate garb, seeking church 'endorsements' for their authority, or for the removal of others (as Grace Mugabe did in November 2017 just before the coup unseated her husband), then it is clear that apoliticism no longer characterises Zimbabwe's multitude of Pentecostal sects and AICs, if indeed it ever did (Chitanda 2020a).[19] With traditional leaders and chiefs sometimes re-forging older claims to autochthony, authority and land through Christian idioms of divine authority – by, for example, assertions that 'criticisms of the President' are forms of 'satanism' as the then new Chief Murinye did in conversation in December 2011[20] – then the growing political salience of peculiarly Christian idioms becomes harder to avoid. Likewise, the prominent role of Baptist Pastor Evan Mawarire in the 2016 #ThisFlag protests,[21] and of others in more recent civil society activities, and the state-sponsored harassment this has often provoked, suggest that charismatic churches may now have picked up the batten of political activism, which, in a much earlier moment, had been carried by those missions and churches who supported Zimbabwe's liberation struggle in the 1960s–70s (Maxwell 1999; McLaughlin 1996; Linden 1980; Bhebe 1979).

Although references to churches, ministries and pastors are repeated frequently in the stories discussed in this book, I have not made analysis of the role of Zimbabwe's diverse Christianities in its politics of the dead a central part of the arguments developed here. This is mainly because I have neither the competence nor the data with which to do this. As with the *gukurahundi*, there are many other scholars better placed to develop these arguments. However, my perspective would assume that

---

[19] 'Zimbabwe: Pastor Chamisa vows will not quit politics, denies ED confrontation at odds with christian beliefs' *Newzimbabwe.com* 12/6/19, accessed 12/6/20; 'Chamisa now a pastor' *Herald* 28/11/16; 'Churches endorse ED' *Herald* 6/3/18; 'Zimbabwe: ED pleads with church to cast out demons afflicting Zimbabwe' *Newzimbabwe.com* 3/2/20, accessed 12/6/20; 'Mnangagwa Offers "indigenous" churches free state land' *Newzimbabwe.com* 2/2/20, accessed 12/6/20; 'Mnangagwa woos apostolic sect' *Standard* 15/7/18; 'Grace Mugabe has again attacked Zim's vice president' *SABC News* 5/11/17, www.youtube.com/watch?v=OljERTx1xnY, accessed 12/6/20; 'Women, pray and intercede for Zimbabwe – Min Mutsvangwa' *Herald* 24/5/21.

[20] Interview with Chief Ephias Murinye, 19/12/11; also Fontein 2015: 297–300.

[21] '"Fight for rights will continue" in Zimbabwe, #ThisFlag movement pastor vows' *NPR* 10/12/17, www.npr.org/sections/parallels/2017/12/10/569757806/fight-for-rights-will-continue-in-zimbabwe-thisflag-movement-pastor-vows, accessed 12/6/20; 'Interview: The man behind #ThisFlag, Zimbabwe's accidental movement for change' *Guardian* 16/5/16; 'A Maverick Citizen conversation with Pastor Evan Mawarire' *Daily Maverick* 18/9/19.

Conclusion

Zimbabwe's diversity of churches, pastors and Christian sects are not immune or separate from its politics of the dead, but rather deeply implicated in it. Pastors and churches of all sorts have been involved in the Fallen Heroes Trust (FHT)'s vernacular exhumations, and in war veteran-led movements to monumentalise massacre sites in Gutu (Mujere et al. 2017), in 'national heroes' funerals and in the complex, precarious life stories of mediums like Rotina Mavhunga and Mai Melissa. In these and other contexts they do encounter the excessive potentialities of human corporeality, the alterity of spirit and the unfinished nature of death that this book has described, even if they have often sought cultural and political as well as vast economic capital by deliberately juxtaposing themselves against mediums and other 'traditionalists' through denunciations of spirit mediumship as nefarious witchcraft or 'demonic possession'. The literature on changing death practices across the region clearly shows that churches of all sorts have been deeply implicated in historical transformations to mortuary culture, and that often this had exactly to do with encounters with problematic material and corporeal substances (Bernault 2006). Engelke (2007), for example, shows how this works with regard to the anxiety provoking, unstable materiality of the Bible for the *Masowe eChishanu* apostolics he worked with in Harare. Likewise Golomski's research on changing funeral culture in Swaziland illustrates how 'prayer healing and perceptions of a healed afterlife' can become 'a material resource for the extension of life itself' (2018a: 80) – one that can be exploited by dubious pastors as recent (much ridiculed) examples of pastors 'raising' people from death surely indicate.[22]

Pastoral fraud aside, it is clear that charismatic Christians of all sorts are in no way immune from the anxieties that the torque of human corporeality, the alterity of spirit, and the uncertain, unfinished, incompleteness of death can provoke. However, it remains for future research to document and analyse the diverse and complex ways that this can manifest. Given all of the above, there are likely to be both changes and continuities, transformations and endurances implicated in these emergent processes. Ranger (2011b: 6) suggested that 'throughout Zimbabwean religious history prophets and radicals have risen to challenge communal establishment and to introduce new ideas of healing', and 'what might first appear as rupture' – a claim that Pentecostals often explicitly make – 'might well be the latest instalment of a long tradition of cyclical cleansing'. 'The idiom has become increasingly Christianized', Ranger continued, 'but the search for personal security – healing, prosperity, fertility – through acts of cleansing has remained a constant' (2011b: 6). The profound but productive uncertainties of death that this book

---

[22] 'Pastor raising man from the dead a hoax – Funeral parlour' 26/2/19 *SABC News* see www.sabcnews.com/sabcnews/pastor-raising-man-from-the-dead-a-hoax-funeral-service, accessed 23/9/19.

has explored, drawn from the uneasy imbrication of excessive human corporealities and the otherness of immateriality are challenges that face everybody, including adherents of Zimbabwe's multitude of diverse Christian sects. The expanding anthropology of Christianity emergent over the last two decades suggest this might become a rich vein for future analysis of death and corporeality in Zimbabwe, and across the region.

New directions for liberation heritage

It is also clear that the particular aspects of the politics of the dead discussed in this book will continue to transform. The massive, and massively problematic, material, corporeal, political and social legacies of the *gukuruhundi* have been a significant aspect of Zimbabwe's politics of the dead over the last two decades, and an important backdrop to the arguments developed here. Much research remains to be done, particularly as it is a situation in much flux under Mnangagwa's 'new dispensation' (Chapter 7). The shape, form and politics of liberation heritage in Zimbabwe and across the region also continue to emerge and transform. This has taken root in many countries which fought for independence or supported such struggles through the former Frontline states (Jopela 2017; Mataga 2019). Tanzania was surprisingly late in the game, given its unrivalled role hosting nationalists and guerrilla armies from across the region, as well as the OAU Liberation Committee, during the 1960s–70s. But, as scholars have increasingly turned their attention to the lives and politics of guerrillas, nationalists and refugees in exile, especially in Tanzanian camps (Lissoni 2008; Lissoni & Suriano 2014; Pallotti 2018; Williams 2013; Houston et al. 2015; Alexander et al. 2017), so too have Tanzanian museum authorities begun to focus attention in this direction.[23] The almost-derelict building that used to house the OAU Liberation Committee in Dar es Salaam is being turned into a liberation heritage centre, and the incredibly promising but still hard-to-access OAU Liberation Committee archives were recently moved to the National Archives in Dodoma, where it is hoped they will one day become accessible to researchers.[24] Mozambique, Angola, Namibia, South Africa and

---

[23] In November/December 2015 and May 2018 I carried out ethnographic fieldwork at former guerrilla camps in Tanzania at Ruvu and Mgagao, as well as in Dar es Salaam. During the first visit it was surprising how little official interest was devoted to the remains of numerous former camps across the country. Any efforts that had been made were due to the energetic activities of Dr Frank Masele, an archaeologist at the University of Dar es Salaam, Field notes, November/December 2015. Three years later his efforts had gained some recognition with museum authorities and the former building of the OAU Liberation Committee in Dar es Salaam was being turned into a Liberation Heritage Centre, Field notes, May 2018.

[24] ibid.

Conclusion

Zambia all have their own 'liberation' or 'freedom' heritage programmes, and old linkages between people and movements dating to the nationalist period are being remade through these heritage processes. As Chipunza explained, various MOUs and other less formal collaborations with NMMZ's partner organisations across the region have been established.[25]

New links are also being made. One surprising new connection that has emerged over recent years is between Zimbabwe and Rwanda, especially as these countries supported different sides in the devastating Congolese war of the late 1990s, but also because the history and context of the violence and killings at the heart of each country's commemorative programmes are so very different. More research needs to be done on these connections, and their emergent form, but they seem to have been at least partly driven by the need for Zimbabwe's vernacular exhumers, as well as for NMMZ, to seek alternative forms of expertise and experience in exhumations and the monumentalisation of mass graves.[26] As Zimbabwe has again begun to make its own 'peace and reconciliation' initiatives under Mnangagwa (Chapter 7), there is also interest in learning from Rwanda's experience with different forms of post-conflict reconciliation (Chigwenya 2019; UNDP no date).[27] Of course, neither in Zimbabwe nor in Rwanda have

---

[25] Interview with Chipunza, 5/3/20.

[26] In developing their own 'vernacular' expertise in exhumations, Rwanda officials visited Germany and the UK several times to talk to forensic experts, companies selling equipment for preserving corpses and to look at memorials (Laure Major pers. com. 2/7/20). Since late 2019, new state-driven 'mass exhumations' have also begun to take place in Burundi, under the auspices of its Truth and Reconciliation Commission. This is already receiving academic attention by scholars such as Jamar and Major (2020: 1) who argue that although the histories of violence and post-violence processes in these neighbouring countries have different trajectories, both involve 'vernacularised forms of forensic practice' using 'techniques that differentiate remains and prepare them for public display but with much other forensic intention and method absent'. In both cases 'efforts are motivated by truth-seeking and reconciliation aspirations but also help to articulate a specific narrative of victimhood and state legitimacy' (Jamar &Major 2020: 1).

[27] There have been various new bilateral governmental initiatives between Rwanda and Zimbabwe recently, not just around the issue of post-conflict resolution and commemoration but also economic development and military co-operation. 'Zimbabwe's minister 'moved' by Rwanda's unity, reconciliation gains' *New Times* 4/10/18;'ED: Zimbabwe Could Learn From The Rwanda Post-Genocide Reconciliation Model' *Pindula News* 5/7/19; 'Zimbabwe can learn from Rwanda: ED' *Bulawayo Chronicle* 5/7/19; 'Zimbabwe: ED Attends Rwanda Liberation Day' *Herald* 4/7/19; 'The Zimbabwe Staff College Students on study tour in Rwanda' no date, see https://urugoli.co/news/the-zimbabwe-staff-college-students-on-study-tour-in-rwanda, accessed 27/6/20. Although many of these bilateral efforts have taken place since the 2017 coup, similar efforts to engage with Rwanda experiences of post-conflict reconciliation were initiated by the ONHRI during the GNU years (2009–11), see UNDP (no date).

these processes been unproblematic (Ingelaere 2016; Major 2015; Burnet 2009; Caplan 2007; Richters et al. 2005; Eltringham 2004; Pottier 2002).

The exhumations of war graves 'thrust'[28] upon NMMZ in the 2000s as part of its liberation heritage portfolio, following the activities of vernacular war veteran exhumers and the ruling party's 'patriotic' politics, have continued; the most recent taking place at Odzi in late 2019.[29] None have achieved the kind of controversy that Chibondo did. National Museums and Monuments has built up considerable experience in these processes, developing working relationships with groups like the FHT, and finding ways of working with the mediums, diviners and 'prophets' associated with them, and the divinatory and spirit possession processes they often espouse. At the same time, it has also acknowledged its need to develop greater forensic expertise and its capacity to identify human remains through other kinds of techniques, practices and technologies, including DNA testing.[30] Suggestions in early 2020 that DNA samples from all human remains exhumed from war graves would be collected into a DNA bank for future cross-referencing, with the assistance of the African Institute of Biomedical Science and Technology (AiBST) based at Wilkins Hospital in Harare,[31] suggest that some of the critiques levelled against the 2011 Chibondo exhumations have been taken on board. Given the costs involved and Zimbabwe's ongoing economic struggles it is not clear when these plans will materialise. Yet these developments do suggest recognition and awareness of the excessiveness of human materials, which demands but ultimately often defies stabilisation into meaning and the 'remaking of the dead' into particular and known kinds of dead, like victims, heroes or ancestors.

As well as new and continuing exhumations of war graves in Zimbabwe and across its borders, NMMZ has also continued to monumentalise other liberation war sites, such as the massacre sites at Hurodzevasikana and Kamungoma in Gutu district (Mujere et al. 2017), the site of Tongogara's deadly road accident in Mozambique, and the new 'Chinhoyi Seven Heroes Monument' commemorating the 1966 battle of Chinhoyi, which is often presented as the first battle of the liberation struggle, in which all the ZANLA guerrillas involved were killed.[32] In 2013 there were similar calls to monumentalise the Chiredzi site of the former Gonakudzingwa detention

---

[28] Interview with Chipunza, 5/3/20.
[29] Ibid.
[30] It is interesting to note that the University of Zimbabwe has recently introduced a new MA in Forensic Archaeology, which as Munyaradzi Elton Sagiya notes, 'could be aimed at capacitating future exhumers' (pers. com. 2/4/21).
[31] 737Ibid. According to Chipunza an MOU has been signed between AiBST and the Ministry of Higher and Tertiary Education.
[32] 'At last, honours for Cde Tongo' *Sunday Mail* 25/3/18; 'Zim pays tribute to its heroes with new attraction' *Daily Southern & East African Tourism Update* (tourismupdate.co.za) 10/1/20.

Conclusion

camp, where nationalist leaders like Joshua Nkomo, Edgar Tekere, Leopold Takawira and others were detained for many years during the 1960s.[33] Museums and exhibitions about the liberation struggle have also been established at the National Heroes Acre and at the former ZANLA base at Chimoio in Mozambique. National Museums and Monuments has continued to try to retain its professionalism and political impartiality, despite the political pressure it has endured and the effects of Zimbabwe's continuing economic crises. Another museum is due to be constructed at the former 'Freedom Camp' in Zambia, where ZIPRA forces were based, to match that at Chimoio. Both NMMZ's commitment to establishing this second museum and the fact that it has not happened yet, reflect the complex politics that liberation heritage has inevitably been immersed in; as with state commemoration and the ruling party's 'patriotic history', priority continues to be granted to ZANLA's history and its contributions to the struggle, whatever NMMZ's own motivations and perspectives.

Undoubtedly the political pressure that NMMZ's archaeologists, curators and heritage managers face continues to be substantial. Rumours of deep divisions between different branches of NMMZ's executive, and allegations of fraud and corruption levied at particular people in top leadership positions, probably reflect how the ruling party's nasty factional politics has swept many of Zimbabwe's civil servants and parastatal organisations along with it.[34] Nevertheless, NMMZ has maintained, against the odds perhaps, its commitment to more conventional forms of heritage and archaeology alongside liberation heritage, and there have been a host of promising new archaeological projects at Great Zimbabwe and elsewhere in close collaboration with archaeologists from the University of Zimbabwe and other international universities.[35] At the same time, however, with Mnangagwa's regime making much noise about the need to 'finally' deal with the legacies of post-independence violence, particularly *gukurahundi*, NMMZ has found itself drawn into proposals by the Zimbabwe Human Rights Commission for new exhumations across Matabeleland and the Midlands. This too, like the exhumations associated with liberation heritage, has been 'thrust' upon NMMZ.[36] Such measures are part of Mnangagwa's efforts to differ-

---

[33] 'Efforts under way to declare Gonakudzingwa national monument' *Bulawayo Chronicle* 23/10/13; 'Gonakudzingwa: A sinking heritage' *Patriot* 7/11/13.

[34] Field notes, March 2020; 'Graft accused National Museums bosses try to gag star witness' *Newzimbabwe.com* 31/12/19; 'NMMZ bosses in 18 000 litres of fuel scandal' *Nehandaradio.com* 21/2/19; both accessed 28/6/20.

[35] Ezekia Mtetwa is conducting fascinating post-doctoral research surveying graves and burial sites in caves around the Boroma hills, south-east of Great Zimbabwe, which early indicators already suggest far pre-date the 19th century 'refuge tradition' that had hitherto been assumed (pers. com. 14/4/20); also Chirikure 2021.

[36] Interview with Chipunza, 5/3/20.

entiate his administration from Mugabe's regime (Chapter 7), and to draw a line under an issue that has become of increasing political salience over the last two decades. It remains to be seen what form and extent these will take, what NMMZ's role will amount to, how these efforts will be received and whether they will indeed have the potential to offer anything like the kind of resolution that is needed and demanded. The arguments developed in this book suggest that although the enormous need to address these problematic legacies of violence and death is undeniable, care will need to be taken about raising expectations that exhumations and reburials can really, in the final count, offer the kinds of justice and resolution often demanded of them.[37] Death, I have argued, always remains potentially incomplete.

Ambuya Nehanda returns?

Even (or perhaps especially) the death of Charwe Nyakasikana, the Nehanda medium hanged in 1898, with whose story this book began and who famously stated 'my bones will rise again', remains in many respects unfinished. This is reflected not only in the continuing emergence of new Nehanda mediums, a recurring phenomena, or the salience that appeals to Nehanda's legacy continue to have in war veterans' understandings of what drove land occupations in the 2000s (Chapter 2), but also in the controversies raised in the mid-2000s when the Harare tree she had allegedly been hanged from was accidently knocked down by a passing truck. More recently, two new projects appear to have been 'thrust' upon NMMZ in the form of, firstly, widely publicised efforts to repatriate corporeal remains held in UK museums that are purported to belong to several key leaders of the first *chimurenga* of 1896/97, including, amongst others, the mediums of Ambuya Nehanda and Sekuru Kaguvi; and secondly, the erection of a statue of Nehanda in central Harare, which dominated news headlines in late 2020 and early 2021. As this book began with Nehanda's famous story it is fitting to include a discussion of these emerging events at its end.

Claims about the presence of these human remains in UK museums first emerged in 2013 through the activities of a group known as 'The Handa Project', or the 'Handa Research Institute', led by Ottoman Magaya, who mobilised various descendants of prominent executed leaders of the 1896/97 rebellions, including Chief Mashayamombe Chinengundu, Chief Chingirai Makoni, Chief Kadungure Mapondera, Chief Mutekdza Chiwashira and Chief Mashonganyika.[38] Given both the significance

---

[37] Interview with Shari Eppel, 11/3/20; Interview with Strike Mkandla 12/3/20; Interview with Mbuso Fuzwayo, 12/3/20.

[38] 'Bring back our heroes', *Patriot*, issue 442, 6–12/3/20; 'A long homecoming for pioneers of the struggle' *Sunday Mail* 23/2/20; 'Over a century later, Mbuya

Conclusion

of Nehanda, Kaguvi and other first *chimurenga* ancestors to nationalist practices and ideologies of anti-colonial struggle, and more recently to ZANU PF's 'chimurenga politics', and very much in the wider context of resurgent efforts since the early 2000s to repatriate human remains (and other cultural heritage, Hicks 2020)[39] acquired under dubious colonial circumstances by museums in the global North, it is not surprising that these demands were quickly taken seriously by the ruling party. A repatriation committee headed by the current Chief Makoni was established, including various 'traditional leaders', representatives of The Handa Project, and of the Ministry of Home Affairs and Cultural Heritage, and ZANU PF's Department of Gender and Culture. National Museums and Monuments was assigned to lead negotiations with UK museum authorities. Discussions began in late 2014, and in 2015 a formal request was made to the UK government for the return of human remains from Zimbabwe held in UK museums.[40]

President Mugabe himself referred to the issue in a speech at Heroes Acre in 2015, asserting that the 'first chimurenga leaders, whose heads were decapitated by the colonial occupying force, were then dispatched to England, to signify British victory over, and subjugation of, the local population'. 'Surely, keeping decapitated heads as war trophies, in this day and age, in a national history museum', Mugabe continued, 'must rank among the highest forms of racist moral decadence, sadism and human insensitivity'.[41] Mugabe's comments about the deeply problematic nature of colonial-era museum collections of human remains were matched by comments from descendants of those whose ancestors' remains were allegedly among those held in the UK. One report cited Donald Kamba, 'a direct descendant of Chief Chingaira and an estate agent from Rusape, in eastern Zimbabwe ... where the headless body of his ancestor is buried', who claimed that 'ever since Chingaira's head disappeared, every subsequent Makoni chief, irrespective of their house, went blind'.[42] Later the current Chief Makoni was quoted as stating:

> It has been close to 40 years after we attained our independence and we still haven't brought back the skulls of our icons and our culture rightly says that if a person is killed in a native land that person can only rest if the body and soul has been united with their roots ... After thorough research, we found that there are about 27 heads that were taken and

---

Nehanda could return home' *Forbes Africa* 1/10/15; 'Zimbabwe: remains of Mbuya Nehanda, Sekuru Kaguvi expected in April from UK' *Newzimbabwe.com* 14/2/20, accessed 19/6/20.

[39] See for example: '2 600 Zim artefacts looted' *Herald* 14/8/15.
[40] 'Robert Mugabe tells Natural History Museum to return human skulls' *Guardian* 13/8/15
[41] Ibid.
[42] 'Over a century later, Mbuya Nehanda could return home' *Forbes Africa* 1/10/15.

The Politics of the Dead

gifted to the British Crown as war medals ... We are very grateful that the repatriation process is now ending and very soon, we would have bought back the remains of our ancestors, so that we can reunite their skulls with their roots because they belong here. Many people might just think the skulls are not important but they are very important, and the white settlers knew that if they take just the head then they have disconnected the connection between the body and the head and the person will not become a spirit medium.[43]

For his part, Godfrey Mahachi, who as Executive Director of NMMZ was tasked with leading negotiations with museums in the UK, was quoted as stating: 'we cannot have other people keep the remains of our ancestors in a cardboard box elsewhere ... There are implications to do with how we treat the deceased; these implications have a bearing on the past, present and future'.[44] Typically vitriolic, Jonathan Moyo, then Minister of Higher and Tertiary Education, added to the affray and 'stirred emotions on Twitter', by saying 'how can we focus on the economy when the skulls of Mbuya Nehanda and Sekuru Kaguvi are displayed in a British museum? These barbarians have been displaying the skulls of our First Chimurenga heroes and heroines in their libraries!'[45]

In the UK the issue was taken seriously, but also cautiously. This is understandable given the sensitivities concerned, especially in the wake of the 2004 Human Tissue Act which introduced new regulations for the display, storage and return of human materials in and from museums, and equally the international prominence that other efforts to repatriate human remains from former colonial museums had achieved, to which there were many references in Zimbabwe's state-owned media.[46] Amongst others, the recent repatriation from German museums of Herero skulls dating to the Namibian genocide, and of Sara Baartman's remains – both of which received much media attention across the region – were particularly referred to as comparative cases by Zimbabwe's media.[47] Despite some confusion about the role of the British Museum, it was quickly established that there are human remains from Zimbabwe being held in London in the Natural History Museum's large collection of human materials, and

[43] 'Zimbabwe: remains of Mbuya Nehanda, Sekuru Kaguvi expected in April from UK' *Newzimbabwe.com* 14/2/20, accessed 19/3/20. For more on the history of controversy around Chief Makoni's skull, see Ranger 1988.
[44] 'Over a century later, Mbuya Nehanda could return home' *Forbes Africa* 1/10/15.
[45] Ibid.
[46] 'Robert Mugabe tells Natural History Museum to return human skulls' *Guardian* 13/8/15; 'Repatriation of First Chimurenga heroes imminent' *Sunday Mail* 1/9/19; 'A long homecoming for pioneers of the struggle' *Sunday Mail* 23/2/20; 'Bring back our heroes', *Patriot*, issue 442, 6–12/3/20.
[47] Ibid.

Conclusion

possible in other museums around the country.[48] Research later identified the human remains of between 11 and 13 individuals from Zimbabwe in the Natural History Museum's collections.[49]

Where there was particular caution, however, was in official responses to the claims made by President Mugabe, Jonathan Moyo and some of the other public figures pushing these events, that these human remains included the remains of prominent figures associated with the first *chimurenga*, and most especially Ambuya Nehanda herself. As *The Guardian* reported:

> The Natural History Museum said it was not clear whether any remains in its collection are related to the skulls referred to by Mugabe. A spokesperson said: 'The Natural History Museum cares for 20,000 human remains in its collection. They are referred to by scientists both at the museum and internationally for research. We have a policy of considering formal requests for return of human remains to their places of origin, under the provisions of Section 47 of the Human Tissue Act 2004, and we have been involved in a series of significant repatriations. This is a thorough process that involves establishing the correct provenance of remains based on complex historical sources. It is not yet clear whether any remains in the Museum collection are related to the events, places or people referred to in President Mugabe's speech this week.'[50]

It is noticeable that in his statements, Godfrey Mahachi too, like his UK museum counterparts, was careful to avoid making claims about the exact identity and provenance of the human remains held in the Natural History Museum's collections. 'It has always been our wish to have those remains back home' he told *Forbes Africa* 'but we have to proceed in this process with much caution. Proper identification and research needs to be conducted so as to ensure that whatever we bring back to Zimbabwe is ours'.[51]

On the one hand, therefore, the statements of Chief Makoni, Donald Kamba and others point to enormous salience of human corporeality in the management of death and the proper transformations it demands, and the long-term repercussions that can result from failed, disrupted or denied funerary practices, thereby reiterating some of the central arguments developed in Chapters 1 and 2 of this book. On the other hand, the measured caution of the museum professionals involved, both in the UK and in Zimbabwe, reflects again the excessivity of human remains which, I have argued, demands but often defies highly technical

---

[48] 'Robert Mugabe tells Natural History Museum to return human skulls' *Guardian* 13/8/15.
[49] Ibid.; 'Repatriation of First Chimurenga heroes imminent' *Sunday Mail* 1/9/19.
[50] 'Robert Mugabe tells Natural History Museum to return human skulls' *Guardian* 13/8/15.
[51] 'Over a century later, Mbuya Nehanda could return home' *Forbes Africa* 1/10/15

or specialised efforts to stabilise or 'remake the dead' into clearly identifiable subjects, ancestors, victims or heroes. Both these related arguments have therefore been reflected in the way the question of the return of Nehanda's and others' remains from the UK emerged in the mid-2010s.

It is also noticeable than after an early splurge of international and local publicity around the question of repatriating the alleged remains of Nehanda, Kaguvi and other first *chimurenga* heroes from the UK in the mid-2010s, the issue went conspicuously quiet. It was only in mid-2019, after the 2017 coup had removed Mugabe from office, that the issue re-appeared in the public sphere, as new reports emerged that plans for the repatriation of these remains were now proceeding quickly.[52] The repatriation committee led by Chief Makoni and NMMZ were now being assisted by members of the Zimbabwean diaspora in the UK, who organised a 'Ambuya Nehanda Repatriation Conference' in Leicester in October 2019, to which Godfrey Mahachi, as NMMZ's Executive Director was invited as guest of honour.[53] In early 2020, just before the corona pandemic interrupted travel plans everywhere, Mahachi was scheduled to make a high-profile – and much publicised – visit to the UK to finalise the repatriation of the remains identified in the Natural History Museum's collections, and to discuss further efforts to locate Zimbabwean human remains in other UK museums. The planned visit was surrounded by a new splurge of reports in the state-owned and ZANU PF-dominated media in Zimbabwe, covering the issue and discussing plans for a 'national funeral' and public reburial of the returning remains before the 2020 Heroes Day celebrations.[54] Little or no mention was made in these recent reports of the continuing uncertainties that exist about the provenance and identity of the remains due to be returned to Zimbabwe.[55]

[52] 'Repatriation of Zimbabwe's First Chimurenga war heroes/royal remains from UK gathers momentum' *News of the South* 14/8/19; 'Repatriation of First Chimurenga heroes imminent' *Sunday Mail* 1/9/19; 'Repatriation of First Chimurenga heroes, heroines in 2 months' *Herald* 15/2/20; see also 'A long homecoming for pioneers of the struggle' *Sunday Mail* 23/2/20; 'Zimbabwe: remains of Mbuya Nehanda, Sekuru Kaguvi expected in April from UK' *Newzimbabwe.com* 14/2/20; 'Zimbabwe: Nehanda, Kaguvi heads found in London, public funeral planned for Chimurenga icons' *Newzimbabwe.com* 6/3/20.

[53] 'Repatriation of Zimbabwe's First Chimurenga war heroes/royal remains from UK gathers momentum' *News of the South* 14/8/19; 'A long homecoming for pioneers of the struggle' *Sunday Mail* 23/2/20.

[54] 'Repatriation of First Chimurenga heroes, heroines in 2 months' *Herald* 15/2/20; 'A long homecoming for pioneers of the struggle' *Sunday Mail* 23/2/20; 'Zimbabwe: remains of Mbuya Nehanda, Sekuru Kaguvi expected in April from UK' *Newzimbabwe.com* 14/2/20; 'Zimbabwe: Nehanda, Kaguvi Heads found in London, public funeral planned for Chimurenga icons' *Newzimbabwe.com* 6/3/20; both accessed 19/6/20.

[55] Information provided by the Natural History Museum (to the BBC reporter

Conclusion

Under the headline 'Bring back our Heroes' a special issue of ZANU PF's newspaper, *The Patriot*, published in March 2020, carried a long article discussing the issue.[56] This report was heavily garnished with well-known historical pictures of Nehanda and Kaguvi before their execution, interspersed with evocative images (of unknown origin) of rows of skulls in storage rooms. Although the article mentioned that procedures (including DNA tests) to confirm the identity of the remains were on going, it revealed no uncertainties about who the remains were or how they had been acquired. 'The remains of Mbuya Nehanda and Sekuru Kaguvi' it claimed without hesitation, 'have been on display at the Westminster Abbey and the National History museums in London'. Furthermore, although 'in August 2015, the British Government acknowledged holding the remains of the heroes and heroines of the First Chimurenga', it had 'been reluctant to release them', and an earlier 'team of experts … on a similar mission … was aborted and no reasons were given'.[57] For now, it concluded:

> Zimbabwe awaits the successful repatriation of the remains of Mbuya Nehanda and other heroes who were decapitated by the British and their heads taken to Britain as trophies for the Queen. Such callous, inhuman and barbaric behaviour by the same people who today preach the gospel of 'human rights' to Africans! Isn't that hypocrisy at its worst?[58]

Clearly for *The Patriot*, at least, like the exhumed remains of Zimbabwe's liberation war dead, Nehanda's bones have indeed arisen.[59] Perhaps they were right. In late June 2020, NMMZ and Harare's city authorities

---

Damian Zane) suggests that 3 of the 11 Zimbabwean skulls in its collections are 'purported to be Matabele' and 'were taken by the donor in 1893 from a place reportedly associated with executions by Lobengula, probably in Bulawayo'; four 'were found or excavated in mining shafts and operations' and 'two of those (one a cranium and the second a cranium with postcrania) found near Bulawayo were donated in 1897' and a further two (postcrania only …) were found in mining operations in Mashonaland before 1919' and 'donated to the museum in 1955'; a further two 'were reportedly found in archaeological contexts in caves: one (a cranium) has no location other than Zimbabwe (the donor inherited from his father and donated in 1961); the second (a cranium) was excavated from a cave in 1943 near Marandellas and given to the Museum in 1958'; one cranium 'is reportedly a Matabele warrior found on an old battlefield at Selukwe, Matabeleland during mining operations in 1894 and was donated to the Museum in 1982'; and the final cranium 'is reportedly Matabele but no location information is available' and 'was given to the Museum in 1968' (pers. com. Damian Zane, 16/10/20).

[56] 'Bring back our heroes', *Patriot*, issue 442, 6–12/3/20.
[57] Ibid.
[58] Ibid.
[59] One article explicitly wrote this, see 'Repatriation of Zimbabwe's First Chimurenga war heroes/royal remains from UK gathers momentum' *News of the South* 14/8/19.

began work in the city centre to erect a statue of Nehanda at the junction of Julius Nyerere Way and Samora Machel Avenue.[60] This led to new controversy after Nelson Chamisa criticised the government's priorities during an e-rally, saying 'you want to commit state resources to build a statue instead of putting money and effort into building buildings and infrastructure', adding that 'our (MDC) government will honour heroes but will not worship any human beings. We will not worship the dead'.[61] This quickly provoked angry responses from the ruling party and government-aligned media, who criticised Chamisa for 'castigating' Mnangagwa 'for honouring the dead', with some claiming that he had said that 'Mbuya Nehanda was not an important person and as such she did not deserve our respects'.[62] According to ZANU PF's Director for Information and Publicity, Tafadzwa Mugwadi, 'by … disrespecting our founding heroes like Mbuya Nehanda, Chamisa has demonstrated a high level of immaturity, and his true colours that the MDC Alliance worships their western masters who imposed sanctions on Zimbabwe'. Chamisa's 'utterances demeaning the dead' he continued, 'are nonsensical and rendered him a nonentity who lacks qualities of a leader'.[63] Meanwhile others speculated that the sudden, unexpected death of Chamisa's mother on the same day, just a few hours later, at her rural home in Gutu, was punishment from the spirits for his 'demeaning' words.[64]

Later in the year the statue raised further controversies. In July, Felix Elijah Shamuyarira, a man claiming to be a 'maternal relative' of the Nehanda medium Charwe Nyakasikana, made an application to Harare's high court to halt the erection of the statue. He argued that 'the government had bypassed traditional rites by not engaging her family' and demanded that 'a cleansing ceremony is conducted in the "dirty" city of Harare', because 'a lot of innocent lives have been lost in recent years'.[65] Naming 'Home Affairs minister Kazembe Kazembe, his Local Government counterpart July Moyo, National Archives of Zimbabwe director Ivan Murambiwa, National Museums and Monuments director

---

[60] 'Work on Mbuya Nehanda memorial statue begins' *Herald* 4/7/20; 'Nehanda statue to cultivate heroism' *Herald* 6/7/20; 'Zimbabwe to honour Mbuya Nehanda' *Sunday Mail* 4/7/20.

[61] 'Nehanda statue: Chamisa blasts govt over poor priorities' *Newzimbabwe.com* 7/7/20.

[62] 'Chamisa slammed for his utterances on Mbuya Nehanda statue' *ZBC News* 7/7/20; 'Obert Gutu and ZANU PF loyalists blast Chamisa for telling govt that Mbuya Nehanda monument is not a priority' *Zimeye.net* 7/7/20, accessed 8/7/20.

[63] Ibid.

[64] 'Was Nelson Chamisa punished for belittling Chimurenga war heroine Mbuya Nehanda?' *News of the South* 7/7/20.

[65] 'Man goes to court over Mbuya Nehanda statue' *NewsdzeZimbabwe* 29/7/20, accessed 24/2/21.

Conclusion

Godfrey Mahachi and National Assembly Speaker Jacob Mudenda as respondents in the court case', Felix Shamuyarira argued that

> the project must be declared unlawful in the absence of a consent document signed by her four 'blood' family members, two representatives of the spirit medium of Mbuya Nehanda, chiefs Chiweshe and Hwata and two other individuals ... since independence in 1980, the government did not bother to meet with or appreciate Charwe's family for the work she had done as a spirit medium during the liberation struggle.[66]

Furthermore,

> 'The family members and Chief Hwata, together with their spirit mediums maintain that the government of Zimbabwe and its leadership made a grave mistake in announcing their mission to the world without first engaging them on such important, national and historical matters that directly affect them,' Shamuyarira said. 'The erection of the statue is of great importance as it is clearly apparent that Charwe did not die a natural death as she was murdered by the colonial regime of the settler British colonialists. As a matter of fact, the Hwata people have since independence remained secretive as the execution of Charwe traumatises them to this present day, hence the need of a healing process for them at national level. According a special day in our calendar to be declared a national holiday and in her name as already directed and pleaded to our authorities with due respect, remains necessary' Shamuyarira argued.[67]

Although that court case rumbled on into 2021,[68] the government's determination to put up a statue to Nehanda was not diminished. Further controversies soon arose. By the end of the year, images of the new bronze statue had been revealed only to cause 'mixed reactions' amongst Zimbabweans, some of whom disapproved of the quality of the work and felt the sculptor, David Mutasa, had not been 'faithful in depicting Mbuya Nehanda'. Others 'applauded the artist for trying to depict Mbuya Nehanda in her prime and not as she appeared in the famous photos'.[69] As a Twitter storm erupted about corporeality of the statue's 'youthful' depiction of Nehanda, one user commented: '*Ko Mbuya nehanda vave nema hips* [Mbuya Nehanda now has hips] so someone just did a statue of their queen not Zim's Mbuya Nehanda'.[70] The row continued until President Mnangagwa himself got involved in the affray, and ordered that the

---

[66] Ibid.
[67] Ibid.
[68] 'Mbuya Nehanda statue court battle rages on' *Daily News* 3/4/21; 'Mbuya Nehanda's relatives warn of disasters if her statue is erected' *Pindula News* 16/4/21, accessed 6/7/21.
[69] 'Mbuya Nehanda's memorial statue causes mixed reactions' *iHarare.com* 19/12/20, accessed 24/2/21.
[70] Ibid.

statue be remade to more closely match a famous picture taken of the medium and Sekuru Kaguvi before they were hanged in 1896. According to the President's spokesperson, George Charamba, it had been at the suggestion of NMMZ officials, who felt that 'the artistic production must convey and communicate vigour, permanence, youthfulness of the spirit which Nehanda incarnates or personifies', that Mutasa had made Nehanda look 'a lot younger to suggest that buoyancy which they wanted to communicate to the onlooker'. But, Charamba continued, 'the President didn't agree' and demanded that 'that youthful face of Nehanda should be put away', and the statue be remade to represent 'a Nehanda who is closer to how the good lady looked in real life, which means a lot more wrinkled, well past middle age, and of course showing the strains and stresses of captivity'.[71]

On 25 May 2021, timed to coincide with *Africa Day*, the reworked bronze statue of Nehanda was erected to much official celebration – with many politicians, regional dignitaries, chiefs and traditional leaders in attendance, and to music provided by well-known musicians like the Mbare Chimurenga Choir and Mbuya Stella Chiweshe – at the junction of Samora Machel Avenue and Julius Nyerere Way in central Harare; near to, it was alleged, a spring where Nehanda herself used to drink water before a Presbyterian Church was constructed over it. 'The colonialists' attempt to destroy the nation's history by closing the springs had not worked' Mnangagwa asserted, vowing, in addition, that his government's efforts to 'repatriate Mbuya Nehanda's skull and the skulls of others from the UK' were continuing and would succeed.[72] To reinforce the Pan-Africanist credentials of Mnangagwa's 'second republic', *The Herald*'s editorial noted the significance of the statue's location, where the 'intersecting roads are … named after Africa's greatest sons of the 20th century – Tanzania and Mozambique's founding fathers'.[73] While the state press went to overdrive in its reporting of the unveiling, announcing that 'Mbuya Nehanda had arisen' and that 'the great continent of Africa has now awakened and will tell its own story for the benefit of both present and future generations',[74] critics of the government responded with outrage, suggesting, for example, that 'if ever there was any insult to Nehanda and her memory, then yesterday's event was the gravest of

---

[71] 'Mnangagwa rejects Mbuya Nehanda statue, work to be redone' *Newzimbabwe.com* 19/12/20.

[72] 'President Mnangagwa unveils Mbuya Nehanda statue in Harare' *Herald* 25/5/21; 'Mbuya Nehanda has risen!' *Herald* 26/5/21;' 'Anger in Zimbabwe at Nehanda statue amid collapsing economy' *Guardian* 26/5/21.

[73] 'Mbuya Nehanda has risen!' *Herald* 26/5/21; 'EDITORIAL COMMENT: Nehanda still talking point in statue form' *Herald* 25/5/21.

[74] Ibid.; 'African story retold by Africans' *Herald* 26/5/21; 'All set for Mbuya Nehanda statue unveiling' *Herald* 25/5/21; Editorial Comment: 'Nehanda statue: We make our own history' *Herald* 26/5/21.

Conclusion

all', and that 'if her "bones" are to "rise", then it hasn't happened yet'.[75] Many critiqued the ZANU PF government for wasting scarce resources amidst the worsening economic crisis, and especially in the middle of the COVID-19 pandemic, and as well as for its 'partisan' use of Nehanda's legacy. As *The Guardian* reported:

> The Zimbabwean novelist Tsitsi Dangarembga said the statue's unveiling on Africa Day, which commemorates the founding of the Organisation of African Unity on 25 May 1963, was 'absurd'. 'The absurdity and misguidedness of co-opting a historical figure as a partisan symbol, and celebrating this symbol in a partisan manner in a way that hinders citizens' right of movement, on a day dedicated to a continental vision is so fundamental that only comprehensive transformation will improve Zimbabwe's prospects,' Dangarembga told the Guardian.[76]

The Guardian also cited another government critic, the Zimbabwean journalist Hopewell Chin'ono, for whom:

> it was a disgrace for the government to squander money on a statue when the country's hospitals were in a state of collapse, short of medicines and reliant on donors during the pandemic. 'Ordinarily, honouring cultural and liberation heroes is a noble thing to do but I think it is a disgrace to do it at a time when Zimbabweans are going to bed on empty stomachs,' Chin'ono said. 'It is a disgrace to do it at a time when Zimbabweans are going to hospitals without medication. It is a serious disgrace when we build statues when our youths do not have jobs.' He said: 'The person being honoured would have wanted people to have access to good medication.'[77]

Meanwhile, Charwe Nyakasikana's alleged descendants, pursuing their opposition to the statue through the high court (including Chief Maxwell Dzapasi-Hwata; Susan Rosi Tirivangani, who claims to be Charwe's granddaughter; and Israel Marufu 'an alleged maternal nephew of Mbuya Charwe') argued that 'ornaments to do with spirit mediums [are] sacred' and warned 'that natural disasters will occur across the country if the government erects the statue without observing traditional rites'.[78]

Nehanda may indeed have arisen, but these recent controversies about the presence of her alleged remains in the UK and about her statue in Harare illustrate how her death and her corporeality remain as

---

[75] 'Mbuya Nehanda didn't sacrifice her life for this pungent rot by Zimbabwe ruling elite – if her "bones" are to "rise", then it hasn't happened yet' *Zimbabwean* 26/5/21.

[76] 'Anger in Zimbabwe at Nehanda statue amid collapsing economy' *Guardian* 26/5/21.

[77] Ibid.

[78] 'Mbuya Nehanda's relatives warn of disasters if her statue is erected' *Pindula News* 16/4/21, accessed 6/7/21.

The Politics of the Dead

contested, uncertain, incomplete and unresolved as they have long been. The same can be said of the uncertain material and immaterial remains and unfinished deaths of so many other Zimbabweans who have never been afforded a statue – from the *gukurahundi*, the liberation struggle and many other troubling periods of Zimbabwe's recent and distant past – which continue to disrupt its postcolonial milieu in diverse, salient and sometimes unexpected ways.

Exhuming Bob?

It is not unexpected that Robert Mugabe's death and burial (Chapter 7) has remained just as incomplete and controversial as Nehanda's. In early May 2021, as discussions about the Nehanda statue were beginning to reach their zenith, reports emerged that Chief Zvimba had summoned Grace Mugabe to his court to answer accusations of having 'improperly' buried Mugabe in Kutama in 2019; and, when she failed to attend (because she was receiving medical treatment in Singapore), that he sought to order his exhumation and reburial at the National Heroes Acre.[79] This provoked a new splurge of rumours, accusations, denials and counter-accusations. Amid initial denials by Chief Zvimba himself,[80] many suspected Mnangagwa's hidden hand in the renewed controversy, having been out-manoeuvred by Grace Mugabe in 2019 over the same issue, with some suggesting that senior police officers and one of the President's aides had delivered the summons to the 'Blue Roof' mansion in Harare.[81] Both Leo Mugabe, the family spokesperson, and Mugabe's nephew, Patrick Zhuwao, blamed Mnangagwa for stoking the renewed dispute, with the latter claiming (from exile in South Africa) that the President wanted:

> to exhume the mortal remains of ... Mugabe ... because he has been looking for what is referred to as *tsvimbo yaMambo/induku yeNkosi* [king's staff], which is really the scepter [sic] that he believes will give him the authority to be the leader of Zimbabwe.[82]

According to *The Zimbabwean*, Zhuwao 'accused Mnangagwa of being an occultist, adding he is going after Mugabe's "non-existent" scepter [sic] because "he is very uncomfortable about the prospects of the 2023 elections, and he believes that he will need to secure those elections

---

[79] Grace Mugabe summoned by Chief Zvimba' *Zimbabwean* 13/5/21; 'Fresh war over Mugabe remains' *Standard* 2/5/21; 'Mugabe exhumation: saga deepens' *Newsday* 14/5/21.
[80] 'Mugabe exhumation: saga deepens' *Newsday* 14/5/21.
[81] Ibid.
[82] 'Mnangagwa wants Mugabe exhumed over "mystic tsvimbo", nephew claims' *Zimbabwean* 13/5/21; 'Mugabe exhumation: Saga deepens' *Newsday* 14/5/21.

Conclusion

through violence"'.[83] Responding on Twitter, ZANU PF and government officials (including George Charamba, the President's spokesperson; Tafadzwa Mugwadi, ZANU PF's director of information; and Nick Mangwana, the government's Permanent Secretary for Information) mocked Zhuwao's comments as 'childish' and 'belittling to Mugabe'.[84]

On 24 May, the day before Nehanda's statue was unveiled, Chief Zvimba issued an order for the exhumation and reburial Mugabe's remains at the National Heroes Acre by 1 July, ahead of National Heroes Day celebrations the following month.[85] As well as being ordered to pay the exhumation and reburial costs, Grace Mugabe was also charged with having failed to oversee the proper redistribution of Mugabe's property after his death, fined five head of cattle and one (some reports claim two) goats, and instructed to 'ensure that Mugabe's property is collected from all over the country before July 1 this year'.[86]

According to *Newsday*, the chief's order had the effect of 'igniting rage from the family and confounding critics who said the country's leadership was neck deep into occultism'.[87] Mugabe's relatives responded by launching a court appeal challenging the chief's instructions,[88] while public commentators, including the lawyer Lovemore Madhuku, questioned the chief's authority to order the exhumation and reburial.[89] Growing increasingly wary of the repeated rumours of Mnangagwa's involvement, and about accusations of government 'occultism' more generally,[90] and likely seeking to avoid further distraction from their

---

[83] 'Mnangagwa wants Mugabe exhumed over "mystic tsvimbo", nephew claims' *Zimbabwean* 13/5/21.
[84] 'Mugabe exhumation: saga deepens' *Newsday* 14/5/21.
[85] 'BREAKING: Chief Zvimba orders mugabe reburial at the National Heroes Acre before 1 July' *iAfrica24.com* 24/5/21, accessed 7/7/21; 'Exhume Mugabe, chief orders' *Newsday* 25/5/21; 'Zimbabwe chief orders Mugabe remains to be exhumed for reburial at heroes' shrine' *Guardian* 25/5/21; 'Robert Mugabe remains must be dug up and reburied at heroes' shrine – Zimbabwe chief' *Guardian* 25/5/21.
[86] 'Exhume Mugabe, chief orders' *Newsday* 25/5/21; 'Zimbabwe chief orders Mugabe remains to be exhumed for reburial at heroes' shrine' *Guardian* 25/5/21; 'Robert Mugabe remains must be dug up and reburied at heroes' shrine – Zimbabwe chief' *Guardian* 25/5/21.
[87] 'Exhume Mugabe, chief orders' *Newsday* 25/5/21.
[88] 'Mugabe children challenge exhumation, reburial order of late father's remains' *VOAZimbabwe.com* 6/6/21; 'Mugabe's children appeal ruling to exhume remains of former leader' *Africanews.com* 8/6/21; 'Zimbabwe: ex-president Mugabe's family vows to challenge exhumation ruling' *Newzimbabwe.com* 25/1/21; all accessed 7/7/21.
[89] 'Mugabe Exhumation. Traditional court has no jurisdiction – Commentator' *eNCA* 29/5/21; 'Zimbabwe Court ruling on Mugabe's reburial described as outrageous' *SABCnews.com* 1/6/21; both accessed 7/7/21.
[90] See for example: 'Upsurge in ritual killings and violent crimes in Zimbabwe

triumphant unveiling of Nehanda's statue just a few days earlier, ZANU PF officials increasingly sought to distance themselves from the whole affair. On 27 May the Information Secretary, Nick Mangwana, told reporters that the 'government had no interest in Mugabe's skeleton'. 'It is a very local matter', he continued, adding:

> I am not sure the chief has jurisdiction on who should be buried at the Heroes Acre or not which is a piece of land outside his dominion. But what I can tell you (please take it as official) is that the Government of Zimbabwe has no interest in this matter at all and we are just observing this local matter with annoyance.[91]

Given the interest that Mnangagwa and his 'second republic' government had previously invested in the controversies surrounding Mugabe's burial in 2019, as well as the double-edged salience of recurring rumours and accusations of its involvement in 'murderous occultism',[92] Mangwana's response and denial seemed to suitably reflect the dangerous (as well as productive) duplicity of rumours discussed in this book (Chapters 3, 4, 7). The resurgence of disputes around Mugabe's burial in 2021 meant that Bob's death has continued to exemplify the unfinished nature of death in Zimbabwe. At the time of completing this book, it remained to be seen if this exhumation and reburial would go ahead.

Meanwhile, as the controversies around Nehanda's statue, her alleged remains in the UK, and Mugabe's unfinished death dominated local news and social media in late May of 2021, at Bhalagwe in Matabeleland South another less reported struggle was also revived. On Sunday 23 May 2021 a *gukurahundi* memorial service was held at Bhalagwe by local chiefs and *Ibhetshu LikaZulu*, a Ndebele civil society group, during which a commemorative plaque to victims of the massacres was unveiled. It was to replace a previous plaque erected there in 2019 but soon after destroyed by 'suspected security agents'.[93] Despite Mnangagwa's previous announcements that *gukurahundi* commemorations could now proceed, the event did not go by unhindered, as 'police blocked roads leading to the camp and detained traditional chiefs and other guests for hours before they were given the go-ahead to proceed with the

---

unsurprising – what are we to expect from a country governed by a leadership embroiled in murderous occultism?' *Zimbabwean* 14/5/21.
[91] 'Govt "annoyed" by links to Mugabe voodoo, exhumation fuss – Mangwana' Newzimbabwe.com 27/5/21, accessed 7/7/21.
[92] 'Upsurge in ritual killings and violent crimes in Zimbabwe unsurprising – what are we to expect from a country governed by a leadership embroiled in murderous occultism?' *Zimbabwean* 14/5/21.
[93] 'Bhalagwe Gukurahundi plaque "stolen"' 26/5/21 CITE, https://cite.org.zw/bhalagwe-gukurahundi-plaque-stolen, accessed 7/7/21.

Conclusion

event while observing Covid-19 regulations'.[94] The following day news emerged that the new plaque had again been 'stolen'. 'We reported it to the officers and they did nothing' claimed Mbuso Fuzwayo, *Ibhetshu LikaZulu*'s secretary general, 'but what they are good at is always trying to ensure that people of Matabeleland do not remember the people who were killed by the government'. 'Honestly speaking the plaque will be erected and we will always remember the victims', he asserted defiantly. Unsurprisingly, for many these events raised further questions about 'the government's sincerity in solving the Gukurahundi atrocities'.[95] 'There is an agreement between the chiefs and the government which gives us the authority to have these meetings and talk about Gukurahundi freely', lamented Chief Fuyane, 'but whenever we want to come to Bhalagwe we are stopped'.[96] Another member of *Ibhetshu LikaZulu*, Effie Ncube, summed up the mood well:

> 'We will continue to strongly mourn for our relatives and in defiance. We will continue to fight for justice, we will never give in to the perpetrator, we owe it to the victims, to those who died, to those who survived the torture camps like Bhalagwe and others. We won't betray our being alive, they died and we survived not just to survive but so that we remain fighting for the causes for which they died,' said Ncube.[97]

Coinciding within a few days of each other (and just before this book's final manuscript was delivered), the concurrence of all these controversies in late May 2021 – Nehanda's disputed statue; the unresolved demands for the return of her skull; Mugabe's contested burial; and the ongoing obstruction of *gukurahundi* commemorations – perfectly epitomised and exemplified the continuing salience, complexity, multiplicity and deeply contested, uncertain, corporeal/material, and emergent nature of the politics of the dead in Zimbabwe; and perhaps (with the inevitable diversity of all particular contexts) everywhere.

---

[94] Ibid.
[95] 'Mat South chiefs question Govt sincerity on Gukurahundi', https://cite.org.zw/mat-south-chiefs-question-govt-sincerity-on-gukurahundi 26/5/21, accessed 7/7/21.
[96] Ibid.
[97] 'Bhalagwe Gukurahundi plaque "stolen"' 26/5/21 CITE, https://cite.org.zw/bhalagwe-gukurahundi-plaque-stolen, accessed 7/7/21.

BIBLIOGRAPHY

Abraham, D.P. (1966). 'The roles of Chaminuka and the Mhondoro cults in Shona Political History', in: E.T. Stokes & R. Brown (eds), *The Zambesian Past* (Manchester: Manchester University Press), 28–46.

Adebanwi, W. (2008). 'Death, national memory and the social construction of heroism', *Journal of African History*, 49(3), 419–44.

Akong'a, J. (1987). 'Rainmaking rituals: A comparative study of two Kenyan societies', *African Study Monographs*, 8(2), 71–85.

Alexander, J. (2006). *The Unsettled Land: State-making & the Politics of Land in Zimbabwe, 1893–2003* (Oxford: James Currey).

___. (2009). 'Death and disease in Zimbabwe's prisons', *The Lancet*, 373, 995–6.

Alexander, J. McGregor, J. & Ranger, T. (2000). *Violence & Memory: One Hundred Years in the 'Dark Forests' of Matabeleland* (Oxford: James Currey).

Alexander, J., McGregor, J. & Tendi, B.-M. (2017). 'The transnational histories of southern African liberation movements', *Journal of Southern African Studies*, 43(1), 1–12.

Allen, L. (2006). 'The polyvalent politics of martyr commemorations in the Palestinian Intifada', *History and Memory*, 18(2), 107–13.

Appadurai, A. (1980). 'The past as a scarce resource', *Man*, 16(2), 201–19.

___. (1998). 'Dead certainty: Ethnic violence in the era of globalization', *Public Culture*, 10(2), 225–47.

Aries, P. (1974). *Western Attitudes toward Death* (Baltimore: Johns Hopkins University Press).

___. (1991). *The Hour of Our Death* (Oxford: Oxford University Press).

Baines, E. (2010). 'Spirits and social reconstruction after mass violence', *African Affairs*, 109(436), 409–30.

Baudrillard, J. (1990). *Fatal Strategies* (New York: Semiotext[e]).

Bender, B. (1998). *Stonehenge: Making Space* (Oxford: Berghahn Books).

Bent, J.T. (1896). *The Ruined Cities of Mashonaland* (London: Longmans, Green & Co).

Bernault, F. (2006). 'Body, power and sacrifice in Equatorial Africa', *The Journal of African History*, 47(2), 207–39.

___. (2010). 'Colonial bones: The 2006 burial of Savorgnan de Brazza in the Congo', *African Affairs*, 109(436), 367–90.

___. (2013). 'Carnal technologies and the double life of the body in Gabon', *Critical African Studies*, 5(3), 175–94.

Bibliography

Bertelsen, B.E. (2004). 'It will rain until we are in power: Floods, elections and memory in Mozambique', in: H. Englund & F.B. Nyamnjoh (eds), *Rights and the Politics of Recognition in Africa* (London: Zed Books), 169–91.

Bhebe, N. (1979). *Christianity and Traditional Religion in Western Zimbabwe, 1859–1923* (Oxford: Longman).

___. (2004). *Simon Vengayi Muzenda & the Struggle for and Liberation of Zimbabwe* (Gweru: Mambo Press).

Bloch, M. (1971). *Placing the Dead: Tombs, Ancestral Villages, and Kinship Organization in Madagascar* (London: Seminar Press).

___. (1988). 'Death and the concept of the person', in: S. Cederroth, C. Corlin & J. Lindström (eds), *On the Meaning of Death* (Stockholm: AUU), 11–30.

Bloch, M. & Parry, J. (eds) (1982). *Death and the Regeneration of Life* (Cambridge: Cambridge University Press).

Boddy, J. (1989). *Wombs and Alien Spirits* (Madison: University of Wisconsin Press).

Bourdillon, M.F.C. (1987a). 'Guns and rain: Taking structural analysis too far?' *Africa*, 57(2), 263–73.

___. (1987b) [1976]. *The Shona Peoples* (Gweru: Mambo Press).

Branch, A. (2011). *Displacing Human Rights* (Oxford: Oxford University Press).

Branch, D. (2010). 'The search for the remains of Dedan Kimathi', *Past & Present*, 206 (Supplement 5), 301–20.

Bratton, M. & Masunungure, E. (2007). 'Popular reactions to state repression: Operation Murambatsvina in Zimbabwe', *African Affairs*, 106(422), 21–45.

Brickhill, J. (1995). 'Making peace with the past: War victims and the work of the Mafela Trust', in: N. Bhebe & T. Ranger (eds), *Soldiers in Zimbabwe's Liberation War* (London: James Currey), 163–73.

Brown, B. (2001). 'Thing theory', *Critical Inquiry*, 28(1), 1–22.

Brown, M.(2007). 'The fallen, the front and the finding: Archaeology, human remains and the Great War', *Archaeological Review from Cambridge*, 22(2), 53–67.

Buchli, V. (2002). *The Material Culture reader* (London: Berghahn Books).

Burnet, J. (2009). 'Whose genocide? Whose truth? Representations of victim and perpetrator in Rwanda', in: A.L. Hinton and K.L. O'Neill (eds), *Genocide: Truth, Memory, and Representation* (London: Duke University Press) 80–110.

Butler, J. (2004). *Precarious Life* (London: Verso).

Buur, L. & Kyed, H.M. (2006). 'Contested sources of authority: Re-claiming state sovereignty by formalizing traditional authority in Mozambique', *Development & Change*, 37(4), 847–69.

Buyandelgeriyn, M. (2008). 'Post-post-transition theories: Walking on multiple paths', *Annual Review of Anthropology*, 37(1), 235–50.

Bibliography

Caplan, P. (2007). 'Never again: Genocide memorials in Rwanda', *Anthropology Today*, 23(1), 20–23.

Carsten, J. (2013). 'Introduction: Blood will out', *Journal of the Royal Anthropological Institute*, 19(1), 1–23.

Casper, M. & Moore, L. (2009). *Missing Bodies: The Politics of Visibility (Biopolitics: Medicine, Technoscience and Health in the 21st Century)* (New York: New York University Press).

Catholic Commission for Justice and Peace (CCJP) (2007). 'Gukurahundi in Zimbabwe: A Report on the Disturbances in Matabeleland and the Midlands 1980–1988'. Available at: http://hrforumzim.org/wp-content/uploads/2010/06/breaking-the-silence.pdf [accessed 28 May 2020].

Chadya, J.M. (2015). 'Where the dead queued for fuel: Zimbabweans remember the fuel crisis and its impact on the funeral industry 1999–2008', in: T.M. Chen & D. Churchill (eds), *The Material of World History* (New York: Routledge), 167–88.

Chambers, K. (2009) 'Zimbabwe's battle against cholera' *The Lancet* 373, 993–4.

Chan, S. (2019). *Robert Mugabe: A Life of Power and Violence* (London: IB Tauris).

Charumbira, R. (2008). 'Nehanda and Gender Victimhood in the Central Mashonaland 1896–97', *History in Africa*, 35(2008), 101–31.

___. (2010) 'Zimbabwe's hanging tree' *Not Even Past*. Available at https://notevenpast.org/zimbabwes-hanging-tree [accessed 27 May 2020].

Chaumba, J., Scoones, I. & Wolmer, W. (2003a). 'From *Jambanja* to planning', *Journal of Modern African Studies*, 41(4), 533–54.

___. (2003b). 'New politics, new livelihoods: Agrarian change in Zimbabwe', *Review of African Political Economy*, 30(98), 585–608.

Chigudu, S. (2019). 'The politics of cholera, crisis and citizenship in urban Zimbabwe: "People were dying like flies"', *African Affairs*, 118(472), 413–34.

Chigumadzi, P. (2018). *These Bones Will Rise Again* (Auckland Park, South Africa: Jacana Media).

Chigwenya, C. (2019). 'Can We Borrow Peacebuilding Mechanisms?' Honours dissertation, University of Johannesburg.

Chipangura, N. (2015). 'Archaeologists and vernacular exhumers in Zimbabwe', paper presented at the conference Legacies of Struggle in Eastern & Southern Africa, British Institute in Eastern Africa, Nairobi, March 2015.

Chirikure, S. (2021). *Great Zimbabwe: Reclaiming a 'Confiscated' Past* (London: Routledge).

Chirisa, I., Nyamadzawo, L., Bandauko, E. & Mutsindikwa, N. (2015). 'The 2008/2009 cholera outbreak in Harare, Zimbabwe', *Reviews on Environmental Health* 30(2), 117–24.

Chitanda, E. (2020a). *Politics and Religion in Zimbabwe* (Oxford: Routledge).

___. (ed.) (2020b). *Personality Cult and Religion in Mugabe's Zimbabwe* (Oxford: Routledge).

Bibliography

Chitukutuku, E. (2017). 'Rebuilding the liberation war base: Materiality and landscapes of violence in Northern Zimbabwe', *Journal of Eastern African Studies*, 11(1), 133–50.

___. (2019). 'Spiritual temporalities of the liberation war in Zimbabwe', *Journal of War and Culture*, 12(4), 320–33.

Chuma, W. (2005). 'Zimbabwe: The media, market failure and political turbulence'. *Ecquid Novi: African Journalism Studies*, 26(1), 46–62.

Chung, F. (1995). 'Education and the war', in: N. Bhebe & T. Ranger (eds), *Society in Zimbabwe's Liberation War* (London: James Currey), 139–46.

___. (2006). *'Re-living the Second Chimurenga: Memories from the Liberation Struggle in Zimbabwe'* (Harare: Weaver Press).

Clark, H.A. (1985). *A Policeman's Narrative of Witchcraft and Murder in Zimbabwe* (Kent Town: Veritas).

Clarke, M. & Nyathi, P. (2016). *Welshman Hadane Mabhena* (Bulawayo: Amagugu Books).

Clarkson Fletcher, H. (1941). *Psychic Episodes of Great Zimbabwe* (Cape Town: Central News Agency South Africa).

Cohen, D. & Odhiambo, E. (1992). *Burying SM* (London: James Currey).

___. (2004). *The Risks of Knowledge* (Athens: Ohio University Press).

Coltart, D. (2016). *The Struggle Continues* (Harare: Jacana Media).

Comaroff, J. (1985). *Body of Power, Spirit of Resistance* (Chicago, IL: University of Chicago Press).

Cook, S.E. (2009). *Genocide in Cambodia and Rwanda* (Piscataway, NJ: Transaction Publishers).

Coombes, A. (2004). *History after Apartheid: Visual Culture and Public Memory in a Democratic South Africa* (Durham, NC: Duke University Press).

Cooper, E. & Pratten, D. (2015). *Ethnographies of Uncertainty in Africa* (London: Palgrave Macmillan).

Copeman, J. (2005). 'Veinglory: Exploring processes of blood transfers between persons', *Journal of the Royal Anthropological Institute*, 11(3), 465–85.

___. (2009). *Veils of Devotion* (New Brunswick, NJ: Rutgers University Press).

Cox, J. (1998). *Rational Ancestors: Scientific Rationality and African Indigenous Religions*. Religions in Africa Series of African Association for the Study of Religions (Cardiff: Cardiff Academic Press).

___. (2005). 'The land crisis in Zimbabwe: A case of religious intolerance?' *Fieldwork in Religion*, 1(1), 35–48.

Crais, C. & Scully, P. (2009). *Sara Baartman and the Hottentot Venus* (Princeton, NJ: Princeton University Press).

Crawford, J.R. (1967). *Witchcraft and Sorcery in Rhodesia* (London: Oxford University Press).

Crossland, Z. (2000). 'Buried lives: Forensic archaeology and the disappeared in Argentina', *Archaeological Dialogues*, 7(2), 146–59.

Bibliography

___. (2009a). 'Of clues and signs: The dead body and its evidential traces', *American Anthropologist*, 111(1), 69–80.

___. (2009b). 'Acts of estrangement: The post-mortem making of self and other', *Archaeological Dialogues*, 16(1), 102–25.

Csordas, T. (1994). *Embodiment and Experience* (Cambridge: Cambridge University Press).

Dande, I & Mujere, J. (2019) Contested histories and contested land claims', *Review of African Political Economy*, 46(159), 86–100.

Daneel, M. (1970). *God of the Matopo Hills* (The Hague: Mouton).

___. [as Mafuranhunzi Gumbo] (1995). *Guerrilla Snuff* (Harare: Baobab Books).

___. (1998). *African Earthkeepers Volume 1* (Pretoria: UNISA Press).

Dangarembga, T., Mabasa, I., Milio, Y., Muchemwa, E., Mujeri., C. & Mukwasi, K. (2014). 'A family portrait: A collection of short stories from the Breaking the Silence project by Zimbabwean writers' (Harare: Icapa Publishing).

Das, V. & Poole, D. (2004). *Anthropology in the Margins of the State* (Oxford: James Currey).

de Witte, M. (2011). 'Of Corpses, clay, and Photographs', in: M. Jindra. & J. Noret (eds), *Funerals in Africa* (London: Berghahn Books), 177–206.

Deleuze, G. & Guattari, F. (1987) [1980]. *A Thousand Plateaus*, translated by B. Massumi (Minneapolis: University of Minnesota Press).

Denich, J. (1994). 'Dismembering Yugoslavia: Nationalist ideologies and the symbolic revival of genocide', *American Ethnologist*, 21(2), 377–81.

Derman, W. (2003). 'Cultures of development and indigenous knowledge', *Africa Today*, 50(2), 67–85.

Dobler, G. (2012). 'Whose skulls? Namibian body parts in a German university collection'. Unpublished seminar paper, CAS, University of Edinburgh, 2 November 2011.

Domańska, E. (2006). 'The return to things', *Archaeologia Polona*, 44(2006), 171–85.

Doran, S. (2017). *Kingdom, Power, Glory: Mugabe, ZANU and the Quest for Supremacy, 1960– 1987* (Midrand, South Africa: Sithatha Media).

Dorman, S., Hammett, D. & Nugent, P. (2007). *Making Nations, Creating Strangers* (London: Brill).

Douglas, M. (1966). *Purity and Danger* (London: Routledge).

Droz, Y. (2011). 'Transformations of death among the Kikuyu of Kenya', in: M. Jindra & J. Noret, *Funerals in Africa* (London: Berghahn Books), 69–87.

Dube, Z. (2018). 'The ancestors, violence and democracy in Zimbabwe', *Verbum et Ecclesia* 39(1), 1–8.

Elias, N. (1995). *The Loneliness of Dying* (Oxford: Blackwell).

Ellis, S. (1989). 'Tuning in to pavement radio', *African Affairs*, 88(352), 321–30.

___. (2008). 'The Okija Shrine: Death and life in Nigerian politics', *Journal of African History*, 49(3), 445–66.

Bibliography

Eltringham, N. (2004). *Accounting for Horror: Post-Genocide Debates in Rwanda* (London and Sterling, VA: Pluto Press).

Engelke, M. (2007). *A Problem of Presence* (Berkeley: University of California Press).

Eppel, S. (2001). 'Healing the dead to transform the living: Exhumation and reburial in Zimbabwe'. Presented at the conference Regional and Human Rights' Contexts and DNA, University of California, Berkeley, 26–27 April 2001.

___. (2004). '"Gukurahundi" The need for truth and reparation', in: B. Raftopoulos & T. Savage (eds), *Zimbabwe: Injustice and Political Reconciliation* (Cape Town Institute for Justice and Reconciliation), 43–62.

___. (2009). 'A tale of three dinner plates: Truth and the challenges of human rights research in Zimbabwe', *Journal of Southern African Studies*, 35(4), 967–76.

___. (2013). 'Repairing a fractured nation: Challenges and opportunities in the post-GPA Zimbabwe', in: B. Raftopoulos, *The Hard Road to Reform: The Politics of Zimbabwe's Global Political Agreement* (Harare: Weaver Press), 211–50.

___. (2014). 'Bones in the forest in Matabeleland, Zimbabwe: Exhumations as a tool for transformation', *International Journal of Transitional Justice*, 8(3), 404–25.

Espirito Santo, D., Kerestetzi, K. & Panagiotopoulos, A. (2013). 'Human substances and ontological transformations in the African inspired ritual complex of Palo Monte in Cuba', *Critical African Studies*, 5(3), 195–219.

Fabian, J. (1972). 'How others die: Reflections on the anthropology of death', *Social Research*, 39(3), 543–67.

Falisse, J.-B., Macdonald, R., Molony, T. & Nugent, P. (2021). 'Why have so many African leaders died of COVID-19?' *BMJ Global Health* 6(5).

Fassin, D. (2007). *When Bodies Remember* (Berkeley: University of California Press).

Feldman, A. (1991). *Formations of Violence* (Chicago, IL: Chicago University Press).

___. (2003). 'Political Terror and the technologies of memory', *Radical History Review, Terror and History*, Winter (85), 58–73.

Fforde, C. (2004). *Collecting the Dead* (London: Duckworth).

Fforde, C., Hubert, J. & Turnbull, P. (2002). *The Dead and their Possessions* (London: Routledge).

Filippucci, P. (2004). 'Memory & marginality: Remembrance of war in Argonne (France)', in: F. Pine, K. Deena & H. Haukanes (eds), *Memory, Politics & Religion* (Münster: Lit-Verlag), 35–7.

___. (2010). 'Archaeology and memory on the Western Front', in: D. Boric, *Archaeology and Memory* (Oxford: Oxbow Books), 171–82.

Bibliography

Filippucci, P., Harries, J., Fontein, J. & Krmpotich, K. (2012). 'Encountering the past: Unearthing remnants of humans in archaeology and anthropology', in: D. Shankland (ed.), *Archaeology and Anthropology: Past, Present and Future* (London: Berghahn Books, ASA Monographs 48), 197–218.

Fontein, J. (2000). 'UNESCO, heritage and Africa: An anthropological critique of world heritage', Occasional Paper No. 80, Centre of Africa Studies, University of Edinburgh.

___. (2004). 'Ambuya VaZarira speaks – Five conversations with a spirit medium in Masvingo Province, Zimbabwe, 2000–2001' Unpublished manuscript.

___. (2006a). *The Silence of Great Zimbabwe: Contested Monuments and the Power of Heritage* (London: UCL Press).

___. (2006b). 'Languages of land, water and "tradition" around Lake Mutirikwi in southern Zimbabwe', *Journal of Modern African Studies*, 44(2), 223–49.

___. (2006c). 'Shared legacies of the war: Spirit mediums and war veterans in Southern Zimbabwe', *Journal of Religion in Africa*, 36(2), 167–99.

___. (2006d). 'Graves, water and chiefs: The articulation of memories and practices of landscape around Lake Mutirikwi'. Unpublished paper, presented at the History seminar, University of Zimbabwe, 2 June 2006.

___. (2009a). 'Anticipating the tsunami: Rumours, planning and the arbitrary state in Zimbabwe', *Africa*, 79(3), 369–98.

___. (2009b). 'The politics of the dead: Living heritage, bones and commemoration in Zimbabwe'. ASA online, www.theasa.org/publications/asaonline/articles/asaonline_0102.shtml [accessed 27 May 2020].

___. (2010). 'Between tortured bodies and resurfacing bones: The politics of the dead in Zimbabwe', *Journal of Material Culture*, 15(4), 423–48.

___. (2011). 'Graves, ruins and belonging: Towards an anthropology of proximity', *Journal of the Royal Anthropological Institute*, 17(4), 706–27.

___. (2013). 'Editorial: The vitality and efficacy of human substances', *Critical African Studies*, 5(3): 115–26.

___. (2015). *Remaking Mutirikwi: Landscape, Water & Belonging in Southern Zimbabwe* (Woodbridge: James Currey).

___. (2018). 'Death, corporeality, and uncertainty in Zimbabwe', in: A. Robben, *A Companion to the Anthropology of Death* (Hoboken, NJ: Wiley-Blackwell), 337–56.

___. (2020). 'Review of Casey Golomski, *Funeral Culture: AIDS, Work, and Cultural Change in an African Kingdom* (Bloomington, Indiana University Press, 2018) in *Human Remains and Violence*, 6(1), 102–5.

___. (2021). 'From "other worlds" and "multiple ontologies" to "a methodological project that poses ontological questions to solve epistemological problems": What happened to *Thinking Through Things*?' *Ethnos*, 86 (1), 173–88.

Bibliography

Fontein J. & Harries J. (2009). 'Report of the "Bones Collective" Workshop, 4–5 December 2008, www.san.ed.ac.uk/__data/assets/pdf_file/0013/29110/Final_Report.pdf [accessed 2 February 2010].

___. (2013) 'The vitality and efficacy of human substances', *Critical African Studies*, 5(3), 115–26.

Forty, A. & Küchler, S. (1999). *The Art of Forgetting* (Oxford: Berghahn Books).

Fry, P. (1976). *Spirits of Protest* (Cambridge: Cambridge University Press).

Gable, E. (2006). 'The funeral and modernity in Manjaco', *Cultural Anthropology*, 21(3), 385–415.

Garbett, K. (1977). 'Disparate regional cults and a unitary field in Zimbabwe', in: R. Werbner, *Regional Cults* (London: Academic Press), 55–92.

___. (1992). 'From conquerors to autochthons', *Social Analysis*, 31(1), 12–43.

Garlake, P. (1983). 'Prehistory and ideology in Zimbabwe', in: J.D.Y. Peel. & T. Ranger (eds), *Past & Present in Zimbabwe* (Manchester: Manchester University Press), 1–19.

Gastrow, C. & Lawrence B.N. (2021). 'Vaccine nationalism and the future of research in Africa', *African Studies Review*, 64: 1, 1–4.

Geary, P. (1986). 'Sacred commodities: The circulation of medieval relics', in: A. Appadurai, *The Social life of Things* (Cambridge: Cambridge University Press), 169–92.

Geertz, C. (1973). 'Thick description: Toward an interpretive theory of culture', in: *The Interpretation of Cultures: Selected Essays* (New York: Basic Books), 3–30.

Gelfand, M. (1959). *Shona Ritual* (Cape Town: Juta).

Gell, A. (1998). *Art & Agency* (Oxford: Oxford University Press).

George, C.B. (2015). *The Death of Rex Nhongo* (London: Quercus Books).

Geschiere, P. (2005). 'Funerals and belonging', *African Studies*, 48(2), 45–64.

___. (2009). *The Perils of Belonging* (Chicago, IL: University of Chicago Press).

Gewald, J.B. (2001). 'El Negro, el Niño, witchcraft and the absence of rain in Botswana', *Pula: Botswana Journal of African Studies*, 16(1), 37–51.

___. (2004). 'Namibia's past in the present: Towards patriotic history?' Unpublished paper, presented at the conference Heritage in Southern and Eastern Africa, Livingstone, 5–8 July 2004.

Gibson, J. (1977). *Perceiving, Acting, Knowing: Towards an Ecological Psychology* (Hillsdale: Lawrence Erlbaum Associates).

Golomski, C. (2018a). *Funeral Culture: AIDS, Work, and Cultural Change in an African Kingdom* (Indiana: Indiana University Press).

___. (2018b). 'Work of a nation: Christian funerary ecumenism and institutional disruption in Swaziland', Journal of Southern African Studies, 44(2), 299–314.

Gosden, C. (2005). 'What do objects want?' *Journal of Archaeological Method and Theory*, 12(3), 193–211.

Government of Zimbabwe (2000). 'A Guide to the Heroes Acre' (pamphlet) (Harare: Ministry of Information, Posts & Telecommunications).

Graeber, D. (2015). 'Radical alterity is just another way of saying "reality": A reply to Eduardo Viveiros de Castro', *HAU: Journal of Ethnographic Theory*, 5(2), 1–41.

Green, J W. (2008). *Beyond the Good Death* (Philadelphia, PA: University of Philadelphia Press).

Gulbrandsen, O. (2012). *The State and the Social* (Oxford: Berghahn Books).

Haddow, G. (2000). *Organ Transplantation and (Dis)Embodiment* (Edinburgh: Edinburgh University Press).

___. (2005). 'The phenomenology of death, embodiment and organ transplantation'. *Sociology of Health and Illness*, 27(1), 92–113.

Hall, R.N. (1905). *Great Zimbabwe, Mashonaland, Rhodesia* (London: Metheun Publishing).

Hallam, E. (2010). 'Articulating bones: An epilogue', *Journal of Material Culture*, 15(4), 465–92.

Hallam, E. & Hockey, J. (2001). *Death, Memory & Material Culture* (Oxford: Berghahn Books).

Hallam, E., Hockey, J. & Howarth, G. (1999). *Beyond the Body: Death and Social Identity* (London: Routledge).

Hamber, B. & Wilson, R.A. (2002). 'Symbolic closure through memory, reparation and revenge in post-conflict societies', *Journal of Human Rights*, 1(1), 35–53.

Hansen, T.B. & Stepputat, F. (2001). *States of Imagination* (Durham, NC: Duke University Press).

___. (2005). *Sovereign Bodies* (Princeton, NJ: Princeton University Press).

Harries, J. (2017a). 'A Beothuk skeleton (not) in a glass case: Rumours of bones and the remembrance of an exterminated people in Newfoundland – the emotive immateriality of human remains', in: J.M. Dreyfus & E. Anstett (eds), *Human Remains in Society* (Manchester: Manchester University Press), 220–48.

___. (2017b). 'A stone that feels right in the hand: Tactile memory, the abduction of agency and presence of the past', *Journal of Material Culture*, 22(1), 110–30.

Harrison, S. (2012). *Dark Trophies* (London: Berghahn Books).

Henare, A., Holbraad, M. & Wastell, S. (2007). *Thinking Through Things* (London: Routledge).

Hertz, R. (1960). *Death and the Right Hand*, translated by R. Needham & C. Needham (New York: Free Press).

Hicks, D. (2020). *The Brutish Museums: The Benin Bronzes, Colonial Violence and Cultural Restitution* (London: Pluto Press).

Hodder, I. (1995). *Interpreting Archaeology* (London: Routledge).

___. (2012). *Entangled: An Archaeology of the Relationships between Humans and Things* (Oxford: Wiley-Blackwell).

Bibliography

Holbraad, M. (2009). 'Ontography and alterity: Defining anthropological truth', *Social Analysis*, 53(2), 80–93.

___. (2011). 'Can the thing speak?' Open Anthropology Cooperative Press. Working Paper Series 7, http://openanthcoop.net/press/2011/01/12/can-the-thing-speak [accessed 14 September 2013].

Holbraad, M. & Pedersen, M.A. (2017). *The Ontological Turn* (Cambridge: Cambridge University Press).

Holland, H. (2012). *Dinner with Mugabe* (Johannesburg: Penguin Random House).

Houston, G., Plaatjie, T. & April, T. (2015) 'Military training and camps of the PanAfricanist Congress of South Africa, 1961–1981', *Historia*, 60(2), 24–50.

Hove, C. (1988). *Bones* (Harare: Baobab Press).

___. (1996). *Ancestors* (London: Picador).

Human Rights Watch (HRW) (2008). '"Bullets for each of you": State-sponsored violence since Zimbabwe's March 29 elections', www.hrw.org/en/reports/2008/06/19/bullets-each-you [accessed 19 June 20].

Huntington, P. & Metcalf, P. (1991). *Celebrations of Death* (Cambridge: Cambridge University Press).

Ingelaere, B. (2016). *Inside Rwanda's Gacaca Court* (Madison: University of Wisconsin Press).

Ingold, T. (1992). 'Culture and the perception of the environment', in: E. Croll & D. Parkin (eds), *Bush Base: Forest Farm* (London: Routledge) 14–32.

___. (2007). 'Materials against materiality', *Archaeological Dialogues*, 14(1), 1–16.

___. (2009). 'The textility of making', *Cambridge Journal of Economics*, 34(1), 91–102.

___. (2016). 'On human correspondence', *Journal of the Royal Anthropological Institute*, 23(1), 9–27.

Jamar, A. & Major, L. (2020). 'Managing mass graves in Rwanda and Burundi: Authoritarian vernaculars of the right to truth', unpublished paper.

James, D. (2007). *Gaining Ground?* (Oxford: Routledge).

James, W. (1972). 'The Politics of rain-control among the "Uduk"', in: I. Cunnison & W. James (eds), *Essays in Sudan Ethnography: Presented to Sir Edward Evans-Pritchard* (London: Hurst), 31–57.

Jedrej, M.C. (1992). 'Rain makers, women, and sovereignty in the Sahel and East Africa', in: L.O. Fradenburg (ed.), *Women and Sovereignty* (Edinburgh: Edinburgh University Press), 290–99.

Jenkins, T. (2010). *Contesting Human Remains in Museum Collections* (London: Routledge).

Jensen, S. (2012). 'Shosholoza: Political culture in south africa between the secular and the occult', *Journal of Southern African Studies*, 38(1), 91–106.

___. (2013). 'Corporealities of violence: Rape and the shimmering of embodied and material categories in South Africa', *Critical African Studies*, 7(2), 99–117.

Jindra, M. (2011). 'The rise of "death celebrations" in the Cameroon Grassfields', in: M. Jindra & J. Noret (eds), *Funerals in Africa* (London: Berghahn Books), 109–29.

Jindra, M. & Noret, J. (eds) (2011) *Funerals in Africa* (London: Berghahn Books).

Jones, A. (2003). 'Technologies of remembrance: Memory, materiality and identity in early Bronze Age Scotland', in H. Williams (ed.), *Archaeologies of Remembrance – Death and Memory in Past Societies* (New York: Kluwer/Plenum), 65–88.

Jones, B. (2007). 'The Teso insurgency remembered: Churches, burials and propriety', *Africa*, 77(4), 500–16.

Jopela, A.P. (2017). 'The Politics of Liberation Heritage in Postcolonial Southern Africa with special Reference to Mozambique'. Unpublished PhD thesis, University of the Witswatersrand.

Kalusa, W.T. & Vaughan, M. (2013). *Death, Belief & Politics in Central African History* (Lusaka: Lembani Trust).

Katanekwa, N. (2004). 'SADC Freedom War heritage in Zambia'. Unpublished paper, presented at Livingston Conference, July 2004.

Kaufman, S.R. & Morgan, L.M. (2005). 'The anthropology of the beginnings and ends of life', *Annual Review of Anthropology*, 34(1), 317–41.

Klaeger, G. (2013). 'Introduction: The perils and possibilities of African roads'. Special issue Ethnographies of the Road, *Africa*, 83(3): 359–66.

Knappett, C. & Malafouris, L. (2008). *Material Agency* (Berlin: Springer).

Krige, E.J. & Krige, J.D. (1943). *The Realm of the Rain Queen* (Oxford: Oxford University Press).

Kriger, N. (1992). *Zimbabwe's Guerrilla War: Peasant Voices* (Cambridge: Cambridge University Press).

___. (1995). 'The politics of creating National Heroes', in: N. Bhebe & T. Ranger (eds), *Soldiers in Zimbabwe's Liberation War* (Harare: University of Zimbabwe; London: James Currey), 148–62.

___. (2003). *Guerrilla Veterans in Post-War Zimbabwe* (Cambridge: Cambridge University Press).

___. (2020). 'Biographies of two "big men" in Zimbabwe: A review essay', *Small Wars and Insurgencies*, 31(5), 1130–6.

Krmpotich, C. (2008). 'Ancestral bones: Creating proximity and familiarity'. Unpublished paper presented to Bones Collective Workshop, 4–5 December 2008.

Krmpotich, C., Fontein, J. & Harries, J. (2010). Preface to Special Issue: 'The substance of bones: The emotive materiality and affective presence of human remains', *Journal of Material Culture*, 15(4), 371–84.

Küchler, S. (1999). 'The place of memory', in: A. Forty & S. Küchler (eds), *The Art of Forgetting* (Oxford: Berghahn Books), 53–73.

Kuklick, H. (1991). 'Contested monuments: The politics of archaeology in Southern Africa', in: G.W. Stocking *Colonial Situations* (Madison: University of Wisconsin Press), 135–69.

Bibliography

Kuper, A. (2005). 'Clueless', *London Review of Books*, 27(8).
Kwon, H. (2006). *After the Massacre* (Berkeley: University of California Press).
Kyed, H.M. & Buur, L. (2006). 'Recognition and democratisation: "New roles" for traditional leaders in sub-Saharan Africa', Working Paper 2006: 11 (Copenhagen: Danish Institute for International Studies).
Lambek, M. (2002a). 'Nuriaty, the saint and the sultan: Virtuous subject and subjective virtuoso of the postmodern colony' in: R. Werbner, *Postcolonial Subjectivities in Africa* (London: Zed Books), 25–43.
___. (2002b). *The Weight of the Past* (New York: Palgrave Macmillan).
Lambek, M. & Strathern, A. (1998). *Bodies and Persons* (Cambridge: Cambridge University Press).
Lambert, H. & McDonald, M. (2009). *Social Bodies* (London: Berghahn Books).
Lamont, M. (2009). 'Interroger les morts pour critique les vivants: Ou exotisme morbide? Encounters with African funerary practices in Francophone anthropology', *Africa*, 79(3), 455–62.
___. (2011). 'Decomposing pollution? Corpses, burials, and affliction among the Meru of Central Kenya', in: M. Jindra & J. Noret (eds), *Funerals in Africa* (London: Berghahn Books), 99–108.
___. (2012). 'Accidents have no cure! Road Death as industrial catastrophe in Eastern Africa', *African Studies*, 71(2), 174–94.
___. (2013). 'Speed governors: Road safety and infrastructural overload in post-colonial Kenya, c. 1963–2013', *Africa*, 83(3), 367–84.
Lan, D. (1985). *Guns & Rain* (London: James Currey).
Langewiesche, K. (2011). 'Funerals and religious pluralism in Burkina Faso', in: M. Jindra & J. Noret (eds), *Funerals in Africa* (London: Berghahn Books), 130–53.
Latour, B. (1999). *Pandora's Hope* (Cambridge, MA: Harvard University Press).
Lawton, J. (2000). *The Dying Process* (Oxford: Routledge).
___. (2001). 'Contemporary hospice care: The sequestration of the unbounded body and "dirty dying"', *Sociology of Health and Illness*, 20(3), 121–43.
Leach, J. (2007). 'Differentiation and encompassment: A critique of Alfred Gell's theory of the abduction of creativity', in: A. Henare, M. Holbraad & S. Wastell (eds), *Thinking Through Things* (London, New York: Routledge), 167–88.
Lee, R. (2011). 'Death on the move: Funerals, entrepreneurs and the rural-urban nexus in South Africa', *Africa*, 81(2), 226–47.
Lee, R. & Vaughan, M. (2008). 'Death and dying in the history of Africa since 1800', *Journal of African History*, 49(3), 341–59.
___. (2012). 'Introduction: Themes in the study of death and loss in Africa', *African Studies*, 71(2), 163–75.
Linden, I. (1980). *The Catholic Church and the Struggle for Zimbabwe* (London: Longman).

Bibliography

Lissoni, A. (2008). 'The South African Liberation Movements in Exile, c. 1945–1970' PhD thesis, SOAS, London, 2008.

Lissoni, A. & Suriano, M. (2014). 'Married to the ANC: Tanzanian women's entanglement in South Africa's liberation struggle', *Journal of Southern African Studies*, 40 (1), 129–50.

Livingston, J. (2008). 'Disgust, bodily aesthetics and the ethic of being human in Botswana', *Africa*, 78(2), 288–307.

Lock, M. (1996). 'Death in technological time: Locating the end of meaningful life', *Medical Anthropology Quarterly*, 10(4), 575–600.

___. (2002). *Twice Dead: Organ Transplants and the Reinvention of Death* (California and London: University of California Press).

Lock, M. & Farquhar, J. (2007). *Beyond the Body Proper* (Durham, NC: Duke University Press).

Lowenthal, D. (1990). 'Conclusion: archaeologists and others' in: P. Gathercole & D. Lowenthal (eds) *The Politics of the Past* (London: Routledge), 302-14.

___. (1998). *The Heritage Crusade and the Spoils of History* (Cambridge: Cambridge University Press).

Lynch, G. (2018). *Performances of Injustice* (Cambridge: Cambridge University Press).

Maalki, L. (1995). *Purity and Exile* (Chicago, IL: University of Chicago Press).

Macdonald, S. (2008). *Difficult Heritage* (London: Routledge).

Mafu, H. (1995). 'The 1991–92 Zimbabwean drought and some religious reactions', *Journal of Religion in Africa*, 25(3), 208–308.

Major, L. (2015). 'Unearthing, untangling and re-articulating genocide corpses in Rwanda', *Critical African Studies*, 7(2), 164–81.

Major, L. & Fontein, J. (2015). 'Editorial: Corporealities of violence in southern and Eastern Africa', *Critical African Studies*, 7(2), 89–98.

Maloka, T. (1996). 'Populism and the politics of chieftaincy and nation-building in the new South Africa', *Journal of Contemporary African Studies*, 14(2), 173–96.

Mamdani, M. (1996). *Citizen & Subject* (London: James Currey).

___. (2002). *When Victims become Killers* (Princeton, NJ: Princeton University Press).

Marongwe, N. (2003). 'Farm occupations and occupiers in the new politics of land in Zimbabwe', in: A. Hammar, B. Raftopoulos & S. Jensen (eds), *Zimbabwe's Unfinished Business* (Harare: Weaver Press), 155–90.

___. (2012). 'Rural Women as the Invisible Victims of Militarised Politics Violence: The Case of Shurugwe District'. PhD thesis, University of the Western Cape.

Marschall, S. (2010). *Landscape of Memory* (Leiden: Brill).

Maringira, G. (2016) 'Soldiering the terrain of war: Zimbabwean soldiers in the Democratic Republic of the Congo (1998–2002)', *Defence Studies*, 16(3), 299–311.

Bibliography

Masunungure, E. (2009). *Defying the Winds of Change* (Harare: Weaver Press and Konrad Adenauer Foundation).

Mataga, J. (2019). 'Unsettled Spirits, performance and aesthetics of power: The public life of liberation heritage in Zimbabwe', *International Journal of Heritage Studies*, 23(3), 277–97.

Matenga, E. (2000). 'Traditional Ritual Ceremony held at Great Zimbabwe', *NAMMO Bulletin, Official Magazine of NMMZ*, 1(9), 14–15.

___. (2011). 'The Soapstone Birds of Great Zimbabwe'. PhD, Uppsala University. Available at: www.dissertations.se/dissertation/e1343c85f2 [accessed 29 May 2020].

Matereke, K.P. & Mungwini, P. (2012). 'The occult, politics and African modernities: The case of Zimbabwe's "Diesel n'anga"', *African Identities*, 10(4), 423–38.

Mattheeuws, C. (2008). 'Do crisps flavoured with chicken tikka have something in common with Central-East Malagasy ancestral bodies?' Unpublished paper, presented at the What Lies Beneath conference, Edinburgh University, December 2008.

Mawere, A. & Wilson, K. (1995). 'Socio-religious movements, the state and community change: Some reflections on the Ambuya Juliana cult of Southern Zimbabwe', *Journal of Religion in Africa*, 25(3), 252–87.

Maxwell, D. (1999). *Christians and Chiefs in Zimbabwe* (Edinburgh: Edinburgh University Press).

___. (2006) *African Gifts of the Spirit* (James Currey: Oxford).

Mazarire, G.C. (2013). 'ZANU PF and the Government of National Unity', in: B. Raftopoulos (ed.), *The Hard Road to Reform* (Harare: Weaver Press), 71–116.

Mbembe, A. (2001). *On the Postcolony* (Berkeley: University of California Press).

___. (2003). 'Necropolitics', *Public Culture*, 15(1), 11–40.

Mbiba, B. (2010). 'Burial at home: Negotiating death in the diaspora and in Harare', in: J. McGregor & R. Primorac (eds), *Zimbabwe's New Diaspora* (London: Berghahn Books), 144–63.

McGregor, J. (2013). 'Surveillance and the city: Patronage, power-sharing and the politics of urban control in Zimbabwe', *Journal of Southern African Studies*, 39 (4), 783–805.

McGregor, J. & Schumaker, L. (2006). 'Heritage in southern Africa: Imagining and marketing public culture and history', *Journal of Southern African Studies*, 32(4), 649–65.

McLaughlin, J. (1996). *On the Front Line: Catholic Missions in Zimbabwe's Liberation War* (Harare: Baobab Books).

Meier, B. (2013). '"Death does not rot": Transitional justice and local "truths" in the aftermath of war in Northern Uganda', *Africa Spectrum*, 48(2), 25–50.

Melber, H., Chiumbu, S.H. & Moyo, D. (eds) (2004). 'Media, public discourse and political contestation in Zimbabwe', *Current African Issues* 27 (Uppsala, Sweden: Nordic African Institute).

Melnick, A. (2013). 'On traffic accident blackspots in Kenya'. Unpublished paper, presented at the European Conference in African Studies, Panel 121 – Spirits of Place, 2013, Lisbon.

Meredith, M. (2003). *Our Votes, Our Guns* (New York: Public Affairs).

Mhanda, W. (2011). *Dzino: Memories of a Freedom Fighter* (Harare: Weaver Press).

Miller, D. (2005). *Materiality* (London: Duke University Press).

Mkhize, N. (2009). 'Nicholas Gcaleka and the Search for Hintsa's Skull', *Journal of Southern African Studies*, 35(1), 211–21.

Mkodzongi, G. (2016). '"I am a paramount chief, this land belongs to my ancestors": The reconfiguration of rural authority after Zimbabwe's land reforms', *Review of African Political Economy*, 43(1) 99–114.

Moore, D. (2011) 'Zimbabwe's media: Between party-state politics and press freedom under Mugabe's rule', in: H. Besada (ed.), *Zimbabwe: Picking up the Pieces* (London: Palgrave), 55–79.

___. (2014) 'The Zimbabwean People's Army moment in Zimbabwean history, 1975–1977: Mugabe's rise and democracy's demise', *Journal of Contemporary African Studies*, 32(3), 302–18.

___. (2018) 'A very Zimbabwean coup: November 13–24, 2017', *Transformation: Critical Perspectives on Southern Africa*, 97, 1–29.

___. (forthcoming A). *Mugabe's Legacy: Coups, Conspiracies, and the Conceits of Power* (London: Hurst).

___. (forthcoming B) 'Unravelling Zimbabwe's January (2019) *Jambanja*: Truth, lies, rumours, conspiracies; coups, context, Cohen', in: C. Brown, D. Moore, B. Rutherford (eds), *South Africa and Zimbabwe Now: Pasts, Presents, Futures* (Kingston, ON and Montreal, QC: McGill-Queen's University Press).

Moyo, D. (2005). 'The "independent" press and the fight for democracy in Zimbabwe: A critical analysis of the banned Daily News', *Westminster Papers in Communication and Culture*, 2(1), 109–28.

Mpofu, S. (2014). 'Public and Diasporic Online Media in the Discursive Construction of National Identity: A Case of Zimbabwe'. PhD Thesis, University of Witwatersrand.

Mubvumba, S. (2005). 'The Dilemma Of Governance: Government Policy on Traditional Authority in Resettlement Areas, 1980–2004: The Case of Guruve'. BA History Honours Dissertation, University of Zimbabwe.

Muchemwa, K.Z. (2010). 'Necropolitan imagination', *Social Dynamics*, 36(3), 504–14.

Mudau, T. & Dylan, Y. (2018). 'Operation restore legacy: An epitome of Mnangagwa anti-Mugabe narrative', *Ubuntu: Journal of Conflict Transformation*, 179–202.

Mujere, J. (2011) 'Land, graves and belonging: Land reform and the politics of belonging in newly resettled farms in Gutu, 2000–2009', *Journal of Peasant Studies*, 38(5), 1123–44.

Bibliography

___. (2012). 'Autochthons, Strangers, Modernising Educationists, and Progressive Farmers: Basotho Struggles for Belonging in Zimbabwe 1930s–2008'. PhD Thesis, University of Edinburgh.

___. (2019) *Land, Migration and Belonging: A History of the Basotho in Southern Rhodesia c. 1890–1960s* (Woodbridge: James Currey).

Mujere, J., Sagiya, M.E. & Fontein, J. (2017). '"Those who are not known, should be known by the country": Patriotic history and the politics of recognition in southern Zimbabwe', *Journal of Eastern African Studies*, 11(1), 1–29.

Mukasa, S.D. (2003). 'Press and politics in Zimbabwe', *African Studies Quarterly*, 7(3), 171–83.

Munguma, C. (2019). 'The role of the Zimbabwe Human Rights Commission in the promotion of fundamental rights and freedoms', in: A. Moyo (ed.), *Selected Aspects of the 2013 Zimbabwean Constitution and The Declaration of Rights* (Lund: Raoul Wallenberg Institute of Human Rights and Humanitarian Law), 242–60.

Mupira, P. (2018). 'Exhuming forgotten fallen comrades at Rusape's "Butcher site"', *Occasional Papers of the National Museums and Monuments of Zimbabwe, Series A, Human Sciences*, 5(1), 149–207.

Murphree, M.W. (1969) *Christianity & the Shona* (London: University of London Press).

Musila, G. (2015). *A Death Retold in Truth and Rumour: Kenya, Britain and the Julie Ward Murder* (Woodbridge: James Currey).

Navaro-Yashin, Y. (2009). 'Affective spaces, melancholic objects: Ruination and the production of anthropological knowledge', *Journal of the Royal Anthropological Institute*, 15(1), 1–18.

Ndlovu, J. (2003). *Breaking the Taboo: Mzilikazi and National Heritage*, Lozikeyi Lecture. Bulawayo National Gallery, Zimbabwe, 7 August 2003.

Ndlovu, R. (2019). In the Jaws of the Crocodile: Emmerson Mnangagwa's Rise to Power in Zimbabwe (Penguin Random House: South Africa).

Ndlovu-Gatsheni, S.J. (2015). *Mugabeism? History, Politics and Power in Zimbabwe* (New York: Palgrave Macmillan).

___. (2017). *Joshua Mqabuko Nkomo of Zimbabwe* (London: Palgrave Macmillan).

Ndlovu-Gatsheni, S. & Willems, W. (2009). 'Making sense of cultural nationalism and the politics of commemoration under the third chimurenga in Zimbabwe', *Journal of Southern African Studies*, 35(4), 945–66.

Ndoro, W. & Pwiti, G. (2001). 'Heritage management in southern Africa: Local, national and international discourse', *Public Archaeology*, 2(1), 21–34.

Niehaus, I. (2007a). 'Death before dying', *Journal of Southern African Studies*, 33(4), 845–60.

___. (2007b). '"A witch has no horn": The subjective reality of witchcraft in the South African Lowveld', *African Studies*, 56(2), 251–78.

___. (2013a). 'Averting danger: Taboos and bodily substances in the South African Lowveld', *Critical African Studies*, 5(3), 115–26.
___. (2013b). *Witchcraft and a life in the New South Africa* (London: Cambridge University Press).
Nkomo, J. (1984). *The Story of My Life* (London: Methuen); reprinted in 2001 (Harare: SAPES Books).
Nugent, P. (2008). 'Putting the history back into ethnicity', Comparative Studies in Society and History, 50(4), 920–48.
Nunez, L. & Makukule, I. (2008). 'Disposal of migrant corpses at South African mortuaries'. Unpublished paper.
Nyamnjoh, F.B. (2017a). 'Incompleteness: Frontier Africa and the currency of conviviality', *Journal of Asian and African Studies*, 52 (3), 253–70.
___. (2017b). *Drinking from the Cosmic Gourd: How Amos Tutuola Can Change Our Minds* (Bamenda, Cameroon: Langaa RPCIG).
Nyamnjoh, H. & Rowlands, M. (2013). 'Do you eat Achu here? Nurturing as a way of life in a Cameroon diaspora', *Critical African Studies*, 5(3), 140–52.
Nyandoro, M. (2011). 'Historical overview of the cholera outbreak in Zimbabwe (2008–2009)', *Journal for Contemporary History*, 36(1), 154–74.
Nyarota, G. (2018). *The Graceless Fall of Robert Mugabe: The End of a Dictator's Reign* (Cape Town: Penguin Books).
Nyathi, L. (2003). 'The Matopos Hills Shrines: A Comparative Study of the Dula, Njelele and Zhame Shrines and their Impact on the Surrounding Communities'. BA History Honours Dissertation, University of Zimbabwe.
Nyathi, P. (2007). 'How does Bulawayo survive?' Unpublished paper, presented at Urban Culture and Urban Crisis – Britain Zimbabwe Society Research Day, Oxford University, 9 June 2007.
Onslow, S. & Plaut, M. (2018). *Robert Mugabe* (Athens: Ohio University Press).
Packard, R. (1981). *Chiefship and Cosmology* (Bloomington: Indiana University Press).
Pallotti, A 2018 'We paid a heavy price for hosting them': Villagers and freedom fighters in Mgagao, Tanzania', *Southern Africa Historical Journal*, 70(1), 168–93.
Papagaroufali, E. (1999). 'Donation of human organs or bodies after death: A cultural phenomenology of "flesh" in the Greek context', *Ethnos*, 27(3), 283–314.
Paperno, I. (2001). 'Exhuming bodies of Soviet terror', *Representations*, 75(1), 89–118.
Parker, J. (2005). 'The cultural politics of death and burial in early colonial Accra', in: D. Anderson & R. Rathbone (eds), *Africa's Urban Past* (Portsmouth, NH: Heineman), 205–21.
Parsons, N. & Segobye, A.K. (2002). 'Missing persons and stolen bodies: The repatriation of "El Negro" to Botswana', in: C. Fforde, J. Hubert & P. Turnbull, *The Dead and their Possessions* (London: Routledge), 245–55.

Perman, T. (2011). 'Awakening spirits: The ontology of spirit, self, and society in Ndau spirit possession practices in Zimbabwe', *Journal of Religion in Africa*, 41(1), 59–92.

Petrovic, M. (2005/06). 'Producing "bodies" – reproducing "persons": Conceiving human remains in Tasmania and the former Yugoslavia', *Cambridge Anthropology*, 25(3), 61–71.

Pinney, C. (2005). 'Things happen: Or, from which moment does that object come?' in: D. Miller (ed.) *Materiality* (Durham, NC: Duke University Press), 256–72.

Posel, D. (2002). 'A matter of life and death: Revisiting "modernity" from the vantage point of the "new" South Africa'. Draft Manuscript, Wits Institute for Social and Economic Research – WISER, Johannesburg.

Posel, D. & Gupta, P. (2009). 'The life of the corpse', *African Studies*, 68(1), 299–309.

Pottier, J. (2002). *Re-imagining Rwanda* (Cambridge: Cambridge University Press).

Potts, D. (2006). 'Restoring order? Operation Murambatsvina and the urban crisis in Zimbabwe' *Journal of Southern African Studies*, 32(2), 272–91.

Primorac, R. (2007). 'The poetics of state terror in twenty-first century Zimbabwe', *Interventions*, 6(3), 434–50.

Raftopoulos, B. (2003). 'The state in crisis: Authoritarian nationalism, selective citizenship and distortions of democracy in Zimbabwe', in: A. Hammer, B. Raftopoulos & S. Jensen (eds), *Zimbabwe's Unfinished Business* (Harare: Weaver Press), 217–42.

___. (2007). 'Nation, race and history in Zimbabwean politics', in: S. Dorman, D. Hammett & P. Nugent (eds), *Making Nations, Creating strangers, States and Citizenship in Africa* (London: Brill), 181–196.

___. (2013) (ed.) *The Hard Road to Reform: The Politics of Zimbabwe's Global Political Agreement* (Harare: Weaver Press).

Ranger, T. (1967). *Revolt in Southern Rhodesia 1896–7* (London: Heineman).

___. (1982a). 'Tradition and travesty: Chiefs and the administration in Makoni District, Zimbabwe, 1960–80', *Africa*, 52(3), 20–41.

___. (1982b). 'The death of Chaminuka: Spirit mediums, nationalism and the guerrilla war in Zimbabwe', *African Affairs*, 324(81), 349–69.

___. (1985). *Peasant Consciousness and Guerrilla War in Zimbabwe* (London: James Currey).

___. (1987). 'Taking hold of the land: Holy places and pilgrimages in twentieth century Zimbabwe', *Past & Present*, 117(1), 158–94.

___. (1988). 'Chingaira Makoni's head: Myth, history and the colonial experience' 18th Annual Hans Wolff Memorial Lecture, 29 March 1988, Indiana University.

___. (1992). 'Afterword: War, violence and healing in Zimbabwe', *Journal of Southern African Studies*, 18(3), 698–707.

___. (1995). *Are We Not Also Men?* (London: James Currey).

Bibliography

___. (1999). *Voices from the Rocks* (Oxford: James Currey).

___. (2003). 'Women and environment in African religion: The case of Zimbabwe', in: J. McGregor & W. Beinart (eds), *Social History & African Environment* (Oxford: James Currey), 72–86.

___. (2004a). 'Historiography, patriotic history and the history of the nation: The struggle over the past in Zimbabwe', *Journal of Southern African Studies*, 30(2), 215–34.

___. (2004b). 'Dignifying death: The politics of burial in Bulawayo', *Journal of Religion in Africa*, 34(1/2), 110–44.

___. (2007a). 'Living ritual and indigenous archaeology: The case of Zimbabwe', in: E. Kyriakidis (ed.), *The Archaeology of Ritual* (Los Angeles: Cotsen Institute of Archaeology, University of California), 123–54.

___. (2007b) 'Scotland Yard in the bush: Medicine murders, child witches and the construction of the occult – A literature review', *Africa*, 77(2), 272–83.

___. (2010a). 'Shaping the heritage landscape: Perspectives from East and Southern Africa'. Unpublished lecture, The British Institute in Eastern Africa, Nairobi, 5 May 2010.

___. (2010b). 'From spirit to body: Violence and memory in Zimbabwe'. Unpublished lecture, University of Illinois, 14 October 2010, Available at: www.youtube.com/watch?v=h0Zz7I4JnlA [accessed 21 May 2020].

___. (2010c). 'Report on the 2010 Britain Zimbabwe Society research days: Day one – African religion', BZS *Zimbabwe Review*, 10(4), November 2010.

___. (2011a). 'A decent death: Changes in funerary rites in Bulawayo', in: M. Jindra & J. Noret (eds), *Funerals in Africa* (London: Berghahn Books), 41–68.

___. (2011b). 'The politics of Zimbabwean Christianity: Histories of interaction with a "dignified" African spirituality', BZS *Zimbabwe Review*, 11(1).

Ranger, T. & Ncube, M. (1996). 'Religion in guerrilla war: The case of Southern Matabeleland', in: N. Bhebe & T. Ranger (eds), *Society in Zimbabwe's Liberation War* (Oxford: James Currey), 35–57.

Renshaw, L. (2010). 'Scientific and affective identification of Republican civilian victims from the Spanish Civil War', *Journal of Material Culture*, 15(4), 449–63.

___. (2011). *Exhuming Loss* (Walnut Creek, CA: Left Coast Press).

Reynolds, P. (1990). 'Children of tribulation: The need to heal and the means to heal war trauma', *Africa*, 60(1), 1–38.

Richters, A., Dekker, C. & De Jonge, K. (2005). 'Reconciliation in the aftermath of violent conflict in Rwanda', *Intervention*, 3(3), 203–21.

Riviera, A. (2009). 'The Masquerading Monster'. Unpublished Dissertation, University of Edinburgh.

Robben, A.C.G.M. (2018). *A Companion to the Anthropology of Death*. (Oxford: Wiley-Blackwell).

Bibliography

Roberts, J. (2011). 'Funerals and fetish internment in Accra, Ghana', in: M. Jindra & J. Noret (eds), *Funerals in Africa* (London: Berghahn Books), 207–26.

Rodlach, A. (2006) *Witches, Westerners and HIV: AIDS and Cultures of Blame in Africa* (Walnut Creek, CA: Left Coast Press).

Rogers, D. (2019). *Two Weeks in November: The Astonishing Untold Story of the Operation that Toppled Mugabe* (Johannesburg: Jonathan Ball Publishers).

Rønning, H. (2003). 'The media in Zimbabwe: The struggle between state and civil society', in: S. Darnolf & L. Laakso (eds), *Twenty Years of Independence in Zimbabwe* (London: Palgrave Macmillan), 196–221.

Rosa, H. (2018). 'The idea of resonance as a sociological concept', *Global Dialogue*, 8(2), http://globaldialogue.isa-sociology.org/the-idea-of-resonance-as-a-sociological-concept [accessed 8 May 2019].

___. (2019). 'Resonant sovereignty? The challenge of social acceleration – and the prospect of an alternative conception'. Unpublished paper presented at the Global Sovereignty conference, University of St Andrews, April/May 2019.

Rosaldo, R. (2004). 'Grief and a headhunter's rage', in: N. Scheper-Hughes & P. Bourgois (eds), *Violence in War and Peace* (London: Wiley-Blackwell), 150–56.

Rousseau, N. (2009). 'The farm, the river and the picnic spot: Topographies of terror', *African Studies*, 68(3), 351–69.

Rousseau, N., Rassool, C. & Moosage, R. (2018). 'Missing and missed: Rehumanisation, the nation and missing-ness', *Kronos*, 44(1), 10–32.

Rowlands, M. (1999). 'Remembering to forget: Sublimation as sacrifice in war memorials', in: A. Forty & S. Küchler (eds) *The Art of Forgetting* (Oxford: Berghahn Books), 129–45.

Rowlands, M. & De Jong, F. (2007). *Reclaiming Heritage* (Walnut Creek, CA: Left Coast Press).

Russ, A J. (2005). 'Love's labour paid for: Gift and commodity at the threshold of death', *Cultural Anthropology*, 20(1), 128–55.

Rutherford, B. (1999) 'To find an African witch', *Critique of Anthropology*, 19 (1).

Sachikonye, L. (2011). *When a State Turns on Its Citizens* (Harare: Weaver Press).

Sagiya, M.E. & Fontein, J. (2021). 'Toward a critical history of the National Museums and Monuments of Zimbabwe: Rethinking pastness and materiality, in: R. Silverman, G. Abungu & P. Probst (eds), *National Museums in Africa: Identity, History and Politics* (London: Routledge), 203–26.

Salpeteur, M. & Warnier, J.-P. (2013). 'Looking for the effects of bodily organs and substances through vernacular public autopsy in Cameroon', *Critical African Studies*, 5(3), 153–74.

Sanders, T. (2008a). *Beyond Bodies* (Toronto: University of Toronto Press).

Bibliography

___. (2008b). 'Buses in Bongoland. Seductive analytics and the occult', *Anthropological Theory*, 8(2), 107–32.

Scheper-Hughes, N. & Wacquant, J. (2002). *Commodifying Bodies* (London: Sage).

Schmidt, H. (1997). 'Healing the wounds of war: Memories of violence and the making of history in Zimbabwe's most recent past', *Journal of Southern African Studies*, 23(2), 301–10.

Schoffeleers, J.M. (ed.) (1979). *Guardians of the Land: Essays on Central African Territorial Cults* (Gweru: Mambo press).

Scott, M. (2005). 'Hybridity, vacuity, and blockage: Visions of chaos from anthropological theory, Island Melanesia and Central Africa', *Comparative Studies of Society and History*, 47(1), 190–216.

Seymour, J.E. (1999). 'Revisiting medicalisation and "natural" death', *Social Science and Medicine*, 49(1), 691–704.

Shanks, M. (2007). 'Symmetrical archaeology', *World Archaeology*, 39(4), 589–96.

Sharp, L. (2000). 'The commodification of the body and its parts', *Annual Review of Anthropology*, 29(1), 287–328.

___. (2001). 'Commodified kin: Death, mourning and competing claims on the bodies of organ donors in the United States', *American Anthropology*, 103(1), 112–33.

Shipton, P. (2009). *Mortgaging the Ancestors* (London: Yale University Press).

Shoko, T. (2006). ''My bones shall rise again': War veterans, spirits and land reform in Zimbabwe' ASC Working Paper No. 68 (Leiden: African Studies Centre).

___. (2007). *Karanga Indigenous Religion in Zimbabwe* (London: Ashgate).

Sibanda, M., Gumbo, S.D. & Moyana, H. (1992). *The African Heritage: History for Junior Secondary School, Book 1*. (Harare: Zimbabwe Publishers House).

Simmons, D. (2000). 'African witchcraft at the milennium: Musings on a modern phenomenon in Zimbabwe', *Journal of the International Institute*, 7(2), 1–6.

Sinclair-Bright, L.T. (2016). 'This Land: Politics, Authority and Morality after Land Reform in Zimbabwe'. PhD Thesis, University of Edinburgh.

___. (2019) 'Ambiguous bonds: Relationships between farm workers and land beneficiaries after Zimbabwe's Land Reform programme', *Journal of Southern African Studies*, 45(5), 927–44.

Sithole, M. (1979). *Zimbabwe: Struggles within the Struggle*, 1st edn (Harare: Rujeko Publishers).

Smith, D., Simpson, C. & Davis, I. (1981). *Mugabe* (London: Sphere Books).

Solidarity Peace Trust (SPT) (2008a). 'Punishing dissent, silencing citizens: The Zimbabwe elections 2008', 21 May, http://solidaritypeacetrust.org/133/punishing-dissent-silencing-citizens [accessed 3 February 2010].

___. (2008b). 'Desperately seeking sanity: What prospects for a new beginning in Zimbabwe?' 29 July, http://solidaritypeacetrust.org/326/desperately-seeking-sanity [accessed 3 February 2010].

Southall, A. (1953). *Alur Society* (Cambridge: Heffer).

Spierenburg, M. (2004). *Strangers, Spirits and Land Reforms* (Leiden & Boston: Brill).

Stadler, J. (2021). *Public Secrets and Private Sufferings in the South African AIDS Epidemic* (Switzerland: Springer Nature).

Steedly, M. (1993). *Hanging without a Rope: Narrative Experience in Colonial and Postcolonial Karoland* (Princeton: Princeton University Press).

Stepputat, F. (2014). *Governing the Dead* (Manchester: Manchester University Press).

Stewart, P.J. & Strathern, A. (2003). *Witchcraft, Sorcery, Rumors and Gossip* (Cambridge: Cambridge University Press).

Stoler, A.L. (2008). 'Imperial debris: Reflections on ruins and ruination', *Cultural Anthropology*, 23 (2), 191–219.

Stoller, P. (1995). *Embodying Colonial Memories* (New York: Routledge).

Straight, B. (2006). 'Becoming dead: The entangled agencies of the dearly departed', *Anthropology and Humanism*, 31(2), 101–10.

Tarlow, S. (2002). 'The aesthetic corpse in 19th century Britain', in: Y. Hamilakis, M. Pluciennik & S. Tarlow (eds), *Thinking Through the Body: Archaeologies of Corporeality* (New York: Kluwer Academic and Plenum Publishers), 85–97.

Taussig, M. (1993). *Mimesis and Alterity* (New York: Routledge).

Taylor, A.C. (1996). 'The soul's body and its states: An Amazonian perspective on the nature of being human', *Journal of Royal Anthropological Institute*, 2(2), 201–15.

Taylor, C. (1999). *Sacrifice as Terror* (New York: Berghahn Books).

Tekere, E.Z. (2007). *A Lifetime of Struggle* (Harare: Sapes).

Tendi, B.M. (2010). *'Making History in Mugabe's Zimbabwe: Politics, Intellectuals and the Media'* (Oxford: Peter Lang).

___. (2016). 'State intelligence and the politics of Zimbabwe's presidential succession', *African Affairs*, 115(459), 203–24.

___. (2020a). *The Army and Politics in Zimbabwe: Mujuru, the Liberation Fighter and Kingmaker* (Cambridge: Cambridge University Press).

___. (2020b). 'The motivations and dynamics of Zimbabwe's 2017 military coup', *African Affairs*, 119 (474), 39–67.

Theuws, J. (1960). 'Naître et mourir dans le rituel Luba', *Zaire*, 14, 115–73.

___. (1968) 'Le styx ambigu', *Problèmes Sociaux Congolais*, p.33.

Tomaselli, K. (2009). '(Re)mediatising HIV/AIDS in South Africa', *Cultural Studies Critical Methodologies*, 9(4), 570–87.

Trouillet, M R. (1995). 'An unthinkable history: The Haitian revolution as a non-event', in: M.R. Trouillet (ed.), *Silencing the Past: Power and the Production of History* (Boston, MA: Beacon Press), 70–107.

Bibliography

Tsintjilonis, D. (2000). 'The sacrifice of signs: "Measuring" the dead in Tana Toraja', *Oceania*, 71(19), 1–17.

___. (2004). 'Words of intimacy: Re-membering the dead in Buntao', *Journal of the Royal Anthropological Institute*, 10(2), 375–93.

___. (2006). 'The death bearing senses in Tana Toraja', *Ethnos*, 72(2), 173–94.

Turner, V. (1969). *The Ritual Process* (London: Routledge).

UNDP (no date) 'Strengthening the National Peace and Reconciliation Infrastructure in Zimbabwe: Key Milestones of the Organ for National Healing, Reconciliation and Integration (2009–2014)', https://erc.undp.org/evaluation/managementresponses/keyaction/documents/download/177 [accessed 1 July 20].

Vambe, M.T. (2008). *The Hidden Dimensions of Operation Murambatsvina* (Harare: Weaver Press).

Vansina, J. (2011). 'Foreword', in: M. Jindra & J. Noret (eds), *Funerals in Africa* (London: Berghahn Books), ix–xii.

Vaughan, M. (2013). 'Big houses for the dead', in: W.T. Kalusa & M. Vaughan, *Death, Belief and Politics in Central African History* (Lusaka: Lembani Trust), 327–54.

Venis, S. (2003). 'The Interview: Shari Eppel', *The Lancet*, 361(9354), 354.

Vera, I. (1993). *Nehanda* (Harare: Baobab Press).

Verdery, K. (1999). *The Political Lives of Dead Bodies* (New York: Columbia University Press).

Wagner, R. (1975). *The Invention of Culture* (Chicago, IL: University of Chicago Press).

Walsh, K. (1992). *The Representation of the Past* (London: Routledge).

Walter, T. (1994). *The Revival of Death.* (London: Routledge).

Warnier, J.-P. (2007). *The Pot King: The Body and Technologies of Power* (Leiden: Brill).

Weate, J. (2003). 'Achille Mbembe and the post colony: Going beyond the text', *Research in African Literatures*, 34(4), 27–41.

Werbner, R. (1989). 'Regional cult of God above: Achieving and defending the macrocosm', in: R. Werbner, *Ritual Passage, Sacred Journey* (Washington: Smithsonian).

___. (1991). *Tears of the Dead: The Social Biography of an African Family* (Edinburgh: Edinburgh University Press).

___. (1998). 'Smoke from the barrel of a gun: Postwars of the dead, memory and reinscription in Zimbabwe', in: R. Werbner (ed.), *Memory and the Postcolony: African Anthropology and the Critique of Power* (London: Zed Books), 67–98.

White, L. (2000). *Speaking with Vampires* (London & Berkeley: University of California Press).

___. (2003). *The Assassination of Herbert Chitepo* (Bloomington: Indiana University Press).

Bibliography

Wilkins, S. (2013). 'Ndira's wake: Politics, memory and mobility among the youth of Mabvuku-Tafara, Harare', *Journal of Southern African Studies*, 39(4), 885–901.

Williams, C. (2013). 'Introduction: Thinking Southern Africa from "the Camp"', *Social Dynamics: A Journal of African Studies*, 39(1), 1–4,

Williams, H. (2004). 'Death warmed up: The agency of bodies and bones in early Anglo-Saxon cremation rites', *Journal of Material Culture*, 9(1), 263–91.

Zimbabwe Human Rights (ZHR) NGO Forum (2009). 'Taking transitional justice to the people – Outreach Report' (Harare: ZHR), www.hrforumzim.org/publications/taking-transitional-justice-to-the-people-outreach-report [accessed 28 May 2020].

Zvobgo, C. (2017). *The Struggle for Zimbabwe 1935–2004: Eddison JM Zvobgo* (Gweru, Zimbabwe: Mambo Press).

INDEX

abductions   98–9, 111, 252–3
accidents   4, 31–2, 36–7, 158–60,180–91
  road   89, 166, 180–3, 254, 300
  black spots   181
  black dog   182
African Union (AU)   261
AIDS/HIV   7, 9, 13, 42, 221, 223, 225,291–2
Alan Wilson Patrol   51, 53, 60
  grave, monument (Matobo), road   51, 53, 256
alterity, otherness   2, 5, 37–8
  of bones and bodies   37–8, 120, 121, 124, 148–51, 180, 184, 195, 244–6, 286–7
  of materiality   36, 124, 148, 152, 157, 245
  of spirits, rumours and the immaterial   38–9, 152, 192–3, 195, 204, 212-17, 238–44, 244–6, 286–7, 297
AMANI Trust   24, 62, 71, 77, 119 n.71, 120, 134, 139, *see also* Ukuthula Trust
Angola   40, 64, 65, 70, 298
archaeology, archaeologists   34, 38, 50–2, 66, 73, 74, 80, 90, 301, *see also* NMMZ
  as emotive practice, like funeral   80–2, 92–4, 148
  excavations   29, 38, 66, 68, 143–5
  exhumations   18, 29,30, 38, 92–4, 95–6, 109, 122–3, 132–7, 143–5
  expertise   18, 29,72, 131, 134, 137, 146
  politics of, and distancing effects of   18, 30, 34, 50–2, 75, 76, 80, 92–3, 95–6, 109
  remaking the dead   148, 150, 193, 287

assassinations   4, 154, 164, 172 n.61, 182-5, 188, 189, 250, 254, *see also* accidents
autopsies   11, 100
  Mujuru, Solomon   167, 169, 176–7
autochthony, belonging   5, 8, 10, 17, 105, n.44, 187, 218, 223, 239, 288, 295, 296
ancestors   *see* spirits

bio-politics   3, 124, 155, 179, 187, *see also* necro-politics
bira ceremonies   68, 74, 213, 219, 232–4, *see also* spirit possession
  mikwerera (rainmaking)   195, 204, 213
Biti, Tendai   167
bodies, corpses, bodily remains and substances   1–5, 8–14, 22–3, 29–32, 35–6, 45–6, 76–83, 84–92, 93–6, 97–112, 121–51, 133, 285–98, 299 n.26, *see also* corporeality
  abandoned   8, 10, 294
  anonymous   8, 17, 77, 294
  commodification   6
  containment   3, 10, 31, 32, 84–5
  dangerous   8, 10, 106, 275, 279–80, 286, 289–90
  disappeared   22, 24, 35, 85, 98, 99, 101, 112, 114, 120, 140, 147, 187, 303
  disgust   10, 106, 291
  dismembered   22, 98, 120, 187
  dumped   35, 79, 85, 88, 98, 99, 110, 112, 114, 138, 147
  as evidence   12, 100, 101, 112, 123, 130, 133, 134, 138, 141–2, 146, 151, 154, 177, 264–5
  leaky   1, 13, 29, 32, 35–6, 83, 84–5, 94–7, 101, 104–5, 108, 118, 120,

Index

123-4, 138-43, 157, 169, 187, 190, 248, 287, 291
pollution 7, 10, 106, 292
tortured 1, 22, 23, 29, 35, 97, 99, 102, 124, 147, 294
transformation of 10, 35, 85, 88, 94-6, 105-6, 108-11, 114, 119-20, 121, 147-8, 157, 187, 265, 280, 305
bones
  affective presence and emotive materiality 2, 29, 34-5, 40, 45-6, 78-9, 84, 93-7, 104-8, 147
  ambiguous or dual agency 34-5, 40, 46, 76-82, 93-7, 147, 240
  collective x, 45, 289 n.6
  as evidence *see* bodies
  repatriation 5, 39, 63, 68, 282, 303-7
  resurfacing 1, 18, 22-3, 29, 35, 74, 77-8, 82, 85-97, 101, 117, 118, 120, 147, 193, 287
  subject/objects 3, 11-12, 31, 34, 36, 46, 78-83, 84-5, 93-5, 111, 124, 143, 146, 147-51, 180, 195, 245, 286-7
Botswana 6, 17, 40, 64, 65
bringing home ceremonies 63, 88, *see also umbuyiso* and *kugadzira*
burials, reburials *see also* graves
  belonging 5, 10, 14
  caves 10, 236, 239, 274, 301 n.35, 307 n.55
  commemoration, liberation heritage 17, 19, 44-5, 49, 61-2, 64-5, 69, 74-5, 90, 92, 127, 274
  gukurahundi 24-8, 62, 77, 119
  problematic, disrupted, in the wrong place 35, 38, 100-3, 117, 145, 146, 194, 237, 245, 265, 286, 293, 294
  reconciliation, healing 6, 24-8, 29, 31-2, 114, 117, 143, 147, 150, 190, 191, 302

Catholic Commission for Justice and Peace (CCJP) 23, 109, 119 n. 71
carnal fetishism 5, 14, 62, 282, 290
cemeteries 58, 72, 142, 294
  Granville, Harare 41
  Lady Stanley, Bulawayo 23, 57-9
  Warren Hill, Harare 100

Central Intelligence Organisation (CIO) 42, 60, 71, 90, 118, 129, 163, 208, 251, 263
Chamiswa, Nelson 206, 255, 257, 259, 295, 308
Chaminuka (ancestor) 6, 50, 206
Changamire Dombo (ancestor) 196-7, 202-3, 213, *see also* diesel *n'anga* and Rotina Mavhunga
Charamba, George, alias Nathaniel Manheru 136, 259, 310, 310, 313
Chauke, Crispin xii, 65, 71-2, 75, 81, 94
Chavunduka, Gordon 103, 117
Chiadzwa, Marange 97, 123, 140, 142, 182, 293
chiefs/chieftainship/clans 1, 43, 53, 54, 62, 63, 68, 75, 92, 105, 126, 207, 211, 212, 263, 296, 309, 310, 314-15
  Charumbira 210, 218
  Kandeya 41-3
  Makoni 206, 302-3, 304 n. 43, 305-6
  Mugabe 54, 76, 80, 105, 210
  Murinye 105 n. 44, 105, 210-13, 226, 241, 296
  Nemanwa 54, 211, 218, 222 n.7, 223-4, 226, 237
  Zvimba 274, 276-7, 312-13
Chigumadzi, Panashe 16, 19, 67, 86, 289
Chikerema, James 60, 186
Chimoio camp (Mozambique) 19 n.18, 30, 64, 66, 67, 81, 88, 301
Chimurenga see also liberation struggle
  1 39, 85, 87, 288, 302, 303-7
  2 15, 85-6, 87, *see also* liberation struggle
  politics 16, 39, 67, 86, 113, 115, 154, 249, 251, 256, 273, 277, 293, 303
Chinoyi 196-9
Chinyani, Anyway 69 n.64, 72, *see also* Fallen Heroes Trust
Chipunza, Kundishora Tungamirai 18, 64, 66, 70-1, 73, 74, 122, n.2, 132-3, 135, 136, 143-6, 150, 247, 280 n.145, 299, 300 n.31
Chitepo, Herbert
  commission 188
  confessions 184, 191

341

Index

murder/assassination 4, 36, 154, 183–5, 188
Chiwenga, General Constantine 160 n.10, 165
  involvement in coup 2017 98, 163, 185, 248,
  name change 248 n. 4
  rumours 163, 164
  vice-president 163, 250, 251
Chokuda, Moses
  murder 103–4
  ngozi 103–4, 117
  refusal to bury 103–4
cholera 291–3
churches
  African Independent Churches (AIC) 69, 216, 217, 222, 227, 295, 296–7
  burial, politics of 42, 69, 297
  catholic 216
  Christianisation 8
  Dutch Reformed 216
  healing 49, 69
  Pentecostalism 69, 227, 295–6
  prophets and pastors 69, 296–7
  war 204 n.47, 205, 208, 285
commemoration 1–3, 5, 9, 15, 17, 19, 21–2, 29–32, 34–6, 40, 46–63, 76–83, 88–94, 121, 129–31, 157, 186, 258–61, 268, 298–302
  monuments 5, 6, 39, 46–8, 51, 119, 280
  renaming and monumentalisation of roads, barracks, camps etc. 7, 17, 18, 33, 40, 44, 54–5, 65, 71, 127, 288, 299–300
  statues 21, 39, 302, 308–12, 313–15
corporeality 1, 3, 11–15, 29, 38, 80, 84, 277, 278, 281, 282, 284, 285–6, 288–9, 290, 295, 305, 309, 311
  ambiguity 108, 147
  excessivity and uncertainty 3, 11, 30–2, 35–6, 121, 124, 143–4, 147–51, 155, 157, 159–60, 180, 188, 191, 193, 245–6, 248, 286, 291, 297–8, 300
  metonymy 11, 149–50, 180
Covid 19 292–3, 311, 315

Dabengwa, Dumiso 56–62, 64–5, 72–3, 78, 127–8, 139, 161
  death and burial 257–60
death and dying
  dignifying 7, 42, 289
  in Africa 5–15, 284–5
  medicalization of 8, 283
  pollution 7, 10, 106, 292
  remaking of 30–2, 37, 85, 96, 109, 117, 120, 121, 147–51, 179, 190, 195, 246, 289, 300
  rupture 10, 38, 179, 246, 286, 309
  unfinished, incompleteness, unresolved 1, 31–2, 36–9, 120, 121, 159, 180–1, 183, 185, 188–91, 192–3, 216, 218, 240, 245–6, 248, 282, 284–5, 291, 297, 302, 312, 314
Democratic Republic of Congo (DRC) 162, 293, 299
diaspora 5, 8, 267, 282, 294, 306
Diesel *n'anga* 34, 37, 193–204, 207, 209, 214, 216, 237, 242, 243, 279, 286, *see also* Mavhungu, Rotina
divination 30, 37, 38, 95, 142, 148, 150–1, 195, 201, 245, 287, *see also* spirit possession

elections 22, 67, 84, 91, 97–9, 101, 109, 110, 112–13, 115–16, 118, 123, 125, 140, 141, 153, 154, 162, 164, 165, 169, 206, 221, 250, 252, 312
Entumbane 20 n.22, 26, 51, 141, 161 n.12, 190
Eppel, Shari 109, 113–14, 116, 119, 127, 129, 133–4, 139, 144, 151, 155, 191, 264–5
excessivity *see also* uncertainty, alterity
  of death *see* death and dying, unfinished, incompleteness, unresolved
  of human remains ix, 3, 11, 30–2, 35–6, 38, 120, 121, 124, 143–4, 147–51, 155, 157, 159, 180, 195–6, 245–6, 248, 283–4, 286–7, 290, 297–8, 300, 305
  of materiality 36, 147–9, 195, 245
  of spirits 37–8, 193, 195–6, 240, 242, 245–6, 248, 283–4, 286–7, 290, 297–8

Index

exhumations 6, 13, 14, 17, 24–5, 27–8, 29, 30–2, 35, 45, 48, 56, 61–2, 74, 77–8, 81–2, 92, 114, 119–20, 190–1, 245, 247–8, 260–2, 264–5, 299–300, 301
  Chibondo 2, 3, 18, 30, 36, 67, 72–3, 74, 121–57, 188, 193, 245, 287
  at former camps *see* Chimoio, Nyadzonia, *and* Freedom camp
  forensic *see* forensic archaeology
  Guinea Fowl Mine 18
  gukurahundi see gukurahundi exhumations
  Herbert Mine 18
  Matombo Six Mine 18
  Monkey William mine *see* Chibondo
  Odzi 18
  Rusape 18, 67, 91, 95, 109
  Tsholotsho 262, 267
  vernacular 3, 18, 75, 90, 92, 122, 287, 297, 299 n. 26

Fabian, Johannes 283–5
Fallen Heroes Trust (FHT) 18–19, 68–74, 95–6, 135, 109, 122, 127, 132–6, 138–9, 142–5, 150, 154, 297, 300
Fast Track Land Reform (FTLR) 10, 33, 43, 198 n.16, 205, 207, 221, 295
  Jambanja 207
forensic sciences, archaeology 11, 12, 18, 30, 38, 75, 94–5, 123, 130, 133, 143, 148, 151, 193, 195, 264–5, 287
  Argentinian forensic team 24, 134, 139, 142
  DNA testing 133
  experts, expertise 30, 72, 73–4, 131, 134, 137, 139, 143, 150, 151, 299 n. 26, 300
  pathology, pathologists, investigations 163, 159, 167, 173–4, 175, 195, 287, 294
  unforensic 123, 131, 133, 142, 153
funerals 5, 7, 8, 13, 19, 42, 47, 81, 88, 94–5, 104, 106–8, 147–8, 187, 246, 268, 280, 291, 293, 297, *see also* bringing home ceremonies, *umbuyiso, kugadzira* and *kurova guva*
  contested, disrupted 22, 29, 31, 35, 42–3, 62, 85, 99–102, 112, 114, 117, 120, 146, 238, 294, 305

funerary expertise, insurance 7–8, 282, 288, 291
Freedom camp (Zambia) 30, 64, 66, 88, 301
Fuzwayo, Mbuso xii, 130, 259, 264–5, 315

Gell, Alfred 34, 79–80, 84–5, 93, 102
genocide 5, 304
  gukurahundi 26, 67, 129, 266
  Rwanda 45 n.15
Global Political Agreement (GPA) 97, 112–13, 116, 125 n.4, 153
Gonakudzingwa (detention camp) 7, 300–1
Gonzalez, Dr Gabriel Alviero (pathologist) 176–8
Government of National Unity (GNU) 24, 25–6, 78, 85, 97, 100, 103–4, 112–20, 127, 131, 143, 144, 153, 166, 182, 253–4, *see also* Organ of National Healing and Reconciliation (ONHR)
graves 43, 52, 55, 76–7, 80, 268, 280, 290, 301 n.35, *see also* burial
  abandoned 18, 82
  and belonging 5, 10, 77, 288, 295
  anonymous, unmarked, unknown 17, 77, 89, 90
  at Bhalagwe 25, 110, 264
  mass graves 18, 22, 24, 25, 27, 29, 30, 32, 45 n. 15, 49, 63, 71, 73, 77, 88, 91, 95, 122, 126–7, 128–30, 139, 146, 151, 292, 299–300
  shallow 29, 49, 61, 63, 64, 76, 77, 88, 92, 112
Great Zimbabwe 18–19, 33, 49–54, 68–9, 205, 208, 212, 215–16, 218, 301
  graves 18, 51, 76, 80, 82, 290, 301 n.35
  liberation heritage 18, 63, 67, 74–5, 79
  psychic séances 53
  Zimbabwe controversy 50–1, 76
gukurahundi xii, 24–5, 27–8, 35, 49, 57, 58, 74, 77, 89, 104, 109–10, 129–30, 128, 129, 146
  announcements about commemorations now permitted, post-2017 2, 24, 25, 27, 28, 38, 77, 78, 119, 146, 190, 260–7, 301

343

Index

Bhalagwe   24, 314–15
Chihambakwe report   26, 190
commemorations, thwarted, obstructed, blocked   24–5, 28, 44, 59–60, 62, 77, 78, 91, 109, 115, 128–30, 137, 264, 293
Dumbutshena Report   26, 141 n. 77, 190
exhumations   24, 25, 62, 77–8, 119, 130, 139
noisy silence   24, 26, 62, 67, 91, 247

Harries, John   x, 11, 13, 45
healing, reconciliation   25–6, 29, 31, 35, 47, 49, 78, 85, 92, 103–4, 109, 112–20, 121, 129, 131–4, 143, 147, 150, 190, 208, 216, 266, 297, 309, *see also* Organ of National Healing and Reconciliation (ONHR)
transitional justice   6, 29, 92, 113, 115–16, 267
heritage   1, 15–19, 25, 33, 34–5, 39, 46–63, 76–82, 303, *see also* liberation heritage
  African heritage   45
  anti-heritage   47–8
  freedom heritage   *see* liberation heritage
  living, intangible, ritual   17, 45, 49, 82
  world heritage   48–9, 56, 69–70
Hertz, Robert   11, 13, 289
Hove, Chenjerai   85, 87–8
human remains   *see* bones, bodies *and* corporeality
Human Tissue Act (UK) 2004   304–5
Hurodzevasikana   7, 71, 300

Ibhetshu LikaZulu (Ndebele civil society group)   130, 264, 314–15, *see also* Fuzwayo, Mbuso
Ingold, Tim   35, 84–5, 94–6, 105, 111, 147–8, 195

Joint Monitoring Committee (JOMIC)   116, 118
Julianna, Ambuya   205, 213–15, 241

Kaguvi, Sekuru   50, 86, 203, 206, 302–4, 306–7, 310, *see also* Nehanda
Kamungoma   7, 71, 300
Kasukuwere, Saviour   127, 133–4, 137, 165
Kenya   5–7, 10, 92, 113, 162, 188, 289, 290
Kewada, Thakor   170, 177, 178
Khupe, Thokozani   255, 257
kugadzira, kurova guva   88, 280, *see also umbuyiso*

Lan, David   105, 204–6, 214
landscapes of terror   181
  black spots   *see* accidents
  militia bases   32, 181, 190, 253
Latour, Bruno   34, 80, 84–5, 93–4, 102, 148
liberation heritage   17–19, 25, 29, 34–5, 40, 44–6, 49, 56, 64–76, 77–82, 90–2, 112, 114, 115, 120, 121–3, 132, 137, 205, 261, 282, 285, 298–302, *see also* exhumations *and* Chibondo
  museums   6, 17, 39, 64–6, 71, 137, 281, 288, 298, 301–7
  regional, SADC   17, 48, 70–1, 298
liberation struggle   15, 16, 22, 30, 35, 40, 49, 53, 56, 57, 59–60, 67, 86, 100, 109, 113, 127, 130, 194, 200, 208, 215, 250, 296, 300, 301

Madagascar   94, 104, 108
Madhuku, Lovemore   41, 173, 313
Mafela Trust   20 n.22, 21, 58, 59, 61–2, 71, 73, 128, 135, 138, 140–1, *see also* ZIPRA War Shrines Committee
Mahachi, Godfrey, Executive Director of NMMZ   137, 181, 304–6, 309
Makoni, Simba   165, *see also Muvambo/Kusile/Dawn* movement
Makumbe, John   130–1, 140, 162–3
mapfupa edu achamuka   66, 85, *see also* Nehanda, Ambuya
Maseko, Owen   26
Masuku, Lookout   57–9, 257
  Death, funeral   58
  grave   57–9
materiality   2–3, 11–15, 34–5, 40, 79–80, 84–5, 93–7, 106, 148–9, 152, 195, 244–5, 284, 288, 297, *see also* Latour, Bruno; Gell, Alfred; Ingold, Tim

344

Index

matter and meaning 9, 11–12, 13, 15, 31–2, 154–5, 180–1, 196
object agency 79, 84
torque of 124, 147–50, 152, 245, 287
Matabeleland Collective 261, 263
Forum 263
Matobo 25, 52, 69
Banyubi graves 52, 55
grave of King Mzilikazi 52, 69
Mwari shrines 49, 69, 192, 213
Matonjeni 69, 213
Njelele 20, 69, 213
Rhodesian monumentalisation 51–2, *see also* Rhodes, Cecil
Mavhungu, Rotina, alias Nomatter Tagarira 37, 193–5, 196–204, 209–16, 242, 297, *see also* diesel *n'anga*
Mbembe, Achille 32, 152, 153, 189, 283
Mhanda, Wilfred, alias Dzino Machingura 19, 160 n.8, 182–3, 186, 207, 253–4 n.28, 289
Mkandla, Strike 266
Miller, Daniel 79, 94, 195, 287
Mnangagwa, Emmerson
coup 38, 160 n.8, 163, 185, 248–9
escape 250
gukurahundi 25, 27, 28, 38, 77, 116, 119, 130, 146, 190, 260–7, 299, 301
Nehanda statue 309–10
poisoning, grenade attack 183, 250–1
presidency 2, 23, 38, 40, 97–8, 100, 251–2, 253–7, 271 n.110, 272–3, 276–7, 301–2
rumours 163, 164–5, 251, 312–14
Mohadi, Kembo 65, 134–5, 160 n.10, 197, 258
Motsi, Comrade Jimmy 69, 72, *see also* Fallen Heroes Trust
Movement for Democratic Change (MDC) 16, 22–5, 29, 38, 41–2, 44, 67, 78, 97, 99–101, 112–13, 115, 123, 125, 127, 129–31, 140–2, 153–4, 165, 200, 206, 253–4, 255, 263, 267, 271
MDC-N 26, 129, 206
MDC-T 130, 131, 165, 255, 257
Mozambique 17, 19, 30, 40, 45 n.15, 63–4, 67, 70, 72, 74–5, 86, 88, 92, 94, 183, 204–5, 218, 220, 223, 224, 226, 228–9, 231–6, 238, 242, 246, 250, 289, 298, 300, 310
Mt Darwin 30, 36, 41, 69, 71, 73, 90, 122–8, 131–2, 135–6, 141, 155, 157, *see also* Chibondo
Mthwakazi Liberation Front (MLF) 127–9, 264
Muchini, Sophia 19 n. 19, 53–4, 195, 208–17, 241, 242, *see also* Nehanda mediums
Mudede, Registrar-General Tobaiwa 198–202
Mugabe, Grace 21, 163–5, 249–51, 256, 273–81, 296, 312–13
Mugabe, Leo 275, 277–8, 312
Mugabe, Robert
biographies of 160 n.7
corporeality 277–81
coup 16, 38, 42, 78, 97–8, 103, 128, 163, 183, 248–51, 273, 275
death 2, 163, 196, 247, 260, 267–81
disputes over burial 21, 38, 267–81
exhumation of 312–14
on exhumations 55–6, 77, 128, 135, 247–8
funeral 272, 275–7, 276–7
ghosts/haunting 89–90, 118, 184, 281
on *gukurahundi* 25, 59, 129, 261
mausoleum 275–7
mugabeism 16, 44, 135, 247, 273
properties, 'blue roof' mansion 275–6, 312
relations with Mujuru, Solomon 32, 158, 164–5, 167, 179
Mugabe, Sally 256, 268, 270, 275, 276
Mujuru, General Solomon, alias Rex Nhongo
autopsy 167, 169,176–7
business dealings 160–2, 166, 185
death 159–69
exhumation, demands for 167
fire 4, 32, 36, 158–9, 160, 166, 168–9, 170–2, 173–7
inquest 169–80
Mugabe, Robert, relations with 32, 158, 164–5, 167, 179

345

Index

Mujuru, Joice 135, 160, 163, 164–5, 167, 172, 185, 249, 279
museums
  Germany 5, 304
  Tanzania 298
  UK 39, 288, 302, 303–7
  Zimbabwe 64–6, 71, 137, 281, 301, *see also* National Museums and Monuments of Zimbabwe (NMMZ)
Mutasa, Didymus 166, 197, 200, 205
Muvambo/Kusile/Dawn movement 165
Muzorewa, Bishop 164, 236 n.31
  Auxiliaries 236, 239
Mzila-Ndlovu, Moses 26, 104, 115, 129

Nambia 5, 17, 45 n.15, 70, 298, 304
n'anga see also spirit mediums
National Archives of Zimbabwe (NAZ) 16 n.13, 66, 73, 308
National Heroes Acre 15, 20, 36, 44, 56, 59–60, 66, 89, 156–7, 167–8, 186, 189, 258, 268, 272–7, 281, 301, 312–13
National Museums and Monuments of Zimbabwe (NMMZ) 6, 17, 18–19, 29–30, 34, 39, 45, 49–51, 64–76, 78, 90, 92–3, 95–6, 120, 122–3, 134–7, 143–6, 208, 261, 298–302, 302–7, 310
  Act 19, 71, *see also* liberation heritage *and* exhumations
National Peace and Resolution Bill/Act 260–1, 264
  Commission (NPRC) 261
necro-politics 3, 31, 32, 100, 104, 121, 124, 153, 155, 179, 184, 187–9, 283, 284, 285, 293, *see also* bio-politics
Ncube, Welshman 206
Ndira, Tonderai 99–100
Nehanda, Ambuya
  ancestor/spirit 1, 50, 53, 85, 86, 89, 109, 203, 209, 213, 216, 279
  remains/skull 39, 302–7, 309–10, 311–12, 315
  corporeality 289, 309–10, 311–12
  Handa Project 302–3
  hanging 1, 66, 85, 86, 89, 203, 206, 288, 302, 310
  in literature 85–6, 288

Mbuya 1, n.1
  mediums of 19, 89, 204, 207–8, 209, 211, 213, 302
Muchini, Sofia 19, 53–4, 195, 208–17, 241, 242
Nyakasikana, Charwe 1, 39, 194
prophesy, 'my bones will rise again' 1, 39, 66, 85, 109, 194, 302
  statue 39, 302, 307–12, 313–14, 315
  tree 288, 302
Nkomo, Joshua 58, 61–2, 67, 160 n.7, 301
  death and burial 20, 25, 59, 261
  statue 21–2
Nyadzonya camp (Mozambique) 30, 75, 81–2, 88
Nyakasikana, Charwe *see* Nehanda, Ambuya
Nyamnjoh, Francis 43, 31, 190, 245, 284–5

OAU Liberation Committee 17 n.14, 298
ontology, ontological 2, 4, 9, 10, 13, 14–15, 31–2, 36, 37, 111, 149, 159, 180, 192, 240, 244, 284
Operation *Murambatsvina* 97, 130, 152, 154–5, 221
Operation Restore Legacy *see* ZANU PF coup
Organ of National Healing and Reconciliation (ONHR) 25, 104, 112–16, 118, 119, 299 n.27

patriotic history 16–17, 20, 30, 34, 40, 45, 60, 70, 86, 123, 151, 206, 247, 250, 293, 301, *see also chimurenga* politics
Capturing a Fading National Memory 16 n.13, 66
cultural galas 16 n.12, 67
Hashim Mbita Documentation Project 16 n.13, 66
Operation *mapfupa achamhuka* 66
Pinney, Chris 31, 124, 148, 149, 152, 245, *see also* materiality, torque of
Provincial Heroes Acres 15, 56, 59, 61, 77, 89

346

Index

Ranger, Terence 6, 7, 11, 16, 42, 52, 89, 193, 204, 205, 240, 282, 287–9, 295, 297
reconciliation *see* healing *and* Organ of National Healing and Reconciliation (ONHR)
repatriation 5, 39, 63, 68, 282, 303–7
Rhodes, Cecil
  grave 51–2, 55–6, 247
  pioneer column 76
  #RhodesMustFall 55
Rutanhire, Comrade George 68, 127, 134, 136, *see also* Fallen Heroes Trust(FHT)

Sekeramayi, Sydney 160, 197
Shiri, Air Marshall Perence 160 n.10, 164
Shorty, Sekuru 37, 218–38, 240–1, 245–6, 291
  death & burial 236, 239, 246
Sithole, Rev. Ndabaningi 60, 164, 186
Solidarity Peace Trust (SPT) 134, 139
South Africa 5, 6, 8, 9, 10, 17, 29, 45 n.15, 46 n.17, 47, 70, 137, 142, 173, 177, 181, 270, 294
  South African Police Service (SAPS) 174
Southern African Development Community (SADC) 17, 45, 49, 66, 70, 97, 112, 249, 273
Spanish civil war, exhumations 6, 13, 150–1
spirits, ancestors 1, 4, 19–20, 29, 31, 34, 37, 50–1, 53–4, 55, 63, 68, 76, 80, 85, 86–9, 94, 105, 108–9, 119, 147–8, 180, 191, 193, 194, 203, 205, 208, 212, 214–15, 286, 287, 300, 303, 306
  alterity of 38, 195, 204, 212–13, 216–17, 238–6, 287, 297
  authenticity 37, 194–5, 203–4, 206, 211–14, 216, 239–40, 243–4
  autonomy of 193, 240, 244
  excessivity, uncertainty 3–4 n.2, 4, 31, 38, 193–6, 212–3, 216, 229, 240, 242–4, 245–6, 286–7
  ghosts 29, 31, 32, 181, 190, 285
  index of 205

Mozambican 88, 220, 222–3, 224, 226, 228–9, 231–4, 236, 238, 242, 246
Ndau 228, 240–2
ngozi 29, 31, 34, 35, 37, 89, 102–5, 117–18, 177, 181, 190–1, 192–3, 213, 237, 239, 280, 287, 289, 291
possession 4, 30, 37, 38, 49, 142, 150, 151, 192–5, 203, 211–15, 219–21, 225–8, 236–7, 239, 240–6, 287, 290–1, 297, 300
shave 196, 211, 213–14, 215
spirit mediums/mediumship
  habitus, habits 203, 241, 243
  politics 4, 180, 192–4, 201, 202–4, 205, 207, 210, 212, 243, 278–9
  precarity/uncertainty 4, 37–8, 180, 192–4, 195, 202–4, 206, 211–12, 213–16, 237, 240, 242–3, 244
Swaziland 7, 8, 15, 42, 291, 297

Tandara, Gift 41–5, 62, 78, 82, 91, 99
Tanzania 17, 40, 45 n.15, 61, 64–5, 70, 256, 298, 310
Tekere, Edgar 128, 186, 250, 257, 301
Tomana, Attorney-General Johannes 169–70
Tongogara, Josiah Magama 7, 256, 300
  death 4, 36, 154, 173, 185
  rumours 4, 89, 154, 183–4, 188
Transitional Justice *see* healing
Tsvangirai, Morgan
  beating 41, 42, 254
  death, burial 38, 187, 206, 254–5, 256–7, 258, 263, 267
  leader, MDC 97, 112, 164
  prime minister, GNU 118, 141–2, 161, 165–6, 254
  MDC violence 254
Tsvangirai, Susan
  death 182, 254

Uganda 6, 102, 117, 119
Ukuthula Trust 119 n.71, 120, 134, 262, 265, *see also* AMANI Trust
umbuyiso 88, 289, *see also* kugadzira, kurova guva

347

Index

uncertainty
  in anthropology 151–2
  of death *see* death and dying
  of human remains 3, 11, 29–32, 121, 139, 147–51, 151–7, 195, 212
  politics, power of 2, 3, 4, 29–32, 37, 38, 121, 124, 151–7, 179–80, 187, 189–91, 195, 253, 285, 287
  of rumours 3 n.2, 4, 121, 152–7, 158–9, 163, 166, 187–9, 250
  of spirits 3–4 n.2, 4, 31, 38, 193–6, 212–13, 216, 229, 240, 242–4, 245–6, 286–7
  of water 195
UNESCO 17, 34, 45, 48–9, 69–70
  world heritage 47–9, 50, 54, 56, 69–70
Ushewokunze, Herbert 209

Vashandi rebellion 160 n.8, 183, 253 n.28, *see also* Mhanda, Wilfred
Vera, Ivonne 86
Verdery, Katherine 2, 45–6, 79, 190
violence
  CIO *see* Central Intelligence Organisation (CIO)
  elections/political *see* elections
  forms, techniques of 109–12
  maborder gezi, militia 61, 99–101, 110, 113, 118, 181, 190, 253
  military, soldiers 6, 24, 41, 58, 123, 132, 163–4, 250–1, 252, 255
  police 23, 41, 74, 82, 99, 101–2, 129, 163, 202, 207, 209, 251
  rape and torture 1, 22, 29, 35, 84, 97–112, 147, 181, 188 n. 137, 252, 253, 294, 315
  resolution of *see* healing, reconciliation
  secondary, post-violence, disrupted funerals 22, 29, 31, 35, 42–3, 62, 84–5, 99–102, 112, 114, 117, 120, 121, 146, 238, 282, 294, 305

war veterans 18–20, 23, 29, 53, 61, 68, 71, 74–5, 79, 86–90, 92–3, 109, 122–3, 126, 127, 136, 142, 207, 249 n.8, 302, *see also* Fallen Heroes Trust (FHT)
Taurai Zvehondo 68, 71

War Veterans Association 20, 71, 75, 77, 89
Zimbabwe Liberators' Platform 183, 207
ZIPRA War Veteran's Trust 133–5, 137 n.55, 141–2
Williams, Jenny 263
witchcraft, occult 6, 31, 37, 69 n.64, 181, 182, 188–9, 192, 228, 237, 278, 279, 280, 291, 297, 312–13
  accusations 183, 227, 279, 297, 313–14
  muti murders 290
  necrophagy 280, 289

Zimbabwe Broadcasting Corporation (ZBC) 142
Zimbabwe Human Rights Commission (ZHRC) 113, 261, 301
Zimbabwe National Traditional Healers Association (ZINATHA) 103, 117, 292 n.10, 293
Zambia 17, 19, 30, 40, 45 n.15, 61, 63, 64–6, 70, 72–3, 88, 92, 183, 205, 239, 299, 301
ZANU PF (Zimbabwe African National Union Patriotic Front) *see also* patriotic history, chimurenga politics, commemoration and elections
  coup/ Military Assisted Transition (MAT) 16, 21, 98, 160 n.8, 140, 163–4, 183, 247 n.2, 248–9, 251
  factionalism 21, 30, 36, 125, 135, 159, 162–4, 166, 182–3, 185, 249, 268, 278
  G40 faction 21, 163, 249, 251, 254 n.29, 271
  post-Mugabe 2, 74, 77, 165, 273, *see also* Mnangagwa, Emmerson
  violence 3, 22–3, 29, 35, 42, 68, 78, 82, 97, 99, 102, 104, 109, 112–13, 115, 118, 123, 140, 144, 146, 187, 252–3, *see also* violence
ZANLA (Zimbabwe National Liberation Army) 32, 56, 123, 154, 158, 161 n.12, 190 n.139, 236 n.31, 300, 301
ZAPU (Zimbabwe African Peoples

Index

Union)   20, 21–3, 25, 57–61, 77, 78, 112, 127–8, 139–40, 258, *see also* Dabengwa, Dumiso
ZIPA (Zimbabwe Peoples' Army)   160, 183, 253 n.28, *see also Vashandi* rebellion *and* Mhanda, Wilfred
ZIPRA (Zimbabwe Peoples' Revolutionary Army)   20–1, 44, 56–60, 65–6, 72–3, 123, 128, 133–5, 137 n.55, 139, 141–2, 182, 236 n.31, 257, 258, 259, 293, 301
ZIPRA War Shrines Committee   20 n.22, 58, 61, *see also* Mafela Trust
Zarira, Ambuya   88, 126, 138, 195, 207, 210, 212, 215–16, 241
Zvobgo, Eddison   61, 160 n.7, 186

Printed in the United States
by Baker & Taylor Publisher Services